POLITICAL CORRUPTION IN AMERICA

An Encyclopedia of Scandals, Power, and Greed

POLITICAL CORRUPTION IN AMERICA

An Encyclopedia of Scandals, Power, and Greed

Mark Grossman

A B C  C L I O

Santa Barbara, California   Denver, Colorado   Oxford, England

This book is dedicated to my good friends Paula Herbst and Carol Hoffman, whose friendship and inspiration continue to be my guiding light; to my parents, who have always been my personal heroes; and to my good friend Audrey Taylor in Great Britain, who loves her pursuit of everything Thomas Paine and is a someone I am glad to have befriended.

Library of Congress Cataloging-in-Publication Data

Grossman, Mark.

   Political corruption in America : an encyclopedia of scandals, power, and greed / Mark Grossman.

     p. cm.

   Includes bibliographical references and index.

   ISBN 1-57607-060-3 (hardcover : alk. paper); ISBN 1-85109-492-X (eBook)

   1. Political corruption—United States—Encyclopedias.   I. Title.

JK2249.G767   2003

973'.03—dc21

2003013127

0605   98765432

This book is also available on the World Wide Web as an eBook. Visit abc-clio.com for details.

ABC-CLIO, Inc.

130 Cremona Drive, P.O. Box 1911

Santa Barbara, California 93116–1911

This book is printed on acid-free paper ∞.

Manufactured in the United States of America

CONTENTS

Introduction, xi

POLITICAL CORRUPTION IN AMERICA

An Encyclopedia of Scandals, Power, and Greed

INTRODUCTION

"Scandal: disgrace, shame, discredit, or other ignominy brought upon a person or persons due to illicit or corrupt wrongdoing."

Oscar Wilde wrote that scandal is gossip made tedious by morality. In England, one form of defamation due to scandal or corruption was called *scandalum magnatum,* or "the slander of great men," usually reserved for the worst of all allegations. It is the scandal of political corruption, corruption that is perpetrated by men and women in elected and appointed offices, that is the focus of this work. Historian Edwin G. Barrows explained:

> Corruption in government—the betrayal of an office or duty for some consideration—is a familiar subject among American historians, but for several reasons the history of corruption as such is not. For one thing, corruption has never denoted a specific kind or form of misconduct, much less a specific crime. No one has ever gone to jail for it. It is essentially only an accusation that encompasses a large and shifting ensemble of determinate abuses—bribery, fraud, graft, extortion, embezzlement, influence peddling, ticket fixing, nepotism—not all of which have always been recognized as improper; some of which continue to be regarded as more consequential than others; most of which have been defined in different ways at different times; and each of which, arguably, deserves a quite different historical treatment.

Despite all this, a comprehensive history of the pervasiveness of corruption in American politics has yet to be written—until now. Corruption, as a study of history, deals also with ethics and how laws and ethics clash. From the Greek *ethika,*

meaning "character," ethics encompass the principles or standards of human conduct, also sometimes called morals. The laws discussed herein set the boundaries of morality, both in the actual law and in the letter of the law, and the violation of them is considered "unethical." Historian Norman John Powell wrote:

> Political corruption has four principal meanings. The first is patently illegal behavior in the sphere of politics; bribery is a prime example. The second relates to government practices that, while legal, may be improper or unethical. To some people, patronage is such a practice—although, it should be noted, patronage can also serve democratic ends and can even be used to combat corruption. A third meaning involves conflicts of interest on the part of public officials—for example, the vote of a legislator who owns oil stock and casts his vote in favor of oil depletion allowances. James Madison made this point in *Federalist No. 10:* "No man is allowed to be a judge in his own cause, because his interest would certainly bias his judgment, and, not improbably, corrupt his integrity." The fourth meaning also has an ethical, rather than a legal, basis: It related to political behavior that is nonresponsive to the public interest. The Watergate scandals provide vivid examples of such corrupt behavior, but the classic formulation of this view remains the one given by John E. E. Dalberg-Acton (Lord Acton): "Power tends to corrupt, and absolute power corrupts absolutely."

Writers from the beginning of America—even before it became a nation, when it was merely a series of colonies, firmly connected to Mother England—have railed against corruption, with disparate results. William Livingston wrote in the latter part of the eighteenth century: "No Man who has projected the Subversion of his Country will employ Force and Violence, till he has, by sowing the Seeds of Corruption, ripen'd it for Servility and Acquiescence: He will conceal his Design, till he spies an Opportunity of accomplishing his Iniquity by a single Blow." Englishman William Cobbett came to America, where he used the art of writing bitterly satirical pamphlets to rail against political corruption and social injustice. The issue of political corruption was also folded into many of the writings of some of America's best politicians: Daniel Webster explained, "Justice is the ligament which holds civilized beings and civilized nations together." Alexander Hamilton, writing in the *Federalist, No. 78,* penned, "[T]here can be but a few men in the society who will have sufficient skill in the laws to qualify them for the stations of judges. And making proper deductions for the ordinary depravity of human nature, the number must still be smaller of those who unite the requisite integrity with the requisite knowledge."

In the years since the end of the Second World War, more than fifty members of Congress have been indicted for various criminal offenses, although many of these have been acquitted. At the same time, however, Congress has imposed stricter and stricter ethics rules on its members, banning honoraria (monetary gifts for speeches) and other gift giving and instituting rigid reporting standards for campaign contributions. In two rare instances since the end of the Civil War, two members have been expelled from the U.S. House of Representatives for corruption.

This is not a history of all corruption in American political history—the sex scandals (which have been recently upon us in the form of the Monica Lewinsky affair) are not included, as the author believed from the outset that these were not scandals of corruption in the pure sense of the word. By the standards set up for use in this work, "political corruption" is defined as "the dishonest use of a position of elected power to gain a monetary advantage." Despite this clear definition, some scandals contained herein fall outside of this, but are included nonetheless: for instance, Watergate, or Iran-Contra, which are considered "political scandals," were used for gains or agendas other than monetary gain. It was also discovered that political corruption is not owned by any one party—in-

cluded in the pages that follow are crooks who were Republicans, Democrats, and third-party members, and reformers who were Republicans, Democrats, and third-party members.

As well, this is not just a history of political corruption in America—it is also the history of reformers, and reform measures, and the laws and court cases that have come down to shape laws in this area. This work is also the history of how ethics has been treated in our nation's history. Senator Paul H. Douglas of Illinois, in discussing the ethics in government, stated in 1951, "[W]hen I once asked a policeman how some of his colleagues got started on the downward path, he replied, 'It generally began with a cigar.'" The state of ethics has radically changed: for instance, in 1832, Representative William Stanbery (D-OH) was censured by the entire House for saying that Speaker of the House Andrew Stevenson's eyes might be "too frequently turned from the chair you occupy toward the White House." However, in 1872, Representative James A. Garfield was not censured, despite admitting that he had illegally accepted stock in the Crédit Mobilier scandal; eight years later, Garfield was elected president of the United States. Mark Twain once wrote that "[t]here is no distinctly native American criminal class except Congress." How a century later his words still have effect is why this work exists.

Historians have been warning about the acidic effects of corruption upon the body politic for many years. In 1787 Scottish historian Alexander Tyler explained,

A democracy cannot exist as a permanent form of government. It can only exist until the voters discover that they can vote themselves largesse from the public treasury. From that moment on, the majority always votes for the candidates promising the most benefits from the public treasury, with the result that a democracy always collapses over loose fiscal policy, always followed by a dictatorship. . . . The average age of the world's greatest civilizations has been two hundred years. These nations have progressed through this sequence: From bondage to spiritual faith; from spiritual faith to great courage; from courage to liberty; from liberty to abundance; from abundance to complacency; from complacency to apathy; from apathy to dependence; from dependence back again into bondage.

Tyler was writing about the fall of Athens some two millennia prior, but his words shine a light on any democracy and the pitfalls of allowing scandal and corruption to go unpunished.

In *The Federalist, No. 51,* James Madison explained, "If men were angels, no government would be necessary. If angels were to govern men, neither external nor internal controls on government would be necessary. In framing a government which is to be administered by men over men, the great difficulty lies in this: you must first enable the government to control the governed; and in the next place oblige it to control itself. A dependence on the people is, no doubt, the primary control on the government; but experience has taught mankind the necessity of auxiliary precautions." It is impossible to document every instance of political corruption in American history—many were small cases, many were local, and some were recorded by contemporary historians but soon forgotten and have faded from public view. I have done my best to unearth as many of these scandals as possible, but, alas, all errors of fact and spelling are mine and mine alone.

I would like to thank the following people and institutions, without whose collections and valuable assistance this work would have remained an idea and not the completed form that it has become: The Library of Congress, and all of the people who aided me during several trips there while I researched and wrote this work; The British Library in London, where I was able to copy many rare volumes dealing with British and American political corruption; Roger Addison in the Legislative Resource Center, Office of the Clerk of the House of Representatives, for his assistance in finding information on Representative "Bud" Shuster of Pennsylvania; The folks at the Oklahoma Department of Libraries, Archives and Records Division, for allowing me access to the Henry S. Johnston Papers, including the record of his impeachment; and the many others who assisted me with information, with photocopies, and with the guiding hand that any author tackling such a diverse and complicated subject always needs.

References: Burrows, Edwin G., "Corruption in Government" in *Encyclopedia of American Political History,* 3 vols. Jack P. Greene, ed. (New York: Charles Scribner's Sons, 1984), I:417; Douglas, Paul H., quoted in *Ethical Standards in Government,* U.S. Senate, Committee on Labor and Public Welfare, *Report of the Special Subcommittee on the Establishment of a Commission on Ethics in Government,* 82d Cong., 1st Sess. (1951), 44; Powell, Norman John, "Corruption, Political" in *Dictionary of American Biography,* 7 vols. (New York: Charles Scribner's Sons, 1976–1978), II:231.

POLITICAL CORRUPTION IN AMERICA

An Encyclopedia of Scandals, Power, and Greed

A

ABSCAM

Major political scandal of the 1970s, involving charges of bribe taking that drove several congressmen and a U.S. senator to resign from office. It all began with an investigation into allegations that organized crime figures were selling stolen securities and art objects. The investigation was directed by Neil J. Welch, head of the Federal Bureau of Investigation (FBI) office in New York, and Thomas P. Puccio, head of the Department of Justice's New York eastern district organized crime task force, and cleared with the approval of Attorney General Benjamin Civiletti.

The operation grew when agents of the FBI disguised themselves as Arab sheikhs and offered bribes to numerous congressmen and senators in exchange for allegedly getting the sheikhs easy entry into the United States to purchase casinos. Setting themselves up under the phony corporation name of "Abdul Enterprises, Ltd.," the FBI agents asked to see the congressmen and senators from Pennsylvania, New Jersey, and Florida, where such casinos would be built and operated. Representative Raymond Lederer (D-PA) became interested in helping the "sheikhs" and volunteered his services in exchange for a hefty bribe. All of those ensnared were Democrats save for one, Representative Richard Kelly (R-FL). All were congressmen save one, Senator Harrison Williams (D-NJ).

All of the men implicated were rising stars or major figures in their respective parties. Michael Myers (D-PA) was in his second term when he became involved in ABSCAM. Born in Philadelphia, he had served in the Pennsylvania state House of Representatives before going to the U.S. House in November 1976 to fill a vacancy caused by the death of Representative William A. Barrett. John M. Murphy (D-NY) had served with honor as an intelligence officer in Korea during the Korean War, winning the Distinguished Service Cross and Bronze Star with V and Oak Leaf Cluster, after which he was in private business before being elected to the U.S. House of Representatives in 1962. Representative John W. Jenrette Jr. (D-SC) had been a city attorney and judge in North Myrtle Beach, South Carolina, and was a member for many years of the South Carolina state House of Representatives. Raymond Lederer had been a probation officer in the Philadelphia Probation Department and member of the Pennsylvania state House of Representatives before his election to the U.S. House of Representatives in 1976. Frank Thompson Jr. (D-NJ) was a decorated war hero during World War II and was a member of the New Jersey state assembly before his election to the U.S. House of Representatives in 1954—among the ABSCAM members, he was the longest serving. Richard Kelly, the sole Republican implicated in the scandal, had served as the senior assistant U.S. attorney for the southern district of Florida (1956–1959) and as a circuit judge for the sixth judicial circuit of Florida (1960–1974) prior to his

Representative Michael Myers speaks to reporters at the Capitol after he was expelled from Congress by fellow house members for taking a bribe in the FBI ABSCAM case. (Bettmann/Corbis)

election to the U.S. House of Representatives in 1974. Harrison Williams, the only U.S. senator involved, had served in World War II in the U.S. Naval Reserve, and had been a successful attorney in New Hampshire and New Jersey before he was elected to the U.S. House of Representatives in 1952 to fill a vacancy caused by the resignation of Representative Clifford Case. In 1958 Williams was elected to the first of four terms in the U.S. Senate.

The "scam" began in 1978, when the FBI established a front. Using a New York contractor, Richard Muffaletto, who was given $6 million to create a phony business, the Olympic Construction Company, it was alleged that phony sheikhs from the Middle East were trying to gain asylum in the United States and at the same time gain a business foothold in the country. One phony sheikh, convicted con man Mel Weinberg, approached Murphy, chairman of the House Merchant Marine and Fisheries Committee, to allow for a merger between the company owned by the "sheikh" and the Puerto Rican Maritime Authority. At a meeting held between the "sheikh" and Murphy at the Hilton Inn at Kennedy International Airport in

New York, cameras videotaped Murphy agreeing to accept payoffs for himself and others of more than $70 million, in exchange for Murphy's support for the merger. Myers was videotaped accepting a bribe in exchange for his introduction in the House of a bill or intervention with the Department of State to allow for the emigration of the phony sheikhs. Lederer was taped taking a paper bag with $50,000 in it (Myers asked for his in an envelope), while Kelly, in one of the more amusing moments of the scandal, asked the "sheikhs" if the money he had shoved inside his suit jacket left noticeable "bulges."

The scam lasted for two years, until the story broke on 2 February 1980. On that day, all seven legislators were indicted on charges of bribery. Other officials, including Mayor Angelo Errichetti of Camden, New Jersey; Harry P. Jannotti, a former councilman in Philadelphia; and George Katz, a businessman and Democratic Party fund-raiser, were also indicted. Murphy told a reporter in denying he had done anything wrong, "I didn't take any actions on behalf of anyone. I merely met with some people who portrayed themselves in a certain light." He called the allegations "lies, damn lies." Frank Thompson used $24,000 of his campaign funds in his own defense, a practice that was legal at the time but which raised serious ethical issues. Jenrette, videotaped accepting a $50,000 bribe from businessman—and FBI informant—John Stowe, said that he merely got a $10,000 loan from Stowe. Another congressman, John P. Murtha (D-PA), offered to push for the legislation, but refused the money, and thus was never charged. Senator Larry Pressler (R-SD) charged out of the room when the money was brought up, and he was later hailed as a hero. Pressler was puzzled at the response: "I turned down an illegal contribution," he said. "Where have we come to if that's considered heroic?"

Despite charges that the sting constituted illegal entrapment—that these officials would never have been involved in corruption had the FBI not offered them bribes—the men went on trial, starting with Myers. In August 1980 he was convicted on all charges, and immediately the U.S. House of Representatives set about having him expelled from that body. On 2 October 1980, Myers was expelled by a vote of 376–30, with a two-thirds vote needed for expulsion. Representatives Jenrette and Thompson abstained in the vote. Myers thus became the first sitting member of the U.S. House of Representatives to be expelled since the Civil War. Myers was not the first to either leave or be forced to leave. After their convictions in court, Jenrette, Murphy, and Thompson all lost their reelection attempts. Kelly was not renominated by the Republicans in 1980 (his conviction was overturned in 1982, but he was not reelected to his old seat), and Lederer resigned his seat on 29 April 1981. Williams was threatened with expulsion from the Senate, and on 11 March 1982, he tearfully resigned his seat.

ABSCAM brought down more members of Congress than any other scandal. Congress established two select committees in 1982 to investigate the allegations of entrapment, but in the end found no wrongdoing by the FBI. ABSCAM remains the quintessential kickback scandal, one to which all others are compared.

See also Myers, Michael Joseph; Williams, Harrison Arlington, Jr.

References: "ABSCAM," in George C. Kohn, *Encyclopedia of American Scandal: From ABSCAM to the Zenger Case* (New York: Facts on File, 1989), 1–2; *Congressional Ethics* (Washington, DC: Congressional Quarterly, 1980), 1–9; *Final Report of the Senate Select Committee to Study Undercover Activities of Components of the Department of Justice,* Senate Report 682, 97th Congress, 2nd Session (1982); Garment, Suzanne, *Scandal: The Crisis of Mistrust in American Politics* (New York: Times Books, 1991), 225; *In the Matter of Representative John W. Jenrette, Jr.,* House Report No. 96–1537, 96th Congress, 2nd Session (1980), 10; *In the Matter of Representative Raymond F. Lederer,* House Report No. 97–110, 97th Congress, 1st Session, (1981), 16; *Law Enforcement Undercover Activities: Hearings Before the Senate Select Committee to Study Law Enforcement Undercover Activities of Components of the Department of Justice,* 97th Congress, 2nd Session (1982); U.S. Congress, House, Committee on Standards of Official Conduct, *In the Matter of Representative Michael J. Myers,* House Report No. 96–1387, 96th Congress, 2nd Session (1980), 5; U.S. Congress, House, Committee on Standards of Official Conduct, *In the Matter of Representative Michael J. Myers: Report of Committee on Standards of Official Conduct (to accompany H. Res. 794)* (Washington, DC: Government Printing Office, 1980).

Adams, Llewelyn Sherman (1899–1986)

Governor of New Hampshire (1949–1953), chief of staff to President Dwight D. Eisenhower (1953–1958), implicated in the famed "Vicuna Coat" scandal of 1958, which forced him from office. Adams was born at the home of his maternal grandparents in East Dover, Vermont, on 8 January 1899, the son of Clyde Adams, a grocer in the village of East Dover, and Winnie (née Sherman) Adams. As an infant he moved with his parents to Providence, Rhode Island, where he attended public schools. Clyde Adams left the family home when his son was young, and Llewelyn was primarily raised by his mother and maternal uncle, Edwin Sherman. He went to Dartmouth College and during World War I entered service in the United States Marine Corps. He returned to Dartmouth and earned his degree in 1920. Adams considered entering medical school and becoming a surgeon, but turned down that option and instead entered private business, working for a series of lumber companies in the village of Healdville, Vermont, in 1921 and 1922 and then in the paper and lumber business in Lincoln, New Hampshire, from 1922 until he entered national politics in 1944. He was also involved in banking concerns.

In 1940 Adams was elected to the New Hampshire state House of Representatives, where he served until 1944. In the 1943 and 1944 sessions, he served as Speaker of the House. According to biographer Kenneth Pomeroy, "[He] helped frame and enact New Hampshire timber tax law, aided in formation of Northeast Forest Fire Compact, and improved forest policy in New Hampshire." Adams, a Republican, rose up the ranks of his party, serving as chairman of the Grafton County Republican Committee (1942–1944) and as a delegate to the party's national conventions in 1944 and 1952. In 1944 Adams was elected to a seat in the U.S. House of Representatives, defeating Democrat Harry Carlson to represent the New Hampshire 2nd District. He declined to run for a second term in 1946, instead unsuccessfully seeking the Republican nomination for governor of New Hampshire against incumbent Charles M. Dale, who was ultimately reelected. Out of office, Adams went to work as a representative of the American Pulpwood Industry in New York City for two years.

Governor Dale was ineligible to run in 1948 after serving for two two-year terms, so Adams ran for his party's gubernatorial nomination and was successful; he went on to defeat Democrat Herbert W. Hill and, in 1950, Democrat Robert P. Bingham, to serve two terms as governor. Historians Robert Sobel and John Raimo wrote, "Governor Adams urged economy on both a public and a personal basis; he also urged appropriations for state aid to the aged, and requested legislation to make New Hampshire citizens eligible for Federal Old Age and Survivors Insurance." Adams also served as chairman of the New England Governors' Conference (1951–1952).

During the 1952 presidential campaign, Adams lent his support to General Dwight D. Eisenhower, the Republican presidential nominee, and was considered a leading candidate for U.S. ambassador to Canada or even secretary of labor. When Eisenhower offered the assistant to the president position (now called the chief of staff) to campaign strategist and New York attorney Herbert Brownell, the New Yorker demurred and asked for the attorney general position. Senator Henry Cabot Lodge of Massachusetts was also considered for chief of staff, but when Eisenhower named him as U.S. ambassador to the United Nations, the new president turned to Adams to fill the

most important position in the White House. In his memoirs, Adams later wrote that Eisenhower wanted him to handle all White House business without much nonsense and to "keep as much work of secondary importance as possible off [your] desk." During his more than five years as chief of staff, Adams defined the modern power of that position, taking control of all aspects of the presidential office. He was an important voice in the advocacy of forest conservation, serving as a speaker to the Fourth American Forest Congress in 1953, and at the Southern Forest Fire Prevention Conference in 1956. Adams maintained control over the White House's daily schedule, deciding who could and who could not meet the president. When Eisenhower had a heart attack in 1955, Adams's influence grew, and he became in effect the president's chief aide, more than Vice President Richard M. Nixon. Following the 1956 election, Adams was retained in his position.

What got Adams in trouble was a policy he had been following for some time, even when he was governor of New Hampshire. To supplement his salary, he accepted gifts and other emoluments from rich friends. This was not uncommon in the days before ethics rules were strictly enforced. A congressional investigation by Representative Oren Harris of Arkansas turned up the fact that Adams had assisted two wealthy New England businessmen—Bernard Goldfine and John Fox—with federal regulators after the two men had given Adams gifts and money. When Fox went bankrupt, he made a deal with the Internal Revenue Service to give damning testimony against both Goldfine and Adams. Extensive investigating found that Goldfine did not give money to any one party—he gave to those who could help him advance his business causes. He had also given money to numerous senators, congressmen, mayors, and governors—among them Senator Henry Styles Bridges of New Hampshire—and Adams. Adams enjoyed being with Goldfine. In his memoirs, years after this relationship cost him his seat of power, Adams explained, "Goldfine was a man with a lot of fun in him and we enjoyed his company." Goldfine had given gifts and money to Adams, contributing to his 1948 and 1950 gubernatorial campaigns. When Adams went to Washington, Goldfine gave him more gifts—including a camel's hair coat (which later was mislabeled in the press as a vicuna coat, giving a name to the entire affair). When Adams traveled, Goldfine picked up the hotel bills. When Goldfine needed help with his business, he called Adams, who intervened with Federal Trade Commissioner Edward F. Howrey to allow Goldfine to import certain woolen items into the United States. In 1956, when the controversy arose again, Adams arranged for Howrey to meet Goldfine. When U.S. House investigator Bernard Schwartz came across memos dealing with Adams's intervention, he leaked them to the *New York Times* and was fired. Among the memos was one detailing how Adams had gotten an aide to call the Securities and Exchange Commission (SEC) to look into an SEC investigation regarding alleged financial report irregularities by Goldfine.

The walls closed in on Adams. When Clark Mollenhoff, Washington correspondent for the *Des Moines Register,* asked Eisenhower at a press conference in April 1958 about the calls Adams had made, the president refused to answer. Fox then testified before a grand jury and specified that Goldfine had given Adams large sums of money and many gifts and had paid his hotel bills in many cities. Facing a potential charge of influence peddling, Adams went before a special House oversight committee on 17 June 1958. He denied any improprieties, saying, "I never permitted any personal relationship to affect in any way any actions of mine in matters relating to the conduct of my office." He denied that he had done anything for Goldfine and also rejected the claim that he intervened with FTC Chairman Howrey, claiming, "The only thing I ever asked Mr. Howrey for was information." He admitted accepting gifts and money from Goldfine, but claimed that these were based on friendship and were not an attempt to get Adams to intervene with state or federal agencies. However, Representative John Moss (D-CA) got Adams to admit that his call to the SEC was not like a regular call from the chief of staff.

The situation for Adams, and by extension Eisenhower, went from bad to worse. Columnist Drew Pearson presented evidence that Goldfine had given money to the president to help refurbish his Gettysburg, Pennsylvania, home. Vice President Nixon, speaking with party leaders, intimated that Adams needed to resign for the good of the party and the administration. Eisenhower agreed and delegated Nixon to ask for Adams's resignation or fire him. Adams might well have been allowed to stay on but for the upcoming midterm elections. In August, at a meeting of the Republican National Committee, party chairman Meade Alcorn was forced to quell a rebellion by party regulars over Adams. Returning to Washington, Alcorn sat down with Adams and told him he must go for the good of the party and the administration. Adams reluctantly agreed and in a nationally televised speech on 22 September 1958, he resigned, steadfastly denying that he had done anything wrong.

Destroyed politically by the Goldfine scandal, Adams returned to New Hampshire, where he wrote and lectured, eventually penning his memoirs. His interest in conservation continued: in 1986, he wrote *The Weeks Act: A 75th Anniversary Appraisal.* He established a ski resort in 1966 and became president and chairman of the board of the Loon Mountain Corporation.

Adams died at his home in Hanover, New Hampshire, on 27 October 1986 at the age of eighty-seven. With his passing, the famed "vicuna coat" scandal once more became front-page news to a new generation.

References: "Adams, Llewelyn Sherman," in Robert Sobel and John Raimo, eds., *Biographical Directory of the Governors of the United States, 1789–1978,* 4 vols. (Westport, CT: Meckler Books, 1978), III:998–999; Adams, Sherman, *Firsthand Report: The Story of the Eisenhower Administration* (New York: Harper, 1961); Pomeroy, Kenneth B., "Adams, Sherman," in Richard H. Stroud, ed., *National Leaders of American Conservation* (Washington, DC: Smithsonian Institution Press, 1985), 24–25.

Addonizio, Hugh Joseph (1914–1981)

United States Representative from New Jersey (1949–1962), mayor of Newark, New Jersey (1962–1970), convicted of charges of taking kickbacks from Mafia figures who were then allowed to control the city. Addonizio was born in Newark, New Jersey, on 31 January 1914. He attended the public schools of that city before graduating from Fordham University in New York in 1939. He then went to work for the A & C Clothing company in Newark, rising to become vice president of the concern by 1946. In 1941, when the United States entered World War II, he volunteered for service in

Hugh Joseph Addonizio, mayor of Newark, NJ (1962–1970). In 1970, Addonizio was convicted of taking kickbacks from Mafia figures. (Library of Congress)

the U.S. Army with the rank of private. He attended Officers Candidate School at Fort Benning, Georgia, and after being commissioned a second lieutenant was assigned to the Sixtieth Infantry of the Ninth Division of the U.S. Army. He saw action in the European theater of operations before he was discharged with the rank of captain in February 1946. A Democrat, Addonizio was elected to a seat in the U.S. House of Representatives, serving in the Eighty-first through the Eighty-seventh Congresses. He resigned his seat on 30 June 1962 to run for mayor of Newark. He defeated the incumbent, Leo Carlin, who had served since 1953, and was reelected to a second term in 1966.

During the early 1960s, the FBI planted wires in the offices of many of New Jersey's top crime figures in an effort to break the hold of the Mafia on that state. During one of the recorded conversations, known Mafia figure Angelo "Gyp" De-Carlo was heard telling an associate, Joseph De Benedictis, "Hughie [a nickname for Addonizio] helped us all along. He gave us the city." This opened the investigation into Addonizio. The FBI soon discovered that in exchange for kickbacks

from the mob, Addonizio had allowed them to virtually run the city unchallenged. The power of the mob's grip on the city was evident when, in 1966, one of Addonizio's challengers was warned by DeCarlo that he would come to harm if he pushed his candidacy.

In 1970 Addonizio and a dozen other state and public officials, including Thomas J. Whelen, mayor of Jersey City; John R. Armellino, mayor of West New York City, New Jersey; and New Jersey Democratic political boss John J. Kenny, were indicted by a federal grand jury. The indictment alleged that Addonizio, as mayor of the nation's thirteenth largest city, had shared $1.5 million in payoffs from the Mafia with the other accused men. Federal prosecutor Frederick B. Lacey said, "The plunder was unmatched by anything in my experience." At the time, Addonizio was looking at serving a third term. However, in the 1970 elections Addonizio was opposed by Democrat Kenneth A. Gibson, a black reformer who promised to clean up city hall. Gibson's election victory must be noted with some irony, as Gibson himself was indicted in 2000 on charges of stealing thousands of dollars from the New Jersey school district. He pled guilty in 2002 and was given five years probation.

On 22 September 1970, Addonizio was convicted, and Judge George H. Barlow sentenced him to ten years in prison and fined him $25,000. During sentencing, Judge Barlow said of Addonizio:

> Weighed against these virtues [of Addonizio's public service] . . . is his conviction by a jury in this court of crimes of monumental proportion, the enormity of which can scarcely be exaggerated and the commission of which create the gravest implications for our form of government . . .
>
> Mr. Addonizio, and the other defendants here, have been convicted of one count of conspiring to extort and 63 substantive counts of extorting hundreds of thousands of dollars from persons doing business with the City of Newark. An intricate conspiracy of this magnitude, I suggest to you, Mr. Hellring [Addonizio's attorney], could have never succeeded without the then-Mayor Addonizio's approval and participation . . .
>
> These were no ordinary criminal acts . . . These crimes for which Mr. Addonizio and the other defendants have been convicted represent a pattern of continuous, highly organized, systematic criminal

extortion over a period of many years, claiming many victims and touching many more lives …

Instances of corruption on the part of elected and appointed governmental officials are certainly not novel to the law, but the corruption disclosed here, it seems to the Court, is compounded by the frightening alliance of criminal elements and public officials, and it is this very kind of totally destructive conspiracy that was conceived, organized and executed by these defendants …

It is impossible to estimate the impact upon— and the cost of—these criminal acts to the decent citizens of Newark, and, indeed, to the citizens of the State of New Jersey, in terms of their frustration, despair and disillusionment.

In 1972 the United States Supreme Court refused to hear Addonizio's appeal (405 U.S. 936). In 1973 the U.S. Parole Commission released new guidelines as to sentencing and ordered that Addonizio be held until the end of his ten-year sentence. The district judge who heard Addonizio's appeal ruled that the Parole Commission's action was illegal and in 1975 reduced Addonizio's sentence to time served. The United States appealed the decision, which was affirmed by a court of appeals, and in 1978 the U.S. Supreme Court granted certiorari (the right to hear the case) on this single issue only. Argued on 27 March 1979, the case was decided on 4 June of that same year. Justice John Paul Stevens held for a unanimous court (Justices William Brennan and Lewis Powell did not participate) that Addonizio's sentence could not be challenged by a district judge. Justice Stevens wrote:

The import of this statutory scheme is clear: the judge has no enforceable expectations with respect to the actual release of a sentenced defendant short of his statutory term. The judge may well have expectations as to when release is likely. But the actual decision is not his to make, either at the time of sentencing or later if his expectations are not met. To require the Parole Commission to act in accordance with judicial expectations, and to use collateral attack as a mechanism for ensuring that these expectations are carried out, would substantially undermine the congressional decision to entrust release determinations to the Commission and not the courts.

Addonizio was released from prison soon after his case was reversed by the U.S. Supreme Court.

He lived in Tinton Falls, New Jersey, until he died in Red Bank, New Jersey, on 2 February 1981, at the age of sixty-seven. He was buried in Gate of Heaven Cemetery in Hanover, New Jersey.

References: *Addonizio v. United States,* 405 U.S. 936 (1972); Anyon, Jean, *Ghetto Schooling: A Political Economy of Urban Educational Reform* (New York: Teachers College Press, 1997), 109; Nash, Jay Robert. *Encyclopedia of World Crime: Criminal Justice, Criminology, and Law Enforcement,* 4 vols. (Wilmette, IL: CrimeBooks, Inc., 1989), I:30–31; *United States v. Addonizio,* 442 U.S. 178 (1979).

Agnew, Spiro Theodore (1918–1996)

Governor of Maryland (1967–1969), vice president of the United States (1969–1973), the second vice president to resign from office and the first because of criminal charges leveled against him. Agnew was born in Baltimore, Maryland, on 9 November 1918, the son of Theodore Agnew, a Greek-born restaurateur who shortened his name from Anagnostopoulos, and Margaret (née Akers) Agnew. Called "Ted" by his friends, Spiro Agnew attended the schools of Baltimore before he went to Johns Hopkins University and studied the law at the University of Baltimore Law School, from which he graduated from in 1947. During World War II, he served in the U.S. Army in France and was decorated with the Bronze Star for heroism. After he graduated from law school, Agnew was admitted to the Maryland bar and opened a practice in Baltimore.

Agnew entered the political realm in 1957 when he won a seat on the Baltimore County Zoning Board. When the county council for Baltimore, dominated by Democrats, apportioned his seat out of existence, he ran instead for county executive and was elected in 1962. He served in this office for four years. In 1966, his political star rising, Agnew was nominated by the Republicans for governor. He defeated Democrat George P. Mahoney to become the governor of Maryland. Agnew's election as governor marked a turn in Maryland politics. Previously the cities had dominated the political agenda, but now the suburban areas, where Agnew had won a majority of his votes and which controlled both houses of the Maryland General Assembly, dominated. Agnew reorganized state government and revised the state tax code. He became the first "law and order" official, speaking

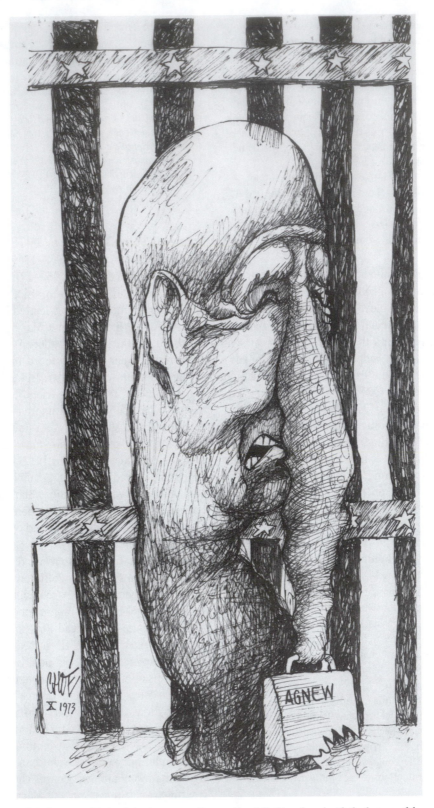

Political cartoon showing Spiro Agnew standing outside a jail cell, endowed with the features of the Republican elephant. Agnew was the second vice president to resign from office and the first to resign because of criminal charges leveled against him. (Library of Congress)

out against protests by students and others against the Vietnam War. Nevertheless, he was considered a moderate politically, standing for strong laws against pollution and signing the first open-housing law south of the Mason-Dixon Line.

As the 1968 election approached, Agnew threw his support behind New York Governor Nelson A. Rockefeller for the Republican presidential nomination. However, when it appeared that former Vice President Richard M. Nixon would receive the party nod, Agnew backed the Californian. In a stunning political move, Nixon chose Agnew as his running mate. Little known outside of Maryland, Agnew took to the stump and campaigned across the nation and was rewarded for his efforts when Nixon won a close victory over Vice President Hubert Humphrey. In eight short years, Agnew went from the Baltimore County Zoning Board to become the thirty-ninth vice president of the United States.

During his first four years in office, Agnew earned a reputation as the administration's "hatchet man," criticizing the press (as "nattering nabobs of negativism") and Vietnam War protestors ("hopeless, hysterical hypochondriacs of history"). In 1972, when Nixon and Agnew were renominated for a second term, *Time* magazine wrote:

> For much of Nixon's first term, the vice president's principal duty seemed to be to go after the Administration's enemies and critics with a spiked mace. In alliterative swings he denounced Democrats, liberals, the Eastern Establishment, even dissident members of his own party, with an assiduousness and acidity that would hardly have been becoming of the President. There were liberal Republicans who though it unbecoming even in a vice president, and who saw in Agnew few qualities that would make him a suitable President of the U.S., should the need arise. They urged Nixon to choose a new running mate for his second term. But the President, secure in the polls and mindful of Agnew's loyal and noisy constituency on the right, decided not to break up a winning combination.

The ticket was reelected in a landslide, and to many it appeared that in 1976 Agnew would be the Republican nominee for president.

Even as he was being reelected, however, Agnew was under investigation by the FBI and a grand jury in Baltimore. Allegations had arisen that Agnew, from his time as county executive through his time as governor and continuing even as he sat a heartbeat away from the presidency, was taking kickbacks from milk producers and others in Maryland. U.S. Attorney George Beall headed up the investigation and ran the grand jury. In 1999 the FBI files on Agnew were released pursuant to a Freedom of Information Act request. One contractor told the grand jury investigating the case, "I just paid off the vice president of the United States," and described how he had given Agnew $10,000 in cash in the White House basement. One person who paid Agnew a kickback of $1,500 cash was allowed to fly on board the vice president's jet to watch an Apollo moon launch. One FBI document reads, "The gist of this background was that [missing information] prior to 1966, when Agnew was the County Executive (Mayor) of Baltimore, [missing information] began making payments to [missing information] of kickbacks from three to five percent of the total of the contracts he received."

Beall traced the corruption to Agnew and called four men who had worked for him before the grand jury, among them Jerome Wolff, a former staffer for Agnew who then headed the Maryland Highway Administration, and Lester Matz, head of an engineering firm. Matz told Beall, "You probably don't want to know about this, but I've been paying off the vice president of the United States." Beall was ready to indict Agnew, when *The Wall Street Journal* broke the story in August 1973. Agnew called Attorney General Elliot Richardson, demanding that leaks of such an investigation be stopped. Behind the scenes, Agnew knew he was finished and negotiated a deal in which he would resign his office and plead no contest to falsifying his tax returns and not reflecting the bribes. On 10 October 1973, less than nine months after he was inaugurated for his second term as vice president, Agnew resigned. That same day, in district court in Baltimore, he pled *nolo contendere* to the single charge and admitted that he had been taking bribes for many years. Agnew was fined $10,000 and sentenced to three years' probation.

In his final years, Agnew became a business consultant. He stayed out of the public eye, except for penning his memoirs, *Go Quietly . . . or Else* (1980). He entered a hospital in September 1996 for heart surgery and died on 17 September at the age of seventy-seven. After his death, it was discovered that he had been suffering from incurable leukemia. His remains were cremated, and the ashes were interred in Dulaney Valley Memorial Gardens in Timonium, Maryland.

It is a common fallacy that Agnew was the first vice president to resign or to face criminal charges—those "honors" go to Aaron Burr, who was charged with treason (and acquitted), and to John C. Calhoun, who resigned on 28 December 1832 to fill a vacancy in the U.S. Senate. Agnew is the first vice president to resign because of charges relating to corruption.

References: Agnew, Spiro T., *Go Quietly . . . Or Else* (New York: Morrow, 1980); Albright, Joseph, *What Makes Spiro Run: The Life and Times of Spiro Agnew* (New York: Dodd, Mead, 1972); Cohen, Richard M., and Jules Witcover, *A Heartbeat Away: The Investigation and Resignation of Vice President Spiro T. Agnew* (New York: Viking Press, 1974); "The Coronation of King Richard," *Time,* 28 August 1972, 17; Hill, Janellen, *Spiro T. Agnew: Tactics of Self-Defense, August 1 to October 15, 1974* (Master's thesis, Arizona State University, 1974); Lucas, Jim Griffing, *Agnew: Profile in Conflict* (New York: Award Books, 1970); Marsh, Robert, *Agnew: The Unexamined Man—A Political Profile* (New York: M. Evans, 1971); "Spiro Agnew: Dishonest Vice President Resigns," in George C. Kohn, *Encyclopedia of American Scandal: From ABSCAM to the Zenger Case* (New York: Facts on File, 1989), 3–4; Weil, Martin, "Former Vice President Spiro T. Agnew Dies at 77," *Washington Post,* 18 September 1996, A1.

Alexander, Lamar

See Blanton, Leonard Ray

Ames, Adelbert (1835–1933)

United States senator from Mississippi (1870–1873) and governor of that state (1868–1870, 1874–1876), impeached and forced to resign because of race riots and corruption of the carpetbag government in the state. Ames was born in Rockland, Maine, on 31 October 1835, the son of Jesse Ames, a mill owner and former sailor, and Martha (née Tolman) Ames. His granddaughter, Blanche Ames, wrote in 1964, "His people were New Englanders descended from the early Pilgrims and Puritans, of English and Scottish descent. They were venturesome people, and many had fought in the Colonial and Revolutionary wars. Some were farmers and teachers and some were seafaring men like Adelbert's father."

Adelbert Ames attended private schools at Farmington and Bucksport near his Maine home and thereafter went to the U.S. Military Academy at West Point, from which he graduated in 1861. When the Civil War exploded in April 1861, Ames volunteered for service, starting with the rank of second lieutenant and rising to the rank of brevet-major general of volunteers in 1866 for bravery in battle. He saw tremendous action and was awarded the congressional Medal of Honor for gallantry at the Battle of Bull Run in 1861. With the end of the war, Ames was assigned as a lieutenant colonel of the Twenty-fifth Infantry during the immediate reconstruction of Mississippi.

General Ulysses S. Grant, as military commander in charge of the region, appointed Ames as the military governor of Mississippi under the Reconstruction Acts passed by Congress. On 15 June 1868, Ames, a Republican, took over from Governor Benjamin Humphreys, a Democrat. In total control of the state, Ames resubmitted to the people of the state a new state constitution that allowed for black suffrage that had been defeated previously. This time, the constitution was overwhelmingly accepted, despite the defeat of a provision barring any person who had supported the Confederacy from holding elective office. In 1870, after just two years as governor, Ames was elected by the overwhelmingly Republican legislature to a seat in the United States Senate. These seats opened up to the former Confederate states when they accepted the Thirteenth and Fourteenth Amendments to the Constitution and were readmitted to the Union. Ames served in the Senate from 23 February 1873 until 10 January 1874. During this short tenure, he served as the chairman of the Committee on Enrolled Bills.

In the 1873 election for governor of Mississippi, Ames's name was advanced, despite the fact that he had already served as governor and was now a U.S. senator in Washington. Despite this, he defeated another Republican, James Lusk Alcorn, and resigned his Senate seat on 10 January 1874 to become governor a second time. It was during this second tenure as governor that Ames was impeached. It is not clear from the history books just why. Ames had been fighting the power of the Ku Klux Klan in the state, but for the first time Alcorn (who had switched to the Democratic Party) and other whites did not assist Ames in battling the Klan. Ames even got mixed signals from Washington and the administration of President Ulysses S. Grant, under whom Ames had once served. Blacks were being murdered, but when Democrats called for a truce until after the 1875 elections for the state legislature, Ames backed down from calling for federal troops to quell the violence. Then, only weeks before the election, the violence began anew, and Ames was powerless to stop it. White Democrats won the elections, having chased or frightened black Republicans away from the polls.

Having endured this outrage, Ames now faced another. Historian Richard N. Current wrote:

> After a vacation in the North, Ames returned to Jackson with his wife and children, to face the new, hostile Democratic legislature in January 1876. "At night in the town here," [Ames' wife Blanche] wrote home, "the crack of the pistol or gun is as frequent as the barking of dogs," and some shots were fired at the [governor's] mansion itself. Undeterred by this, Ames in his first message to the new legislature denounced it as an illegal body, a product of force and fraud. Promptly the legislature responded with the first steps toward an impeachment of the governor. The impeachers had no difficulty in trumping up charges against him—that he absented himself from the state, pardoned criminals, degraded the judiciary, and the like. There was no charge of corruption. "Nothing is charged beyond political sins," Ames explained to a New York friend; "of course, with them that is a sin which to Republicans is of the highest virtue. Their object is to restore the Confederacy and reduce the colored people to a state of serfdom. I am in their way, consequently they impeach me."

Ames struck a deal with the Democrats: he would resign if the impeachment was dropped. In the end, the Democrats broke their promise—Ames did resign, but the Democrats published the charges and hailed their getting rid of the governor. Ames resigned on 29 March 1876 and moved to New York City. Lieutenant Governor A. K. Davis, an Ames ally, was also forced to resign. With the resignation of both men, State Senator John Marshall Stone (1830–1900), a Democrat, became governor.

Ames eventually moved to Lowell, Massachusetts, where he was engaged in the flour mill busi-

ness, with the mills in Minnesota. When the Spanish-American War broke out in 1898, he was recalled to military duty and served as brigadier general of volunteers until 1899. He then retired to Lowell. Ames died at his winter home in Ormond, Florida, on 12 April 1933, at age ninety-seven. He is one of only nineteen state governors in American history to have been impeached.

References: "Ames, Adelbert," in Robert Sobel and John Raimo, eds., *Biographical Directory of the Governors of the United States, 1789–1978*, 4 vols. (Westport, CT: Meckler Books, 1978), III:816–817; Ames, Blanche Ames, *Adelbert Ames, 1835–1933: General, Senator, Governor* (New York: Argosy-Antiquarian, 1964), 1; Benson, Harry King, "The Public Career of Adelbert Ames, 1861–1876" (Ph.D. dissertation, University of Virginia, 1975); Buice, S. David, "The Military Career of Adelbert Ames," *Southern Quarterly*, 2 (April 1964), 236–246; "The Carpetbagger as Man of Conscience: Adelbert Ames," in Richard N. Current, *Three Carpetbag Governors* (Baton Rouge: Louisiana State University Press, 1967), 91–92; Lord, Stuart B., "Adelbert Ames, Soldier Politician: A Reevaluation," *Maine Historical Society Quarterly*, 13 (Fall 1973), 81–97; *The Testimony in the Impeachment of Adelbert Ames, as Governor of Mississippi* (Jackson: Power & Barksdale, 1877).

Ames, Oakes (1804–1873)

Congressman from Massachusetts (1863–1873), a leading figure in the Crédit Mobilier scandal that disgraced the Grant administration and brought down Vice President Schuyler Colfax. Born in Easton, Massachusetts, on 10 January 1804, Oakes was the eldest son of Oliver Ames Sr. and Susanna (née Angier) Ames. The Ames family could trace their ancestry back to one William Ames, who left Bruton, England, in 1635 to flee religious persecution, arriving in Plymouth in the Massachusetts Bay Colony. Four Mayflower pilgrims are among Ames's ancestors, including John Alden. Oliver Ames Sr. founded the Oliver Ames and Sons Shovel Works in North Easton, turning it over to his sons Oliver Jr. and Oakes in 1844. Oakes, the subject of this biography, attended local public schools and the Dighton (Massachusetts) Academy. He worked in his father's company, taking control of the concern with his brother in 1844. In 1860 Oakes Ames entered the political realm when he was elected as a member of the executive council of Massachusetts.

Two years later, Ames was elected as a Republican to a seat in the U.S. House of Representatives,

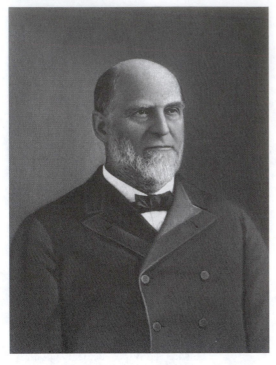

Oakes Ames (1804–1873), American financier and politician involved in the Crédit Mobilier scandal. (Bettmann/Corbis)

serving in the Thirty-eighth through Forty-second Congresses (4 March 1863–3 March 1873). As a member of the House Railroad Committee, he immediately became a major lobbyist for the railroad concerns that sought to construct a transcontinental railroad. Oakes's brother Oliver became the president of the Union Pacific Railroad, and through his influence in Congress Ames was able to get appropriations directed to the Union Pacific for the construction of the project. One of the major towns through which the railroad passed in Iowa was named Ames to honor Oakes's assistance in the project. To assist in the construction, Ames and other stockholders of the Union Pacific Railroad established the Crédit Mobilier of America as a shell corporation into which congressional appropriations could be sent. Thus, as head of the Crédit Mobilier, the stockholders, including Ames, were able to negotiate with Congress for money with which to pay themselves in stock options. In 1867 Ames sold contracts to seven stockholders in Crédit Mobilier to build the last 667 miles of railroad—these contracts were worth more than $7 million each.

Ames was able to conceal these deals for years, but by 1869, when the Union Pacific was reporting heavy losses amid the huge appropriations Congress had bestowed on it, he needed more to cover his tracks. He approached numerous members of Congress and offered them stock in the Crédit Mobilier at reduced prices; he wrote to his friend Henry S. McComb that he had positioned the stock "where it will produce the most good to us." With the correspondence, Ames forwarded a list of the congressmen and senators who had received shares. This correspondence and list came back to haunt Ames and his cohorts.

During the presidential campaign of 1872, McComb, incensed for some reason, released the important Crédit Mobilier correspondence to Charles A. Dana, editor of the *New York Sun* and avowed political enemy of the Grant administration. Included on the fateful list were the names of Vice President Schuyler Colfax, who was not running for reelection, and Senator Henry Wilson, who was Grant's running mate in 1872, as well as other high-ranking Republican congressmen and senators. Dana blew the whistle on the scheme. Starting with the edition of 4 September 1872, in blazing headlines, he called attention to "the King of Frauds—How the Crédit Mobilier Bought Its Way Through Congress." Ames and the others named by the *Sun* denied the entire affair. In December 1872 when Congress assembled (as was the practice during that time), Speaker of the House James G. Blaine, himself implicated, called upon Representative Samuel S. Cox of New York, who had run unsuccessfully in the 1872 election as a liberal Republican, to take the Speaker's chair and name a congressional panel to investigate the allegations. Cox named Luke Poland of Vermont to head a five-man committee to investigate. On 18 February 1873, the Poland Committee reported back to the House. It found that Ames and Representative James Brooks (D-NY) were indeed guilty and asked that both men be expelled from the House. However, some Democrats refused to go along with the recommendation, and in the end Ames and Brooks were merely censured. Ames, who had not been a candidate for reelection in 1872 because of the allegations, left Congress under this ethical cloud.

Returning to Massachusetts, Ames felt the sting of the congressional censure. On 8 May 1873, two months after he left Congress, Ames died in Easton at the age of sixty-nine and was buried in the Unity Cemetery in North Easton. Despite the ignominious manner in which he left the House, Ames is remembered more today for his work than his corruption. In 1883 the Massachusetts state legislature passed a resolution calling attention to his work and petitioned the U.S. Congress to do the same. The previous year, in 1882, the Union Pacific Railroad erected a pyramid near Laramie, Wyoming, in honor of Ames's work in the transcontinental railroad completion. Ames's son, Oliver Ames (1831–1895), served as governor of Massachusetts (1887–1890).

> **See also** Brooks, James; Crédit Mobilier Scandal
> **References:** "Ames, Oakes," in *The National Cyclopaedia of American Biography,* 57 vols. and supplements A-N, (New York: James T. White & Company, 1897–1984), II:199–200; Crawford, J. B., *The Crédit Mobilier of America—Its Origin and History, Its Work of Constructing the Union Pacific Railroad and the Relation of Members of Congress Therewith* (Boston: C. W. Calkins & Co. Publishers, 1880).

Archbald, Robert Wodrow (1848–1926)

United States district judge, implicated in a scandal in which he "took advantage of his official" position for profit, for which he was impeached by the U.S. House of Representatives and convicted by the U.S. Senate. Little is known of Archbald. He was born in Carbondale, Pennsylvania, on 10 September 1848, the son of James and Augusta (née Frothingham) Archbald. He studied the law in Scranton, Pennsylvania, in the offices of a local law firm, Hand & Post. He received his bachelor's degree from Yale in 1871, was admitted to the bar in 1873, and practiced law in Scranton. He served as a judge from 1885 to 1888, when he was named as the presiding judge of the Forty-fifth Judicial District of Pennsylvania, where he served until 1901. A Republican, Archbald was appointed as a U.S. district judge for the Middle District of Pennsylvania by President William McKinley on 29 March 1901. In 1910 President William Howard Taft named him to be a judge of the Third Circuit Court of Appeals and on 1 February 1911, additionally to the U.S. Commerce Court, which heard commercial cases.

Following allegations that Archbald had been involved in numerous acts of corruption, includ-ing influence peddling, Attorney General George W. Wickersham appointed one Wrisley Brown a special investigator to examine the allegations. Among these were accusations that Archbald, while sitting as a member of the Commerce Court, "induced" the Erie Railroad Company to sell him certain properties owned by a subsidiary corporation at a cheap price, despite the fact that the railroad had cases pending before the court on which Archbald sat; that he influenced a litigant before the Commerce Court to lease him land with large coal deposits on it; and that he purchased stock in a gold mining concern from a litigant who had business before his court, after which he ruled in the litigant's favor. Finding these allegations to be true, Brown sent his report to the attorney general, who forwarded it to Congress for consideration. On 23 April 1912, Representative (later Senator) George Norris of Nebraska introduced a resolution calling for the House Judiciary Committee to examine Brown's findings and report back to the full House. On 8 July 1912, the Judiciary Committee recommended that the full House impeach Judge Archbald and included thirteen articles of impeachment. The articles were debated and all were adopted by the House on 11 July 1912.

The Senate trial of Judge Archbald began on 16 July, just five days after the House voted. Norris was one of the House managers, along with Henry D. Clayton of Alabama, Edwin Y. Webb of North Carolina, John C. Floyd of Arkansas, John W. Davis of West Virginia, John A. Sterling of Illinois, and Paul Howland of Ohio. The managers argued that Archbald "improperly argued his influence as a judge to enter into business dealings with potential litigants before his court ... [used his influence in the] improper acceptance of gifts from litigants, [and used his influence in the] improper appointment of a jury commissioner." As in the impeachment trial of Judge Charles H. Swayne, none of the thirteen articles dealt with indictable offenses; Archbald's counsel, Alexander Simpson Jr., made a point of this detail in his arguments before the Senate. In fact, Archbald never denied the facts contained in the impeachment articles—his claim was that such conduct was part of his duties as a judge on a court hearing cases involving commerce. Norris argued that the allegations added up to a usurpation of power and "the entering and enforcement of orders beyond his jurisdiction."

On 13 January 1913, the Senate voted to convict Archbald on articles 1, 3, 4, 5, and 13, the last being a "super article" in which all of the charges were consolidated into one charge: "During his time as a district judge and as a judge assigned to the Commerce Court, Archbald wrongfully sought to obtain credit from and through persons who were interested in litigation over which he presided. He speculated for profit in the purchase and sale of various coal properties, and unlawfully used his position as judge to influence officers of various railroad companies to enter into contracts in which he had a financial interest, which such companies had litigation pending in his court." Simpson, Archbald's counsel, concluded that the message sent by the Senate in convicting Archbald was that it was "determined that a judge ought not only to be impartial, but he ought so to demean himself, both in and out of the court, that litigants will have no reason to suspect his impartiality; and that repeatedly failing in that respect constituted a 'high misdemeanor.'" Simpson also charged that many senators did not sit through the trial testimony, instead relying on the *Congressional Record*. After the guilty verdict was announced, the Senate voted to remove Judge Archbald from office. Then, by a vote of thirty-nine to thirty-five, it disqualified him from holding any office under the United States in the future. House manager Norris said that in convicting Archbald, the Senate had adopted "a code of judicial ethics for the first time in American history." Only months later, Congress abolished the Commerce Court. Justice Felix Frankfurter of the United States Supreme Court later wrote, "The impeachment of Judge Archbald justly cast no reflection against the Court as an institution nor any of its other members. Hence we find that during the final stage of the movement for [the] abolition of the Court, the Archbald impeachment does not figure in the debate. Yet the mere fact of the impeachment was a weighty, even if inarticulate, factor. For the conviction of one of the judges (because it involved the use of his influence to secure favors from carriers litigating before him, confirmed the widespread claim of railroad bias and partisanship deemed inevitable in the very nature of so specialized and concentrated a tribunal as the Commerce Court."

After being forced to leave the bench, Archbald returned to his home in Scranton. He died there on 19 August 1926, three weeks shy of his seventy-eighth birthday.

References: Biographical information on Archbald in Harold Chase, et al., comps., *Biographical Dictionary of the Federal Judiciary* (Detroit, MI: Gale Research Company, 1976), 9; Frankfurter, Felix, and James Landis, *The Business of the Supreme Court: A Study in the Federal Judicial System* (New York: Macmillan, 1928), 171; Hoogenboom, Ari, and Olive Hoogenboom, *A History of the ICC: From Panacea to Palliative* (New York: W. W. Norton, 1976), 68; "Robert Archbald: Unworthy of Public Office," in George C. Kohn, *Encyclopedia of American Scandal: From ABSCAM to the Zenger Case*" (New York: Facts on File, 1989), 12–13; Simpson, Alexander, Jr., *A Treatise on Federal Impeachments, With an Appendix Containing, Inter Alia, an Abstract of the Articles of Impeachment in all of the Federal Impeachments in this Country and in England* (Philadelphia: Law Association of Philadelphia, 1916); United States Senate, *Proceedings of the United States Senate and the House of Representatives in the Trial of Impeachment of Robert W. Archbald, Additional Circuit Judge of the United States from the Third Judicial Circuit and designated a Judge of the Commerce Court*, 3 vols. (Washington, DC: Government Printing Office, 1913.).

Archer, Stevenson (1827–1898)

United States representative from Maryland (1867–1875), Maryland state treasurer (1886–1890), convicted and sent to prison for four years for embezzling more than $132,000 in state funds. The son of Stevenson Archer Sr. (1786–1848), who served in Congress from 1811 to 1817 and 1819 to 1821, as well as serving as a justice on the Mississippi Territorial Supreme Court and the Maryland Court of Appeals, Stevenson Archer Jr. was born at "Medical Hall" near the village of Churchville, Maryland, on 28 February 1827. He attended the prestigious Bel Air Academy in Maryland, then entered Princeton College (now Princeton University) in New Jersey, graduating in 1848. He studied law and was admitted to the Maryland state bar in 1850.

In 1854 Archer was elected to the Maryland state house of delegates, where he served for a single one-year term. A Democrat, he was elected to a seat in the U.S. House of Representatives from Maryland's Second District in 1866 and served in the Fortieth through the Forty-third Congresses, from 4 March 1867 until 3 March 1875. He was defeated for the Democratic nomination in 1874 and retired from political life. However, in 1885 he was elected Maryland state treasurer, overseeing the handling of public funds. Before this time there was no hint of Archer being involved in corruption of any kind. However, it is possible that a lifetime of public service that had brought him little financial comfort, coupled with having the financial account of the entire state of Maryland within his power, was too much of a temptation for Archer. By early 1890 serious allegations had arisen that state money had gone missing under Archer's control. After an investigation, it was discovered that more than $132,000 could not be accounted for. Archer was arrested, removed from office by Governor Elihu E. Jackson, a fellow Democrat, and charged with embezzlement. Archer, apparently chagrined at being caught, plead guilty before the court. He told the judge in a written statement, "No part of the State's money or securities was ever used by me in gambling, stock speculation, or for political purposes; nor have I at this time one dollar of it left." Archer was sentenced to five years in prison; however, he began to suffer from ill health soon after the beginning of his sentence. In May 1894, after less than four years in prison, he was pardoned by Governor Frank Brown, also a fellow Democrat. Archer returned home in disgrace. He lived for four years following his release, dying in the Baltimore City Hospital on 2 August 1898 at the age of seventy-one. He was buried in the Presbyterian Cemetery in Churchville, Maryland. Despite his career of service, which ended in a jail term, Archer's name is virtually forgotten.

References: *Biographical Directory of the American Congress, 1774–1996* (Alexandria, VA: CQ Staff Directories, 1996).

Austin v. Michigan Chamber of Commerce, 494 U.S. 652 (1990)

United States Supreme Court decision holding that state regulations banning the use of certain corporate funds for campaign purposes are constitutional. In 1976 the Michigan legislature enacted Section 54(1) of the Michigan Campaign Finance Act, which prohibited corporations from making contributions and/or independent expenditures to candidates for election in the state. In this case, the only question was whether the ban on independent expenditures was constitutional. The act defined an "expenditure" as "a payment, donation, loan, pledge, or promise of payment of money or anything of ascertainable monetary value for goods, materials, services, or facilities in assistance of, or in opposition to, the nomination or election of a candidate." In June 1985 Michigan scheduled a special election to fill a vacancy in the state house of representatives. The Michigan Chamber of Commerce, a nonprofit organization in the state with more than 8,000 members, sought to use contributions to fund an independent advertising campaign during the election. State law allowed for such expenditures if it came from a separate campaign fund not connected with the corporation's general fund, but in this case the Chamber desired to use monies from its general treasury to pay for the campaign. As such an act was a felony, the Chamber challenged the law in the federal district court for the Western District of Michigan, arguing that restrictions on expenditures was an unconstitutional infringement under the First and Fourteenth Amendments. The district court upheld the statute (643 F. Supp. 397 (W.D. Mich. 1986)), and the Chamber of Commerce appealed to the U.S. Court of Appeals for the Sixth Circuit. This court struck down the statute, holding that because the Chamber was a nonprofit corporation, the law could not be applied to it without infringing on the First Amendment rights of its members (856 F. Supp. 783 (1988)). The U.S. Supreme Court agreed to hear the case, which took place on 31 October 1989.

On 27 March 1990, Justice Thurgood Marshall wrote the opinion for a six-to-three majority (Justices Antonin Scalia, Anthony Kennedy, and Sandra Day O'Connor dissented) that the limitations on corporate expenditures were constitutional:

The Chamber argues that this concern about corporate domination of the political process is insufficient to justify a restriction on independent expenditures. Although this Court has distinguished these expenditures from direct contributions in the context of federal laws regulating individual donors (it has also recognized that a legislature might demonstrate a danger of real or apparent corruption posed by such expenditures when made by corporations to influence candidate elections ... Regardless of whether this danger of "financial quid pro quo" corruption ... may be sufficient to justify a restriction on independent expenditures, Michigan's regulation aims at a different type of corruption in the political arena: the corrosive and distorting effects of immense aggregations of wealth that are accumulated with the help of the corporate form and that have little or no correlation to the public's support for the corporation's political ideas.

Marshall then addressed the concerns of the three justices in the minority:

The Act does not attempt "to equalize the relative influence of speakers on elections," at 705 (KENNEDY, J., dissenting); see also at 684 (SCALIA, J., dissenting); rather, it ensures that expenditures reflect actual public support for the political ideas espoused by corporations. We emphasize that the mere fact that corporations may accumulate large amounts of wealth is not the justification for 54; rather, the unique state-conferred corporate structure that facilitates the amassing of large treasuries warrants the limit on independent expenditures. Corporate wealth can unfairly influence elections when it is deployed in the form of independent expenditures, just as it can when it assumes the guise of political contributions. We therefore hold that the State has articulated a sufficiently compelling rationale to support its restriction on independent expenditures by corporations.

Axtell, Samuel Beach (1819–1891)

Governor of Utah Territory (1874–1875) and New Mexico Territory (1875–1878), implicated in, but never charged with, corruption that led to a range war. Axtell was born in Franklin County, Ohio, on 14 October 1819, the son of a farmer and the grandson of a veteran of the War of 1812. He attended local schools, then went to Western Reserve College (now Case Western University) in Oberlin, Ohio, after which he was admitted to the Ohio bar. In 1851 he left Ohio for California, where he worked in the gold mines that sprouted up in that territory. When California became a state in 1854, Axtell was elected as the district attorney for Amador County and served for three terms. In 1860 he moved to San Francisco and for a time practiced law there. In 1866 Axtell, a Democrat, was elected to a seat in the U.S. House of Representatives, serving in the Fortieth and Forty-first Congresses from 4 March 1867 until 3 March 1871. His service there was undistinguished, and he did not seek a third term in 1870. During his final term in Congress, he sided more with the Republican administration of President Ulysses S. Grant than his own Democratic Party.

In 1874, when Utah Territorial Governor George L. Woods was not reappointed, Axtell was named in his stead. Axtell had had little administrative experience, but nonetheless Grant placed him in this position. His time in Utah was short, however: he was criticized by the anti-Mormon faction in the territory for his closeness to the Mormon Church. One of his most controversial acts was to deliver the certificate of election to George Q. Cannon. Cannon had just been elected to the U.S. House of Representatives, but because he was a Mormon, Territorial Governor George Woods had refused to sanction his seating. Because Axtell had sided with Cannon, he was nicknamed "Bishop Axtell." In 1875 Grant decided to move him out of Utah. Following the death of New Mexico Territorial Governor Marsh Giddings on 3 June 1875, Grant named Axtell as his replacement.

Starting soon after his appointment in 1875, Axtell got into trouble in New Mexico. The *New York Times* headlined a story on numerous unexplained charges leveled against Axtell: "There have been published in this city for the last thirty days incessant attacks upon Gov. Axtell, the newly appointed Governor, who has been in the Territory about that length of time. Charges have also been telegraphed to the press in regard to him, which, he asserts, are false in every particular. It is not believed that there is any dissatisfaction among the public with regard to his course." However, Axtell was indeed involved with a gang of land thieves known as the Santa Fe Ring. Working with landowner (and future U.S. senator from New Mexico) Thomas B. Catron, the ring controlled territorial land affairs through intimidation that exploded in the so-called Colfax County War. There were numerous shootings and vigilante killings. In 1878, declaring the entire Colfax County to be in insurrection, President Rutherford B. Hayes sent a federal investigator, Frank W. Angel, to look into the matter. Angel concluded that Catron and Axtell, through massive corruption and intimidation, had allowed the war to go on unimpeded. Angel also discovered that the local U.S. attorney and the territorial surveyor general were also involved in the corruption. However, because Axtell's role was cloudy at best and little actual evidence existed of his corruption, Hayes decided to merely remove the governor from his post. In 1878 Hayes removed Axtell and replaced him with General Lew Wallace, famed for his book *Ben Hur: A Tale of the Christ.* However, Axtell remained in New Mexico Territory, and just four years after Hayes removed him he was appointed by Territorial Governor Lionel Allen Sheldon as chief justice of the New Mexico Territorial Supreme Court. He served in this position until he resigned in 1885.

Samuel Axtell remained a leading politician in New Mexico, rising to be elected to the position of chairman of the Territorial Republican Committee in 1890. He died while in Morristown, New Jersey, on 7 August 1891 at the age of seventy-one.

See also Catron, Thomas Benton

References: "Axtell, Samuel Beach," in McMullin, Thomas A. and David Walker, *Biographical Directory of American Territorial Governors* (Westport, CT: Meckler Publishing, 1984); *Biographical Directory of the American Congress, 1774–1996* (Alexandria, VA: CQ Staff Directories, 1996); Duran, Tobias, "Francisco Chalvez, Thomas B. Catron, and Organized Political Violence in Santa Fe in the 1890s," *New Mexico Historical Review,* 59 (July 1984), 291–310; Jacobsen, Joel K., "An Excess of Law in Lincoln County: Thomas Catron, Samuel Axtell, and the Lincoln County War," *New Mexico Historical Review* 68 (April 1993), 133–151; "Malicious Attacks on Gov. Axtell. A Case of Contempt of Court. Another Escape of Prisoners from the Penitentiary," *New York Times,* 9 March 1875, 7.

B

Baker, Robert Gene (1928–)

Secretary to the Senate majority leader (1955–1963), "Bobby" Baker was convicted of tax evasion and defrauding the government and was implicated in, but never charged with, corrupt use of his office for personal financial gain. His case led to the establishment of the Senate Committee on Ethics and Standards. Although his case was widely reported, little is known about Baker himself. Born in Pickens, South Carolina, in 1928, the son of a mill worker, he attended local schools. In 1942 Senator Burnet Maybank (D-SC) appointed the fourteen-year-old Baker a page for the United States Senate. Two years later, he was named as chief page. He then became part of the Senate's clerical staff.

It was there that Baker's career took off. He became an assistant for Senator Robert S. Kerr (D-OK). However, he was noticed by another senator, Lyndon Baines Johnson of Texas. When Johnson became the minority whip in 1951, he named his protégé Baker as minority secretary. Johnson later told people that Baker "is the first person I talk to in the morning and the last one at night." When Johnson became minority leader in 1953, Baker was at his side. Two years later, when Johnson became the majority leader, Baker was there to reap the rewards of his association with this up-and-coming political star and was named secretary to the majority leader. He stuck by Johnson so much that he became known as "Little Lyndon." As his

power grew, many referred to Baker as "the 101st senator." No one knew that as his boss advanced, Baker was using his position to buy and sell influence. In 1960 Johnson was elected vice president, and when he took office in January 1961, Senator Mike Mansfield (D-MT) became Baker's boss. Baker continued his backdoor deals, which were not exposed for three years.

On 12 September 1963, allegations arose that Baker had used his position for personal and financial gain. The *Washington Post* published a story that Baker had demanded payoffs of $5,000 from a man to get the man's vending machines into government offices. As the allegations piled up against him, Baker resigned his office on 7 October 1963, although he faced no criminal charges. He had financed—with his own money (he was making only $19,612 a year)—the purchase of a hotel in Ocean City, Maryland, where he wined and dined congressional friends and cronies. Then Baker bought a home for his wife and children for $124,500. Senator John James Williams (R-DE) asked the Senate to conduct an investigation into how Baker could afford these purchases. Because the Senate did not have a committee on ethics, the charges were referred to the Rules Committee for hearings. A month after Baker resigned, President John F. Kennedy was assassinated, and Johnson was elevated to the presidency. Over the next year, the Senate Rules Committee uncovered evidence that became highly embarrassing for President

Johnson, as Baker's use of his office for personal gain was exposed. Williams found witnesses were unwilling to go public with stories about Baker's wild spending sprees.

Historian Jay Robert Nash explained:

> At hearings held by the Senate committee in 1964, witnesses gave some damning testimony against Baker, who was accused of helping a friend sell Johnson expensive life insurance policies (more than $200,000 worth) in the 1950s, in return for the friend's agreement to buy advertising time on Mrs. Johnson's Texas radio station. Baker was also accused of giving an alleged $100,000 payoff to Johnson for pushing through a $7 billion TFX plane contract for the Texas-based General Dynamics Corporation. Besides this, Baker was also accused of receiving an illegal $25,000 payment, allegedly from Democratic National Committee chairman Matthew H. McCloskey, to be channeled into the 1960 Kennedy-Johnson campaign fund. Members of the committee were unable to get much out of Baker when he appeared before them in February 1964; he said nothing to hurt his friends in high places, and invoked the Fifth Amendment to the Constitution, against self-incrimination. The hearings ended on March 25, 1964.

Despite the pile of evidence against Baker, the Rules Committee hesitated to find that one of the Senate's own had committed any crimes, holding that he had merely committed "gross improprieties," and closed the hearings without any action being taken. Williams, outraged, took the investigation further, backed by public approval of his actions. Senator Barry Goldwater (R-AZ), running for president against Johnson in 1964, called attention to the Baker matter in some of his campaign speeches.

Johnson was reelected in a landslide in November 1964, and the Baker issue went away for a time. However, Department of Justice attorneys, investigating Baker's role in the sale of influence, and without White House intervention, indicted Baker in 1966 on charges of tax evasion and defrauding the government. He was convicted in 1967 and after a series of appeals went to prison in January 1971. He was released in June 1972 after serving only seventeen months. As of this writing he is a retired real estate developer in St. Augustine, Florida.

Baker's case led to the establishment of the Senate Committee on Standards and Ethics and a series of rules governing the behavior of members and officers of Congress and their employees, most notably financial disclosure rules for all groups who work or serve Congress.

See also Williams, John James

References: Baker, Bobby, with Larry King, *Wheeling and Dealing: Confessions of a Capitol Hill Operator* (New York: W. W. Norton, 1978); "Bobby Baker: Wheeler-Dealer with High-level Machinations," in George C. Kohn, *Encyclopedia of American Scandal: From ABSCAM to the Zenger Case* (New York: Facts on File, 1989), 18–19; U.S. Congress, Senate, Committee on Rules and Administration, *Financial or Business Interests of Officers and Employees of the Senate. Hearings, 88th Congress, Pursuant to Senate Resolution 212, Parts 1–27* (Washington, DC: Government Printing Office, 1964), 20.

Barry v. United States ex rel. Cunningham, 279 U.S. 597 (1929)

United States Supreme Court decision holding that the U.S. Senate was within its authority "to exclude persons asserting membership who either had not been elected, or, what amounts to the same thing, had been elected by resort to fraud, bribery, corruption, or other sinister methods having the effect of vitiating the election." In November 1926 Republican William S. Vare appeared to have defeated Democrat William B. Wilson for the United States Senate seat from Pennsylvania. However, Wilson appealed to the Senate with charges that irregularities in the voting should disqualify Vare from being seated.

The Senate opened an investigation into the allegations. The Senate Committee on Privileges and Elections went to Pennsylvania to question witnesses and examine documents. However, one Thomas Cunningham refused to testify. He had served as a member of an organization that supported Vare in the Republican primary and the general election and allegedly had given the chairman of the group $50,000 in two installments to be used for Vare's election. In February 1927 Cunningham was called before the U.S. Senate committee, but again refused to testify. In March 1928 the Committee reported to the Senate, including the refusal of Cunningham to testify, and urged that he be found in contempt of the committee and the Senate. The Senate, instead, enacted a resolution instructing the president of the Senate to issue a warrant commanding the sergeant-at-arms of the Senate, or his deputy, to take Cunningham into custody and bring him "before the bar of the Senate, then and there or elsewhere, as it may direct, to answer such questions pertinent to the matter under inquiry as the Senate, through its said committee, or the President of the Senate, may propound, and to keep the said Thomas W. Cunningham in custody to await further order of the Senate." Cunningham was taken into custody, whereupon he filed for a writ of habeas corpus in the federal district court for the Eastern District of Pennsylvania. He claimed that he was illegally found to be in contempt of the Senate and that it had no authority to issue a warrant for his arrest.

The district court denied Cunningham's writ and ordered him into the custody of the sergeant-at-arms. Cunningham appealed to the U.S. Circuit Court of Appeals for the Second Circuit. This court reversed the district court, holding that the information Cunningham was required to give—regarding monetary donations to Vare's campaign that the Senate was not supposed to investigate—was not relevant, and thus his refusal to answer could not be the basis for a contempt charge. The Senate appealed to the U.S. Supreme Court. Arguments were heard on 23 April 1929.

A month later, on 27 May 1929, Justice George Sutherland spoke for a unanimous Court in reinstating Cunningham's arrest and holding that the Senate had a firm constitutional right to question witnesses before it and punish those who refused to answer:

> Generally, the Senate is a legislative body, exercising in connection with the House only the power to make laws. But it has had conferred upon it by the Constitution certain powers, which are not legislative, but judicial, in character. Among these is the power to judge of the elections, returns, and qualifications of its own members. Article 1, 5, clause 1. "That power carries with it authority to take such steps as may be appropriate and necessary to secure information upon which to decide concerning elections." *Reed v. County Commissioners,* 277 U.S. 376, 388, 48 S. Ct. 531. Exercise of the power necessarily involves the ascertainment of facts, the attendance of witnesses, the examination of such witnesses, with the power to compel them to answer pertinent questions, to determine the facts and apply the appropriate rules of law, and, finally, to render a judgment that is beyond the authority of

any other tribunal to review. In exercising this power, the Senate may, of course, devolve upon a committee of its members the authority to investigate and report; and this is the general, if not the uniform, practice. When evidence is taken by a committee, the pertinency of questions propounded must be determined by reference to the scope of the authority vested in the committee by the Senate. But undoubtedly the Senate, if it so determines, may in whole or in part dispense with the services of a committee and itself take testimony, and, after conferring authority upon its committee, the Senate, for any reason satisfactory to it and at any stage of the proceeding, may resume charge of the inquiry and conduct it to a conclusion, or to such extent as it may see fit. In that event, the limitations put upon the committee obviously do not control the Senate; but that body may deal with the matter, without regard to these limitations, subject only to the restraints imposed by or found in the implications of the Constitution. We cannot assume, in advance of Cunningham's interrogation at the bar of the Senate, that these restraints will not faithfully be observed. It sufficiently appears from the foregoing that the inquiry in which the Senate was engaged, and in respect of which it required the arrest and production of Cunningham, was within its constitutional authority . . .

It is said, however, that the power conferred upon the Senate is to judge of the elections, returns, and qualifications of its "members," and, since the Senate had refused to admit Vare to a seat in the Senate, or permit him to take the oath of office, that he was not a member. It is enough to say of this that upon the face of the returns he had been elected, and had received a certificate from the Governor of the state to that effect. Upon these returns and with this certificate, he presented himself to the Senate, claiming all the rights of membership. Thereby the jurisdiction of the Senate to determine the rightfulness of the claim was invoked and its power to adjudicate such right immediately attached by virtue of section 5 of article 1 of the Constitution. Whether, pending this adjudication, the credentials should be accepted, the oath administered, and the full right accorded to participate in the business of the Senate, was a matter within the discretion of the Senate. This has been the practical construction of the power by both houses of Congress; and we perceive no reason why we should reach a different conclusion. When a candidate is elected to either house, he of course is elected a member of the body; and when that body determines, upon presentation of his credentials, without first giving him his seat, that the election is void, there would seem to be no real substance in a claim that the election of a "member" has not been adjudged. To hold otherwise would be to interpret the word "member" with a strictness in no way required by the obvious purpose of the constitutional provision, or necessary to its effective enforcement in accordance with such purpose, which, so far as the present case is concerned, was to vest the Senate with authority to exclude persons asserting membership, who either had not been elected or, what amounts to the same thing, had been elected by resort to fraud, bribery, corruption, or other sinister methods having the effect of vitiating the election.

Barry is the controlling case in American law when it comes to the power of the Senate to investigate its own members. The U.S. Supreme Court has not backed away at all from its decision in this case in more than seven decades.

See also Vare, William Scott
References: *Barry v. United States ex rel. Cunningham,* 279 U.S. 597, at 614–615.

Barstow, William Augustus (1813–1865)

Governor of Wisconsin (1854–1856), implicated but never charged in massive bribery during his tenure, resigned due to possible election improprieties in the 1856 state election. Despite the numerous allegations against him, Barstow was never tried, and he later served with distinction in the U.S. Civil War. Born in Plainfield, Connecticut, on 13 September 1813, he was the son of a farmer, William Augustus Barstow, who served in the American Revolution, and his second wife, Sally. William Barstow received only a limited education in the common schools of Plainfield. He left school at age sixteen to become a clerk in a store run by his older brother, Samuel Barstow, in Louisville, Connecticut. In 1834 William Barstow moved to Cleveland, Ohio, where he became part of a flour-milling business with his brother Horatio Barstow. When the business failed in the depression of 1837–1838, Barstow headed for Wisconsin, where he settled in the village of Prairieville, near Waukesha. There, Barstow went into a partnership with one John Gale of Milwaukee in another flourmill, this one on the Fox River. At the same time that he was an active businessman, Barstow also became involved in local politics, serving in a number of local offices, including as a member of the Milwaukee Count Board and as postmaster of Prairieville.

In 1849, Barstow, a Whig, was nominated by the state party for secretary of state, running on the same ticket with Governor Nelson Dewey, who was running for reelection. Barstow went on to victory. However, while serving as secretary of state, allegations of corruption in his office first surfaced. As a member of the Public Lands Commission, Barstow approved the sale of tracts of land to certain people—these were later found to be speculators who never bid for the land, as was established by law. Barstow was also a member of the board of the State Printing Commission, and here, too, allegations of the sale of state printing contracts to some of Barstow's friends came out, although no charges were ever leveled in either case. However, the charges were serious enough to cause Barstow to lose his reelection bid in 1851.

Two years later, the Whig party dead, Barstow switched to become a Democrat. Remarkably, despite the allegations that had been floating around him, the Democrats named Barstow as their gubernatorial candidate that year. He went on to defeat the Free Soil (antislavery) candidate, Edward D. Holton, and the Whig candidate, Henry Baird. The corruption that had been hinted at when Barstow was secretary of state followed him into the governor's office. As historians Robert Sobel and John Raimo explain:

> While he was governor, Barstow, along with eight legislators and A. T. Gray, the Secretary of State, organized the St. Croix and Lake Superior Railroad Company with Barstow as president. Barstow also owned stock in the Fox-Wisconsin River Improvement Group. He threatened to veto any bill calling for an investigation of the latter company's handling of its land grants. Barstow was also implicated in bribery, and other maneuvers, involving the trading of land grants between the St. Croix and Lake Superior Railroad, and the La Cross and Milwaukee Railroad Company. No investigation resulted and no charges were ever brought, but Barstow's reputation suffered nonetheless.

In 1854, Barstow, under fire for his business practices, ran for a second term. He was opposed by Coles Bashford, the candidate of the new Republican Party, and a sitting Wisconsin state senator. Barstow did not get full support from his own party, but he won the election, albeit barely, that November. Almost from the start, allegations of massive vote rigging by Barstow and his cronies led Bashford to challenge the election results. However, after an investigation by the Democratically controlled State Board of Canvassers, Barstow was declared the winner by 157 votes and allowed to take the oath of office for a second term. Even with this result, the state Republican Party took the case to the Wisconsin state supreme court. Facing a potential challenge, Barstow resigned on 21 March 1856. The state supreme court eventually upheld Bashford's challenge, but Barstow's resignation made the case moot.

Barstow returned to private business, including his flour mill. In 1861 when the Civil War exploded, he volunteered for service in the Third Wisconsin Cavalry, starting off as a colonel. He served as the provost marshal general for the state of Kansas and saw action in one battle in 1863, but illness forced his retirement. He later served as an officer in the military courts in St. Louis until the end of the war. Following his discharge, he moved to Leavenworth, Kansas, but succumbed to his illness on 13 December 1865, two months after his fifty-second birthday.

References: "Barstow, William Augustus," in Robert Sobel and John Raimo, eds., *Biographical Directory of the Governors of the United States, 1789–1978*, 4 vols. (Westport, CT: Meckler Books, 1978), IV:1719–1720; Martin, Jennie McKee, "The Administration of Governor Barstow" (Bachelor's thesis, University of Wisconsin, 1921); *The Trial in the Supreme Court, of the Information in the Nature of a Quo Warranto Filed by the Attorney General on the Relation of Coles Bashford vs. Wm. A. Barstow, Contesting the Right to the Office of Governor of Wisconsin* (Madison, WI: Calkins & Proudfit, and Atwood and Rublee, 1856).

Belknap, William Worth (1829–1890)

Secretary of war (1869–1876) in the administration of President Ulysses S. Grant, implicated in a bribery scandal and impeached, but found not guilty by the Senate because he had resigned, setting a precedent in impeachment law that remains to this day. Born in Newburgh, New York, on 22 September 1829, Belknap was the son of a military officer who later gained fame in the Mexican War. He attended Princeton College (now Princeton

University) in New Jersey, then studied the law in Washington, D.C., and was admitted to the District bar in 1851. He then moved west, settling in Keokuk, Iowa, and opened a law practice in that city. In 1856, running as a "Douglas" Democrat—a member of the antislavery wing of the party—he was elected to a single two-year term in the Iowa state legislature. When the Civil War broke out in 1861, Belknap received a commission as a major with the Fifteenth Iowa Infantry and saw action at the battles of Shiloh, Corinth, and Vicksburg. In 1864 he was promoted to the rank of brigadier general and put in charge of the Fourth Division of the XVII Corps, working to help General William Tecumseh Sherman battle the Confederates in Georgia and the Carolinas. After leaving the service at the end of the conflict, Belknap served from 1865 until 1869 as the collector of internal revenue for the state of Iowa.

After becoming president in 1869, Ulysses S. Grant named one of his chief aides, John Aaron Rawlins, as secretary of war. Rawlins, however, was dying of tuberculosis and succumbed to the disease on 9 September 1869, less than six months into his tenure. Grant wanted to name General William T. Sherman, a hero of the Civil War, Rawlins's successor, but Sherman merely acted in a caretaker capacity until a permanent replacement for Rawlins could be found. Grant then approached Belknap, who offered to fill the vacant cabinet portfolio. After Senate confirmation, he took office as the thirtieth secretary of war. Belknap's tenure has been largely forgotten save for his final few months in office, when the cloud of scandal erupted around him.

Belknap was not the only figure engulfed in corruption at that time—his was among a multitude of shameful episodes in American history at that time. Crédit Mobilier, the Sanborn Contracts, the Whiskey Ring, the Indian Ring, "Boss" Tweed—all were in the news in the mid-to-late 1870s. But Belknap became the first cabinet official directly implicated in corruption. The story of this scandal begins in 1870, when Congress enacted a law authorizing the secretary of war "to permit one or more trading establishments to be maintained at any military post on the frontier not in the vicinity of any city or town, when he believes such an establishment is needed for the accommodation of emigrants, freighters, or other

THE DAYS' DOINGS.

Illustrating Extraordinary Events of the Day.

Entered according to the Act of Congress, in the year 1876, by the Publisher of The Days' Doings, in the office of the Librarian of Congress, at Washington.

No. 408.—VOL. XVI. | NEW YORK, MARCH 18, 1876. | 13 Weeks, $1.00. 34 Yearly. | PRICE, 10 Cents.

THE NATIONAL DISGRACE.

AN AFFECTING EPISODE OF THE *EXPOSE* OF THE CRIME OF SECRETARY BELKNAP.—THE WIFE OF THE RUINED SECRETARY GOES, WITH HER INFANT, THROUGH THE STORMY NIGHT TO THE RESIDENCE OF MR. BLACKBURN, AND MAKES A PITEOUS APPEAL IN BEHALF OF HER HUSBAND.—See Next Page.

Illustration showing wife of Secretary William Belknap, at the home of Mr. Blackburn, pleading to save her husband's honor. During a period of abundant political scandals, Belknap became the first cabinet official directly implicated in corruption. (Library of Congress)

citizens. The persons to maintain such establishments shall be appointed by him, and shall be under protection and control as camp-followers." Historian George Kohn, writing about Belknap, explained:

> Belknap's annual salary of $8,000 as Secretary of War was evidently not enough for him and his wife, who desired to live and entertain in a grand style. She communicated with a wealthy friend of hers, a New York contractor named Caleb P. Marsh, to whom she proposed a deal: she would secure for him the lucrative Indian trading post at Fort Sill, Oklahoma, if he agreed to pass on to her some of the profits. At the time the post was held by one John S. Evans, who refused to relinquish it because of the large investment and profitability to him, but he agreed to pay Marsh $12,000 annually if he could keep the tradership. The agreement was made, and Marsh gave half of his yearly payments to the acquisitive Mrs. Belknap. After her death, the monies were sent to Belknap himself, who subsequently received nearly $25,000 in "kickbacks" from the Fort Sill trader.

In 1875, with scandals exploding in all sections of the Grant administration, congressional investigators looking into corruption in trading posts came across the evidence that Belknap was on the take. The investigators also found that, unconnected to Belknap's corruption, the president's brother, Orville, was cashing in the same way. The story broke in the American press in February 1876, when the *New York Herald* printed an exposé on the corrupt practices of one of Grant's cabinet members. Other newspapers, such as the *New York Times,* followed. Belknap's career was finished. On 2 March 1876, Belknap resigned from the cabinet. Grant wrote to his friend that he accepted the resignation "with great regret."

Alas, Belknap was not free of responsibility just because he had resigned his office. On 14 January 1876, Representative William Ralls Morrison (D-IL) introduced a resolution calling for the Committee on Expenditures to investigate several cabinet departments, including the Department of War. Citing the bribes, the Committee recommended on 2 March 1876 that Belknap be impeached. The secretary resigned that same day. However, the House moved forward with the impeachment inquiry, appointing the Judiciary Committee to draft articles of impeachment. On 3 April 1876, the Committee reported to the whole House five articles of impeachment, which were then adopted. Article 1 alleged that "on October 8, 1870, Belknap appointed Caleb P. Marsh to maintain a trading post at Fort Sill. On the same day, Marsh contracted with John S. Evans for Evans to fill the commission as posttrader at Fort Sill in exchange for a yearly payment to Marsh of $12,000. On October 10th, at the request of Marsh, Belknap appointed Evans to maintain the trading establishment at Fort Sill. On 2 November 1870, and on four more occasions over the next year, Belknap unlawfully received $1,500 payments from Marsh in consideration of allowing Evans to maintain a trading establishment at Fort Sill." The other articles alleged the same improprieties, except for article 4, which listed in 14 distinct sections, each payment made by Marsh to Belknap.

The first cabinet officer ever to be impeached, Belknap hired a coterie of experienced Washington hands to defend him: Matthew Carpenter, an experienced Washington lawyer; Jeremiah S. Black, former secretary of state and former attorney general, who had been turned down by the Senate for a seat on the U.S. Supreme Court; and Montgomery Blair, former postmaster general under Abraham Lincoln. The Senate opened the trial on 3 April 1876. The three attorneys representing Belknap strangely did not argue Belknap's innocence—instead, they maintained that Belknap's resignation made an impeachment trial, designed to remove a corrupt officer from office, moot. Belknap even refused to enter a plea. Despite these moves, the trial opened on 5 April 1876, a month after his resignation. Interspersed in the testimony on Belknap's malfeasance were arguments that as a private citizen Belknap could not be impeached. As time went on, this mere fact overrode any and all evidence against him. On 1 August 1876, the Senate voted, with twenty-five senators holding out for acquittal. Lacking the two-thirds majority required to convict, the Senate found Belknap not guilty. Afterwards, twenty-two of the senators who voted to acquit reported that their vote was based on the fact that they had no jurisdiction over a private citizen.

Belknap was never tried criminally for taking bribes, and he became an attorney of some note in Washington, D.C. On 13 October 1890, after visiting with U.S. Supreme Court Justice Samuel Freeman Miller, Belknap collapsed at his home and died, presumably of a heart attack. He was sixty-one years old. Despite his corrupt activities and being the only cabinet officer up to that time to be impeached, Belknap, for his wartime service, was laid to rest in Arlington National Cemetery. Needless to say, his marker does not mention his ignominious governmental career.

References: "Belknap's Fall. Exposure of Flagrant Corruption and Malfeasance. Shameful Traffic in the Patronage of the War Department," *New York Herald,* 3 March 1876, 3; "Belknap Scandal: He Followed in his Wife's Path," in George C. Kohn, *Encyclopedia of American Scandal: From ABSCAM to the Zenger Case* (New York: Facts on File, 1989), 26–27; "Belknap, William Worth," in *The National Cyclopaedia of American Biography,* 57 vols. and supplements A-N (New York: James T. White & Company, 1897–1984), IV:23–24; Bell, William Gardner, *Secretaries of War and Secretaries of the Army: Portraits and Biographical Sketches* (Washington, DC: United States Army Center of Military History, 1982), 78; "The Case of Gen. Belknap. Sentiment in Washington," *New York Times,* 4 March 1876, 1; "Death of General Belknap. The Ex-Secretary, Stricken Down Suddenly, Alone, in His Office," *Evening Star* (Washington, DC), 13 October 1890, 1; Ingersoll, Lurton D., *A History of the War Department of the United States, With Biographical Sketches of the Secretaries* (Washington, DC: Francis B. Mohun, 1879), 566–571; Prickett, Robert C., "The Malfeasance of William Worth Belknap, Secretary of War, October 13, 1869 to March 2, 1876," *North Dakota History,* 17:1 (January 1950), 5–51, and 17:2 (April 1950), 97–134; United States Congress, Senate, *Proceedings of the Senate Sitting for the Trial of William W. Belknap, Late Secretary of War, on the Articles of Impeachment Exhibited by the House of Representatives, Forty-Fourth Congress, First Session,* 4 vols. (Washington, DC: Government Printing Office, 1876).

Biaggi, Mario (1917–)

United States Representative from New York (1969–1988), resigned before he could be expelled after he was implicated in a financial and kickback scandal. Born in New York City on 26 October 1917, Biaggi attended city schools before earning his law degree from the New York Law School in 1963, after which he was admitted to the New York state bar. He became a senior partner in the law firm of Biaggi, Ehrich & Lang in New York City. Leaving the practice of the law, he joined the New York state Division of Housing as a community re-

lations specialist and as an assistant to the secretary of state. Biaggi served in these positions from 1961 to 1965.

Prior to entering law school, Biaggi had worked as a police officer with the New York City Police Department (NYPD). During a twenty-three year career as a cop, Biaggi received multiple gunshot wounds, but was highly respected by his colleagues. He retired in 1965 with full disability, holding the department's medal of honor plus twenty-seven other commendations and decorations. Later elected to the National Police Officers Association of America Hall of Fame, Biaggi served as president of the association in 1967.

In 1968 Biaggi ran for and was elected to a seat in the U.S. House of Representatives as a Democrat, taking his seat on 3 January 1969 in the Ninety-first Congress and serving until 1988. Biaggi was a staunch Democrat, siding with his party on many of the important issues of the day. He was highly popular in Congress and his district and was reelected nine times.

Biaggi got into trouble when he tried to make money off the stock of Wedtech. Wedtech, a manufacturer of equipment for the Department of Defense, went public in 1983 with shares of its stock. At that time, 112,500 shares of stock were issued to Richard Biaggi, brother of Mario; an additional 112,500 shares were issued to Bernard Ehrlich, a former law partner of Mario Biaggi. Richard Biaggi was also a partner of this law firm. In 1987 it was alleged that Richard Biaggi, Mario Biaggi, and others conspired to use to stocks as a payoff to Biaggi in exchange for his influence to secure Department of Defense contracts for Wedtech using Small Business Administration (SBA) loans. Mario Biaggi was also accused of having the stock for him from Wedtech placed under the names of his brother and law partner so that he could circumvent the House of Representatives restrictions on outside earnings by members. On 16 March 1987, Mario Biaggi, his brother, Ehrlich, and former Brooklyn Democratic leader Meade Esposito were indicted by a federal grand jury. Richard Biaggi was also indicted for knowingly filing false tax returns for 1983, when he accepted the stocks, and 1985, when he sold them at a profit. Esposito was indicted for paying Biaggi's expenses for trips made by the congressman to St. Maarten and a Florida health spa. In August 1988 Biaggi was convicted of racketeering, extortion, bribery, mail fraud, filing a false tax return, and false financial disclosure. (Richard Biaggi, Ehrlich, and Esposito were also convicted; Richard Biaggi's convictions on bribery and fraud were reversed on appeal, but those involving tax fraud were allowed to stand.) Mario Biaggi was sentenced to eight years in prison. On 5 August 1988, he resigned his seat, after it appeared that he faced almost certain expulsion by the full House.

On appeal to the Second Circuit Court of Appeals, Mario Biaggi's conviction was upheld. He eventually served twenty-six months in prison, but was able to draw a congressional pension of $44,000, outraging many. In 1992 he ran unsuccessfully for his old seat in Congress, but was not even nominated by the Democrats. Fighting ill health, he settled in the Bronx, New York.

References: *Biographical Directory of the American Congress, 1774–1996* (Alexandria, VA: CQ Staff Directories, Inc., 1996), 657; *In the Matter of Representative Mario Biaggi,* House Report No. 100-506, 100th Congress, 2nd Session (1988); "Mario Biaggi: A Senior Congressman's Sudden Comedown," in George C. Kohn, *Encyclopedia of American Scandal: From ABSCAM to the Zenger Case* (New York: Facts on File, 1989), 32–33.

Bilbo, Theodore Gilmore (1877–1947)

United States senator (1934–1947) from Mississippi, refused admittance to the Senate in 1947 when allegations of bribery in the election of another senator arose. Bilbo was never cleared or charged and died before his case could be adjudicated. Born on a farm in Juniper Grove, Mississippi, on 13 October 1877, Bilbo attended local schools before he received a secondary education at Peabody College and Vanderbilt University in Nashville, Tennessee, and the University of Michigan in Ann Arbor, after which he worked as a teacher in Mississippi. He became an active Baptist lay preacher when he was just nineteen years old. In 1908, after studying the law, he was admitted to the Mississippi bar. That same year, on a platform that advocated white supremacy, Bilbo was elected to the Mississippi state senate. Two years later, allegations arose that Bilbo took a bribe to help elect a fellow Democrat to the U.S. Senate, but he dismissed the allegation by claiming that he had taken the "gift" to trap the person offering the

bribe. The state senate attempted to oust him, but in running for reelection Bilbo went back to his district and told his constituents that he was the victim of a vicious political smear. He was overwhelmingly reelected. In 1911 he ran for lieutenant governor and was elected with Democrat Earl L. Brewer.

In 1915 Brewer stepped aside, and Bilbo was nominated by the Democrats for governor of Mississippi. His opposition in a one-party state was token: Socialist J. T. Lester, who was defeated by Bilbo by 46,000 votes out of some 50,000 cast. Bilbo served this single term (1916–1920), but in 1927 he ran to succeed Governor Dennis Murphree and was again elected, serving from 1928 to 1932.

In 1934 Bilbo was elected to the United States Senate, where he became one of the leading spokesmen for the populist stand against civil rights for blacks. Bilbo was for more than denying blacks the right to vote: he was a segregationist of the most extreme sort. In 1940, for instance, he told a crowd during his reelection campaign, "I want to make it impossible for the Negro to vote and thus guarantee white supremacy." In the Senate, he was the chairman of the Committee on [the] District of Columbia, and, later, the chairman of the Committee on Pensions.

In December 1946, following Bilbo's reelection to a third Senate term, Senator Glen H. Taylor, Democrat of Idaho, demanded that the Senate investigate allegations of financial impropriety against Bilbo. Bilbo's fellow Southern Democrats threatened a filibuster if Bilbo were not allowed to take his seat. Bilbo, suffering from cancer, returned home to Mississippi and made a deal with Senate Majority Leader Alben Barkley that he would not take his seat until he returned. A Senate panel then opened an inquiry into allegations that Bilbo had used his office for war contractors in return for financial favors. During the investigation, Bilbo admitted that he had received "gifts" from certain people in exchange for promoting the candidacy of Democratic Senate candidate Wall Doxey, but Bilbo claimed that these gifts were not improper. Another committee examined allegations that Bilbo had used his influence to block blacks from voting in Mississippi in the 1946 election. This committee found that while Bilbo did appeal to racist impulses, he did not commit any illegal acts.

The second committee, however, found that Bilbo had taken tens of thousands of dollars of campaign contributions from war contractors and converted them to his private use. The Senate seemed on the verge of expelling Bilbo as soon as he would return to the Senate.

Bilbo, however, would not return. In Mississippi, he discovered that stomach cancer had advanced, and a series of operations in New Orleans in 1947 could not save his life. On 21 August 1947, he succumbed at the age of sixty-nine and was buried in Poplarville, Mississippi. The reports of the two committees were tabled, and nothing further was done about the allegations.

References: "Bilbo, Theodore Gilmore," in John A. Garraty and Mark C. Carnes, gen. eds., *American National Biography* (New York: Oxford University Press; 24 vols., 1999); *Biographical Directory of the American Congress, 1774–1996* (Alexandria, VA: CQ Staff Directories, Inc., 1996); "Death of a Demagogue," *American Heritage* (July-August 1997), 99–100; Morgan, Chester, *Redneck Liberal: Theodore G. Bilbo and the New Deal* (Baton Rouge: Louisiana State University Press, 1985); Smith, Charles P., "Theodore G. Bilbo's Senatorial Career: The Final Years, 1941–1947" (Ph.D. dissertation, University of Southern Mississippi, 1983).

Hiram Bingham, U.S. senator from Connecticut (1924–1933), censured by the Senate in 1929 for hiring a lobbyist to write tariff legislation that would aid Bingham's business. (Library of Congress)

Bingham, Hiram (1875–1956)

United States Senator from Connecticut (1924–1933), censured by the Senate in 1929 on charges of placing a lobbyist on his payroll. Bingham was better known for his famed explorations of the Incan ruins at Machu Picchu. Bingham was born in Honolulu, Hawaii, on 19 November 1875, the son of Hiram Bingham and Minerva Clarissa (née Brewster). He was descended from Deacon Thomas Bingham, who had emigrated to the American colonies from England in 1650 and settled in Connecticut. Hiram Bingham (1789–1869), grandfather of the subject of this biography, was the first Protestant missionary to the Hawaiian Islands, and his son, also named Hiram (1831–1908), was a missionary to the Hawaiian Islands and the Gilbert Islands. The young Hiram Bingham was brought up in Hawaii and received his education at the Punahou School and at Oahu College from 1882 to 1892. He then moved to the United States, where he attended the prestigious Phillips Andover Academy in Andover, Massachusetts, Yale University, the University of California at Berkeley,

and Harvard University, graduating from the latter institution in 1905. After graduation, Bingham became a professor of history and politics, first at Harvard and then at Princeton University.

Gradually, Bingham became a leading scholar in the civilizations of Central and South America. Starting in 1906, he went to South America to follow the route that Simon Bolivar took in 1819. In 1909, he published his notes from the journey in *Journal of an Expedition across Venezuela and Colombia*. He was a delegate to the First Pan American Scientific Congress at Santiago, Chile, in 1908. Three years later he served as the head of a Yale University expedition to Peru, where he began the first intensive search for the ruins of the lost Incan cities of Machu Picchu and Vitcos. On this journey, he became the first Westerner to ascend Mt. Coropuma, 21,763 feet high. The following year, on a return trip, Bingham did indeed find the ruins of Machu Picchu. Many of his explorations are famous, and many consider him the model for the famous motion picture hero and explorer "Indiana" Jones.

Following these discoveries, Bingham entered the political and military realm. In 1916, during World War I, he served as a captain in the Connecticut National Guard. He became an aviator and helped organize the United States Schools of Military Aeronautics in May 1917. Bingham also served in the Aviation Section of the U.S. Signal Corps and eventually moved up to the rank of lieutenant colonel. Near the end of the conflict, from August to December 1918, he commanded the flying school at Issoudun, France.

A Republican, Bingham attended the 1916 and 1920 Republican National Conventions as an alternate delegate. In 1922 he was nominated by the Democrats for Connecticut lieutenant governor, and was elected with Republican Governor Charles A. Templeton. Bingham served loyally under Templeton for the two years of his term. When Templeton chose not to run for a second term, Bingham was nominated by the Republicans. He defeated Democrat Charles Morris and appeared ready to assume office. However, Senator Frank B. Brandegee committed suicide on 14 October 1924, and on 16 December 1924, Bingham was elected to fill the open seat for the term ending on 3 March 1927. Bingham did serve as governor of Connecticut for a few days, until he resigned to go to Washington to take his seat in the Senate. Reelected in 1926, he served as chairman of the Committee on Printing (Seventieth Congress) and the Committee on Territories and Insular Possessions (Seventeeth–Seventy-second Congresses).

Bingham got into trouble with ethics when he hired Charles L. Eyanson, a secretary to the president of the Connecticut Manufacturers' Association, as an assistant to help write tariff legislation. Placing a lobbyist to help write legislation that could aid his business sector brought repudiation to the explorer. Senator George W. Norris (R-NE) placed before the Senate a resolution:

> The action of the Senator from Connecticut in placing Charles L. Eyanson, then an officer in the Manufacturers Association of Connecticut, on the official rolls of the Senate, at the time and in the manner set forth in the report of the subcommittee of the Committee on the Judiciary, is contrary to good

morals and senatorial ethics and tends to bring the Senate into dishonor and disrepute, and such conduct is hereby condemned.

The Senate then began debate on Bingham's punishment, during which senators added language stating that Bingham's hiring of Eyanson was "not the result of corrupt motives." Despite the lack of support, Bingham refused to see the error of his ways and apologize to his Senate colleagues. His son, Alfred Bingham, wrote in a biography of his father:

> Believing in his own moral rectitude he took the floor in his own defense, insisting that what he had done was neither immoral nor dishonorable. "My only desire," he said, "was to secure the best possible information on a difficult and intricate subject, particularly as it related to the people who elected me to the United States Senate." At most he acknowledged that "my judgment in the way in which I endeavored to use this tariff expert may have been at fault." He insisted on his purity of motive and refused to concede that appointing a lobbyist as a paid expert was improper.

On 4 November 1929, the Senate voted fifty-four to twenty-two to censure Bingham, making him one of only twelve senators to be the subject of a censure motion and one of only ten to actually be censured. Eighteen senators, including Bingham, did not vote.

In 1932 Bingham lost a narrow reelection race to Democrat Augustine Lonergan. As Bingham's son Alfred explains, "[His election loss] was less because of the lingering disgrace of having been censured than as a consequence of the deepening depression." Bingham remained in Washington and was engaged in banking and literary exploits. During World War II, he lectured at naval training schools and from 1951 to 1953 served as chairman of the Civil Service Commission's Loyalty Review Board, ferreting out potential Communists. Bingham died in Washington on 6 June 1956 at the age of eighty. Because of his service to his nation, he was laid to rest in Arlington National Cemetery in Virginia.

References: "Bingham Accuses Senators of Plot to Besmirch Him, Norris to Ask for Censure," *New York Times,* 29 October 1929, 1; Bingham, Alfred M. "Raiders of the Lost City," *American Heritage,* 38 (July/August 1987), 54–64; Bingham, Alfred M., *Portrait of an*

Explorer: Hiram Bingham, Discover of Machu Picchu (Ames: Iowa State University Press, 1989); Bingham, Hiram, *An Explorer in the Air Service* (New Haven: Yale University Press, 1920); Bingham, Woodbridge, *Hiram Bingham: A Personal History* (Boulder: Bin Lan Zhen Publishers, 1989); *Biographical Directory of the American Congress, 1774–1996* (Alexandria, VA: CQ Staff Directories, Inc., 1996), 662; *Congressional Ethics* (Washington, DC: Congressional Quarterly, 1980), 27; Miller, Frank L., "Fathers and Sons: The Binghams and American Reform, 1790–1970" (Ph.D. dissertation, Johns Hopkins University, 1970).

Blaine, James Gillespie (1830–1893)

United States representative (1863–1876) and senator (1876–1881) from Maine, accused, but never tried or convicted, of corruption in the so-called Mulligan letters controversy, which probably cost him the presidency of the United States. Blaine was born in West Brownsville, Pennsylvania, on 31 January 1830, and after attending local schools graduated from Washington College in Washington, Pennsylvania, in 1847. He taught school for several years, including at the Western Military Institute in Blue Lick Springs, Kentucky, before he returned to Pennsylvania and studied law. He finished his teaching career at the Pennsylvania Institution for the Blind in Philadelphia from 1852 to 1854. In 1854 Blaine relocated to Maine, a state with which he would be identified for the remainder of his life. There, he became the editor of the *Portland Advertiser* and the *Kennebec Journal.* In 1858 he entered the political realm, running for a seat in the Maine state house of representatives, and serving from 1859 to 1862, the last two years as Speaker of that body. In 1862 Blaine gave up this seat to run for a seat in the U.S. House of Representatives from the Third Maine district. He defeated a Democrat named Gould and took his seat in the Thirty-eighth Congress on 4 March 1863. Blaine would serve in this seat until his resignation on 10 July 1876, through the Forty-fourth Congress. From 4 March 1869 through 1 December 1873, Blaine served as Speaker of the House, becoming one of the most powerful politicians in the United States. Because of his service as Speaker and his oratorical skills, many Republicans considered him a potential presidential candidate.

In 1876 Blaine was considered the leading Republican to succeed Ulysses S. Grant as president. But an episode from his past came to light and ruined his chances that year. In 1876 the U.S. House began to investigate a number of allegations of corruption in their midst. Rumors had swirled around Blaine for a long time, but he was initially cleared when no evidence was found. However, on 31 May 1876, this all changed. James Mulligan, a bookkeeper who worked for a businessman, Warren Fisher Jr., testified before the House Judiciary Committee that Blaine, while Speaker, had used his position to profit financially. Working with Fisher, Blaine had secured the renewal of a land grant for the use of the Little Rock & Fort Smith Railroad of Arkansas, and in return Fisher sold that railroad's bonds to Blaine at a cut-rate price. When the railroad went bankrupt, Blaine sold the worthless bonds to the Union Pacific Railroad and earned a large commission. Blaine denied that this happened, but Mulligan testified that he had incriminating evidence—the letters Blaine had sent to Fisher regarding the transaction. Mulligan testified that Blaine knew of the corruption he was committing; in his letters to Fisher, he had concluded each one with the phrase "Burn this letter." Before Mulligan had a chance to present these letters, Blaine cajoled him into giving the Maine congressman a look at them and then claimed that he had taken control of private correspondence. On 5 June 1876, Blaine went before the whole House and in a moment of high drama read redacted portions of the letters. This move did not help Blaine, but instead of bowing out he went to Cincinnati to the Republican National Convention where his name was put into nomination. However, the Mulligan letters episode scared some of Blaine's allies, and the party nominated Ohio Governor Rutherford B. Hayes for president instead. Robert Ingersoll's nominating speech for Blaine was best remembered for the nickname he bestowed on Blaine: "The Plumed Knight." In the end, because Blaine had all of the Mulligan letters, and no other evidence existed against him, the House Judiciary Committee did not accuse him of any crime, and there the matter rested. Blaine was elected to the U.S. Senate.

In 1880 Blaine was once again a potential candidate for the Republican presidential nomination, but again he was denied. He threw his weight behind a friend, Ohio Representative James A. Garfield, who went on to capture the nomination.

For his support, Blaine was named secretary of state by Garfield when he became president. Because of the Mulligan letters controversy, Blaine's nomination was controversial, but he won Senate confirmation. However, his term in office was short. On 2 July 1881, Blaine was at a train station with Garfield when an assassin shot the president. Garfield lingered a few months and died from his wounds on 19 September 1881. Soon after Garfield's successor, Chester A. Arthur, took office, Blaine resigned as secretary of state and went into private life. He wrote his memoirs, *Twenty Years of Congress* (2 vols., 1884–1886).

In 1884 Blaine's turn had come. Despite the Mulligan letters and other rumors of corruption by Blaine, the former Speaker and senator was nominated by the Republicans for the presidential race. He selected General John A. Logan as his running mate. Liberal Republicans and civil service reformers were disgusted and stormed out of the party, forming a group called the "Mugwumps" that supported the Democratic presidential candidate, New York Governor Grover Cleveland. Despite Cleveland's admission of having a child out of wedlock with a young girl, these reformers stood by Cleveland's side. However, Blaine appeared to lead the race. It was not until a Presbyterian clergyman, the Reverend Samuel D. Burchard, spoke at a Blaine campaign stop in New York that he ran into trouble. Burchard said of the Democratics that theirs was "the party whose antecedents are rum, Romanism, and rebellion." The reference to "Romanism" was aimed directly at Irish immigrants in New York, all of whom were Roman Catholic. Blaine's failure to disavow Burchard's remarks cost him dearly. On election day Cleveland carried New York state by just 1,149 votes out of more than 1 million cast. Because Blaine lost New York, Cleveland won the electoral vote and was elected the twenty-second president. It was a stunning loss for Blaine, made all the worse by rumors of his corruption and a badly timed remark.

In 1888 Cleveland was vulnerable, and the Republicans prepared to nominate Blaine a second time. However, Blaine's heart was not in another race, and he threw his support behind Senator Benjamin Harrison of Indiana. Harrison lost the popular vote, but a combination of wins in the western states threw the electoral vote to him, the second such election in the nineteenth century. For a second time, because of his support, Blaine was named secretary of state. Again, his nomination was controversial, but he was confirmed. During his tenure, 1889–1892, Blaine fostered closer relations between the United States and Latin America, leading the way to the first Pan-American Congress. Blaine also concluded a treaty with the British over fur-sealing in Canadian waters near Alaska.

Three days before the Republican National Convention in 1892, Blaine resigned as secretary of state over policy differences with Harrison. He unsuccessfully fought his former boss for the presidential nomination, but the party stuck with Harrison, who was defeated by former President Cleveland that November. Blaine was sick and dying at the time. On 27 January 1893, he succumbed to numerous ailments, four days before his sixty-third birthday. His remains were initially interred in the Oak Hill Cemetery in Washington, D.C.; however, in 1920, at the request of the state of Maine, they were removed to be reburied in the Blaine Memorial Park in Augusta, Maine.

References: "James G. Blaine, Republican," in Lillian B. Miller, et al., *"If Elected . . ." Unsuccessful Candidates for the Presidency, 1796–1968* (Washington, DC: Smithsonian Institution Press, 1972), 247–249; "Mulligan Letters," in George C. Kohn, *Encyclopedia of American Scandal: From ABSCAM to the Zenger Case* (New York: Facts on File, 1989), 236–237; Muzzey, David Saville, *James G. Blaine: A Political Idol of Other Days* (New York: Dodd, Mead & Company, 1935).

Blanton, Leonard Ray (1930–1996)

United States Representative from Tennessee (1967–1973) and governor of Tennessee (1975–1979), removed from the governorship amidst allegations that he sold pardons and that he and his cronies profited, a crime for which he served nearly two years in prison. Blanton was born on his family's farm in Hardin County, Tennessee, on 10 April 1930 and attended the public schools of Hardin County. He graduated with a Bachelor of Science degree from the University of Tennessee at Knoxville in 1951 and three years later, with his father and his brother, established the B & B Construction Company in Knoxville.

In 1964 Blanton entered politics, running as a Democrat and winning a seat in the Tennessee House of Representatives, representing McNairy and Chester Counties. Two years later, Blanton ran for a seat in the U.S. House of Representatives, representing the seventh congressional district, and defeated Republican Julius Hurst. Blanton served from the Ninetieth through the Ninety-second Congresses. In 1972 he gave up his seat to run for the U.S. Senate, but was defeated by Republican Howard Baker Jr.

Two years after his senatorial defeat, Blanton was nominated for governor by the Democrats and defeated Republican Lamar Alexander to become the chief executive of the state of Tennessee. As governor, Blanton pushed for equality for blacks and women, and he established the Department of Tourism, making Tennessee the first state to have a government-level department to capitalize on the benefits of tourism.

During his campaign for office, Blanton had run on a law-and-order platform, particularly against the excesses of the Watergate scandal. Once in office, though, Blanton felt he had a blank check to do as he pleased, and he did just that. Six aides, including the governor's legal counsel, Thomas Sisk, and a former Democratic committeeman from Hamilton County, Tennessee, William Aubrey Thompson, came up with a plan to demand payoffs from people in prison in order to get pardons from the governor. Blanton and his cronies rapidly collected huge sums from wealthy men in prison who could pay a price for their freedom. What sunk Blanton and his scheme was a woman named Marie Ragghianti. Serving as chair of the state Parole Board, Ragghianti opposed some of the pardons Blanton was granting (without her knowing that Blanton was being paid for them) and, when she spoke out against them, was fired. Outraged by Blanton's use of raw power to get his way, Ragghianti hired Tennessee attorney Fred Dalton Thompson to represent her in court against Blanton and the state government in a bid to get her job and good name back. Thompson helped expose the cash-for-pardons scheme that Blanton had been conducting and won a legal victory for Ragghianti. The FBI began an inquiry and soon was secretly recording various Blanton administration figures offering pardons for cash. One, Charles Taylor, a former highway patrolman on Blanton's staff, told an undercover FBI agent, "These people I'm fronting for have a product to sell."

A grand jury was convened, and on 18 December 1978, Blanton was called before it. He had not been a candidate for reelection that year, and Republican Lamar Alexander had won a stunning victory and was preparing to take office in just a few weeks' time. Based on the grand jury hearings, it was discovered that Blanton was still selling pardons, and it appeared he would do so until his last day in office. Even the arrest of two of his aides on charges of extortion and conspiracy to sell pardons, paroles, and commutations did not deter Blanton from continuing to sell pardons up until the moment he left office. The U.S. attorney involved in the case told Governor-elect Alexander that illegal activities were continuing and suggested that he take office immediately. Alexander went to the state attorney general, who allowed Alexander to take office on 16 January 1979, three days before his term legally began. That day, in a somber proceeding before a small crowd, Alexander was sworn in as governor by Tennessee state supreme court chief justice Joe Henry. After the ceremony, the state attorney general called Blanton to inform him that his term was over and that he must vacate his office immediately. Alexander sent a staff member to lock up the governor's office, who found a Blanton aide trying to leave with a stack of pardons to be signed by Blanton. Blanton, in the last hours of his term, had signed commutations or pardons for twenty-four convicted murderers and twenty-eight others convicted of other serious offenses. On 22 January 1979, the *Washington Post* editorialized, "The year is young, but we are almost ready right now to give the 1979 Award for Last-Minute Abuse of Power by an Outgoing State Executive to Ray Blanton." The editorial concluded, "Tennesseans . . . can at least count themselves lucky that Tennessee law permits the moving up of the inauguration date. And they can take considerable comfort in the fact that the state's other top Democratic officials were quick to recognize the need to limit the damage by cooperating in the effort to replace their fellow Democrat with his Republican successor as quickly as possible."

In 1980 Blanton was indicted, not for illegally selling pardons, but for selling liquor licenses and skimming 20 percent of the sales of the licenses for himself and others. Blanton was indicted on nine counts of mail fraud, one count of violating the Hobbs Act, a federal law against extortion or conspiracy to commit extortion that interferes with interstate commerce, and one count of conspiracy in violation of 18 U.S.C. § 371. Because all of the circuit judges in the Middle District of Tennessee knew Blanton, they recused themselves from the case. A Judge Peck was brought in, later to be replaced by a Judge Brown. On 9 June 1981, Blanton was convicted of all of the counts against him, and his two aides were convicted of mail fraud and conspiracy. Blanton was sentenced to three years in prison and a fine of $11,000.

Blanton appealed, but his conviction was sustained. However, in 1983, a three-judge panel of the U.S. Court of Appeals for the Sixth Circuit overturned the conviction, holding that the voir dire (juror questioning) process had been flawed (*United States v. Blanton,* 700 F.2d 298 (6th Cir. 1983)). When the full court heard the appeal, it overruled the three judges and reinstated the conviction (*United States v. Blanton,* 719 F.2d 815 (6th Cir. 1983)). The U.S. Supreme Court refused to hear the case in 1984.

In 1987 the U.S. Supreme Court narrowed the statutes under which Blanton and his aides had been convicted in the case of *McNally v. United States,* 483 U.S. 350 (1987), so Blanton asked for his conviction to be thrown out. A district judge granted the motion in respect to the mail fraud conviction, but he allowed to remain in place the conviction for violation of the Hobbs Act. In 1991 Blanton appealed, saying that his attorney was incompetent in allowing Blanton to testify when he knew the former governor was intoxicated. On 28 August 1996, Blanton's case before the U.S. Court of Appeals for the Sixth Circuit was decided: in *Blanton v. United States* (Case #95-6141), the court held that Blanton was denied effective counsel, but allowed his convictions to stand. At the time of the decision, Blanton was dying of kidney disease. He succumbed to the ailment on 22 November 1996, at the age of sixty-six, and was interred in the Shiloh Church Cemetery in Shiloh, Tennessee.

Ray Blanton may well have been the most corrupt state governor in American history. His case gave rise to many stories, including those of Marie Ragghianti and Fred Thompson. After she was cleared by a jury, Marie's case became the subject of the book *Marie, a True Story,* by Peter Maas. When it was to be made into a motion picture in 1985, the producers were so impressed with Marie's attorney, Thompson, that they cast him in the film as himself. This gave rise to a major motion picture career for Thompson and, in 1994, to his election to the United States Senate, where he became the chairman of the committee that investigated the campaign finance violations of the Clinton/Gore campaign in the 1996 campaign.

References: "Blanton, Ray," in John Raimo, ed., *Biographical Directory of the Governors of the United States, 1978–1983* (Westport, CT: Meckler Publishing, 1985), 291–293; Hillin, Hank, *FBI Codename TENNPAR: Tennessee's Ray Blanton Years* (Nashville, TN: Pine Hall Press, 1985).

Brehm, Walter Ellsworth (1892–1971)

United States representative from Ohio (1943–1953), convicted of unlawfully accepting a campaign contribution of $1,000 from one of his clerks. Despite the conviction, Brehm's sentence was suspended, and he never served any time in prison. He was born in Somerset, Ohio, on 25 May 1892, attending the public schools of that area. He later went to Boston University in Massachusetts and Ohio Wesleyan University, a religious school, in Delaware, Ohio, before graduating from the Ohio State University Dental School in Columbus, Ohio, in 1917. After graduating high school Brehm worked in a series of odd jobs and served for five years (1908–1913) as a member of Company D of the Seventh Regiment of the Ohio Infantry. Starting in 1921 and continuing for the next twenty-two years, Brehm worked as a dentist in the town of Logan, Ohio.

A Republican, Brehm served as the treasurer of the Republican Executive Committee of Hocking County, Ohio, and as a member of the Logan City Council from 1936 to 1938. In the latter year he was elected to a seat in the Ohio state house of representatives, serving until 1942. In 1942 Brehm ran for a seat in the U.S. House of Representatives, representing the Eleventh Ohio congressional district. He defeated a Democrat, Harold Claypool, and entered the Seventy-eighth Congress on 3 January 1943. Brehm was reelected in 1944, 1946, 1948, and 1950. In 1951 Brehm was indicted by a federal grand jury in Washington, D.C., on charges that he willingly and unlawfully accepted a contribution of $1,000 from his own clerk, Emma Craven, and the same amount from another clerk,

Clara Soliday. On trial, Brehm told the jury that no matter how he tried, "money just kept turning up no matter how often he refused it, appearing in filing cabinets" where his wife found it, as crime historian Jay Robert Nash explained. Brehm was convicted of taking the contribution from Craven, but acquitted of taking it from Soliday. On 11 June 1951 he was sentenced to five to fifteen months in prison and fined $5,000. However, Judge Burnita Shelton Mathews suspended the sentence, explaining that Brehm had led an exemplary life before this incident. The U.S. Court of Appeals later upheld the conviction, but Brehm was undaunted, even though he did not run for reelection in 1952. He returned to Ohio and to work as a dentist. After he retired he worked for a dental supply company. Brehm died in Columbus, Ohio, on 24 August 1971 at the age of seventy-nine.

References: *Biographical Directory of the American Congress, 1774–1996* (Alexandria, VA: CQ Staff Directories, Inc., 1996); Nash, Jay Robert, *Encyclopedia of World Crime: Criminal Justice, Criminology, and Law Enforcement,* 4 vols. (Wilmette, IL: CrimeBooks, Inc., 1989), I:484.

Brewster, Daniel Baugh (1923–)

United States representative (1959–1963) and senator (1963–1969) from Maryland, convicted of accepting an illegal gratuity as senator, although the conviction was later reversed by a high court. Daniel Baugh Brewster was born in Baltimore County, Maryland, on 23 November 1923, and was educated at a public school in Baltimore. He attended St. Paul's School in Concord, New Hampshire, before going to Princeton University and Johns Hopkins University, although he never earned a degree from either institution. In 1942 Brewster enlisted as a private in the United States Marine Corps, rising to be commissioned as a second lieutenant in 1943 and serving until 1946. He saw action in Europe during World War II. After returning to the United States, he attended the University of Maryland Law School and earned a law degree from that institution in 1949. That same year he was admitted to the Maryland bar and opened a practice in the town of Towson, Maryland.

In 1950 Brewster ran for and won a seat in the Maryland House of Delegates, serving from 1950

to 1958. In the latter year, he ran for a seat in the U.S. House of Representatives, representing the Second Maryland district. Brewster defeated his Republican rival to win the seat, and he took office on 3 January 1959 in the Eighty-sixth Congress. He was reelected in 1960. However, in 1962 he refused to run for a third term. Instead, he ran for the U.S. Senate to succeed the retiring Senator John Marshall Butler, a Republican. Brewster won the Democratic primary, then defeated his Republican rival, Edward T. Miller, by nearly 200,000 votes. Brewster would serve only one term in the U.S. Senate.

In 1968 Brewster came under investigation for allegedly taking an "illegal gratuity" while serving in the Senate. The following year, he was indicted, tried, and convicted. However, this conviction was reversed upon appeal; in 1975, Brewster decided to plead guilty to one charge of accepting an illegal gratuity. He had left the Senate in 1969, and, after serving a short prison term, he returned to his home in Maryland, where he continues to live as of this writing.

References: *Biographical Directory of the American Congress, 1774–1996* (Alexandria, VA: CQ Staff Directories, Inc., 1996), 706.

Brooks, James (1810–1873)

United States representative (1849–1853, 1863–1866, 1867–1873) from New York, censured by the House for his role in the Crédit Mobilier scandal. Born in Portland, Maine, on 10 November 1810, the son of James and Elizabeth (née Folsom) Brooks, he attended the public schools in that city and the academy at Monmouth, Maine. His father was killed at sea during the War of 1812, leaving the family in poverty and forcing Brooks to work as a storekeeper. He became a teacher at a school in Lewiston, Maine. He graduated from Waterville (Maine) College in 1831, after which he studied law and edited the *Portland Advertiser,* becoming that paper's Washington, D.C., correspondent in 1832.

In 1835 Brooks was elected to a seat in the Maine state house of representatives, where he sat for a single one-year term. The following year he was the Whig nominee for a seat in the U.S. House of Representatives, but was defeated by Democrat Francis O. J. Smith. Brooks moved to New York after his defeat and established the New York *Daily Express,* serving as editor-in-chief of the paper until his death. He was elected to the New York state assembly in 1847.

In 1848 Brooks was elected as a Whig to the U.S. House of Representatives representing the Sixth District. Serving in the Thirty-first and Thirty-second Congresses, he was not a standout politician, although he did support Senator Henry Clay's resolutions to head off civil war over slavery. In 1852 Brooks was redistricted into the Eighth New York District and lost reelection to Democrat Francis B. Cutting. He resumed his newspaper writing, flirting for a time with the American, or "Know Nothing," Party, an alliance that advocated laws against immigrants and Catholics. As his views changed, Brooks moved from the Whigs to the Democrats and in 1862 ran for a seat in the U.S. House. He won over a candidate with an unknown party backing and entered the Thirty-eighth Congress. In 1864 he beat Republican William E. Dodge by 150 votes, but when he presented his credentials, a House investigation handed the seat to Dodge. In 1866 Dodge refused to run for reelection, and Brooks ran again, beating Republican Legrand B. Cannon to reclaim his old seat. Brooks would hold this seat until his death. He served on the Ways and Means Committee, and twice was the Democrats' candidate for Speaker of the House.

In 1868 Brooks was a stern critic of the Congress's attempts to impeach President Andrew Johnson and, in recognition of his loyalty to Johnson, was named by the president as the government director of the Union Pacific Railroad on 1 October 1867. It was in this position that Brooks used his influence to enrich himself with stock from the Crédit Mobilier corporation. When the scandal broke in 1872, revealing how politicians were bribed by Representative Oakes Ames of Massachusetts, Brooks was caught in the tangled web of intrigue. An investigation uncovered Brooks's role, and the committee investigating the scandal recommended that Brooks be expelled. Instead, Brooks and Ames were censured by the House on 27 February 1873. The vote for censure for Brooks was 174 yeas, 32 nays, and 34 not voting.

Brooks was in poor health when he was censured. A trip to India in 1872 had left him with a serious fever, and the strain of the investigation and ultimate censure sapped his strength. On 30 April 1873, just two months after he was formally disgraced, Brooks died in Washington, D.C., at the age of sixty-two. He was buried in Greenwood Cemetery in Brooklyn, New York.

See also Ames, Oakes; Crédit Mobilier Scandal
References: Crawford, J. B., *The Crédit Mobilier of America—Its Origin and History, Its Work of Constructing the Union Pacific Railroad and the Relation of Members of Congress Therewith* (Boston: C. W. Calkins & Co., 1880); "The King of Frauds. How the Crédit Mobilier Bought Its Way Through Congress. Colossal Bribery," *The Sun* (New York), 4 September 1872, 1, 2; Nevins, Allen, "Brooks, James," in Allen Johnson and Dumas Malone, et al., eds., *Dictionary of American Biography,* 10 vols. and 10 supplements (New York: Charles Scribner's Sons, 1930–1995), II:77–79.

Buckley v. Valeo, 424 U.S. 1 (1976)

Landmark Supreme Court decision holding that the expenditure provisions of the Federal Elections Campaign Act of 1971 violated the First Amendment. The challenge to the law was brought by James L. Buckley, a U.S. senator from New York who was running for reelection in 1976, and several other politicians. A three-judge panel of the federal district court declined to find the act unconstitutional, but the case went up to the U.S. Court of Appeals for the District of Columbia Circuit for review. A majority of that court also rejected the plaintiffs' arguments. As the Supreme Court later noted:

The [appeals] court found "a clear and compelling interest" . . . in preserving the integrity of the electoral process. On that basis, the court upheld, with one exception, the substantive provisions of the Act with respect to contributions, expenditures, and disclosure. It also sustained the constitutionality of the newly established Federal Election Commission. The court concluded that, notwithstanding the manner of selection of its members and the breadth of its powers, which included nonlegislative functions, the Commission is a constitutionally authorized agency created to perform primarily legislative functions. The provisions for public funding of the three stages of the Presidential selection process were upheld as a valid exercise of congressional power under the General Welfare Clause of the Constitution, Article I, Section 8.

The United States Supreme Court agreed to hear the issues in the case, and arguments were heard on 10 November 1975.

On 30 January 1976, the Court, in a unanimous *per curiam* opinion (having no identifiable author—Justice John Paul Stevens did not participate) that ran for ninety-four pages, upheld all of the provisions of the 1971 act except for the limitation on expenditures, which the Court said violated the Constitution. The justices wrote:

> In summary, we sustain the individual contribution limits, the disclosure and reporting provisions, and the public financing scheme. We conclude, however, that the limitations on campaign expenditures, on independent expenditures by individuals and groups, and on expenditures by a candidate from his personal funds are constitutionally infirm. Finally, we hold that most of the powers conferred by the Act upon the Federal Election Commission can be exercised only by "Officers of the United States," appointed in conformity with Article II, [Section] 2, [Clause] 2, of the Constitution, and therefore cannot be exercised by the Commission as presently constituted.

The Supreme Court's decision in *Buckley* set the stage for a question pointed straight at the heart of future campaign finance reform: because the Court equated money with speech, how could the asking of donations be curtailed? In *Federal Election Commission v. National Conservative Political Action Committee,* 470 U.S. 480 (1985), the Court extended the holdings in *Buckley* to apply to "independent" expenditures made by political committees. Even as the present debate over the passage of comprehensive and updated campaign reform measures takes place, the long shadow of *Buckley v. Valeo* is cast over it and tempers the ideas of many who advocate reform. The Court further upheld limits on contributions in *Nixon v. Missouri PAC,* 528 U.S. 377, 145 L. Ed. 2d 886 2000).

See also Federal Elections Campaign Act of 1971; *Federal Election Commission v. National Conservative Political Action Committee; Nixon v. Missouri PAC*

Bullock, Rufus Brown (1834–1907)

Reconstruction era governor of Georgia (1868–1871), tried but acquitted on charges of political corruption and embezzlement. Born in Bethlehem, New York, on 28 March 1834, Bullock was the son of Volckert Veeder Bullock and Jane Eliza (née Brown) Bullock. He attended local schools and graduated from the Albion Academy in 1850. Bullock became an expert in the field of telegraphy and helped supervise the construction of telegraph lines between New York state and Southern states. In 1859 he became a representative of the Adams Express Company in Augusta, Georgia. Although he was a Republican and opposed to slavery and secession, Bullock offered his services to the Confederate government when the Civil War exploded in 1860. During the war, he was a lieutenant colonel in the Confederate army and at the end of the war was serving as acting assistant quartermaster general.

Bullock returned to Augusta, where he helped organize the First National Bank of Augusta and in 1867 was elected president of the Macon and Augusta Railroad. Although he had served in the Confederate army, Bullock was a Republican and was allowed to run for governor of Georgia, then still under martial law. In a popular vote in which former Confederates were not allowed to participate, Bullock defeated Democrat John B. Gordon by 7,000 votes out some 160,000 cast. Following the removal of Governor Thomas Howard Ruger by General George C. Meade, military commander of the Third Military District, Bullock was inaugurated governor on 21 July 1868. The state then came under civilian control. Despite capturing control of the majority of the Georgia state government, Bullock's tenure was dogged by a series of events he could not control, including the siding of many moderate Republicans with Democrats to block his legislative agenda. The legislature refused to elect his choice for the United States Senate and against his wishes expelled all of the black members of the legislature. After the national Democratic ticket of New York Governor Horatio Seymour won Georgia in the 1868 election and the Ku Klux Klan began operating in the state, Bullock appealed to Congress to "reconstruct" Georgia a second time. With Bullock working to reinstitute military rule, the legislature threatened to impeach him. Despite the threat, Bullock went to Washington and, receiving the backing of numerous Republicans, had both houses pass the bill, which was signed by President Ulysses S. Grant.

Contingent upon its ratification of the Fifteenth Amendment, Georgia would not be allowed readmittance to the Union and would remain under military rule.

The legislature quickly ratified the Fourteenth and the Fifteenth Amendments, but the cost to Bullock's party and reputation was high: In the next state elections, the Democrats took control of the state legislature and began investigations of alleged corruption and wrongdoing by Bullock. Allegedly, Bullock allowed his friends to buy stock in the state-owned Western and Atlantic Railroad cheaply, and he profited as well. Democrats also accused him of paying off newspapers to side with him editorially, of selling pardons and taking funds from the state prison account, and of encouraging extravagance in every bureau of state government that he controlled. With the likelihood of impeachment and a criminal indictment pending, Bullock resigned as governor on 23 October 1871 and left the state, leaving the problems to his successor, Benjamin F. Conley, the president of the state senate. The Democrats continued their vendetta against Bullock by targeting Conley and forcing a new election, which was won by Democrat James M. Smith. Conley, ironically, was the last Republican governor of Georgia before Sonny Perdue was elected in 2002.

The Democratic press had a field day with the Bullock allegations. The *Sun* of New York wrote, "The committee appointed by the Legislature of Georgia to investigate the financial transactions of Gov. Bullock have secured evidence confirming the worst reports of fraud and robbery which have gained currency. Bullock, it will be remembered, fled from the State to avoid prosecution, and has judiciously kept out of sight until the present time." Bullock remained in exile until 1876, when the Democrats in Georgia succeeded in bringing an indictment against the former governor and ordering his arrest and forced return to the state. Bullock was tried on numerous counts of embezzlement, but the jury acquitted him of all charges. Despite being hounded out of office, Bullock then remained in Georgia, serving as president of the Atlanta Cotton Mills and the local chamber of commerce, as well as director of the Union Pacific Railroad. Bullock died on 27 April 1907, one month past his seventy-third birthday.

References: Abbott, Richard H., "The Republican Party Press in Reconstruction Georgia, 1867–1874," *The Journal of Southern History,* LXI:4 (November 1995), 725–760; "Bullock, Rufus Brown," in Robert Sobel and John Raimo, eds., *Biographical Directory of the Governors of the States, 1789–1978,* 4 vols. (Westport, CT: Meckler Books; 1978), I:301; Cook, James F., *The Governors of Georgia, 1754–1995* (Macon, GA: Mercer University Press, 1995), 153; "[Editorial:] The Georgia Frauds," *The Sun* (New York), 9 August 1872, 2; Smith, W. Calvin, "The Reconstruction 'Triumph' of Rufus B. Bullock," *The Georgia Historical Quarterly,* LII:4 (December 1968), 414–425.

Bundling

Campaign donation practice in which small donations are combined into a "bundle," usually by a small political action committee (PAC), and then delivered to one or many campaigns, thus acting as one large, single contribution instead of numerous small contributions. The practice starts when a contributor directs his or her money to a specific political party or candidate. This money is then earmarked by the contributor for a political action committee. Contributions are gathered together into a bundle by a conduit, or intermediary, who delivers or forwards the bundled contributions to the candidate or political committee specified. These contributions are used to circumvent the contribution limits, which are $1,000 to each candidate per election cycle, $5,000 to each PAC, and $20,000 to each political party. Bundled funds are used as either "soft money," given to parties instead of candidates, or as independent expenditures, which have no limits, as per the 1976 U.S. Supreme Court decision *Buckley v. Valeo.*

The practice of bundling allows interest groups and PACs to stay just within the legal limits of campaign finance laws, yet also demonstrate their political and money-raising power. The campaign finance legislation known as McCain-Feingold, sponsored by Senator John McCain of Arizona and Russ Feingold of Wisconsin, bans most forms of bundling.

References: Utter, Glenn H., and Ruth Ann Strickland, *Campaign and Election Reform: A Reference Handbook* (Santa Barbara, CA: ABC-CLIO, 1997).

Burton, Joseph Ralph (1852–1923)

United States senator (1901–1906) from Kansas, convicted of illegally accepting compensation for services before a federal agency and forced to resign before he could be expelled from the Senate. Born on his father's farm near the village of Mitchell, Indiana, on 16 November 1852, Burton was the son of Allen and Elizabeth (née Holmes) Burton. His great-grandfather, John P. Burton, came to America from England about 1750. Joseph Burton gained an education in local district schools and the Mitchell Academy, which had been founded by his father. After attending Franklin College in Franklin, Indiana, he entered DePauw University, but due to illness left in his senior year without receiving his degree. When he recovered, he read the law in an office in Indianapolis and was admitted to the Indiana bar in July 1875.

Almost immediately, Burton entered the political arena, working for the Republican National Committee during the election of 1876 as a speaker in Indiana. However, two years later he moved west, settling in Abilene, Kansas. There he formed, with local attorney John H. Mahan, the law firm of Mahan & Burton. Burton became a leading lawyer in Kansas, rising to such prominence that in 1882 he was elected to a seat in the Kansas state legislature. He became interested in railway legislation and, working with several other legislators, helped to form the first railway commission in Kansas history. He also served as a member of the House Judiciary Committee. In 1886 he narrowly lost the Republican nomination for a seat in the U.S. House of Representatives, instead winning his state house seat that year and in 1888. In 1891 Burton took part in a series of debates on political issues with state Senator William A. Peffer, which resulted in Burton's nomination for a seat in the U.S. House of Representatives in 1892. The Fifth District from which he ran was a hotbed of populism, and Burton was defeated by People's Party candidate John Davis. In 1894 he was considered for the Republican nomination for the U.S. Senate, but was defeated by Lucien Baker. Two years later, when the other U.S. Senate seat opened up, Burton defeated incumbent Senator John J. Ingalls for the Republican nomination, but as the legislature (which chose U.S. Senators prior to the passage of the Seventeenth Amendment to the U.S. Constitution) was controlled by the Democrats, William A. Smith was elected. It was not until 1900 that Burton was elected to the U.S. Senate, defeating incumbent Senator Lucien Baker. In

the Senate, he was a consistent Republican, despite his opposition to the allowance of Cuba joining the United States.

Burton's troubles began two years after he was elected to the Senate. Burton was accused and convicted of taking a bribe in the sum of $2,500 from the Rialto Grain & Securities Company of St. Louis, Missouri, in exchange for Burton's work to help the company in a proceeding before the Post Office Department. Burton intervened with the Post Office Department, although it is not known if he was successful in his venture. The following year, in 1903, a grand jury in St. Louis indicted Burton for violating Section 1782 of the Revised Statutes, that "no Senator, Representative, or Delegate, after his election and during his continuance in office, and no head of a department, or other officer or clerk in the employ of the government, shall receive or agree to receive any compensation whatever, directly or indirectly, for any services rendered, or to be rendered, to any person, either by himself or another, in relation to any proceeding, contract, claim, controversy, charge, accusation, arrest, or other matter or thing in which the United States is a party, or directly or indirectly interested, before any department, court-martial, bureau, officer, or any civil, military, or naval commission whatever." He was tried in the Eastern District of Missouri and convicted of six counts. Burton appealed the conviction, and in 1905 the U.S. Supreme Court struck down the conviction as improper. Burton was tried a second time on the charge that Rialto merely paid Burton, without alleging that he received the bribe. Again, Burton was convicted, and he again appealed. The U.S. Supreme Court heard arguments and on 21 May 1906 upheld Burton's conviction and the constitutionality of Section 1782, giving Congress the right to ban the taking of bribes and other illegal solicitations by its members. On 4 June 1906, faced with expulsion by the Senate, Burton resigned. He returned to Abilene, where he worked in the newspaper business for a number of years, rising to control the Central Kansas Publishing Company with his wife.

On 27 February 1923, Burton died while in Los Angeles, California, at the age of seventy. He was cremated, and his remains were for a time deposited in the columbarium of the Los Angeles Crematory Association. In 1928 the ashes were removed, taken to Kansas, and buried in the Burton family plot in the Abilene Cemetery in Abilene, Kansas.

See also *Burton v. United States*

References: *Biographical Directory of the American Congress, 1774–1996* (Alexandria, VA: CQ Staff Directories, Inc., 1996), 752; Butler, Anne M., and Wendy Wolff, *United States Senate Election, Expulsion and Censure Cases, 1793–1990* (Washington, DC: Government Printing Office, 1995), 275–276; Byrd, Robert C., *The Senate, 1789–1989: Historical Statistics, 1789–1992,* 4 vols. (Washington, DC: Government Printing Office, 1993), IV:667.

Burton v. United States, 202 U.S. 344 (1906)

Supreme Court decision holding that Congress has the right to enact legislation outlawing the taking of, or solicitation of, bribes. In 1903 Senator Joseph Ralph Burton of Missouri was indicted in the District Court for the Eastern District of Missouri and found guilty of violating Section 1782 of the Revised Statutes by agreeing "to receive compensation ([in] the sum of $2,500, for services to be rendered by him for the Rialto Grain & Securities Company (in relation to a proceeding, matter, and thing, in which the United States was interested, before the Post Office Department." Section 1782 proscribes that "no Senator, Representative, or Delegate, after his election and during his continuance in office, and no head of a department, or other officer or clerk in the employ of the government, shall receive or agree to receive any compensation whatever, directly or indirectly, for any services rendered, or to be rendered, to any person, either by himself or another, in relation to any proceeding, contract, claim, controversy, charge, accusation, arrest, or other matter or thing in which the United States is a party, or directly or indirectly interested, before any department, court-martial, bureau, officer, or any civil, military, or naval commission whatever." Burton appealed the conviction on the grounds that the alleged crime did not take place in Missouri, where he was tried. In *Burton v. United States,* 196 U.S. 283 (1905), the Supreme Court held that Burton was improperly tried in Missouri and remanded the case for another trial. Burton was again tried in Missouri, where the government presented an indictment more generally written (for example, that Rialto had simply paid

Burton, and not stating where he received the money). Burton was convicted a second time and appealed on the grounds that Section 1782 "was repugnant to the Constitution." The United States Supreme Court agreed to hear the parties on a direct appeal, and arguments were heard on 3 and 4 April 1906.

On 21 May 1906, Justice John Marshall Harlan delivered the six-to-three decision of the court (Justices David J. Brewer, Edward White, and Rufus Peckham dissented) in upholding Burton's second conviction. Justice Harlan wrote, "We cannot doubt the authority of Congress by legislation to make it an offense against the United States for a senator, after his election and during his continuance in office, to agree to receive or to receive compensation for services to be rendered or rendered to any person, before a department of the government, in relation to a proceeding, matter, or thing in which the United States is a party or directly or indirectly interested."

See also Burton, Joseph Ralph

References: *Burton v. United States,* 196 U.S. 283 (1905).

Bustamante, Albert Garza (1935–)

United States representative from Texas (1985–1993), convicted and sentenced to three years in prison for influence peddling. Bustamante at one time was one of the most powerful Hispanic politicians in the U.S. House. Born in Asherton, Texas, on 8 April 1935, he attended the public schools of the area before entering the U.S. Army as a paratrooper in 1954, where he served for two years. He returned to Texas, where he studied at San Antonio College before receiving a degree in secondary education from Sul Ross State College in Alpine, Texas, in 1961. He then served as a teacher and coach from 1961 until 1968.

In 1968 Bustamante went to work as an assistant to Representative Henry Gonzalez (D-TX). Three years' work with Gonzalez gave Bustamante the experience to go into politics on his own. By this time, Hispanics were becoming a growing force in Texas politics, and Bustamante was elected as a member of the Bexar County Commission in 1972, serving from 1973 to 1978. In that latter year, he was elected as a judge for Bexar (pronounced "Bear") County and served until 1984. At that time, he ran for a seat in the U.S.

House of Representatives, representing the Twentieth District. He ran unopposed and took his seat in the Ninety-ninth Congress on 3 January 1985. He would serve through the 102nd Congress, until 3 January 1993. He was a leading Hispanic voice in the House.

In 1992 Bustamante was indicted by a federal grand jury on federal bribery and racketeering charges, as well as influence peddling. Prosecutors accused him of engaging in a pattern of corruption, including accepting a $35,000 bribe in exchange for helping a friend's company gain a food service contract with the air force, accepting illegal gifts, and using his office for personal gain, including obtaining an illegal loan to buy stock in a television station. In 1992 these allegations served to destroy Bustamante as a candidate: he was challenged by Republican Henry Bonilla, a Hispanic reporter from San Antonio. Bustamante, angered at his opponent, called the Republican a "eunuch for the plantation owners" for failing to support a minimum wage increase. But Bustamante was the focus of the campaign, and in November 1982 Bonilla defeated him, by a vote of 59 to 38 percent. Bustamante went on trial in 1995, was convicted of influence peddling, and was sentenced to forty-two months in prison. On 9 February 1998, after nearly three years in prison, Bustamante walked out of federal prison to finish his sentence in a halfway house in San Antonio. When he returned to San Antonio, a mariachi band and his supporters greeted him. "It feels good to be back with my family and friends," he said.

References: *Biographical Directory of the American Congress, 1774–1996* (Alexandria, VA: CQ Staff Directories, Inc., 1996), 755.

Butler, David C. (1829–1891)

Governor of Nebraska (1867–1871), impeached and removed from office for taking state money for his personal use. Despite his having been the governor of a state, little is known of Butler—in fact, state sources do not even have a record of his middle name. He was born on his family's farm in Lincoln, Indiana, on 15 December 1829. His father died when he was a youngster, and he was forced to balance his education with the care of his family. He engaged in several areas of business, including farming, mercantile entrepreneurship, and cat-

tle dealing, and acquired a sizable fortune that he lost in the financial panic of 1857. Two years later he moved from Indiana to Pawnee City, Nebraska, and after studying the law was admitted to the Nebraska bar in 1861. He operated a mercantile business at the same time he practiced law.

The same year that he began his law practice, 1861, Butler was elected to a seat in the Nebraska territorial legislature, and two years later to a seat in the Nebraska territorial senate. On 1 March 1867, Nebraska was admitted into the Union, and the legislature elected Butler as the first state governor over Democrat Julius Sterling Morton, the former territorial secretary of Nebraska. Butler was reelected in 1868 and 1870, running unsuccessfully for a seat in the U.S. Senate in 1870.

In 1870, after he won a third term, allegations of financial improprieties surfaced against Butler. Historians believe that these emanated from his assisting in the move of the territorial (and later state) capital from Omaha to Lincoln in 1867. However, the official historical record shows that Butler was impeached because he allegedly loaned out state funds targeted for education "improvidently, recklessly, and without any authority of law."

In all, eleven articles were drawn up and approved against Butler, alleging other improprieties as well. On 1 March 1871, the house managers appeared before the state senate and announced that Governor Butler had been impeached and in a formal call asked that the charges be heard in an impeachment trial. On 7 March, Butler appeared with his counsel, Clinton Briggs, John I. Redick (who later served as an associate justice on the New Mexico Supreme Court), and Turner Mastin Marquette (later a U.S. Representative [1867]), to answer the charges. The trial started one week later, on 14 March. It continued through the remainder of March, all of April, and all of May. On 2 June 1871, the state senate voted: it acquitted Butler on every article save the first one, which alleged that Butler had taken funds that came from the sale of public lands in Nebraska and "corruptly and unlawfully intermingle[d] the same with his own private funds and used the same for his own personal benefit." Butler was removed from office, and Secretary of State William Hartford James, who had been serving as governor until the disposition of the impeachment could be concluded, was confirmed as acting governor. He would serve out the remainder of Butler's term, giving way in 1873 to fellow Republican Robert W. Furnas.

Butler became a cattle farmer. On 15 February 1877, the state senate voted to expunge his impeachment from the official record, the only time such an occurrence had happened in American history. Just five years later, in 1882, Butler was elected as an Independent to the state senate that had convicted him and in 1888 he ran as a member of the Union Labor Party for governor, but came in a poor third place. Just three years later, on 25 May 1891, Butler died on his farm near Pawnee City, Nebraska, at the age of sixty-one.

References: "Butler, David," in *The National Cyclopædia of American Biography,* 57 vols. and supplements A–N (New York: James T. White & Company, 1897–1984), XII:1; "Butler, David C.," in Robert Sobel and John Raimo, eds., *Biographical Directory of the Governors of the United States, 1789–1978,* 4 vols. (Westport, CT: Meckler Books, 1978), III:1; *Impeachment Trial of David Butler, Governor of Nebraska, at Lincoln. Messrs. Bell, Hall and Brown, Official Reporters* (Omaha, NE: Tribune Steam Book and Job Printing House, 1871).

Butler, Roderick Randum (1827–1902)

U.S. representative from Tennessee (1867–1875, 1887–1889), censured by the Congress in 1870 for corruption. Butler was born in Wytheville, Virginia, on 9 April 1827. It does not appear that he received any primary or secondary education. He was bound as an apprentice at an early age and learned the trade of a tailor. At some unknown time, he moved to Taylorsville (now Mountain City), Tennessee, where he attended night school and studied the law. He was admitted to the bar in 1853 and opened a practice in Taylorsville. Soon after he was appointed postmaster of the town by President Millard Fillmore.

Butler rose to become a major in the First Battalion of the Tennessee militia. He served as a member of the Tennessee state senate from 1859 to 1863. His militia training was put to use during the Civil War, when he served in the Thirteenth Regiment of the Tennessee Volunteer Cavalry, with the rank of lieutenant colonel. Serving from 5 November 1863 until 25 April 1864, he saw limited action and was honorably discharged. He served as a delegate to the Republican National Convention that same year and also attended the 1872

and 1876 conventions. He served as well as a delegate to the Tennessee state constitutional convention in 1865 and that same year was named as a county judge and then judge of the first judicial circuit of Tennessee. After the war, Butler became chairman of the first state Republican Executive Committee of Tennessee.

In 1866 Butler was elected to a seat in the U.S. House of Representatives, serving in the Fortieth and three succeeding Congresses, from 4 March 1867 until 3 March 1875. During this tenure, he served as chairman of the Committee on the Militia (Forty-third Congress).

In 1870 Butler got caught up in a wide-ranging scandal that implicated several congressmen in selling appointments to the U.S. Military Academy at West Point and the U.S. Naval Academy at Annapolis in exchange for political favors or payoffs. Along with Butler, these men were John Thomas Deweese of Florida and Benjamin Franklin Whittemore of South Carolina, all Republicans. Deweese and Whittemore, prior to any congressional action, resigned their seats, while Butler was subjected first to an expulsion motion, and then, when that failed, a censure motion, which passed.

Hind's Precedents, a collection of rulings from Congress, reported regarding the move first to expel Butler, and then to censure him:

On March 16, 1870, Mr. William L. Stoughton, of Michigan, as a question of privilege, submitted a report of the Committee on Military Affairs, recommending the adoption of the following resolution: "Resolved, That the House declares its condemnation of the action of Hon. Roderick R. Butler, Representative from the First district of Tennessee, in nominating Augustus C. Tyler, who was not an actual resident of his district, as a cadet at the Military Academy at West Point, and in subsequently receiving money from the father of said cadet for political purposes in Tennessee, as an unauthorized and dangerous practice." This report was signed by 4 members only, but it was explained that 6 members had concurred in the vote on it, thus making it the report of the majority of the committee. The minority also presented views, signed by 4 Members, recommending the adoption of this resolution as a substitute:

"Resolved, that Roderick R. Butler, a Representative in Congress from the First Congressional district of Tennessee, be, and he is hereby, expelled from his seat as a Member of this House." When the resolution recommended by the majority came up for consideration, Mr. John A. Logan, of Illinois, moved to amend by substituting the minority resolution. This amendment was agreed to, yeas 101, nays 68—a majority vote. The amendment having been agreed to, the question recurred on agreeing to the resolution as amended, which had thereby become a resolution of expulsion. The Speaker stated that under the Constitution a two-thirds vote would be required. There were yeas 102, nays 68—not a two-thirds vote—and the resolution was rejected. Mr. Stoughton then offered a resolution which was the resolution originally reported by the majority of the committee, with the addition of these words: "and he is hereby censured therefor" . . . The resolution of censure was then agreed to, yeas 158, nays 0.

Despite this censure, Butler was reelected in 1870 and 1872, but lost his seat in 1874. He returned to Tennessee, where he served as a member of the state house of representatives from 1879 to 1885. In 1886 he made a political comeback, getting elected again to a seat in the U.S. House of Representatives and serving a single term until 3 March 1889. He did not run for reelection. He then returned to Tennessee, where he died in Mountain City on 18 August 1902 at the age of seventy-five. He was buried in the Mountain View Cemetery in Mountain City.

References: *Biographical Directory of the American Congress, 1774–1996* (Alexandria, VA: CQ Staff Directories, Inc., 1996), 757; Hinds, Asher Crosby, *Hinds' Precedents of the House of Representatives of the United States, Including References to Provisions of the Constitution, the Laws, and Decisions of the United States Senate,* 8 vols. (Washington, DC: Government Printing Office, 1907–1908), II:832–833.

C

Caldwell, Alexander (1830–1917)

United States senator (1871–1873) from Kansas, forced to resign from the Senate before he was expelled for bribing legislators to vote for him in his 1871 senatorial contest. Born in the town of Drake's Ferry, Pennsylvania, on 1 March 1830, Caldwell was the son of James Caldwell, the owner of an iron foundry, and Jane Matilda (née Drake) Caldwell. James Caldwell's father, Alexander, was a native of County Donegal, Ireland, and he and his son James immigrated to America. Jane Drake Caldwell was a descendant of the noted English explorer Sir Francis Drake. Alexander Caldwell, the subject of this biography, attended local public schools and worked as a store clerk and bank officer. His father enlisted in the United States Army to serve in the Mexican War and was killed in the battle of Chapultec. Alexander Caldwell then joined his father's unit, Company M of the Second Regiment of the Pennsylvania Volunteer Infantry, and saw action at such battles as Contreras, Churubusco, Monterey, National Bridge, and the entry into Mexico City. He returned to Pennsylvania and worked in the First National Bank of Columbia as a clerk.

In 1861 Caldwell moved west and settled in Leavenworth, Kansas, where he served for a time as a contractor hired by the United States government to move army supplies to military posts west of the Monroe River. He formed A. Caldwell & Company and eventually employed some 5,000 men in his efforts. When several railroads were built that made his company's work obsolete, he changed his company's emphasis and turned first to supplying the railroads and then to constructing the roads themselves, assisting in the building of the Missouri Pacific Railroad from Kansas City to Leavenworth. He helped to form the Kansas Central Railroad Company and served as vice president of the company.

Caldwell did not seem destined for a political career, especially when in early 1870 he refused a nomination from the Republican Party for a seat in Congress. However, in January 1871, when the Kansas state legislature met to name a successor to U.S. Senator Edmund G. Ross, who had voted to acquit President Johnson of impeachable offenses in 1868 and was refused another nomination by the Republicans, Caldwell was persuaded to throw his hat into the ring. Caldwell was not the only potential candidate: many considered Representative Sidney Clarke, a Republican who had been defeated for reelection in 1870, and Samuel J. Crawford, the thirty-six-year-old governor of Kansas to be worthy of the nomination. Clarke was soon ousted when the legislature met on 10 January 1871, and he threw his support behind Caldwell. Another potential candidate, former Governor Thomas Carney, also threw his support behind Caldwell. Over the next fifteen days, a vicious fight between Democrats and Republicans ensued, but on 25 January Caldwell was elected with eighty-seven votes. Crawford received thirty-four votes and Democrat Wilson Shannon Jr. received two. In the Senate, Caldwell was a devout Republican, speaking against Southern abuses against freed blacks and supporting the Enforcement Act of 1871, which used the law against the Ku Klux Klan. He was named to the Senate committees on naval affairs, the District of Columbia, and mines and mining.

Almost from the start, however, there were rumors that Caldwell and his backers had paid off state legislators to win his election. In fact, there were similar charges against the other U.S. senator from Kansas, Samuel Clarke Pomeroy. After a year of charges and countercharges, the Senate authorized the Senate Committee on Privileges and Elections to investigate and issue a report. Former Representative Sidney Clarke, who had been Caldwell's confidant and had assisted in his election, testified that he was told that Caldwell and his close friends would pay $250,000 to secure votes in the legislature for Caldwell. Former Governor Carney, who had withdrawn from the race and backed Caldwell, testified he was paid $15,000 to do just that. Several friends of Caldwell said that he had admitted that the race had personally cost him $60,000.

An angry Caldwell confronted the Senate committee, demanding to know what authority they had to investigate a state matter, and then dismissing all of the evidence against him as coming from bitter foes and other politicians who were jealous of his election. Despite his attitude, on 17 February 1873, the committee sent to the full Senate a report asking either for Caldwell's election to be voided or for him to be expelled, reporting that he had not been "duly and legally elected" to his seat. A debate broke out in the Senate. Caldwell hired Kansas attorney Robert Crozier as his defense counsel. Many in the Senate felt that the U.S. Senate as a body could not invalidate the action of a state legislature, no matter how crooked it may have been. This had been the opinion of three of the reporting committee's members: John Logan of Illinois, Matthew H. Carpenter of Wisconsin, and Henry B. Anthony of Rhode Island. Even as Caldwell's case was being debated, that of Senator Powell Clayton of Arkansas was being discussed.

Senator Orris S. Ferry (R-CT) took to the floor on 21 March and declared in a moving speech that Caldwell's bribery for his seat forced the Senate to expel him. "The crime of bribery," Ferry explained, "goes down to the very foundations of the institutions under which we live. We all know it and . . . we shall stifle our own consciences if we do not vote to expel." Senators Frederick T. Frelinghuysen of New Jersey and Timothy O. Howe of Wisconsin were of the opinion that Caldwell should not be expelled for a crime of which he had not been convicted in a court of law. However, when these two men surveyed the rest of the Senate, they found that ten to twelve senators were prepared to vote with Caldwell, while the rest would expel him. On 23 March, a resolution to delay a vote on Ferry's motion to expel was tabled. Later that day, seeing the handwriting on the wall, Caldwell submitted his resignation. It was Vice President Schuyler Colfax (who himself was later implicated in political corruption) who announced to a stunned Senate the following morning that Caldwell had made any attempt at expulsion moot. In a tremendous irony, attorney Robert Crozier, who had served as Caldwell's counsel during the expulsion hearings, was elected by the Kansas legislature to fill the vacancy left by Caldwell's resignation.

Caldwell returned to Kansas to live out his life in obscurity. He served as the head of a company that manufactured wagons and carriages from 1877 until 1897 and, in the latter year, became the president of the First National Bank of Leavenworth, where he served until 1915. He died two years later, on 19 May 1917, at the age of eighty-seven, and was buried in the Mount Muncie Cemetery in Leavenworth.

Historian Robert S. Laforte wrote of Caldwell and his times, "Senator Caldwell deserves more coverage than he has thus far received. His election, resignation, and activities as a senator reveal a great deal about politics in the immediate post–Civil War period in Kansas and the United States. Caldwell's place in the Senate's past confirms the older, negative opinion of 'progressive historians,' not the current upbeat views expressed by historical revisionists of the Gilded Age. If nothing else, the senator's experiences bolster Henry Adams's well-known lament that 'one might search the whole list of Congress, Judiciary, and Executive during the twenty-five years [from] 1870–1895, and find little but damaged reputation.'"

See also Pomeroy, Samuel Clarke

References: Butler, Anne M., and Wendy Wolff, *United States Senate Election, Expulsion and Censure Cases, 1793–1990* (Washington, DC: Government Printing Office, 1995), 174–177; Harris, Thomas LeGrand, "Caldwell, Alexander," in Allen Johnson and Dumas Malone, et al., eds., *Dictionary of American Biography*, X vols. and 10 supplements (New York: Charles Scribner's Sons, 1930–1995), II:405–406; LaForte, Robert S., "Gilded Age Senator: The Election, Investigation, and Resignation of Alexander Caldwell, 1871–1873," *Kansas History*, 21:4 (Winter 1998–1999), 234–255; "S.C. Pomeroy and Alexander Caldwell," in George S. Taft, *Compilation of Senate Election Cases From 1789 to 1885* (Washington, DC: Government Printing Office, 1885), 376.

Campaign Finance Scandal 1996

Financial corruption, implicating the Clinton-Gore administration in unethical and potentially illegal conduct in campaign fundraising during the 1996 election cycle. In the final report of the Senate Governmental Affairs Committee's investigation into the scandal, it was noted:

> In mid-1995, the President and his strategists decided that they needed to raise and spend many millions of dollars over and above the permissible limits of the presidential campaign funding law if the President was going to be reelected. They devised a legal theory to support their needs and proceeded to raise and spend $44 million in excess of the Presidential campaign spending limits.
>
> The lengths to which the Clinton/Gore campaign and the White House–controlled Democratic National Committee were willing to go in order to raise this amount of money is essentially the story of the 1996 Presidential campaign scandal. The President and his aides demeaned the offices of the President and Vice President, took advantage of minority groups, pulled down all the barriers that would normally be in place to keep out illegal contributions, pressured policy makers, and left themselves open to strong suspicion that they were selling not only access to high-ranking officials, but policy as well. Millions of dollars were raised in illegal contributions, much of it from foreign sources. When these abuses were discovered, the result was numerous Fifth Amendment claims, flights from the country, and stonewalling from the White House and the DNC.

Following the election debacle in 1994, when Republicans took control of both houses of Congress, President Bill Clinton, staring at low approval ratings, a failed health care initiative, and now the threat of his entire agenda stalled in Congress, looked to be an easy target when he ran for re-election in 1996. Clinton, frightened by the prospect, called in his old friend Dick Morris, a political adviser when Clinton was the governor of Arkansas, to advise him on a course to win re-election. Morris told Clinton that he needed to raise millions of dollars in "soft money" donations—those not covered by campaign finance laws—and outspend his opponent in the 1996 race. Clinton did just this, taking in money from "coffees" he held at the White House, from entertaining contributors in the Lincoln Bedroom in the White House, and collecting funds from overseas sources, such as the Lippo Group, headed by an old Clinton friend, James Riady, an Indonesian businessman. His Vice President Al Gore also collected questionable donations, making calls from his office and visiting a Buddhist temple in Los Angeles to collect funds.

When the 1996 campaign started in early 1996, Clinton was on the air, utilizing his multi-million-dollar war chest to paint any potential rival with a broad brush. As the Republican primaries moved forward, and Senate Majority Leader Robert J. Dole of Kansas looked more and more likely to be the Republican nominee, Clinton and the Democratic Party began to air advertisements on television castigating Dole as an obstructionist who worked with House Speaker Newt Gingrich to hurt Americans. Dole, fighting hard in the primaries, did not have the funds to respond, and the allegations went unchallenged. When the primaries had ended and Dole stood as the nominee, his campaign was penniless, and Clinton's ads continued. It was not until the Republican convention in August, when Dole got a fresh infusion of cash as the party nominee, that he was able to go on television with his own ads. By then, however, it was too late—the impression of him as an evil ogre (Clinton and the DNC aired commercials of a threatening looking Dole in black and white) had settled with the American people. Down in the polls, Dole could not rise to challenge Clinton.

By October, as the campaign began to wind down, it became apparent that Clinton was sailing

Cartoon shows President Bill Clinton sitting on an altar in the lotus position and Vice President Al Gore holding a pot in which he collects money from a line of visitors for the opportunity to whisper into the president's ear. (Library of Congress)

to a double-digit popular vote victory and a landslide in the Electoral College. However, reports soon began to appear that the Democratic National Committee had received some $425,000 in donations from an Indonesian couple, Arief and Soraya Wiriadinata, with ties to Riady's Lippo Group. The Wiriadinatas were residents of Jakarta, Indonesia. As the reports spread, the DNC admitted that it had also accepted $260,000 from a South Korean company. Even though both donations were returned, the story grew bigger as Clinton's ties to Riady were fully explored. More donations, from Asians or Asians in the United States who were not legal citizens (and thus could not make donations to campaigns), were uncovered. On 17 October, *The Wall Street Journal* reported that after a visit by Vice President Gore, members of the Hsi Lai Buddhist Temple (who were monks and had taken vows of poverty) had contributed some $50,000 to the DNC. Five days later, Gore said that he was not aware that the temple event was a fundraiser, a claim later contradicted by memos sent to him. Another Clinton friend, John Huang (pronounced "Wong"), was found to have solicited

money from the Communist government in Beijing, money that ended up in DNC accounts. When a subpoena was issued for Huang's arrest, he fled the country. He later appeared when Judicial Watch, a conservative legal group, handed him a court order.

On 30 October, bowing to pressure from the press (and with Clinton's numbers sinking in the polls), the DNC released a partial list of its donors. That same day, Huang testified that he met numerous times with President Clinton and his wife in the White House. White House logs showed Huang being admitted 78 times in the 15 months before the scandal was uncovered that month. On 5 November, Clinton was re-elected, although by much smaller margins than he had been leading by in the polls just a few weeks earlier; as well, the Democrats, leading in the race to capture the House and Senate, again fell short, and the burgeoning scandal was blamed. In the two months after Clinton's re-election, hundreds of news stories appeared, highlighting each instance of the massive fund-raising program Clinton and his administration had been involved in.

On 13 November, the Justice Department denied a request by Senator John McCain, Republican of Arizona, to have the attorney general appoint an independent counsel to investigate the charges against Clinton. New terms entered the American lexicon: "coffees" and "Lincoln Bedroom stay-overs." Clinton had used the White House as a base for his fundraising parties, in which he served his guests coffee as he asked them to help him raise more and more money. Clinton admitted in January 1997, shortly before his second inauguration, that he rewarded donors with overnight stays in the Lincoln Bedroom.

On 11 March 1997, the Senate voted unanimously to authorize the Senate Governmental Affairs Committee to conduct "an investigation of illegal or improper activities in connection with 1996 Federal election campaigns." A deadline of 31 December 1997 was imposed on the committee to wrap up its work. During its hearings, over a total of 33 days in July, September, and October 1997, the committee heard from 70 witnesses who testified in public, with 200 witness interviews conducted and 196 depositions taken under oath. The delays encountered by the committee were extraordinary: after its authorization, Democrats argued over jurisdiction, claiming that alleged campaign finance violations by the Dole campaign should be investigated as well. Quarrels over the committee's budget and how to approach potential witnesses who exerted their Fifth Amendment rights to keep silent bogged the committee down in senseless minutiae. In the end, 23 witnesses, many of them key to the investigation, asserted this right. Other witnesses demanded a grant of immunity, which either the panel's Democrats or the Justice Department did not support granting. 10 witnesses who were called before the committee fled the United States, including Yah Lin "Charlie" Trie, another old friend of Clintons who had raised money for the DNC, Ted Sioeng, and Pauline Kanchanalak, all foreign money raisers for Clinton/Gore 1996 and for the Democratic National Committee. In all, the committee collected more than 1.5 million documents.

On 5 March 1998, the committee's final report was released. In ten volumes, it dissected the 1996 campaign, criticized both parties for fundraising abuses, but singled out the Clinton/Gore campaign for wanton violations. Eight members, all Republicans, approved the majority report; seven Democrats angrily dissented in the minority report.

In the frenzied drive to raise such large amounts of campaign money, the Democratic Party dismantled its own internal vetting procedures, no longer caring, in effect, where its money came from and who was supplying it. Worse, their campaign eviscerated federal fundraising laws and reduced the White House, key Administration offices, and the Presidency itself, to fundraising tools. For the U.S. political process as a whole, the DNC and White House's reckless fundraising disregarded an obvious risk— the danger that powerful foreign nationals, or even governments, would attempt to buy influence through campaign contributions. The result of all this was foreseeable, including: the erosion of safeguards in U.S. election law designed to guard against political corruption, and unprecedented amounts of illegal foreign contributions making their way into Democratic coffers. The Committee uncovered strong circumstantial evidence that the Government of the People's Republic of China (PRC) was involved in funding, directing, or encouraging some of these foreign contributions.

President Clinton has attempted to distance himself from these scandals by trying to distinguish his own "official" re-election campaign (Clinton/Gore '96) from the abuses the DNC carried out. Based on the evidence compiled by the Committee, however, this distinction is untenable. Indeed, no one has done more to erode this very distinction than the President himself, who with his staff effectively seized control of DNC operations and ran all Democratic party campaign and fundraising efforts out of the White House. During the 1996 campaign, the DNC was the alter ego of the White House.

In the end, nothing came from the entire affair. Attorney General Janet Reno refused to name an independent counsel to investigate the Clinton/Gore campaign, and the Department of Justice secured a few indictments and convictions only against some of the lesser-known characters in this scandal.

See also Clinton, William Jefferson; Gore, Albert Arnold, Jr.; Thompson, Fred Dalton

References: Bedard, Paul, and Donald Lambro, "Fund-Raising Woes Turn Off Many Democratic Donors; DNC Official Cites 'Chilling Effect' of Probes," *The Washington Times,* 11 June 1997, A4; Sandalow, Marc, "The Campaign Finance Controversy: Everything You Wanted to Know about the Fuss over Fundraising— But Were Afraid to Ask," *The San Francisco Chronicle,*

17 March 1997, A3; United States Senate, Committee on Governmental Affairs, *Final Report of the Investigation of Illegal or Improper Activities in Connection with 1996 Federal Election Campaigns, Together with Additional and Minority Views,* 10 vols.(Senate Report 105–167, 105th Congress, 2nd Session) (Washington, DC: Government Printing Office, 1999).

Catron, Thomas Benton (1840–1921)

Delegate (1895–1897) and U.S. senator (1912–1917) from New Mexico, implicated but never charged in the corruption and land fraud in the Colfax County War in New Mexico in the 1870s. Despite being identified with New Mexico, Catron was actually born near Lafayette, Missouri, on 6 October 1840, and he attended the common schools there. He attended and then graduated from the University of Missouri at Columbia in 1860, then joined the Confederate army and saw action during the Civil War. At the close of the conflict, he moved west to New Mexico, where he studied the law, and was admitted to the bar in 1867. He opened a practice in Las Cruces. Before he had earned his law degree, Catron was elected district attorney of the third New Mexico district, serving from 1866 to 1868. In 1869 he was appointed attorney general of New Mexico Territory; he resigned when he was appointed U.S. attorney by President Ulysses S. Grant.

Although he was born and raised a Democrat, Catron saw that power lay in the hands of the Republican Party in New Mexico, and he switched party affiliations as a way to rise politically in the territory. Catron served as a member of the New Mexico Territorial Council in 1884, 1888, 1890, 1899, 1905, and 1909.

Starting in the 1870s, Catron invested heavily in land in Colfax County, New Mexico. The University of New Mexico, in introducing his papers, writes, "To his friends, he was a financial genius and a great leader; to his enemies, he was a greedy land-grabber and a ruthless politician." As an attorney, he was able to use a loophole in the law and requested that his legal fees be paid with land rather than money; by this method, Catron was able to string together tracts of land to make himself a major landowner in New Mexico. And as a leading landowner, Catron was also deeply involved in the politics of the territory. When he acted as counsel to help certain area creditors collect debts against another landowner, John Chisum, the beginnings of what became the "Lincoln County War" were shaped. A number of local businessmen and landowners took sides, either with Chisum or against him. One of these men was Alexander Mc-Sween, who hired Billy the Kid, as well as other outlaws, for protection from Chisum's men. The territorial government, led by Governor Samuel Axtell, allowed this situation to fester while members of Axtell's administration were buying land and influence in Lincoln County. This situation mirrored what occurred in Colfax County from 1875 to 1878. From 1878 to 1881 a shooting war exploded in Lincoln County, leaving many people dead, but others wealthier from their land buying and corruption. When the war first started, President Rutherford B. Hayes declared Lincoln County to be in insurrection and sent Frank W. Angel, a federal investigator, to examine the state of affairs there. Angel discovered that Axtell, Catron, and many other high-ranking officials of the territorial government were implicated in the war. These officials were dubbed the "Santa Fe Ring." Almost all of these men were also Republican Party officials. On Angel's recommendation, Hayes removed Axtell and Catron from positions of power; General Lew Wallace (author of the famed *Ben Hur: A Tale of the Christ*) was named in Axtell's place and helped clean up the situation, so by 1881 calm had settled on both Lincoln and Colfax Counties.

Despite being implicated in corruption and fraud on a massive scale, Catron's political career was barely dented. Although he was defeated in a congressional run in 1892, just two years later he was elected as a delegate to Congress, serving in the Fifty-fourth Congress from 4 March 1895 until 3 March 1897. Defeated for reelection, he resumed the practice of law in Santa Fe. When New Mexico was admitted to the Union as the forty-sixth state in 1911, the legislature selected Catron as one of the first two senators it was entitled to send to Washington. Ironically, the other senator was Albert Bacon Fall, who later, as secretary of the interior in the Harding administration, was convicted and sent to prison for his role in the Teapot Dome scandal.

In 1916 Catron came up for reelection, but decided, at age seventy-six, not to be a candidate. He returned to Santa Fe, where he died on 15 May

1921 at the age of eighty. He was buried in the Fairview Cemetery in that city. Although today he is barely known, Catron may have been one of the most corrupt politicians in the history of the United States.

See also Axtell, Samuel Beach

References: Chamberlain, Kathleen Egan, "Catron, Thomas Benton," in John A. Garraty and Mark C. Carnes, eds., *American National Biography*, 24 vols. (New York: Oxford University Press, 1999), 4:581–582; Duran, Tobias, "Francisco Chalvez, Thomas B. Catron, and Organized Political Violence in Santa Fe in the 1890s." *New Mexico Historical Review* 59 (July 1984), 291–310; Jacobsen, Joel K. "An Excess of Law in Lincoln County: Thomas Catron, Samuel Axtell, and the Lincoln County War." *New Mexico Historical Review* 68 (April 1993), 133–151; Westphall, Victor, *Thomas Benton Catron and His Era* (Tucson: University of Arizona Press, 1973).

Caudle, Theron Lamar

See Income Tax Scandal, Department of Justice (1951–1952)

Censure

An act of a legislature defined as a move "to criticize severely; blame; to express official disapproval of" a certain government official. Censure is considered a lesser form of punishment than impeachment, and many historians and legal authorities consider this to be equal in status with a "rebuke." *Black's Law Dictionary* defines *censure* as "the formal resolution of a legislative, administrative, or other body reprimanding a person, normally one of its own members, for specified conduct."

Under the Constitution, the Senate or House may officially discipline any member for misconduct, and each chamber may specify that misconduct. The U.S. Supreme Court, in case after case, has held that the power to discipline members of the legislature is exclusive to the legislature and beyond judicial review. In *In re Chapman*, 166 U.S. 661 (1897), the Court held that the Senate had the authority to demand subpoenaed testimony in its investigative process. In *United States v. Brewster*, 408 U.S. 501 (1972), the Court held that "[t]he process of disciplining a Member of Congress . . . is not surrounded with the panoply of protective shields that are present in a criminal case. An ac-

cused Member is judged by no specifically articulated standards, and is at the mercy of an almost unbridled discretion of the charging body . . . from whose decisions there is no established right of review."

Four times in American history, the Congress has censured a sitting president: in 1834, Andrew Jackson for illegally removing Bank of the United States deposits; in 1842, John Tyler for unknown reasons; in 1848, James K. Polk for refusing to disclose a "secret" fund in the State Department; and in 1864, Abraham Lincoln for unknown reasons. In 1999 the Senate came close to censuring Bill Clinton for his role in the Monica Lewinsky affair, but Republican opposition caused this punishment to fail of a majority. Jackson's censure is perhaps the most famous: in 1834, the Senate, under control of the opposition Whig party, censured Jackson for removing the deposits from the Bank of the United States, an authority that the Congress had granted solely to the secretary of the treasury, at that time William J. Duane. When Duane refused to go along with Jackson's plan, he was summarily fired; in his place, Jackson named Roger B. Taney, who acceded to the president's plan of action against the bank. Enraged that the president was defying the Congress and its original intent for the bank's deposits, the Senate enacted a resolution: "Resolved, that the President, in the late Executive proceedings in relation to the public revenue, had assumed upon himself authority and power not conferred by the Constitution and laws, but in derogation of both." The word "censure" was never formally utilized, but the slap against the president was just as hard. Jackson condemned the action; in a letter to the Senate he said:

Without notice, unheard and untried, I thus find myself charged on the records of the Senate, and in a form hitherto unknown in our history, with the high crime of violating the laws and Constitution of my country . . . when the Chief Executive Magistrate is, by one of the most important branches of the Government in its official capacity, in a public manner, and by its recorded sentence, but without precedent, competent authority, or just cause, declared guilty of a breach of the laws and Constitution, it is due to his station, to public opinion, and to a proper self-respect [to] promptly expose the wrong which has been done. . . . [I am] perfectly convinced that the discussion and passage of the

In 1834, the Senate censured President Andrew Jackson for removing the deposits from the Bank of the United States. In this political cartoon of the day, United States Bank officials run for cover as President Jackson overthrows the bank by vetoing the renewal of its charter. (Corbis)

above-mentioned resolution were not only unauthorized by the Constitution, but in many respects repugnant to its provisions and subversive of the rights secured by it to other . . . departments, [I should] maintain the supremacy of that sacred instrument and the immunities of the department intrusted to my care. . . . It is alike due to the subject, the Senate, and the people that the views which I have taken of the proceedings referred to, and which compel me to regard them in the light that has been mentioned should be exhibited at length and with the freedom and firmness which are required by an occasion so unprecedented and peculiar. . . . In every other respect each of [the three branches of government] is the coequal of the other two, and all are the servants of the American people, without power or right to control or censure each other in the service of their common superior, save only in the manner and to the degree which that superior has prescribed. . . . The responsibilities of the President are numerous and weighty. He is liable to impeachment for high crimes and misdemeanors . . . the resolution of the Senate is wholly unauthorized by the Constitution,

and in derogation of its entire spirit. It assumes that a single branch of the legislative department may for the purposes of a public censure, and without any view to legislation or impeachment, take up, consider, and decide upon the official acts of the Executive. But in no part of the Constitution is . . . any such power conferred on either branch of the Legislature.

The Senate refused to accept Jackson's protest, and it was only published in the Washington newspaper *Niles' Weekly Register.* The response of Jackson led just five years later to a stunning reversal of fortune: when the Jacksonians took control of the Senate, they had the censure motion expunged from the Senate records, as if it never happened. Historians still debate whether Jackson was actually censured, whether the Senate had the power to censure him, and whether the Jacksonians had the power to expunge the censure. The censure motions against the three other presidents all stand.

The use of censure was specifically allowed for the Congress to punish its own members. Congress also expanded the power to include members not in Congress but in the executive branch of the government. In 1822, Congress censured Major Christopher Van Devanter, the chief clerk of the War Department, for awarding a construction contract to his brother-in-law, Elijah Mix, who in turn sold a quarter interest in the contract back to Van Devanter. The so-called Mix Contract scandal resulted in the contract being revoked and Van Devanter fired. The move by Congress paved the way for the use of censure in future proceedings. Twenty-seven years later, the House censured Secretary of the Treasury William M. Meredith and Attorney General Reverdy Johnson for approving the paying out of interest on a loan by the War Department in which Secretary of War William H. Crawford had a direct financial interest. The House also enacted three distinct resolutions calling the interest payment "improper." In 1859, during a corruption investigation, the House censured Isaac Toucey, secretary of the navy, for awarding contracts to cronies; a minority of the House committee investigating the frauds held that Toucey had acted with the approval of President Buchanan, and they thus demanded that Buchanan be censured also. This did not happen, however. In 1862 the House censured Secretary of War Simon Cameron over alleged corruption in the awarding of contracts for army supplies on which Cameron's cronies profited. A censure resolution was introduced in 1874 by Representative Charles Foster (R-OH) against William A. Richardson, secretary of the treasury, for his alleged failure to supervise contracts handed out by a tax collector, John Sanborn, leading to the so-called Sanborn Contracts scandal. However, Richardson resigned his office and the censure resolution was never formally voted on. In 1892 a House Committee ordered that President Benjamin Harrison's chief of the Bureau of Pensions, Green B. Raum, be removed for using his office for private gain. In the twentieth century, the censure motion has been used only sparingly against noncongressional officials, most notably against members of the Harding and Coolidge administrations in relation to the Teapot Dome scandal.

In the history of the Congress, very few members have faced censure: the total is nine in the Senate and twenty-two in the House. Of the nine senators, four—Hiram Bingham, Thomas J. Dodd, Herman E. Talmadge, and David F. Durenberger—were due to allegations of corruption. In the House, seven of the twenty-two censures of members were because of corruption. However, rules have changed regarding censure in the past century. In Congress today members may also be "denounced," "condemned," "reprimanded," and "rebuked" for their violations of ethics. Historians and legal scholars continue to debate whether these punishments rise to the level of "censure." As well, both houses have held that a member may be censured for acts not related to his or her "official" duties. For example, Representative Adam Clayton Powell was censured by the House, even though it held that the ethics violations he was accused of committing did not bear upon his official duties.

References: *Black's Law Dictionary* (St. Paul, MN: West Publishing Company, 1990), 224; Fisher, Louis, *Constitutional Conflicts between Congress and the President* (Lawrence: University Press of Kansas, 1997), 54–55; Richardson, James D., ed., *A Compilation of the Messages and Papers of the Presidents, 1789–1907,* 9 vols. and 1 appendix (Washington, DC: Government Printing Office, 1896–1900), III:69–93; Schultz, Jeffrey D., *Presidential Scandals* (Washington, DC: CQ Press, 2000), 62–64; *Speech of Mr. Black, of Georgia, on The Right of Members to Their Seats in the House of Representatives. Delivered in the House of Representatives, February 12, 1844* (Washington, DC: Printed at the Globe Office, 1844); Striking of Jackson censure in Register of Debates, 24th Congress, 2nd Session (1837), 379–418, 427–506; Woodward, C. Vann, *The Responses of the Presidents to Charges of Misconduct* (New York: Delacorte Press, 1974), 41.

Chinagate

Financial scandal, concerning alleged payoffs to the 1992 and 1996 election campaigns of President Bill Clinton by corporations doing business in China, which Clinton approved despite national security concerns. The scandal in "Chinagate" grew out of the use of campaign finances to allow technology to be sent to China. In 1994 Bernard L. Schwartz, a longtime Democratic fund-raiser and chairman of the Loral Corporation, a major satellite technology company, wrote a check for $100,000 to the Democratic National Committee (DNC). At the same time, Schwartz asked to be included as a member of a trade mission coordinated by then-Secretary of Commerce Ronald H.

Brown to aid American businesses overseas. Brown's intention on forming these trade missions was to use American government wherewithal to open markets overseas for American businesses. However, it was later discovered, Brown and the DNC made donations to the party a prerequisite to go on these junkets.

Schwartz's desire to be included on the Brown trade mission to China grew out of Loral's desire to be a part of China's expanding market for satellite delivery services for its growing telecommunications sector. China's desire to have Loral make sure its satellites could be launched safely into orbit was teamed with its further desire to gain American expertise in launching rockets—those carrying satellites, as well as those carrying nuclear missiles. A long-standing American policy had infringed on China's ability to launch satellites. In 1992 the United States discovered secret Chinese missile sales to Pakistan, then under American sanctions for their nuclear weapons program. A year later, the new administration of Bill Clinton ordered that no American satellite with sophisticated technology could be launched on board a Chinese rocket. However, the head of the Hughes Company's satellite division, C. Michael Armstrong, wrote two letters to Clinton outlining his past and continued support for the Democratic Party—some $2.5 million in contributions from 1991 to 1993 alone. Armstrong told Clinton that European satellite launchers were profiting from having the American firms excluded from the Chinese market. Two years later, Loral's Schwartz went on a junket with Commerce Secretary Brown. On the trip, Brown helped Schwartz meet with Chinese communications officials. Schwartz later said that the junket "helped open doors that were not open before." While in China, Schwartz signed a lucrative deal with the Chinese government allowing for Loral to provide China with a mobile telephone network. Schwartz now told top Democrats that more contributions would flow into the party's coffers in exchange for loosening the regulations. Within two years, the Clinton administration ended all sanctions on China relating to American satellites, and control over transfers of American satellite technology was moved from the Department of State, where support for keeping the sanction was strong, to the Department of Commerce, where Brown, former head of the DNC, favored

ending the sanctions. Schwartz later called the donations and the waivers "coincidence."

What exposed the so-called Chinagate scandal was a rather unintentional rocket launch on 15 February 1996. The Chinese launched a Long March 3B rocket carrying an American-built Intelsat 708 satellite from the Xichang launch center in China. However, just twenty-two seconds after launch, the rocket strayed off its course and, before it could be destroyed, slammed into a nearby neighborhood, killing unknown numbers of people. One witness later reported that "thousands of corpses were loaded in dozens of trucks and buried in mass graves." The technicians for Loral, the company that made the rocket, examined the remains and found a glitch in the guidance control system that could only be fixed by using American technology that had never been sanctioned for foreign use by the American government. Despite the restrictions, Loral went ahead and used the patch. What no one knew was that China used the Long March 3B not only for satellite launches, but also for their intercontinental ballistic missiles—many of them aimed at the United States. Thus, an American company had assisted the Chinese in making sure their missiles could be aimed better at the American nation. The Cox Report, which later examined the scandal as part of its mandate to investigate Chinese donations to the Democratic Party and spying in the United States, concluded:

> Although Loral and Hughes were well aware that a State Department license was required to provide assistance related to the guidance system of a PRC [People's Republic of China] rocket, neither company applied for or obtained the required license. Loral was warned of the need for a license at the time it agreed to participate in the investigation, but took no action.
>
> Loral and Hughes also failed to properly brief participants in the failure investigation of U.S. export requirements, failed to monitor the investigation as it progressed, and failed to take adequate steps to ensure that no prohibited information was passed to the PRC.

When word began to leak out that Loral had used its Chinese contract to fix the satellites with American technology, the Pentagon launched an investigation. After a year, these investigators concluded that U.S. national security had been harmed. It was at this same time that allegations of campaign finance violations by the 1996 Clinton-Gore campaign came to light and were being investigated. The fact that Clinton had taken campaign donations from a company that aided the Chinese in making their nuclear missiles more reliable was a stunning development that rocked the nation's capital. In February 1997, however, Clinton added insult to injury by signing an order making wholly legal the transfer of technology that Loral had done—without U.S. government approval or waiver. A writer for the magazine *Human Events* wrote, "The greatest scandal of the Clinton administration is that the President of the United States has sold out the national security interests of our country to Communist China."

As outrage in Congress grew, a resolution was enacted on 18 June 1998 establishing the Select Committee on U.S. National Security and Military/Commercial Concerns with the People's Republic of China to investigate the claims against Loral and Hughes and to ascertain whether the laws were loosened because of campaign donations. The final report was issued on 25 May 1999. In it the committee explained that because other congressional committees—including the Senate Governmental Affairs Committee, chaired by Senator Fred Thompson (R-TN)—were investigating campaign finance abuses by the Clinton campaign, they were limited in their investigative sphere. Every witness that the committee called exerted their Fifth Amendment rights against self-incrimination, and no firm evidence could be found linking the donations with the waivers.

In the end, no one from Loral or Hughes went to prison, and the ties between Clinton and the donations were never conclusively established.

See also Clinton, William Jefferson; Cox Report; Gore, Albert Arnold, Jr.

References: Chapman, Michael, "An Inside Job at Commerce? Satellite Secrets Left Department with Official," *Investor's Business Daily,* 19 June 1998, A1, A28; Gertz, Bill, *Betrayal: How the Clinton Administration Undermined American Security* (Washington, DC: Regnery Publishing, 1999); Marcus, Ruth, and John Mintz, "Big Donor Calls Favorable Treatment a 'Coincidence,'" *Washington Post,* 25 May 1998, A1; Timperlake, Edward, and William C. Triplett II, *Year of the Rat: How Bill Clinton Compromised U.S. Security for Chinese Cash* (Washington, DC: Regnery Publishing, 1998).

Choate, Joseph Hodges (1832–1917)

American lawyer and diplomat, a leader against the Tweed Ring and corruption in Tammany Hall in New York City. The youngest son of Dr. George Choate and Margaret Manning (née Hodges), Joseph Choate was born in Salem, Massachusetts, on 24 January 1832. He was descended from a long line of New England pioneers, his distant relative John Choate emigrating from England in 1643 and settling in Massachusetts. George Choate was a graduate of Harvard, so he sent his sons there, including Joseph, who graduated in 1852. That same year, Joseph entered the Harvard Law School and two years later earned a law degree. He spent time finishing his education in the Boston office of Hodges and Saltonstall (of which his cousin was a partner), and in October 1855 he was admitted to the Massachusetts bar. He moved to New York City and joined the law firm of Butler, Evarts & Southmayd. Because of his legal acumen, within three years he was invited to become a partner in the firm, renamed Evarts, Choate, Sherman and Léon.

Lawyer and diplomat Joseph Hodges Choate. Choate, a member of the Committee of Seventy, spoke out against the excesses of the Tweed Ring and corruption in New York City's Tammany Hall. (Library of Congress)

A Republican, Choate became one of the first persons with influence to be heard to speak out against the excesses of the ring of politicians around William M. Tweed. At a meeting of luminaries at the city's Cooper Union on 4 September 1871, Choate called for the formation of a council to oppose the Tweed Ring. Thus, Choate became a member of the so-called Committee of Seventy, formed by seventy major personalities from all walks of life in New York City to call for an end to the reign of Tweed and his cronies. Because of his work in helping to bring down Tweed and his gang, Choate became not only a legal luminary but a political one as well. In 1894 when Tammany Hall again reared its corrupt head in the form of "Boss" Richard Croker, Choate once again stepped forward when he acted as a member of the "Committee of Thirty" in opposition to Croker's rule. And although he was a Republican, he was not against speaking out against corruption in his own party. In 1903 when Senator Thomas C. Platt (R-NY) was up for reelection, Choate consented to run as a protest candidate in opposition to Platt and "bossism." Choate knew that Platt wielded absolute authority in the party, and his reelection was a foregone conclusion—but Choate desired to run anyway. As his biographer, Theron George Strong, later wrote, Choate said, "I told them I would run if I only got one vote. In fact I got seven, and I regarded that as a real triumph." Choate never held an elective office, but because of his long career, he was named by President William McKinley as the U.S. ambassador to the Court of St. James (now called the ambassador to Great Britain) where he served from 1899 until 1905.

Choate is considered one of America's finest legal minds. He served as president of the American Society for the Judicial Settlement of International Disputes and vice president of the Carnegie Endowment for International Peace. He argued numerous cases before the United States Supreme Court, including that of *In re Neagle* (135 U.S. 1), in which the Court exonerated a man who had killed a judge to protect a justice of the Supreme Court, and the famed *Income Tax Cases* (57 U.S. Y29; 158 U.S. 601) before the court in 1895. In 1907 he was one of two American representatives at the Second Peace Congress at The Hague, the Netherlands. When World War I broke out, he harshly criticized President Wilson for refusing to enter the war, but he later apologized. Choate worked right up until his death on 14 May 1917 at the age of eighty-five.

References: Martin, Edward Sandford, *The Life of Joseph Hodges Choate, As Gathered Chiefly from His Letters*, 2 vols. (New York: Charles Scribner's Sons, 1920); Strong, Theron George, *Joseph Choate, New Englander, New Yorker, Lawyer, Ambassador* (New York: Dodd, Mead & Company, 1917), 88.

Cianci, Vincent A, Jr. (1941–)

Mayor of Providence, Rhode Island, (1991–2002) indicted and convicted of racketeering conspiracy in 2002 for his role in corruption uncovered in city contracts. Cianci, despite his conviction, remains a popular politician in Providence. Born in that city on 30 April 1941, he is the son of Dr. Vincent A. Cianci. He was educated at the Moses Brown School in Providence and later earned a bachelor's degree in government at Fairfield University in Fairfield, Connecticut, a master's degree at Villanova University, and a J.D. degree from the Marquette University School of Law. In 1966 Cianci entered the U.S. Army, serving in the Military Police Corps until 1969 and until 1972 served in the U.S. Army Reserves, Civil Affairs Branch.

In 1967, while serving in the army, Cianci was admitted to the Rhode Island bar. Two years later, he was named a special assistant attorney general and in 1973, when he left the army, he became the main prosecutor of the Rhode Island attorney general's Anti-Corruption Strike Force, investigating political corruption in the state. He was holding that position in 1974 when he ran for and was elected mayor of Providence, Rhode Island, at the age of thirty-three, defeating a very popular incumbent, Joe Doorley. He was reelected in 1978 for a second four-year term and in 1982 for a two-year term after the city constitution was changed. In 1984, after three terms, Cianci did not run for reelection when he admitted to assaulting a contractor after having had an affair with the man's wife. Cianci returned to private life, resumed his law practice, and for a time hosted a popular radio talk show in Providence. In 1990, however, after six years out of power, Cianci once again ran for mayor and was elected. He was reelected in 1992, 1994, 1996, and 1998.

During his tenure as mayor, disturbing allegations of political corruption against Cianci arose.

In 1998 the federal government initiated Operation Plunder Dome to investigate corruption in the Providence City Hall. In July 1999 Cianci's former chief of staff, Frank Corrente, was indicted on charges of extortion. Cianci, denying any ties to the charges, told reporters, "I'm saddened by it. Frank is a friend of mine—I have a tremendous amount of sympathy for him and his family. I just can't believe—I don't want to believe he did anything wrong, because I've never known him to do anything wrong."

The Operation Plunder Dome investigation closed in on Cianci. On 2 April 2001, a federal grand jury indicted Cianci on charges of extortion, conspiracy, racketeering, money laundering, and tampering with a witness. The indictment ran for ninety-seven pages. Cianci took a devil-may-care attitude at a press conference: "It's ninety-seven pages," he said. "It goes on and on. I'm not afraid of this. Ninety-seven plus zero still equals zero."

On 17 April 2002, Cianci went on trial with two other defendants: Corrente, his former chief of staff; and Richard Autiello, a member of the Providence Towing Association and owner of an automobile company in Providence, who had been indicted the same day as Corrente on charges of racketeering conspiracy. (Cianci's attorney, Richard Egbert, had also served as counsel for another politician indicted for political corruption: Rhode Island Governor Edward DiPrete.) In closing arguments, Assistant U.S. Attorney Richard W. Rose told the jury that Cianci, using a local businessman, sold entry to city hall. "The evidence shows that the price of admission was often $5,000. . . . Want a job? Five thousand. Want to be on the [city's official] tow list? Five thousand. Want to grease the chairman of the tax board? Five thousand. It was a city for sale, where anything could be had for a price." On 24 June 2002, after nine days of deliberations, the jury found Cianci, Corrente, and Autiello guilty of racketeering conspiracy. Cianci was acquitted on eleven additional charges. Corrente was convicted of six of sixteen counts, while Autiello was convicted of three of seven counts. Following the verdict, Cianci maintained his usual attitude. "That stain [of corruption] hasn't stuck on my jacket yet."

Racketeering conspiracy carries a maximum penalty of twenty years in prison and/or $250,000 in fines. In September 2002 Cianci was sentenced to 64 months in prison and fined $100,000.

References: The author wishes to thank journalist Brian Mooney for his assistance in writing this entry; "Convicted Providence Mayor Won't Run Again," *USA Today,* 26 June 2002, A3; Ferdinand, Pamela, "Providence Mayor Is Found Guilty," *Washington Post,* 25 June 2002, A2; Mooney, Brian C., "Cianci Found Guilty of Conspiracy: R.I Mayor Says He Has No Plan to Quit Office," *The Boston Globe,* 25 June 2002, A1.

Civil Service Act

See Pendleton Civil Service Act

Civil Service Reform

See Curtis, George William; Eaton, Dorman Bridgman; Pendleton, George Hunt; Pendleton Civil Service Act.

Claiborne, Harry Eugene

See Claiborne v. United States

Claiborne v. United States, 465 U.S. 1305 (1984)

Supreme Court ruling decided on the narrow grounds of whether a "sitting federal judge may . . . be criminally prosecuted before being removed from office by impeachment" by the U.S. Senate. Judge Harry E. Claiborne, a federal judge on the District Court for the District of Nevada, was indicted in December 1983 for taking bribes (violations of 18 U.S.C. § 201[c] and 18 U.S.C. § 1343). To forestall going to jail before impeachment proceedings could be brought against him, Claiborne sought a ruling from the Ninth Circuit Court of Appeals "that a sitting federal judge may not be criminally prosecuted before being removed from office by impeachment, and that the government prosecuted him in order to punish him for decisions made as a federal judge." The court denied his appeal. Chief Justice Rehnquist (who was serving in rotation on the Ninth Circuit as a circuit judge) denied the appeal, simply explaining, "I do not believe that four Justices of this Court would vote to grant certiorari to review any one of these claims at the present stage of this litigation, and I therefore deny the application." After

Claiborne was impeached, the U.S. Supreme Court held that a sitting federal judge could be impeached and removed for taking bribes.

References: "Claiborne, Harry E.," in Jay Robert Nash, *Encyclopedia of World Crime: Criminal Justice, Criminology, and Law Enforcement,* 4 vols. (Wilmette, IL: CrimeBooks, Inc., 1989), II:717; Geer, Carri, "Ex-Judge's Trial Rings Familiar: The Trial of Former District Judge Gerard Bongiovanni Parallels the Plight of a Past U.S. District Court Jurist," *Las Vegas Review-Journal,* 30 November 1997, A1; *United States v. Claiborne* 727 F.2d 842 (1984).

Clark, William Andrews (1839–1925)

United States senator (1899–1900, 1901–1907) from Montana, resigned from the Senate when accused of electoral misconduct and bribery, but was reelected the following year to the same seat. Born on his family's farm near the town of Connellsville, Pennsylvania, on 8 January 1839, Andrews was the son of Scotch-Irish immigrants John and Mary (née Andrews) Clark. He attended the common schools of the area, as well as the Laurel Hill Academy, but much of his education was interrupted to work on his family's farm. In 1856 the Clarks moved to Iowa, and William Clark furthered his education there at an academy in Birmingham and studied law at the Iowa Wesleyan University in Mount Pleasant. He never received a degree from either of these institutions, but he did teach while he studied the law.

In 1862 Clark moved to Central City, Colorado, where he worked in the quartz mines nearby. A year later, he moved again, this time settling in Bannack, Montana, a state with which he would be identified for the remainder of his life. He worked as a placer miner in that town for two years, later engaging in business pursuits in the mercantile trade in the cities of Blackfoot and Helena, and in banking in Deer Lodge. In 1877 he was named to a state battalion with the rank of major, which pursued Chief Joseph and the Nez Perce Indians to the Bear Paw Mountains. A Democrat, Clark served as president of the state constitutional convention in 1884 and of another convention in 1889 that considered amendments to the state constitution.

In 1898 Clark was elected to the U.S. Senate for the term commencing on 4 March 1899. Soon there were allegations that he had used his financial wherewithal to assist in his election. The Sen-

ate Committee on Privileges and Elections took up the case in 1899. The *Literary Digest,* a summary of contemporary journalistic thinking and writing in America in the latter nineteenth century and early twentieth century, editorialized, "The testimony now being given before the Senate Committee on Privileges and Elections in the hotly contested case of Senator Clark of Montana 'is revealing the seamy and corrupt side of Montana politics,' says the Chicago *Evening Post,* 'in a manner calculated to produce general disgust.' The Washington correspondent of the Boston *Transcript* says that it 'shows what a war between two not overscrupulous multimillionaires can accomplish for the political degradation of a commonwealth.'" The Senate Committee's decision to strip Clark of his seat was leaked, and, on 15 May 1900, Clark resigned before this could formally occur. However, to express outrage at the Senate's decision to force Clark out, Montana Governor Robert Burns Smith, a Democrat, named Clark to fill the vacancy caused by his own resignation, and Clark returned to the Senate, the only time in American history in which this situation has occurred. However, the Senate once again stated that Clark could not hold his seat and declared it vacant. In 1901 the Montana legislature elected Clark to fill this "vacancy," and this time he was seated, serving a full six-year term until 3 March 1907. He was not a candidate for reelection. This time, there were no allegations of impropriety, or perhaps the Senate was tired to trying to strip Clark of the seat.

After leaving the Senate, Clark resumed his business interests, which included banking, copper mining, and railroading. He moved to New York, where he died on 2 March 1925 at the age of eighty-six and was buried in Woodlawn Cemetery there. The William Andrews Clark Memorial Library, on the campus of the University of California at Los Angeles, was named in his honor by his son, a noted book collector of the early twentieth century.

References: Butler, Anne M., and Wendy Wolff, *United States Senate Election, Expulsion and Censure Cases, 1793–1990* (Washington, DC: Government Printing Office, 1995), 170–173; Foot, Forrest L., "The Senatorial Aspirations of William A. Clark, 1898–1901: A Study in Montana Politics" (Ph.D. dissertation, University of California, 1941); Malone, Michael P., "Midas of the West: The Incredible Career of William Andrews Clark." *Montana: The Magazine of Western History* 33

(Autumn 1983), 2–17; "The Montana Senatorial Scandal," *The Literary Digest,* XX:3 (20 January 1900), 74; Phillips, Paul Chrisler, "Clark, William Andrews," in Allen Johnson and Dumas Malone, et al., eds., *Dictionary of American Biography,* (New York: Charles Scribner's Sons, 1930–1995), II:144–146.

Clayton, Powell (1833–1914)

Governor of Arkansas (1868–1871), United States senator (1871–1877) from Arkansas, investigated for, but cleared of charges of corruption while he was governor. Born in Bethel, Pennsylvania, on 7 August 1833, he was the son of John Clayton, a surveyor, and Ann (née Clark) Clayton. He received his education in the common schools of the area and at the Partridge Military Academy in Bristol, Pennsylvania. He studied civil engineering in Wilmington, Delaware, and after he moved to Kansas in 1855 he made that field his life's work, being appointed as the city engineer for Leavenworth, Kansas, in 1857. (Some sources list this as 1859, but his official congressional biography gives the 1857 date.)

When the Civil War broke out, Clayton volunteered for service as a captain in the First Kansas Infantry, rising to the rank of colonel in the Fifth Kansas Cavalry. He was sent to Missouri and Arkansas and saw action at Little Rock. For his work in Arkansas, he was given the rank of brigadier general and mustered out of the Union army on 24 August 1865. He then settled in Arkansas and became a gentleman cotton planter in the town of Pine Bluff.

When a new constitution was promulgated for Arkansas, an election for governor was ordered. During the war, Governor Harris Flanigan, a Confederate sympathizer, had been removed from office by Union forces, and Isaac Murphy, a Democrat and Unionist, was installed as provisional governor, serving from 20 January 1864. Under the new election laws, former Confederates were barred from voting. Clayton, a Republican, ran unopposed because the entire Democratic party in the state had been run by Confederates. Despite having no opposition, Clayton campaigned on the "doctrines of loyalty, freedom, Negro rights, economic development, and free public education for both races alike." With his election as governor, and with a Republican legislature, Arkansas was readmitted to the Union after ratifying the Thirteenth and Fourteenth Amendments to the Constitution. Dubbed a "carpetbagger" by his opponents, Clayton went after them with a vengeance. He declared martial law in the state and called out a militia, composed of freed slaves, to hunt down the Ku Klux Klan.

It was while he was governor that allegations arose against Clayton that he had used state bonds to finance railroads to be built in the state and that he had fraudulently won the 1868 election. Clayton was able to blunt any impeachment proceedings because his party controlled the state senate, and conviction was out of the question. Clayton wrote in his 1915 memoirs, *The Aftermath of the Civil War, in Arkansas,* "The primary object of the impeachment proceedings was to cause my suspension from office, the induction of Lieutenant-Governor [J. M.] Johnson to the Gubernatorial chair, and such delay in the prosecution of the impeachment that I would have remained indefinitely out of office, while my enemies worked out their ulterior purposes. The disastrous failure of this whole conspiracy greatly strengthened me with my party, as is shown by the results of my second election to the United States Senate, which occurred on March 15, 1871, when I received a two-thirds majority on [a] joint ballot: all Republicans—18 votes in the Senate—and 42 in the House." Despite the allegations against him, it was never proved that Clayton ever did anything wrong.

Clayton served in the U.S. Senate from 4 March 1871 until 3 March 1877, which is one full six-year term. There, he served as the chairman of the Committee on Enrolled Bills (Forty-third Congress) and of the Committee on Civil Service Retrenchment (Forty-fourth Congress). After refusing a second term, he left politics and served as a member of the Republican National Committee. In 1897 President William McKinley named him U.S. minister to Mexico, replacing Matt W. Ransom, who had served in the previous administration. Clayton was promoted to ambassador in 1898 and remained in Mexico until 26 May 1905, when he was replaced by Edwin H. Conger. He returned to Arkansas, where he remained until moving to Washington, D.C., in 1912. He died there two years later, on 25 August 1914, less than three weeks after his eighty-first birthday. For his wartime service to his nation, Clayton was laid to rest in Arlington National Cemetery in Fort Myer, Virginia.

References: Butler, Anne M., and Wendy Wolff, *United States Senate Election, Expulsion and Censure Cases, 1793–1990* (Washington, DC: Government Printing Office, 1995), 170–173; Clayton, Powell, *The Aftermath of the Civil War in Arkansas* (New York: Neale Publishing, 1915), 319–328; Driggs, Orval Truman, Jr., "The Issues of the Powell Clayton Regime, 1868–1871," *Arkansas Historical Quarterly,* 8 (Spring 1949), 1–75; "Powell Clayton," in Timothy P. Donovan, Willard B. Gatewood, Jr., and Jeannie M. Whayne, eds., *The Governors of Arkansas: Essays in Political Biography* (Fayetteville: University of Arkansas Press, 1995), 46–57; Swinney, Everette. "United States v. Powell Clayton: Use of the Federal Enforcement Acts in Arkansas." *Arkansas Historical Quarterly* 26 (Summer 1967): 143–154; Thomas, David Y., "Clayton, Powell," in Allen Johnson and Dumas Malone, et al., eds., *Dictionary of American Biography,* X vols. and 10 supplements (New York: Charles Scribner's Sons, 1930–1995), II:187–188; Westwood, Howard C. "The Federals' Cold Shoulder to Arkansas' Powell Clayton." *Civil War History* 26 (September 1980): 240–256.

Clean Politics Act of 1939
See Hatch Act

Clinton, William Jefferson (1946–)

Forty-second president of the United States (1993–2001) and only the second president in American history to be impeached, in this case for allegedly lying before a federal grand jury investigating charges of obstruction of justice. Investigated for much of his time in office for such scandals as Whitewater, Travelgate, Filegate, Chinagate, and an affair with an aide, Monica Lewinsky, which led to his impeachment, Clinton left office still popular with the American people. He finished his scandal-ridden tenure by issuing numerous pardons, many of which became highly controversial, leading to the scandal known as Pardongate. Clinton was born William Jefferson Blythe IV in Hope, Arkansas, on 19 August 1946, the son of William Jefferson Blythe III, a traveling salesman who was killed in an automobile accident three months before his son was born, and Virginia (née Cassidy) Blythe. Virginia Blythe left her son with her parents in Hope while she went to New Orleans to finish her training to become a nurse anesthetist. In 1950 William joined her in Hot Springs, Arkansas, where she had moved after marrying Roger Clinton. When he was fifteen years old, William Blythe took the name of his stepfather, despite the fact that Clinton was an alcoholic who regularly beat William's mother.

From an early age, Bill Clinton was interested in student government, and in 1963, at age seventeen, he was able to journey to Washington, D.C., as part of Boy's Nation, a student government and public affairs organization, where he met Senator James William Fulbright of Arkansas, and, in a moment caught on film, shook the hand of President John F. Kennedy. The following year, Clinton went to Georgetown University in Washington, D.C., and at the same time earned tuition money working for Senator Fulbright. Clinton graduated from Georgetown in 1968 with a bachelor of science degree in international affairs. He won a Rhodes Scholarship and went to Oxford University in England, where he studied government, but did not earn a degree. It was during his time at Oxford that he received a draft notice, but he decided to enter the Reserve Officers' Training Corps (ROTC) instead. He then asked to be let out of ROTC. Charges that he dodged the draft in this fashion would later come back to haunt Clinton. After two years at Oxford and his chances of being drafted had ended, Clinton returned to the United States, where he began law school at Yale University. While attending Yale, he worked for the election of Joseph I. Lieberman to the U.S. Senate and met a fellow student, Hillary Rodham, whom he later married.

After receiving his law degree from Yale in 1973, Clinton returned to Arkansas, where for a time he taught law at the University of Arkansas at Fayetteville. In 1974 he decided to enter politics and ran for a seat in the U.S. House of Representatives from Arkansas' Third District. His outlook seemed bright: the resignation of President Richard M. Nixon, caught in the wake of the Watergate scandal, made the country sour on Republicans. However, Clinton challenged a strong Republican incumbent, Representative John Paul Hammerschmidt, and lost that race. However, Clinton finished with 48.5 percent of the vote, losing by the narrowest margins ever against the popular Hammerschmidt. The experience gave Clinton new impetus to continue in Arkansas politics.

In 1975 he decided to run for state attorney general. Defeating a field of strong candidates and capturing the Democratic nomination with 56 percent of the vote, Clinton was able to avoid a runoff and, with no Republican opposition, was elected. In 1976 he served as the coordinator for Jimmy Carter's presidential campaign in Arkansas. Just two years later, Clinton decided to run for governor. Only thirty-two years old, he nonetheless campaigned as a populist, opposing a tax cut. He defeated Republican State Chairman Lynn Lowe in the general election and became, with the exception of John Seldon Roane (1849–1852), the youngest governor in Arkansas history. In his first term, Clinton set out an ambitious agenda of fixing roads, increasing teacher salaries, and instituting a system of health care in Arkansas. However, a series of events beyond his control, as well as one within his control, doomed his tenure. Riots by Cuban refugees, housed by the U.S. government at Fort Chafee, Arkansas, and a number of natural disasters plagued the state. But Clinton's raising of taxes on common goods, in the midst of a national economic slowdown, cost him support. In 1980, running for reelection, he was upset by Republican businessman Frank White.

In 1982 Clinton decided to make a comeback. He aired television commercials in which he apologized for the errors he made in his first term and asked for the forgiveness of the voters. The tactic worked: Clinton won the Democratic nomination, and, with 55 percent of the vote, defeated White to become the first governor in Arkansas history to return to office after being voted out. Having learned the lessons that led to his defeat in 1980, Clinton decided to push a more moderate and less ambitious agenda, this time emphasizing slower but more attainable goals in education, environmental protection, and siding against tax raises on gas and diesel fuel (his veto was overridden by the state legislature). This slower, more moderate approach won the voters over, and Clinton was reelected to another two-year term in 1984. In 1986 with the state constitution changed to allow for a four-year term, Clinton was reelected and became a rising star in the Democratic Party. Despite his dreadfully long speech (for which he was booed) at the 1988 Democratic National Convention in Atlanta, Clinton's star continued to rise. After his reelection in 1990, many believed that Clinton would run for president, despite his promise that he would serve out his term as governor.

On 3 October 1991, Clinton announced that he would seek the Democratic nomination for president. Many considered the move folly, mainly because President George H. W. Bush, the incumbent, stood at record high numbers in public approval polls after the Persian Gulf War. Nonetheless, Clinton entered the race. As the American economy sputtered, and Bush's numbers dropped, the battle for the Democratic presidential nomination heated up between Clinton, former U.S. Senator Paul Tsongas of Massachusetts, and Senator Robert Kerrey of Nebraska. Clinton's chances seemed to take a hit when two scandals enveloped his campaign: the idea that he may have dodged the draft during the Vietnam War, and allegations that he had been having a long-time relationship with a lounge singer, Gennifer Flowers. Clinton denied both stories, but they bit into his poll numbers. He slid into second place in New Hamshire, a critical state, but he recovered, went on to win a series of important primaries and in August 1992 accepted the nomination of his party to be president. He selected Senator Albert A. Gore Jr. of Tennessee as his running mate, defying political wisdom by selecting another Southerner to be on the ticket. Republican President Bush and billionaire businessman H. Ross Perot, running on a third-party ticket, attacked Clinton and his handling of Arkansas during his tenure. They pointed to more than 120 tax increases in ten years, with results showing Arkansas at the bottom of every economic and educational measurement scale in the nation. Bush characterized Clinton as a "failed governor of a small state." Despite these charges Arkansas had made steady progress in many areas, with Clinton's initiatives in education and health leading the way. The American economy was the key issue of the 1992 campaign, and with the nation in recession, the voters looked for an alternative. On 3 November 1992, Clinton won the election, garnering 43 percent of the vote in a three-way race, besting Bush's 38 percent and Perot's 19 percent, the second largest vote for an independent candidate in American history. Clinton, at forty-six years old, was one of the youngest men to become president. However, in order to win the election, Clinton had made several back room deals,

BALANCE

BUDGET

Editorial cartoon showing President Bill Clinton walking a tightrope by using the budget on one hand and Monica Lewinsky on the other. (Library of Congress)

particularly with foreign sources, and these would come back to haunt his entire administration.

Soon after taking office, Clinton was forced to deal with allegations that he and his wife had profited illegally from a series of investments in a land scheme called Whitewater. Although he resisted pressure to do so for a long time, in the end he relented and asked that Attorney General Janet Reno appoint an independent counsel to clear up the matter. Soon, another scandal hit, when Paula Corbin Jones, a former Arkansas state employee, filed a sexual harassment suit against Clinton, alleging that as governor, Clinton had demanded sexual favors from her in exchange for better positions in the state government. The case went to the U.S. Supreme Court, which eventually allowed the case to proceed while Clinton was in office. Clinton was also hit with the so-called Chinagate scandal. In 1994 allegations arose that Clinton's administration was giving favorable treatment to companies that had given his campaign financial support in exchange for loosening regulations on shipping sensitive technology to Communist China. This scandal led to an independent counsel investigation of Clinton's secretary of commerce, Ron Brown, and the congressional investigation that culminated in the release of the Cox Report.

Dissatisfaction with Clinton's efforts to solve the nation's health care crisis and tax hikes passed by Democrats in Congress led to the Republicans taking control of both houses of Congress after the midterm elections in 1994. Clinton feared that his reelection in 1996 was not at all assured.

Advised that he needed to raise as much money as possible and go on the attack against his Republican opponents as early as possible, Clinton went on a crusade to collect campaign donations from every conceivable source. As later documented in an investigation by the Senate Governmental Affairs Committee, Clinton and Vice President Gore used fund-raising methods that even Clinton's defenders called embarrassing: offering overnight stays in the Lincoln Bedroom in the White House to big dollar donors; holding meetings (called "coffees") in the White House during which donations were solicited; making calls from government offices to ask for donations; taking money from foreign sources, particularly from the Chinese; allowing Secretary of Commerce Ron Brown (who was killed in a plane crash in 1995) to take donors on "trade missions" where they could get official American backing for expanding their businesses overseas. At the same time these events were occurring, Clinton was carrying on a secret affair with a young White House intern, Monica Lewinsky.

Clinton went on to a landslide reelection victory in November 1996 and became the first Democrat since Franklin Delano Roosevelt to win a second term. Prior to this victory, however, stories began to leak out about Chinese money making its way into Clinton's 1996 campaign. These stories may well have cost the Democrats control of the House of Representatives that year. Just after Clinton was inaugurated a second time, stories of the overnight stays, Chinese money, and other questionable fund-raising tactics hit the press. Clinton told reporters that he had remained "within the letter of the law," but questions persisted. In 1997 the Senate Governmental Affairs Committee, led by Senator Fred Dalton Thompson, Republican of Tennessee, investigated the allegations that Clinton had funded his 1996 campaign with illegal Chinese contributions. This investigation, as well as that conducted by the Select Committee on U.S. National Security and Military/Commercial Concerns with the People's Republic of China, also known as the Cox Committee, demonstrated that Clinton had both solicited and accepted illegal foreign funds for his 1996 race and was allowing American firms to aid China with missile technology in exchange for campaign donations as well. The allegations also tarred Vice President Gore. In the end, neither man faced prosecution for the alleged crimes. Critics contend this was because Attorney General Janet Reno, in charge of the investigations relating specifically to campaign finance abuses, refused to name a special counsel to look into the matter.

In January 1998 the Monica Lewinsky affair broke in the press and nearly led to Clinton's removal. Clinton had been carrying on an affair with a White House intern; however, when questioned about it in relation to a lawsuit by former Arkansas worker Paula Jones, he denied it. Jones had appealed all the way to the U.S. Supreme Court to be able to continue her lawsuit for sexual harassment during Clinton's term in office, and the Supreme Court had agreed in a landmark decision. Clinton underwent strict questioning by Jones's attorneys, and under oath he lied about matters relating to Lewinsky and gifts he had given her.

Kenneth W. Starr, the independent counsel who was investigating the Whitewater affair, was charged by Attorney General Reno to investigate whether Clinton had suborned perjury and obstructed justice in the Lewinsky matter. At first, Clinton denied having an affair with Lewinsky, asking her to lie, or to cover up or obstruct any investigation. Clinton's supporters accused Starr, a Republican who had served as solicitor general in the George Bush administration, of conducting a vendetta against Clinton. But during months of investigation, Starr was able to ascertain that Clinton indeed did have an affair with Lewinsky, and he charged Clinton with lying under oath and obstructing justice.

As per the statute, when an independent counsel finds evidence of an impeachable offense, he or she must make a report to the U.S. House of Representatives spelling out the charges in preparation for an impeachment inquiry. Starr did just this, and for the first time since Andrew Johnson in 1868, an impeachment inquiry was begun against a sitting American president. The American public became disenchanted with the investigation, and in November 1998 handed Democrats a large number of congressional seats in the midterm elections. Despite this, the Republican majority went forward with impeachment hearings and on 19 December 1998, impeached Clinton on four articles alleging perjury and obstruction of justice. For the first time in American history, an elected president underwent an impeachment trial in the U.S. Senate, at that time led by Republicans by a fifty-five to forty-five margin.

However, Democrats held firm in their belief that Clinton was not guilty of impeachable offenses, making conviction by the required two-thirds vote—or sixty-seven senators—an impossibility. On 12 February 1999, the Senate acquitted Clinton on both charges. However, a federal judge hearing the Jones case found Clinton to be in contempt of court and fined him $90,000 for giving false testimony before a federal judge, making Clinton the first president to be so cited.

As Clinton prepared to leave office, a final scandal erupted that tainted him and First Lady Hillary Rodham Clinton, who had been elected to a U.S. Senate seat from New York in 2000. Part of a presi-

dent's power is that of granting pardons. On his final day in office, 20 January 2001, Clinton pardoned numerous felons, including Marc Rich, a financier who had fled the country and was hiding in Europe from charges of illegal commodities trading, as well as trading with enemies of the United States, and Carlos Vignali, a drug dealer who was serving a long sentence in prison for importing drugs. After Clinton left office, it was discovered that Rich's wife, as well as Vignali's father, had given large amounts of cash both to the Democratic Party and to the Clinton Presidential Library in Arkansas. An uproar ensued, and further allegations that tied in Hillary Clinton's brother, Hugh Rodham, and Clinton's brother, Roger Clinton, in taking kickbacks for pardons, were uncovered. The *Kansas City Star* was one of a number of American newspapers that editorialized against the pardons, "Of all Bill Clinton's questionable actions during his eight years in office, his last-minute pardon of fugitive commodities trader Marc Rich stands as one of Clinton's most abhorrent abuses of presidential power."

In August 2001, after being out of the spotlight since leaving office, Clinton signed a $10 million book deal with Alfred A. Knopf, the largest advance for a nonfiction book. He remains one of the Democratic Party's luminaries and is expected in the coming years to speak out and write on many issues.

See also Campaign Finance Scandal; Chinagate; Cox Report; Gore, Albert Arnold, Jr.; "Filegate"; Pardongate; Starr, Kenneth Winston; Tucker, James Guy, Jr.; Whitewater

References: "[Editorial:] Marc Rich Deserved No Mercy," *Kansas City Star,* 27 January 2001, C1; Gertz, Bill, *Betrayal: How the Clinton Administration Undermined American Security* (Washington, DC: Regnery, 1999); Timperlake, Edward, and William C. Triplett II, *Year of the Rat: How Bill Clinton Compromised U.S. Security for Chinese Cash* (Washington, DC: Regnery, 1998); U.S. Congress, Senate, *Proceedings of the United States Senate in the Impeachment Trial of President William Jefferson Clinton,* 4 vols. (Washington, DC: Government Printing Office, 1999), I:18–19; "William Jefferson Clinton," in Timothy P. Donovan, Willard B. Gatewood Jr., and Jeannie M. Whayne, eds., *The Governors of Arkansas: Essays in Political Biography* (Fayetteville: University of Arkansas Press, 1995), 261–275.

Code of Official Conduct

Series of rules, promulgated by Congress in 1999 and published as Rule 23 of the *House of Represen-*

tatives Rules Manual (House Document 106-320). The code reads:

Rule XXIII—Code of Official Conduct

There is hereby established by and for the House the following code of conduct, to be known as the "Code of Official Conduct":

1. A Member, Delegate, Resident Commissioner, officer, or employee of the House shall conduct himself at all times in a manner that shall reflect creditably on the House.

2. A Member, Delegate, Resident Commissioner, officer, or employee of the House shall adhere to the spirit and the letter of the Rules of the House and to the rules of duly constituted committees thereof.

3. A Member, Delegate, Resident Commissioner, officer, or employee of the House may not receive compensation and may not permit compensation to accrue to his beneficial interest from any source, the receipt of which would occur by virtue of influence improperly exerted from his position in Congress.

4. A Member, Delegate, Resident Commissioner, officer, or employee of the House may not accept gifts except as provided by clause 5 of rule XXV.

5. A Member, Delegate, Resident Commissioner, officer, or employee of the House may not accept an honorarium for a speech, a writing for publication, or other similar activity, except as otherwise provided under rule XXV.

6. A Member, Delegate, or Resident Commissioner–

(a) shall keep his campaign funds separate from his personal funds;

(b) may not convert campaign funds to personal use in excess of an amount representing reimbursement for legitimate and verifiable campaign expenditures; and

(c) may not expend funds from his campaign account that are not attributable to bona fide campaign or political purposes.

7. A Member, Delegate, or Resident Commissioner shall treat as campaign contributions all proceeds from testimonial dinners or other fund-raising events.

8. (a) A Member, Delegate, Resident Commissioner, or officer of the House may not retain an employee who does not perform duties for the offices of the employing authority commensurate with the compensation he receives.

(b) In the case of a committee employee who works under the direct supervision of a member of the committee other than a chairman, the chairman may require that such member affirm in writing that the employee has complied with clause 8(a)

(subject to clause 9 of rule X) as evidence of compliance by the chairman with this clause and with clause 9 of rule X.

(c)(1) Except as specified in subparagraph (2) a Member, Delegate, or Resident Commissioner may not retain his spouse in a paid position; and an employee of the House may not accept compensation for work for a committee on which his spouse serves as a member.

(2) Subparagraph (1) shall not apply in the case of a spouse whose pertinent employment predates the One Hundred Seventh Congress.

9. A Member, Delegate, Resident Commissioner, officer, or employee of the House may not discharge and may not refuse to hire an individual, or otherwise discriminate against an individual with respect to compensation, terms, conditions, or privileges of employment, because of the race, color, religion, sex (including marital or parental status), disability, age, or national origin of such individual, but may take into consideration the domicile or political affiliation of such individual.

10. A Member, Delegate, or Resident Commissioner who has been convicted by a court of record for the commission of a crime for which a sentence of two or more years' imprisonment may be imposed should refrain from participation in the business of each committee of which he is a member, and a Member should refrain from voting on any question at a meeting of the House or of the Committee of the Whole House on the state of the Union, unless or until judicial or executive proceedings result in reinstatement of the presumption of his innocence or until he is reelected to the House after the date of such conviction.

11. A Member, Delegate, or Resident Commissioner may not authorize or otherwise allow an individual, group, or organization not under the direction and control of the House to use the words "Congress of the United States," "House of Representatives," or "Official Business," or any combination of words thereof, on any letterhead or envelope.

12. (a) Except as provided in paragraph (b), an employee of the House who is required to file a report under rule XXVI may not participate personally and substantially as an employee of the House in a contact with an agency of the executive or judicial branches of Government with respect to nonlegislative matters affecting any nongovernmental person in which the employee has a significant financial interest.

(b) Paragraph (a) does not apply if an employee first advises his employing authority of a significant financial interest described in paragraph (a) and obtains from his employing authority a written waiver stating that the participation of the employee in the activity described in paragraph (a) is necessary. A copy of each such waiver shall be filed with the Committee on Standards of Official Conduct.

13. Before a Member, Delegate, Resident Commissioner, officer, or employee of the House may have access to classified information, the following oath (or affirmation) shall be executed:

"I do solemnly swear (or affirm) that I will not disclose any classified information received in the course of my service with the House of Representatives, except as authorized by the House of Representatives or in accordance with its Rules."

Copies of the executed oath (or affirmation) shall be retained by the Clerk as part of the records of the House. The Clerk shall make signatures a matter of public record, causing the names of each Member, Delegate, or Resident Commissioner who has signed the oath during a week (if any) to be published in a portion of the *Congressional Record* designated for that purpose on the last legislative day of the week and making cumulative lists of such names available each day for public inspection in an appropriate office of the House.

14. (a) In this Code of Official Conduct, the term "officer or employee of the House" means an individual whose compensation is disbursed by the Chief Administrative Officer.

(b) An individual whose services are compensated by the House pursuant to a consultant contract shall be considered an employee of the House for purposes of clauses 1, 2, 3, 4, 8, 9, and 13 of this rule. An individual whose services are compensated by the House pursuant to a consultant contract may not lobby the contracting committee or the members or staff of the contracting committee on any matter. Such an individual may lobby other Members, Delegates, or the Resident Commissioner or staff of the House on matters outside the jurisdiction of the contracting committee.

References: *House Rules Manual* (House Document No. 106-320), 107th Congress (1999), 861–865.

Coelho, Anthony Lee (1942–)

United States representative from California (1979–1989) implicated in potential ethics violations involving campaign finance and a "junk bond" deal, who resigned his seat before an ethics investigation could begin. Coelho was also involved in shady dealings that cast a shadow over his short tenure as general chairman of the Al Gore for President Campaign in 2000. Coelho was born in the town of Los Banos, California, on 15 June 1942, the grandson of Portuguese immigrants. He was raised on his parents' dairy farm in the central valley region of California. He attended the schools of another town, Dos Palos, before he entered Loyola University and received his bachelor of arts degree in 1964, becoming the first member of his family to attend college. Out of college, he worked for the entertainer Bob Hope, who saw promise in the young man and urged him to go to work for the local congressman. Coelho had been diagnosed as an epileptic, and this affliction prevented him from entering the priesthood. (The 1917 Code of Canon Law states, "Qui epileptici vel amentes vel a daemone possessi sunt vel fuerent"—meaning that those with epilepsy or possessed by the devil would not be subject to ordination.) Thus politics seemed the best route for the young man. The following year, Coelho began serving on the staff of Representative Bernie Sisk of California, where he worked until 1978, rising to become Sisk's administrative assistant in 1970. From 1971 to 1972, Coelho served as the staff director of the House Agriculture Committee's Subcommittee on Cotton. He also served as the staff coordinator for the House Subcommittee on Broadcasting of the House Rules Committee and on the House Select Committee on Professional Sports. A Democrat, he served as a delegate to the Democratic National Convention in 1976, 1980, 1984, and 1988. Of his congressional staff work, Coelho said in a 1988 interview, "I fell in love with [it] . . . I fell in love with the fact that you could really change people's lives. I realized I could do much more in this job that I could as a priest."

In 1978 Sisk declined to run for reelection, and Coelho ran for and won the seat in the U.S. House of Representatives, representing California's Fifteenth Congressional District. He served from 3 January 1979 until his resignation on 15 June 1989. He rose to become a star in his party, serving as head of the Democratic Congressional Campaign Committee (DCCC) from 1981 to 1986, and assisting his party in raising millions of dollars to help elect Democrats to Congress. He changed the focus of fund-raising; despite being a liberal,

Coelho appealed to business groups as opposed to only labor groups. But as chairman of the DCCC, Coelho stretched the bounds of ethics. He became the first congressional campaign fundraiser to accept "soft money"—that is, unregulated donations from persons, corporations, or unions that do not fall under limits imposed by federal law. For assisting the Democrats to hold their majority in the 1986 and 1988 elections, Coelho was chosen as Majority Whip in the 101st Congress (1989–1991).

Starting in 1987, questions about Coelho's financial dealings began to surface. They culminated in a story in *Newsweek* magazine alleging that Coelho had violated House rules and federal law in his dealings with a savings and loan bank in Texas. As head of the DCCC in 1986, Coelho used the bank's yacht for DCCC fundraisers costing $25,184. House rules put a cap on such gifts at $100. As well, federal law prohibits a political committee from receiving more than $15,000 from any one source. Coelho refused to comment on the *Newsweek* story. Another allegation involved a purchase in 1986 of a $100,000 "junk bond" by Coelho from Thomas Spiegel, the chairman of the Columbia Savings & Loan Association, a California institution that was in financial trouble. An investigation revealed that Spiegel had purchased the bond in his own name and then offered it to Coelho at below-market rates and that Coelho then failed to report the loan on his financial disclosure form that was filed with the government. The Department of Justice started an investigation into the allegations. Sensing that he was in trouble, Coelho resigned from Congress on 15 June 1989, and the Department of Justice later ruled that it would not bring charges against the Californian. Coelho was privately destroyed by the allegations and his resignation, having been considered a leading candidate to become Speaker of the House someday. Friends rallied around Coelho, and a few months later he went to work for Wertheim Schroder & Co., a New York investment bank.

For the next several years, Coelho worked in the private sector. One of his actions was to serve as head of the American mission to the 1998 World Exposition in Lisbon, Portugal. It was here that Coelho came under additional fire: while serving as head of the mission, Coelho allegedly used his position to negotiate a loan for $300,000 that he never reported on his federal financial disclosure report. The loan, obtained from the president of Banco Espirito Santo, a bank in Lisbon, was to help Coehlo manage the work of the Luso-American Wave Foundation, which Coelho formed in April 1998. This foundation's aims were to raise funds to build "The Wave," a huge blue-tiled and stainless-steel sculpture to be exhibited at the U.S. Pavilion at the World Exposition. Under the Ethics in Government Act, Coelho was required to list the loan on his financial disclosure report. The law is clear that "failing to report required information" is a crime, committed by one "who knowingly and willfully fails to file or report any information required." This information was not made public until 1999, when Coelho was already serving as the campaign manager for Vice President Al Gore's 2000 election campaign. In October 1999 the State Department's Office of Inspector General released a report criticizing not only the loan, but Coelho's management of the world's fair pavilion. It harshly criticized the loan, which went unpaid; as well, Coelho had leased for himself (at government expense), a four-bedroom, $18,000-a-month waterfront condominium in Lisbon, the records for which were destroyed prior to the government examination. The audit also discovered numerous "questionable payments" that Coelho had doled out to people working on the pavilion, including airline tickets provided at government expense and the hiring of Coelho's niece by the pavilion at $2,500 a month to assist Coelho's deputy.

On 11 May 1999, to assist his flagging presidential campaign, Gore had selected Coelho to serve as his campaign manager. Coelho was known as the "king of soft money donations" during his reign from 1981 to 1986 as the chairman of the Democratic Congressional Campaign Committee. On 2 October 1999, the allegations by the State Department were leaked by the Center for Public Integrity, a political watchdog group. Gore, appearing on CBS's *Face the Nation* the following day, reacted to the report by strongly backing Coelho. "I haven't seen the report," Gore said, "but I know him, and he is going to continue doing the terrific job he's been doing as my campaign chair." However, as Gore's campaign continued to sag in the polls, and the heat of the State Department investigation continued, Gore looked for an easy way to be rid of his campaign manager. On 15 June 2000, after being hospitalized with stomach pains,

Coelho announced that he was stepping down as campaign manager, to be replaced by Secretary of Commerce Bill Daley. "My doctors have told me that I need to slow down, eat better and travel less for a period of time," Coelho said in a statement.

References: *Biographical Directory of the American Congress, 1774–1996* (Alexandria, VA: CQ Staff Directories, Inc., 1996), 839; Connolly, Ceci, "Daley to Chair Gore Campaign, Commerce Secretary Steps in after Coelho Quits, Citing Health," *Washington Post,* 16 June 2000, A1; Lavelle, Marianne, and Kenneth T. Walsh, "Al Gore's Risky Asset: Tony Coelho's Controversial Business Life May Prove to be a Liability," *U.S. News & World Report* 127:23 (13 December 1999), 31–36; United States Information Agency, Office of Inspector General, *Report of Audit, Review of Planning and Management of Lisbon Expo 98* (Washington, DC: Government Printing Office, 1999).

Colfax, Schuyler, Jr. (1823–1885)

Vice president of the United States (1869–1873) implicated but never charged in the Crédit Mobilier scandal, although he lost the vice presidency because of the allegations. Colfax was born in New York City on 23 March 1823, the son of Schuyler Colfax Sr. and Hannah (née Stryker) Colfax. Schuyler Colfax Jr. (he was never called "Junior" by any of his contemporaries, and biographies of him do not mention this addition to his name) came from a family of distinguished members. His grandfather, a veteran of the American Revolution and a friend of George Washington, married Hannah Schuyler, the daughter of General Philip Schuyler. They named one of their sons Washington and another Schuyler. Schuyler Colfax Sr. became a bank teller in New York City and married Hannah Stryker, a widow who ran a boardinghouse. When she was pregnant with their son, Schuyler Colfax Sr. developed tuberculosis and died, two months before his son, named after him, was born. The junior Colfax attended public schools in New York City, quitting at age ten to go to work as a clerk in a retail store to help support his mother and grandmother. In 1836 his mother married George W. Matthews, owner of a store in New Carlisle, Indiana, and that year Colfax and his mother joined her new husband there. Schuyler Colfax would be identified with Indiana for the remainder of his life.

In 1841 Colfax entered the political realm. His stepfather Matthews was elected county auditor for Joseph County (South Bend), Indiana, and he named Colfax as his deputy. The young Colfax watched the debates in the state legislature and became an expert in parliamentary matters. At the same time, Colfax desired to become a journalist and he wrote to Horace Greeley, the famed editor of the *New York Tribune*, asking to become a correspondent for Greeley's paper. Greeley decided to include Colfax's writings on the Indiana legislature, and the two men also began a friendship that would last until Greeley's death in 1872. Colfax also reported on the doings in the state legislature for the *Indiana State Journal* and, when he was nineteen, was asked to become the editor of the Whig journal *The South Bend Free Press*. In 1844 Colfax married, purchased the *Free Press* outright, and renamed it the *St. Joseph Valley Register*. It espoused Whig principles, particularly the beliefs of Senator Henry Clay, Whig of Kentucky. In 1848 Colfax served as a delegate to the National Whig Convention and as a representative to the state convention in 1849 that drafted a new state constitution for Indiana. In 1851 Colfax was nominated by the Whigs for a seat in the U.S. House of Representatives from the Ninth Indiana District, but lost narrowly to the incumbent, Democrat Graham Newell Fitch. By 1852 Colfax was disenchanted with the proslavery leanings of the Whig Party (particularly the party's stand on forcing Nebraska into the Union as a proslavery state). In 1854 he ran for a seat in Congress under the "Anti-Nebraska" banner. (Some congressional histories list Colfax as the Republican candidate in that particular election.) Winning easily over the pro-Nebraska Democrat, Colfax took his seat in the Thirty-fourth Congress (4 March 1855). He would win reelection six more times, serving until 3 March 1869. In Congress, Colfax was an amiable man; his colleagues dubbed him "Smiler" Colfax. Although some historians consider it a mark of affection, others consider it a gibe. He joined the Republican Party, and rose in that party's hierarchy, serving as chairman of the Post Office Committee. In November 1863 Representative Galusha A. Grow (R-PA), who had been Speaker of the House, was defeated. The following month when the House convened, Colfax was elected Speaker. He would hold the position through the remainder of the Civil War and until the end of the first session of the Fortieth Congress.

During his more than five years as Speaker, Colfax was a Radical Republican, helping the House to pass a number of measures that imposed strict Reconstruction on the postwar South. He clashed with President Andrew Johnson over Reconstruction policy and presided over the impeachment vote that led to the first impeachment of a president in the nation's history. Colfax was a strong supporter of the railroads and led a congressional tour of the nation of the railroads at the behest of President Abraham Lincoln shortly before Lincoln's assassination. It was this interest that led to Colfax's downfall. He was a leader in pushing for massive congressional appropriations to help construct a transcontinental railroad. The company that was reaping the rewards from government largesse, the Union Pacific Railroad, was being funded by a company called the Crédit Mobilier of America. What few outside of government knew was that the Crédit Mobilier was merely a shell corporation, designed to funnel a large amount of the government funds to rich benefactors. To keep the congressional leaders quiet, one of the members of the Crédit Mobilier, Representative Oakes Ames (R-MA), was offering stock in the Union Pacific to these leaders. One of those who benefited was Colfax. Over the years, he built up a tidy fortune in stock, which went up in value as he voted for more congressional appropriations for the railroad.

As the 1868 election drew near, Colfax considered running for a seat in the U.S. Senate or for governor of Indiana, but decided to hold his congressional seat and remain Speaker. At the Republican National Convention in Chicago, General Ulysses S. Grant was nominated unanimously on the first ballot. Then the party turned to the vice presidential nomination. Senator Benjamin Wade of Ohio led in the balloting, followed by Governor Reuben E. Fenton of New York, Senator Henry Wilson of Massachusetts, and Colfax last. Over the next four ballots, Fenton and Wilson faded, leaving Wade in a battle with Colfax. On the fifth ballot, Fenton and Wilson backers moved their support to Colfax, and, on the sixth ballot, Colfax won the nomination overwhelmingly. The man who was born two months after the death of his father and who had left school at age ten to work as a clerk had been nominated for vice president of the United States. The election in November was a landslide: Grant defeated Democrat Horatio Seymour, former Governor of New York, by 214 electoral votes to 80, and Colfax became the vice president of the United States. At that time, he married Ellen Wade, niece of Senator Benjamin Wade.

During his four years as vice president, Colfax served as the Senate president pro tem in the silent role given the vice president by law. A history of the office, written by the U.S. Senate Historical Office, explains, "The first Speaker of the House ever elected vice president (a previous former Speaker, James K. Polk, had won the presidency in 1844), Colfax moved easily to the Senate chamber as a man long familiar with the ways of Capitol Hill. The Senate proved an easier body to preside over, leaving him with time on his hands to travel, lecture, and write for the press. The Indianapolis *Journal* observed that 'the Vice Presidency is an elegant office whose occupant must find it is his principal business to try and discover what is the use of there being such an office at all.'" Despite the lack of duties for Colfax, many inside and outside the Republican Party believed that Grant would step aside in 1872 and allow Colfax to be nominated for president, with Senator Charles Sumner of Massachusetts as his running mate.

By 1871, however, rumbles about the Crédit Mobilier began to come back to haunt the vice president. Rumors that he had been one of those who had received stock in the Crédit Mobilier, at that time ready to go bankrupt, caused many Republicans to rethink having him on a national ticket. The Grant administration was mired in numerous scandals, but Grant decided he should run for a second term and replace Colfax with Senator Henry Wilson of Massachusetts. To outsiders, it appeared when Wilson replaced the forty-nine-year-old Colfax that simple politics was at play. Near the end of the campaign, a list of the senators and congressmen who received stock was handed over to the *New York Sun,* a Democrat-leaning newspaper that published the list and correspondence from Representative Ames. On the list were Colfax and Senator Wilson, as well as many other high-ranking Republicans. Ames and the others denied any role in the Crédit Mobilier affair. After the election, however, which was won by Grant, an investigation was begun in both houses of Congress. Speaker of the House James G. Blaine, implicated himself, was forced to step aside. A committee, chaired by Representative Luke Poland of Vermont, investigated the allegations against the House members, including those against Colfax, which were alleged to have happened while he was a member of the House. On 7 January 1873, while still sitting as vice president, Colfax appeared before the Poland committee to testify. Despite the fact that the committee had correspondence from Ames showing that Colfax was paid in stock, whose dividends he later used to buy more stock, Colfax denied to the end that any stock was not paid for from his own funds. Colfax, when shown a check with his signature on it, claimed that Ames had forged his signature. When the check, for $1,200, was corresponded with a deposit in the same amount into Colfax's bank account, he claimed that he had received $1,200 in funds from other people, including $1,000 from a contributor, George F. Nesbitt, who had since died. This opened the way for the investigation into how Nesbitt was able to get a lucrative contract for supplying the government with envelopes—a contract that came from the House Post Office Committee, chaired by Colfax. Immediately, plans were drawn up for the impeachment of Colfax. However, as Colfax had just a few weeks remaining in his term, the House refused to impeach him on a strict party-line vote. Colfax's political career was over.

Disgraced, Colfax became a writer and lecturer and in his last years made more money in these positions than he did as vice president. He was in Mankato, Minnesota, on a lecture, when he suddenly died, probably of heart failure, at the age of sixty-one. His body was returned to Indiana, and he was buried in the City Cemetery in South Bend. His gravestone reads: "Schuyler Colfax, Vice President of the United States, 1869 to 1873. Statesman and Beloved Citizen. South Bend Post 50, American N. Legion Acknowledges the Service He Rendered His Country." Colfax counties in Nebraska and New Mexico are named in his honor.

References: Crawford, Jay Boyd, *The Crédit Mobilier of America: Its Origin and History, Its Work of Constructing the Union Pacific Railroad and the Relation of Members of Congress Therewith* (Boston: C. W. Calkins, 1880), 148–185; "Schuyler Colfax," in Wolff, Wendy, ed. *Vice Presidents of the United States, 1789–1993* (Washington, DC: Government Printing Office, 1997), 227; Smith, Martin, and Edward Winslow, *The Life and Public Services of Schuyler Colfax, Together with His Most Important Speeches* (New York: United States Publishing Company, 1868), 11–19; Willard, Harvey, "The Political Career of Schuyler Colfax to His Election as Vice President in 1868." (Ph.D. dissertation, Indiana University, 1939).

Colorado Republican Federal Campaign Committee v. Federal Election Commission, 116 S. Ct. 2309, 518 U.S. 604 (1996)

Supreme Court case, in which the court held that an independent expenditure not directed toward or for a particular candidate was not a violation of the Federal Election Campaign Act of 1971 and was protected by the First Amendment to the United States Constitution. In 1986 the Colorado Republican Federal Campaign Committee paid for radio advertisements that criticized Representative Timothy Wirth, a Democrat who was seeking his party's nomination for the United States Senate. The Republican Party, however, did not itself have a nominee for the seat. The Colorado Democratic Party filed a complaint against the Republicans with the Federal Election Commission (FEC), which decided that the ad violated the "Party Expenditure Provision" of the Federal Election Campaign Act of 1971 (2 U.S.C. § 431, at § 441a[d][3]), which imposed limits on contributions to candidates for federal offices. The FEC said that the expenditure came from a "coordinated" party effort and thus violated the law. The agency filed suit in federal district court in Colorado; the Republican Committee argued that the ad was not made in conjunction with any particular campaign and thus was not in violation of the law. The district court agreed with the Republicans, but on appeal the United States Court of Appeals for the Tenth Circuit reversed, holding that because the ad was directed *at,* and not necessarily *for,* a particular candidate, it did violate the law and that banning such advertising did not violate the First Amendment. The Republican Committee appealed to the U.S. Supreme Court, and arguments were heard in the case on 15 April 1996.

On 26 June 1996, the justices held seven to two that the advertisement did not violate the Federal Election Campaign Act and that banning such advertising violated the First Amendment. Justice

Stephen Breyer announced the decision of the court, which was joined by Justice Sandra Day O'-Connor. Chief Justice William H. Rehnquist was joined by Justices Anthony Kennedy, Antonin Scalia, and Clarence Thomas in concurring with part of the majority opinion and dissenting on other parts. Justices John Paul Stevens and Ruth Bader Ginsburg dissented completely. Justice Breyer wrote:

Because this expenditure is "independent," the Court need not reach the broader question argued by the Colorado Party: whether, in the special case of political parties, the First Amendment also forbids congressional efforts to limit coordinated expenditures . . . Section 441a(d)(3) cannot withstand a facial challenge under the framework established by *Buckley v. Valeo*, 424 U.S. 1 (per curiam). The anticorruption rationale that the Court has relied on is inapplicable in the specific context of campaign funding by political parties, since there is only a minimal threat of corruption when a party spends to support its candidate or to oppose his competitor, whether or not that expenditure is made in concert with the candidate. Parties and candidates have traditionally worked together to achieve their common goals, and when they engage in that work, there is no risk to the Republic. To the contrary, the danger to lies in Government suppression of such activity.

References: *Colorado Republican Federal Campaign Committee v. Federal Election Commission*, 116 S. Ct. 2309, 518 U.S. 604 (1996); "Colorado Republican Federal Campaign Committee v. Federal Election Commission," in William C. Binning, Larry Esterly, and Paul A. Sracic, *Encyclopedia of American Parties, Campaigns, and Elections* (Westport, CT: Greenwood Press, 1999), 53.

Colvin, Harvey Doolittle (1815–1892)

Mayor of Chicago (1873–1875, 1876), a reformer who apparently tried to clean up the corruption in the Windy City but lost his office because of his efforts. Little is known of Colvin. He was born in Herkimer County, New York, on 18 December 1815, the son of two British immigrants. His father may have been a farmer. Harvey Colvin attended local schools and, after marrying a girl from the town of Little Falls in Herkimer County, he opened a boot factory there. He also held a series of local offices, including town supervisor. In 1854, working as a resident agent for the U.S. Express Company—later to be known as American Express—Colvin was transferred to Chicago, and he made that town his adopted home. Despite being a Democrat, he supported the Northern cause during the Civil War, and in fact became a Republican in 1864. However, by 1873, he had returned to the Democratic Party.

Chicago in post–Civil War America was a rough town, filled with saloons and houses of prostitution. In 1873 Mayor Joseph E. Medill tried to close the saloons on Sundays, igniting the ire of the German immigrants who ran them. These Germans joined the Populist Party and the Democratic Party, which named Colvin as their fusion candidate for mayor. Colvin, opposing the saloon-closing attempt, did not realize that corrupt city officials involved in the liquor business also backed him. However, Colvin himself was clean, and he defeated Republican and Union candidate Lester Legrand Bond, who had served as interim mayor since Medill's resignation because of the clash with the Germans. Taking office on 1 December 1973 as Chicago's twenty-second mayor, Colvin dropped all efforts to close saloons on Sundays, but instead was faced with more pressing problems. Just weeks into his administration, the city treasurer defaulted on all city loans, throwing the entire city economic structure into anarchy. When a new city charter that centralized city control over the police and fire departments was offered to the people, Colvin opposed it. It narrowly passed, and Colvin became highly unpopular because of his opposition. The final straw against Colvin came when Illinois state officials changed the length of the terms of city officials; Colvin claimed that this extended his own term to 1877. However, elements of opposition in Chicago nominated real estate magnate Thomas Hoyne, and an election was held on 18 April 1875 without Colvin participating. When Hoyne won, Colvin claimed that the election was illegal and he refused to relinquish his office. For two months, Chicago had two mayors and two sets of administrations running city affairs. Finally, state courts struck down the 1875 election as illegal, and Colvin was allowed to retain his office on 5 June 1876. An election was held on 7 July 1876, but Colvin did not run and left office when his successor took over.

Despite all of this turmoil during his term of office, many historians who have studied Colvin believe he was an honest administrator who tried to better the city. However, following his death on 16 April 1892 in Jacksonville, Florida, Colvin was soon forgotten by a city that went on to elect William Hale Thompson, acknowledged as one of the most crooked mayors in American history.

See also Thompson, William Hale

References: Barrett, Paul, "Colvin, Harvey Doolittle," in Melvin G. Holli and Peter d' A. Jones, *Biographical Dictionary of American Mayors, 1820–1980: Big City Mayors* (Westport, CT: Greenwood Press, 1981), 74–75.

Coman, Thomas (1836–1909)

Mayor of New York City (1868), indicted and convicted (the conviction was later dismissed) for his role in the Tweed frauds in city contracts. Coman has been forgotten by historians, and little is known about him. He was born in Ireland sometime in 1836 and immigrated to New York as a small child with his parents. He earned a living by working for James Gordon Bennett's *New York Herald* and then with the Post Office. However, that last position ended when Coman was accused of embezzlement. He then went to work as a fireman, serving with Eagle Engine Company No. 13. During the draft riots in New York City in 1863, Coman led fireman in helping to quench fires and suppress riots.

In 1865 Coman was elected an alderman from New York City's second district, which encompassed the fourth and sixth ("The Bloody Ould") wards. He served in this position until 1869. A year later he was elected as alderman-at-large, serving until 1872. In 1868, when Mayor John T. Hoffman left office to go to Albany after being elected governor of New York state, Coman stepped in and served for a short time as acting mayor until Abraham Oakey Hall took over as the city's chief executive. Coman served as president of the New York board of aldermen from 1868 to 1870, becoming one of the most powerful politicians in the city.

As New York historian Leo Hershkowitz wrote, "Coman's political world tumbled, along with that of many others, after the denunciation of Boss William M. Tweed by the *New York Times* beginning in July 1871. In June 1872, the *Times* involved Coman on unprosecuted charges of having, as acting mayor, fraudulently signed several warrants. Coman insisted that such bills had been approved by others and had only needed his official signature; moreover, Mayor John T. Hoffman was never away from his office longer than six days, and under the law Coman was never really acting mayor. He issued a statement of disgust with the new 'Tammany Hall Management' in June 1872 and lost a fight to become president of the aldermen again." For a year, Coman staved off being implicated further in the Tweed frauds; however, in June 1873 he was indicted on six counts of bribery and a warrant was issued for his arrest. Instead of turning himself in, Coman fled to Canada. In October 1874 he returned. In June 1875 the state of New York sued him and the other implicated officials for some $400,000 in stolen funds. After a lengthy trial, all of the men (except Tweed, who had fled to Europe) were found guilty, but on appeal Coman's conviction was tossed out, and he was never retried. Coman then retired from politics, instead going to work for the Equitable Life Insurance Society selling insurance.

Coman died in New York on 22 October 1909. Among the Tweed defendants who stole untold millions from New York City, Coman's name is today almost wholly forgotten.

References: Hershkowitz, Leo, "Coman, Thomas," in Melvin G. Holli and Peter d'A. Jones, *Biographical Dictionary of American Mayors, 1820–1980: Big City Mayors* (Westport, CT: Greenwood Press, 1981), 75; Hershkowitz, Leo, *Tweed's New York: Another Look* (Garden City, NY: Anchor Press/Doubleday, 1977).

Common Cause

American political reform and public interest group, founded by John Gardner, a former secretary of health, education, and welfare in the cabinet of President Lyndon Baines Johnson, in 1970. After leaving office, Gardner desired to have a watchdog group oversee elections, campaign committees, and other election operations, and report to the media and the American people on their findings. On 18 August 1970, he formed Common Cause, explaining, "We are going to build a true 'citizens' lobby—a lobby concerned not with the advancement of special interests but with the well-being of the nation. . . . We want public officials to have literally millions of American citizens looking over their shoulders at every move they make. We want phones to ring in Washington and state capitols and town halls. We want people watching and influencing every move that government makes."

As the organization explains, "Gardner envisioned a movement propelled by the focused and concerted grassroots lobbying activities of Common Cause members and reinforced with professional lobbying on Capitol Hill." In 2002 it had more than 200,000 members and is financed completely by the dues and donations of its members. It does not accept money from special interest groups or corporations. In July 1999 Scott Harshbarger, a former Democratic candidate for governor of Massachusetts, was elected president of the organization.

References: "Common Cause," in William C. Binning, Larry Esterly, and Paul A. Sracic, *Encyclopedia of American Parties, Campaigns, and Elections* (Westport, CT: Greenwood Press, 1999), 54; the Common Cause website at www.commoncause.org

Congressional Ethics Code

Rules enacted by Congress on 11 July 1958, as part of an ethics package that "should be adhered to by all Government employees, including officeholders."

The code, as it was enacted, reads:

CODE OF ETHICS FOR GOVERNMENT SERVICE
Any person in Government service should:

1. Put loyalty to the highest moral principals and to country above loyalty to Government persons, party, or department.

2. Uphold the Constitution, laws, and legal regulations of the United States and of all governments therein and never be a party to their evasion.

3. Give a full day's labor for a full day's pay; giving to the performance of his duties his earnest effort and best thought.

4. Seek to find and employ more efficient and economical ways of getting tasks accomplished.

5. Never discriminate unfairly by the dispensing of special favors or privileges to anyone, whether for remuneration or not; and never accept for himself or his family, favors or benefits under circumstances which might be construed by reasonable persons as influencing the performance of his governmental duties.

6. Make no private promises of any kind binding upon the duties of office, since a Government employee has no private word which can be binding on public duty.

7. Engage in no business with the Government, either directly or indirectly which is inconsistent with the conscientious performance of his governmental duties.

8. Never use any information coming to him confidentially in the performance of governmental duties as a means for making private profit.

9. Expose corruption wherever discovered.

10. Uphold these principles, ever conscious that public office is a public trust.

In 1977 Congress amended this code by setting standards on all ethical conduct, as well as limited congressional honoraria (outside income) gifts and fees.

See also Honoraria

References: United States Congress, House, Committee on Post Office and Civil Service, *Display of Code of Ethics for Government Service: Report to Accompany H.R. 5997* (Washington, DC: Government Printing Office, 1980); United States Congress, Senate, Special Committee on Official Conduct, *Senate Code of Official Conduct: Report of the Special Committee on Official Conduct, United States Senate, to Accompany S. Res. 110* (Washington, DC: Government Printing Office, 1977).

Connally, John Bowden, Jr. (1917–1993)

Governor of Texas (1963–1969), secretary of the treasury (1971–1972), implicated but acquitted in a milk price-fixing scandal that was alleged to have occurred while he was the governor of Texas. Many considered Connally a potential president of the United States in the image of Lyndon B. Johnson, but Connally's star faded before he could achieve that high office. He was born on his family's farm near Floresville, Texas, on 27 February 1917, one of eight children of John Bowden Connally Sr. and Lela (née Wright) Connally. The younger Connally attended local schools in San Antonio, before he entered the University of Texas in 1933. He received his law degree from the University of Texas Law School in 1921. He had passed his bar exam in 1938 and, although he aimed to become an attorney, instead entered government service, starting in 1939 as a legislative assistant to Representative Lyndon B. Johnson, then a rising star in the Democratic Party. The two men would become close friends, and Johnson ultimately became Connally's benefactor.

In 1941 Connally left government service to enter the U.S. Naval Reserve. Commissioned, he served as a fighter director aboard several aircraft carriers during World War II and saw major action in the Pacific theater of operations. At the end of the war, serving on the USS *Essex,* he overcame fifty-two hours of kamikaze attacks by Japanese planes. At the end of the conflict he was sent back to civilian life with the rank of lieutenant commander. Back in Texas, Connally joined a group of war veterans who purchased radio station KVET. Connally did not return to government service: instead, he joined a law firm in Austin. However, in 1946 he returned to politics and served as the campaign manager for Lyndon Johnson's reelection that year to Congress. Two years later, when Johnson ran for a U.S. Senate seat, Connally once again served as his campaign manager. Despite rumors of suspicious activity by Connally—he was alleged to have concocted late votes that swung the narrow election to Johnson—the election results stood. Once Johnson was elected to the Senate, Connally went to Washington and served as his aide until 1951. That year, he became the legal counsel for Texas oilman Sid Williams Richardson (1891–1959), serving in this capacity until Richardson's death in 1959.

In 1960 Johnson, now Senate majority leader, decided to run for the Democratic presidential nomination. Once again, John Connally was there to serve as his campaign manager. Although Johnson did not win the party's presidential nod, he did come in a close second, and when he was offered the vice presidential slot on the ticket by Senator John F. Kennedy, Johnson jumped at the chance. The ticket's election in November 1960 guaranteed Connally's continued presence in Washington. To reward him for sticking with the ticket, Connally was named as secretary of the navy in January 1961. At one time this prestigious post had been a cabinet position, but now it was one of four major positions under the secretary of defense. Connally took the post at the height of the Cold War, and in his year in the job he improved naval morale and garnered increased appropriations for the service. He resigned the office in 1962 to run for governor of Texas. The field of Democrats vying for the office was large—it included sitting Governor Price Daniel Sr., who had already served three terms. Despite low ratings in the polls when he began, Connally used his Texas connections, his association with now-Vice President

Lyndon Johnson, and his charm to stage a comeback. He won the Democratic nomination, which in those days was tantamount to winning the election. Connally took office as governor of Texas, and his political star seemed to be on the rise. Then came the events of 22 November 1963.

Politics in Texas had become rather nasty during Connally's term. President Kennedy had become unpopular in the state aside from having Johnson at his side, and the thought of losing the Lone Star State to the Republicans in 1964 sent shivers up the Democrats' spines. In November 1963 Kennedy slated a major trip to Texas, with Connally at his side, to calm the fears of local Democrats and try to repair the interparty split that was fracturing the state Democrat Party. On 22 November, Connally rode next to Kennedy in Dallas, as both men went to attend a luncheon. Shots rang out, and Kennedy was assassinated. Connally, sitting next to him, was seriously wounded in the arm. Despite being nearly killed, Connally ran for a second term in 1964 and won easily. He won in a similar style in 1966.

In 1969, when he left the governorship, Connally went to work for Vinson and Elkins, a prestigious Houston law firm. He also became a close friend of President Richard Nixon, a Republican who had succeeded Johnson as president that same year. Nixon named Connally in 1969 to the President's Foreign Intelligence Advisory Board to counsel the president on foreign policy matters. As such, Connally's star rose in the Republican administration. When Secretary of Treasury David M. Kennedy resigned on 11 February 1971, Connally was named as his successor. A year later, Connally headed up Democrats for Nixon, and helped the Republican carry Texas for the GOP. In April 1973, three months after his mentor Lyndon Johnson died, Connally switched parties, becoming a Republican. Later that year, when a bribery scandal forced Vice President Spiro Agnew to resign from office, many speculated that Nixon would name Connally as his replacement. As it was, Democrats objected and claimed they would "destroy" the Texan if he were named. Nixon was forced to pass him over for Representative Gerald Ford of Michigan.

Connally left office and returned to his law firm in Houston. That was when his world collapsed. Connally was indicted for allegedly taking bribes when he was governor, using his influence to fix milk prices. The trial began and ended in April 1975, with weak evidence tying Connally to any wrongdoing. On 17 April 1975, he was acquitted of all charges. However, his good name was damaged, and he never recovered from the trial. He did not run for president in 1976.

In 1980, however, Connally made one last run at the Republican presidential nomination. He was the only Republican who refused to take public money, instead financing his campaign with private contributions only. He raised and spent $11 million, but received only one delegate. When former California Governor Ronald Reagan won the nomination, Connally was one of several names he considered for the second slot on the ticket before he went with former CIA chief George Bush.

In the 1980s Connally left law and politics and decided to invest his money in real estate. For a time, he was a wealthy man, until the bottom dropped out of the Texas real estate market, and he lost everything, eventually declaring bankruptcy. In his final years, he made a slight comeback, earning a living by serving on the corporate boards of several major American corporations. Connally died of pulmonary fibrosis while in the Methodist Hospital of Houston on 15 June 1993 at the age of seventy-six. He was remembered more for his few moments sitting next to President Kennedy as he was assassinated than for his years of government service or his alleged corruption.

References: Connally, John B., with Mickey Herskowitz, *In History's Shadow: An American Odyssey* (New York: Hyperion, 1993); Reston, James, *The Lone Star: The Life of John Connally* (New York: Harper and Row, 1989).

Connelly, Matthew J. (1907–1976)

Appointments secretary to President Harry S. Truman, indicted and convicted in 1956 of tax-fraud conspiracy during his time in the White House, spending two years in prison. Little is known of Connelly—even his middle name remains a mystery to even his closest associates. He was born in Clinton, Massachusetts, on 19 November 1907. He attended local schools before entering Fordham University in the Bronx, in New York, from which he earned a degree in 1930. For a time, he worked as a stockbroker in New York City, even as the

Great Depression was raging. However, in 1933, when Franklin D. Roosevelt was elected president and began his New Deal programs to help end the depression, Connelly went first to Boston and then Washington, D.C., to aid federal work and food relief agencies. This service lasted from 1933 until 1938.

In 1939 Connelly decided to leave relief work and enter government service. He took a post as a member of the Democratic staff of the U.S. House of Representatives Committee on Appropriations. A year later he became a staff member with the U.S. Senate Special Committee to Investigate [the] National Defense Program, headed by then-U.S. Senator Harry S. Truman. This work would take Connelly to the upper reaches of power, culminating in his working for Truman when the Missourian became president of the United States in 1945. As Connelly later said in an oral history interview:

I did not meet the then-Senator Truman until the day I walked into his office. I was recommended by Senator Lister Hill of Alabama. I was purposely trying to establish another relationship which Senator Hill had suggested as a trouble-shooter for the White House. Senator Hill called me one afternoon and said he would like to see me and to call him off the Senate floor. I made that appointment, and Senator Hill took me back to his office in the Senate Office Building and there he said, "We just had a meeting today of the Military Affairs Committee," of which he was a member and of which Senator Truman was a member. Senator Hill told me that Senator Truman was going to have to have a very important investigation, and he wanted me to work on his committee. I was not very happy about it because of the original understanding I had with Senator Hill, however, I kept the appointment with Senator Truman on the following morning. I walked into his office; I had never met him, as I said before, so he said, "Come in." He said, "I know all about you. I know what you did in Missouri, Chicago, and other committees you've been on. We have a very peculiar situation here. I have been authorized to become chairman of this committee, however, it has not been determined what our appropriations are going to be. I do not know what I can pay you, but I will say this to you, if you go along with me, you will never have any reason to regret it."

In 1945, when Truman became vice president of the United States, Connelly went to work as his assistant. Just three months after becoming the number-two man in government, Truman was advanced to president when Franklin D. Roosevelt died suddenly. Matthew Connelly was named as the new president's appointments secretary. Connelly would serve in this position until the end of Truman's administration on 20 January 1953.

Connelly explained his role as appointments secretary to the president:

> Officially, I was appointments secretary[;] I handled all the appointments for the President. In addition, I had to act as a sort of contact man for the politicians from all over the states. Every politician who came into Washington could not get in to see him, it would be impossible, so that job fell on me with the result they could go home and say, "Well, no I didn't see the President, but I talked to his secretary and he's going to get me some help," because it saves face for them in their home state, or have dinner with them or go to a cocktail party for a state delegation and that was all left to me just to keep politics a little bit smooth. I handled all the politics in the White House except for Truman and at his own level and their level, he would handle it. And we maintained a liaison with the national committee, to see about political things—working together is part of the game—it is a game.

While serving under Truman, Connelly accepted illegal gifts from one Irvin Sachs, a St. Louis, Missouri, wholesaler, who was later found guilty of evading $128,721 in income taxes and fined $40,000. After Connelly left government, he and T. Lamar Caudle, the general counsel to the Internal Revenue Service (IRS), were indicted in 1955 for accepting gifts—such as oil royalties—from Sachs in exchange for pressuring the IRS and the Justice Department not to prosecute Sachs, and, when he was prosecuted, for trying to limit his sentence. Connelly and Caudle were tried together and in 1956 both were convicted of conspiracy to defraud the government and commit bribery and perjury, of knowingly making false statements, and of violating the internal revenue code. Both men were sentenced to two years in prison and both appealed their sentences. Finally, in May 1960, when his appeals ran out, Connelly entered prison, ultimately serving six months, being paroled in November 1960.

Connelly's former boss, Harry Truman, felt that the prosecution of Connelly and Caudle was railroaded and he appealed for a pardon from President John F. Kennedy. In January 1962 Truman wrote to Attorney General Robert Kennedy:

> Some time ago I wrote you about Matthew Connelly, another Massachusetts Irishman who has been abused and wofully [sic] mistreated by an old Judge in my State. This old Judge threatened to persecute me and Senator [Stuart] Symington [of Missouri] through the Grand Jury under his control.
>
> Matt Connelly has been abused and mistreated as told you in my original letter. I want him pardoned and his full rights restored.
>
> I've never spoken to your brother about this and I don't intend to—But if you think I enjoy mistreatment and injustice to one of my employees, you are mistaken.
>
> So don't smile at me any more unless you want to do justice to Matt Connelly, which is the right thing—a full pardon.
>
> P.S.—This has nothing to do with my relations with your brother.

On 22 November 1962, President Kennedy gave Connelly a full pardon, restoring his citizenship and voting rights in full. The move was applauded by his old boss, now in retirement in Independence, Missouri.

Connelly lived for less than fourteen years following his pardon, dying in Oak Park, Illinois, on 10 July 1976 at the age of sixty-eight. He was one of nine former Truman administration officials who served prison time for corrupt acts in office.

References: "Matt Connelly Is Given Pardon," *The Kansas City Times,* 23 November 1962, 14; Matthew J. Connelly Official File, Harry S Truman Library, Independence, Missouri (including Truman to Robert Kennedy, 24 January 1962); Matthew J. Connelly Oral History Interview, 28 November 1967, Courtesy Harry S Truman Library, Independence, Missouri.

Contempt of Congress

Power of Congress, used by that body to force a response to any action that may serve to obstruct the legislative or investigative process of Congress. Contempt as it now stands is a federal crime and can result in prison time. It can be invoked when a person is called before Congress to respond to an inquiry or a hearing and either ignores the sub-

Seven Hollywood writers and directors walk up the steps of federal court in Washington, D.C. (1950), to face trial charges of contempt of Congress for their defiance of the House Un-American Activities Committee. (Library of Congress)

poena or goes before Congress and refuses to answer questions.

However, the refusal to answer a question or provide a document demanded by Congress is not necessarily considered contempt. William Holmes Brown, the former House parliamentarian, wrote:

The statute which penalizes the refusal to answer in response to a congressional subpoena provides that the question must be "pertinent to the question under inquiry." 2 U.S.C. 192. That is, the answers requested must (1) relate to a legislative purpose which Congress may constitutionally entertain, and (2) fall within the grant of authority actually made by Congress to the Committee. . . . In a prosecution for contempt of Congress, it must be established that the committee or subcommittee was duly authorized and that its investigation was within the scope of delegated authority. (*United States v. Seeger,* C.A.N.Y. 303 F2d 478 [1962]). A clear chain of authority from the House to its committee is an essential element of the offense. (*Gojack v. United States,* 384 U.S. 702 [1966]). . . . In contempt proceedings brought under the statute, constitutional claims and other objections to House investigatory procedures may be raised as a defense. (*United States v. House of Representatives* (556 F. Supp. 150 [1983]). The courts must accord the defendant every right "guaranteed to defendants in all other criminal cases."

Watkins v. United States, 354 U.S. 178 (1957). All elements of the offense, including willfulness, must be proven beyond a reasonable doubt. *Flaxer v. United States,* 358 U.S. 147 (1958).

References: Clarke, Mary Patterson, *Parliamentary Privilege in the American Colonies: Essays in Colonial History Presented to Charles McLean Andrews* (New Haven, CT: Yale University Press, 1943); Dimock, Marshall Edward, *Congressional Investigating Committees* (Baltimore, MD: Johns Hopkins University Press, 1929); May, Thomas Erskine, Lord Farnborough, *A Treatise on the Law, Privileges, Proceedings and Usage of Parliament* (London: Butterworths, 1873), 83–97; Rozell, Mark J., *In Contempt of Congress: Postwar Press Coverage on Capitol Hill* (Westport, CT: Praeger Publishers, 1996); Shapansky, Jay R., *Congress' Contempt Power,* Congressional Research Service Report No. 86–83A, 28 February 1986.

Corrupt Practices Act, 36 Stat. 822 (1910)

Act of Congress, enacted 25 June 1910, which provides:

No candidate for Representative in Congress or for Senator of the United States shall give, contribute, expend, use, or promise, or cause to be given, contributed, expended, used, or promised, in procuring his nomination and election any sum, in the aggregate, in excess of the amount which he may lawfully give, contribute, expend, or promise under the laws of the state in which he resides: Provided, that no candidate for Representative in Congress shall give, contribute, expend, use, or promise any sum, in the aggregate, exceeding five thousand dollars in any campaign for his nomination and election; and no candidate for Senator of the United States shall give, contribute, expend, use, or promise any sum, in the aggregate, exceeding ten thousand dollars in any campaign for his nomination and election:

Provided further, that money expended by any such candidate to meet and discharge any assessment, fee, or charge made or levied upon candidates by the laws of the state in which he resides, or for his necessary personal expenses, incurred for himself alone, for travel and subsistence, stationery and postage, writing or printing (other than in newspapers), and distributing letters, circulars, and posters, and for telegraph and telephone service, shall not be regarded as an expenditure within the meaning of this section, and shall not be considered any part of the sum herein fixed as the limit of expense and need not be shown in the statements herein required to be filed.

The most notable case to which this law applied was that of Senator Truman H. Newberry, who lost his Senate seat but was ultimately acquitted of all charges. The act, the first to reform campaign finance laws, was overturned by the United States Supreme Court in 1925. At that time, it was repassed as the Federal Corrupt Practices Act, but again was weakened because it did not cover primary elections. This 1925 act was the prevailing congressional campaign finance law until 1971, when the Federal Election Campaign Act (FECA) was enacted.

See also: *Newberry v. United States*
References: Baltimore Reform League, *Special Report of the Executive Committee of Baltimore Reform League as to the Statements of Candidates and Others, Filed Under Provisions of the Corrupt Practices Act Subsequently to the Primary Election for Representatives in Congress, Held August 30, 1910* (Baltimore, MD: The League, 1910); "Federal Corrupt Practices Act of 1910 and 1911," in William C. Binning, Larry E. Esterly, and Paul A. Sracic, *Encyclopedia of American Parties, Campaigns, and Elections* (Westport, CT: Greenwood Press, 1999), 169.

Corrupt Practices Acts (Congressional)

See Federal Corrupt Practices Act of 1925; Federal Election Campaign Act of 1971; Hatch Act; Pendleton Civil Service Act; Publicity Act of 1910; Tillman Act of 1907

Coughlin, John Joseph (1860–1938)

Chicago alderman, known as "Bathhouse John," allied with fellow alderman Michael "Hinky Dink" Kenna to reign over a graft operation that lasted for more than forty years. Coughlin was born in Chicago on 15 August 1860, the son of Irish immigrants Michael Coughlin, from County Roscommon, and Johanna (née Hanley), of County Limerick. Little is known of John Coughlin's upbringing or education—only that his mother died in childbirth when he was a youngster, and he was raised by a stepmother. He went to work as a "rubber," or someone who rubbed items to a sheen, in the Palmer House Baths in the poorer area of Chicago. It was there that he got his nickname "Bathhouse John." He opened his own bathhouse in that same area.

Bathhouse John Coughlin might have been wholly forgotten by history had he not joined with Michael Kenna, an alderman of the First Ward of Chicago, known as "Hinky Dink" or "the Little Fellow" in 1893. Coughlin and Kenna went on to form one of the most corrupt organizations in nineteenth-century Chicago. Under the auspices of Kenna, who used his powerful office as a front, the men sold protection to gambling houses and houses of prostitution in the First Ward, also called "The Levee" because southern gamblers populated the area, and in the South a "levee" was the worst part of town. These two men thus became known as the "Lords of the Levee." In exchange for their protection, the two men employed lawyers who instantly appeared to defend bootleggers or prostitutes who had the ill fortune to be arrested.

In 1890, with the huge growth in Chicago's population, Mayor Carter Harrison moved the Levee from the First Ward to the Second. Normally, a politician needs merely to reach out to his or her new constituents, but Kenna and Coughlin were now losing the people they were being paid to protect. Kenna pushed a plan to redistrict the Second Ward, to reinclude the Levee back into the First Ward. The Second Ward alderman, William

Hale Thompson (who later became mayor of Chicago and who himself was corrupt), did not want the area in his district, so he supported Kenna's plan. In exchange for this support, Thompson received Kenna and Coughlin's backing to run for mayor. By the turn of the century, the "New Levee," as it was designated by many in Chicago, was populated by gambling houses and an extensive red light district. In the midst of this district, Coughlin, Kenna, and Thompson centered their power.

The "New Levee" in fact gave birth to the movement that was its destruction. The Columbian Exposition in 1893 gave Chicago its first major exposure as a large city, bringing thousands of people to that metropolis for the first time. One of these was William T. Stead, an English reformer and editor of the magazine *Review of Reviews,* a collection of contemporary editorial opinion in major journals. Stead, wandering around the city, saw firsthand the conditions in the "New Levee," and, appalled, returned to England, where in 1894 he published *If Christ Came to Chicago,* an exposé of the area that condemned the Democratic Party for its vise grip on the denizens of the poverty-stricken section. Stead's tome flashed a light on the conditions of Coughlin and Kenna's district, leading to the founding of the Civic Federation (CF), the first major reformist organization in Chicago. The CF called for an improvement of conditions in the "New Levee," lessening Coughlin and Kenna's power base. The changing political system and the crackdown on widespread political corruption by a new mayor, Carter Harrison, led to Coughlin and Kenna's downfall. Under assault by Harrison, Coughlin stepped aside as alderman after forty-six years in power.

As Coughlin's biographers, Lloyd Wendt and Herman Kogan, note, Coughlin died in poverty, besieged by piling debts in his last years. He died in Chicago on 8 November 1938 at the age of seventy-eight, remembered for his power, but also for his brand of corruption that was rampant in many nineteenth-century urban centers.

References: Nash, Jay Robert. *Encyclopedia of World Crime: Criminal Justice, Criminology, and Law Enforcement,* 4 vols. (Wilmette, IL: CrimeBooks, Inc., 1989), I:798; Wendt, Lloyd, and Herman Kogan, *Lords of the Levee: The Story of Bathhouse John & Hinky Dink* (Indianapolis, IN: Bobbs-Merrill Company, 1943).

Covode, John (1808–1871)

United States representative from Pennsylvania (1855–1863, 1867–1869), responsible for the Covode investigation of campaign finance practices of the James Buchanan administration and for introducing the impeachment resolution against President Andrew Johnson. Born on his father's farm near West Fairfield, Pennsylvania, on 17 March 1808, John Covode was the son of Jacob Covode and his wife, whose first name is unknown. He attended public schools in the area and then worked for several years on his father's farm and as an apprentice blacksmith, before going to work in a woolen mill as a laborer. He eventually purchased the mill and engaged in other business pursuits, such as owning outright or with partners the Pennsylvania Canal, the Pennsylvania Railroad, and the Westmoreland Coal Company.

Covode was a product of the political machine of Pennsylvania Senator Thaddeus Stevens, and he ran as a Whig for a seat in the U.S. House of Representatives, representing the Nineteenth Congressional District of that state. Defeating a Democrat, Covode served in the Thirty-fifth, Thirty-sixth, and Thirty-seventh Congresses, during which time he served as chairman of the Committee on Public Expenditures, on which he earned the sobriquet "Honest John." An opponent of slavery, Covode joined the infant Republican Party in 1856 and was elected to his third term in Congress that year. Gradually, he became identified with the Radical Republicans, a group from that party who demanded an end to slavery and complete emancipation and citizenship for blacks.

On 5 March 1860, amid allegations that President James Buchanan had bribed two House members to vote for the so-called Lecompton Constitution that had been passed by proslavery members of the Kansas legislature, Buchanan charged that Covode had won his 1858 race by bribing voters. Covode took to the floor of the House to condemn the accusation and to ask for an investigation into the Lecompton bribery allegations. Covode soon became Buchanan's worst political enemy, going after the president on every ground possible. Historian Edward Chester explained:

On Saturday, October 8, 1859, John Covode spoke to a gathering of some 400 to 500 people at Lafayette Hall, in Pittsburgh. . . . In this speech, according to an account printed in the Pittsburg *Post,* Covode attempted to implicate President Buchanan in certain printing frauds which he had helped to uncover while serving as a member of a Congressional committee the previous winter. A letter which James Buchanan wrote to the President of the Pittsburg Centenary Celebration of 1858 may have incited Covode to make his attack. In this letter Buchanan charged that the Republicans had employed money in an illegal manner to carry certain districts in Pennsylvania in the election of 1856. The exchange between Buchanan and Covode quickly began to attract the interest of other parties. A typical reaction was the charge made on December 12, 1859, by Congressman John Hickman of Pennsylvania, a former Douglas Democrat who ran as a Republican in 1860, that President Buchanan had tried to bribe him.

With these allegations in hand, Covode introduced a resolution calling for the establishment of a special House committee to investigate. Covode was named chairman of this committee—other members included Republicans Abram B. Olin of New York and Charles Train of Massachusetts and Democrats Warren Winslow of North Carolina and James Robinson of Illinois. On 29 March 1860, seven days after the special committee convened, Buchanan sent a letter of protest, calling into question Covode's judgment, and denouncing a "blanket inquiry." Documents showing that Democrats had given immigrants naturalization papers so that they could vote in state elections were introduced; when Representative Winslow looked into allegations of Republican frauds in the state, he could find no evidence. John Forney, a Pennsylvania Democrat who later turned Republican and went to work for the Lincoln administration, wrote the committee that Buchanan paid off people for good press in the state.

On 17 June 1860, the committee's majority and minority reports were released. Writing for the three Republican members, Representative Charles Train charged that the president had deliberately tried to enter Kansas as a slave state in violation of the law and that he had bribed members of Congress to gain their votes to pass the Lecompton Constitution allowing the state to enter the Union. In the minority report, Representative Warren Winslow wrote that evidence was lacking, but he did not refute the allegation that Buchanan had tried to bribe members in the Kansas statehood question. Representative James Robinson, despite being a Democrat, later said that he concurred in the majority report although he did not sign it.

The Covode Committee's report became a campaign issue in the 1860 campaign; Republicans used it in their local pamphlets, while Democrats barely mentioned it. It may have helped to gain Pennsylvania for the Republicans, won by Republican Abraham Lincoln in the election that year. Covode himself won reelection in 1860 easily.

During the Civil War, Covode became a member of the wing of the Republican Party known as the Radical Republicans—standing for a quick end to slavery, establishment of the Freedman's Bureau, and passage of the Reconstruction Acts imposing a harsh peace on the defeated Southern states, as well as the Civil Rights bills that were vetoed by President Andrew Johnson. Covode was a chief voice in the House for the impeachment of Johnson in 1868.

After a close election victory in 1868 in which the House ultimately sided with him over his Democratic opposition, Henry D. Foster, Covode decided not to run for reelection in 1870. The decision was perhaps based on his declining health. Covode never got a chance to live a life after his career ended: on 11 January 1871, before his term could end, he died in Harrisburg, Pennsylvania, at the age of sixty-two and was buried in the Methodist Episcopal Cemetery in West Fairfield, Pennsylvania. Although his investigation into potential fraud and corruption never reached the heights of the ABSCAM investigation or the Keating Five in the late twentieth century, his committee's work is still cited by historians for its investigative thoroughness.

References: Chester, Edward W., "The Impact of the Covode Congressional Investigation," *Western Pennsylvania Historical Magazine,* 42 (December 1959), 343–350; Cotterill, Robert Spencer, "Covode, John," in Allen Johnson and Dumas Malone, et al., eds., *Dictionary of American Biography,* X vols. and 10 supplements, (New York: Charles Scribner's Sons, 1930–1995), II:470; Dodds, Archibald J., "'Honest John' Covode" (Master's thesis, University of Pittsburgh, 1933); Stanchak, John E. "Covode, John," in Faust, Patricia L., ed., *Historical Times Illustrated Encyclopedia of the Civil War* (New York: Harper and Row, Publishers, 1986), 187–188.

Cox, Charles Christopher (1952–)

United States representative from California (1989–), chairman of the Select Committee on U.S. National Security and Military/Commercial Concerns with the People's Republic of China, also known as the Cox Committee. He was born in St. Paul, Minnesota, on 16 October 1952, and attended St. Gregory's School and the St. Thomas Academy, both in St. Paul, before he headed west and received his bachelor's degree *magna cum laude* after just three years of study from the University of Southern California in 1973. He moved east to earn his master's of business administration degree from Harvard Business School in 1977 and his law degree from Harvard Law School that same year, both with honors. During his time at Harvard he had also served as the editor of the *Harvard Law Review.* Immediately out of law school Cox was hired as a law clerk to Judge Herbert Y. C. Choy, a member of the U.S. Court of Appeals for the Ninth Circuit in San Francisco. After leaving that post in 1978, Cox returned home to work for his father, who had founded a publishing firm that put out an English-language version of *Pravda,* the Soviet newspaper from Moscow. In 1978 Cox went to work for the international law firm of Latham & Watkins, as a partner in charge of their Orange County, California, office, specializing in venture capital and corporate finance. He took time off in 1982 to spend two years teaching business administration at Harvard Business School.

In 1986 Cox entered the political realm, when he was appointed senior associate counsel to President Ronald Reagan. At just thirty-four years of age, Cox was a bright young face among Reagan's staff. He assisted in advising the president on numerous policy matters and helped to write the tax legislation for Reagan's Budget Process Reform Act.

In 1988 Cox returned to California and ran for a seat in the U.S. House of Representatives. Representative Robert Badham, Republican of California's Forty-seventh Congressional District, declined to run for a sixth term, and Cox entered a field of fourteen candidates. Despite this, and his being little known in the district, he recruited Republican firebrands Representative Robert Dornan and former U.S. Supreme Court nominee Robert Bork to campaign for him. Cox won the Re-

publican primary, and garnered 67 percent of the vote in the general election to win the House seat. In his first term, he was named a member of the House Budget Committee. In 2000 Cox introduced the measure he had written for President Reagan, the Budget Process Reform Act, and it received its first floor vote, although it was not enacted into law.

Following allegations that the Clinton administration had assisted the People's Republic of China in obtaining missile technology in exchange for campaign contributions from leading American satellite launchers, in addition to other allegations relating to China, the U.S. House of Representatives on 18 June 1998 established the Select Committee on U.S. National Security and Military/Commercial Concerns with the People's Republic of China to examine the allegations and make recommendations. Cox was a natural to serve as the chairman of the committee—the *Los Angeles Times* called him "an expert in foreign affairs." Starting from scratch, Cox was able to form a committee that held thirty-four total meetings over a 6-month period, including 22 separate meetings and more than 200 hours of testimony heard from over 75 different witnesses, as well as more than 700 hours of interviews. On 25 May 1999, after several delays, the Cox Committee report was released. It alleged that China had used a systematic campaign of intelligence gathering to assemble a growing military machine. In releasing the report, Cox explained, "[China's] targeting of sensitive U.S. military technology is not limited to missiles and satellites, but covers other military technologies. . . . Sensitive U.S. military technology has been the subject of serious [Chinese] acquisition efforts over the last two decades, and continues today. A significant reason for the creation of the Select Committee was to determine whether Space Systems/Loral and Hughes were responsible for the transfer of technology that damaged the national security of the United States. Based on unclassified information, we have found that national security harm did occur. We have investigated these questions more thoroughly than any other part of the U.S. Government." He added, "These transfers are not limited to satellite and missile technology, but cover other militarily significant technologies. . . . Rather quickly, our investigation led to even more serious problems of [Chinese] technology acquisition efforts targeted at the United States. The seriousness of these findings, and their enormous significance to our national security, led us to a unanimous report."

Cox's work on the committee, as well as the respect he has garnered from both sides of the political aisle in the House, make him a leading candidate to become Speaker of the House, if not another high office, before his political career is finished. In 2001 President George W. Bush considered Cox for a seat on the U.S. Court of Appeals for the Ninth Circuit in San Francisco, but Cox begged off because the Senate was in Democratic control and Cox did not want a bruising confirmation battle.

See also Chinagate; Cox Report
References: *Biographical Directory of the American Congress, 1774–1996* (Alexandria, VA: CQ Staff Directories, Inc., 1996), 871; Clines, Francis X., "Republicans' New Man in the Middle," *New York Times,* 21 May 1998, 26; "Cox, Christopher," in Clifford Thompson, ed., *Current Biography 1999* (New York: H. W. Wilson & Co., 2000), 18–19; United States Congress, House, Select Committee on U.S. National Security and Military/Commercial Concerns with the People's Republic of China, *U.S. National Security and Military/Commercial Concerns with the People's Republic of China. Submitted by Mr. Cox of California,* 3 vols. (Washington, DC: Government Printing Office, 1999).

Cox Report

Narration of the United States Congress, issued 25 May 1999, which detailed the acquisition by the People's Republic of China of American nuclear secrets through espionage and other illicit means. Following a number of stories regarding Chinese missile technology, missile tests in China, campaign donations to the campaigns of President Bill Clinton by American satellite companies that were then allowed by the American administration to sell sensitive technology to China, and the story of Los Alamos, New Mexico, scientist Wen Ho Lee, who was accused (but later cleared) of selling nuclear secrets to China, the U.S. Congress established the Select Committee on U.S. National Security and Military/Commercial Concerns with the People's Republic of China, pursuant to House Resolution 462, which was adopted on 18 June 1998. The resolution, which explained the committee's jurisdiction, stated that:

The Select Committee shall conduct a full and complete inquiry regarding the following matters and report such findings and recommendations, including those concerning the amendment of existing law or the enactment of new law, to the House as it considers appropriate:

(1) The transfer of technology, information, advice, goods, or services that may have contributed to the enhancement of the accuracy, reliability, or capability of nuclear-armed intercontinental ballistic missiles or other weapons of the People's Republic of China, or that may have contributed to the enhancement of the intelligence capabilities of the People's Republic of China.

(2) The transfer of technology, information, advice, goods, or services that may have contributed to the manufacture of weapons of mass destruction, missiles, or other weapons or armaments by the People's Republic of China.

(3) The effect of any transfer or enhancement referred to in paragraphs (1) or (2) on regional security and the national security of the United States.

(4) The conduct of the executive branch of the United States Government with respect to the transfers or enhancements referred to in paragraphs (1) or (2), and the effect of that conduct on regional security and the national security of the United States.

(5) The conduct of defense contractors, weapons manufacturers, satellite manufacturers, and other private or government-owned commercial firms with respect to the transfers or enhancements referred to in paragraphs (1) or (2).

(6) The enforcement of United States law, including statutes, regulations, or executive orders, with respect to the transfers or enhancements referred to in paragraphs (1) or (2).

(7) Any effort by the Government of the People's Republic of China or any other person or entity to influence any of the foregoing matters through political contributions, commercial arrangements, or bribery, influence-peddling, or other illegal activities.

(8) Decision-making within the executive branch of the United States Government with respect to any of the foregoing matters.

(9) Any effort to conceal or withhold information or documents relevant to any of the foregoing matters or to obstruct justice, or to obstruct the work of the Select Committee or any other committee of the House of Representatives in connection with those matters.

(10) All matters relating directly or indirectly to any of the foregoing matters.

The committee was given the mandate to investigate these concerns from July 1998, when they first met in session, until December 1998. Representative Christopher Cox (R-CA) was named committee chairman (hence the committee being called the Cox Committee); Representative Norman Dicks (D-WA), was named as the ranking Democrat. The other committee members were: Representative Porter Goss, vice chairman (R-FL); Representative Doug Bereuter (R-NE); Representative James V. Hansen (R-UT); Representative John M. Spratt Jr. (D-SC); Representative Curt Weldon (R-FL); Representative Lucille Roybal-Allard (D-CA); and Representative Bobby Scott (D-VA).

The committee focused on several narrow matters: it started with the allegations that Loral and Hughes, two major American satellite manufacturers, had given large campaign donations to the Clinton campaigns in 1992 and 1996, and in exchange U.S. government restrictions of the sale of satellite technology to China were relaxed. Several launch failures of Chinese rockets, which were then fixed with American technology from Loral, highlighted these concerns. Other matters investigated included American government involvement in allowing high-performance computers to be legally exported to China; the role of alleged Chinese espionage in American nuclear facilities; the role of Chinese-owned companies in the United States and the part they played in this alleged espionage and the transfer of technology from the United States to China; and U.S. government oversight (or lack thereof) regarding this transfer. One part of H. Res. 463 that was highly controversial was allowing an investigation into the role that alleged Chinese campaign donations might have had on Clinton administration responses to the relaxation of technology restrictions. Given that other committees were investigating such campaign violations by the 1992 and 1996 Clinton presidential campaigns, the Cox Committee could not go far with the inquiry into this area. Several witnesses were contacted by the committee, but all of them exerted their Fifth Amendment rights against self-incrimination, and in the end the Cox Committee Report did not go into great depth on its findings regarding such campaign contribution violations and their role in the whole Chinese matter.

The committee delved into the task quite heavily: the members received numerous briefings and met with various government officials, from Department of Energy experts to Central Intelligence Agency (CIA) staffers. During their six months of investigating, the committee met 34 times to hear testimony and conduct committee business, hearing more than 150 hours of testimony from 75 witnesses. Over 500,000 pages of evidentiary material was reviewed, and, after issuing 21 subpoenas, the committee heard from 150 additional individuals and conducted more than 700 hours of interviews. In four instances, immunity was granted so that testimony could be heard.

The committee wrapped up its work by the end of 1998 as scheduled and prepared to release its report on 3 January 1999. However, several disputes and the redacting of sensitive material led to delays that pushed official public release to 25 May 1999. In the end, the three-volume, 900-page report painted a picture of an advancing nation, China, which sought by all means necessary to acquire nuclear secrets from the United States. The committee report alleged that Chinese operatives, working in U.S. nuclear laboratories and other facilities, gathered information starting in the 1970s and accelerating in the 1990s, of missile technology and were able to steal the plans for the W-88 warhead, known better as the Trident II. The report also charged that these same Chinese spies had gathered information on guidance systems for American missiles and jet fighters and electromagnetic weapons technology that was being studied for use in the National Missile Defense (NMD) program, known better as "Star Wars." It also alleged that China was using its more than 3,000 commercial ventures in the United States as fronts to gather information to use in China. The committee explained that although the Clinton administration had relaxed restrictions on the sale of high-technology computers to China in 1996, there was no way to learn if this had come about because of campaign donations, or if the computers were used in China's military or commercial sector. The committee did allege that the Hughes Electronics Corp. and Loral Space and Electronics, Ltd. Did illegally assist China with satellite and rocket technology, which was used in their own military missile program, and that the Clinton administration had relaxed oversight standards on the two companies.

The Cox Committee report was a bombshell when released in May 1999 and was denounced by the Chinese government as a propaganda tool. The report did force the U.S. Department of Energy to tighten its regulations and security for the first time in many years.

References: Eilperin, Juliet, and Vernon Loeb, "Panel Says Chinese Arms Used U.S. Data," *Washington Post*, 25 May 1999, A1; Laris, Michael, "China Says It Can Build Neutron Bomb, Beijing Attempts to Discredit Cox Report on Theft of U.S. Secrets," *Washington Post*, 15 July 1999, A1.; United States Congress, House, Select Committee on U.S. National Security and Military/Commercial Concerns with the People's Republic of China, *U.S. National Security and Military/Commercial Concerns with the People's Republic of China. Submitted by Mr. Cox of California*, 3 vols. (Washington, DC: Government Printing Office, 1999).

Cranston, Alan MacGregor (1914–2000)

United States senator from California (1969–1993), implicated in the so-called Keating Five financial scandal and receiver of the harshest punishment of the five U.S. senators so involved. Cranston was born in Palo Alto, California, on 19 June 1914. He attended the public schools of Los Altos, California, before attending Pomona College (Pomona, California), the University of Mexico, and Stanford University, graduating from the latter institution in 1936. Out of school, Cranston got a job as a reporter with the International News Service (now part of UPI, the United Press International), covering the growing threat of war in England, Germany, Italy, and Ethiopia from 1937 to 1938. Sensing the danger posed by German leader Adolf Hitler, Cranston, with a former editor for Hearst newspapers, Amster Spiro, published a version of Hitler's manifesto, *Mein Kampf* ("My Struggle") with explanatory notes that were plainly anti-Nazi. Hitler sued Cranston to stop publication of the work in the United States, but by the time he got a court injunction to cease, more than 500,000 copies had been sold. Cranston then became the chief of the foreign language division of the Office of War Information in the U.S. Department of War, serving in that position from 1940 to 1944. In 1944 he enlisted in the U.S. Army as a private and served in an infantry unit in the United States, finishing the conflict as the editor of *Army Talk Magazine.* He was discharged in 1945. That year, he published *The Killing of the Peace,* his thoughts on

the U.S. Senate's decision in 1919 not to join the League of Nations.

Cranston soon became involved in the political arena. He had worked in Washington in 1939 as a member of the Common Council for American Unity, a left-leaning group that urged nondiscrimination in immigration and naturalization. After the war, he served as national president of the United World Federalists, a group that advocated one world government. But Cranston was also involved in business. In 1947 he became the head of Cranston Co., a real estate concern in Palo Alto that had been established by his father. In 1958 Cranston entered California politics with his election as state comptroller, and he was reelected in 1962. In 1968 he ran for and was elected to the United States Senate, defeating Republican Max Rafferty. A member of the Senate Committee on Veterans, Cranston would rise to become chairman of that panel in the 95th and 96th and 101st and 102nd Congresses. He would also advance to become Democratic whip, serving from 1977 to 1991. In 1984 he ran a spirited but disastrous campaign for the Democratic presidential nomination.

One of the most far-reaching ethics cases in U.S. Senate history was exposed in 1990. Cranston, along with fellow Senators Dennis DeConcini (D-AZ), John McCain (R-AZ), John Glenn (D-OH), and Donald W. Riegle Jr. (D-MI), was revealed to have given assistance to savings and loan operator Charles H. Keating Jr. in his attempts to stave off government oversight, in exchange for campaign contributions. Keating had approached senators from California and Arizona, where his savings and loans were located, in an effort to get their help in stopping federal banking investigators from looking into the financial affairs of the institutions, which were slowly going bankrupt. Several other politicians were contacted, but refused to help: Governor Bruce Babbitt of Arizona, after looking into the Keating matter, told Cranston specifically that Keating was "a crook." Nonetheless the Californian aided the thrift operator, to his detriment.

Hearings into the actions taken by these senators opened on 15 November 1990 before the Senate Select Committee on Ethics (it had changed its name from the Select Committee on Standards and Conduct in 1977). A special outside counsel, Washington attorney Robert S. Bennett, who had investigated Senator Harrison Williams in the ABSCAM scandal and would be the committee's counsel against Senator David F. Durenberger, was retained. What followed were televised hearings (available to a startled nation for the first time in American history) and thirty-three hours of closed-door deliberations over six weeks, culminating on 27 February 1991. Bennett and the committee found that of the five senators involved, Cranston was most culpable for committing the most egregious violations. In his final report to the committee, Bennett cited four specific occasions when Cranston worked to assist Keating, after Keating had either delivered campaign donations to Cranston, or had solicited donations for him. The committee report, released on 19 November 1991, stated:

The Committee finds that in connection with his conduct relating to Charles H. Keating, Jr., and Lincoln Savings and Loan Association, Sen. Alan Cranston of California engaged in an impermissible pattern of conduct in which fundraising and official activities were substantially linked. . . . It is further resolved:

1. That Sen. Cranston's impermissible pattern of conduct violated established norms of behavior in the Senate, and was improper conduct that reflects upon the Senate.

2. That Sen. Cranston's conduct was improper and repugnant.

3. In reviewing the evidence available to it, the committee finds that Sen. Cranston: violated no law or specific Senate rule; acting without corrupt intent; and did receive nor intend to receive personal financial benefit from any of the funds raised through Mr. Keating.

4. Further, the committee finds that extenuating circumstances exist, including the following:

a. That Sen. Cranston is in poor health.

b. That Sen. Cranston has announced his intention not to seek reelection to the Senate.

5. Sen. Cranston's improper conduct deserves the fullest, strongest, and most severe sanction which the committee has the authority to impose.

Therefore, the Senate Select Committee on Ethics, on behalf of and in the name of the Senate, does hereby and severely reprimand Sen. Alan Cranston.

Prior to the hearings, Cranston announced that he was suffering from prostate cancer and would not be a candidate for reelection in 1992. He left the Senate on 3 January 1993, and returned to private business. He continued to speak out and write on foreign policy matters and in 1996 became the chairman of the Gorbachev Foundation USA, a think-tank named after the former Soviet Communist Party chairman.

On 30 December 2000, Cranston died at his home in Los Altos, California, at the age of eighty-six. He was remembered by his former colleagues and intimates as a man of principle, but his obituaries were tinged with the words "Keating Five."

See also Keating Five

References: *Biographical Directory of the American Congress, 1774–1996* (Alexandria, VA: CQ Staff Directories, Inc., 1996), 877; *Congressional Ethics: History, Facts, and Controversy* (Washington, DC: Congressional Quarterly, 1992), 44–45; Fowle, Eleanor, *Cranston, the Senator from California* (San Rafael, CA: Presidio Press, 1980); United States Congress, Senate, Select Committee on Ethics, *Investigation of Senator Alan Cranston: Report of the Select Committee on Ethics, United States Senate*, 2 vols. (Washington, DC: Government Printing Office, 1991).

Crédit Mobilier Scandal

One of the most widespread cases of political corruption in American history, implicating several U.S. congressmen and senators, as well as the vice president of the United States, Schuyler Colfax, in taking monies from a railroad to get legislation favorable to that railroad enacted.

The entire scandal started when Thomas Durant, vice president of the Union Pacific Railroad Company, was able in 1864 to acquire the controlling interest in the Pennsylvania Fiscal Agency, which was controlled by the Crédit Mobilier of America. The Crédit Mobilier was established in the early 1860s to build a transcontinental railroad. Things started out badly, as the heads of the railroad concern named their company after a French corporation that had defrauded French investors of millions of French francs in the 1850s. When the Crédit Mobilier started building the railroad at ridiculous cost, Durant and his friends made millions of dollars. To keep Congress from investigating their extravagant profit making, Durant showered certain congressmen with stock from the Crédit Mobilier. Utilizing the talents of Representative Oakes Ames of Massachusetts as a

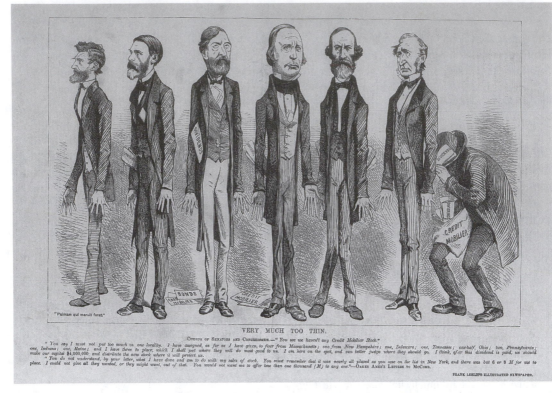

VERY MUCH TOO THIN.

These senators and congressmen denied taking railroad stock from Crédit Mobilier as bribes. (Bettmann/Corbis)

middleman, the company gave stock to Representatives James Brooks of New York, James A. Garfield of Ohio, William D. Kelley of Pennsylvania, John Bingham of Ohio, and John A. Logan of Illinois. Senators James W. Patterson of New Hampshire and Henry Wilson of Massachusetts, and Vice President Schuyler Colfax, among others, also received the gifts. These illicit payments went on for many years. One of the men who was able to escape all accusations from the scandal was Representative William Almon Wheeler of New York, who was offered stock by Ames but refused on the grounds that such stock offers were illegal. Wheeler, the chairman of the House Committee on Pacific Railroads, even resigned his chairmanship so as to avoid any appearance of wrongdoing. For his scruples, Wheeler was later rewarded with the second spot on the Republican ticket in 1876 and served as vice president from 1877 to 1881 under Rutherford B. Hayes.

By 1869, however, the Union Pacific Railroad was reporting heavy financial losses, and congressional patience for covering these with increased appropriations was growing thin. Ames plied some congressmen and senators with more stock. To a friend, Henry S. McComb, Ames sent a list of these politicians, almost bragging about how he had covered himself. Three years passed and up came a presidential election. The country had been mired in the scandals of the first four years of the administration of President Ulysses S. Grant, and the time seemed ripe for Grant to lose the White House to the Democrats. However, nothing could be pinned on Grant himself, until McComb came forward with Ames's list. Passing it along to Charles A. Dana, editor of the *New York Sun* and a political opponent of Grant, McComb let loose a torrent. On 4 September 1872, in the middle of the presidential campaign, the charges against Ames, Brooks, Blaine, and Grant's vice president (who had been shoved aside for Senator Henry Wilson, who was also implicated in the scheme) were aired on the front pages of the *Sun*. Ames and the others denied the charges vehemently, and Grant was able to coast to an easy reelection victory over New York journalist and newspaper editor Horace

Greeley, nominated by the Democrats and a liberal faction of the Republican Party.

In December 1872 Congress met in session (as they did at that time), and the seriousness of the charges were addressed. Speaker of the House James G. Blaine, implicated in the scandal, in an extraordinary move selected Representative Samuel S. Cox of New York (who, running as a liberal Republican, had lost his 1872 reelection effort) to chair the whole House and to assemble a congressional committee to investigate the allegations of bribery. Cox then named Representative Luke Poland (R-VT), who had lost his reelection attempt in 1872, to head a committee in the house. Members of this committee included Nathaniel P. Banks of Massachusetts, James B. Beck of Kentucky, William E. Niblack of Indiana, and George W. McCrary of Iowa. The Poland Committee reported back to the House on 18 February 1873, prior to the end of the congressional session, implicating Representatives Ames and James Brooks (D-NY), and asking that both men be expelled from the House. The others were exonerated, despite the evidence against them. Many believe that Ames and Brooks were "sacrificial lambs," thrown to the wolves to absolve the House as a whole of the massive corruption scandal. Many Democrats refused to vote for expulsion for either man, and in the end all they received was a censure. (Both men had lost their seats in 1872, making either an expulsion or censure measure rather moot.)

The House named a second committee, headed by Representative J. M. Wilson of Indiana, to investigate whether any of the persons who bought stock in the Crédit Mobilier or Union Pacific Railroad could be held criminally liable. Members of this committee included Samuel Shellabarger of Ohio, George F. Hoar of Massachusetts, Thomas Swann of Maryland, and H. W. Slocum of New York. No charges ever came out of this committee's findings.

Representative James Garfield of Ohio, one of the largest purchasers of shares from Ames, escaped unscathed and was elected simultaneously to the U.S. Senate and to the presidency in 1880, a feat not since repeated. Garfield was assassinated in mid-1881. Blaine resumed the speakership and was nominated for president by the Republicans in 1884, but his ties to the Crédit Mobilier scandal, as well as another dubbed the Mulligan Letters scandal, caused many reformist Republicans to flee the party to Democrat Grover Cleveland, who defeated Blaine. Blaine later served twice as secretary of state. Vice President Schuyler Colfax, forced off the Republican ticket in 1872 because of the Crédit Mobilier scandal, never recovered his good name and died in 1885.

Historian George Kohn writes of this scandal,

The Crédit Mobilier scandal, with its almost incredible waste, crime, and corruption of basic principles, shook the country, set many weak organizations toppling, and made cynical the average American affected by it. The weak congressional discipline in the affair hardly frightened financier Jay Gould, who had fronted a similar holding-construction company while he controlled the building of the Northern Pacific Railroad (1870–73). In the Panic of 1873, that construction stopped, and the wily Gould escaped with his gains untouched by even minor congressional concern.

See also Ames, Oakes; Brooks, James; Colfax, Schuyler, Jr.; Garfield, James Abram; Patterson, James Willis

References: Butler, Anne M., and Wendy Wolff, *United States Senate Election, Expulsion and Censure Cases, 1793–1990* (Washington, DC: Government Printing Office, 1995), 189–195; Crawford, Jay Boyd, *The Crédit Mobilier of America: Its Origin and History, Its Work of Constructing the Union Pacific Railroad and the Relation of Members of Congress Therewith, by J. B. Crawford* (Boston, C. W. Calkins, 1880); "Crédit Mobilier Scandal," in George C. Kohn, *Encyclopedia of American Scandal: From ABSCAM to the Zenger Case* (New York: Facts on File, 1989), 77–78; Hazard, Rowland, *The Crédit Mobilier of America: A Paper Read Before the Rhode Island Historical Society, Tuesday Evening, February 22, 1881, by Rowland Hazard* (Providence: S. S. Rider, 1881).

Croker, Richard (1841–1922)

Known as the "Boss of New York politics" as head of the Tammany organization from 1886 to 1902, implicated in, but never convicted of, serious financial misconduct. In an era when immigrants found political power for the first time in American history, Richard Croker was ably suited and situated to rise to the top of the crooked and powerful Tammany organization in the last decades of the nineteenth century. He was born in Cloghnakilty, Ireland, on 23 November 1841, the son and one of nine children of one Eyre Coote Croker.

When Richard was three, in 1844, the family emigrated to America, settling in New York City, where Richard Croker attended public school. However, when he was only thirteen, he began to work as a machinist, and from that time his education ended and his work history began. During his teens, Croker was also an amateur prizefighter.

By the time he was eighteen, Croker had joined the Tammany Hall society, a machine of political cronies that ran New York City. Initially appointed an attendant in the supreme court, he moved over to become an engineer in the New York fire department. By this time, about 1868, Tammany was splitting into two factions: those led by William Magear Tweed, known as "Boss" Tweed, leader of Tammany, and the "Young Democracy," a reformist wing of the machine led by "Honest John" Kelly and opposed to the crookedness of Tweed and his cronies. As a member of this latter group, Croker ran for a seat on the board of aldermen, and, after being elected, on 20 March 1870, signed a manifesto declaring that he, along with all the other members of the "Young Democracy," would refuse to push any measure affecting the city without the express support of the group. Tweed disagreed with Croker's attitude against municipal corruption and in 1870 helped to enact a law in the New York state legislature getting rid of Croker's aldermanic seat. But Tweed's power was limited in Albany, and he could not fight Croker's subsequent appointment by the state comptroller to a post in the city government in Manhattan. Tweed's fall from power in 1871 following an investigation by several newspapers, including the *New York Times,* left Croker in a powerful position. "Honest John" Kelly succeeded Tweed, and Croker was named as New York coroner. When a political opponent of Croker's was murdered on election day 1874, Croker was initially charged with the crime and spent one month in jail, but the case was later dismissed due to lack of evidence. Years later Croker admitted that one of his friends was the real killer, having committed the crime in self-defense when Croker himself was attacked by the victim.

Croker returned to his coroner's position, later promoted to fire commissioner by Mayor Franklin Edison. In 1886 Croker, still a leader in the movement to bring reform to city politics, succeeded "Honest John" Kelly as head of Tammany Hall. It was at this point that Croker, emboldened by the power of the Tammany organization, became chairman of the Tammany Finance Committee and became a virtual dictator over Democratic Party politics until 1902. As the Tammany leader, Croker could elect a mayor, or help defeat a candidate he did not support. This is shown in the elections of Hugh Grant in 1888, Thomas F. Gilroy in 1892, and Robert Van Wyck in 1897 to the mayoralty. In 1886 Croker helped to defeat the reform candidate for mayor, Theodore Roosevelt, instead helping to install Abram S. Hewitt. Investigations failed to dislodge Croker, known (ironically) as "Boss" Croker: in 1893–1894, the Lexow Committee, looking into police corruption and ties to Tammany Hall, could not find evidence against Croker; in 1899 the Mazet Committee investigated political corruption in Tammany Hall, but again Croker was not charged with a crime.

In 1893 Croker's hold on the Tammany organization began to break. The election of William L. Strong as mayor came about because of the Lexow Committee investigation that caused clean elections to be instituted and Croker's role diminished. The chief counsel of the Lexow Committee, Democratic attorney John Goff, ran as Strong's running mate. His leadership tarnished, Croker left the United States and went to England into forced exile. The Tammany organization was taken over by John C. Sheehan, who could not stop Republican William McKinley from carrying the city in 1896. Croker returned and pushed Robert C. Van Wyck for mayor in 1897; Van Wyck battled the anti-Tammany candidate, Seth Low. As soon as Van Wyck was inaugurated, Croker moved in and named all of the new mayor's staff positions. This, and the news that Croker had paid hundreds of thousands of dollars for property in the United States and England led to another run by Low in 1901, this time successful. Croker's hold over Tammany and New York politics was broken. He again moved to England, living for a time at Wantage, afterwards transferring to an estate, Glencairn, near Dublin, Ireland. In these, his final years, Croker spent his time as a dapper Englishman instead of the rough-and-tumble politico that he had been for years.

Croker's contribution to American politics is in fact large: prior to his leadership of Tammany Hall, the organization was an anti-Catholic and anti-immigrant group. By the time Croker came to head it up, he saw that Catholics and immigrants (mostly Irish) were populating the cities, and their support was key to his and Tammany's continued popularity. Croker later wrote, "Think of the hundreds of thousands of foreigners dumped into our city. . . . They are alone, ignorant strangers, a prey to all manner of anarchical and wild notions. . . . And Tammany looks after them for the sake of their votes, grafts them upon the Republic, makes citizens of them, in short. . . . If we go down into the gutter it is because there are men in the gutter, and you have to go down where they are if you are to do anything with them."

Many historians believe that Croker intended one day to return to New York and take up the mantle of leadership, but he never did. In early 1922, as he lay dying in his bed in Ireland, someone told him that he was going to a better place on the "other side." "I doubt it," Croker said. After his death, his children fought each other bitterly for years for control of his property.

References: "Croker, Richard," in Harold Zink, *City Bosses in the United States* (Durham, NC: Duke University Press, 1930), 128–146; "Croker, Richard," in Jay Robert Nash, *Encyclopedia of World Crime: Criminal Justice, Criminology, and Law Enforcement,* 4 vols. (Wilmette, IL: CrimeBooks, Inc., 1989) II:827; Croker, Richard, "Tammany Hall and the Democracy," *North American Review,* 154:423 (February 1892), 225–230; *Essays in the History of New York City: A Memorial to Sidney Pomerantz* (Port Washington, NY: Kennikat Press, 1978); Lewis, Alfred Henry, *Richard Croker* (New York: Life Publishing Company, 1901), 4–12; Stoddard, Lothrop, *Master of Manhattan: The Life of Richard Croker* (New York: Longmans, Green and Company, 1931).

Crosby, William (c. 1690–1736)
See Zenger, John Peter

Curley, James Michael (1874–1958)
Member of the Massachusetts State House of Representatives (1902–1903), U.S. representative from Massachusetts (1911–1914, 1943–1947), mayor of Boston (1914–1917, 1922–1925, 1930–1933, 1946–1949), governor of Massachusetts (1935–1937), head of the powerful Democratic machine in that city and the first to organize Irish immigrants into a powerful political force in the United States.

Born in Boston on 20 November 1874, Curley was the son of Michael Curley and Sarah (née Clancy) Curley, both Irish immigrants. Michael Curley was killed in an accident when his son James was twelve, and James's mother was forced to go to work as a maid. James Curley attended the public schools of Boston, leaving school early to go to work for the baking and confectionery concern of Logan, Johnston & Co. Later, Curley was involved in the selling of real estate and insurance. However, he soon found Boston Irish politics in his blood. Despite the fact that his father had once worked for P. J. "Peajacket" Maguire, ward boss of the Seventh Boston Ward, in 1898 James Curley ran for a seat on the Boston City Council against a "Peajacket"-endorsed candidate. Despite his loss, he ran again the next year and, employing the same rough tactics of his opponents, he won, and took his council seat at age twenty-six. In 1902, he decided to run for a seat in the Massachusetts state legislature. Elected, he served until 1903. At that time he returned to Boston and ran for a position on the Boston Board of Aldermen. When he was caught taking a civil service examination for a friend, he was sent to jail for sixty days, from which he campaigned. Despite this, he was elected, and served on the board from 1904 to 1909. Curley later served as a member of the Boston City Council from 1910 to 1911.

In 1910 Curley ran for a seat in the U.S. House of Representatives, representing Massachusetts's Twelfth District. A Democrat, he served two undistinguished terms, until his resignation on 4 February 1914. In 1913 Curley ran for mayor of Boston. Facing the political machine of "Honey Fitz" Fitzgerald—the maternal grandfather of President John F. Kennedy—Curley defeated Fitzgerald's candidate, Thomas J. Kenny. Curley then threw out all the machine politicians who ran the city and instituted his own system of cronyism. Opening up city coffers, he spent lavishly on city projects such as hospitals, parks, and roads. However, he alienated many in the business community and when he ran for reelection in 1917 he was defeated by a powerful ward boss, Martin Lomasney.

Despite this defeat, Curley plotted a comeback. In 1921, he defeated three candidates in the Democratic primary to win a second nonconsecutive term. Once again, he spent city funds, this time to create jobs and end unemployment. In 1924 he ran for governor, but lost. In 1926 he was again defeated as mayor, but four years later he again made a comeback and served in that same office from 1930 to 1934. In 1934 Curley ran for governor of Massachusetts, becoming the chief executive of that state. In 1936 he ran for the United States Senate, but he lost to Republican Henry Cabot Lodge Jr. He ran again unsuccessfully for mayor of Boston in 1937, for governor in 1938, and for mayor in 1940. He was elected to a seat in the U.S. House of Representatives in 1942 and reelected in 1944, and served a fourth term as mayor of Boston from 1945 to 1949. In 1957 he served in his final office, that of appointed head of the Massachusetts State Labor Commission.

Curley's career was marked by repeated allegations of corruption, and two times he was convicted. As biographer Stanley Schultz explained, in 1937 in his race for governor Curley accepted a bribe for helping to settle an insurance claim against the city of Boston in exchange for political support. Found guilty, he was ordered to repay the city the amount of $42,629. In 1941 Curley served as the president of Engineers Corp., a military firm that used Curley's name to get war contracts prior to the American entry into World War II. Although Curley only served in this capacity for six months and was never paid for his work, in 1945 he was indicted by the U.S. Department of Justice and charged with taking $60,000 through influence peddling. Found guilty, he was sentenced to eighteen months in prison. Sickly, he served only four months before President Harry S. Truman gave him executive clemency. Out of prison, he recovered and once again served as mayor of Boston. In 1950, Truman gave him an unconditional pardon.

James Michael Curley is considered one of the most unusual and colorful characters in the history of Massachusetts politics. Author Edwin O'-Connor based his fictional political boss Frank Skeffington on Curley when he penned *The Last Hurrah* (1956). Curley wrote his own memoirs, *I'd Do It Again: A Record of All My Uproarious Years,* in 1957. Curley died in Boston on 12 November 1958 and was laid to rest in Old Cavalry Cemetery in that city.

References: Beatty, Jack, *The Rascal King: The Life and Times of James Michael Curley* (Reading, MA: Addison-Wesley Publishing Co., 1993); *Biographical Directory of the American Congress, 1774–1996* (Alexandria, VA: CQ Staff Directories, Inc., 1996), 892–893; Curley, James Michael, *I'd Do It Again: A Record of All My Uproarious Years* (Englewood Cliffs, NJ: Prentice-Hall, 1957); Dinneen, Joseph F., *The Purple Shamrock: The Honorable James Michael Curley of Boston* (New York: Norton, 1949); "James M. Curley Dies in Boston, Colorful Democratic Boss was 83," *New York Times,* 13 November 1958, 1; Jones, Peter d'A., "Curley, James Michael," in Melvin G. Holli and Peter d'A. Jones, *Biographical Dictionary of American Mayors, 1820–1980: Big City Mayors* (Westport, CT: Greenwood Press, 1981), 86–88; Schultz, Stanley K., "Curley, James Michael," in Allen Johnson and Dumas Malone, et al., eds., *Dictionary of American Biography,* X vols. and 10 supplements (New York: Charles Scribner's Sons, 1930–1995), 6:138–141.

Curtis, George William (1824–1892)

American writer and reformer, editor (1863–1892) of *Harper's Weekly,* commissioner and advocate of civil service reform in the latter part of the nineteenth century. Born on 24 February 1824 in Providence, Rhode Island, Curtis was the scion of a wealthy family. In 1836, his father, George Curtis, a banker, took a position with Continental Bank; he moved his family and his wife, Mary Elizabeth Curtis, to New York. There, George Curtis was educated at a exemplary boarding school and by private tutors. He later moved with his brother Burrill to the Brook Farm commune in West Roxbury, Massachusetts, south of Boston. Curtis moved to Boston, becoming friends with such literary giants as Ralph Waldo Emerson, Henry David Thoreau, and Nathaniel Hawthorne. It was his association with these men, as well as a trip through Europe with his brother between 1846 and 1850 that led him on a path of writing and journalism. His time spent in Europe, particularly in Rome and Berlin, as well as in Egypt and Syria in the Middle East, led him to publish his first book, *Nile-Notes of Howadji,* in 1850.

After his return to the United States in 1850, Curtis went to work as a travel writer for Horace Greeley's *New York Tribune,* at that time perhaps the most influential newspaper in the United States. Soon after, however, in 1852 Curtis left the *Tribune* to help start *Putnam's Monthly,* a new magazine that was, unfortunately, short-lived. Nonetheless, within a year Curtis went to work for

Harper's Monthly Magazine as a contributor, commencing the highly successful column "The Easy Chair," and, after that, *Harper's Weekly*, where he penned "The Lounger," another successful column. *Harper's* was one of the most influential publications in America at that time, and Curtis became the editor in chief of *Harper's Weekly* in 1857.

Biographer Gordon Milne, in assessing Curtis's rise from mere columnist to political reformer, explained Curtis's work after 1873:

> Curtis kept the attention of his *Weekly* readers focused during the next decade principally on the problem of civil service reform. If he had a favorite cause this was it, and almost all of his political activity in subsequent years revolved around his efforts in behalf of the reform. The Curtis household was strewn with civil service tokens, the Curtis library was filled with books and pamphlets relating to the cause, the Curtis-written editorial pages of *Harper's Weekly* were devoted time and time again to discussions of the question.

A staunch Republican, Curtis nonetheless was a critic of the scandals of the administration of Ulysses S. Grant, and in the pages of the *Weekly* he called for reform by Congress. He also used the *Weekly* to savage Democrats—he hired cartoonist Thomas Nast to savage New York political boss William M. "Boss" Tweed, leading to Tweed's downfall. However, in 1884, when the Republicans nominated Senator James G. Blaine for president, Curtis and Nast left the Republican Party and used the pages of their paper to lambaste Blaine. Curtis became one of the leaders of the so-called Mugwump movement, consisting of disaffected Republicans who refused to back Blaine and, in some cases, crossed over and voted for Democrat Grover Cleveland for president.

In 1873 President Grant formed the United States Civil Service Commission and named Curtis as one of the commissioners. Although the panel did not last long, lacking a congressional mandate for reform, Curtis remained at the forefront of the movement. The scandals of the Grant administration led to the passage in 1883 of the Civil Service Reform Act, or the Pendleton Act after its sponsor, Senator George H. Pendleton of Ohio. With the establishment of a new Civil Service Commission, President Chester A. Arthur named Curtis as the chairman of the panel. He finished his life's work in this capacity, having also established the New York Civil Service Reform Association and the National Civil Service Reform League.

George Curtis died at his home on New York's Staten Island on 31 August 1892 at the age of sixty-seven. Despite his work for the last twenty years of his life to enact civil service reform, he is better remembered for his columns and editorials in *Harper's Weekly* and his many pithy sayings.

See also Eaton, Dorman Bridgman; Pendleton Civil Service Act

References: Cary, Edward, *George William Curtis* (Boston: Houghton, Mifflin, 1894); Curtis, George William, *Orations and Addresses of George William Curtis,* ed. Charles Eliot Norton (New York: Harper & Brothers, 1894); Hellman, George S., "Curtis, George William," in Allen Johnson and Dumas Malone, et al., eds., *Dictionary of American Biography,* X vols. and 10 supplements (New York: Charles Scribner's Sons, 1930–1995), II:614–616; Milne, Gordon, *George William Curtis & the Genteel Tradition* (Bloomington: Indiana University Press, 1956), 150.

D

Daugherty, Harry Micajah (1860–1941)

United States attorney general (1921–1924), the first of two attorneys general to get into ethical trouble while in office. Daugherty was also a well-known Ohio attorney who served as the campaign manager for Senator Warren G. Harding at the 1920 Republican National Convention. He was born in Washington Court House, Ohio, on 26 January 1860. After attending local schools, he received his law degree from the University of Michigan in 1881. He returned to the place of his birth and established himself as an important local attorney. His hallmark was getting his clients relief through political connections—a means he would use later to his own and to others' political advantage.

Daugherty, despite his political connections, served only briefly in local Ohio politics—first as the township clerk, then for two terms in the Ohio state legislature (1890–1894). A year before leaving the state legislature, Daugherty moved his law practice from Washington Court House to Columbus. Over the next several years he built up a client base, mainly of Ohio corporations, and became a wealthy man. In 1895 he ran unsuccessfully for state attorney general and two years later ran a similar unsuccessful race for governor of Ohio. This final defeat led Daugherty to conclude that he was better representing people than running the show himself. This led him to a rising star in Ohio politics, Warren G. Harding. Harding was a news-

paper publisher in his hometown of Marion, Ohio. In 1902, after having served in the Ohio state senate (1899–1903), Harding ran for lieutenant governor—and Harry M. Daugherty served as his campaign manager. Because of his connections, Daugherty was able to secure a victory for the bashful Harding. Daugherty became his chief backer. The attorney used his influence in the Republican Party to get Harding plum speaking roles, including one at the 1912 Republican National Convention in which he introduced President William Howard Taft. This led Daugherty to help Harding obtain the Republican nomination for the U.S. Senate in 1914 and be elected to that body. In the Senate, Harding was a quiet man who spoke little and supported even less legislation. Despite this, he was personally popular, and Daugherty made friends with the right people to further advance his friend's career.

In 1920 several candidates stepped forward to compete for the Republican presidential nomination. When the convention deadlocked over these candidates, Daugherty, sitting in a back room (later dubbed "the smoke-filled room")jammed with the influential leaders of the party, suggested the bland and wholly uncontroversial Harding as a potential nominee. This proposal seemed more than intriguing, and Harding was nominated on the next ballot. Governor Calvin Coolidge of Massachusetts, also a colorless figure with little in his record to find controversial, was given the second place on the ticket. Daugherty ran Harding's campaign, keeping him away from contentious issues such as the League of Nations. In the end, Harding won a landslide victory against Ohio Governor James Cox—the first time two men from the same state ran against each other—with 60 percent of the vote. Soon after his victory, Harding named his political benefactor Harry M. Daugherty as the next attorney general. Confirmed by the Senate, Daugherty took office on 5 March 1921.

During his tenure as the chief law enforcement officer in the U.S. government, which ended on 28 March 1924, Daugherty became the first of two attorneys general to face criminal charges regarding actions he took in office. (The other, John Mitchell, in fact went to prison.) Daugherty was alleged to have been involved in the scandal known as Teapot Dome, in which U.S. national oil reserves under the control of Secretary of the Navy Edwin Denby and Secretary of the Interior Albert B. Fall were sold off in exchange for bribes. What few historians write about is that Daugherty in fact did take a bribe—but not in connection with Teapot Dome. Instead, Daugherty accepted a bribe from the American Metal Company, a concern confiscated from a German company when America entered World War I. The company bribed Daugherty so that action allowing the German parent company to reacquire its American subsidiary could be speeded up. As well, Daugherty was accused by Congress of failing to investigate several individuals accused of defrauding the U.S. government during the war. When Daugherty apparently did not move fast enough in these investigations, Representative Oscar O. Keller (R-MN) introduced an impeachment resolution in Congress, but it did not go anywhere. Although he had been a close friend of theirs, Harding was destroyed by his officials' apparent corruption. Harding is alleged to have yelled, "My God, this is a hell of a job! I can take care of my enemies all right. But my friends—my God damn friends, they're the ones that keep me walking the floor nights!" In August 1923 Harding suddenly died while on a trip to Alaska and California and was succeeded by his vice president, Calvin Coolidge.

Daugherty was soon under fire for the American Metal Company matter. On 25 January 1923, Representative Robert Young Thomas Jr. (D-KY) wrote part of the minority report on Daugherty after a House committee investigation of the attorney general:

> It was strongly intimated if not directly contended by several members of the committee that the Attorney General could not be impeached except for an indictable offense. I think this view is absolutely incorrect. Impeachment is an extraordinary remedy born in the parliamentary procedure of England, and the principles which govern it have long been enveloped in clouds of uncertainty ... by usage of the English Parliament so far back that the memory of man runneth not to the contrary, offenses were impeachable which were not indictable or punishable as crimes at common law. Therefore the phrase "high crimes and misdemeanors" must be broad and extended as the offense against which the process of impeachment affords protection. Every case of impeachment must stand alone, and while certain general principles control the judgement and conscience, the Senate alone must determine the issue.

In 1924, when word spread of how the Teapot Dome and Elk Hills reserves had been sold off, the United States Senate opened an investigation, establishing the Senate Select Committee on Investigation of the Attorney General, which looked into Daugherty's conduct in running the Department of Justice. Through a number of hearings, the senators discovered that not only had Secretary of the Interior Albert Fall been heavily involved in the selling of the reserves in exchange for bribes, but that Secretary of the Navy Edwin Denby had acquiesced to the scheme, and that Daugherty had been aware of it but had done nothing to stop it, even though there was no evidence he himself had taken any bribes. The Senate hired two special prosecutors—one Democrat and one Republican—to oversee a more thorough investigation. After a period, these men, Deputy Attorney General Owen J. Roberts and former U.S. Senator Atlee Pomerene of Ohio, concluded that Daugherty had not been aware of the frauds and had not taken any bribes. Despite being cleared by the special investigations, Daugherty's name was still tarnished within the context of the entire Teapot Dome scandal. On 28 March 1924, President Coolidge, seeking to put an end to the scandal, asked for and received Daugherty's resignation. He quickly replaced him with Harlan Fiske

Stone, the dean of the Columbia Law School and a man of impeccable character.

Despite being cleared in the Teapot Dome matter, Daugherty was still under an ethical cloud for his role in the American Metal Company situation. Two different grand juries heard the evidence in the case, but both times these juries failed to indict the former attorney general. Although he never formally faced criminal charges relating to any of the scandals in which he was allegedly involved, Daugherty's good name was ruined, and he spent the rest of his life trying to repair his damaged reputation. In 1932 he penned *The Inside Story of the Harding Tragedy,* in which he tried to claim innocence. In 1940, in declining health, Daugherty gave an interview to a magazine in which he once again proclaimed his innocence. "What I did was done in the interest of the American people and my action was sustained by the courts," he wrote. "Notwithstanding the abuse I received, I can say now that given the same circumstances I would not change an official or personal act of mine while I was Attorney General. That's a clear conscience for you." Daugherty died on 12 October 1941 at the age of eighty-one, his name still tied to the scandals that rocked his leadership of the Justice Department and the Harding administration as a whole.

See also *McGrain v. Daugherty*

References: Cognac, Robert Earl, "The Senatorial Career of Henry Fountain Ashurst" (Master's thesis, Arizona State University, 1953); Daugherty, Harry M., and Thomas Dixon, *The Inside Story of the Harding Tragedy* (New York: The Churchill Company, 1932); "Daugherty Is Denounced in the Senate as Letting Friends Sell Immunity; Name of a Senator on Brokers' Books," *New York Times,* 20 February 1924, 1; Forth, William S., "Wesley L. Jones: A Political Biography" (Ph.D. dissertation, University of Washington, 1962); Giglio, James M., "The Political Career of Harry M. Daugherty" (Ph.D. dissertation, Ohio State University, 1968); "Harry Daugherty: The Appearance of Evil," in George C. Kohn, *Encyclopedia of American Scandal: From ABSCAM to the Zenger Case* (New York: Facts on File, 1989), 82–83; Remarks of Rep. Thomas in House Report 1372, 67th Congress, 4th Session (1923).

Delaney, Denis W.

See Income Tax Scandal, Department of Justice (1951–1952)

Democracy: An American Novel

Popular work of literature written in 1880, the first major piece of fiction in American literature to deal with political corruption at the highest points in American government.

When *Democracy* appeared in 1880, Henry Adams, scion of the famed Adams family, was considered to be its author. Set in Washington, it concerned the widow Madeleine Lee, a rich woman from New York who, as the author explained, came to Washington "to see with her own eyes the action of primary forces; to touch with her own hand the massive machinery of society; to measure with her own mind the capacity of motive power. She was bent upon getting to the heart of the great American mystery of democracy and government." Mrs. Lee bought a house on Lafayette Square and invited many of the city's rich and famous, including politicians, to come to her home each afternoon for tea and sandwiches. Historians who have examined the book over the years have concluded that Adams based the character Mrs. Lee on his own wife, Clover Adams, who, with her husband, lived on Lafayette Square and dined with Washington's rich and powerful.

Mrs. Lee falls in love with the rich and powerful Senator Ratcliffe, but just before she is to marry him, another politician reveals that Ratcliffe is a corrupt and unethical scoundrel, and the wedding is canceled. Many believe that Adams based Ratcliffe on Senator James Gillespie Blaine, a former Speaker of the U.S. House of Representatives and U.S senator implicated in a railroad scandal in 1876 that would in 1884 cost him the presidency. The novel was a smash hit, the first such work to mix genteel politics with corruption in Washington, broaching that subject for the very first time.

Over the years, some historians have questioned whether Henry Adams penned this work at all. In 1923 Henry Holt, Adams's publisher, wrote that Henry Adams indeed was its author. However, some people believe that Adams's wife, Clover, was the real author and that she based the novel on her own observations of Washington society. Despite its questionable authorship, *Democracy* was the first work of fiction to portray Washington awash in corruption and power.

See also *Mugwumps*

References: Conroy, Sarah Booth, "The Earlier D.C. 'Anonymous'," *Washington Post,* 5 February 1996, C3.

Denby, Edwin (1870–1929)

Secretary of the navy (1921–1924), implicated in the Teapot Dome scandal but never charged, although his reputation was destroyed by the affair. Denby came from a family long involved in politics. Born in Evansville, Indiana, on 18 February 1870, Denby went to China with his father, Charles Denby, a noted American diplomat to that Asian country. Edwin Denby received his education in China, mostly from private tutors. From 1887 until 1894 he served in the Chinese Maritime Customs Service. When he returned home, he entered the University of Michigan, from which he earned a law degree in 1896. After he passed the Michigan bar, Denby went to work with the Detroit law firm of Chamberlin, Denby, Webster and Kennedy. Two years later, when the Spanish-American War broke out, Denby left the firm and volunteered for service in the United States Navy. He rose to the rank of gunner's mate second class while serving on the USS *Yosemite*. He saw action during the conflict at Guantanamo Bay in Cuba, in Puerto Rico, and at Manila Bay when American forces under Admiral Dewey attacked Spanish warships. After the war, he returned to the practice of law.

In 1903 Denby ran for and was elected to a seat in the Michigan state house of representatives. He served in that seat for less than two years: in 1904, he ran for a seat in the U.S. House of Representatives, representing the First Congressional District. He defeated Democrat Alfred Lucking and served in the Fifty-ninth, Sixtieth, and Sixty-first Congresses from 4 March 1905 until 3 March 1911. A staunch Republican, Denby supported his party in virtually all his votes. In 1910 he was defeated by Democrat Frank Doremus. He then entered private business, serving in banking and other work. He was a founder of the Hupp Motor Company, as well as the Federal Motor Truck Company and the Detroit Motor Bus Company. From 1916 until 1917, he served as head of the Detroit Board of Commerce. In 1917, following the United States' entry into World War I, Denby again volunteered for service and, despite being nearly fifty years old, was accepted for duty as a private in the United States Marines. Instead of serving in Europe, however, Denby served as a training officer at Parris Island, South Carolina. By the end of the war, he had advanced to the rank of major and continued after the end of the conflict in the Marine Corps Reserve.

In 1920 Senator Warren G. Harding (R-OH) was elected president. In selecting his cabinet, Harding reached out to all factions of the Republican Party—and in doing so called upon Edwin Denby to serve as his secretary of the navy. Despite his limited experience with the military, Denby was chosen on a recommendation of Senator John Wingate Weeks of Massachusetts. He was easily confirmed by the U.S. Senate and took office on 6 March 1921.

In his three years in office, Denby became known as perhaps one of the worst—and most corrupt—secretaries of the navy. From the start, he was intimately involved in the scandal that later became known as Teapot Dome. On 4 June 1920, the U.S. Congress ordered that the national oil reserves located at Elk Hills, California, and Teapot Dome, Wyoming, were to be moved from the control of the secretary of the interior to that of the secretary of the navy. However, on 31 May 1921, President Harding signed an executive order that placed the administration of the reserves under Secretary of the Interior Albert B. Fall. Fall then entered into secret deals with oilmen who were able to buy the oil in exchange for bribes to Fall. However, because Congress had given the ultimate authority over the reserves to Denby, Fall needed his signature on all of the contracts, and it is impossible to believe that Denby was not knowledgeable about what Fall was doing. The United States Supreme Court later catalogued exactly what Denby's involvement was: in a 1927 decision, *Pan American Petroleum & Transport Co. v. United States,* 273 U.S. 456 (1927), Justice Pierce Butler explained:

> Denby was passive throughout, and signed the contracts and lease and the letter of April 25, 1922, under misapprehension and without full knowledge of their contents. [On] July 8, 1921, Fall wrote [oilman Edward] Doheny: "There will be no possibility of any further conflict with Navy officials and this department, as I have notified Secretary Denby that I should conduct the matter of naval leases under the direction of the President, without calling any of his force in consultation unless I conferred with himself personally upon a matter of policy. He understands the situation and that I shall handle matters exactly as I think best and will not consult with any officials of any bureau in his department, but only with himself, and such consultation will be

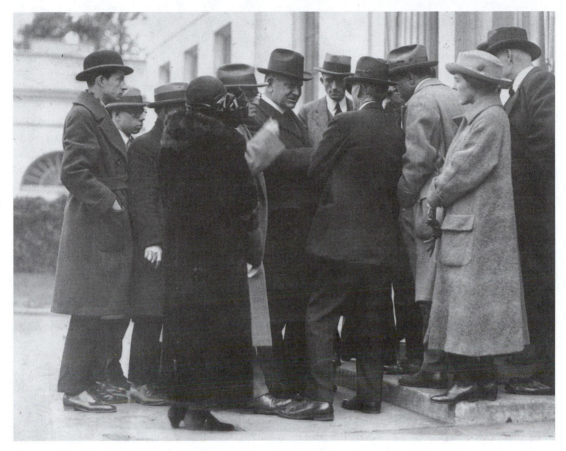

Secretary of the Navy Edwin Denby surrounded by reporters at the White House as he announces he would not resign from the Cabinet as a result of the Teapot Dome investigation. (Library of Congress)

confined strictly and entirely to matters of general policy.

Despite being implicated in the scandal that came to light in 1924, Denby was not criminally implicated; in other words, there was no evidence that Denby had taken bribes. Perhaps his worst crime was naivete and stupidity. No one will ever know—no records exist, and Denby never spoke about it. He resigned his office on 10 March 1924 after the Senate demanded that President Calvin Coolidge, who succeeded Harding upon the latter's death in August 1923, remove Denby. He left Washington and returned to private life in Detroit.

Edwin Denby died in his sleep on 8 February 1929, having the Teapot Dome scandal still hanging over his head. Although Fall went to prison, Denby was never tried, but never really cleared, and historians tie him in with the corruption of the scandal.

References: "Criminal Prosecution of Fall Looms; Denby Scored as 'Partner'; McAdoo Gives Up His Doheny Retainer," *New York Times,* 8 February 1924, 2; Grossman, Mark, *Encyclopedia of the United States Cabinet,* 3 vols. (Santa Barbara, CA: ABC-CLIO, 2000), II:496–498; Justice Butler's remarks in *Pan American Petroleum & Transport Co. v. United States,* 273 U.S. 456, 509 (1927); "Oil Scandal Broadens as Senate Vote Nears on the Ousting of Secretary Denby," *New York Times,* 9 February 1924, 2; Woods, John Kent, "Denby, Edwin," in John A. Garraty and Mark C. Carnes, gen. eds., *American National Biography,* 24 vols. (New York: Oxford University Press, 1999), 6:429–430.

Dever, William Emmett (1862–1929)

Mayor of Chicago (1923–1927), defeated by Al Capone's organization, who helped to reinstall the crooked "Big" Bill Thompson and end Dever's cleanup of city corruption. A Democrat, Dever was born in Woburn, Massachusetts, on 13 March

1862, one of six children of Patrick Dever, a leather manufacturer. William Dever attended public schools in Woburn, before he graduated from high school in 1870 and went to work in his father's business. Afterwards, he worked for a major tannery in the town of Olean, New York, and then in Chicago. After attending law school at the Chicago College of Law, he received his law degree in 1890. He also entered the political realm as a staunch Democrat.

In 1902 Dever, pushed by numerous reformers who desired a change of city government in Chicago, ran for a seat as an alderman in Chicago's Seventeenth Ward and won. He served until 1910, when he resigned to run for a judgeship on the Cook County Superior Court. Reelected in 1916, he served until 1923. He also served as a member of the Illinois Appellate Court.

In 1923 Dever ran for mayor of Chicago. For years governed by a weak mayorship and numerous aldermen who ran their wards like fiefdoms, Chicago had become a patchwork of weak and ineffective government. By 1923 the mayor, "Big" Bill Thompson, was seen as the corrupt arm of many of the crooks in Chicago—including the crime boss Al Capone. Selected by the Democrats in their February primary, Dever defeated Republican Arthur C. Lueder and Socialist William A. Cunnea on 3 April 1923 to become the thirty-fourth mayor of Chicago. During his single four-year term, Dever was seen as being a mildly effective reformer whose plans were stymied by the entrenched powers. Historian Andrew Prinz wrote, "Dever's administration was characterized by high-quality appointments, plans, and programs for physical growth, and a vigorous campaign for law and order. Chicago's first zoning ordinance was passed while he was mayor, and the double-deck Wacker Drive was completed. In addition, the Chicago River was straightened, Union Station was finished, traffic lights installed in the downtown Loop, and extensive paving of streets and alleys took place. Dever's zeal to enforce Prohibition antagonized many voters and contributed to his defeat" in 1927. Another factor that led to his defeat was his strong crackdown on organized crime. He shut down The Four Deuces, the gambling casino owned by Johnny Torrio, and had the police raid suspected alcohol establishments. As Dever stated on the issue of alcohol, "I am just as sure that this miserable traffic with its toll of human life and morals can be stamped out as I am that I am mayor, and I am not going to flinch for a minute."

In 1927, with a strong record of accomplishment behind him, Dever ran for reelection on a platform of "Dever and Decency." Republicans put forward "Big" Bill Thompson, who had the backing of elements siding with Al Capone. Because of Capone's backing, and Dever's strong Prohibition record, Thompson defeated him by nearly 80,000 votes out of some 1 million cast. Thompson immediately ordered that the crackdown on liquor establishments end, helping Capone continue to build his empire.

Dever left office and became the vice president of the Bank of America (BOA). However, a year later, his health suddenly declined, and he retired. Suffering from cancer, he died on 3 September 1929 at the age of sixty-seven.

See also: Thompson, William Hale
References: Prinz, Andrew K., "Dever, William Emmett," in Melvin G. Holli and Peter d'A. Jones, *Biographical Dictionary of American Mayors, 1820–1980: Big City Mayors* (Westport, CT: Greenwood Press, 1981), 101–102; Schmidt, John R., *The Mayor Who Cleaned Up Chicago: A Political Biography of William E. Dever* (DeKalb: Northern Illinois University Press, 1989).

Deweese, John Thomas (1835–1906)

United States representative from North Carolina (1868–1870), censured by the House for corruption in appointments to the United States Military and Naval Academies. Born in Van Buren, Arkansas, on 4 June 1835, he was educated at home, where he read the law. He was admitted to the state bar in 1856, but moved to Henderson, Kentucky, where he opened a practice. Deweese then moved around, living in Denver, Colorado, for some time before he settled in Pike County, Indiana, in 1860. When the Civil War broke out, he volunteered for service in the Union army and was commissioned as a second lieutenant with Company E of the Twenty-fourth Regiment of the Indiana Volunteer Infantry on 6 July 1861. He served with that unit until his resignation on 15 February 1862; he was then moved to Company F of the Indiana Volunteer Infantry, with the rank of captain. He was eventually promoted to the rank of colonel and after the war, moved to North Carolina. When the army was reorganized after the war, Deweese was appointed a second lieutenant to the Eighth United States Infantry on 24 July 1866.

Deweese resigned his rank on 14 August 1869, after he had been elected to Congress. In 1868 he served for a short time as register in bankruptcy (in effect, a bankruptcy judge) for North Carolina. When the state was readmitted to the Union under Reconstruction, Deweese ran for and won a seat in the U.S. House of Representatives, representing the Fourth North Carolina District. Running as a Republican, he defeated conservative candidate Sion H. Rogers. Deweese entered the House in the Fortieth Congress on 6 July 1868 and served until his resignation on 28 February 1870. He served as chairman of the Committee on Expenditures in the Department of the Interior and as chairman of the Committee on Revolutionary Pensions.

In 1870 Deweese came under fire after it was alleged that he had sold appointments to the United States Military Academy at West Point and the United States Naval Academy at Annapolis. Part of a congressman's responsibility is to nominate persons in his district for spots at these academies, but Deweese, along with several other congressmen, were accused of selling these spots for money. An investigation ensued, and it was discovered that the allegations against Deweese were in fact true. Historian Hubert Bruce Fuller wrote in 1909, "John T. DeWeese [*sic*], a member from North Carolina, sold cadetships to the naval academy for five hundred dollars and was 'found out.' To avoid expulsion he resigned. Even his confreres, his fellow carpet-baggers, bitterly denounced him, not because of his dishonesty; not even because of his clumsiness in being detected; but because he had hurt the market. They had been charging, and receiving too, from one to two thousand dollars for each cadetship. He had cut the rate."

On 1 March 1870, Representative John A. Logan of Illinois, a member of the Committee on Military Affairs, reported the following resolution:

> Resolved, That John T. Deweese, late a Representative in Congress from the Third Congressional district of North Carolina, did make an appointment to the United States Naval Academy in violation of law, and that such appointment was influenced by pecuniary considerations, and that his conduct in the premises has been such as to show him unworthy of a seat in the House of Representatives, and is there-

fore condemned as conduct unworthy of a Representative of the people.

Hinds' Precedents then reported that "Mr. Logan explained that the committee would have reported a resolution of expulsion had not the House by its action in a previous case decided against expelling a Member who had resigned. The resolution was then agreed to, yeas 170, nays 0." Deweese thus became one of only a handful of congressmen in the history of the House who have been the subject of expulsion measures. In the end, he was merely censured, but because he resigned his seat this punishment had no substance.

Deweese returned to the practice of law, remaining in Washington. He lived there for the remainder of his life, dying on 4 July 1906, one month past his seventy-first birthday. Because of his military service, he was buried in Arlington National Cemetery.

References: *Biographical Directory of the American Congress, 1774–1996* (Alexandria, VA: CQ Staff Directories, Inc., 1996), 936; Fuller, Hubert Bruce, *The Speakers of the House* (Boston: Little, Brown, and Company, 1909), 171; Hinds, Asher Crosby, *Hinds' Precedents of the House of Representatives of the United States, Including References to Provisions of the Constitution, the Laws, and Decisions of the United States Senate,* 8 vols. (Washington, DC: Government Printing Office, 1907–108), II:796.

Dewey, Thomas Edmund (1902–1971)

Governor of New York (1943–1955), Republican presidential candidate (1944, 1948), known for his work as a prosecutor in New York in which he broke the back of organized crime and prosecuted political corruption cases. Born in Owosso, Michigan, on 24 March 1902, Dewey attended local schools before he entered the University of Michigan, graduating from that institution in 1923. He moved to New York, where he studied at the Columbia University School of Law, earning a law degree in 1925. He was admitted to the New York bar the following year.

Practicing on his own for a short time, Dewey was named as chief assistant to the U.S. attorney for the Southern District of New York, George Medalie, in 1931. It was under Medalie's tutelage that Dewey grew in stature as a crime fighter. For two years starting in 1935, Dewey, as a special

Thomas E. Dewey, speaking before microphones at a press conference in New York, following his upset loss to President Truman.
(Library of Congress)

prosecutor fighting organized crime, obtained seventy-two convictions out of seventy-three cases tried, a record yet to broken. At the end of his run, in 1937, Dewey ran for district attorney for New York County and was elected. (He was also the Republican candidate for governor against Herbert H. Lehman, but Lehman was easily reelected at the same time Dewey was winning the district attorney position.) During his tenure in that position from 1938 to 1943, Dewey earned the name "racket buster" because of his work to break the organized crime families led by "Lucky" Luciano and "Dutch" Schultz. He also went after Tammany boss James J. Hines for running numbers rackets in Harlem, and sent Louis "Lepke" Buchalter to the electric chair. In 1942, emboldened by his status as a crime fighter and honest politician, Dewey ran for governor of New York and was elected over Democrat John J. Bennett Jr. and several third-party candidates. During his tenure as governor, 1943–1955, Dewey became the leading Republican in the nation. Only a year after becoming governor, Dewey was nominated by the Republicans for president at their national nominating convention in Chicago. However, the country was in the midst of war, and President Franklin Delano Roosevelt was easily reelected to a fourth term. Roosevelt died soon after his fourth term began, and immediately Dewey was once again the leading Republican candidate for president. In 1948 the Republicans at their convention in Philadelphia once again nominated him for president, and though Dewey was heavily favored to win, the nation narrowly gave the election to the incumbent, Harry S. Truman. Dewey never ran for national office again, becoming one of the few men to twice be the nominee of his party for president in losing campaigns.

Dewey was still the leader of his party, however. In 1952 he led the group of eastern moderates in the party that threw the presidential nomination not to Senator Robert Taft of Ohio, a conservative, but to the more moderate General Dwight D. Eisenhower. Remaining as governor of New York until 1955, Dewey was known for his steadfast honesty, his reforms toward efficiency in state government, and his establishment of the first state agency in the United States to handle employment discrimination cases. After he left state government, Dewey returned to the private practice of law, serving in an informal basis as an adviser to Republican presidents Eisenhower and Nixon. In 1969, when Chief Justice of the U.S. Supreme Court Earl Warren retired from the Court, Nixon offered the post to Dewey, but in declining health, the former two-time presidential candidate refused.

Thomas Dewey died in Bal Harbour, Florida, on 16 March 1971, eight days shy of his sixty-ninth birthday. He was remembered for his honesty, integrity, and drive in prosecuting political corruption and criminal figures both in and out of government.

References: Beyer, Barry K., "Thomas E. Dewey, 1937–1947: A Study in Political Leadership," (Master's thesis, University of Rochester [New York], 1962); "Dewey, Thomas Edmund," in Robert Sobel and John Raimo, eds., *Biographical Directory of the Governors of the United States, 1789–1978,* 4 vols. (Westport, CT: Meckler Books, 1978), III:1103–1104; Dewey, Thomas E., *Twenty against the Underworld* (New York: Doubleday, 1974); Stolberg, Mary M., *Fighting Organized Crime: Politics, Justice, and the Legacy of Thomas E. Dewey* (Boston: Northeastern University Press, 1995).

Diggs, Charles Coleman, Jr. (1922–1998)

United States representative from Michigan (1955–1980), the first congressman censured by the House of Representatives since 1921 because of a court conviction involving charges of mail fraud and falsifying payroll forms. Diggs was born in Detroit, Michigan, on 2 December 1922, the son of Charles Coleman Diggs Sr. The senior Diggs, a member of the Michigan state senate, was convicted in 1944 of taking bribes and sent to prison when his son was in his twenties. Charles Diggs Jr. was educated in the public schools of Detroit and studied at the University of Michigan at Ann Arbor before moving to Fisk University in Tennessee in 1942. In 1943 he volunteered for service in the U.S. Army Air Forces, and entered the service as a private in February of that year. He rose to the rank of second lieutenant before he wad discharged on 1 June 1945. He entered the Wayne (Michigan) College of Mortuary Science in Detroit three months after leaving the service, earning a degree in June 1946 and becoming a licensed mortician. He opened his own business, Diggs, Inc. He later studied law and graduated from the Detroit College of Law in 1951.

While still a law student, Diggs ran for and was elected to a seat in the Michigan state senate, where he served from 1951 to 1954. In the latter year, he challenged incumbent Democratic U.S. Representative George D. O'Brien, who had served three consecutive terms representing Michigan's Thirteenth Congressional District, which encompassed Detroit and many of its surrounding poor neighborhoods. Diggs defeated O'Brien in the Democratic primary and went on to score a victory over Republican Landon Knight to win the seat. Taking his seat on 3 January 1955, Diggs sat on the Interior and Insular Affairs Committee as well as on the Veterans' Committee. He was a consistent liberal, supporting increases in the minimum wage and advocating a federal agency to assist handicapped people obtain work much the same way the Civilian Conservation Corps helped the jobless during the Great Depression. He backed policies that assisted in aiding nations in Africa except for South Africa, and he criticized the latter's apartheid government. In 1963 he became a member of the Committee on the District of Columbia and advanced to become the committee chairman after Representative John L. McMillan of South Carolina was defeated for reelection in 1972. Whereas McMillan had blocked home-rule measures for the District, Diggs became a firm advocate of them. Because of Diggs's work, on 24 December 1973, President Richard M. Nixon signed the District of Columbia Self-Government and Governmental Reorganization Act, allowing the District's residents to elect a mayor and city council for the first time since 1874. Diggs rose to become the most senior and most respected black member of Congress. In 1969 he became the first chairman of the Congressional Black Caucus, serving until 1971.

Starting sometime in the 1970s, Diggs started to file false payroll forms to the House. In 1978 he was indicted on eleven counts of mail fraud and eighteen counts of filing the false forms. Evidence was presented showing that between 1973 and 1977 he had skimmed some $66,000 from the paychecks of the people who worked in his congressional office, giving them large raises so that the income would not be missed. During his trial, Diggs insisted that he had done nothing wrong and that his was a "selective prosecution" that was being pursued only because of the color of his skin. The jury, however, did not buy his racial argument and on 7 October 1978 convicted him of all twenty-nine counts. During his appeals, the U.S. House of Representatives heard charges against Diggs in the Committee on Standards of Official Conduct, which recommended in a report in 1979 that Diggs be formally censured by the House. On 31 July 1979, the House voted to censure Diggs, marking the first time that punishment was used since Thomas L. Blanton was censured in 1921. He was also stripped of all of his committee and subcommittee chairmanships. Diggs retained his seat, however, during his appeals. When the U.S. Supreme Court refused to his hear his appeal, Diggs resigned his seat on 3 June 1980, and began serving his sentence of three years at the federal prison at Maxwell Air Force Base in Alabama. He eventually served seven months before he was paroled.

Diggs returned to the Washington, D.C., area, settling in Hillcrest Heights, in Maryland. He earned a political science degree from Howard University in Washington, D.C., and opened a funeral home. In 1998 Diggs suffered a stroke and on 24 August 1998, he died in a hospital in Washington, D.C., at the age of seventy-five.

References: "Charles Diggs: Censured Congressman," in George C. Kohn, *Encyclopedia of American Scandal: From ABSCAM to the Zenger Case* (New York: Facts on File, 1989), 88–89; *Congressional Ethics* (Washington, DC: Congressional Quarterly, 1980), 29–30; Nash, Jay Robert, *Encyclopedia of World Crime: Criminal Justice, Criminology, and Law Enforcement*, 4 vols. (Wilmette, IL: CrimeBooks, Inc., 1989), II:943; Pearson, Richard, "Charles Diggs Dies at 75," *Washington Post*, 26 August 1998, B6; U.S. Congress, House, Committee on Standards of Official Conduct, *"In the Matter of Representative Charles C. Diggs, Jr.: Report, Together with Supplemental Views to Accompany H. Res. 378*, 2 vols. (Washington, DC: Government Printing Office, 1979).

Dodd, Thomas Joseph (1907–1971)

United States representative (1953–1957) and senator (1959–1971) from Connecticut, censured by the U.S. Senate in 1967 for the misuse of campaign and office funds for personal use. Dodd was born in Norwich, Connecticut, on 15 May 1907, the son of Thomas Joseph Dodd, a contractor, and Abigail Margaret (née O'Sullivan) Dodd. He attended the public schools, including the Norwich Free Academy, and then graduated from the prestigious St. Anselm's Preparatory School in 1926. To finish his education, he attended Providence College in New Hampshire, graduating with a degree in philosophy in 1930, and Yale Law School, from which he received a law degree in 1933. After getting his law degree, he was hired by the Federal Bureau of Investigation (FBI) as a special agent and served until 1934. His most notable work for the FBI was his service in setting a trap to capture outlaw and criminal John Dillinger in Rhinelander, Wisconsin, from which Dillinger escaped by shooting his way out.

After leaving the FBI, Dodd went to work as the Connecticut director of the New Deal's National Youth Administration, serving until 1945. From 1938 to 1945 he served as a special assistant to the Office of the Attorney General in the U.S. Justice Department, serving under five attorneys general: Homer S. Cummings, Frank Murphy, Robert H. Jackson, Francis Biddle, and Tom C. Clark. In his sphere of responsibility in the Justice Department, Dodd established the first civil rights division, and helped to prosecute cases of Ku Klux Klan violence in South Carolina and, during World War II, cases of industrial espionage. In 1945, when former Attorney General Jackson, now an associate justice on the U.S. Supreme Court, was named as the chief U.S. prosecutor at the Nuremberg War Crimes trial of former Nazi leaders in Germany, Jackson requested that Dodd be named as his executive trial counsel. For his work during the trial, Dodd was awarded the Medal of Freedom from President Harry S. Truman.

After the war, Dodd returned to Hartford, Connecticut, and was engaged in the practice of the law until 1953. A Democrat, in 1952 he ran for a seat in the U.S. House of Representatives, representing the First Congressional District. Defeating Republican John Ashmead, Dodd took his seat in the Eighty-third Congress. Reelected in 1954, he gave up this seat in 1956 to run for a seat in the U.S. Senate, but was defeated by Republican Prescott S. Bush, whose son and grandson later became president. Two years later, Dodd challenged incumbent Senator William Arthur Purtell, a Republican. Dodd won by 140,000 votes out of some 960,000 cast, and took his seat in the Senate. A famous story recounts that when he got to Washington, Dodd made a deal with Senate Majority Leader Lyndon Baines Johnson (D-TX) that, in exchange for a seat on the Senate Foreign Relations Committee, Dodd would vote to abolish Senate Rule 22, which required a two-thirds vote to cut off a Senate filibuster. Despite Dodd's keeping his end of the bargain, Johnson gave the Foreign Relations seat to Senator Albert Gore of Tennessee, breaking his promise. Dodd eventually did make it to that committee. In the Senate he had a mixed record, supporting liberal civil rights laws, but at the same time delivering addresses for the American Security Council, a right-wing group that sought to expose communists in American life.

In 1964, after the senate majority leader's secretary, "Bobby" Baker, was exposed for having used his office for personal business interests, the U.S. Senate formed the Select Committee on Standards and Conduct to investigate ethics questions in that body. Two years later, that committee's first inquiry was into the conduct of Senator Thomas Dodd. Starting on 24 January 1966 and continuing for several weeks, journalists Drew Pearson and Jack Anderson, in their hard-hitting newspaper columns, alleged that Dodd had used his personal Senate expense fund to pay for his Senate reelection campaign in 1964; that he had billed the government twice for personal travel expenses; and that he had done improper business with Julius Klein, a representative of West German business interests. The investigation was based on some 4,000 documents that four former Dodd aides had stolen from his Senate office. On 26 February 1966, Dodd asked the Committee on Standards and Conduct to investigate the Klein allegation. However, based on the seriousness of the Pearson-Anderson allegations, the committee opened an investigation into all three accusations. Dodd testified on the matters. He claimed that the money in his Senate fund, which were proceeds from testimonial dinners, he "truly believed" to be "gifts from friends." As to the charge regarding double billing for travel expenses, he cited "sloppy bookkeeping" and said that his aide, Michael O'Hare, who had assisted Pearson and Anderson, was "a liar." On the third allegation, Dodd said that his relationship with Klein was as a mere friend. At the time these allegations became public, President Lyndon Johnson, seeing the danger in aligning himself with Dodd, was asked about the senator's predicament at a news conference. "I have had no information about any dinners held for anyone to obtain funds for personal use," Johnson stated. "I didn't know that it was for personal, or political, or local campaign [*sic*], or national [campaigns]."

On 27 April 1967, the Senate Select Committee on Standards and Conduct released its report on the Dodd case. It recommended that Dodd be censured for spending campaign contributions on personal matters and for double billing the government for travel expenses. As to the third charge, the Senate called the relationship "discreet" and said there was no evidence of wrongdoing. After debate, on 23 June 1967, the Senate voted forty-five to forty-one not to censure on the double-billing charge, but voted ninety-two to five to censure Dodd "for having engaged in a course of conduct . . . from 1961 to 1965 of exercising the influence and favor of his office as a United States Senator . . . to obtain, and use for his personal benefit, funds from the public through political testimonials and a political campaign, deserves the censure of the Senate; and he is so censured for his conduct, which is contrary to accepted morals, derogates from the public trust expected of a Senator, and tends to bring the Senate into dishonor and disrepute." Dodd, who was stunned by the action, took to the floor after the vote and said that he held no bitterness toward any of the ninety-two senators who voted to censure him. "They are all honorable men, decent men, and I do not think they intended to visit any injustice on me." However, he added, "But I think a grave mistake has been made, and I am the one who must bear the scar of that mistake for the rest of my life."

Dodd, running for reelection in 1970, lost the Democratic nomination to Joseph Duffey. Despite this setback, Dodd ran as an Independent, and in the general election came in a distant third behind Duffey and the victor, Republican Lowell Weicker.

Destroyed by his censure and defeat, Dodd returned home to Connecticut. On 24 May 1971, he suffered a fatal heart attack and died. Only eight days earlier he had celebrated his sixty-fourth birthday. Dodd was buried in St. Michael's New Cemetery in Pawcatuck, Connecticut. His son, Christopher Dodd, currently serves as a U.S. senator from Connecticut and in 1997 was himself tainted by the campaign finance scandal surrounding the 1996 election because he had served as cochairman of the Democratic National Committee.

References: *Biographical Directory of the American Congress, 1774–1996* (Alexandria, VA: CQ Staff Directories, Inc., 1996), 950; "[Editorial]: Censure for Mr. Dodd," *New York Times*, 24 June 1967, 28; "Ex-Senator Dodd Is Dead at 64, Censured in 1967 by Colleagues," *New York Times*, 25 May 1971, 1, 43; Garment, Suzanne, *Scandal: The Crisis of Mistrust in American Politics* (New York: Times Books, 1991), 32; Kenworthy, E. W., "Dodd Censured by Senate, 92–5, on Fund Count," *New York Times*, 24 June 1967, 1, 14; "Thomas Dodd: Censured Senator," in George C. Kohn, *Encyclopedia of American Scandal: From ABSCAM to the Zenger Case* (New York: Facts on File, 1989), 90–92; United States Congress, Senate, Select Committee on Standards and Conduct, *Investigation of Senator Thomas J. Dodd. Hearings, Eighty-Ninth Congress, Second Session, on Allegations Against Senator Thomas J. Dodd, Pursuant to Senate Resolution 338, 88th Congress*, 2 vols. (Washington, DC: Government Printing Office, 1966–1967).

Dorsey, Stephen Wallace (1842–1916)

United States senator from Arkansas (1873–1879), implicated but acquitted for his role in the Star Route frauds of the 1880s. Despite his being linked with Arkansas, Dorsey was born in Benson, Vermont, on 28 February 1842. When Dorsey was a teenager, he and his family moved to Oberlin, Ohio, where Dorsey went to work as a house painter. He had attended local schools in Vermont and continued his education by attending Oberlin College in Ohio.

In April 1861, with the outbreak of the Civil War, Dorsey volunteered for the Union army, enlisting in the First Ohio Light Artillery. He caught the attention of some of his superiors and was assigned to the staff of General James A. Garfield (who became president of the United States in 1881). Dorsey saw action at Shiloh, Perryville, Stone River, Chattanooga, and Missionary Ridge. Near the end of the conflict he was transferred to the Army of the Potomac, serving under General Ulysses S. Grant at the battles of Cold Harbor and the Wilderness. In 1865, when Dorsey was mustered out of the service, he had attained the rank of captain. In 1867 he was awarded a commission with the rank of lieutenant colonel—strictly an honorary rank—for "meritorious service." Dorsey returned to Ohio, settling in the town of Sandusky. There he went to work for a local firm that manufactured tools. The company, Allen, Tenny & Dorsey, later to become the Sandusky Tool Company, became a large concern, and Dorsey rose to become company president. A Republican, Dorsey became involved in local politics, serving as a member of the Sandusky city council. He served as a delegate to the 1868 Republican National Convention that nominated his former commander, General Ulysses S. Grant, for president.

In 1871 Dorsey became the president of the Arkansas Central Railroad and soon after moved with his wife and two children to Helena, Arkansas. Personally enriched by the sale of his share of the Sandusky Tool Company, Dorsey was able to concentrate on helping to build up the Arkansas Central Railroad. In 1871 he wrote *Statistical and Other Facts Relating to Narrow Gauge Railways, Compiled by S. W. Dorsey,* which he took with him to London to sell railway bonds to wealthy British investors. After his return, he was hailed for aiding in the building of this important rail link through the state. For this, he was elected by the state legislature in 1872 to a seat in the United States Senate. Dorsey served one term, 4 March 1873 to 3 March 1879, and, not being a candidate for reelection, returned to Arkansas. During his time in the Senate, he served as the chairman of the Committee on [the] District of Columbia.

While in the Senate, in 1876, Dorsey became a member of the Republican National Committee. A year later, he went to New Mexico, where he had purchased a large tract of land in the northeastern part of the territory, called Uña de Gato. Dorsey became good friends with the territorial governor, Samuel B. Axtell. It was at this time, however, that Dorsey got himself into ethical trouble in Washington. He involved his brother, John Dorsey; his brother-in-law, John M. Peck; John Miner, a former coowner of the Sandusky Tool Company; and Jim Bosler, a miner with land holdings in Texas and Nebraska, in a scheme that had been introduced to Dorsey by Thomas J. Brady, the second assistant postmaster general. Brady had told Dorsey that there was money to be made in Star Routes. These routes, so called because on official post office reports they were marked with an asterisk or a star, were mail routes that were not serviced officially by the U.S. Post Office because no train or ship came near them, and thus private contractors delivered the mail. These routes were quite lucrative,

but the whole system was open to abuse. Contractors claimed increased population in uninhabited areas cost them more and they asked for higher appropriations from the U.S. government, without any oversight. The firm of Miner, Peck and Company, with backing from Stephen and John Dorsey, filed applications for some of these routes.

In 1878 charges arose that the firm was making money illegally from the Star Routes they controlled, and the fact that Stephen Dorsey, a sitting United States senator, was involved in the corruption came to light. Dorsey managed to convince congressional investigators that his ties to the firm were negligible at best and that he had no knowledge of illegalities. However, when his Senate term ended in 1879, Dorsey in fact became more involved in the business of his brother and brother-in-law. In 1880 his old friend James A. Garfield was nominated for president of the United States by the Republicans, and Dorsey was named secretary of the Republican National Committee in charge of the campaign. Dorsey concentrated on Indiana, spending what was later called illegal campaign funds. Indiana went for Garfield, and he was elected president.

After Garfield was inaugurated, he named Thomas Lemuel James, a noted reformer, as postmaster general. James came across the Star Route scheme and Dorsey's role in it and brought the facts of the matter to the attention of the new president. The *New York Times* got the story and published an article entitled "Star Route Corruption" that alleged, "The amount known to have been pocketed by the Stephen W. Dorsey gang in excess of the amount called for by their original bids is not less in round figures than $412,000." It was now open season on Dorsey and his "gang." The former senator was dubbed "Star Route Stephen."

When a congressional investigation later looked into the Star Route frauds, Postmaster General James stated:

> In the early part of June [1881] ex-Senator Powell Clayton of Arkansas, called on me at the Department and said that he had been visited by Montfort C. Rerdell, clerk and superintendent of the Dorsey combination, who, he said, desired to make a 'clean breast' of his relations to ex-Senator Dorsey and the star-route contracts. I suggested that the Attorney-General was the proper person for Mr. Rerdell to see, but was informed that Mr. Rerdell preferred to

see me. [James then explained that Rerdell did not wish to be seen at the Department, and the two men arranged to meet in Arlington, Virginia, in the evening.] Many of his statements were substantiated by papers then produced. The following is substantially the statement as Mr. Rerdell made it. He said that he had come to the conclusion to make a clean breast of his connection with the star-route contracts; that he was secretary to Mr. Dorsey, of Arkansas, while Mr. Dorsey was Senator; that he prepared the proposals; that they were sent in bulk to the West, and after being partially filled up were brought back to be executed; that after the proposals were accepted he attended to getting up influence, petitions, etc., for expedition, and after the contracts were expedited he managed the business of the combination, which consisted of S. W. Dorsey, John W. Dorsey, Miner, Peck, and Boone, the last named being frozen out to make room for [H. M.] Vaile. He showed me transcripts he made of the books, and said during the Congressional investigation he shammed sickness for fear of being summoned before the Congressional committee. During the time of his feigned sickness a book was copied from the original, with the exception that the money charged in that book to the petition names of Smith and Jones were there entered under the head of profit and loss. Smith represented Brady, and Jones Turner, of the Contract Office. Brady received 33 1/3 per cent, as his share of the expedition for one year, and 50 per cent, of the remissions of the fines and decorations.

Following the release of this surprising information, Dorsey threatened the Republicans that if he were targeted he would release information that Indiana was carried for the party in 1880 by members of the Star Route "frauds" and that the Republican National Committee was aware of this. Then Garfield was shot and he later died from his wounds. Vice President Chester A. Arthur became president. Dorsey asked to meet with him, but Arthur refused. On 4 March 1882, based on the information from Rerdell and James, a grand jury handed down indictments against all of the Star Route suspects, including Thomas Brady and Stephen Dorsey. The men were charged with conspiracy to defraud the government through nineteen mail routes.

Dorsey retained noted attorney Robert Green Ingersoll, who also defended Brady. The trial of all the Star Route defendants began on 1 June 1882. Historian J. Martin Klotsche explained:

One hundred and fifteen witnesses were examined and 3,600 exhibits were presented to the jury during the course of the trial. Witnesses for the government were for the most part people from the West who had intimate knowledge of the workings of particular routes—special agents, postmasters and sub-contractors. The defense, on the other hand, insisting that the postal irregularities were the incidents of a liberal postal policy, hoped to vindicate the action of the department on the grounds that the western constituencies needed mail service. Hence, they offered the testimony of congressmen and other government officials. The court finally had to decide that "no offender against the law can screen himself by producing [a] postmaster-general or Senators or Representatives who urge a certain policy upon him."

Ingersoll, in his closing argument, thundered, "That is the end of this route, as far as the indictment is concerned. Second, that Dorsey made and Rerdell filed false petitions. There is no proof that any of the petitions were false, no proof that any were forged, and no proof that John W. Dorsey or M. C. Rerdell had anything to do with that route one way or the other." Despite the massive evidence against all the men, including Dorsey, on 11 September 1882, Miner and Rerdell were found guilty, and Peck and Turner acquitted. Regarding the two Dorsey brothers, the jury could not agree on a verdict, and the judge ordered a mistrial. There were allegations of bribery of the jurors, but no evidence of this was found. The judge set aside the guilty verdicts, arguing that their "general unreasonableness" demanded a second trial. This second trial began on 1 December 1882, and stretched into 1883. Ingersoll tried to raise the issue that Dorsey was suffering from Bright's disease (a malady of the kidneys), but his pleas to have Dorsey excluded from the courtroom were refused. Right after the trial started, Dorsey resigned as secretary of the Republican National Committee. By this time, the public and the newspapers, which just two years earlier had demanded repayment of the money fraudulently taken from the government, now drifted to other matters. On 14 June 1883, all of the defendants were found not guilty. This was not the only Star Route case—others had been held in 1882 that also resulted in not-guilty verdicts—but the Dorsey trials were the most high profile. Under President Grover Cleveland, additional charges were brought forward, but in the end, only two lower officials were convicted. The cases, however, were fodder for the reformers, who worked together to deny Republican James G. Blaine the presidency in 1884. That same year, a congressional investigation reopened the Star Route controversy, and Dorsey's role in the fraud was raised. No further charges were ever pursued, however.

After his acquittal, Dorsey returned to New Mexico, engaging in cattle ranching and mining there and in Colorado. He later moved to Los Angeles, California, where he resided until his death on 20 March 1916, just a month past his seventy-fourth birthday. He was buried in the Fairmont Cemetery in Denver.

> **See also** Ingersoll, Robert Green; Star Route Frauds
> **References:** Caperton, Thomas J., *Rogue! Being an Account of the Life and High Times of Stephen W. Dorsey, United States Senator and New Mexico Cattle Baron* (Santa Fe: Museum of New Mexico Press, 1978); Klotsche, J. Martin, "The Star Route Cases," *The Mississippi Valley Historical Review*, XXII:3 (December 1935), 415; Lowry, Sharon K., "Mirrors and Blue Smoke: Stephen Dorsey and the Santa Fe Ring in the 1880s," *New Mexico Historical Review,* 59 (October 1984), 395–409; Lowry, Sharon K., "Portrait of an Age: The Political Career of Stephen W. Dorsey, 1868–1889" (Ph.D. dissertation, North Texas State University, 1980); *Proceeding in the Second Trial of the Case of the United States v. John W. Dorsey, John R. Miner, John M. Peck, Stephen W. Dorsey, Harvey M. Vaile, Montfort C. Rerdell, and Thomas J. Brady, for Conspiracy,* 4 vols. (Washington, DC: Government Printing Office, 1883); "[Obituary:] Stephen W. Dorsey," *Arkansas Gazette,* 22 March 1916, 5.; Testimony of Postmaster General Thomas L. James in U.S. Congress, House, *Testimony Relating to Expenditures in the Department of Justice: The Star Route Cases,* House Miscellaneous Document No. 38, Part II, 48th Congress, 1st Session (1884), 6.

Duer, William (1747–1799)

Assistant secretary of the treasury (1789–1790), implicated in stealing more than $200,000 from the treasury to speculate wildly. Secretary of the Treasury Alexander Hamilton was likewise implicated in Duer's scandal, but never faced prosecution. Duer was born in Devonshire, England, on 18 March 1747, the son of John Duer, a wealthy landowner, and Frances (née Frye) Duer. William Duer, the third son of this union, underwent preparatory studies, then attended Eton College in England. In 1765, he became an aide-de-camp to Lord Robert Clive, the Governor General of India. Unable to adapt to the harsh Indian climate, he returned to England. Three years later, however, when his father died, Duer, now the inheritor of some of his father's land holdings in the New World, moved to the West Indies. In 1768, he visited New York to purchase some timber for the British navy, where he met Philip Schuyler, a member of the New York assembly and later a general in the Revolutionary War. Schuyler convinced Duer to purchase a large tract of land near Saratoga, New York. In 1773, interested in making the colonies his home, Duer returned to England, settled his financial affairs, and returned to New York, settling in the town of Fort Miller.

Duer made his presence known quite quickly in his adopted home: in his first year in the colonies, he was appointed a justice of the peace for his town. In 1775 he served as a delegate to the Provincial Congress, being appointed at the same time as deputy adjutant general of the troops of New York, with the rank of colonel. In June 1776 Duer was named a delegate to the New York constitutional convention and in the early part of 1777, served in the state senate. He was then elected to a seat in the Continental Congress, but served for only a short time. On 8 May 1777, he was appointed a judge of common pleas of Charlotte (now Washington) County, New York, a position he held until 1786. He was a signer of the Articles of Confederation, the document that formed the loose coalition of states into the earliest form of union.

In 1783 Duer moved to New York City, where he helped to establish the Bank of New York the following year. He had become a rich man helping to buy and furnish supplies to the Continental Army, and he used his wealth to ingratiate himself into New York society. From this wealth in 1787 Duer and a group of investors sought to purchase massive tracts of land in the areas of what would become the western United States. This scheme was called the Scioto Speculation after the area in Ohio they sought to purchase.

In 1789, when the U.S. government was organized and the Department of the Treasury established, Duer's friend Alexander Hamilton was named the first secretary of the treasury. Duer, in turn, was appointed assistant secretary. Whereas

Hamilton was honest and sought to work for the betterment of his country, Duer took his usually speculative ways to the Treasury Department, headquartered then in New York. Historian Jeffrey D. Schultz wrote, "Using his power [at Treasury], Duer speculated with public money, and Hamilton asked him to resign. However, Hamilton did not attempt to recover the money—more than $200,000—that Duer had stolen from the Treasury. The comptroller of the Treasury brought suit against Duer, and his downfall was one of the chief causes of the financial panic that struck the nation in 1792." One of his speculations involved the national debt. During the years prior to the founding of the national government, individual states had racked up tremendous debt, and Hamilton looked for a way to resolve this issue by having the national government assume it. Duer decided to speculate in this area as well. How the debt would be refinanced and paid off could become lucrative to the right investor—so when Henry Lee, a friend of Hamilton's, asked about details of the plan, he was told that nothing could be said. However, William Bingham, a close friend of Duer's, borrowed some £60,000 to speculate on the federal debt based on what Duer had told him. Duer had resigned from the Treasury after just six months in office rather than adhere to strict standards against speculation by Treasury employees, and went into business with Alexander Macomb, one of New York's richest citizens. Duer used Macomb's money to speculate on stock from the Bank of New York on a rumor Duer heard at Treasury that the bank was to be taken over by the Bank of the United States. Duer used Macomb's money to buy the stock, at the same time secretly selling the stock from his own account—thus, if the bank sold, he and Macomb would profit, but if it did not, he would personally stand to profit. Hamilton, his former boss, became aware of what Duer was up to, and wrote to him on 2 March 1792, "'Tis time, there must be a line of separation between honest Men & knaves, between respectable Stockholders and dealers in the funds, and mere unprincipled gamblers."

Duer became seriously involved in speculation, and soon he was spending more than he could cover, putting him into massive debt. He borrowed $203,000 from Walter Livingston, scion of the famed Livingston family. The suit by the comptrol-ler general to recover the funds Duer stole from the U.S. government also hurt. Duer's end came on 23 March 1792, when he was arrested for debt and sent to debtor's prison. Because Duer had his hands in so many areas of selling and buying stocks, a financial panic ensued, leaving many people broke. However, Hamilton stepped in and, with the aid of U.S. securities that he ordered to be printed and sold, helped quickly end the panic and keep solvent vital financial institutions.

Hamilton intervened for Duer and assisted in getting him out of debtor's prison for a time, but Duer's speculation got him sent back again and he died there on 7 May 1799 at the age of fifty-two. He was buried in the Duer family vault under the old church of St. Thomas in New York City; later, his remains were moved and reinterred in Jamaica, on Long Island.

References: Jones, Robert F., "The Public Career of William Duer: Rebel, Federalist Politician, Entrepreneur and Speculator 1775–1792" (Ph.D. dissertation, University of Notre Dame, 1967); Jones, Robert F., "William Duer and the Business of Government in the Era of the American Revolution," *William and Mary Quarterly,* 3rd Series, 32:3 (July 1975), 393–416; Knott, H. W. Howard, "William Duer," in Allen Johnson and Dumas Malone, et al., eds., *Dictionary of American Biography,* X vols. and 10 supplements (New York: Charles Scribner's Sons, 1930–1995) III:486–487; Marshall, James V., *The United States Manual of Biography and History* (Philadelphia: James B. Smith & Co., 1856), 136; Schultz, Jeffrey D., *Presidential Scandals* (Washington, DC: CQ Press, 2000), 7; "William Duer, Entrepreneur, 1747–1799," in Joseph Stancliffe Davis, *Essays in the Earlier History of American Corporations* (Cambridge: Harvard University Press, 1917).

Durenberger, David Ferdinand (1934–)

United States senator from Minnesota (1978–1995), denounced by the Senate in 1990 for unethical conduct, one of only nine senators ever censured, condemned, or denounced in American history. Durenberger was born in St. Cloud, Minnesota, on 19 August 1934. He attended public schools in the nearby town of Collegeville, and graduated from St. John's Preparatory School in Collegeville. He later attended St. John's University in Collegeville, graduated from that institution in 1955, and received his law degree from the University of Minnesota Law School four years later. Admitted to the bar in 1959, he began a practice in St.

Paul. In 1956 Durenberger volunteered for service in the U.S. Army and served in the military until 1963. Afterwards, he returned to the practice of law.

Following the death of Senator (and former Vice President) Hubert H. Humphrey, a special election was held on 7 November 1978 to fill his vacant seat. Durenberger entered the race and won the Republican nomination; he then easily defeated Democrat/Farmer Labor candidate Robert E. Short. Four years later, running for a full term of his own, Durenberger defeated chain-store magnate Mark Dayton (who later won this seat in the 2000 election), also the Democrat/Farmer Labor candidate. A member of the Select Committee on Intelligence, Durenberger rose to chair that committee in the Ninety-ninth Congress (1985–1987).

Starting in 1983, a series of financial transactions in which Durenberger was involved led first to his denouncement by the Senate and ultimately the loss of his Senate seat. From August 1983 until November 1989, Durenberger appeared to be renting a Minneapolis condominium from a friend. In fact, Durenberger owned this property. He owned both a home in McLean, Virginia, and the condominium and decided he could not afford both on his Senate salary. He then sold the home in Virginia and changed his official residence to his parents' home in Avon, Minnesota. He was not allowed to charge the rent of the condominium he owned, so he transferred title to a friend, Roger Scherer, a political backer, and then when he stayed in the residence, billed the U.S. government for expenses. The second set of actions revolved around a book deal of questionable character. In 1984 Durenberger collected a work of white papers on foreign policy, *Neither Madmen Nor Messiahs,* which was published by an obscure house, Piranha Press of Minneapolis. Piranha was owned by Gary L. Diamond, a close friend of Durenberger's who published pieces for the restaurant and hospitality industries. In 1986 Piranha released a second work by Durenberger, *Prescription for Change,* which was a collection of the senator's speeches on health care issues. Starting in 1985, Piranha Press paid Durenberger $100,000 in quarterly installments of $12,500. At the same time, Durenberger traveled across the country and promoted his books, making 113 appearances in all.

In 1989 the Senate Select Committee on Ethics opened an investigation into allegations that Durenberger had improperly billed the government for his travel expenses and had violated the Senate's rules on honoraria. The committee hired, as special outside counsel, Washington attorney Robert S. Bennett, who had been the committee's counsel on the Harrison Williams (ABSCAM) investigation and would later be famed for his similar investigation of the Keating Five and his defense of President Bill Clinton during the Paula Jones sexual harassment case. Bennett issued 198 subpoenas for documents and other evidence, conducted 240 interviews with witnesses, and presided over 75 depositions. Durenberger's attorney, Michael C. Mahoney, had asked the Federal Elections Commission (FEC) if Durenberger's arrangement with Piranha Press had broken any laws, and the agency issued an opinion that the senator was in the clear. However, Bennett concluded, Durenberger's appearances to promote his book were to earn his honoraria outside the limits of the Senate's rules. In his report to the committee, Bennett stated, "This very hungry fish, Piranha Press, was allowed to engage in a feeding frenzy on responsible organizations who thought they were sponsoring traditional events, and unfortunately, the evidence shows that Senator Durenberger . . . allowed himself and the stature of his office to be used as the bait, and he got $100,000 for his trouble." (Ironically, Durenberger was prosecuted by a little-known Justice Department employee named Jackie M. Bennett Jr.—no relation to Robert Bennett—who later served on the staff of Independent Counsel Kenneth W. Starr in the Whitewater/Monica Lewinsky investigation opposing Robert Bennett, who was serving as President Clinton's personal counsel.)

Durenberger repaid the government $11,005 in reimbursement expenses; the committee ordered him to repay an additional $29,050. He was also ordered to give to charities the amount he had earned from honoraria that broke Senate rules: approximately $95,000. The committee also asked the full Senate to denounce Durenberger for his actions. On 25 July 1990, the Senate voted ninety-six to zero to do just this, the ninth time a senator had been so punished. (The others were censured, condemned, or denounced, but Senate historians consider all three punishments to be equal in strength.) The only senator who rose in Durenberger's defense was fellow Minnesotan Rudy Boschwitz. Both Boschwitz and Durenberger voted "present" during the denouncement vote, and two other senators were absent.

Durenberger did not run for reelection in 1994. He became a senior counselor with APCO Associates, a consulting firm in the District of Columbia, soon after leaving the Senate in 1995.

References: Berke, Richard L., "Fellow Senators Vote to Denounce Durenberger, 96–0, Rare Disciplinary Move," *New York Times,* 26 July 1990, A1, A17; *Biographical Directory of the American Congress, 1774–1996* (Alexandria, VA: CQ Staff Directories, Inc., 1996), 973; *Congressional Ethics: History, Facts, and Controversy* (Washington, DC: Congressional Quarterly, 1992), 33–35; United States Congress, Senate, Senate Select Committee on Ethics, *Investigation of Senator David F. Durenberger: Report of the Select Committee on Ethics and the Report of Special Counsel on S. Res. 311* (Washington, DC: Government Printing Office, 1990).

Dwyer, R. Budd (1939–1987)

Pennsylvania politician, state senator (1970–1985), and state treasurer (1985–1987), who committed suicide on television before he was to be indicted on bribery and other acts of malfeasance in office. The story of R. Budd Dwyer is known by few people, but his death, carried out while cameras were rolling on a near-psychotic press conference held by Dwyer to condemn his treatment by the justice system, became one of the leading news stories of 1987. Born in St. Charles, Missouri, on 21 November 1939, Dwyer was elected to a seat in the Pennsylvania state house of representatives in 1964 and served from 1965 until 1970. In that latter year, he was elected to the state senate. In 1985 he was named as Pennsylvania state treasurer. It appeared that Dwyer was doing a good job.

However, following an investigation, Dwyer and former state Republican Party Chairman Robert B. Asher were indicted by a federal grand jury on charges that Dwyer had offered a state contract to a California computer company without taking bids; the company's officers testified that they had received the contract after paying Dwyer a $300,000 bribe. Asher, the state party official, came across the scheme and instead of reporting it demanded that a portion be given to the state party's fund. The two men went on trial and in December 1986 were both convicted on all charges. They both faced sentencing on 23 January 1987. State Attorney General Leroy Zimmerman announced that Dwyer would be removed from office.

On 22 January 1987, the day before he faced a sentence of up to fifty-five years in prison, Dwyer held a press conference in Harrisburg, Pennsylvania. In front of a barrage of reporters, Dwyer gave a short speech condemning the verdict, declaring his innocence, and calling the potential sentence "medieval." He then spoke with some aides and moved in front of the cameras with a manila envelope. He handed out a statement to the reporters, then pulled a .357 Magnum gun from the envelope and stuck it into his mouth. To cries of "Budd, don't do it!" Dwyer pulled the trigger on live television and blew his brains out. He was killed instantly. In his letter to reporters, he praised Governor Bill Casey and asked that his wife be named as his replacement as state treasurer.

References: "Dwyer, R. Budd," in Jay Robert Nash, *Encyclopedia of World Crime: Criminal Justice, Criminology, and Law Enforcement,* 4 vols. (Wilmette, IL: CrimeBooks, Inc., 1989), II:1049.

E

Eaton, Dorman Bridgman (1823–1899)

Attorney and civil service reformer who drafted the Pendleton Act (1883), which regulated certain government finance laws for more than a century. Born in Hardwick, Vermont, on 27 January 1823, Eaton was educated in local schools before graduating from the University of Vermont in 1848. He then entered Harvard University and graduated from that institution in 1850. That same year, despite an absence of any legal training, he was admitted to the New York state bar, serving for a time as a law partner of one William Kent in New York City. Although he was interested in running for a political office, he never did. During the 1860s and 1870s, Eaton spent several years traveling in Europe, most notably spending his time studying the civil service systems in European governments and writing about how such a system could be utilized in the United States. Eaton also was an expert in municipal government. He helped to draft the Metropolitan Health Law, which established the modern health system in New York in 1866, and also aided in the formation of the New York Fire and Police Departments.

In 1873, when Eaton returned to the United States, President Ulysses S. Grant named him as chairman of the U.S. Civil Service Commission in an effort to establish a civil service system. Working with fellow commissioners Carl Schurz (later secretary of the interior in the Rutherford B. Hayes administration) and George W. Curtis, editor of *Harper's Weekly*, Eaton helped to push for reform of the system under which government officials and officers were hired. Eaton also assisted Senator George Pendleton in drafting the legislation that became the Civil Service Reform Act of 1883, also known as the Pendleton Act. This landmark act, discussed elsewhere in this book, radically overhauled the system of hiring workers for government positions and ended much of the patronage that had dominated American politics for the first century of its existence.

President Chester A. Arthur appointed Eaton chairman of the United States Civil Service Commission, an office he held from 1881 until 1886. Ever interested in studying foreign civil service systems, Eaton went to Europe in 1885. Two years later President Rutherford B. Hayes asked Eaton to brief him personally on the British Civil Service system. Eaton's work, *Civil Government in Great Britain* (1880), is considered one of the foremost non-British works on that country's government.

Dorman Eaton died in 1899, forgotten even at the time of his death.

References: *Dorman B. Eaton: 1823–1899* (New York: Privately Published, 1900); Ward, Sir Adolphus William, et al., eds., *The Cambridge History of English and American Literature*, 18 vols. (New York: G. P. Putnam's Sons, 1907–1921), 17:28–29.

Edwards, Edwin Washington (1927–)

Governor of Louisiana (1972–1980, 1984–1988, 1992–1996), convicted in 2000 of using his influence to sell boating licenses in exchange for kick-backs. A Cajun, Edwards was born near the village of Marsville, Louisiana, on 7 August 1927, the son of Clarence W. Edwards and Agnes (née Brouillette) Edwards, both sharecroppers. He attended local schools before entering the Naval Air Corps during World War II. When he returned to the United States, Edwards entered the Louisiana State University Law School, from which he earned a law degree in 1949. From that year until 1964, he served in private law practice with a law firm in the city of Crowley, Louisiana. In that city, he became successful by conducting business in both English and French.

In 1954 Edwards, a Democrat, entered the political realm by winning election to the Crowley City Council, serving in this capacity for a decade. In 1963 he decided to run for a seat in the Louisiana state senate, taking on an opponent with twenty years incumbency. However, Edwards was able to defeat this senator and in the state senate became a leader in his party. On 1 July 1965, when U.S. Representative Theo Ashton Thompson was killed in an auto accident, Edwards threw his hat into the ring for the nomination to succeed him. Defeating four other Democrats in the primary, which in those days was tantamount to winning election outright. Edwards entered Congress in 1965, representing the Seventh Louisiana District. Edwards remained in Congress for nearly seven years, winning reelection three times and serving as a member of the Public Works, Judiciary, and Internal Security Committees. Despite being from a fairly conservative state, Edwards compiled a liberal record in the House.

In 1971 Edwards decided to forego another term in the House to run for governor of Louisiana. In late 1971 he won the Democratic nomination by defeating state Senator—and future U.S. Senator—J. Bennett Johnston. He then defeated Republican David Treen in the general election by 57 to 43 percent to become governor, winning a majority of the Cajun and black vote. This was the first of three separate terms for Edwards as governor. In his first term, he oversaw the writing of a new state constitution and changed the tax structure imposed on crude oil pumped in Louisiana, a change that brought in more revenue to the state. As governor, Edwards appointed more blacks to high state offices than previous state ex-

ecutives. Although there were rumors of corruption, much of it implicating Edwards himself, he avoided any culpability. One of these scandals was the Korean Gift Scandal. In 1976 Edwards was questioned on receiving gifts from former Korean government agent Tongsun Park, but he was not indicted. Edwards became one of the most powerful chief executives in Louisiana state history since Huey Long, who had served as governor before his assassination in 1935.

After serving two terms, Edwards was constitutionally unable to run for a third and left the governor's office in 1980. In 1983, however, he once again ran for the office and defeated his former opponent Treen, who had succeeded him in 1980. Edwards took office for the second time in 1984. Promising to spend more time on state problems than his own, Edwards called for a state income tax increase to fund education. However, a depressed state economy led to low approval ratings, and his effectiveness was diminished.

In 1985 Edwards was indicted by a federal grand jury on charges of conspiracy and racketeering. Federal prosecutors alleged that Edwards and a group of cronies had plotted to use his influence as governor to sell hospital certificates in the state, earning Edwards and his friends some $10 million. In December 1985 Edwards's first jury trial ended in a mistrial; in May 1986 he was acquitted of all charges. But this vindication did not end the scrutiny of Edwards's business practices. In October 1986 he was called before a federal grand jury to answer questions relating to allegations that he had sold pardons to cronies. Edwards was also investigated for allegedly selling land in Louisiana to the Texaco Corp. in exchange for campaign contributions. However, in all of these affairs, Edwards was never charged.

In 1987 Edwards sought an unprecedented fourth term. However, the years of allegations against him made him a prime target, not just of Republicans but of other Democrats. A number of well-known state and federal politicians lined up to oppose him, including Representative Billy Tauzin (a Democrat who later switched to the Republican Party) and Representative Bob Livingston (a Republican who nearly became Speaker of the House in 2000). However, Edwards's chief rival was Representative Charles "Buddy" Roemer, a conservative Democrat from northern Louisiana. Roemer, calling Edwards's administration a "sinkhole of dirty corrupt politics," won the October 1987 primary, the first time Edwards had ever lost an election. Despite the possibility of a run-off, Edwards saw the potential of Roemer's victory and bowed out. It appeared that his political career was over, and he returned to his law practice.

Four years later, in 1991, Roemer had failed to deliver his reformist agenda and faced numerous opponents in his bid for reelection. One of these was former Ku Klux Klan Grand Wizard David Duke. When Duke entered the contest as a Republican—despite being barred from running on his party's ticket—Edwards threw his hat into the ring. In October 1991 Edwards won a primary of all candidates, with Duke coming in a close second and Roemer a distant third. The election held in January 1992 pitted the allegedly corrupt Edwards against the racist Duke. A coalition of business leaders, fearing that a Duke win could devastate the Louisiana economy because of boycotts, reluctantly backed Edwards, who won by a 61 to 39 percent margin to a fourth term as governor. During this term, 1992–1996, Edwards spent his time backing casino gambling legislation for his state. However, this support proved to be the issue that eventually brought him down.

In 1999 Eddie DeBartolo, the owner of the San Francisco 49ers of the National Football League, testified before a grand jury in Louisiana that in 1997 Edwards had demanded a bribe of approximately $400,000 in exchange for getting DeBartolo a casino license in the state. Others, including Ecotry "Bobby" Guidry, who was a close friend of Edwards's and a member of the state gaming control board, also testified that Edwards, as well as Louisiana state Senator Greg Tarver and four other state officials, had also demanded payoffs for a gambling license. In all, as was later stated by federal prosecutors, Edwards and his cronies shook people down for about $3 million. Edwards was indicted on 6 November 1999, along with Guidry, Tarver, cattleman Cecil Brown, Edwards aide André Martin, Edwards's friend Bobby Johnson, and Edwards's own son Stephen. The indictment alleged that the men violated the Racketeer Influenced and Corrupt Organizations (RICO) Act, committed extortion, mail fraud, wire fraud, money laundering, interstate travel and communications in aid of racketeering, false statements, il-

legal wiretapping, and conspiracy. Edwards answered DeBartolo's charge that he had extorted $400,000: "If I was in a position to extort a spoiled kid who'd inherited $600 million, do you think I would ask for $400,000? I'd have hit him up for maybe $40 million!"

Edwards's trial began with jury selection starting on 11 January 2000. From the start, prosecutors, utilizing secretly made audiotapes and other documentary evidence as well as the testimony of DeBartolo and some other men who were asked for payoffs, laid out a case that grew stronger against Edwards. Writer Ken Ringle of the *Washington Post* later explained that "federal prosecutors unreeled hours of taped telephone and office conversations detailing payoff and money-laundering schemes that Edwards sought unsuccessfully to portray as harmless efforts to disguise his role as a legitimate if controversial consultant to casino license seekers."

On 9 May 2000, after two weeks of deliberations, the jury returned with guilty verdicts on seventeen of the twenty-six charges against Edwards (he was acquitted of nine charges) and eighteen counts against Stephen Edwards. The jury found Brown and Martin guilty on all counts and Johnson on nine counts. Tarver and Guidry were acquitted. On 10 May 2000, following Edwards's conviction, the *New York Times* stated, "After a picturesque career lived at the edge of the law, the hayride ended for Edwin W. Edwards today as a federal court jury in Baton Rouge, La., convicted the former Louisiana governor of racketeering, conspiracy and extortion charges related to the awarding of state riverboat casino licenses." On 8 January 2001, Edwards was sentenced to ten years in prison and fined $250,000. Although he called the decision a "death sentence," his appeals were all denied.

References: *Biographical Directory of the American Congress, 1774–1996* (Alexandria, VA: CQ Staff Directories, Inc., 1996), 984; Bridges, Tyler, *Bad Bet on the Bayou: The Rise of Gambling in Louisiana and the Fall of Governor Edwin Edwards* (New York: Farrar, Straus & Giroux, 2001); Draper, Robert, "Elegy for Edwin Edwards, Man of the People," *GQ*, (July 2000), 160–167, 184–186; Duggan, Paul, "Ex-Louisiana Governor Gets 10 Years, Fine," *Washington Post*, 9 January 2001, A11; "Edwin Washington Edwards," in Marie Marmo Mullaney, *Biographical Directory of the Governors of the United States, 1988–1994* (Westport, CT: Greenwood Press, 1994), 155–163; Ringle,

Kentucky, "Former La. Governor Edwards Found Guilty of Fraud; Louisiana Legend Faces Prison Term," *Washington Post,* 10 May 2000, A1.

Edwards, Francis Smith (1817–1899)

United States representative from New York (1855–1857), accused of corruption and the subject of an expulsion hearing in the House in 1857. Born in Windsor, New York, on 28 May 1817, Edwards completed studies in preparation for higher education, after which he attended Hamilton College in Hamilton, New York. However, he did not receive a degree. Instead, he studied the law and was admitted to the New York bar in 1840, opening a practice in the town of Sherburne, New York. In 1842 Edwards was appointed master and examiner in chancery for Chenango County, New York. In 1851 he moved to the town of Fredonia, New York, and continued his law career there. Two years later he was appointed a special county surrogate for Chautauqua County, New York, serving until 1 November 1855.

Edwards became a member of the American, or "Know Nothing," Party, so named because its platform of excluding Catholics and immigrants was so controversial that its members claimed to "know nothing" if asked about it. He ran for a seat in the U.S. House of Representatives in 1854 and won, representing the Thirty-third New York District. Edwards served less than a full two-year term. Entering Congress on 4 March 1855, he resigned his seat on 28 February 1857. The record to this day remains hazy as to what crime Edwards was charged with—contemporary sources do not report on it, and *Hinds' Precedents* merely explains that Edwards, along with Representatives William Augustus Gilbert and William Welch were all accused of the same crime, with Edwards and Gilbert being targeted for the worst punishment. (See the entry on William Augustus Gilbert.) Because he had been defeated the previous November in his attempt at reelection, Edwards left Congress just a few days before his term was to end anyway. He never ran for national office again.

After leaving Congress, Edwards settled in the town of Dunkirk, New York, and resumed the practice of law. He served as that town's city attorney for nine years, before retiring in 1892. However, in his retirement he was elected a police justice and

served in this capacity until ten days before his death. Edwards died in Dunkirk on 20 May 1899, eight days shy of his eighty-second birthday. He was buried in the Forest Hill Cemetery in Fredonia, New York.

References: *Biographical Directory of the American Congress, 1774–1996* (Alexandria, VA: CQ Staff Directories, Inc., 1996), 984–985; Hinds, Asher Crosby, *Hinds' Precedents of the House of Representatives of the United States, Including References to Provisions of the Constitution, the Laws, and Decisions of the United States Senate,* 8 vols. (Washington, DC: Government Printing Office, 1907–1908), II:833–836; United States Congress, House, Joint Committee on Congressional Operations, *House of Representatives Exclusion, Censure and Expulsion Cases from 1789 to 1973,* 93rd Congress, 1st Session (Washington, DC: Government Printing Office, 1973).

Eilberg, Joshua (1921–)

United States representative from Pennsylvania (1967–1978) who pled guilty in 1979 to charges that he illegally accepted a bribe to help a Philadelphia hospital get a $14.5 million grant. Eilberg was born in Philadelphia, Pennsylvania, on 12 February 1921, and received his education in local schools. He graduated from the prestigious Wharton School at the University of Pennsylvania, and then the Temple University School of Law, and was admitted to the Pennsylvania bar. During World War II Eilberg served in the United States Naval Reserve, after which he returned to Philadelphia and practiced law. In 1952 he was named assistant district attorney for the city of Philadelphia, serving until 1954, when he was elected to a seat in the Pennsylvania General Assembly, where he served until 1966. From 1965 to 1966, he served as majority leader in the assembly. A delegate to several Democratic national conventions, he served as the Democratic ward leader for the Fifty-fourth Ward of Philadelphia.

In 1966 Eilberg was elected to a seat in the U.S. House of Representatives from Pennsylvania's Fourth District, easily defeating Republican Robert Cohen. Eilberg would serve in the U.S. House of Representatives until 3 January 1979, from the Ninetieth through the Ninety-fifth Congresses. He is most remembered for serving on the House Judiciary Committee when that committee drafted articles of impeachment against President

Richard M. Nixon in 1974 and for his introduction of a bill to reform the way grand juries work.

Eilberg may have remained an influential representative had it not been revealed in January 1978 that he had used fraud to end an investigation against him. In 1977 U.S. Attorney David W. Marston, a Republican holdover from the Nixon and Ford administrations, was investigating several allegations against two Pennsylvania Democrats—Dan Flood and Joshua Eilberg. Somehow Eilberg got wind of the investigation and personally phoned President Carter to ask that the president remove Marston and replace him with a Democrat—without explaining that Marston was investigating Eilberg. Carter, unaware of the investigation, ordered his attorney general, Griffin Bell, to remove Marston and replace him. This was done in November 1977, but it was not until the following January that the story leaked. The embarrassment for Carter came from his being unaware of Martson's investigation. The leaking of the story opened the floodgates against Eilberg. In October 1978 he was indicted by a federal grand jury on several charges of conflict of interest, including unlawful influence in having Marston removed. The scandal caused his political downfall—in November 1978, Eilberg was defeated by Republican Charles S. Dougherty in a landslide. Afterwards, Eilberg pled guilty and served some time in prison. Released, he returned to his home state of Maryland, where he lives as of this writing. Eilberg was the only member of the House Judiciary Committee to vote for impeachment charges against President Richard Nixon who was later implicated in political corruption.

References: Burnham, David, *Above the Law: Secret Deals, Political Fixes and Other Misadventures of the U.S. Department of Justice* (New York: Charles Scribner's Sons, 1996), 62–66; *In re Grand Jury Investigation Into Possible Violations of Title 18,* 587 F.2d 589 (3d Cir. 1978); *United States v. Eilberg,* 465 Fed. Supp. 1080 (E.D. Pa. 1979); *United States v. Eilberg,* 507 Fed. Supp. 267 (E.D. Pa. 1980); *United States v. Eilberg,* 536 Fed. Supp. 514 (E.D. Pa., 1982).

English, George Washington (1868–1941)

District judge for the U.S. District Court for the Eastern District of Illinois, impeached by the House of Representatives in 1925 on five articles, including charges of "abus[ing] his office through tyranny and oppression, thereby bringing the administration of justice in his court into disrepute," as well as misusing the power to appoint judges to appear before him in order to enrich himself. English resigned before a Senate trial could take place. He was born in Johnson County, Illinois, on 9 May 1868, the son of Manuel and Rebecca (née Smith) English. He was educated at Ewing College in Illinois and studied law at Illinois Wesleyan University, graduating in 1891. Admitted to the Illinois bar, he practiced in the town of Vienna with fellow attorney H. M. Ridenhower until 1896. A Democrat, English was elected to the Illinois state legislature in 1906, 1908, and 1910. In 1913, when Democrat Woodrow Wilson became president, English went to Washington and served as an attorney in the Treasury Department. He served there until 1918, when Wilson appointed him a district judge for the United States District Court for the Eastern District of Illinois.

On 1 April 1926, the U.S. House of Representatives impeached Judge English on five articles. For years, complaints about the manner in which Judge English ran his courtroom and allegations about his profiting from appointing certain attorneys had made their way to the House. On 13 January 1925, Representative Harry Bartow Hawes (D-MO) introduced a resolution calling on the Judiciary Committee to open an investigation into Judge English's conduct. Representative George Scott Graham (R-PA), chairman of the Judiciary Committee, introduced a joint resolution on 10 February 1925, calling for a similar investigation by three members of the Judiciary Committee, formed as a special committee. A report from these members was submitted on 19 December 1925. On 12 January 1926, Judge English was allowed to testify before the committee. In the end, the special committee found truth to the allegations and drafted five articles of impeachment. The first article accused English of disbarring attorneys who had appeared before him without any notice or hearing and of using the power of the bench to summon certain state and local officials before him in order to harass and threaten them, using "a loud and angry voice" and "profane and indecent language," denouncing them without naming an act of misconduct and threatening to

Judge George English (second from left) appears before the U.S. Senate in impeachment proceedings. (Library of Congress)

remove them from their office." It was also alleged in this first article that English "intend[ed] to coerce the minds of certain jurymen by telling them he would send them to jail if they did not convict a defendant whom the judge said was guilty." The second article alleged that Judge English "engaged in a course of unlawful and improper conduct, 'filled with partiality and favoritism,' in connection with bankruptcy cases within [his] district." English was charged with appointing a friend, attorney Charles B. Thomas, as a referee for bankruptcy cases and "unlawfully changing the rules of bankruptcy for the district to allow Thomas both to appoint friends and relatives as receivers and to charge the cost of expensive office space to the United States and the estates in bankruptcy," and "allowing Thomas to hire English's son at a large compensation to be paid out of funds of the es-

tates in bankruptcy." Article 3 alleged that English received an illegal gratuity of $1,435 from Thomas so that Thomas could be appointed the attorney of a defendant before English, who was given a more lenient sentence when Thomas took over his case. Article 4 alleged simply that "in conjunction with Thomas, English corruptly and improperly deposited, transferred, and used bankruptcy funds for the pecuniary benefit of himself and Thomas." Article 5 alleged that English "repeatedly treated members of the bar in a course, indecent, arbitrary, and tyrannical manner, so as to hinder them in their duties and deprive their clients of the benefits of counsel."

In 1913 the Senate had impeached Judge Robert Archbald; now the senators would be handed the case of another judge accused of abusing his authority. However, on 4 November 1926,

Judge English suddenly resigned from the bench. The House managers, who had been selected and were preparing their case, reported that Judge English's resignation "in no way affects the right of the Senate" to hear the evidence and come to a conclusion. Despite this, these same House managers recommended that the Senate not hold an impeachment trial. On 13 December 1926, the Senate voted seventy to nine to accept the recommendation, and all charges relating to the impeachment were dropped.

English fell into a void of ignominy after his forced resignation—so much so that when he died in Ft. Lauderdale, Florida, in July 1941, his death was unreported by almost every newspaper in the United States.

References: Chase, Harold, et al., comps., *Biographical Dictionary of the Federal Judiciary* (Detroit, MI: Gale Research Company, 1976), 85; English, George W. (impeachment) File 69B-A1, in *Records of Impeachment Proceedings, 1st–90th Congress (1789–1968), General Records of the United States House of Representatives, 1789–1988*, RG 233, National Archives, Washington, DC; Nash, Jay Robert, *Encyclopedia of World Crime: Criminal Justice, Criminology, and Law Enforcement*, 4 vols. (Wilmette, IL: CrimeBooks, Inc., 1989), II:1097; *Proceedings of the United States Senate in the Trial of Impeachment of George W. English, District Judge of the United States for the Eastern District of Illinois* (Senate Document No. 177, 69th Congress, 2nd Session, 1926), 2, 78.; U.S. House of Representatives, *Conduct of George W. English, United States District Judge, Eastern District of Illinois: Hearing Before the Special Committee of the House of Representatives Pursuant to House Joint Resolution 347*, 2 vols. (Washington, DC: Government Printing Office, 1925).

EPA (Environmental Protection Agency) Scandal (1983)
See Morrison v. Olson

Espy, Michael Albert (1953–)
United States representative from Mississippi (1987–1993), secretary of agriculture (1993–1994), tried but acquitted of charges of influence peddling and accepting illegal gifts while secretary from companies doing business before the Department of Agriculture. Espy was born 30 November 1953, in Yazoo City, Mississippi, the poorest section of the state. After attending local schools, he went to Howard University in Washington, D.C., where he earned his bachelor's degree in 1975. Three years later, he earned his law degree from the University of Santa Clara Law School in California. Intending to give something back to the community from whence he came, Espy returned to his home state and became an attorney with Central Mississippi Legal Services, an agency that assists the poor to pay for legal assistance. During this period, 1978 to 1980, Espy also served as assistant secretary of state and then chief of Mississippi Legal Services, the statewide organization. In 1980 Espy was named by Governor William Winter, a Democrat, to be assistant secretary of the Public Lands Division for the state of Mississippi. Four years later, Winter named Espy assistant attorney general.

In 1986, with little experience in the political field but with strong backing from the black community, Espy ran for a seat in the U.S. House of Representatives, representing Mississippi's Second District. Espy was elected over Republican Webb Franklin, and he took his seat in the 100th Congress on 3 January 1987. Espy became a rising star in the Democratic Party, having been elected at age thirty-two as the first black representative from Mississippi since Reconstruction. He was a conservative voice in the Congressional Black Caucus, a member of the National Rifle Association (NRA), and a proponent of capital punishment.

In 1992 Espy supported the presidential campaign of Arkansas Governor William Jefferson Clinton. When Clinton got into trouble for criticizing the lyrics of a rap singer, Espy embraced Clinton and stood by his side. Espy saw Clinton as the new moderate leader of a party swinging between the northeastern liberal element and the more conservative South. On 24 December 1992, President-elect Clinton named Espy the first black and first southerner to serve as secretary of agriculture. At first, Espy was praised by watchers of the department. He trimmed unneeded staff and cut waste. He supported a plan pushed by his predecessor—a Republican—to cut some 1,100 department field offices across the nation. He also examined and oversaw closely investigations into cases of tainted foods.

After a little more than a year in office, Espy was rocked by allegations that he had illegally accepted gifts from the nation's largest chicken producer,

Tyson Foods of Arkansas, and that these gifts had interfered with his oversight responsibility regarding the company. These allegations were first aired in an article that appeared in the *Wall Street Journal,* which questioned why Tyson had received preferential treatment from the Department of Agriculture under Espy's watch. The paper outlined how Tyson owner Don Tyson, who had close ties to Clinton when he was governor of Arkansas, had hosted Espy on several trips paid for at company expense, giving him free air travel and tickets to sporting events. Based on these allegations, the Agriculture Department's inspector general investigated Espy's ties to Tyson, then reported on the charges to the Justice Department. On 9 August 1994, Attorney General Janet Reno asked the U.S. Court of Appeals for the District of Columbia to name an independent counsel to investigate these allegations. The news was a stunning blow, not only to Espy, who was considered a potential candidate for governor of Mississippi once he left office, but to Clinton, then in the midst of his own ethical problems arising out of the Whitewater scandal. On 9 September 1994, a panel from this court named Los Angeles attorney Donald C. Smaltz as the independent counsel in the Espy investigation. The court's mandate gave Smaltz the authority to investigate whether Espy "committed a violation of any federal law . . . relating in any way to the acceptance of gifts by him from organizations or individuals with business pending before the Department of Agriculture." On 3 October 1994, less than a month after Smaltz was named, Espy announced his resignation. Smaltz continued his investigation.

In December 1994 *Time* magazine reported that Smaltz had uncovered what he believed to be massive corruption. As part of his investigation of Espy, Smaltz examined closely the fact that Espy had delayed and suspended department regulations on poultry makers like Tyson and considered whether Espy had done this because of the gifts he had received from the company. Smaltz asked for records regarding a meeting in 1993 between Espy, Espy's chief of staff Ronald Blackley, and Tyson lobbyist Jack Williams. Smaltz desired to call Blackley before a grand jury. In addition to receiving permission to do this, Smaltz was given the green light to investigate other areas involving Espy previously off limits—including allegations that Espy had received donations from other com-

panies; that Espy's brother Henry, who had run for Espy's congressional seat after Espy was named as secretary of agriculture, was given illegal campaign contributions; and that Blackley, himself a former lobbyist for agricultural concerns, had improperly interceded in matters relating to these concerns.

Smaltz's expansion of the Espy matter led him down many trails—overall, he was able to get more than a dozen criminal convictions or pleas of guilty from numerous companies, including Tyson Foods and Sun-Diamond Growers of California, also implicated in giving Espy illegal gratuities. (The Sun-Diamond conviction was later overturned by the D.C. Court of Appeals, and that decision was upheld by the U.S. Supreme Court in 1999.) Tyson agreed to pay a $6 million fine for giving Espy contributions; Blackley was found guilty by a federal jury in the District of Columbia and sentenced to twenty-seven months in prison.

On 27 August 1997 Espy was indicted by a federal grand jury on thirty-eight separate charges that he accepted some $35,000 in gifts in exchange for lessening the regulations on companies that the Department of Agriculture did business with or oversaw. Although the judge overseeing the trial initially threw out three of the charges against the former cabinet secretary, a federal appeals court reinstated them on 16 June 1998. On 1 October 1998 Espy went on trial. Smaltz himself prosecuted Espy instead of having a subordinate do it for him. During two months of testimony, accusations that Espy, along with a girlfriend, his brother, and his aides at the Agriculture Department, accepted gifts were presented. Espy's defense countered that despite accepting the gifts, he did not do anything in return for them.

On 2 December 1998, after Judge Ricardo Urbina had thrown out eight of the charges for lack of evidence, a Washington, D.C., jury acquitted Espy of the remaining thirty charges. Despite spending some $17 million in the Espy case, Smaltz later said that he had nabbed more than a dozen other people, including gathering a guilty plea from Tyson Foods and gaining some $11 million in fines. "The actual indictment of a public official may in fact be as great a deterrent as a conviction of that official," Smaltz said in a statement.

Espy, his career in tatters, returned to Mississippi after resigning his office.

References: Devroy, Ann, and Susan Schmidt, "Agriculture Secretary Espy Resigns," *Washington Post,* 4 October 1994, A1; Lewis, Neil A., "Espy Is Acquitted on Gifts Received while in Cabinet; Finish to 4-Year Inquiry," *New York Times,* 3 December 1998, A1; Locy, Toni, "Ex-Agriculture Secretary Indicted," *Washington Post,* 28 August 1997, A1; Locy, Toni, "Major Agricultural Co-Op Charged with Trying to Influence Espy," *Washington Post,* 14 June 1996, A27; Miller, Bill, "Espy Acquitted in Gifts Case," *Washington Post,* 3 December 1998, A1.

Ethics in Government Act, Public Law 95-521 (1978)

Congressional enactment (1978) that bars members of Congress, as well as "officers and employees of the executive, legislative, and judicial branches," from soliciting or accepting anything of value from any person or corporate concern that does business with Congress or the other branches. The act also established the office of special prosecutor, or independent counsel, to investigate all allegations involving violations of this law and all others in government. This latter portion of the law laid out a specific series of actions for the attorney general to take and for a special panel of the Court of Appeals for the D.C. Circuit to appoint an independent counsel. The third portion of the law requires the filing of financial disclosure reports (FDRs), which release information on the types and sources of all income of congressmen and related offices, as well as any candidates for the U.S. House of Representatives. Under title 1 of the Ethics in Government Act (now at 5 USC § 101), these reports are filed with the clerk of the U.S. House of Representatives and retained on file for six years after filing.

The act has been amended several times, most notably by the Ethics Reform Act of 1989.

See also Ethics Reform Act of 1989
References: Ethics in Government Act, Public Law 95-521 (1978).

Ethics Reform Act of 1989, Public Law 101-194 (1989)

Congressional enactment, 30 November 1989, that revised the financial disclosure requirements for Congress first set forth in the Ethics in Government Act of 1978. The rules regarding honoraria and disclosure requirements were strengthened.

As part of 18 USC § 207(e), the act broadened the list of officials subject to honoraria requirements. Prior to the 1989 revisions, only certain matters and certain people were subject to the restrictions. The act also for the first time restricted gifts and honoraria that could be received after an individual left office, whereas previously only current officeholders were covered. The act also named the Office of Government Ethics, located in Washington, D.C., as the "supervising ethics office" for the entire U.S. government.

When President George Bush signed the act into law on 30 November 1989, he stated:

> Today I have signed into law H.R. 3660, the Ethics Reform Act of 1989, which contains important reforms that strengthen Federal ethical standards. It is based on the legislation that I sent to the Congress last April, the recommendations of the President's Commission on Federal Ethics Law Reform, and the report of the House Bipartisan Ethics Task Force.
>
> Key reforms in the Act include: the extension of post-employment "revolving door" restrictions to the legislative branch; a ban on receipt of honoraria by Federal employees (except the Senate); limitations on outside earned income for higher-salaried, noncareer employees in all branches; increased financial disclosure; creation of conflict-of-interest rules for legislative branch staff; and limitations on gifts and travel.

In 1995 the United States Supreme Court struck down part of the 1989 act as unconstitutional—that part that prohibited honoraria for executive branch employees. In *United States v. National Treasury Employees Union,* 115 S. Ct. 1003, 513 U.S. 454 (1995), the Court held that this provision violated the First Amendment of the U.S. Constitution since honoraria allows for free speech.

See also Ethics in Government Act
References: Text of act at Public Law 101-194; Bush statement courtesy of the George Bush Presidential Library, Texas A&M University, College Station, Texas.

Executive Privilege

In government affairs, the right of a president to keep certain documents—secret papers, reports, etc.—from public or congressional examination. The antecedents of what is now known as "executive privilege" started with George Washington,

'DON'T PUT UP ANY RESISTANCE! JUST KEEP IN STEP'

A small man, labeled "Congress," is being hustled away from the Capitol by three hulking men in fedoras and black coats. All three men have President Richard Nixon's features and are labeled "Executive Privilege," "Impounding of Funds," and "Veto Power." In 1972 Nixon extended the principle of executive privilege, refusing to allow members of his staff to testify before congressional committees, most notably the Watergate Committee. (Library of Congress)

who refused to give Congress the secret instructions that he transmitted to the American diplomats whom he sent to negotiate the so-called Jay Treaty with Great Britain in 1794. The first president to formally invoke a privilege to keep private papers not associated with government was Thomas Jefferson. In 1807 Jefferson received a letter from a military officer who was a close friend of his. At the time, former Vice President Aaron Burr was on trial for treason. The court trying Burr claimed that the letter Jefferson had received had "relevant evidence" relating to the Burr trial. Jefferson relied on the advice of Chief Justice John Marshall, who told Jefferson that if the letter did in fact contain such "relevant evidence," Jefferson was compelled to turn it over to the court. The Burr trial ended before the issue was ever taken up.

Presidents from Andrew Jackson through Abraham Lincoln to Franklin D. Roosevelt have invoked the right of presidents to withhold certain documents from scrutiny, whether they be for congressional investigations or for public disclosure of certain government policies. During the Civil War, Abraham Lincoln refused to give to the War Department certain dispatches sent by Lincoln to the commander of Fort Sumter. In 1954 President Dwight D. Eisenhower first used the term "executive privilege" when he ordered his chief of staff, Sherman Adams, not to testify before the committee led by Senator Joseph McCarthy (R-WI) on matters regarding suspected communists in the government. Eisenhower told Adams that "Congress has no right to ask [White House advisers] to testify in any way, shape, or form about the advice that they were giving me at any time on any subject." McCarthy never pressed the matter, so Eisenhower's invocation was never formally challenged.

But executive privilege was rarely an issue until the administration of Richard Nixon. When the Watergate affair exploded, Special Prosecutor Archibald Cox demanded certain White House tapes. On 15 August 1973, Nixon said, "If I were to make public these tapes, containing as they do blunt and candid remarks on many different subjects, the confidentiality of the office of the president would always be suspect from now on." Judge John Sirica, presiding over the trial of the Watergate burglars, refused to listen to Nixon's pleas and ordered that the tapes be handed over to Cox. When he initially dismissed the claims of Nixon as to privilege over the tapes, Sirica asked publicly, "What distinctive quality of the presidency permits its incumbent to withhold evidence?" Nixon ordered Attorney General Eliott Richardson to fire Cox; when Richardson refused, he resigned, as did his deputy, William Ruckelshaus, and it was left to Acting Attorney General Robert H. Bork to fire Cox. A new special prosecutor, Leon A. Jaworski, was hired, but he picked up where Cox had left off and demanded the same tapes. Jaworski took the case to the U.S. Supreme Court, which held in *United States v. Nixon*, 418 U.S. 683 (1974), that although a president did indeed possess a so-called executive privilege, such right was limited. "The President's need for complete candor and objectivity from advisers calls for great deference from the courts," the Court explained in its decision. However, it set the bounds for such a privilege, holding that if evidence was needed in a criminal or civil case, such records must be turned over to a court or investigator. A certain threshold must be met before a claim of executive privilege can be honored. Chief Justice Warren Burger explained:

> In this case we must weigh the importance of the general privilege of confidentiality of Presidential communications in performance of the President's responsibilities against the inroads of such a privilege on the fair administration of criminal justice. The interest in preserving confidentiality is weighty indeed and entitled to great respect. However, we cannot conclude that advisers will be moved to temper the candor of their remarks by the infrequent occasions of disclosure because of the possibility that such conversations will be called for in the context of a criminal prosecution.

> On the other hand, the allowance of the privilege to withhold evidence that is demonstrably relevant in a criminal trial would cut deeply into the guarantee of due process of law and gravely impair the basic function of the courts. A President's acknowledged need for confidentiality in the communications of his office is general in nature, whereas the constitutional need for production of relevant evidence in a criminal proceeding is specific and central to the fair adjudication of a particular criminal case in the administration of justice. Without access to specific facts a criminal prosecution may be totally frustrated. The President's broad interest in confidentiality of communications will not be vitiated by disclosure of a limited number of conversations preliminarily shown to have some bearing on the pending criminal cases.

> We conclude that when the ground for asserting privilege as to subpoenaed materials sought for use in a criminal trial is based only on the generalized interest in confidentiality, it cannot prevail over the fundamental demands of due process of law in the fair administration of criminal justice. The generalized assertion of privilege must yield to the demonstrated, specific need for evidence in a pending criminal trial.

Nixon was forced to hand over the tapes and, when evidence on one tape revealed that he had impeded justice in the Watergate case, he was forced to resign.

During the Clinton administration (1993–2001), executive privilege was invoked numerous times. When Independent Counsel Donald Smaltz demanded certain papers relating to Agriculture Secretary Mike Espy, the Clinton White House invoked executive privilege—but a court ruled that although a president and an administration does in fact have the right of executive privilege, it can only invoke it when it deals with "governmental business." The White House also used this tactic when asked to provide papers in the so-called Filegate scandal, when presidential counsel Jack Quinn refused to turn over some 2,000 documents to the House Government Reform and Oversight Committee.

President George W. Bush has used the right of executive privilege to shield papers from energy meetings held by Vice President Dick Cheney from being released. In 2003, a federal court held that the vice president did not have to turn over the papers.

See also Espy, Michael Albert

References: Berger, Raoul, *Executive Privilege: A Constitutional Myth* (Cambridge, MA: Harvard University Press, 1974); Keighton, Robert Laurie, "The Executive Privilege and the Congressional Right to Know: A Study of the Investigating Powers of Congressional Committees" (Master's thesis, University of Pennsylvania, 1961); Mitchell, Jack, *Executive Privilege: Two Centuries of White House Scandals* (New York: Hippocrene Books, 1992); *United States v. Nixon,* 418 U.S. 683, 711–712 (1974).

Expulsion

Political decision to expel, or remove, a member from a political body for alleged or proved crimes contrary to the rules for that members' seating in that body. Officially defined as "the act of depriving a member of a body politic, corporate, or of a society, of his right of membership therein, by the vote of such body or society, for some violation of his duties as such, or for some offence which renders him unworthy of longer remaining a member of the same," the act of expulsion for the two houses of Congress is crafted in Article 1, Section 5, clause 2 of the U.S. Constitution, which holds that "each house may determine the rules of its proceedings, punish its members for disorderly behaviour, and, with the concurrence of two-thirds expel a member."

The decision—and ability—to expel a member of either the U.S. House of Representatives or the U.S. Senate is one made with great deliberation, owing to both political and supportive considerations. Usually expulsion is in the hands of the majority; the minority party usually has little say one way or the other, unless the member to be expelled is from the majority party and the move to expel is politically popular. In 1797 William Blount of Tennessee became the first U.S. senator to be expelled, after the Senate found that he had been involved in a conspiracy with former Vice President Aaron Burr that the Senate found was "inconsistent with his public trust." In the Senate, a total of fifteen members have been expelled, all but Blount for supporting the Confederate rebellion. No senator has ever been expelled for political corruption; however, four senators—James

Simmons (1862), Joseph Burton (1906), Truman Newberry (1922), and Harrison Williams (1982)—all resigned because of corruption, and most likely would have been expelled. One other, James Patterson (1873), had his term expire before he could be expelled or resign. Only five members of the U.S. House of Representatives have ever been expelled. However, only two of the five were expelled for political corruption. The other three were for supporting the Confederate rebellion during the Civil War. The Senate has considered expulsion in sixteen additional instances, all leading to censure or some other punishment. The House has considered it in twenty-two additional instances, fourteen of which dealt with the issue of political corruption.

The grounds for expulsion have changed since the Senate first convened. When Senator John Smith was expelled in 1808, the committee that recommended expulsion reported "that the senate may expel a member for a high misdemeanor, such as a conspiracy to commit treason. Its authority is not confined to an act done in its presence. . . . That a previous conviction is not requisite, in order to authorize the senate to expel a member from their body, for a high offence against the United States." However, in 1980, when the House expelled Mike "Ozzie" Myers, the fact that he had been convicted of conspiracy in the ABSCAM scandal was the sole reason many voted to expel him. Representative James Traficant (D-OH) was expelled in 2002 when a federal jury in Ohio convicted him of bribery and other offenses. Myers and Traficant are the only congressmen to be expelled; however, several others have faced the punishment of expulsion, only to resign before the House acted. This list includes Representative Mario Biaggi (D-NY) and Benjamin F. Whittemore (R-SC).

Representative Horace H. Harrison (R-TN) took to the floor of the House in December 1873 and gave an impassioned explanation of the history of expulsion as a power of punishment:

The framers of the Constitution of the United States, in prescribing or fixing the qualifications of Members of Congress, must be presumed to have been dealing with the question with reference to an obvious necessity for uniformity in the matter of the qualifications of Members, and with a jealous desire to prevent, by the action of either House of Congress, the establishment of other or different qualifications of Members.

It was appropriate and proper—in fact, necessary—that the power should be given to each House to judge of the elections, returns, and qualifications of its Members; that is, to judge of the constitutional qualifications of its Members.

The exercise of this power requires only a majority vote. But the House possesses another power, to decide who shall and who shall not hold seats in that body. It is altogether distinct, in origin and character, from that to which I have just referred. It is the power of expulsion, which requires a two-thirds vote for its exercise. It is conferred by the following clause of the Constitution:

"Each House may determine the rules of its proceedings, punish its Members for disorderly behavior, and, with the concurrence of two-thirds, expel a Member."

This power of expulsion conferred by the Constitution on each House of Congress was necessary to enable each House to secure an efficient exercise of its powers and its honor and dignity as a branch of the National legislature.

It was too dangerous a power to confer on either House without restriction, and hence it was expressly provided in the Constitution that there must be a concurrence of two-thirds of the Members to expel.

Under this power, guarded as it has been by the constitutional provision requiring a vote of two-thirds, there have been but a very few instances of expulsion since the organization of the Government, and it would seem that a power so rarely exercised does not require the agency of a standing committee.

In April 2002, following the conviction of Representative James A. Traficant Jr. (D-OH), many House members demanded that Traficant either resign his House seat or face expulsion. He was finally expelled on 24 July 2002, the second such action in the House since the Civil War.

See also Censure; Smith, John; Traficant, James A., Jr.

References: Bouvier, John, *A Law Dictionary, Adapted to the Constitution and Laws of the United States of America, and of the Several States of the American Union: with References to the Civil and other Systems of Foreign Law,* ed. Daniel Angell Gleason (Philadelphia: G. W. Childs, Printer, 1868); Butler, Anne M., and Wendy Wolff, *United States Senate Election, Expulsion, and Censure cases, 1793–1990* (Washington, DC: Government Printing Office, 1995); Byrd, Robert C., *The Senate, 1789–1989: Historical Statistics, 1789–1992,* 4 vols. (Washington, DC: Government Printing Office, 1993), IV:669–670; United States Congress, House, Committee on Standards of Official Conduct, *In the Matter of Representative Michael J. Myers: Report of Committee on Standards of Official Conduct (to accompany H. Res. 794)* (Washington, DC: Government Printing Office, 1980).

F

Fall, Albert Bacon (1861–1944)

United States senator (1912–1921) from New Mexico, secretary of the interior (1921–1923), implicated in the Teapot Dome oil scandal, one of only two sitting cabinet members ever to go to prison (the other being John Mitchell, President Richard Nixon's attorney general). Fall was born in Frankfort, Kentucky, on 26 November 1861, and attended local schools. He did not get a secondary education. He earned a living by teaching in local schools, at night reading the law. In 1881 Fall moved to Clarksville, Texas, where he went to work for a time as a bookkeeper. He also served as a cowboy, but he returned to Clarksville and worked in a general store before he married. He moved farther west, eventually working as a miner in Mexico, slowly becoming fluent in Spanish. While in the town of Kingston, New Mexico, he met a local businessman who changed his life, for good and for bad. This man was Edward L. Doheny. Because of Doheny's power to make fortunes, Fall decided to follow him and moved his family to Kingston. Eventually he set up his business in the city of Las Cruces, New Mexico, where he intended to use his legal training and become an attorney. Instead, pushed by Doheny and pressing issues in the New Mexico territory, Fall entered the political scene. He began by purchasing a local newspaper and renaming it the *Las Cruces Independent Democrat.* He turned the journal into a voice against the dominating hold of the regular Democratic Party in the territory. In 1890 Fall was elected to a seat in the territorial legislature. He left that position when he was elected to a seat on the territorial council in 1892. A leading Democrat, Fall came to the attention of President Grover Cleveland, himself an independent Democrat. In 1893, Cleveland named Fall an associate justice on the New Mexico territorial supreme court. Fall served in this capacity until 1895. He later served as territorial attorney general, as well as having repeat stints in the territorial legislature and territorial council.

The son of a Confederate soldier, Fall was a lifelong Democrat until President Theodore Roosevelt's progressive Republican stands made Fall switch to the Republican Party. It was at that time a dangerous thing to do politically. Democrats ran New Mexico, and being from an opposing party could spell political death. However, Fall embraced the new party, serving as a delegate to the 1908 Republican National Convention. In 1912, when New Mexico was granted statehood as the forty-seventh state, it was entitled to send two new United States senators to Washington. Fall was elected to one of these two seats and became one of the most important men in New Mexico politics. He slowly became more conservative during his time in the Senate, standing in opposition to many of the policies of President Woodrow Wilson, a Democrat, including Wilson's plan to bring peace to Europe at the end of World War I. While in the Senate, Fall became close friends—they played cards together

HIS LITTLE TEA PARTY.

Secretary of the Interior Albert Fall, shown sitting holding a cup of tea, was convicted of taking a bribe to sell the rich oil reserves at Teapot Dome, Wyoming. (Library of Congress)

regularly—with Senator Warren G. Harding of Ohio. In 1920 Harding shocked the political world by gaining the Republican Party's presidential nomination in the midst of a tight contest between several candidates. What few people knew was that one of his chief speechwriters was his good friend Senator Fall. Fall did not campaign for the Ohioan, however. When Harding was elected, he asked Fall to serve as secretary of state; regular Republicans, still suspicious of Fall being a former Democrat, protested, and a former associate justice of the U.S. Supreme Court, Charles Evans Hughes, was named for that post instead. Taking into account Fall's western experience, work on the land, and ability to speak Spanish, Harding instead offered him the post of secretary of the interior. Fall was confirmed quickly and settled into office.

Fall's connections with Doheny, a major businessman in the West, should have aroused suspicion, but Fall was allowed to continue communicating with his old friend even while at the Interior Department. Just three months after taking over at Interior, Fall met with Doheny, who was now the president of the Pan-American Petroleum Company, as well as Harry F. Sinclair, the chief of the Mammoth Oil Company. In 1921 the United States owned two major oil reserves at Elk Hills, California, and Teapot Dome, Wyoming, established to aid the American oil market if there was some national emergency or cause for shortfall. Both men desired to have the rights to the oil reserves transferred from U.S. government control to that of their companies. Without Fall's assistance, this was impossible. To get Fall to move their way, the men allegedly paid Fall a bribe—estimated at $100,000, with an additional $300,000 in stock from Sinclair's company. Because government control over the oil reserves lay with the secretary of the navy—in this case, Edwin Denby—Fall interceded with Denby, who convinced President Harding to sign an executive order transferring control of the reserves to the Department of the Interior. With the transfer complete, Fall then signed secret leases with Doheny and Sinclair.

What might have been labeled as simple bureaucratic blundering instead led to scandal. As part of the transfer scheme, Fall had the U.S. Forestry Service moved from the Department of Agriculture to Interior so that he could also sell tracts of preserved forest land to the highest bid-

der. However, Harry Slattery, a bureaucrat in the U.S. Forestry Service, began to investigate the forestry deal and came across the secret oil leases given to Doheny and Sinclair. Slattery took the evidence he collected to Senator Robert LaFollette, a Progressive Republican from Wisconsin, who introduced a resolution to initiate an inquiry. A select committee in the Senate was established, with Senator Thomas Walsh (D-MT) as chairman.

Fall came under scrutiny for the Teapot Dome and forestry decisions, and, following a firestorm of protest against him, he resigned on 4 March 1923 and returned to New Mexico. The Walsh committee, however, expanded its investigation. Forced to testify under oath, Fall denied that Doheny or Sinclair bribed him and claimed that the $100,000 payment was a loan from newspaper publisher Edward L. McLean. The committee did not believe Fall and continued their inquest. Appeals to the courts voided the leases, and in 1929 Fall was indicted for receiving a bribe. Fall was put on trial with Doheny and Sinclair. Doheny was acquitted of paying Fall the bribe, Sinclair was convicted of contempt of Congress, but Fall was convicted of taking the bribe, the first cabinet officer ever to be convicted of a crime. Fall was already in ill health when he began his prison sentence and served only a year before being released. His health and wealth sapped, he was mired in poverty until his death. Fall died in the Hotel Dieu Hospital in El Paso, Texas, on 30 November 1944 at the age of eighty-three. His ranch in New Mexico had been confiscated by the government in 1936.

See also Teapot Dome Scandal

References: *Biographical Directory of the American Congress, 1774–1996* (Alexandria, VA: CQ Staff Directories, Inc., 1996), 1013; "Fall Loan Reprehensible in Last Degree, Is Declared by the Walsh Committee," *Santa Fe New Mexican,* 5 June 1924, 1; Grossman, Mark, *Encyclopedia of the United States Cabinet,* 3 vols.(Santa Barbara, CA: ABC-CLIO, 2000), I:356–358; Werner, Morris Robert; and John Starr, *Teapot Dome* (Clifton, NJ: A. M. Kelley, 1950).

Fauntroy, Walter Edward (1933–)

Delegate to Congress from the District of Columbia (1971–1991), pled guilty in 1995 to lying on a financial disclosure form. Born in Washington, D.C., on 6 February 1933, Fauntroy attended the public schools of the nation's capital, then earned his bachelor's degree at Virginia Union University in Richmond, Virginia, in 1955. Three years later, having studied theology with the intention of becoming a minister, Fauntroy was awarded a bachelor of divinity degree from the Yale University Divinity School in Connecticut. He then took the position of pastor of the New Bethel Baptist Church in 1959.

In 1960 Fauntroy, dedicated to gaining civil rights for black Americans, joined the Southern Christian Leadership Conference (SCLC), headed by the Reverend Dr. Martin Luther King Jr. From 1960 until 1971 Fauntroy served as director of the SCLC's Washington, D.C., bureau. During this same period, from 1966 to 1972, he also served as the founder, and then the director, of the Model Inner City Community Organization in Washington. In 1967 Fauntroy was named vice chairman of the District of Columbia City Council, serving until 1969, and in 1969 served as the national coordinator of the Poor People's Campaign to bring attention to poverty in America. He also served as chairman of the board of directors of the Martin Luther King Jr. Center for Social Change in Atlanta, Georgia, (1969–), and as a member of the Leadership Conference on Civil Rights from 1961 to 1971.

A Democrat, Fauntroy was elected in a special election to the U.S. House of Representatives as a delegate from the District of Columbia (the District has only nonvoting delegates, not regular representatives, as the states do), serving in the 92nd to the 101st Congresses from 23 March 1971 until 3 January 1991. During his time in Congress, Fauntroy was an outspoken advocate for civil rights and for full voting rights for the District residents he served.

In 1990 Fauntroy decided to run for Washington, D.C., mayor, and did not run for reelection to his House seat. He did not win the mayoralty and retired from public life. However, it was soon discovered that he was under investigation by the Department of Justice for allegedly lying on a financial disclosure form regarding a charitable contribution to his congressional campaign. In March 1995 he pled guilty to making false statements on a congressional financial disclosure form in violation of the False Statements Statute, 18 USC § 1001, a felony that could have sent him to prison for up to five years. However, because the United States Supreme Court changed the way

such cases could be proved, the government was forced to make a plea bargain. Fauntroy pled guilty in federal court on 9 August 1995 to a misdemeanor and was sentenced to two years' probation. He occasionally appears on television to discuss political issues.

References: *Biographical Directory of the American Congress, 1774–1996* (Alexandria, VA: CQ Staff Directories, Inc., 1996), 1018; "Fauntroy Pleads Guilty to Filing False Congressional Report," *Washington Post,* 25 March 1995, B2; Locy, Toni, "Fauntroy Fined for False Disclosure; Ruling in Other Case Saves Ex-Delegate from Felony Conviction," *Washington Post,* 10 August 1995, B1.

Federal Corrupt Practices Act of 1910
See Publicity Act of 1910, 36 Stat. 822

Federal Corrupt Practices Act of 1925, 43 Stat. 1070; 2 U.S.C. § 241 (1925)

Congressional legislation, enacted 28 February 1925, that adjusted the spending limits for U.S. House and U.S. Senate candidates and mandated disclosure of campaign receipts and expenditures. The U.S. Congress enacted this legislation following the U.S. Supreme Court decision in *Newberry v. United States* and the Teapot Dome affair, two finance-related scandals that had hit Washington in the previous three years. Specifically, this legislation repealed the 1910 Publicity Act and the 1911 amendments to the Publicity Act and to the 1907 Tillman Act and mandated that all contributions of fifty dollars and higher to any candidate for the U.S. House or U.S. Senate be reported to the government. Any offer of contracts or patronage in exchange for the contribution were outlawed, as was plain bribery or the acceptance of such bribes.

This act was repealed by the act of 7 February 1972 (86 Stat. 20).

Federal Election Campaign Act of 1971, Public Law 92–225, 86 Stat. 3, 2 USC § 431 et seq. (1971)

Congressional legislation, enacted 1971, that for the first time set strict standards for campaign finance reporting and monitoring. The law had four distinct goals: (1) it limited political contributions by individuals to single candidates to $1,000 per year, and by political action committees (PACs) to $5,000 to single candidates; (2) it limited gifts from individuals and groups "relative to a clearly defined candidate" to $1,000 per election; (3) it required political committees to retain and file with the government detailed records of campaign contributions and expenditures, including the name and address of each contributor; and (4) it established an eight-member commission to monitor and oversee elections expenditures and contributions. The U.S. Court of Appeals for the D.C. Circuit, in upholding its decision in *Buckley v. Valeo,* stated that this act was "by far the most comprehensive reform legislation [ever] passed by Congress concerning the election of the President, Vice President, and members of Congress." In *Federal Election Commission v. Akins* (1998), the same court stated, "The Federal Elections Campaign Act of 1971 seeks to remedy corruption of the political process."

Following the reporting of numerous campaign finance abuses by the Nixon reelection campaign in 1972, the Congress sought to reform the law, passing in 1974 the so-called Federal Election Campaign Act Amendments. The main portion of this secondary law established the Federal Election Commission (the 1971 law established an independent agency, but it was struck down by the U.S. Supreme Court and was reinstituted to meet constitutional scrutiny), an independent agency designed to enforce all campaign finance laws, monitor elections and campaign contributions and spending, and fine those candidates who did not follow the law. Following the U.S. Supreme Court's decision in *Buckley v. Valeo* (1975), the Congress again reformed the law in 1976 (Public Law 94-283, 90 Stat. 492, 11 May 1976), and in 1980 amended it to compact and streamline disclosure procedures (Public Law 96-187, 93 Stat. 1354, 8 January 1980).

Several high-profile cases have challenged different sections of the 1971 act and its revisions. In *Buckley,* the U.S. Supreme Court upheld the contribution limits, disclosure requirements, and public financing for presidential elections, but struck down the expenditure limits and declared the Federal Election Commission as it was established in the 1971 law unconstitutional. In *Colorado Republican Federal Campaign Committee v. Federal Election Commission* (1996), the U.S. Supreme Court

held that so-called independent expenditures, those made by state parties or independent groups aside from national parties, were not subject to the spending limits imposed by the 1971 law and its amendments.

See also *Buckley v. Valeo; Colorado Republican Federal Campaign Committee v. Federal Election Commission;* Federal Election Commission; *Federal Election Commission v. National Right to Work Committee*
References: Bartholomew, Paul C., "Corrupt Practices Acts," in *Dictionary of American History,* 7 vols. (New York: Charles Scribner's Sons, 1976–1978), II:232–233; "Federal Election Campaign Act of 1971," in William C. Binning, Larry Esterly, and Paul A. Sracic, *Encyclopedia of American Parties, Campaigns, and Elections* (Westport, CT: Greenwood Press, 1999), 170; Public Law 86 Stat. 3.

Federal Election Campaign Act Amendments of 1974, 88 Stat. 1263 (1974)

See Federal Election Campaign Act of 1971

Federal Election Commission (FEC)

Independent federal agency established to oversee the spending of all congressional and national campaigns and to make sure that no violations of law go unpunished. After allegations of massive campaign financing abuses by the Nixon campaign in the 1972 election, Congress amended the Federal Election Campaign Act of 1971, which had established the FEC as a government body to oversee the collection and distribution of the Presidential Primary Matching Payment Account, the funds collected when Americans check off the small box on their income tax returns for this purpose.

Following the allegations in the Watergate scandal, the FEC was empowered to oversee "the public financing of presidential elections by certifying Federal payments to primary candidates, general election nominees, and national nominating conventions." The amendment, contained presently in 2 U.S.C. § 437(c), gives the commission "exclusive jurisdiction in the administration and civil enforcement of laws regulating the acquisition and expenditure of campaign funds to ensure compliance by participants in the Federal election process. It's chief mission is to provide public disclosure of campaign finance activities and effect voluntary compliance by providing the public with information on the laws and regulations concerning campaign finance." The commission is composed of six commissioners, all appointed by the president with the advice and consent of the U.S. Senate.

The FEC has made many controversial decisions over the years and has been taken to court to advance or block certain campaign financial moves.

The chairman of the FEC in 2000 was Danny Lee McDonald, a Democrat placed on the commission by President Ronald Reagan.

> **See also** *Colorado Republican Federal Campaign Committee v. Federal Election Commission; Federal Election Commission v. National Conservative Political Action Committee; Federal Election Commission v. National Right to Work Committee*
>
> **References:** "Federal Election Commission," in *The United States Government Manual, 2000/2001* (Washington, DC: Government Printing Office, 2001), 411–413; "Federal Election Commission," in William C. Binning, Larry Esterly, and Paul A. Sracic, *Encyclopedia of American Parties, Campaigns, and Elections* (Westport, CT: Greenwood Press, 1999), 173–174.

Federal Election Commission v. Massachusetts Citizens for Life, Inc., 479 U.S. 238 (1986)

United States Supreme Court decision holding that a Federal Election Commission ban on corporate expenditures in political campaigns did not extend to nonprofit organizations. In September 1978 Massachusetts Citizens for Life, Inc. (MCFL), a nonprofit advocacy group calling for the abolition of abortion and enforcing the rights of the unborn, prepared a "special edition" pamphlet for the election that year, identifying each official in the state and showing their views on abortion. Thirteen particular candidates were identified as "pro-life" in the publication. A complaint was filed with the Federal Election Commission that the publication violated Section 316 of the Federal Election Campaign Act (FECA), which prohibited corporations from using general treasury funds "in connection with" any advocacy in an election and required that any advertising come from voluntary funds given exclusively to a separate fund used for campaign advocacy only. The FEC held that the "special edition" violated Section 316 and asked

for a civil penalty and relief. The MCFL was a nonprofit advocacy group and as such it appealed to a district court in Massachusetts that Section 316 was an unconstitutional infringement on its First Amendment rights. The District Court held that Section 316 did not apply to the MCFL, but that if it did the rule itself was wholly unconstitutional. The FEC appealed to the U.S. Court of Appeals for the First Circuit, which held that Section 316 was constitutional but did not apply to the MCFL. The FEC appealed to the U.S. Supreme Court, and arguments were heard on 7 October 1986.

On 15 December 1986, the Court held that Section 316 applied to the MCFL, but that as it was written, it was unconstitutional. Writing for a majority of the justices, many of whom agreed to parts of the judgment and dissented from others, Justice William Brennan explained that "Section 316's restriction of independent spending is unconstitutional as applied to appellee, for it infringes protected speech without a compelling justification for such infringement. The concern underlying the regulation of corporate political activity—that organizations that amass great wealth in the economic marketplace not gain unfair advantage in the political marketplace—is absent with regard to appellee. Appellee was formed to disseminate political ideas, not to amass capital. It has no shareholders or other persons having a claim on its assets or earnings, but obtains its funds from persons who make contributions to further the organization's political purposes. It was not established by a business corporation or a labor union, and its policy is not to accept contributions from such entities." Discussing the difference between corporate advocacy and individual group advocacy, Brennan wrote:

> We have consistently held that restrictions on contributions require less compelling justification than restrictions on independent spending.... It may be that the class of organizations affected by our holding today will be small. That prospect, however, does not diminish the significance of the rights at stake. Freedom of speech plays a fundamental role in a democracy; as this Court has said, freedom of thought and speech "is the matrix, the indispensable condition, of nearly every other form of freedom." Our pursuit of other governmental ends, however, may tempt us to accept in small increments a loss that would be unthinkable if inflicted

all at once. For this reason, we must be as vigilant against the modest diminution of speech as we are against its sweeping restriction. Where at all possible, government must curtail speech only to the degree necessary to meet the particular problem at hand, and must avoid infringing on speech that does not pose the danger that has prompted regulation. In enacting the provision at issue in this case, Congress has chosen too blunt an instrument for such a delicate task.

In 2000 the Court reinstated many of the restrictions used by campaign finance reform in *Nixon v. Shrink Missouri PAC.*

See also *Nixon v. Missouri PAC*

References: *Federal Election Commission v. Massachusetts Citizens for Life, Inc.,* 479 U.S. 238 (1986).

Federal Election Commission v. National Conservative Political Action Committee, 470 U.S. 480 (1985)

United States Supreme Court decision that held on narrow grounds that a political party does not have standing to bring an action against another party to ask if violations of the Federal Elections Campaign Act of 1971 have been committed. Under the Presidential Election Campaign Fund Act (Fund Act), a candidate may receive public financing of his or her campaign; however, under 26 U.S.C. § 9012(f), it becomes a criminal offense for an independent "political committee" to expend more than $1,000 to further that candidate's election. Believing that the National Conservative Political Action Committee (NCPAC) intended to spend more than the allowed $1,000 on the reelection of President Ronald Reagan in the 1984 election, the Democratic National Committee (DNC) filed suit in the United States District Court for the Eastern District of Pennsylvania to request that 26 U.S.C. § 9012(f) be declared constitutional. The court held that, although it felt the DNC had standing to file suit, Section 9012(f) was unconstitutional on its face because "it violated First Amendment freedoms of speech and association." The United States Supreme Court agreed to hear the appeal of NCPAC, with the plaintiffs being named as both the DNC and the FEC. Arguments were heard on 28 November 1984, shortly after the presidential election.

On 18 March 1985, the Supreme Court held that the Democrats had no standing to challenge a po-

litical action committee's spending schemes. Speaking for a divided court, Justice William H. Rehnquist, however, did not strike down Section 9012(f) as unconstitutional, holding that while it "abridges First Amendment freedoms of speech and association, that it is substantially overbroad, and that it cannot permissibly be given a narrowing construction to cure the overbreadth . . . the court did not . . . find [the act] unconstitutional because the PACs had not filed a counterclaim requesting such a declaration." As to the actual issue in the case, whether the DNC had standing to sue, Justice Rehnquist explained, "It seems highly dubious that Congress intended every one of the millions of eligible voters in this country to have the power to invoke expedited review by a three-judge district court with direct appeal to this Court in actions brought by them against other private parties. The DNC is obviously not just another private litigant, and it would undoubtedly be a worthy representative of collective interests which would justify expedited review had Congress so provided; but Congress simply did not draft the statute in a way that distinguishes the DNC from any individual voter." He added, "The plain language of [the relevant sections] of the Federal Election Campaign Act of 1971 (FECA)—which provides that the FEC 'shall administer, seek to obtain compliance with, and formulate policy with respect to' the Fund Act and confers on the FEC 'exclusive jurisdiction with respect to the civil enforcement' of the Act—clearly shows that the Democrats have no standing to bring a private action against another private party." Justices John Paul Stevens, Byron White, William Brennan, and Thurgood Marshall dissented in whole or in part.

References: *Federal Election Commission v. National Conservative Political Action Committee,* 470 U.S. 480 (1985).

Federal Election Commission v. National Right to Work Committee, 459 U.S. 197 (1982)

United States Supreme Court decision that held that certain corporations and unions were prohibited by the Federal Election Campaign Act of 1971 from spending campaign funds. Under the Federal Election Campaign Act (FECA) of 1971, corporations and labor unions were prohibited from making contributions with regard to national political parties. However, the law allowed these entities to establish separate funds that could be used for federal elections; these funds were also tightly controlled by the FECA. One loophole in the law, which became the central issue in this case, allowed a corporation without "capital stock" to solicit contributions to a fund for political purposes from members of that specific corporation. In 1976 the National Right to Work Committee (NRWC), an organization that fought against the power of labor unions but did not have "capital stock," solicited monies from people outside the organization for use in the 1976 federal campaign. The Federal Election Commission held that the NRWC violated that specific section of the FECA and sought an injunction against the group in court. A district court held for the Federal Election Commission, but the U.S. Court of Appeals for the D.C. Circuit reversed, holding that the rule violated free speech. The U.S. Supreme Court granted certiorari (the right to hear the case), and arguments were held on 1 November 1982.

On 13 December 1982, six weeks after arguments were heard, the Supreme Court overturned the appeals court decision and upheld the right of the FEC to apply this provision of FECA. Holding for a unanimous court, Justice William H. Rehnquist explained:

> In order to prevent both actual and apparent corruption, Congress aimed a part of its regulatory scheme at corporations. The statute reflects a legislative judgment that the special characteristics of the corporate structure require particularly careful regulation.... While 441b [the relevant section] restricts the solicitation of corporations and labor unions without great financial resources, as well as those more fortunately situated, we accept Congress' judgment that it is the potential for such influence that demands regulation. Nor will we second-guess a legislative determination as to the need for prophylactic measures where corruption is the evil feared. As we said in *California Medical Assn. v. FEC,* 453 U.S. 182, 201 (1981), the "differing structures and purposes" of different entities "may require different forms of regulation in order to protect the integrity of the electoral process."
>
> To accept the view that a solicitation limited only to those who have in the past proved "philosophically compatible" to the views of the corporation must be permitted under the statute in order for the prohibition to be constitutional would ignore the teachings of our earlier decisions. The governmental interest in preventing both actual corruption and the appearance of corruption of elected representatives has long been recognized ... and there is no reason why it may not in this case be accomplished by treating unions, corporations, and similar organizations differently from individuals.

References: *Federal Election Commission v. National Right to Work Committee,* 459 U.S. 197, at 210.

Ferguson, James Edward (1871–1944)

Governor of Texas (1915–1917), impeached and removed from office by the Texas state legislature for financial improprieties. He later directed his wife's election to the same office, but her two terms were likewise tainted by allegations of pardons sold for influence and other financial irregularities, although she was not impeached. Born in Salado, Texas, on 31 August 1871, Ferguson was the son of James Edward Ferguson, a farmer, and Fannie (née Fitzpatrick) Ferguson. The elder Ferguson died when his son was four, and within just a few years James Ferguson was working the fields of his farm. He received some primary education, but was allowed to enter Salado College, a local preparatory school, when only twelve. This educational period ended when he was expelled for disobedience. Ferguson left home at age sixteen and for the next several years drifted across the American West, living hand to mouth. He returned to Bell County in his mid-twenties and, while working as a farmer and on a railroad bridge gang, studied the law. He was admitted to the Texas bar in 1897 and he commenced a practice in the town of Belton, Texas.

In 1899 Ferguson married Miriam Wallace. He was able to use the proceeds from his law practice to purchase tracts of land and invest in insurance companies, becoming a part owner of the Farmers Bank of Belton and a member of the Texas Banker's Association. At the same time, Ferguson began to enter the political realm. In 1902 he served as the campaign manager for Robert L. Henry in his campaign for Congress, as well as several others, including the gubernatorial campaign of Democrat Oscar B. Colquitt in 1912. Colquitt did not seek reelection in 1914. The Democrats had split into prohibitionist and antiprohibitionist wings, and when the antiprohibitionists met they nominated Ferguson for governor, despite the fact that he did not ask for the nomination or even campaign for it. Ferguson was able to consolidate his support among the party as a whole and was nominated as the Democratic candidate. Running in a nearly one-party state, Ferguson was easily elected over Republican John W. Philip and Socialist E. R. Meitzen and took office on 19 January 1915. During his first term, Ferguson strongly supported increased aid to rural schools, the building of state colleges and the Austin State School for the Feebleminded, and larger appropriations for education as a whole in the state. Ferguson was easily reelected for a second term in 1916, defeating Republican R. B. Creager by more than 250,000 votes out of some 300,000 cast. During this campaign, however, many critics of Ferguson raised charges that he had misappropriated state funds. After he was sworn in for a second term, Ferguson raised the ire of the state legislature by vetoing the school appropriation bill for the University of Texas. Ferguson demanded that certain members of the school's faculty whom Ferguson disliked be dismissed. Instead of dismissing these members, the school and its supporters in the legislature opened up the old charges of misappropriation of funds and leveled new charges. A grand jury was convened in Travis County, Texas, and on 21 July 1917 Ferguson appeared before it. A few days later, the grand jury indicted Ferguson on nine counts, including misapplication of public funds and embezzlement. Ferguson posted bond, went back to being governor, and announced that he would seek a third term in office.

Because of Ferguson's dismissive attitude toward the indictment against him, the Speaker of the Texas state house of representatives called for a special session to consider impeachment articles. Ferguson outdid the legislature and called a special session to consider a new appropriations bill for the University of Texas. Instead, the house began an impeachment inquiry. After a lengthy investigation, the house approved twenty-one separate articles of impeachment, each alleging financial misconduct by Ferguson. Calling the entire process a "kangaroo court" and claiming that the legislature did not have the power to impeach him, Ferguson resigned on 25 August 1917. Five days later, however, the state senate opened the impeachment trial, and, after three weeks of testimony, convicted Ferguson on ten of the twenty-one articles. Five of the articles alleged that Ferguson had failed to enforce the banking laws of the state, and one charged that he had received an illegal gratuity of $156,500 that was found in his bank account and that Ferguson refused to justify. The senate then voted to deny Ferguson the right ever to hold public office in Texas again. Despite this setback, Ferguson remained politically active. He pushed to gain the Democratic nomination for governor in 1918, but was defeated by William P. Hobby. In 1920 he ran on the obscure American, or Know-Nothing, Party ticket for president, but received few votes. In 1922 he was an unsuccessful candidate for the United States Senate.

In 1924 Ferguson turned the tables on his opponents and had his wife enter the field for the Democratic gubernatorial nomination. He ran his wife's campaign against fellow Democrat Judge Felix Robertson, who was supported by the Ku Klux Klan. Remarkably, Miriam Amanda Ferguson received the party nomination and defeated Republican George C. Butte, winning with the slogan "Two Governors for the Price of One!" She thus became the first woman elected governor of a state in the United States (Nellie Taylor Ross of Wyoming, the first female governor, succeeded her husband into office following his death). Known as "Ma" Ferguson (her husband was known as "Pa" Ferguson), Miriam Ferguson spent much of her term vindicating her husband. She helped to pass a prohibition against the wearing of masks in public, a law aimed directly at the Ku Klux Klan. However, she was alleged to have dabbled in the same corruption that caused her husband's downfall, and it was because of this that in 1926 she was defeated in the Democratic primary by state Attorney General Dan Moody, who went on to be elected governor. Four years later, attempting to make a comeback, "Ma" Ferguson entered the Democratic primary again, but was defeated by Ross Sterling. In 1932, promising to cut taxes as the Great Depression worsened, she took on now-Governor Sterling and defeated him in the Democratic primary. She was elected over token Republican opposition and served a second term as chief executive. Her promise to cut taxes died in the state legislature, but she did continue her policy of granting pardons, breaking state records. She left office in 1934. She attempted a final comeback in 1940 when she tried to unseat Governor Lee O'-Daniel, but she failed.

James Ferguson died in Austin on 21 September 1944, three weeks after his seventy-third birthday. His grave in the Texas State Cemetery in Austin simply reads, "He loved his fellow man and was generous to a fault." His widow lived until 1961.

References: DeShields, James T., *They Sat in High Places: The Presidents and Governors of Texas* (San Antonio, TX: Naylor Company, 1940); "Ferguson, James Edward," in Robert Sobel and John Raimo, eds., *Biographical Directory of the Governors of the United States, 1789–1978*, 4 vols. (Westport, CT: Meckler Books, 1978), IV:1532–1533; Nalle, Ouida Ferguson, *The Fergusons of Texas, Or, "Two Governors for the Price of One": A Biography of James Edward Ferguson and his wife, Miriam Amanda Ferguson, ex-Governors of the State of Texas* (San Antonio, TX: Naylor Company, 1946); "Record of Proceedings of the High Court of Impeachment on the Trial of Hon. James E. Ferguson, Governor, Before the Senate of the State of Texas, Pursuant to the State Constitution and Rules Provided by the Senate during the Second and Third Called Sessions of the 35th Legislature. Convened in the City of Austin, August 1, 1917, and Adjourned Without Day, September 29, 1917." Published by Authority of the Legislature, T. H. Yarbrough, Journal Clerk, Senate (Austin: A. O. Baldwin and Sons, State Printers, 1917); Rutherford, Bruce, *The Impeachment of Jim Ferguson* (Austin, TX: Eakin Press, 1983).

Ferguson, Miriam Amanda Wallace (1875–1961)

See Ferguson, James Edward

"Filegate"

Political scandal in which officials in the White House during the administration of President Bill Clinton received through various means the FBI files of numerous Republicans, many of whom had formerly worked at the White House, to be used for unknown purposes. On 30 May 1996, reports leaked to the press that Clinton administration officials had requested through FBI channels the confidential files of some 400 people, most if not all Republicans who had served in the previous administration of President George Bush. The House Committee on Government Reform and Oversight

came across the potential scandal while investigating White House behavior in the case of Billy Dale, an employee in the White House Travel Office who had been mysteriously fired soon after Clinton came to power and later charged but acquitted of stealing from the White House Travel Office fund. In January 1996 Representative William Clinger (R-PA), chairman of the House committee, sent a subpoena to the White House asking for all relevant files on Dale and the other Travel Office employees who were fired. The White House reported that it had no documents on Dale. When Clinger moved to have the White House held in contempt of Congress, and a vote was taken on 9 May 1996, Dale's file mysteriously appeared on Capitol Hill on 30 May. However, President Clinton declared executive privilege to prevent the disclosure of more than 2,000 pages of documents relating to the Travel Office requested by the committee.

Inside the file given to the committee was a White House request, dated 20 December 1993, asking the FBI for a copy of Dale's confidential file. This had happened some seven months after Dale had been fired, but before he was tried by the FBI for allegedly stealing from the Travel Office fund. This story leaked to the press, and a firestorm erupted—requesting such files violated the Privacy Act of 1974. On 5 June 1996, White House Special Counsel to the President Jane Sherburne issued a statement claiming that Dale's file had been "mistakenly" requested. That same day, FBI Director Louis Freeh released a statement that he and his office had never been informed by the White House of the file requests. On 6 June, a White House staffer stated that the White House did not request Dale's file—the Government Accounting Office (GAO) did, in the midst of an investigation. The GAO denied ever asking for the files.

More gasoline was poured on the fire of scandal, when it was learned that Dale's file was not the only one asked for by the White House—but that it was one of at least 338, all of Republicans who had worked in the White House in the Reagan or Bush administrations. On 10 June, Sherburne explained that because some of the former Republican officials had tried to gain access to the White House, their files were necessary to get them a security clearance to the building. Nine days later, the House Committee on Government Reform and

Oversight held its first hearing on the issue. Prior security programs from administrations back for thirty years, both Democratic and Republican, were examined. The committee was told by investigators that in these prior instances a careful process was instituted by each administration to gain security information and that the Clinton administration, for the first time, handed these duties to political operatives and college-age interns lacking security clearances.

As the press focused on the story, the White House tried to limit growing political damage. On 13 June this increased when the FBI reported that seventy-one files not heretofore discussed had also been requested by the White House; these also were of Republican officials from the Reagan and Bush administrations. On 14 June, the official FBI report, titled "Report on the Dissemination of FBI File Information to the White House," disclosed that a total of 408 files had been requested by the White House. Director Freeh reported that these requests had been "without justification," and that "the prior system of providing files to the White House relied on good faith and honor." Among the files requested by the White House were those of Billy Dale and Barnaby Brasseux, another Travel Office employee. The House committee charged that Craig Livingston, in charge of White House security, had been behind the files requests. His own file showed that White House counsel Bernard Nussbaum had told the FBI that Livingston had been placed in his job by First Lady Hillary Rodham Clinton. Livingston had been aided by a former military officer, Anthony Marceca. Neither of these men had ever been given a security clearance to see such information, much less to request it from the FBI.

On 18 June 1996, Judge Kenneth Starr, the independent counsel in the Whitewater case, reported that he felt he did not have the proper jurisdiction to oversee the FBI files case. Attorney General Janet Reno announced that she would ask the court that named Starr to expand his authority over the FBI files case. This was done on 20 June 1996, and the court approved the order the following day.

The press reaction to the growing scandal was scathing, as it appeared that the files were requested to be used against President Clinton's political enemies, potential and real. Such FBI files contained raw data on each subject's background, and the information could be used in many ways. William Safire, a columnist for the *New York Times* and an avowed political enemy of the Clinton administration, wrote on 4 July 1996, "Just as Watergate was first dismissed as a 'caper,' the growing protest at the invasion of privacy of nearly 1,000 Americans by the cesspool of snoopery, sudden death and obstruction known as the Clinton Office of White House Counsel is being characterized as a mere 'flap.'"

Livingston was placed on paid administrative leave, but he never returned to the White House. Senate hearings were conducted in the Senate Judiciary Committee, but White House stonewalling—including the use of executive privilege—limited the inquiry. Although one of the impeachment charges against President Richard Nixon was that he misused FBI files, such charges were never brought against Clinton or any of his aides. In the House committee official report, the majority members reported, "In general, the FBI files issue shows a lack of respect by the Clinton administration for proper security procedures to protect both the President of the United States and the national security. This is all the more so since the White House ignored recommendations from a Democratic committee chairman of the U.S. Senate to take security precautions in response to reported security irregularities in the first years of the Clinton administration. . . . The Clinton White House displayed a lack of respect for the privacy and confidentiality of private citizens. The mere fact that individuals lacking in professional skills and discretion were put in charge demonstrates the cavalier approach of the Clinton administration toward sensitive security matters."

References: Larson, Ruth, "Treasury Official Admits Destroying Filegate Documents," *The Washington Times* (National Edition), 16 November 1997, 1; *Report of the FBI General Counsel on the Dissemination of FBI File Information to the White House,* issued on June 14, 1996, by FBI General Counsel Howard M. Shapiro; U.S. House of Representatives, Committee on Government Reform and Oversight, *Investigation into the White House and Department of Justice on Security of FBI Background Investigation Files,* House Report 104-862, 104th Congress, 2nd Session, 28 September 1996; "U.S. Requests Dismissal of FBI Files Suit White House Got Data on Employees," *Washington Post,* 24 May 1997, A11; "The White House's FBI

Blunder," *The Weekly Standard,* I:40 (24 June 1996), 9–10.

Flood, Daniel John (1903–1994)

United States representative from Pennsylvania (1949–1953; 1955–1980), indicted and later pled guilty to charges of conspiracy involving payoffs, for which he served a year's probation. Flood was born in Hazleton, Pennsylvania, on 26 November 1903. He attended the public schools of the area, particularly in Wilkes-Barre, and later in St. Augustine, Florida. In 1924 he graduated from Syracuse University in Syracuse, New York, after which he attended Harvard Law School before earning his law degree from the Dickinson School of Law in Carlisle, Pennsylvania, in 1929. He was admitted to the Pennsylvania state bar in 1930 and opened a practice in Wilkes-Barre.

During the Great Depression, Flood worked in private practice and in 1934 and 1935 as an attorney for the Home Owners' Loan Corporation, which assisted with loans for home buyers in Pennsylvania. He left this position in 1935, when he was named deputy attorney general for the Commonwealth, and at the same served as counsel for the Pennsylvania Liquor Control Board until 1939. From 1941 to 1944, Flood served as director of the State Bureau of Public Assistance Disbursements and as executive assistant to the state treasurer.

In 1944 Flood was elected as a Democrat to a seat in the U.S. House of Representatives in the Seventy-ninth Congress (1945–1947). In 1946 he was defeated for reelection by Republican Mitchell Jenkins and he resumed the practice of law. Two years later, in 1948, when Jenkins did not run for a second term, Flood entered the race and defeated Republican Robert H. Stroh to take back his old seat. Flood sat in the Eighty-first and Eighty-second Congresses (1949–1953). In 1952 he again lost his seat, this time to Republican Edward J. Bonin. Once again, Flood returned to the practice of law. In 1954 Flood defeated Bonin and held his seat until his resignation on 21 January 1980. Flood was known as much for "bringing home the pork" to his constituents as he was for his flowing handlebar moustache.

In 1978 Flood was indicted on thirteen separate criminal charges. They alleged that he con-

spired with his former chief assistant, Stephen B. Elko, to collect bribes from several businessmen in exchange for Flood's assistance in getting the businessmen grants or contracts from federal agencies. The Justice Department had investigated all of the men, and several agreed to cooperate in the investigation or sought immunity for their testimony against Flood. One of these men, Lieb Pinter, a rabbi from Brooklyn, New York, pled guilty to charges that he paid Flood more than $5,000 in bribes. Flood pled not guilty to the charges. In 1978 he was reelected despite the indictment hanging over his head. Flood's attorneys asked to stay his trial, as a question involving bribery indictments against a sitting congressman was then before the U.S. Supreme Court. In that case, involving Representative Henry Helstoski (D-NJ), the Court was asked to decide whether the Speech or Debate Clause of the Constitution precluded any investigation into how a congressman worked, or what legislation he introduced, despite bribes that may have been given to get that work or legislation enacted. Judge Oliver Gasch ruled against Flood's motion to stay the trial, after prosecutors claimed that legislation Flood may have worked on was not at issue, but rather his pushing federal agencies for contracts for those who had bribed him. Flood's trial began on 15 January 1979, after two of the bribery charges were dropped. On 3 February, Judge Gasch ruled a mistrial after the jury reported back that it was hopelessly deadlocked on the remaining counts. A second trial was set to begin on 4 June, but on 30 May Flood collapsed and had to be hospitalized. The retrial was put off indefinitely. Facing this second trial, and potential ethics investigations in the House, Flood resigned his seat on 31 January 1980. A new trial date of 8 April 1980 was set, when Judge Gasch held that Flood was mentally competent to stand trial. Fighting cancer and a host of other diseases that his lawyers claimed made him unfit to stand trial, Flood pled guilty on 26 February to a single charge of defrauding the government when he solicited an illegal campaign contribution in exchange for his support of obtaining a government contract, and was sentenced to one year's probation. More serious charges were dropped in exchange for the plea bargain. After his plea, Flood told reporters, "The terrible burden of this case has been damaging to my health and I need peace from it. . . . I deny with all my heart that I have committed any criminal offense."

Flood retired to Wilkes-Barre, Pennsylvania, where he died on 28 May 1994 at the age of ninety.

References: *Biographical Directory of the American Congress, 1774–1996* (Alexandria, VA: CQ Staff Directories, Inc., 1996), 1039; *Congressional Ethics* (Washington, DC: Congressional Quarterly, 1980), 26–28.

Florida Right to Life, Inc. v. Lamar, 233 F. 3d 1288 (11th Cir. 2001)

United States court of appeals decision that upheld the right of certain organizations to make monetary contributions to political groups. Florida Right to Life, Inc. (FRL), an antiabortion group, desired to raise money from certain political candidates and groups to further their message. However, Florida law (Fla. Stat. Ann. § 106.08(5)) prohibited this, stating that "[c]andidates . . . may not . . . make contributions to any religious, charitable, civic, or other causes or organizations established primarily for the public good." The FRL sued Lawson Lamar, the Florida state attorney, in district court in Florida, claiming that the law violated the organization's First Amendment right to free speech. The district court, however, upheld the law as constitutional under both the First and Fourteenth Amendments. The FRL appealed to the Court of Appeals for the Eleventh Circuit. Following arguments, the court handed down its decision on 28 November 2001. In striking down the decision, Judge Stanley Birch, speaking for a unanimous three-member court, wrote that § 106.08(5) plainly violated the First Amendment of the U.S. Constitution. He wrote:

> We have concluded that the plain language of § 106.08(5) creates a blanket rule forbidding political candidates from making any donations out of personal or campaign funds to an organization, unless one of the three exceptions applies. Florida concedes that if this is the proper interpretation of § 106.08(5), the provision is facially unconstitutional. Thus, we hold that § 106.08(5) is facially unconstitutional in that it infringes upon basic First and Fourteenth Amendment rights of expression and association held by organizations like FRL....
> In this appeal, we have concluded that § 106.08(5), Florida Statutes, cannot be narrowly construed in a manner that avoids constitutional infir-

mities. As a result, we have decided that the provision is facially unconstitutional under the First and Fourteenth Amendments. Accordingly, we REVERSE the district court's ruling that § 106.08(5) is susceptible to a narrowing construction that survives constitutional scrutiny, and we remand for further proceedings consistent with this opinion.

The case was not appealed to the U.S. Supreme Court.

References: *Florida Right to Life, Inc. v. Lamar,* 233 F. 3d 1288 (2001).

Fortas, Abraham (1919–1982)

Lawyer and jurist, associate justice of the United States Supreme Court (1965–1969), implicated in a financial scandal for which he was forced to resign from the Court. Born on 19 June 1919 in Nashville, Tennessee, he was the son of a Jewish cabinetmaker who had emigrated from England. He attended local schools in Memphis, working to enter Southwestern College in Memphis, from which he earned a bachelor's degree in 1930. In 1933 he graduated from the Yale Law School, having served during his law studies as the editor of the *Yale Law Review.* For four years after earning his law degree, Fortas taught at the Yale Law School. During this period, he also worked while on leave from Yale for the Agricultural Adjustment Administration (AAA), a New Deal agency established by President Franklin D. Roosevelt. When one of his law professors, William O. Douglas, was named to the Securities and Exchange Commission, Fortas went to work as one of his advisers. In 1938, when Douglas was named to the U.S. Supreme Court, Fortas became general counsel of the Public Works Administration. He moved over to the Department of the Interior, rising to become first director of the Division of Electric Power and then in 1942 undersecretary of the interior. In 1945 Fortas left the government and went to work for a private law firm, Arnold and Fortas. For many years, he practiced corporate law in Washington, D.C., defending numerous clients, including several McCarthy hearings suspects and Clarence Earl Gideon, whose appeal to the U.S. Supreme Court in *Gideon v. Wainwright* led the court to mandate legal counsel for all suspects, even indigent ones. One of his lesser-known clients was

Abe Fortas waits outside the Senate Judiciary Committee that is considering his nomination for Supreme Court Justice. Later Fortas was implicated in a financial scandal for which he was forced to resign from the court. (Library of Congress)

Lyndon Johnson, an up-and-coming Texas politician who retained Fortas as counsel for his 1948 Senate race. Because of Fortas's work for Johnson, the two men became close friends.

In 1960 Johnson was elected vice president, and Fortas became one of his closest advisers. On 22 November 1963, following the assassination of President John F. Kennedy, Johnson made his first official call as president to Fortas. He used Fortas to help name important Washington officials to the Warren Commission, headed by Supreme Court Chief Justice Earl Warren. In 1965, when the United States became caught up in the crisis in the Dominican Republic, it was Fortas who gave Johnson advice how to handle the emergency.

In 1964 Fortas refused Johnson's request to become attorney general. When Arthur Goldberg resigned from the U.S. Supreme Court to become the U.S. ambassador to the United Nations, Fortas again turned down his friend. Johnson wanted Fortas in the seat; he called his friend to the White House, told him he would be naming him to the seat whether Fortas wanted it or not. Fortas reluctantly accepted. Nominated on 28 July 1965, he was confirmed on 11 August 1965. In his three-plus years on the Court, Fortas became a reliable liberal vote, voting with the majority in the famed *Miranda* decision, which required police to read arrested suspects their rights, and in *Witherspoon v. Illinois,* which held that people who had a religious view against capital punishment could not be excluded from juries.

On 13 June 1968, Chief Justice Earl Warren sent his letter of resignation to President Johnson. Thirteen days later, Johnson named Fortas as his replacement and Judge Homer Thornberry of the U.S. Court of Appeals for the Fifth Circuit to replace Fortas as associate justice. If Fortas had been confirmed, he would have become the first Jew to serve as chief justice. Fortas's connections with Johnson (as well as Thornberry's longtime friendship with the president) made both of their nominations contentious. Nonetheless, Fortas appeared before the Senate Judiciary Committee for his confirmation hearing. Despite harsh questions from many Republicans on his liberal rulings on the Court, it appeared that Fortas had enough votes to gain confirmation.

However, it was not to be. That September, prior to a Senate vote on his nomination, Fortas's world came apart. A news source disclosed that month that Fortas had received some $15,000 a month in payments for teaching a course for nine weeks at the American University Law School in the summer of 1968. What made the payments suspicious was that they came not from the school, but through one of Fortas's former law partners from five businessmen, one of whom had a son involved in a criminal case before the federal courts. This story did not altogether stop Fortas's nomination: on 17 September, it was reported out of the Senate Judiciary Committee by a vote of eleven to six. However, a coalition of Republicans and conservative Democrats sought to block the nomination through a filibuster. When Democrats backing Fortas tried to end the debate by a cloture—or cutting off—motion, the motion failed, and Fortas's nomination was dead. Chief Justice Warren asked Fortas to withdraw his name from consideration, and he did, with Warren agreeing to remain on the Court until the new president could name his successor. Fortas remained on the court as an associate justice.

On 4 May 1969, *Life* magazine reporter William Lambert reported on another Fortas scandal. The journal disclosed that in January 1966 Fortas had accepted a payment of $300,000 from the foundation of Louis E. Wolfson, an industrialist. Fortas had returned the money that December after Wolfson was indicted on stock fraud charges. Fortas denied accepting the money from Wolfson for any other reason other than "research and writing services." He declared that he had not intervened for Wolfson in any federal proceeding relating to his criminal case. Despite Fortas's denials, members of Congress began to demand Fortas's resignation. On 11 May 1969, according to *Newsweek* magazine, Attorney General John Mitchell allegedly visited with Chief Justice Warren and warned him that the Department of Justice had uncovered even more damaging allegations, and that these would become public soon. Warren went to Fortas and told him that for the sake of the Court he needed to resign. Fortas did resign on 14 May, admitting that he had made an arrangement with Wolfson in 1965 to pay Fortas $20,000 a year for the rest of his life for unnamed services for the Wolfson Foundation. These services were never spelled out by Fortas, and he reiterated that he had returned the money in December 1966 as he had stated.

In his letter to Chief Justice Warren, Fortas wrote,

It is my opinion, however, that the public controversy relating to my association with the Foundation is likely to continue and adversely affect the work and position of the Court, absent my resignation. In these circumstances, it seems clear to me that it is not my duty to remain on the Court, but rather to resign in the hope that this will enable the Court to proceed with it vital work free from extraneous stress.

There has been no wrongdoing on my part. There has been no default in the performance of my judicial duties in accordance with the high standards of the office I hold. So far as I am concerned, the welfare and maximum effectiveness of the Court to perform its critical role in our system of government are factors that are paramount to all others. It is this consideration that prompts my resignation which, I hope, by terminating the public

controversy, will permit the Court to proceed with its work without the harassment of debate concerning one of its members.

Fortas thus became the first justice to resign from the Supreme Court under fire in the Court's 178-year history. On 20 May 1969 the American Bar Association's Committee on Professional Ethics determined that Fortas's conduct was against the canons of judicial ethics. Despite this, the Department of Justice never released any further information on Fortas and never prosecuted him for any crime.

Abe Fortas spent the remainder of his life as a disgraced lawyer, working in Washington, D.C. He died there of a ruptured aorta on 5 April 1982.

References: Abe Fortas Oral History Interview, Lyndon Baines Johnson Library, 14 August 1969; "Abe Fortas: Quit Supreme Court Under Public Pressure," in George C. Kohn, *Encyclopedia of American Scandal: From ABSCAM to the Zenger Case* (New York: Facts on File, 1989), 118–119; Greenhouse, Linda, "Ex-Justice Abe Fortas Dies at 71; Shaped Historic Rulings on Rights," *New York Times,* 7 April 1982, A1; Witt, Elder, *Congressional Quarterly's Guide to the U.S. Supreme Court* (1990), 874.

Foulke, William Dudley (1848–1935)

Lawyer and public official, noted for his work for political reform, including as a member of the National Civil Service Reform League (for which he served as president) and the Civil Service Commission. Foulke remains an obscure figure. What is known about him is that he was born in New York City on 20 November 1848 and apparently attended the local schools of New York. He earned a bachelor's degree from Columbia College (now Columbia University) in 1869 and two years later earned a law degree from the Columbia School of Law. He practiced law in New York City until 1876.

In 1876 Foulke moved to Richmond, Indiana, where he went to work as a corporate attorney for the Pittsburgh, Cincinnati & St. Louis Railroad. A Republican, Foulke was elected to a seat in the Indiana state senate in 1882 and served until 1886.

While in the Indiana state senate, Foulke became an advocate of civil service reform, at that time one of the leading issues. In 1885 he introduced a bill to establish a civil service system in

Indiana. At that time, he also established the Indiana Civil Service Reform Association and was named president of the organization. In 1886, after he left the state senate, he was named president of the American Woman Suffrage Association. He stopped practicing the law in 1889, spending the remainder of his life in the cause of reform. For the National Civil Service Reform League, he worked in 1889 and 1890 to investigate conditions in the federal civil service system. In 1901 he was named to the U.S. Civil Service Commission by President Theodore Roosevelt. In 1907 he was one of the key advocates behind a law that prohibited the solicitation of political contributions from employees in state offices, a precursor of the Hatch Act of 1939. After leaving the commission, he returned to Indiana, where he served as the editor of the *Evening Item,* a Republican newspaper that preached reform. In 1910 he was named president of the National Municipal League, serving until 1914.

In his last years, Foulke published a number of works, including *Fighting the Spoilsmen: Reminiscences of the Civil Service Reform Movement* (1919) and *A Hoosier Autobiography* (1922). From 1923 to 1924, he served as president of the National Civil Service Reform League. Until his death, he continued to speak on behalf of civil service reform.

Foulke died in Richmond, Indiana, on 30 May 1935 at the age of eighty-six.

References: William Dudley Foulke Papers (biographical note) Library of Congress, Washington, DC; "Foulke, William Dudley," in *The National Cyclopædia of American Biography,* 57 vols. and supplements A-N (New York: James T. White & Company, 1897–1984), XXVI:429–430.

G

Garcia, Robert (1933–)

United States representative from New York (1978–1990), implicated and convicted for his role in a kickback scandal after he took a $75,000 bribe. A rising star in the Democratic Party who was ironically elected to Congress as a Republican, Garcia was one of several congressmen brought down by allegations of corruption at the end of the 1980s and beginning of the 1990s. Born in the Bronx, in New York, on 9 January 1933, Garcia attended public schools in New York before attending the City College of New York (CCNY) in 1957. He also went to the Community College of New York that same year. In 1950 he had left school to volunteer with the Third Infantry Division of the U.S. Army, seeing action during the Korean War (1950–1953). After returning to the United States, Garcia completed his education. In 1957 he entered private business and worked as a computer engineer for several years.

In the 1960s increasing Hispanic political power and Garcia's growing interest in politics led him to run for and win a seat in the New York state assembly (1965–1966) and the New York state senate (1966–1978). A Democrat, he served as deputy minority leader in the state senate from 1975 to 1978. In 1978, following the resignation of Representative Herman Badillo of New York, Garcia threw his hat into the race to succeed him, but registered as a liberal Republican. He was elected on that ticket on 14 February 1978, but a week after he took his seat he reregistered as a Democrat. Garcia would later serve until his resignation on 7 January 1990.

Garcia was implicated, with his wife, in the so-called Wedtech scandal. He was indicted for demanding kickbacks from that company in exchange for his assistance in gaining federal contracts for it. Garcia was tried and convicted, and he resigned his office on 7 January 1990 before he could be sentenced. On appeal, his conviction was overturned. He was tried a second time and again convicted. However, this second conviction was also overturned, and in the end Garcia never served any prison time.

References: *Biographical Directory of the American Congress, 1774–1996* (Alexandria, VA: CQ Staff Directories, Inc., 1996); French, Howard W., "U.S. Says Mariotta Paid Garcia a $75,000 Bribe," *New York Times*, 19 July 1988, B3; Lynn, Frank, "Facing Sentencing, Rep. Garcia Resigns," *New York Times*, 3 January 1900, A1; U.S. House of Representatives, Committee on Standards of Official Conduct, "Summary of Activities" 101st Congress, House Report No. 101–995, 101st Congress, 2nd Session (1990) ("In the Matter of Representative Robert Garcia"), 12–13.

Garfield, James Abram (1831–1881)

U.S. representative from Ohio (1863–1880), twentieth president of the United States (1881), implicated, but never charged, in the Crédit Mobilier scandal. Garfield's discussion of political ethics

James A. Garfield, U.S. representative from Ohio (1863–1880) and twentieth president of the United States. During his time in Congress, Garfield was implicated, but never charged, in the Crédit Mobilier scandal. (Library of Congress)

and morality also attracts the interest of historians. Born in the town of Orange, Ohio, on 19 November 1831, Garfield attended local schools before becoming a driver and helmsman on the Ohio canal. As many people did in those days, Garfield entered a religious life, attending the Geauga Seminary in Chester, Ohio. However, he did not follow through with his religious studies and soon left to teach at a local district school. He continued his education, attending the Eclectic Institute in Hiram, Ohio, from 1851 to 1854, and graduating from Williams College in Williamstown, Massachusetts, in 1858. For a time he served as a professor of ancient languages and literature at Hiram College; from 1857 until 1861 he served as that college's president.

A Republican, Garfield entered the political realm in 1859 when he served as a member of the Ohio state senate. He left that office, however, to study law and was admitted to the Ohio state bar in 1860. When the Civil War began in 1861, Garfield volunteered for service in the Union army as a lieutenant colonel in the Forty-second Regiment of the Ohio Volunteer Infantry. He saw action at numerous battles, rising to the rank of major

general by the end of 1863, when he resigned his commission. In March 1863 he had been elected to a seat in the U.S. House of Representatives, but because he did not take his seat immediately he did not serve in the first part of the Thirty-eighth Congress. Garfield served in this seat from 5 December 1863 until he resigned on 8 November 1880, from the Thirty-eighth through the Forty-sixth Congresses. A leader in his party, Garfield served as a member of the Electoral Commission that decided the electoral vote count in the 1876 election between Republican Rutherford B. Hayes and Democrat Samuel Tilden.

In 1870 Garfield became involved in a famous exchange with Representative Ebon C. Ingersoll (R-IL) over the meaning of the word "ethical." The exchange came during the debate over a resolution to allow Democrat John Coggswell Conner of Texas to take his seat in the House. Conner had been accused of whipping and abusing black soldiers under his command in 1868 and the following year had bragged that he would be acquitted by a military court by bribing all the witnesses against him. Garfield, speaking on the House floor on 31 March 1870, said, "Allow me to ask . . . if anything in the Constitution of the United States . . . forbids that a 'moral monster' shall be elected to Congress?" Representative Ingersoll replied, "I believe that the people may elect a moral monster to Congress if they see fit, but I believe that Congress has a right to exclude that moral monster from a seat if they see fit." Nonetheless, Conner was allowed to take his seat.

During his time in Congress, Garfield apparently took money and other fees from several companies that did business before the Congress, including the Crédit Mobilier. Despite the fact that many congressmen and senators—including Garfield's fellow Republicans James G. Blaine and Schuyler Colfax—were politically ruined by the scandal, Garfield remained untouched, and even to this day his name is rarely mentioned in connection with these episodes. Historians have simply passed over his corruption.

In 1880 Garfield became the first—and, as of this writing, the last—man to be nominated to a seat in the U.S. Senate and at the same time for president of the United States. These days, few candidates for the presidency come from the U.S. House of Representatives, but in Garfield's day his leadership led his party to do just that, merging him on the party ticket with Chester A. Arthur, a little-known New York politician who had served in the customs office. Looking at the ticket from modern standards, it may have been perhaps the most inexperienced in the history of American politics. On 4 November 1880, Garfield was elected president and also won his Senate race, a seat he naturally declined to accept. He thus became the last man to be elected directly from the House of Representatives to the White House. His time in office was short—only six months. On 2 July 1881, while standing in a train station in Washington, D.C., he was shot by Charles J. Guiteau, a psychotic who felt that his assistance in the 1880 election was the key to Garfield's election and that he had not been remunerated properly for his work. Garfield, wounded seriously, clung to life, and after a few weeks was moved from the White House to a seaside town in New Jersey. There he died—more from the ineptitude of his physicians than from his wound, which could have been treated properly—on 19 September 1881, the second American president to be murdered.

References: Balch, William Ralston, *The Life of James Abram Garfield, Late President of the United States. The Record of a Wonderful Career* (New York: William H. Shepard, 1881); Conner exchange in "Congressional Ethics" (Washington, DC: Congressional Quarterly, 1980); Peskin, Allan, *Garfield: A Biography* (Kent, OH: Kent State University Press, 1999); Thayer, William Makepeace, *From Log-Cabin to the White House* (Boston: J. H. Earle, 1881).

Gaynor, William Jay (1848–1913)

Lawyer and politician, nominated by Tammany Hall for mayor of New York and then turned around and struck out against corruption, particularly against Tammany. He died from the effects of an assassination attempt. Born in Whitesboro, New York (some sources report it as being in Oneida, New York), on 2 February 1848, he was the son of a blacksmith and farmer. He attended two local religious academies—considered proper areas for higher learning—after which he entered the Roman Catholic order as a novice in 1863. For the next four years, he taught in religious schools in Baltimore and St. Louis. In 1868 Gaynor decided against life in the ministry and left it to pursue a career in the law, studying in Utica, New York, and being admitted to the New York state bar in 1871. He moved to Boston and may have practiced there. After what can be called a short stay in Boston, Gaynor again moved, this time to Brooklyn, New York, where he married about 1873. This marriage ended in divorce in 1881, and he remarried in 1886.

Despite having a law license, Gaynor worked in Brooklyn as a reporter for the *Brooklyn Argus* newspaper and, when that paper ended production, in the same capacity for *The Sun* of New York. Sometime in the 1870s, Gaynor did in fact return to the law and by the 1880s was a noted New York attorney. His most important contribution at this time was his stand for municipal reform and his outspoken lectures against political corruption, most notably that of the bosses from Tammany Hall, the leading New York political organization. Although he was a Democrat, Gaynor did not shy away from criticizing the corruption of officials who were fellow Democrats. Because of these stands, Gaynor's popularity rose and in 1893 running as a Republican, he was elected to the seat of justice of the New York state supreme court, then an elected office. He remained in this seat for twelve years. In 1905 Gaynor was named to the appellate division of the New York state supreme court. Despite being an outspoken advocate of reform in political life, he was critical of those he felt pushed reform too far, including social reformers.

By the middle of the first decade of the twentieth century, many saw Gaynor as a possible political candidate. However, to win in New York City, a candidate had to be supported by Tammany Hall, an organization that Gaynor had a long history of criticizing. However, by 1909 Tammany was in deep trouble. Years of scandal, from the Tweed Ring to incessant corruption inside the organization, led many in the group to look for a candidate who was "clean." Tammany chief Charles F. Murphy saw such a candidate in Gaynor, and he tapped the reformer to be the Tammany candidate for mayor in 1909. The combination of Gaynor's long record of reform and Tammany's political strength made his candidacy an attractive one. Because Tammany was a machine of the Democratic Party, the Republicans opposed him with Otto T. Bannard, an unknown banker who had a long record of being a supporter of charities. He had also served as a delegate to the Republican National

Convention in 1908. An independent group, The Civil Alliance, shying away from both parties, named *New York Journal* publisher William Randolph Hearst as their candidate. Hearst had once backed Gaynor, but turned on the reformer for allying himself with the hated Tammany Hall. The election was tight, but in the end Gaynor was victorious, capturing more than 250,000 votes, with Bannard in second with more than 177,000 and Hearst in third with nearly 154,000. Because Gaynor was running on a Tammany ticket, the forces of Bannard and Hearst elected much of the ticket below Gaynor, making Gaynor the only Tammany candidate to win.

Immediately, Gaynor set to work to implement his reformist agenda, angering many in Tammany who saw him as a pliant tool. He set the stage at the beginning of his tenure: on 1 January 1910, inauguration day, he walked from his home in Brooklyn to City Hall in Lower Manhattan. About 1,500 people were assembled to hear him take the oath of office. He told the crowd, "I enter upon this office with the intention of doing the very best I can for the City of New York. That will have to suffice; I can do no more." Starting with hiring, Gaynor filled city offices not with Tammany-approved candidates but with civil service workers, ending patronage. Political abuses that involved the subways were ended when he refused to expand the system, thereby ending debate. Although historians who have examined his plan for reform almost unanimously consider him a failure as a mayor, nonetheless his ideas for reform and his stands against his former allies at Tammany made him immensely popular. There were calls for his nomination for governor of New York in 1910 and whispers that he would be a leading candidate for the 1912 Democratic presidential nomination.

This talk all ended on 9 August 1910. Gaynor was boarding a ship to go on a European vacation, when a disgruntled dock worker, James J. Gallagher, shot Gaynor in the throat. Although the wound was not fatal, Gaynor's health was compromised, and future political plans were ended. It took two months for Gaynor to recover from his wounds, after which he returned to office. The bullet remained in his throat, never to be removed, and caused a decline in his health. His final two years were spent battling forces that either wanted no reform or reforms Gaynor could not support.

In 1913 Gaynor was not renominated for mayor by either Tammany or the Republicans, although an independent group did name him as their mayoral candidate. Six days after he was nominated, Gaynor was on board the steamship *Baltic* on his way to another European vacation when he suddenly died of a heart attack, believed brought on by the bullet wound he never fully recovered from. Dead at sixty-five, Gaynor was buried in the Greenwood Cemetery in Brooklyn near his home.

References: Cerillo, Augustus, Jr. "Gaynor, William Jay," in John A. Garraty and Mark C. Carnes, gen. eds., *American National Biography,* 24 vols. (New York: Oxford University Press, 1999), 8:816–817; Pink, Louis Heaton, *Gaynor, the Tammany Mayor Who Swallowed the Tiger: Lawyer, Judge, Philosopher* (New York: International Press, 1931); Smith, Mortimer Brewster, *William Jay Gaynor, Mayor of New York* (Chicago: H. Regnery Co. 1951).

Gilbert, William Augustus (1815–1875)

U.S. representative from New York (1855–1857), accused of corruption and the subject of an expulsion hearing in the House in 1857. Born in Gilead, Connecticut, on 25 January 1815, William Gilbert moved with his parents to Champion, New York. He attended the public schools in that town, afterwards studying the law, and was admitted to the New York bar in 1843. He opened a practice in Adams, New York. Gilbert served as a member of the New York state assembly in 1851 and 1852.

In 1854 Gilbert was elected as a Whig to a seat in the U.S. House of Representatives, representing the Twenty-third New York District. He entered the Thirty-fourth Congress, serving from 4 March 1855 until his resignation on 27 February 1857. Apparently, Gilbert became embroiled in some degree of political corruption. However, the record is vague and does not explain what Gilbert's true crime was. He was brought to the bar of the House along with several other House members, including William W. Welch, Orsamus B. Matteson, and Francis S. Edwards, all of whom were accused of corruption and censured in 1857. *Hinds' Precedents* explains the record of the investigation into Gilbert and the others:

On February 19, 1857, the committee made several reports affecting severally the following Members: William A. Gilbert, of New York; William W. Welch, of Connecticut; Francis S. Edwards, of New York, and Orsamus B. Matteson, of New York. Each report was accompanied by resolutions for the expulsion of the Member. Mr. [William Henry] Kelsey [of New York] submitted a minority report, in which he dissented from the several reports on the ground that, according to the rules of the House and parliamentary law, the committee had no power to institute proceedings against any Member of the body under the resolution by which the committee was appointed. He quoted the rule of Jefferson's Manual: "When a committee is charged with an inquiry, if a Member prove to be involved, they can not proceed against him, but must make a special report to the House; whereupon the Member is heard in his place, or at the bar, or a special authority is given to the committee to inquire concerning him."

In their replies the accused Members insisted on this rule, quoting the opinions expressed at the time of the investigation of the Graves-Cilley duel. They also insisted that, as they had not been present when the testimony against them was given, they had been deprived of the proper opportunities for confronting their accusers. When the case of Mr. Gilbert was taken up in the House, on February 25, these objections of the accused were considered at length. It was urged by Mr. Schuyler Colfax, of Indiana, among others, that the accused should not be expelled without a public trial at the bar of the House. Mr. Samuel A. Purviance, of Pennsylvania, moved this resolution as an amendment to the resolutions of expulsion: "Resolved, That this House will forthwith proceed with the trial of Hon. W. A. Gilbert, and that the Sergeant-at-Arms be directed to summon F. F. C. Triplett, James R. Sweeney, and other witnesses to the bar of the House; and that the said Gilbert be heard by himself or counsel."

Mr. Henry Winter Davis spoke at length in defense of the procedure of the committee, and cited as a controlling precedent the action of the Senate in the case of John Smith in 1807, quoting the entire report of Mr. John Quincy Adams in that case. He also quoted the precedents in the [Preston] Brooks case in the House. Mr. Purviance's resolution was disagreed to on February 27 by a vote of 110 nays to 82 yeas. The resolutions of expulsion were then considered, and Mr. Gilbert, by unanimous consent, addressed the House, and concluded his remarks by sending to the Clerk's desk to be read a paper in which he protested against the action of the House, impeached the proceedings, and finally announced that he resigned his seat in the House. Mr. James L. Seward, of Georgia, protested against the putting of the paper in the Journal. The Speaker said:

"The paper will not go upon the Journal unless by direct order of the House. The only thing that will appear on the Journal will be the fact stated by the Member from New York, in his place, that he resigned his seat as a Member of this House."

Mr. Gilbert having resigned, the resolutions of expulsion, which recited also the charges, were laid on the table.

Gilbert thus became one of only a handful of representatives to be censured by the House in the history of that body.

After leaving Congress, Gilbert returned to New York, where he served as president of the village of Adams in 1859 and 1860, thereafter working in the banking business. He died in Adams on 25 May 1875 at the age of sixty and was buried in the Rural Cemetery in that town.

References: *Biographical Directory of the American Congress, 1774–1996* (Alexandria, VA: CQ Staff Directories, Inc., 1996), 1090; Hinds, Asher Crosby, *Hinds' Precedents of the House of Representatives of the United States, Including References to Provisions of the Constitution, the Laws, and Decisions of the United States Senate,* 8 vols. (Washington, DC: Government Printing Office, 1907–1908), II:833–836; United States Congress, House, Joint Committee on Congressional Operations, *House of Representatives Exclusion, Censure and Expulsion Cases from 1789 to 1973,* 93rd Congress, 1st Session (Washington, DC: Government Printing Office, 1973).

Goebel, William (1856–1900)

Governor of Kentucky (1900), assassinated by political opponents in a bid to hold the power of the state. Few historians note the name of Goebel, the only state executive ever assassinated in the history of the United States. He was born in Sullivan County, Pennsylvania, on 4 January 1856, the son of German parents who had emigrated to the United States. He received little primary education, but worked as a jeweler's apprentice, then studied the law under former Governor John W. Stevenson before he went to the Cincinnati Law School and graduated in 1877. Goebel's father had fought in the Civil War; soon after, he moved his family from Pennsylvania to Kentucky, where Goebel grew up. Despite the fact that his father had fought in the Civil War and was a vigorous opponent of slavery, William Goebel became a Democrat in the years after the war. He joined Stevenson's law firm in Kentucky (of whom future Secretary of the Treasury and Speaker of the House John G. Carlisle was also a member) and, in 1887, was elected to the Kentucky state senate. William Goebel was a strong partisan Democrat: in 1895, he challenged one of his political enemies, John Stanford, to a duel and shot the man dead. Although he was never charged with a crime, Goebel earned the wrath of many in the state. He rose to become the leader in the state senate, with Democrats in firm control.

In 1898 Goebel, anticipating a run for the governorship, pushed through the legislature the so-called Goebel Election Law, an enactment that established a Board of Election Commissions named by the senate leader—Goebel—whose sole duty was to judge the fairness of all gubernatorial elections. Governor William O. Bradley, a Republican, vetoed the measure, but Goebel cobbled together enough Democrats to override the veto in both houses. Many conservative Democrats and Republicans opposed Goebel and saw him as a ruthless dictator, hell-bent on winning the governorship at all costs.

In 1899 Goebel used all of his power to get the Democrats' nomination for governor. However, in doing so he angered enough old-line Democrats that they bolted from the regular party and formed the Honest Election League, a third party. The Republicans nominated William S. Taylor, the state attorney general. The election that year was close—a margin of approximately 2,400 votes separated the men. It was so close, in fact, that the contest was thrown before Goebel's own Board of Election Commissioners, all handpicked by Goebel himself. Thus, the people of Kentucky were shocked when the board reported that Taylor, and not Goebel, had been elected as governor. Taylor was inaugurated as the second Republican to head the state.

Goebel, however, was not satisfied. The Democratic majority in the lower house, the general assembly, voted to initiate an investigation into whether Taylor had committed fraud in his victory. Ignoring any sense of justice, the Democrats named a panel with ten of the eleven members being Democrats. Republican outrage boiled over when it was learned that the committee would immediately throw out enough ballots to swing what had been a close election to Goebel, vacate the

election's first results, and name William Goebel, and not William Taylor, as governor of Kentucky.

On 20 January 1900, Goebel and two supporters marched toward the general assembly to accept the committee's findings that he should be the governor. As he approached the building, shots rang out, and Goebel fell to the sidewalk, mortally wounded. The bullet had slammed into his chest at a downward angle, ripping through his lung and lodging in his spine. Governor Taylor called out the militia and ordered the general assembly to disband to a safer location. When Democrats refused, Taylor ordered the militia to bar the doors to prevent their meeting there. The Democrats then moved to a local hotel where, without any Republicans present, they accepted the lopsided panel's recommendation and declared on 31 January 1900 that William Goebel was the rightful governor of the state. Democratic leaders in the state House and Senate went to Goebel's bedside and had him sworn in as the state's thirty-third governor. Mortally wounded, Goebel ordered that the militia disband and that the legislature reassemble in their normal place. When this militia refused to move from the places that Governor Taylor had placed them, Goebel supporters established their own militia and faced the official militia head on. For nearly a month, Republicans refused to accept Goebel as governor, and Democrats accepted Goebel as the state's chief executive. Kentucky came close to a repeat of the civil war that had torn the state asunder less than forty years earlier.

On 3 February 1900, William Goebel succumbed to his wounds after serving as governor for only three days. He thus became the first, and so far only, governor in American history to die at the hands of an assassin. Governor Taylor was ordered to be arrested on charges of conspiracy to commit murder, but he fled to Indiana before the arrest could be done, and Lieutenant Governor John Crepps Wickliffe Beckham, a Democrat, became the governor of Kentucky. (In a side story, Republicans refused to allow Beckham to serve in the governor's mansion, taking the case to the U.S. Supreme Court, which refused to act in May 1900, forcing Republicans to back down and allow Beckham to serve as governor.) Seven Taylor supporters were arrested and charged with the murder, including Caleb Powers, the state secretary of state (who was initially sentenced to death before his sentence was reduced to life). Two of the men were eventually convicted of the murder, and five others, including Powers, were convicted of conspiracy. On 13 June 1908, Governor Augustus E. Willson pardoned Taylor (who had become a wealthy executive in Indiana) and Powers for any role they might have played in the Goebel murder. In 1909 he pardoned all of the remaining conspirators save for one, Henry Youtsey, whom Willson stated was the actual murderer of Goebel. Powers later ran for a seat in the U.S. House of Representatives, serving four terms from 1911 to 1917. Taylor died in Indiana in 1928, never returning to Kentucky.

References: "Goebel, William," in Robert Sobel and John Raimo, eds., *Biographical Directory of the Governors of the United States, 1789–1978*, 4 vols. (Westport, CT: Meckler Books, 1978), III:534; Klotter, James C., *William Goebel: The Politics of Wrath* (Lexington: University Press of Kentucky, 1977); Powers, Caleb, *My Own Story: An Account of the Conditions in Kentucky Leading to the Assassination of William Goebel, Who Was Declared Governor of the State, and My Indictment and Conviction on the Charge of Complicity in His Murder, by Caleb Powers* (Indianapolis: Bobbs-Merrill Company, 1905); Short, Jim, *Caleb Powers and the Mountain Army: The Story of a Statesman from Eastern Kentucky* (Olive Hill, KY: Jessica Publications, 1997).

Gore, Albert Arnold, Jr. (1948–)

United States representative (1977–1985) and U.S. senator from Tennessee (1985–1993), vice president of the United States (1993–2001), implicated but never charged in the campaign finance scandal of the 1996 campaign, in which he claimed that "no controlling legal authority" had power over his decision to make campaign phone calls from his office. Born in Washington, D.C., on 31 March 1948, Gore is the son of Albert Arnold Gore Sr., who served Tennessee as a U.S. representative (1939–1944, 1945–1953) and U.S. senator (1953–1971), and Pauline (née LaFon) Gore. Albert Gore Sr. had already served eight years in Congress before Albert Jr. was born, and in 1952 he was elected to the U.S. Senate, where he soon became, with Senator Estes Kefauver, one of the powerhouses of Tennessee politics. His son grew up in privilege, attending private schools (including St. Albans School) and staying in the Washington, D.C., hotel where his father lived. He entered Harvard University and graduated in 1969 with a bachelor's de-

gree in government. His father, an opponent of the Vietnam War, was in deep political trouble with his constituents in Tennessee, so his son, straight out of college, volunteered for service in the U.S. Army in Vietnam. The junior Gore saw no action (he was in fact a reporter for the U.S. Army publication *Stars and Stripes* and spent much of his time in the South Vietnamese capital, Saigon), and he returned home after four months to assist in his father's reelection attempt in 1970. When the senior Gore lost to Republican Bill Brock, his son felt destroyed by the loss and turned to his first love, journalism. Thus, when a close family friend, John Siegenthaler, editor of the *Tennessean*, the main newspaper in Nashville, offered him a position as a reporter, Gore took it. While working at the paper, Gore also studied philosophy at the Vanderbilt University School of Religion from 1971 to 1972 and at that college's school of law from 1974 to 1976.

In 1976 Gore entered the political realm and won a seat in the U.S. House of Representatives as a Democrat representing Tennessee's Fourth District. He served in the Ninety-fifth through Ninety-eighth Congresses, from 3 January 1977 to 3 January 1985. In 1984 he have up his seat to run for the U.S. Senate vacancy left by the resignation of Senator Howard Baker, who had become chief of staff to President Ronald Reagan. Gore won the seat easily, beating Republican Victor Ashe, and he soon became a leader in such areas as environmental issues and national security. In 1988, just four years into his Senate term, and at the age of only forty-three, Gore made then huge leap to run for the Democratic presidential nomination. His relative youth and inexperience in national affairs, however, cost him, and he won only five southern states overall at the Democratic National Convention. The nomination went to Massachusetts Governor Michael Dukakis. Gore remained in the Senate, winning reelection in 1990. It seemed as if he would make another run for the White House in 1992, but he announced early in that campaign that he would decline to run because his son had been critically injured in a car accident. That year he authored *Earth in the Balance: Healing the Global Environment,* in which he called for a government aid program to change the way the world was allegedly abusing the environment. "I have come to believe that we must

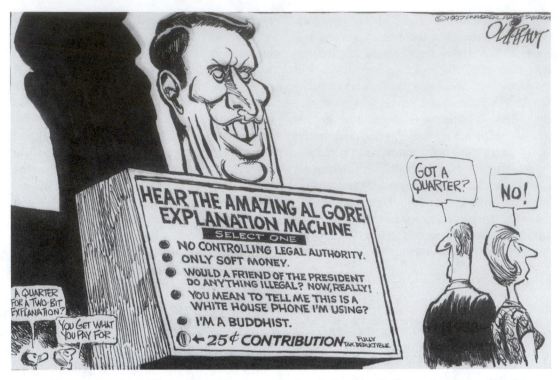

A man and woman pass a bust of Vice President Al Gore atop an "explanation" machine; for 25 cents the machine will explain fundraising calls made during the 1996 presidential campaign. (Library of Congress)

take bold and unequivocal action," he wrote. "We must make the rescue of the environment the central organizing principle for civilization."

When Governor Bill Clinton of Arkansas won the Democratic presidential nomination in 1992, he selected Gore as his running mate, defying political wisdom—one usually selects a running mate from another part of the country or from a different political persuasion within one's party—and launching the ticket to success in defeating President George Bush. Gore became one of the most important vice presidents in modern history, helping to push the North American Free Trade Agreement (NAFTA) through Congress and becoming a leader in environmental policy inside the administration. Following Clinton's reelection victory in 1996, it was considered a given that Gore would try for his party's presidential nomination in 2000, and as the incumbent vice president, he was favored against inconsequential opposition inside the Democratic Party.

What got Al Gore in trouble were campaign finance improprieties he committed during the 1996 campaign. During that contest, Gore used a

White House phone in his vice presidential office to call contributors, a violation of the Hatch Act. Gore also told these contributors that the money they contributed would go not to the Clinton/Gore campaign, which would be so-called hard money, but to the Democratic Party, and thus would be so-called soft money. In fact, it was later learned that a large portion of these funds found their way into the Clinton/Gore official campaign account, again a violation of campaign finance laws. Gore also made the calls using a credit card—although he later said that this was a Democratic National Committee credit card, papers given to the Senate Governmental Affairs Committee related that this was in fact a Clinton/Gore 1996 credit card. Gore told reporters that he made about forty-eight calls—evidence later showed that it was seventy-five.

Gore was also implicated in the foreign money scandal that enveloped the Clinton campaign—millions of dollars from foreign sources, particularly Chinese, flowed into the Democratic coffers, violative of campaign finance laws. Gore, while in California, had visited the Hsi Lai Buddhist temple on 29 April 1996, where he had received illegal campaign contributions from nuns who had taken a vow of poverty. On 22 October 1996, prior to the election, Gore tried to quiet critics of this fundraiser by saying he thought at the time that it was "community outreach."

On 3 March 1997, amid the uproar over the calls and their implications for his potential presidential campaign, Gore held a hastily called press conference at the White House to explain his situation. In the parley, Gore brought more controversy onto himself when he said that "no controlling legal authority" proscribed the kind of calling he had done. The phrase would haunt him later:

> My counsel advises me that there is no controlling legal authority or case that says that there was any violation of law whatsoever in the manner in which I asked people to contribute to our reelection campaign. I have decided to adopt a policy of not making any such calls ever again, notwithstanding the fact that they are charged to the Democratic National Committee as a matter of policy. We're continuing our review of this matter, and I think the entire episode constitutes further reasons why there should be campaign finance reform. The President and I strongly support campaign finance reform, and we hope it is adopted.

The commotion over Gore's apparent dismissal of the seriousness of the charges against him and the Clinton/Gore 1996 campaign led to pressure on the Department of Justice and the Senate Government Affairs Committee to open simultaneous investigations. On 3 September 1997, Attorney General Janet Reno announced that the Department of Justice would open what is called a "preliminary review" of the charges against Gore. Under the Independent Counsel Law then in effect, the attorney general then had thirty days to determine whether the charges were "specific and credible," and if so, to ask to have an independent counsel named. Eventually, she decided against calling for an independent counsel, earning great enmity from Republicans who saw her decision as covering for fellow Democrat Gore.

As the 2000 election neared, more controversy dogged Gore. A special investigator hired by the Department of Justice to look into the campaign finance controversy, Robert J. Conrad Jr., interviewed Gore in his office on 18 April 1998. In the interview, Gore appeared belligerent and gave inconsistent answers regarding all of the controversies. With respect to the Buddhist temple fundraiser, Gore said, "I sure as hell don't recall having—I sure as hell did not have any conversations with anyone saying 'This is a fund-raising event.'" Conrad asked him, "You were aware in late February [1998], were you not, that there was a goal of raising $108 million by the DNC [Democratic National Committee]?" Gore answered, "Yes." "Then, a couple of months later, there is a DNC-sponsored event at the temple, and it didn't raise any fund-raising issues in your mind?" "I did not know it was a fundraiser," Gore answered. On 23 August 2000, Reno decided for the third time not to name an independent counsel to investigate Gore. In her press conference giving her reasons for the decision, she said, "The transcript [between Gore and Conrad] reflects neither false statements nor perjury . . . I've concluded that there is no reasonable possibility that further investigation would produce evidence to warrant charges." *The Economist* wrote at the time, "He was so deeply involved in the campaign-finance scandals of 1996 that he was widely known as the 'solicitor-in-chief,' hosting 23 White House 'coffees,' phoning more than 50 potential donors and even writing a memo volunteering to do more of the same."

Gore's apparent lack of truth-telling may have cost him the votes of many who had once supported him and Clinton. (In May 2001, a think tank released a report showing that an analysis of polling numbers done during the 2000 campaign showed that Gore's numbers dropped because people did not believe he was telling them the truth.) Despite having won the popular vote, Gore lost the presidential election in the electoral college. He conceded defeat and on 20 January 2001, he left office and was out of politics for the first time since 1977. Gore went on to teach at several universities and as of this writing has only begun to reenter politics, speaking out on environmental and other issues. In June 2002 he criticized his own 2000 campaign, blaming his loss on "handlers" and "pollsters." He claimed that if he ran for president again, he would just "let 'er rip." Gore was considered already a candidate for his party's 2004 presidential nomination, but he pulled out of the campaign in December 2002.

References: Baker, Peter, "White House Seeks to Protect Gore in Temple Inquiry," *Washington Post*, 3

September 1997, A1; Cockburn, Alexander, *Al Gore: A User's Manual* (London: Verso, 2000); Dionne, E. J., and William Kristol, eds., *Bush v. Gore: The Court Cases and the Commentary* (Washington, DC: Brookings Institution Press, 2001); "In Search of the Real Man," *The Economist*, 356:8183 (12 August 2000), 22–24; Marcus, Ruth, "GOP Hits Gore on Temple Fund-Raiser, Senate Draft Report Accuses Democrats of Violating Campaign Laws," *Washington Post*, 10 February 1998, A1; Zelnick, Bob, *Gore: A Political Life* (Washington, DC: Regnery Publishing, 1999).

Grover, La Fayette (1823–1911)

Governor of Oregon (1870–1877), United States senator from Oregon (1877–1883), implicated but never charged in a vote-rigging scheme to throw the presidency to Democrat Samuel Tilden in the controversial 1876 presidential election. Born in Bethel, Maine, on 29 November 1823, La Fayette Grover was the son of John Grover, a wealthy manufacturer and Maine politician who served as a member of the Maine state constitutional convention and later in that state's legislature. Despite his wealth, La Fayette Grover attended what were called "common" schools (usually those schools that were not specialized academies), although he did receive some schooling at the prestigious Gould's Academy in Maine. He entered Bowdoin College in Maine in 1844, but after two years he departed without a degree. Settling in Philadelphia, Grover studied law in the offices of a local attorney, Asa Fish, and attended legal orations and addresses at the Philadelphia Law Academy. He was admitted to the Pennsylvania bar in 1850.

In 1850 Grover gave up a growing law practice and moved west to Oregon. A fellow Maine politician, Samuel Thurston, had himself moved to Oregon, was in charge of the Democratic Party apparatus in the new territory, and offered Grover a chance to start in the formation of a new state party. Grover had intended to start a law practice with Thurston, but shortly after Grover arrived in Salem, Thurston unexpectedly died. In 1851 Grover was named clerk of the U.S. district court in Salem and within a year became the prosecuting attorney for the city, as well as serving as the auditor of public accounts for the entire territory. During a series of wars against Indian tribes in the area, Grover served as a recruiter for militia soldiers. After the war, Grover was named a legal expert to settle claims by white homesteaders who had been attacked by these Indian tribes. In 1853 he entered the political realm, serving the first of two (1853, 1855) terms in the territorial legislature. In 1854 he was named by the Department of the Interior to serve as a special commissioner to inspect the spoliation claims that arose from the Rogue River Indian War. In 1857 he served as a delegate to the state constitutional convention, where he assisted in the drafting of a bill of rights for the citizens of Oregon. In 1859, when Oregon was admitted to the union, Grover became the state's first congressman. However, because of the timing of the admission of the state and when congressmen were to be sent to Washington, Grover served only seventeen days before his single term ended. A different faction in the Democratic Party, led by Joseph Lane, prevented Grover's renomination to a second term. He left public life, returning to the practice of the law and investing in the Willamette Woolen Mills, a major concern and one of the new state's largest enterprises.

In 1870 Grover was elected governor of Oregon, defeating Republican Joel Palmer in a narrow victory. Grover was reelected in 1874 and ultimately served from 14 September 1870 until 1 February 1877. He left office on 1 February 1877 when he resigned, having been elected to the United States Senate. He entered the Senate on 4 March 1877 and served until the end of his term on 3 March 1883. Even before he took his seat, his political enemies both in Oregon and Washington accused him of working illegally to secure Oregon's electoral votes for Democrat Samuel Tilden in the controversial 1876 election. On election night of that contest, it appeared that Tilden had edged out Republican Rutherford B. Hayes by winning several small states, including Oregon and Louisiana. However, Hayes contested the election, and an Electoral Commission, composed of representatives, senators, and members of the U.S. Supreme Court, went over each contested state and decided the election in the end for Hayes. When Grover took his seat, it was alleged that he had used illegal means, such as the certification of votes known to be illegal and the illegal delivery of voting lists, to push the state's electoral votes for Tilden. One of the leaders behind the movement to deny Grover his seat was Senator John Hipple Mitchell, who was to become Oregon's senior senator. Mitchell presented a petition from the citizens of Oregon demanding that Grover be denied his seat. (Ironically, Mitchell would later be implicated in a land fraud scheme in Oregon, and would be convicted before his death in 1905.) Grover demanded an investigation into the charges in an attempt to clear his name.

On 15 June 1878, the Committee on Privileges and Elections, after a year-long investigation, released its report, exonerating Grover of all charges. Had he been found guilty, Grover would have been expelled. Instead, he retained his seat, and finished his term in 1883, after which he returned to the practice of law. Grover died on 10 May 1911 at the age of eighty-seven.

See also Mitchell, John Hipple

References: *Biographical Directory of the American Congress, 1774–1996* (Alexandria, VA: CQ Staff Directories, Inc., 1996), 1130–1131; Butler, Anne M., and Wendy Wolff, *United States Senate Election, Expulsion and Censure Cases, 1793–1990* (Washington, DC: Government Printing Office, 1995), 211–212; Higgens-Evenson, R. Rudy, "Grover, La Fayette," in John A. Garraty and Mark C. Carnes, gen. eds., *American National Biography,* 24 vols. (New York: Oxford University Press, 1999), 9:672–673.

Grunewald, Henry W.
See King, Cecil Rhodes

H

Hague, Frank (1876–1956)

Mayor of Jersey City, New Jersey (1917–1947), accused but never convicted of wholesale corruption, allegations that forced his ouster from a seat on the Democratic National Committee (DNC). Born in Jersey City, New Jersey, on 17 January 1876, Hague was the son of Irish immigrants. Hague grew up in poverty and had little education, leaving public school when he had finished only the sixth grade. He then worked in a series of odd jobs, including as a prizefighter.

From the time of Hague's birth, Jersey City was, like many other large American cities at the end of the nineteenth century, a bastion ruled by immigrants—in Jersey City's case, Irish immigrants like Hague's parents. Jersey City was also a one-party town, and for any up-and-coming politician it was a necessity to be a Democrat or forget political advancement. Hague entered the political arena in 1889, running for constable in the Second Ward of the city. He advanced slowly up the ladder of the Democratic Party.

In 1913 Jersey City established a commission form of city government. Hague, running as a reformer, was elected to one of the commission seats. He spent much of his term working to expose police corruption. He also opposed Mayor Mark Fagan, the lone Republican elected in the city. In 1917 Hague opposed Fagan for mayor and, with the backing of the Democratic machine, was elected. Hague was reelected every four years until he left office after thirty years in power. As mayor, Hague built a huge political machine. In 1919 his candidate for governor, Edward I. Edwards, was easily elected. In 1922, when Hague was elected to a seat on the Democratic National Committee (DNC), he became the most important politician in New Jersey. That same year, he decided to have Edwards run for a U.S. Senate seat, which Edwards won with Hague's help. Hague then handpicked George S. Silzer to be Edwards's successor as governor of New Jersey. Silzer was easily elected. In 1924 Hague became vice chairman of the DNC.

At the presidential level, Hague was also a force to be reckoned with. He backed the candidacy of Governor Alfred E. Smith of New York in 1928, but four years later moved away from Smith and backed Smith's rival, Governor Franklin Delano Roosevelt of New York, for president. Roosevelt's election brought Hague even more power. Although his candidates lost the gubernatorial elections of 1928 and 1934—to Morgan F. Larson and Harold Hoffman, respectively—Hague did help in electing Democrats A. Harry Moore and Charles Edison to the governorship. The election of these latter two men allowed Hague to avoid prosecution for various corruption charges. Hague's absolute wielding of power in Jersey City led to investigations by state officials. In 1937 Hague told a reporter that "I am the law"—as to payoffs, bribes, and other allegations. Fortunately for Hague, he was able to fend off these inquiries by using his influence. Historian Robert Fishman wrote,

> Protected from investigation, Hague never scrupled to hide a lifestyle that bore no relationship to his mayor's salary, which never exceeded $7,500 [a year]: a fourteen-room duplex in Jersey City's most fashionable apartment house; a grand summer house at the Jersey shore; and rented villas every winter in Miami or Palm Beach. Tall, well dressed, imperious, he lived like a millionaire but never lost the swagger and grammar of the slums.

Hague did lose a case in federal court in 1939 when an ordinance he had passed banning certain speech was set aside, but this was his only defeat in the court of law.

During the New Deal economic recovery program of President Franklin Roosevelt, millions of dollars in federal monies were funneled into Jersey City through Hague's office, and it is alleged he siphoned off some of that money for himself and his cronies to hold on to power. However, because he was never indicted or formally tried for any crime, allegations against Hague must remain that—allegations.

The end of Hague's reign of power began in 1941, when Governor Charles Edison pushed through a series of judicial and constitutional reforms that crushed Hague's power. Hague persisted in allowing the Irish to hold the power Jersey City, pushing out other growing minorities. In 1947, facing a rupture in his machine, Hague suddenly quit and gave the office to his nephew, Frank Hague Eggers. However, this set off an interparty struggle, and in 1949 John V. Kenny, commissioner of the Second Ward, put together a ticket of disaffected Democrats and Republicans and won a majority of commission seats. When Republican Alfred E. Driscoll was elected governor of New Jersey in 1947 and reelected in 1949, Hague saw the change in power and resigned as Democratic leader in the state. In 1952 he resigned as the DNC's national committeeman and vice chairman.

In 1953 Hague attempted a comeback, trying to back Democrat Elmer Wene for governor—Wene lost in the Democratic primary—and failed to lodge John V. Kenny from leading the Jersey City commission. Frank Hague Eggers's death in July 1954 put an end to Hague's career. He died unremembered in New York City on 1 January 1956, three weeks shy of his eightieth birthday.

References: Connors, Richard J., "Hague, Frank," in Allen Johnson and Dumas Malone, et al., eds., *Dictionary of American Biography,* X vols. and 10 supplements (New York: Charles Scribner's Sons, 1930–1995), 6:265–266; Fishman, Robert, "Hague, Frank," in John A. Garraty and Mark C. Carnes, gen. eds., *American National Biography,* 24 vols. (New York: Oxford University Press, 1999), 9:794–795; McKean, Dayton, *The Boss: The Hague Machine in Action* (New York: Houghton Mifflin, 1940).

Hall, Abraham Oakey (1826–1898)

Mayor of New York City (1868–1872), known as "Boss Tweed's Mayor," tried but acquitted for his role in the Tweed Ring scandals. Known as A. Oakey Hall, he was born in Albany, New York, on 26 July 1826, the son of an English immigrant, Morgan James Hall, who had come to America and settled in upstate New York. There, he married Elsie Lansing Oakey, the daughter of Abraham Oakey, a former state treasurer for the state of New York. In 1830 Morgan Hall died, leaving his widow with two children. She moved to New York City, where her elder son, Abraham, attended local schools and then went to New York University. After graduating in 1844, he went to the Harvard Law School, but after one year at that institution he departed, instead going to New Orleans where he was privately tutored in the law. In 1846 Hall was admitted to the Louisiana bar, and, returning to New York City, opened a law practice with one Aaron J. Vanderpool. In a short time, Hall became a prosperous attorney.

In 1849 Hall was named assistant district attorney for the city and three years later was elected district attorney, holding the office from 1852 until 1860. Although he had been elected as a Republican, Hall became disenchanted with the way he felt the Republicans were harming civil liberties to fight the Civil War, and soon after the war began he switched to the Democratic Party. In 1864 he joined Tammany Hall, then dominating New York politics with a combination of largesse and greed. Just four years after joining Tammany, Hall was nominated as the Tammany candidate for mayor. He defeated Colonel F. A. Conkling by getting over 75,000 of 96,000 votes cast to become mayor. During his tenure, which lasted until 1872, Hall became an integral member of the "Tweed" Ring, run by state senator and Tammany leader William M. Tweed. With Hall's signature on all city documents, he was able to orchestrate a program of corruption and graft unseen in American history then or since. Millions upon millions of dollars were siphoned off from the city budget, landing in the pockets of Tweed or his associates. It is unknown whether Hall himself profited from Tweed's corruption. Historian George Kohn wrote:

> The Tweed Ring, which began operation in 1866, was the first modern city machine in New York, and Tweed was the nation's first real 'boss.' He and his colleagues Peter Sweeny (city chamberlain), Oakey Hall (mayor of New York), and Richard Connolly (city comptroller) comprised the inner circle of the ring that dominated New York City politics for the next five years. Though Tweed's Tammany Hall never proposed a broad remedy to New York's enormous problems of poverty, education, and housing, his ring gained the support of immigrants by giving them patronage jobs, of Catholics by giving city and state money for parochial schools and private charities, and of workers by encouraging unions to organize and allowing them to strike.

By 1871 questions began to rise regarding city finances, and Republicans and writers for the *New York Times* began to look into the situation with earnest. Soon, stories of vast corruption were being aired, and Hall did not run for a second term. Instead, he was tried twice—a mistrial in the first trial led to a second, where mysteriously he was acquitted of all charges in October 1872.

Hall did not return to politics or the law—instead, he spent several years trying to be an actor on the stage. When his first wife died in 1897, Hall married a widow, Mrs. John Clifton. Just seven months after he wed, on 7 October 1898, Hall collapsed and died from heart failure at the age of seventy-two. He was buried in the Hall family vault in Trinity Cemetery in New York City.

A. Oakey Hall in history is labeled as being part of the Tweed Ring, despite the fact that he was the only one of the major players who escaped prison.

References: "A. Oakey Hall on Trial. One Warrant for $39,000 Said to Be a Forgery," *The Sun* (New York), 25 October 1872, 1; "'Boss' Tweed: Corrupt 'Tammany Tiger'," in George C. Kohn, *Encyclopedia of American Scandal: From ABSCAM to the Zenger Case* (New York: Facts on File, 1989), 331; Clinton, Henry Lauren, *Celebrated Trials* (New York: Harper and Brothers, Publishers, 1897); Hershkowitz, Leo, "Hall, Abraham Oakey," in Melvin G. Holli and Peter d'A. Jones, *Biographical Dictionary of American Mayors, 1820–1980: Big City Mayors* (Westport, CT: Greenwood Press, 1981), 146–147; "The Trial of Mayor Hall," *The Sun* (New York), 29 October 1872, 1.

Hanna, Richard Thomas (1914–2001)

United States representative (1963–1974), implicated in the Koreagate scandal to which he pled guilty to charges that he accepted a $200,000 bribe to help influence members of Congress. Born in the city of Kemmerer, Wyoming, on 9 June 1914, Hanna attended local schools before he graduated from Pasadena Junior College in Pasadena, California, and later earned a bachelor's degree and a law degree from the University of California at Los Angeles. For a time after he earned his law degree and was admitted to the California bar, Hanna practiced the law. However, in 1942, after the United States entered World War II, he volunteered for service and became a member of the United States Navy Air Corps, serving until 1945. After returning to the United States, he resumed the practice of the law.

In 1955 Hanna was elected as a Democrat to a seat in the California state assembly, serving from 1956 until 1962. He served as a delegate from California to the Democratic National Convention held in Los Angeles. In 1962, again running as a Democrat, he was elected to a seat in the U.S. House of Representatives, representing California's Thirty-fourth District. Entering the Eighty-fifth Congress, Hanna was reelected five additional times, serving from 3 January 1963 until 31 December 1974.

During the 1970s, Hanna allegedly accepted more than $200,000 in payments from agents of Korean President Tongsun Park and Korean religious figure Sun Myung Moon, in exchange for increased Korean influence on Capitol Hill. Allegedly, approximately 115 congressmen accepted money from the Korean agents. However, when the scandal broke, the investigation was narrowed to only a few of those involved, and only one— Richard Hanna—was ever prosecuted (Representative Otto E. Passman [D-LA] was charged but never put on trial due to ill health). Hanna was charged by a federal grand jury of accepting bribes from the Koreans and later pled guilty. He was sentenced to six to thirty months in prison, ultimately serving twelve months before he was paroled.

Hanna never held political office again. He died in Tryon, North Carolina, on 9 June 2001 on his eighty-seventh birthday. His family scattered his ashes in the Atlantic Ocean.

See also Koreagate.

References: *Biographical Directory of the American Congress, 1774–1996* (Alexandria, VA: CQ Staff Directories, Inc., 1996); Boettcher, Robert, *Gifts of Deceit: Sun Myung Moon, Tongsun Park, and the Korean Scandal* (New York: Holt, Rinehart and Winston, 1980), 61–73; Robinson, Timothy S., and Charles R. Babcock, "Ex-Rep. Hanna Pleads Guilty in Influence Case," *Washington Post,* 18 March 1978, A1, A12; Thompson, Dennis, *Ethics in Congress: From Individual to Institutional Corruption* (Washington, DC: The Brookings Institution, 1995), 46; U.S. House of Representatives, Committee on Standards and Conduct, *Manual of Offenses and Procedures: Korean Influence Investigation, Pursuant to House Resolution 252* (Washington, DC: Government Printing Office, 1977).

Hastings, Alcee Lamar (1936–)

United States district judge of the Southern District of Florida (1979–1989), impeached and convicted of soliciting a bribe to help fix a case. Born in the village of Altamonte Springs, Florida, on 5 September 1936, Hastings attended local schools before he graduated from Crooms Academy in Sanford, Florida, and earned a bachelor's degree from Fisk University in Nashville, Tennessee, in 1958. He later attended the Howard University School of Law from 1958 to 1960, and Florida A&M University, the latter institution awarding him his juris doctor, or law, degree in 1963. Hastings was admitted to the Florida bar the following year. Opening his own law office, Hastings was in private practice from 1964 until 1977. In that latter year, he was elected a judge of the circuit court of Broward County, Florida, in the southern portion of the state. Two years later, he was named by President Jimmy Carter as the U.S. district judge for the Southern District of Florida.

On 29 December 1981, after only two years on the bench, Hastings was indicted by a grand jury in Miami for conspiring to accept a $150,000 bribe. The indictment charged that Hastings, using his friend William A. Borders Jr., as a go-

between, offered to reduce the prison sentence of two racketeers whose cases had come before him in exchange for the bribe. Much of the evidence against Hastings and Borders, both tried separately, was circumstantial, and Hastings maintained that he was never in on the deal and that Borders's promises to the racketeers to have their sentences reduced could not be carried out. The key prosecution evidence was a satchel full of $100 bills found on Borders that he said was the payoff to Hastings. Two years later, in 1983, Borders was convicted on all counts, but Hastings was acquitted. Following the acquittal, two U.S. district judges, who felt that Hastings had lied in order to avoid conviction, filed a complaint with the U.S. Court of Appeals for the Eleventh Circuit, alleging that Hastings had "engaged in conduct prejudicial to the effective and expeditious administration of the business of the courts." As required by law, the chief judge of the circuit reviewed the complaint and then referred it to a special committee to investigate the charges. In 1986, after three years of investigation, this committee returned a report that concluded that Hastings had lied in his trial and had manufactured evidence to avoid conviction. The Judicial Council of the Eleventh Circuit accepted and approved the report and in September 1986 reported to the United States Judicial Conference (the policy-making branch of the American federal judiciary) that Hastings had engaged in conduct that was potentially grounds for impeachment and removal from office. The Judicial Conference agreed and on 17 March 1988, in a rare move, Chief Justice of the United States Supreme Court William H. Rehnquist wrote to the U.S. House of Representatives that Hastings had "engaged in conduct which might constitute one or more grounds for impeachment."

Starting in May 1988 and continuing through June 1988, a subcommittee of the House Judiciary Committee held hearings over the Hastings case, and on 7 July 1988 unanimously adopted seventeen articles of impeachment. The subcommittee was led by Representative John Conyers, a black Democrat from Michigan. When Hastings charged that the proceedings were political revenge against an outspoken black Democrat who had opposed the policies of the Reagan administration, Conyers replied, "A black public official must be held to the same standard any and every other public official

Federal Judge Alcee Hastings addresses his supporters outside the Capitol in the midst of his ongoing impeachment hearing before the Senate. Hastings was eventually convicted of soliciting a bribe. (Bettmann/Corbis)

is held to." The full House Judiciary Committee adopted these seventeen articles on 26 July 1988. On 3 August, the House voted 413 to 3 to impeach Judge Hastings, and, 6 days later, the Senate received the articles from the House managers, who, according to tradition, demanded that the Senate prepare for a trial to hear the charges. Hastings filed a contest to the impeachment, claiming that his acquittal of the charges in a criminal trial barred any Senate trial on those charges due to double jeopardy and that any remaining charges must be thrown out because he would be prejudiced by the span of time between the alleged crime and the trial. He also argued that impeachment Article 17, alleging that "Hastings, through a corrupt relationship with Borders, giving false testimony under oath, fabricating false documents, and improperly disclosing confidential information acquired by him as the supervisory judge of a wiretap, undermined confidence in the integrity and impartiality of the judiciary and betrayed the trust of the people of the United States, thereby bringing disrepute on the Federal courts and the administration of justice by the Federal courts," be

dismissed because it failed to allege a particular "high crime and misdemeanor" within the meaning of the U.S. Constitution. On 15 March 1989, the U.S. Senate heard from Hastings and his counsel on these matters, as well as from the House managers, and, after meeting in closed session to deliberate, voted ninety-two to one to reject the motion to dismiss Articles 1 through 15 and voted ninety-three to zero to reject the motion to dismiss Article 17.

Hastings's impeachment trial opened on 19 July 1989 and lasted until 3 August of the same year. Instead of the full Senate hearing the evidence, a trial committee of twelve senators listened instead to the account of the case against Hastings. On 2 October 1989, this committee reported to the full Senate, and the following day, the full Senate met in closed session to hear the findings of the committee of twelve. On 20 October 1989, the Senate met in open session to vote on the articles. Prior to a vote, the senators agreed that if Hastings were acquitted on Article 1, a summary motion to acquit him on Articles 2–7 would be entered, as all of them related to the same matter. On the first article, the vote was sixty-nine guilty and twenty-six not guilty, convicting Hastings. On Article 6, the vote was forty-eight guilty to forty-seven not guilty, and as a two-thirds vote is needed for conviction, he was acquitted on this article. Votes were taken on the other articles except for Articles 10–15, as it was deemed unnecessary with the prior guilty votes. Hastings was immediately stripped of his judicial office. However, the Senate did not vote to bar him from holding further office.

Hastings then appealed his conviction, a move most legal scholars consider beyond the scope of the courts. Hastings was joined by Judge Walter L. Nixon Jr., who had also been impeached and convicted by the Senate. The men argued that having a Senate panel, and not the full Senate, hear the impeachment trial was a violation of their constitutional rights. Nixon's case was dismissed by the courts, but Judge Stanley Sporkin ruled in *Hastings v. United States,* 802 F. Supp. 490 (District Court of Appeals 1992), that Hastings's case could be examined by the courts. Citing the fact that Hastings had been previously acquitted by a petit jury, he felt that the judge deserved to have his case heard by the full Senate. Sporkin ordered that Hastings's Senate conviction be overturned and a new impeachment trial ordered. This was a shocking development in American constitutional law, a decision never before reached by any court in the history of the American nation. However, soon after Sporkin's milestone ruling, the U.S. Supreme Court held separately in *Nixon v. United States* that the courts could not review impeachment trial outcomes emanating from the U.S. Senate. Sporkin at that point reversed his ruling and held against Hastings. The conviction of the judge and his removal from office stood, unchallenged.

Hastings remained popular in the black community, and many saw his Senate impeachment conviction as a political and racial move. In 1992 Hastings ran for a seat in the U.S. House of Representatives from the Twenty-third District of Florida. The district is heavily populated by blacks and other minorities, and Hastings won easily. He took his seat in a Congress among people who just a few years earlier had voted to impeach him. Despite this, he was accepted as a member of the Congressional Black Caucus, and over the years he has become a leading spokesman for black concerns.

On 20 January 2001, in his last hours in office, President Bill Clinton pardoned Hastings's codefendant William Borders Jr. for his crimes.

See also Impeachment

References: *Biographical Directory of the American Congress, 1774–1996* (Alexandria, VA: CQ Staff Directories, Inc., 1996), 1177; Connolly, Ceci, "Impeached Ex-Judge Revisits History," *Washington Post,* 28 December 1998, A8; Cooper, Kenneth, "Hastings Joins His Former Accusers," *Washington Post,* 6 January 1993, A10.

Hatch Act, 53 Stat. 1147 (1939)

Congressional legislation, enacted 2 August 1939, officially called "an Act to Prevent Pernicious Political Activities," also called "the Clean Politics Act of 1939," designed to prevent federal employees from being involved in federal elections. Prior to the passage of this act, federal employees were sometimes pressured into working for the campaigns of the administration in power, whether they agreed with that administration's policies or not. In addition, federal employees were often working for the election of an administration when they should have been working on the business of their positions. This act was initiated when allegations were aired that the Democratic Party used officials of the Works Progress Administration (WPA) to solicit contributions and votes for the party. Senator Carl Atwood Hatch (D-NM) introduced the legislation to end this practice. The enactment passed the Congress in 1939 and was signed into law by President Franklin D. Roosevelt. It was amended in 1940. (This legislation is sometimes confused with another Hatch Act, introduced by Representative William Henry Hatch of Missouri and enacted in 1887, which pertained to the study of scientific agriculture.)

The Hatch Act, or Clean Politics Act, made it illegal: 1) to threaten, intimidate, or coerce voters in national elections; 2) for administrators in civil service positions to interfere with the nomination or election of candidates for federal office; 3) to promise or withhold any employment position as a reward, or a punishment, for contributing to, or refusing to contribute to, political activity; and 4) to solicit political contributions from those on federal relief (an action pertinent during the Great Depression). On 19 July 1940, the act was amended (54 Stat. 767) to allow for a $5,000 limit on annual individual contributions to any one candidate in any one campaign, at the same time limiting the amount a political committee could receive and spend in one year to $3 million.

In 1942 a case came before the U.S. Supreme Court that tested the constitutionality of the act. In *United States v. Malphurs,* 316 U.S. 1 (1942), a federal employee was coerced to vote a certain way or lose his job, but the high court remanded the case back to the lower court and never ruled on its merits. The lower court ruled that the men involved were indicted for violating the Hatch Act.

References: Bartholomew, Paul C., "Corrupt Practices Acts," in *Dictionary of American History,* 7 vols. (New York: Charles Scribner's Sons, 1976–1978), II:232–233; Fowler, Dorothy Ganfield, "Precursors of the Hatch Act," *The Mississippi Valley Historical Review,* XLVII:2 (Sept 1960), 247–262; Porter, David, "Senator Carl Hatch and the Hatch Act of 1939," *New Mexico Historical Review,* 48 (April 1973), 151–161.

Hays, Wayne Levere (1911–1989)

United States representative (1949–1976), powerful chairman of the House Administration Committee and the Democratic National Congressional Committee (DNCC), implicated in a "sex and public payroll" scandal for which he was forced to resign from the House. Born in Bannock, Ohio, on 13 May 1911, Hays attended the public schools of Bannock and the nearby village of St. Clairsville. He graduated from Ohio State University in Columbia in 1933 and spent some time studying at Duke University in Durham, North Carolina, in 1935. He returned to Ohio, where he served as a teacher in the towns of Flushing and Findlay. For a time he was involved in agricultural pursuits.

In 1939 Hays entered the political arena and served as mayor of Flushing until 1945. He also served in the Ohio state senate in 1941 and 1942, and, after leaving the mayorship, as commissioner of Belmont County from 1945 to 1949. Having joined the Officers' Reserve Corps of the U.S. Army in 1933, Hays remained on inactive service until called to active duty on 8 December 1941, following the Japanese attack on Pearl Harbor in Hawaii. Commissioned a second lieutenant, Hays served until he was given a medical discharge in August 1942. Returning home, he finished his service as mayor of Flushing, Ohio, at the same time working

as chairman of the board of directors of the Citizens National Bank in Flushing.

A Democrat, Hays served as a delegate to the party's national nominating conventions in 1960, 1964, and 1968. He also served as chairman of the U.S. House of Representatives' delegation to the North Atlantic Treaty Organization's Parliamentarians' Conference and as president of the conference in 1956 and 1967. In 1948 Hays ran for and won a seat in the U.S. House of Representatives from the Eighteenth Ohio District, defeating Republican Earl Lewis. Hayes would retain this seat until he resigned on 1 September 1976. Rising through the ranks of the leadership of congressional Democrats, he eventually became chairman of the Committee on House Administration. Hays became one of the most powerful politicians on Capitol Hill. In 1971, when Majority Leader Carl Albert (D-OK) was elected Speaker, Hays was one of those to throw his hat into the ring to succeed Albert as majority leader—among these were Hale Boggs (D-LA), Morris Udall (D-AZ), B. F. Sisk (D-CA), and James O'Hara (D-MI). Boggs was the eventual winner.

Hays's career began to unravel in 1976. Two years earlier he had hired a woman, Elizabeth Ray, as a typist on his staff, and paid her $14,000 a year. What no one knew was that Ray was hired not for her typing skills but because she was Hays's girlfriend. Finally, Ray became disgusted at her situation and went to the *Washington Post,* which exposed her story in a front-page article entitled "Closed Session Romance on the Hill." When the article appeared in the *Post* on 23 May 1976, official Washington was stunned. Even Hays was thrown for a loop: his first reaction, when asked why he kept a mistress, was to say, "Hell's fire! I'm a very happily married man." The House Ethics Committee, having a month earlier voted to investigate the alleged financial misconduct of Representative Robert L. F. Sikes of Florida, proceeded to vote to look into whether Hays had used public money to pay off his mistress. Hays stuck by his story that Ray, who was on the staff of the House Administration Committee, was making the story up, but the allegations took a strange turn when Ray, in an interview, claimed that "I can't type, I can't file, I can't even answer the phone." Finally, on 25 May 1976, before the House Ethics Committee, Hays admitted that he had had a "personal relationship" with Ms.

Ray; however, he denied that she was his mistress or that he had hired her and paid her with public funds so that she could be by his side. That same day, 25 May 1976, Hays requested in writing that the Ethics Committee investigate the allegation that he had paid off Ray with public funds, and twenty-eight members of Congress, in a letter to Ethics Committee chairman John J. Flynt Jr. (D-GA), asked for the committee to investigate. On 2 June 1976, the Ethics Committee voted eleven to zero to initiate an investigation. The Department of Justice and the Federal Bureau of Investigation secretly began to look into the corruption aspects, and on 26 May 1976 a grand jury in Washington, D.C., was empaneled to see if Hays had broken any laws.

With allegations such as these—using public funds for immoral purposes—comes pressure to remove oneself from positions of power, and Hays was not spared. On 3 June he voluntarily stepped down as chairman of the Democratic Congressional Campaign Committee and, just fifteen days later, similarly removed himself as chairman of the Committee on House Administration. That year, Hays ran for reelection, capturing the Democratic Party nomination, but he withdrew before the general election so that another candidate could take his place. Hays was never charged with a crime and, after returning to Ohio, served as a member of the Ohio state house of representatives from 1978 to 1980. Hays retired to the village of St. Clairsville, Ohio. He was in Wheeling, West Virginia, on 10 February 1989 when he died of a heart attack at the age of seventy-seven.

References: *Biographical Directory of the American Congress, 1774–1996* (Alexandria, VA: CQ Staff Directories, Inc., 1996), 1188–1189; "A Capitol Sex Scandal," *Washington Post*, 2 September 1999, C13; "[The Case of] Rep. Wayne L. Hays," in *Congressional Ethics* (Washington, DC: Congressional Quarterly, 1980), 22–23; Clark, Marion, and Rudy Maxa, "Closed Session Romance on the Hill: Rep. Wayne Hays's $14,000-a-Year Clerk Says She's His Mistress," *Washington Post*, 23 May 1976, A3.

Hayt, Ezra Ayres (1823–1902)

Commissioner of Indian Affairs (1877–1880), implicated but never charged with gross irregularities in the Indian Office during his tenure. Hayt remains an obscure figure. He was born in Patterson, New York, on 25 February 1823. His education is unknown; what is known is that he went into the dry goods business when he was about twenty-one years of age and made a good living—so much so that he retired in 1868 with a fortune. A religious man, he was a member of the Board of Foreign Missions of the Reformed Church. It was as a member of this congregation that Hayt was recommended for an appointment to the Board of Indian Commissioners, a panel established by Congress in 1869 made up of famous and rich men and other people who could oversee Indian affairs in the United States and make recommendations to the government. In May 1874, in a clash with the Department of the Interior's program for Indians, the entire board resigned. President Ulysses S. Grant named Hayt to the board on 15 August 1874 to fill one of these vacancies. Hayt served as the head of the purchasing committee, buying and overseeing the purchase of supplies for Indian tribes. According to all historical sources, Hayt did his job thoroughly and without any hint of corruption.

Because of his work on the Board of Indian Commissioners, he was recommended and nominated to succeed John Quincy Smith as the Commissioner of Indian Affairs, the highest ranking officer dealing with Native American affairs in the U.S. government. During his tenure, he handled several conflicts with Indians in the western United States, as well as the massacre of troops under the command of General George Armstrong Custer.

Starting in 1878, Hayt was answering allegations that he was involved in shady beef deals. Secretary of the Interior Carl Schurz, his superior, opened an investigation. The *New York Times* also looked into allegations that Hayt had used his office for nepotism—hiring his son as an Indian agent, for instance—and that monies set aside for certain tribes had not reached them. A riot by the White River Utes of Colorado, which led to the death of an Indian agent, exposed massive corruption. When Schurz asked Hayt for information about the rations allegedly sent to the San Carlos Indians in Arizona, Hayt refused to offer the records, and Schurz demanded his resignation. Hayt stepped down, although he was never formally charged with any crime. Many historians consider him, however, the most corrupt of the commissioners of Indian Affairs.

Hayt returned to New York, where a series of business failures cost him his fortune. He died in poverty on 12 January 1902, six weeks shy of his seventy-ninth birthday.

References: Grossman, Mark, *The ABC-CLIO Companion to the Native American Rights Movement* (Santa Barbara, CA: ABC-CLIO, 1996), 152–153; Meyer, Roy W., "Ezra A. Hayt," in Robert M. Kvasnicka and Herman J. Viola, *The Commissioners of Indian Affairs, 1824–1977* (Lincoln: University of Nebraska Press, 1979), 155–156; Priest, Loring B., *Uncle Sam's Stepchildren* (New Brunswick, New Jersey: Rutgers University Press, 1975).

Helstoski, Henry (1925–1999)

United States representative from New Jersey (1965–1977), indicted for taking bribes (but never formally tried), whose name graces one of the most important U.S. Supreme Court decisions dealing with congressional ethics and the rights of congressmen to speak on matters before the House. Henry Helstoski was born in Wallington, New Jersey, on 21 March 1925 and attended the public schools of Wallington and nearby Rutherford. During World War II, he served in the U.S. Army Air Corps as an instructor and as a radio technician. After the war, he attended Paterson State College and, after going to the Montclair State Teachers' College, he graduated from the latter institution with a bachelor of arts degree in 1947 and a master's degree two years later. From 1949 until 1962, Helstoski served as a teacher, a high school principal, and the superintendent of schools for Bergen County, New Jersey.

Helstoski, a Democrat, entered the political realm in 1956 when he was elected a councilman for East Rutherford, New Jersey. The following year he was elected mayor of the city, serving until 1965. In 1964 he was elected to a seat in the U.S. House of Representatives from the Ninth New Jersey District, taking his seat in the Eighty-ninth Congress on 3 January 1965. Helstoski would ultimately serve until 3 January 1977. During his six terms, he became an influential congressman who consistently voted with his party.

In 1974 the U.S. Department of Justice began investigating allegations that Helstoski had taken bribes from certain people in return for pushing immigration waivers allowing them to remain in the United States. This investigation lasted for nearly two years. In June 1976 a grand jury indicted Helstoski on twelve counts, including accepting bribes for the purpose of "being influenced in the performance of official acts, to wit: the introduction of private bills in the United States House of Representatives." Helstoski had refused to cooperate during the grand jury hearings, claiming that the "Speech or Debate Clause" of the U.S. Constitution shielded him from any examination of his work in the House. The provision of the Constitution, located at Article 1, Section 6, says that "for any Speech or Debate in either House, they [senators and representatives] shall not be questioned in either place." Constitutional scholars had long questioned the precise meaning of this phrase, and up until this case the U.S. Supreme Court had ruled on its meaning in only one case, *United States v. Brewster* (1972). After Helstoski's indictment, the trial court ruled that no evidence of his work in the House could be introduced in trial—in effect assuring that no case could be brought. In a rare move, the U.S. government appealed the judge's decision, going before the U.S. Court of Appeals for the Third Circuit. The Court of Appeals ruled for Helstoski, holding that no legislative work by Helstoski could be introduced at trial. The U.S. government appealed a second time, this time to the U.S. Supreme Court. At the same time, Helstoski sued the trial judge for refusing to dismiss the indictment. On 18 June 1979, after three years of appeals, the U.S. Supreme Court held that the "Speech or Debate Clause" was a proper shield for Helstoski to use to block any introduction of his legislative record into court. Ultimately, because of a lack of evidence arising from this landmark decision, the charges against Helstoski were dismissed, and he never stood trial.

Despite his court victory (his lawsuit against the judge was initially dismissed), Helstoski's political career was ruined. In 1976, he was defeated for the Democratic nomination to retain his seat, and he ran unsuccessfully as an independent in the 1978 general election. In 1980, in his last run for office, he failed to gain the Democratic nomination for Congress. In his last years, Helstoski served as the superintendent of the North Bergen School District (1981–1985) and as a public relations consultant. Henry Helstoski died in Wayne, New Jersey, on 16 December 1999 at the age of seventy-four.

See also *United States v. Brewster; United States v. Helstoski; United States v. Johnson.*

References: *Biographical Directory of the American Congress, 1774–1996* (Alexandria, VA: CQ Staff Directories, Inc., 1996), 1195–1196; *Congressional Ethics* (Washington, DC: Congressional Quarterly, 1980), 24.

Helstoski v. Meanor

See United States v. Helstoski

Henderson, John Brooks (1826–1913)

United States senator from Missouri (1862–1869), named as the first "special prosecutor"—the forerunner of the modern independent counsel—to investigate the Whiskey Ring frauds. Born near Danville, Virginia, on 16 November 1826, Brooks moved with his parents to Lincoln County, Missouri, when he was young, and it was with this state that he was identified for the remainder of his life. He worked as a farmhand and later taught school; at the same time he studied law and was admitted to the Missouri bar in 1844. He opened a practice, but it is unknown where. Initially a Democrat, Henderson was elected to the Missouri state House of Representatives in 1848 and served two nonconsecutive terms: 1848–1850, and 1856–1858.

When the Civil War began in 1861, Henderson volunteered for service in the Missouri state militia and was commissioned a brigadier general in that outfit. However, when Senator Trusten Polk, a Democrat, resigned his Senate seat in 1862 to protest the war, Missouri Governor Hamilton R. Gamble, who had just taken office himself, named Henderson to the vacant seat. Henderson had moved from being a Democrat to a Unionist, which meant he was from a slave state but supported the Union during the war. Henderson was elected by the state legislature to the seat and was reelected in 1863 for a full six-year term. He ultimately served from 17 January 1862 until 3 March 1869, acting as chairman of the Committee to Audit and Control the Contingent Expense and the Committee on Indian Affairs. In 1868 he decided not to stand for reelection.

For several years after he left the Senate, Henderson, now a Republican and a respected former member of the Senate, practiced the law in Washington, D.C. However, in 1875 he was called upon for the start of two important services for the government. First, he was asked personally by President Ulysses S. Grant to prosecute the so-called Whiskey Ring fraud cases. Grant had become embarrassed by a series of investigations by the press that uncovered massive fraud in the collection of whiskey revenue taxes, particularly in St. Louis. The ring of thieves was led by none other than Orville E. Babcock, Grant's personal secretary. On 1 June 1875, to stem the flow of bad press, Grant named Henderson special U.S. attorney to investigate the fraud. Working with the U.S. attorneys in Missouri, Henderson brought indictments against Babcock; John D. MacDonald, the supervisor of revenue for the District of Missouri (who had, allegedly with Babcock's full knowledge, gotten whiskey distillers to pay less federal tax and bribe MacDonald and Babcock for the privilege); and several others. Henderson went to St. Louis and personally prosecuted MacDonald and obtained a conviction. During this period, Henderson came across damning evidence against Babcock and set about to prosecute him as well. Grant, fearing that Henderson would indict his own secretary, appointed a special military board to investigate the allegations against Babcock. This special panel then asked Henderson to turn over to it all evidence in the Babcock case. Henderson refused, and in December 1875 got a St. Louis grand jury to indict Babcock. During the trial, Henderson told the jury in his closing argument that President Grant himself had worked to obstruct the investigation: "What right has the President to interfere with the honest discharge of the duties of the Secretary of the Treasury? None, whatsoever. What right has he to interfere with the discharge of the duties of Commissioner Douglas? None."

Grant immediately fired Henderson, calling his statements "an impertinence." He named a new special prosecutor, James Broadhead, who immediately had the trial of Babcock to deal with, as well as other Whiskey Ring matters.

Two years after being fired from the Whiskey Ring matter, Henderson was named by President Rutherford B. Hayes to serve as a commissioner to deal with several tribes of Indians at war with the United States. Henderson used his experience as chairman of the Senate Committee on Indian Affairs in this position.

In 1888 Henderson moved permanently from Missouri to Washington, where for several years he was a writer. He died in Washington on 12 April 1913 at the age of eighty-six. Although he had no connection with New York State during his life, his remains were laid to rest in the Greenwood Cemetery in Brooklyn, New York.

See also Independent Counsel Statute; Whiskey Ring Scandal

References: *Biographical Directory of the American Congress, 1774–1996* (Alexandria, VA: CQ Staff Directories, Inc., 1996); Mattingly, Arthur H. "Senator John Brooks Henderson, United States Senator from Missouri." (Ph.D. dissertation, Kansas State University, 1971); Roske, Ralph J. "The Seven Martyrs?" *American Historical Review* 64 (January 1959): 323–330.

Hobbs Act, 18 U.S.C. § 1951 (1946)

Federal statute, enacted 3 July 1946, that outlaws robbery and extortion and is used mainly against those public officials involved in political corruption.

The statute reads:

Whoever in any way or degree obstructs, delays, or affects commerce or the movement of any article or commodity in commerce, by robbery or extortion or attempts or conspires so to do, or commits or threatens physical violence to any person or property in furtherance of a plan or purpose to do anything in violation of this section shall be fined under this title or imprisoned not more than twenty years, or both.

In *McCormick v. United States,* 500 U.S. 257 (1991), the U.S. Supreme Court held that political contributions per se are not a violation of the Hobbs Act provisions.

References: Hobbs Act, 18 U.S.C. 1951.

Hoeppel, John Henry (1881–1976)

United States representative from California (1933–1937), convicted and sentenced to prison in 1936 for conspiring to sell an appointment to West Point. Hoeppel was born near Tell City, Indiana, on 10 February 1881. He attended a grammar school in Evansville, Indiana, but he never received any secondary education. When the Spanish-American War started, Hoeppel enlisted in the U.S. Army on 27 July 1898, entering with the rank of private and rising to the rank of sergeant. After the war, he remained in the service, eventually serving with the U.S. Army in France during World War I. He was released from the service in 1921 with an honorable discharge.

In 1919 Hoeppel moved to Arcadia, California, where he served as the postmaster of that city from 1923 to 1931. He also worked as a journalist, serving as the editor of *National Defense* magazine in 1928. A Democrat, in 1932 Hoeppel was elected to a seat in the U.S. House of Representatives from the Twelfth California District. That election heralded the influx of so-called New Deal Democrats into the federal government, and as such, Hoeppel was a staunch supporter of President Franklin D. Roosevelt, also elected in 1932. Hoeppel took his seat in the Seventy-third Congress and served from 4 March 1933 until 3 January 1937. He served as chairman of the Committee on War Claims in the Seventy-fourth Congress.

In 1936, just as he was preparing to run for a third term in Congress, Hoeppel was indicted on charges of conspiring to sell an appointment to West Point. One of a congressman's duties is to recommend constituents for empty spaces at the military academies, including West Point in New York state. Hoeppel was quickly tried and found guilty on all charges. Although he was sentenced to prison, Hoeppel ran for reelection that same year, but lost the Democratic nomination to Jerry Voorhis. While running, Hoeppel had put out a pamphlet that he said explained how he was set up by the political system: "My staunch refusal to be a 'yes man' [is] responsible for my difficulties. The black hand of [Postmaster General James] Farley and [Senator William Gibbs] McAdoo [of California is] evident. The unethical and dishonest attitude of the prosecuting attorney exposed. The 11-juror verdict was one of persecution, not of justice. Official records show my distinguished Army service wherein I saved the Government thousands of dollars overseas by exposing graft."

Hoeppel served a short time in prison before being paroled. In 1946 he was the Prohibition Party candidate for the U.S. House, but was easily defeated. Hoeppel then retired to Arcadia, where he remained for the rest of his life. He never received a presidential pardon for his crime. Hoeppel died at his home in California on 21 September

1976 at the age of ninety-five and was buried in Resurrection Cemetery in San Gabriel, California.

References: *Biographical Directory of the American Congress, 1774–1996* (Alexandria, VA: CQ Staff Directories, Inc., 1996), 1223; "Congressman Hoeppel's Statement of His Political Persecution," in *Remarks of Hon. John H. Hoeppel of California in the House of Representatives, Wednesday, June 17, 1936* (Washington, DC: Government Printing Office, 1936); "Hoeppel, John Henry," in Jay Robert Nash, *Encyclopedia of World Crime: Criminal Justice, Criminology, and Law Enforcement,* 4 vols. (Wilmette, IL: CrimeBooks, Inc., 1989), III:1153.

Hoffman, Harold Giles (1896–1954)

United States representative from New Jersey (1927–1931) and governor of New Jersey (1935–1938) found to have embezzled state funds, a fact not uncovered until after his death. Born in South Amboy, New Jersey, on 7 February 1896, the son of Frank Hoffman and Ada Crawford (née Thom) Hoffman, Harold Hoffman attended the public schools of South Amboy, but after he graduated from South Amboy High School in 1913, he never received any further education. He worked for several newspapers, including the *Perth Amboy Evening News,* before he enlisted on 25 July 1917 to serve in the American Expeditionary Force sent to France in World War I. Serving as a private in Company H of the Third Regiment of the New Jersey Infantry, Hoffman rose to the rank of captain and saw action in the Meuse-Argonne campaign before he was released from the service in 1919.

When he returned to South Amboy, Hoffman went to work as an executive with the South Amboy Trust Company, where he worked until 1942. During this time, he also served as city treasurer from 1920 to 1925 and, in 1923 and 1924, as a member of the New Jersey state house. In 1925 he was elected mayor of South Amboy, serving until 1926. A Republican, he was a delegate to the Republican National Convention in 1936.

In 1926 Hoffman was elected to a seat in the U.S. House of Representatives, representing New Jersey's Third District. He served in the Seventieth and Seventy-first Congresses (1927–1931) and although quite popular, refused to run for a third term. Instead, he returned to New Jersey to accept the position of New Jersey's commissioner of motor vehicles. To all political spectators this move seemed odd—a backward step for a man who could have advanced in Washington politics. What no one knew was that Hoffman, as head of the South Amboy Trust Company, had started in the early 1920s slowly removing small amounts of cash from numerous inactive accounts and putting the funds into his own account. When he moved back to New Jersey in 1931, he not only continued siphoning money in South Amboy, but now, as head of the motor vehicles division in Trenton, he could siphon money from that agency's accounts as well.

In 1934 the Republicans, unaware that Hoffman was leading a secret life of thievery, nominated him for governor. He defeated Democrat William L. Dill by 12,000 votes out of some 1.3 million cast and succeeded Democrat A. Harry Moore as the governor of New Jersey on 15 January 1935. Historians Robert Sobel and John Raimo wrote:

> Hoffman's administration was marked by continual strife between the governor and the legislature over methods to meet the cost of the state's contribution for [the] relief of the poor. The passage of a 2 percent sales tax, in part intended to provide funds for state unemployment benefits, was later repealed. Also while Hoffman was governor the New Jersey Compensation Commission and the Banking Advisory Board were created; the Highway Commission of four members was abolished and replaced by a single commissioner appointed by the governor; provisions were made for uniform policies to cover accident and health insurance; and anthracite coal entering the state by truck was required to bear a certificate of origin.

Hoffman became unpopular right after taking office for openly expressing doubts about the guilt of Bruno Richard Hauptmann, the key suspect in the kidnapping of Charles Lindbergh Jr. Hauptmann, a German immigrant, had been tried and convicted of the horrendous crime and sentenced to die in the electric chair. In order to satisfy his own doubts about the case, Hoffman granted a stay to Hauptmann so that he could investigate the case. An uproar from the citizens of New Jersey led to his retraction of the stay when Hoffman was outvoted on the Board of Pardons to issue a permanent stay. Hoffman told reporters:

I have never expressed an opinion upon the guilt or innocence of Hauptmann. I do, however, share with hundreds of thousands of our people the doubt as to the value of the evidence that placed him in the Lindbergh nursery on the night of the crime; I do wonder what part passion and prejudice played in the conviction of a man who was previously tried and convicted in the columns of many of our newspapers.

After a single term in office, Hoffman left the governorship on 18 January 1938 because of a New Jersey law limiting the governor to a single term. His successor, A. Harry Moore (the man Hoffman had himself succeeded), appointed the former governor as executive director of the New Jersey Employment Compensation Commission (ECC). Hoffman served until 15 June 1942, when he was granted leave to serve as a major in the U.S. Transportation Corps during World War II. He was promoted to the rank of colonel and held this rank when he was discharged on 24 June 1946. He then returned to serving as executive director of the ECC.

In 1954, following several discoveries of missing funds, Governor Robert B. Meyner opened an investigation into allegations that Hoffman had stolen millions of dollars from the state over a twenty-year period. Hoffman was suspended from his position as head of the EEC and claimed that he was completely innocent. He never got a chance to prove it: on 4 June 1954, Hoffman suffered a heart attack and died in a New York City hotel room at the age of fifty-eight. After his death, the state probe uncovered Hoffman's career of massive theft, including some $300,000 from the South Amboy Trust Company and more than $1.2 million in state disability funds that he used to cover up the bank fraud. It is estimated that Hoffman may have stolen as much as $600,000 in his lifetime, although none of this money was ever found after his death.

References: "Harold Hoffman: Embezzling Public Official," in George C. Kohn, *Encyclopedia of American Scandal: From ABSCAM to the Zenger Case* (New York: Facts on File, 1989), 153–154; "Hoffman, Harold Giles," in Robert Sobel and John Raimo, eds., *Biographical Directory of the Governors of the United States, 1789–1978,* 4 vols. (Westport, CT: Meckler Books, 1978), III:1040–1041; New Jersey, Department of Law and Public Safety, *Final Report on the Investigation of the Division of Employment Security,* *Department of Labor and Industry to Robert B. Meyner, Governor, State of New Jersey. With Foreword* (Trenton: State of New Jersey Official Report, 1955).

Hoffman, John Thompson (1828–1888)

Mayor of New York City (1866–1868), governor of New York (1869–1873), destroyed politically by his ties to the administration of "Boss" William M. Tweed, although he was never accused of any impropriety. Born in Sing Sing (later Ossining), New York, on 10 January 1828, Thompson was the son of a doctor and was distantly related to Philip Livingston, a signer of the Declaration of Independence. Thompson attended the prestigious Mount Pleasant Academy in New York, afterwards graduating with honors from Union College in Schenectady, New York, in 1846. He then studied the law with Judge Albert Richmond and Representative Aaron Ward and was admitted to the New York bar in 1849. He formed a law partnership with two local attorneys, Samuel M. Woodruff and William M. Leonard.

A Democrat, Thompson became a member of the New York State Democratic Central Committee in 1848 and, just six years later, became a member of the Young Men's Tammany Hall General Committee. In 1859 he became a full member of the Tammany Society. Tammany was the leading political organization in New York City, controlling patronage and, in effect, the entire political system that ran the city. Joining this society was the only way a politician could gain any semblance of power. Once he had joined Tammany, Thompson was elected to citywide office, starting as recorder of New York City in 1860. The youngest man ever to hold that office at that time (he was only thirty-two), Thompson was forced to deal with the New York Draft riots that hit the city in 1863 in the midst of the Civil War. In 1865, barely five years into his political career, Thompson was nominated by the Democrats for mayor. Opposed by Republican Marshall O. Roberts—as well as John Hecker, a flour magnate who was the Citizens' Union candidate, and C. Godfrey Gunther, who was the anti-Tammany candidate—Thompson was elected with a slim majority over Roberts. In 1867 he was elected to a second term. In 1866 he was nominated by the Democrats for governor of New York, but the support of President Andrew Johnson, who was widely unpopular for his stand against Reconstruction, helped Republican Reuben Fenton defeat Thompson, who returned to his duties in New York City.

In 1868 the Democrats again nominated Thompson for governor, and this time he defeated Republican John A. Griswold to become the state's chief executive. Hoffman had been strongly supported by Tammany and by "Boss" William M. Tweed. At Tweed's request, Governor Thompson named several Tweed allies to state judgeships. Thompson had never been close to Tweed—he was merely an ally in the Tammany organization as mayor—but when allegations of gross fraud and mismanagement came to light against Tweed, Thompson was stained by the accusations. Thompson himself was always considered honest and trustworthy, but as stories leaked out about the millions of dollars stolen by the so-called Tweed Ring of men who worked in collaboration with the Tammany leader, Thompson too became dishonored. Before the allegations arose, many in the Democratic Party were saying that Thompson was likely to be nominated for president in 1872; however, at the party's convention in Baltimore in July 1872, Thompson was merely an attendee and was passed over for Horace Greeley, a former Republican who had started a liberal Republican faction. That year, Thompson did not run for a second term, leaving office on 1 January 1873.

In his last years, Thompson returned to the practice of law. His health began to decline and he went abroad to find treatment. He was in Wiesbaden, Germany, when he died suddenly on 24 March 1888 at the age of sixty.

See also Tweed, William Magear

References: Calkins, Hiram, and Dewitt Van Buren, *Biographical Sketches of John T. Hoffman and Allen C. Beach: The Democratic Nominees for Governor and Lieutenant-Governor of the State of New York. Also, a Record of the Events in the Lives of Oliver Bascom, David B. McNeil, and Edwin O. Perrin, the Other Candidates on the Same Ticket* (New York: Printed by the New York Printing Company, 1868); Hershkowitz, Leo, "Hoffman, John Thompson," in Melvin G. Holli and Peter d'A. Jones, *Biographical Dictionary of American Mayors, 1820–1980: Big City Mayors* (Westport, CT: Greenwood Press, 1981), 166; Hoffman, John Thompson, *Law and Order* (New York: United States Publishing Company, 1876); "Hoffman, John Thompson," in Robert Sobel and John Raimo, eds., *Biographical Directory of the Governors of the United States, 1789–1978*, 4 vols. (Westport, CT: Meckler Books, 1978), III:1085–1086.

Holden, William Woods (1818–1892)

Governor of North Carolina (1868–1870), impeached and removed from office in 1870 in a corruption scandal. Holden was one of seven southern governors (all Republicans) impeached during the Reconstruction period following the American Civil War. Holden was born out wedlock near the town of Hillsborough, North Carolina, on 24 November 1818, the son of Thomas Holden, a miller, and Priscilla Woods. At the age of six, he was removed from his mother's custody and placed in his father's home along with his father's ten legitimate children. He was educated at what was called an "old field school" near his home, but left school at age ten and became a printer's devil (an apprentice in a print shop, whose duties included setting the type for the printing press and putting the type back into the case) for one Dennis Heartt of the Hillsborough (North Carolina) *Recorder*. Holden later worked for newspapers in Milton, North Carolina, and Danville, Virginia, before he returned to Hillsborough. In 1837 he moved to Raleigh, where he worked as a printer and studied the law. Licensed to practice in 1841, it appears that he never became an attorney and remained a printer until he entered the political realm.

In 1843 Holden was offered the prestigious post of editor of the *North Carolina Standard* on the condition that he become a Democrat and agree with the paper's stands. Holden accepted these conditions and turned the paper into the most influential in the state. While serving as editor, and then as a member of the state house of commons (the lower house of the state legislature) from 1846 to 1847, Holden took an extreme prosecessionist stance. In 1858 he ran for the Democratic nomination for governor, but lost to John Willis Ellis, an attorney, who went on to victory and served as governor until his death in 1861. That same year, 1858, Holden was also unsuccessful in two attempts to capture a U.S. Senate seat, losing to Thomas H. Bragg and David Settle Reid. In 1860 Holden served as a delegate to the Charleston and Baltimore Democratic National Conventions, where the party broke into two separate wings;

Holden backed the "Southern" wing, led by former Vice President John C. Breckinridge.

After the election of Republican Abraham Lincoln to the presidency, Holden was sent to a secession convention held in Raleigh. Although he went to the convention still backing the Union, he changed his support and became an ardent secessionist. As the war expanded and the likelihood of a Confederate victory waned, Holden became more and more estranged with the cause he once trumpeted, and when he expressed his sentiments in the *North Carolina Standard* the paper's presses were wrecked. In 1864 Holden decided to run as a Peace candidate against incumbent Governor Zebulon Baird Vance. Holden had once been a firm supporter of Vance, but in this campaign he called for the state's secession from the Confederacy, so that it could sue for a separate peace with the United States. Vance easily won, capturing more than 58,000 votes out of some 72,000 cast. Holden's political defeat would, in normal times, have spelled the end of any future political career, but the days of the Confederacy were numbered. With the collapse of the Southern insurgent government, Holden formed a secret party, known as "The Heroes of America" or "The Red Strings." The goal of this movement was to make a peace deal with the U.S. government and then take control of the North Carolina state government machinery. On 29 May 1865, after the surrender of the Confederacy, President Andrew Johnson, who had assumed the presidency after the assassination of President Abraham Lincoln, ordered Vance to be removed as governor of North Carolina and appointed Holden the provisional governor. In October 1865, at the direction of President Johnson, Holden convened a state convention to pass a new constitution, which gave blacks voting and other civil rights, so that North Carolina could be readmitted to the Union. The convention, which enacted the new constitution, caused such bitterness that when a new election for governor was set for late October 1865, Holden was easily defeated by the Democrat, Jonothon Worth. Johnson nominated Holden in 1866 to be the U.S. minister to San Salvador, but the United States Senate, already at odds with Johnson in a row that would lead to Johnson's impeachment in 1868, refused to confirm the appointment. Holden returned to his editor's position at the *North Carolina Standard*.

As editor, Holden took an opposite stand from his previous editorials: after his first term as governor, he stood for the ratification of the Fourteenth Amendment and defended Reconstruction. In 1867 he was one of the organizers of the state's Republican Party. Under the new constitution that he had helped to bring about, he was nominated by his party for governor and was elected over Thomas Ashe by a sizeable vote, mainly because former slaveowners and other whites were prohibited from voting because their citizenship had been revoked for supporting the Confederate insurrection. The military removed Governor Jonothon Worth, who had been legally elected governor, and replaced him with Holden. With his support, the legislature passed the Ku Klux Klan Acts and ratified the Thirteenth and Fourteenth Amendments to the U.S. Constitution. There were widespread accusations of abuse of power and corruption, although there was never any evidence that Holden himself personally profited from any of it.

Holden's downfall came in 1869 and 1870 when, amid reports of outrages by Klan members, he called on the legislature to grant him broad powers to declare a county in insurrection. He proclaimed Alamance and Caswell Counties to be centers of Klan violence and dispatched a state guard to put down the outrages. When this guard instead arrested political opponents of Holden's and newspaper writers who were critics of Holden's administration, he timidly backed down and released all involved from incarceration. In 1870 the Democrats were able to force black and white Republicans from the polls, resulting in a major Democratic victory in taking control of the state legislature. Their first order of business was to impeach Holden and remove him from office. Although some Democrats feared that the U.S. government might step in and declare the 1870 election void, they decided it was worth the chance if they could be rid of Holden. On 9 December 1870, a resolution calling for Holden's impeachment for "high crimes and misdemeanors" was introduced in the state house, and just ten days later the full house voted on eight articles that had been agreed to by the Judiciary Committee. They charged Holden with illegally dispatching troops to put down the Ku Klux Klan, illegally paying these troops from state coffers, refusing to obey a writ of habeas corpus, and illegally arresting one Josiah Turner in the Klan sweep. When the full house voted to accept the articles and officially impeach Holden on 14 December 1870, he was removed from office, and Lieutenant Governor Tod R. Caldwell, a Republican, assumed the governorship. The trial started on 30 January 1871, with former North Carolina Governors William Graham and Thomas Bragg sitting as Holden's counsel. After a few days of testimony, as Holden wrote in his memoirs (published in 1911):

> In a few days I left for Washington City. In the course of a day or two I called in to see President Grant. He asked me if I knew that a number of my triers [sic], members of the Senate, were Ku Klux. I told him I supposed they were, but that was a matter for his Attorney-General and my two Senators. I had heard soon after my impeachment from a Democrat of character that the Dems had decreed my impeachment. In regard to my power as Commander-in-chief of the Militia of the State, I relied for power to pursue the course I did on the act known as the Shoffner Act, which passed in January, 1870. This act provided in express terms that the Governor "when in his judgment it was proper to do so, could proclaim counties in insurrection, thereby suspending the operation of the civil law." I had never heard the constitutionality of this act questioned.

While in Washington, Holden was able to convince Grant of the necessity of federal legislation to stop the Klan, and Grant sent several acts to Congress. In North Carolina, Holden's counsel brought in 113 witnesses to the impeachment managers' 61. Despite this, the trial was a foregone conclusion: on 22 March, Holden was acquitted on the first two articles dealing with his calling troops illegally to put down Klan violence. But on the articles dealing with sending a force with state funds to arrest suspected Klan members and paying these troops with state funds, he was found guilty. A resolution removing him from office and ever holding state office again was passed. Holden thus became the first state governor to be convicted in an impeachment trial.

Holden moved to Washington, D.C., where he became the editor of the *Washington Daily Chronicle,* a post he held until 1872. He declined an appointment from President Grant in 1872 to become the U.S. minister to Peru, instead accepting a position as postmaster of Raleigh in 1873. He remained a stalwart Republican until he quit the party in 1883 over the issue of suffrage for blacks and a tariff. Holden died in Raleigh on 1 March 1892 at the age of seventy-three and was buried in the Oakwood Cemetery in Raleigh.

Holden had become the symbol of everything critics of Reconstruction hated: the advocacy of black emancipation and suffrage, excesses by white Republicans in leading the former Confederate states after the end of the Civil War, and corruption in state government. Thomas Dixon, the Southern writer famed for his work *The Clansmen,* which later became the 1915 film *The Birth of a Nation,* used Holden as the model for his corrupt governor Amos Hogg, who crushed the Ku Klux Klan in the book *The Leopard's Spots: A Romance of the White Man's Burden, 1865–1900* (1902).

References: Ewing, Cortez A. M., "Two Reconstruction Impeachments," *The North Carolina Historical Review,* XV:3 (July 1938), 204–225; Holden, William Woods, *Memoirs of W. W. Holden* (Durham, NC: The Seeman Printery, 1911), 67; "Holden, William Woods," in Robert Sobel and John Raimo, eds., *Biographical Directory of the Governors of the United States, 1789–1978,* 4 vols. (Westport, CT: Meckler Books, 1978), III:1138–1139; Raper, Horace Wilson, "William Woods Holden: A Political Biography" (Ph.D. dissertation, University of North Carolina at Chapel Hill, 1951), 285–409; State of North Carolina, Legislature, *Articles against William W. Holden,* Document No. 18, 1870–1871 Session (Raleigh: James H. Moore, State Printer, 1871); Zuber, Richard L., *North Carolina during Reconstruction* (Raleigh: State Department of Archives and History, 1996).

Honoraria

Payment, given to a politician, usually for a speech or some other work not related to his or her congressional duty, including writing books and articles for journals or magazines. The law at 5 USC § 505(3), states:

> The term "honorarium" means a payment of money or any thing of value for an appearance, speech or article (including a series of appearances, speeches, or articles if the subject matter is directly related to the individual's official duties or the payment is made because of the individual's status with the Government) by a Member, officer or employee, excluding any actual and necessary travel expenses

incurred by such individual (and one relative) to the extent that such expenses are paid or reimbursed by any other person, and the amount otherwise determined shall be reduced by the amount of any such expenses to the extent that such expenses are not paid or reimbursed.

The history of offering honoraria to politicians is somewhat murky. Historian Mildred Amer writes that the practice appears to have begun in the early nineteenth century, when politicians were paid to deliver lengthy lectures. A lecture bureau was established in 1873 to help politicians find opportunities to speak for the highest compensation possible. The Chautauqua movement, in which politicians and other speakers went to upstate New York to deliver speeches and addresses on various subjects of national interest, helped to promote the careers of politicians and other speakers. As Amer explained, "By the 1950s payment[s] to members of Congress for speeches was a widespread practice and cause for concern, as evidenced in the 1951 report of Senator Paul H. Douglas's Senate Subcommittee on Ethical Standards in Government." But Douglas's report (discussed elsewhere in this book) did not end honoraria, and the practice continued to constitute a major source of politicians' salaries. The post-Watergate reforms of Congress, most notably the Federal Election Campaign Act Amendments of 1974 (88 Stat. 1263), for the first time limited honoraria and established a salary ceiling of $15,000 per year for speeches, and a limit of $1,000 per speech, book, or article. The Senate voted to exclude itself from these restrictions—it was not until 1983 that that body limited honoraria.

During the 1970s and 1980s, honoraria became highly controversial. Critics of the practice saw it as a back door for the corruption of politicians and other officials. As the press reported more and more stories of politicians accepting honoraria for books, speeches, and they even accepted dinners, the outrage among the public grew. But Congress remained loathe to cut off this cash cow, so vital for many politicians not only to receive additional money aside from their salaries, but also for them to get their views out to the public through spoken and written means.

In 1989, however, Congress enacted the Ethics Reform Act (103 Stat. 1716), to end the practice of accepting honoraria or at least to rein it in. In the act, in which Congress stated that "substantial outside earned income creates at least the appearance of impropriety and thereby undermines public confidence in the integrity of government officials," section 501(b) of the Ethics in Government Act of 1978 was amended, prohibiting honoraria to be accepted while any person is a member, an officer, or an employee of the U.S. government. This is called the "section 505(3) ban." Immediately, several groups of government employees challenged the ban, citing a potential violation to their First Amendment right to free speech. The leader in this lawsuit was the National Treasury Employees Union (NTEU). A district court hearing their suit ruled that section 505(3) was "unconstitutional insofar as it applies to Executive Branch employees of the United States government." On appeal, the Court of Appeals for the District of Columbia Circuit affirmed, calling the section a burden on free speech. Again, the government appealed, this time to the United States Supreme Court. On 22 February 1995, that court held six to three (Justice Sandra Day O'Connor concurred with and dissented from various parts of the majority opinion) that 505(3) did in fact violate the free speech rights of government employees. Prior to this action, the U.S. Senate enacted the 1992 Legislative Branch Appropriations Act (Public Law 102-90), which contained a provision ending honoraria for senators.

Although the U.S. Supreme Court has held that banning honoraria for public employees is violative of the U.S. Constitution, the provision that it applied to the U.S. House of Representatives and U.S. Senate were allowed to stand, and as of this writing honoraria remains banned for those officers.

References: Amer, Mildred Lehmann, "Honoraria," in Donald C. Bacon, Roger H. Davidson, and Morton Keller, eds., *The Encyclopedia of the United States Congress*, 3 vols. (New York: Simon and Schuster, 1995), II:1048–1049; Ethics in Government Act, 5 U.S.C. 505(3); *United States v. National Treasury Employees Union*, 115 S. Ct. 1103, 513 U.S. 454 (1995).

Hopkinson, Francis (1737–1791)

Author and judge, impeached by the assembly of Pennsylvania for accepting illegal fees, but acquitted. Due to his long service to the nation, this episode of Hopkinson's life has been forgotten. Born in Philadelphia, Pennsylvania, on 2 October 1737, Hopkinson was the son of an English-born lawyer. Hopkinson was in the first class of the College of Philadelphia (later the University of Pennsylvania) in 1757, receiving his master's degree in 1760 from that school. He studied the law with famed attorney Benjamin Chew, who served as attorney general for Pennsylvania, and was admitted to the Pennsylvania bar in 1761. He was not successful as an attorney, instead working as a secretary to the Pennsylvania Indian Commission in 1761, helping to make treaties with several tribes in the colony. In 1763 he was named customs collector for Salem, New Jersey. He later opened a dry goods business in Philadelphia.

Having traveled to England and made close friends with Lord North, he was named to the royal council of New Jersey. He was elected an associate justice of the New Jersey Supreme Court, but declined. He was a vestryman and layman in the Christ Church in Philadelphia. But Hopkinson was not just an attorney—he was also a brilliant author and musician. He published numerous works and essays and played the harpsichord.

In 1776 Hopkinson served as a delegate to the Constitutional Congress, serving on the committee that drafted the Articles of Confederation. In 1779 he was elected a judge of the admiralty court for Philadelphia. It was on this seat that Hopkinson allegedly committed the crimes that got him impeached. According to a little-known report on the impeachment, on 22 November 1790 a report was presented to the speaker of the house of the Pennsylvania legislature, charging Hopkinson with specific crimes. The report stated:

> That having a power by law to appoint an agent for unrepresented shares belonging to absent seamen, and others, he offered and proposed to appoint Mr. Blair M'Clenachan, agent for a number of such shares belonging to seamen, who had failed on board the privateer *Holker,* upon the condition, that he the said Blair M'Clenachan would make a present of a suit of cloaths [*sic*]; and, this condition not being complied with, he appointed others in his stead;
>
> Receiving presents from persons interested in the condemnation of prizes, previous to their condemnation; particularly a cask of wine from on board the prize brigantine *Gloucester,* presented to

him by the captors before any condemnation, sale or distribution;

> Conniving at, and encouraging the sale of prizes before condemnation, contrary to law, and maliciously before the honourable the Supreme Executive Council; in the instance of the prize ship *Charlotte;* issuing a write of sale, of the cargo of a prize, declaring in the same writ that it was testified to him, that the same cargo was in danger of waste, spoil, and damage, when in fact and in truth no such testimony or return was ever given, or made to him;—in the instance of the cargo of the prize ship *Albion.*

In short, these charges accused Hopkinson of using his influence to sell captured ships ("prizes") and their cargo when their ownership was in question, or for Hopkinson's own personal benefit. Tried before the Pennsylvania state senate, Hopkinson was acquitted of all charges.

These events did not end Hopkinson's career—in fact, he was appointed to a federal judgeship by President George Washington in 1790. However, on 9 May 1791, Hopkinson suffered an attack of apoplexy and died, aged only fifty-three. The mention of his impeachment merited only one line of one his biographies.

References: *An Account of the Impeachment and Trial of the Late Francis Hopkinson, Esquire, Judge of the Court of Admiralty for the Commonwealth of Pennsylvania* (Philadelphia: Printed by Francis Bailey, at Yorick's Head, 1795), 3–4; Ward, Harry M., "Hopkinson, Francis," in John A. Garraty and Mark C. Carnes, gen. eds., *American National Biography,* 24 vols. (New York: Oxford University Press, 1999), 11:190–192.

House of Representatives Banking Scandal

Scandal that arose in 1992 after it was discovered that numerous congressional representatives had used the House of Representatives bank for check overdrafts. Two members—Mary Rose Oakar of Ohio and Thomas Downey of New York—lost their reelection campaigns because of the scandal, and Oakar later pled guilty to using the bank to funnel money from fake campaign donors. In effect, the House "bank" was not a bank at all—it was actually a credit union, run by the House chamber's sergeant at arms, where members could deposit their paychecks, campaign funds, and other monies and withdraw from the accounts via official checks. They were allowed to write over-drafts, if they promised to return the money at a future time. Such overdrafts were not penalized with fines, as at regular banks.

By 1991, many members had simply written a string of bad checks and had not paid back the money, and although taxpayer funds were never in jeopardy, the story that broke left many citizens outraged at the conduct of their elected represen-tatives. One representative, with a paper bag over his head, went to the floor of the House and admit-ted that he, too, had bounced many checks, but told his colleagues that for the good of the institu-tion all the names of all of those involved needed to be revealed. The congressman was Representa-tive Jim Nussle (R-IA), who was reelected the fol-lowing year. On 27 March 1992, Attorney General William Barr named retired Judge Malcolm R. Wilkey as special counsel to investigate the House banking scandal. The following month, in April 1992, the House Ethics Committee released the names of 325 current and former House members who had abused their banking privileges.

The shockwaves of the scandal reached far and wide. The sergeant at arms, Jack Russ, resigned his office in disgrace, later pleading guilty to numer-ous counts of wire fraud and filing false financial statements with the House of Representatives. He was sentenced to two years in prison. Representa-tive Louis Stokes (D-OH), a member of the House Ethics Committee, had to recuse himself from any investigation after it was found he had 551 bounced checks. Representative Oakar was later cleared of her role in the House banking scandal, but a subsequent investigation showed that she used the bank to funnel campaign funds to fake donors; Representative Downey lost his 1992 re-election effort, due in good part to his own check writing in the scandal. The House task force re-sponsible for initiating charges relating to the bank scandal also nabbed Representative Carroll Hubbard, Jr. (D-KY), former Representative Carl C. Perkins (D-KY), and Perkins's secretary, Martha Amburgey.

References: Cooper, Kenneth J., "House Bank Subpoena Is Pressed, Early Inquiry, Said to Show Evidence of Check-Kiting Scheme," *Washington Post,* 28 April 1992, A1; "[Editorial:] The House Bank (Cont'd)," *Washington Post,* 28 April 1992, A14; House Resolution 236, 3 October 1991; LaFraniere, Sharon, "Barr Takes Center Stage at Justice Department with New Script," *Washington Post,* 5 March 1992, A19; "Rehnquist Refuses to Bar Bank Probe," *Washington Post,* 7 May 1992, A14; *United States v. Oakar,* Appellees (No. 96–3084), U.S. Court of Appeals for the DC Circuit, 111 F. 3d 146 (1997); United States Congress, House of Representatives, Committee on Standards of Official Conduct, "Inquiry into the Operation of the Bank of the Sergeant-at-Arms of the House of Representatives: Report of the Committee on Standards of Official Conduct, House of Representatives, Together with Minority Views (to accompany H. Res. 393)" (Washington, DC: Government Printing Office, 1992).

House of Representatives Committee on Standards of Official Conduct

Congressional committee, established 13 April 1967, to oversee ethics in the U.S. House of Repre-sentatives. The committee's jurisdiction is strictly the ethically behavior of the members of the House of Representatives, and is allowed to study, investigate, and recommend action to the full House.

The committee's main responsibilities are to:

A) Recommend administrative actions to establish or enforce standards of official conduct;

B) Investigate alleged violations of the Code of Official Conduct or of any applicable rules, laws, or regulations governing the performance of official duties or the discharge of official responsibilities. Such investigations must be made in accordance with Committee rules;

C) Report to appropriate federal or State author-ities substantial evidence of a violation of any law applicable to the performance of official duties that may have been disclosed in a Committee investiga-tion. Such reports must be approved by the House or by an affirmative vote of two-thirds of the Com-mittee;

D) Render advisory opinions regarding the pro-priety of any current or proposed conduct of a Member, officer, or employee, and issue general guidance on such matters as necessary; and

E) Consider requests for written waivers of the gift rule.

The committee's rules state:

The Ethics in Government Act (EIGA) designates the Committee on Standards of Official Conduct as the "supervising ethics office" for the House of

Representatives and charges the Committee with duties and responsibilities for Financial Disclosure Statements (Title I) and for Outside Employment (Title V) with respect to Members, officers, and employees of the House of Representatives.

The statute also charges the Committee with duties and responsibilities with regard to (1) the Financial Disclosure Statements of candidates for the House, and (2) the Financial Disclosure Statements and Outside Employment of officers and employees of certain legislative branch agencies, including the Library of Congress, the Congressional Budget Office, the Government Printing Office, the Architect of the Capitol, and the United States Botanic Garden. However, the Committee has delegated much of its authority with regard to the officers and employees of those agencies to the heads of those agencies.

The most recent investigation regarding ethics that the committee handled was that of former Representative James A. Traficant (D-OH), who was expelled from the House in 2002.

References: United States Congress, House of Representatives, Committee on Standards of Official Conduct, *Ethics Manual for Members and Employees of the U.S. House of Representatives. Prepared at the Direction of the Committee on Standards of Official Conduct, 96th Congress, 1st Session* (Washington, DC: U.S. Government Printing Office, 1979); United States Congress, House of Representatives, Committee on Standards of Official Conduct, *Rules of Procedure: Committee on Standards of Official Conduct* (Washington, DC: Government Printing Office, 1987).

House of Representatives Post Office Scandal

Scandal in the U.S. House of Representatives, 1992–1995, which exposed several members and former members of that body to allegations of profiteering and obstruction of justice. The first sign of trouble came on 19 March 1992, when House Postmaster Robert V. Rota resigned. Rota, who had worked at the House post office for two decades, resigned without explanation. The departure sent shockwaves through the House and the media. Suddenly, allegations of cash shortages, profiteering, and obstruction of justice came to light. U.S. Attorney Jay B. Stephens, investigating the allegations, uncovered a pattern of obstruction of justice. In his initial probe, starting on 11 June 1991, Capitol Hill police were refused entry to the

offices until 9 July 1991, when federal investigators ordered records to be handed over. These investigators found that Rota had allowed postal employees to cash checks for House members and redeem them with stamps, allowing these members to circumvent campaign spending and donation rules. One of the members accused of doing this was Representative Dan Rostenkowski (D-IL), a powerful member and chairman of the House Ways and Means Committee. A federal grand jury, run by Stephens, subpoenaed three members of Congress. On 24 July 1992, Rostenkowski and the two other members—Representative Austin J. Murphy (D-PA) and Representative Joseph Kolter (D-PA)—all stated that they would refuse to answer any questions regarding the post office matter and would invoke their Fifth Amendment rights against self-incrimination.

The press frenzy over the scandal exploded. The *New York Times,* the *Washington Times,* and the *Washington Post* all covered it with huge headlines. Especially Rostenkowski's own hometown paper, the *Chicago Tribune,* made light of the scandal. On 10 September 1992, a federal grand jury indicted former House post office manager Joanna G. O'Rourke on charges that she conspired to make post office funds available for the personal use of congressional members. House postmaster Robert Rota pled guilty in 1993 to charges that he embezzled money from the House post office. On 31 May 1994, Rostenkowski was indicted on seventeen counts of embezzling public and campaign funds, mail and wire fraud, conspiracy, and obstruction of justice. In 1994 he lost his bid for reelection and, on 9 April 1996, pled guilty to two counts of mail fraud and was sentenced to seventeen months in prison and fined $100,000. Joseph Kolter pled guilty in May 1996 to pocketing $9,300 from the House post office and was sentenced to six months in prison because of ill health.

The House post office scandal cost only a few members their honor and/or positions, Rostenkowski most notably—but it was a turning point in how the American public looked at Congress.

See also Rostenkowski, Daniel David
References: Cooper, Kenneth J., "House Postmaster Resigns; New Allegations Raised on Policies," *Washington Post,* 20 March 1992, A1; Cooper, Kenneth J., "Possible Obstruction Probed in House Post Office,"

Washington Post, 26 March 1992, A1; Locy, Toni, "Ex-Congressman Kolter Indicted in House Post Office Probe," *Washington Post,* 19 October 1994, A6; McAllister, Bill, "House Gives Up Its Post Offices," *Washington Post,* 19 October 1995, A4; Pincus, Walter, "House Postal Cash Went for Loans; Ex-Workers Tell Probe of Regular Shortages," *Washington Post,* 27 March 1992, A1; York, Michael, "Ex-Manager of House Post Office Indicted; Grand Jury Charges Conspiracy to Use Tax Funds to Benefit Members of Congress," *Washington Post,* 11 September 1992, A3.

Housing and Urban Development (HUD) Scandal

Scandal uncovered in 1989 that implicated several members of Ronald Reagan's administration in corruption in the Department of Housing and Urban Development (HUD), but in which Secretary Samuel Pierce Jr. was never implicated by the work of two independent counsels. The HUD scandal investigation ranks with the Iran-Contra investigation and the Whitewater investigation as one of the longest independent counsel inquiries in American history.

The Department of Housing and Urban Development, established in 1965 by Congress under the direction of President Lyndon Johnson's "Great Society" of social programs for the poor and underprivileged, was from its very inception a grand idea interspliced with the corruption of the body politic. Secretary after secretary, under each new administration, found a morass of waste, corruption, and gross fraud in the way housing was constructed, maintained, and provided for the poorer citizens of the nation. And with each new administration calls would come for a cleaning up of the problem. New congressional oversight, new administrative measures, new offices—all were sent down to end the corruption. But with each new administration it was discovered that the cleanups only made the problems worse. In fact, in 1994, the General Accounting Office named the department the only one in the federal government "a high risk" for fraud, waste, and corruption. One of the programs established inside the department was called "Section 8," a fund from which housing vouchers were issued to the poor to rent or lease housing. Unfortunately, this fund was controlled by the secretary of the department himself, in what was essentially an unchecked slush fund.

This program went on for years without any oversight by Congress.

When Ronald Reagan came into office in 1981, he appointed the well-respected Judge Samuel Pierce Jr. as his secretary of housing and urban development. Despite his having no expertise in housing matters, Pierce's history of honesty seemed to be the one thing the department needed most: an honorable leader. Pierce had a solid character and was later cleared of any wrongdoing, but his hands-off style led to massive thievery by friends and cronies of Reagan administration officials. Pierce, in congressional testimony, later said that the department when he found it was open to "improper and even criminal conduct." A lack of congressional oversight was part of the problem, but the structure of HUD and billions of dollars at the department's disposal for housing was another. Many lobbyists and friends of HUD officials were able to put in for loans from the Section 8 fund, and the fund was drained of untold millions of dollars. The true toll of theft is unknown.

Pierce and the scandal surrounding HUD did not surface until he was out of office. In April 1989, three months after Pierce had departed, Paul Adams, the HUD inspector general, issued a report that showed that Section 8 had become an unmitigated disaster of fraud and abuse. The portion of the program that he targeted for concern was the Moderate Rehabilitation Program (called MRP or Mod Rehab). Congress had created MRP as part of the Housing and Community Development Act of 1978. Initially, the act forced the secretary of housing and urban development to distribute MRP funds evenly across the nation, regardless of need. In 1984, however, Congress changed the law so that the secretary could, on his own, send funds where he felt they were needed most. Pierce took full advantage of this change, Adams charged in his report. He documented that ten states received more than 50 percent of MRP funds from 1984 to 1988, the last being Pierce's last full year in office. Pierce's successor, former Representative Jack F. Kemp, ended the program as soon as these abuses came to light.

With the issuance of Adams's report, Congress acted. The House Subcommittee on Employment and Housing, of the House Committee on Government Operations, opened hearings on

Some thousand homeless and their supporters gather at the Washington Monument on 7 October 1989 to demand an end to homelessness and restoration of billions of dollars slashed from scandal-scarred HUD. (Bettmann/Corbis)

the allegations that Pierce and numerous staff members serving under him had engaged in widespread corruption. The hearings, chaired by Representative Tom Lantos (D-CA), got bogged down in partisan wrangling; however, the majority report of the committee stated, "During much of the eighties, HUD was enveloped by influence peddling, favoritism, abuse, greed, fraud, embezzlement, and theft." Based on the early committee findings in late 1989, the majority asked Attorney General Dick Thornburgh to appoint an independent counsel to investigate the matter. In March 1990 Arlin Adams, a former judge on the U.S. Court of Appeals for the Third Circuit and a lawyer in Philadelphia, was named by a three-judge panel in Washington. Adams began his investigation, which he told the court that appointed him that he felt he could wrap up in a few months, by looking at the documentary evidence presented to the House committee. As his probe expanded, so did the cost of the investigation; by the time it was finished, it cost more than $28 million. Adams found a widespread array of fraud and corruption, ranging from a scheme by the

U.S. ambassador to Switzerland, Philip D. Winn, a former assistant secretary of HUD, to pay bribes to HUD officials to steer lucrative Section 8 contracts to his Denver-based housing development company, to 250 units of housing being "given" as a severance package to DuBois Gilliam, a Pierce aide. Deborah Gore Dean, Pierce's chief assistant, was later indicted and convicted of receiving a bribe of $4,000. In all, the investigation produced seventeen convictions and led to more than $2 million in fines. More than $10 million in housing grants was recovered and returned to the federal government. Former Secretary of the Interior James Watt later pled guilty to withholding documents and information from a grand jury investigating his role in lobbying HUD officials in a scheme to get housing grants.

In 1995 Adams stepped aside and was replaced by Larry D. Thompson as the independent counsel. Thompson's work lasted for three additional years, until his final report was released in October 1998. The two men concluded that high HUD officials engaged in a "monumental and calculated abuse of the public trust." The investigators discovered "a pervasive pattern of improper and illegal behavior."

The report went on:

> High-ranking HUD officials put their own interests ahead of those of the members of the public they were charged to serve and protect: the poor and homeless of this nation. . . . At a time of dramatic cutbacks in federal funding—cutbacks that many of these officials publicly supported—increased vigilance was essential to ensure that the scarce remaining funds were put to the best possible use. Instead, a pattern of greed, criminal conduct and systematic corruption of the government process by HUD officials emerged.

In the end, Pierce was never charged with a crime. He was offered a way out if he told prosecutors whether he did in fact foster an environment in which HUD officials were involved in "improper and even criminal conduct." Once Pierce made this admission, he was allowed to walk away from the scandal. But he was not unscathed. When he died in November 2000, obituaries remembered him not for his lifetime of public service, but for the massive scandal in his department that may have cost between $2 billion and $8 billion.

References: Cooper, Kenneth J., "Pierce Misled Hill, Panel Concludes," *Washington Post*, 2 November 1990, A23; *Final Report of the Independent Counsel in re: Samuel R. Pierce, Jr. Arlin M. Adams, Larry D. Thompson, Independent Counsels,* 6 vols. (Washington, DC: U.S. Court of Appeals for the District of Columbia Circuit, Division for the Purpose of Appointing Independent Counsels, 1998); "Samuel Pierce, HUD Secretary," in Jeffrey D. Schultz, *Presidential Scandals* (Washington, DC: CQ Press, 2000), 405–407; Smith, J. Y., "HUD Secretary Samuel Pierce, Jr., 78, Dies, Influence-Peddling Scandal Tainted the Legacy of Reagan Cabinet Member," *Washington Post*, 4 November 2000, B7; "Special Counsel Urges End to 'Impasse,'" *Washington Post*, 3 August 1990, A6.

Hubbard, Carroll, Jr. (1937–)

United States representative from Kentucky (1975–1993) who pled guilty in 1994 to conspiring to defraud the Federal Elections Commission by illegally spending campaign funds for personal uses, and to the theft of government property. Born in Murray, Kentucky, 7 July 1937, he attended the public schools of the area. He received first his bachelor's degree from Georgetown (Kentucky) College in 1959 and then his law degree from the University of Louisville Law School in 1962. Admitted to the Kentucky bar that same year, he opened a practice in the town of Mayfield. He served in the Kentucky Air National Guard from 1962 to 1967, and in the Kentucky Army National Guard from 1968 to 1970.

A Democrat, Hubbard ran for a seat in the Kentucky state senate in 1967 and was elected, serving until 1975. In 1974 he had run for a seat in the U.S. House of Representatives, eventually serving in that body from 3 January 1975 until 3 January 1993. In 1979 he ran unsuccessfully for the Democratic nomination for governor of Kentucky.

Hubbard got into ethical trouble when he was accused of using campaign funds for personal items, including paying for his cable television bill directly from these funds, as well as his wife's hairdressing bills. He was also accused of spending an additional $154,000 on his congressional staff for personal favors. When congressional investigators opened an investigation into the alleged spending irregularities, Hubbard staged a phony burglary at his congressional office in Paducah, Kentucky, later claiming that the documents that had been asked for by the investigators had been stolen. This set off a deeper investigation, one that led directly to Hubbard's corrupt behavior. In 1992, under suspicion, he failed to win his party's nomination for Congress, and he left that body on 3 January 1993. A year later, in 1994, Hubbard pled guilty to conspiring to defraud the Federal Elections Commission of campaign funds, as well as to the theft of government property relating to the faked break-in in his office. Sentenced to three years in prison, Hubbard nonetheless was allowed to collect his congressional pension—$45,000 a year. His wife, Carol Brown Hubbard, also pled guilty to a misdemeanor and was sentenced to probation. Carroll Hubbard ultimately served two years in prison and was released in 1996.

In October 2001 Hubbard's law license was returned by a unanimous opinion of the Kentucky Supreme Court, despite the fact that the Kentucky Bar Association Board of Governors voted unanimously (sixteen to zero) to reject his reapplication.

See also Perkins, Carl Christopher
References: *Biographical Directory of the American Congress, 1774–1996* (Alexandria, VA: CQ Staff Directories, Inc., 1996), 1248; *Hubbard v. United States,* 115 S. Ct. 1754, 514 U.S. 695 (1995).

Hubbell, Levi (1808–1876)

Associate justice (1848–1853) and chief justice (1851) of the Wisconsin Supreme Court who resigned due to alleged malfeasance relating to bribes paid to judicial officers. Hubbell later served as the U.S. attorney for the Eastern District of Wisconsin (1871–1875), but again was forced to resign when allegations of corruption surrounded him. He died in disgrace and is the only judge in the history of Wisconsin to face impeachment over political corruption. Little is known about his life: he was born in the town of Ballston, New York, on 15 April 1808, graduated from Union College in Schenectady, New York, read the law in Canandaigua, New York, and was admitted to that state's bar in 1827. He joined the Whig Party and served as a member of the New York state assembly for a single term. He was the editor of a small newspaper, the *Ontario (New York) Messenger,* for a short period of time.

In 1844 Hubbell moved from New York to Wisconsin, settling in Milwaukee and joining a law firm in that city that was run by Asahel Finch and William Pitt Lynde, two leading local attorneys. In 1848, when Wisconsin entered the Union as a state, Hubbell was elected a circuit judge for the Second Judicial Circuit. His position was advanced when a state supreme court was established and he was named to it, serving as a justice from 1848 to 1853, and as chief justice in 1851. Because the state's terms of office had not been settled, justices drew lots and Hubbell was assigned a three-year term. In 1851 he ran for reelection, this time allowed a six-year term. However, press reports from the nominating convention in 1851 show that Hubbell was not popular in his first term, and his former law partner, Asahel Finch, was named to run against him. One case over which Hubbell had presided as a justice became the main objection to his candidacy: he had cleared a local attorney accused of political corruption when the attorney pled ignorance of the law. Despite press hostility, Hubbell easily won the 1851 race. However, the Democratic Party split into three factions: pro-Hubbell, anti-Hubbell, and a third led by William Barstow, a crooked politician who was later elected governor of Wisconsin. Edward G. Ryan, a local judge and political strongman, led the anti-Hubbell faction.

In the 1853 elections to the state supreme court, Hubbell's political enemies gathered around and denied him a nomination. Ryan, incensed at some of Hubbell's decisions, moved to have Hubbell impeached in the state assembly, accusing the judge of taking bribes and hearing cases in which he had a vested interest. On 22 March 1853, eleven separate charges containing more than seventy specific allegations were lodged against Hubbell in the state assembly. In all, Hubbell was charged with accepting bribes, presiding over cases in which he had an economic interest, using court funds for his own personal uses, and showing prejudice against some persons before him based upon their political connections. Hubbell pled not guilty, and his trial opened on 13 June 1853. Edward G. Ryan acted as the prosecutor, despite the fact that assembly managers for the impeachment had been selected. Hubbell assisted his two attorneys and made an impassioned plea before the court of impeachment. Ryan savaged Hubbell. In one lengthy accusation, he said of the judge:

> [He is] a judge of easy virtue; approaching and retreating by turns, with a rare mockery of judicial virtue on his tongue; promising to set aside verdicts; hinting the vacating of judgments; suggesting settlements for his friends; dissolving injunctions before they are issued; chambering in private with jurors in the jury room; divorcing women and instructing them in the principles of divorcing in sacred privacy; promising to bring on causes for trial, when the paper evidences on which they were founded were lost; tampering with the penal judgments of the law; when money was payable into court, offering to receive part into his own private pocket, instead of the whole into the court, as required by law; refusing to hear argument in court in order to keep his promise made in private.

Hubbell's attorneys argued that he had never committed any illegal offense. Hubbell himself told the court of impeachment, "I trust that such will be the judgment of this court as to satisfy the people, whose name has been used to sanctify this impeachment, and such as to satisfy posterity; that it has been, both in its beginning and in its end, the work of public justice, and not the work of private malice or of a diseased imagination."

Hubbell was ultimately acquitted on all charges, with only half of the senators agreeing to convict. (A two-thirds vote is required for conviction.) Despite the judicial clearance, Hubbell was not wholly exonerated, and his reputation was ruined. He resigned his court position.

For the remainder of his life, Levi Hubbell was marked as the man who suffered the first (and, as of this writing, the only) impeachment in Wisconsin history. In 1863, however, he was elected to a seat in the Wisconsin state assembly, serving for one one-year term. Despite being a Democrat, in 1871 he was named by President Ulysses S. Grant to be the U.S. attorney for the Eastern District of Wisconsin, serving until 1875. It was in this office that again Hubbell was tainted by whispers of political corruption. In 1875 Hubbell was suspended from the U.S. attorney position when several of his associates were implicated in the nationwide Whiskey Ring frauds, a series of swindles of government money by whiskey revenue agents. Hubbell himself was never found to be involved directly in the frauds, but again his name was ruined, and he returned to private law practice in Milwaukee.

Only a year after being removed from the U.S. attorney position, Levi Hubbell died in Milwaukee on 8 December 1876 after falling and being severely injured; he was sixty-eight.

References: Grant, Marilyn, "Judge Levi Hubbell: A Man Impeached," *Wisconsin Magazine of History,* 64:1 (Autumn 1980), 28–39; State of Wisconsin, State Senate, *Trial of Impeachment of Levi Hubbell, Judge of the Second Judicial Circuit, by the Senate of the State of Wisconsin, June 1853. Reported by T.C. Leland* (Madison, WI: B. Brown, 1853).

Hunt, (Harold) Guy (1933–)

Governor of Alabama (1987–1993), convicted of misusing campaign funds and removed from office. Hunt became one of the few governors in the history of the United States to be removed from office for corruption. Born in Holly Pond, Alabama, on 17 June 1933, he is the son of William Otto Hunt and Fances Orene (née Holcombe) Hunt. He attended local schools, studying to be a farmer. He served as president of the local chapter of the Future Farmers of America. However, when the Korean War broke out, Hunt volunteered for service, and, as a member of the 101st Airborne Division and the First Infantry Division, he saw major action, and was awarded the Certificate of Achievement for Outstanding Performance of Military Duty.

When he returned home from the war, Hunt gave up his dream of becoming a farmer and instead entered the ministry. He was ordained a Baptist minister in 1958. However, within four years, he decided to enter politics in Alabama. Athough Alabama was a one-party state, ruled by Democrats from the highest office to the lowest, Hunt became a Republican. In 1962 he ran unsuccessfully for a state senate seat. Two years later, he was elected a probate judge for Cullman County, a seat he held until 1974. In 1976, when former California Governor Ronald Reagan ran for president, Hunt served as his state campaign manager. He also served as chairman of the state delegation to the Republican National Convention in Kansas City that year.

In 1978 Hunt decided to run for governor. However, his opponent was the popular Democrat, Fob James, and Hunt was defeated in a landslide by more than 350,000 votes out of some 750,000 cast. Hunt again served as Reagan's campaign manager in Alabama in 1980 and went to the party's national convention in Detroit. His longtime support for Reagan was rewarded, for when Reagan was elected president, Hunt was appointed state executive director of the Agricultural Stabilization and Conservation Service (ASCS), a post in the U.S. Department of Agriculture. Hunt held this office from 1981 to 1985.

Hunt resigned to make a second run for governor. Again, he stood little chance of being elected—the state had not sent a Republican to the state executive mansion since 1874. When Governor George Wallace decided not to run for reelection, it was assumed that whichever Democrat entered the race and won the party primary would automatically be elected. Hunt won the Republican primary. It appeared that he would face Democratic state Attorney General Charles R. Graddick, who won his party's primary, but Graddick was stripped of the nomination when it was discovered he had called on Republicans to illegally cross over to vote for him. The courts named Graddick's opponent, Lieutenant Governor Bill Baxley, as the nominee, but Graddick threw a wheel in the political spokes when he announced as an independent. However, when his support grew thin, he bowed out of the race, but the split in the Democratic Party helped Hunt. On 4 November 1986, Hunt defeated Baxley, 56 to 44 percent, making him the first Republican governor of Alabama since David Peter Lewis held the office from 1872 to 1874. However, Democrats controlled every other state office, diluting Hunt's power and making it appear he won only because of the Democratic Party split.

During his term, Hunt used his office to attract industry to the state. However, when Democrats in control of the state legislature blocked his agenda, Hunt came off as a sympathetic figure. In 1990 he won reelection by defeating Democrat Paul Hubbert. However, soon after he was sworn in a second time, allegations surfaced that Hunt had violated state ethics laws. Historian Marie Marmo Mullaney explained,

> As a Primitive Baptist preacher, Hunt used state planes for trips to church meetings where he received cash offerings. In small fundamentalist Primative Baptist churches, ministers are not paid salaries but are given donations by churchgoers. Consequently, the state attorney general convened a special grand jury to review allegations of ethics violations against [Hunt]. In response, Hunt wrote the state a personal check to cover the costs of the flights and agreed to stop using state planes to travel to preaching engagements.

Despite this, Hunt was indicted in December 1992 on thirteen charges of ethics violations. Although twelve of these were eventually thrown out, the one that stood alleged that Hunt had misused monies from his 1987 inaugural. Hunt became the eighth governor in American history to be indicted while in office, and the first Alabama governor to be so charged. Hunt was politically dead, despite the fact that he was limited by law to two terms in office. However, when his trial opened in April 1993, the allegations grew when it was shown that he diverted some $200,000 from the 1987 inaugural committee to pay for personal charges. Hunt was convicted on one charge of ethics violations and removed from office on 22 April 1993. Lieutenant Governor James E. Folsom Jr. was sworn into office that same day. Hunt was given five years' probation and ordered to repay the $211,000 and perform 1,000 hours of community service.

Hunt appealed his conviction. Although it was never overturned, the Alabama Board of Pardons and Paroles ruled in 1998 that Hunt was illegally denied the right to vote and restored the right. Hunt immediately announced his candidacy for governor. However, he was defeated in the Republican primary by Winton Blount, a businessman, and left politics forever.

References: "Hunt, Guy," in Marie Marmo Mullaney, *Biographical Directory of the Governors of the United States, 1983–1988* (Westport, CT: Greenwood Press, 1988), 9–11; "Hunt, Guy," in Marie Marmo Mullaney, *Biographical Directory of the Governors of the United States, 1988–1994* (Westport, CT: Greenwood Press, 1994), 3–9.

I

Impeachment

Act of Congress (or other legislative body) to remove government officials who commit "high crimes and misdemeanors," although the exact definition of that phrase has been widely interpreted since it was written into the U.S. Constitution in 1787. The history of impeachment, however, reaches back to England, when it was established as a tool of the English Parliament to punish officers under the authority of the king who had committed a list of various offenses. Historians differ on the exact date that the practice of impeachment began. Some say 1376, while historian Alexander Simpson Jr. believes that the first use of impeachment was actually in 1283. In his *Treatise on Federal Impeachments,* Simpson explained:

> The writers on the judicial history of England disagree as to when the English impeachments began. Stephens in his *History of the Criminal Law of England* says that the first case was against David, the brother of Llewellyn in 1283. Pike in his *Constitutional History of the House of Lords* says that it was against Richard Lyons, a merchant of London, in 1376. Hallam in his *Constitutional History of England* and Anson in his *Law and Custom of the Constitution* agree with Pike that it was in 1376, but say that it was against Lord Latimer.

Historian Elizabeth Hallam writes that the so-called Good Parliament of 1376, which met under the leadership of King Edward III, "was of great importance because of the development of impeachment, which rested upon the basic assumption that the king's ministers, as public officials, were accountable not just to the king but to parliament which represented the whole community of the realm." Thus, under this standard, the first official impeachment was of Lord William Latimer in 1376. The passage of the impeachment statute in the laws of Henry IV in 1399 codified the impeachment action into law. Sir James Fitz-James Stephen, Bart., wrote in 1883, "From 1459 to 1621, a period of 162 years, no impeachment appears to gave taken place. . . . It was not till Parliament reasserted itself under James I and Charles I that it became natural or perhaps possible to use impeachment for the punishment of ministers considered corrupt or oppressive." The English used impeachment quite frequently for a number of centuries; however, by the time of American independence, it had become a rare event. The last two British impeachments were of Warren Hastings in 1787 and Lord Melville in 1805.

In the American colonies, impeachment became a tool of the colonial governments, and in 1635 John Harvey, the Royal Governor of Virginia, was removed from office. However, it was thereafter used only sparingly, because opposition from London precluded any further removals from office without the consent of the king. Because of this lack of authority, from 1700 until

1750 impeachment was used only four times. With the American Revolution, control from London ended, and some state impeachments were initiated, including a threat against Governor Thomas Jefferson of Virginia for failing to prepare for the British invasion of his state. John Adams, in his *Thoughts on Government* (1776), penned, "For misbehaviour the grand inquest of the Colony, the House of Representatives, should impeach [officials] before the Governor and Council, where they should have time and opportunity to make their defence, but if convicted should be removed from their offices, and subjected to such other punishments as shall be thought proper."

When the Founding Fathers gathered in Philadelphia in 1787 to compose the document that became the federal constitution, they decided to insert a clause on impeachment based on the British model. In *Federalist No. 65,* Alexander Hamilton, writing under the pseudonym Publius, later wrote:

> A well-constituted court for the trial of impeachments is an object not more to be desired than difficult to be obtained in a government wholly elective. The subjects of its jurisdiction are those offenses which proceed from the misconduct of public men, or, in other words, from the abuse or violation of some public trust. They are of a nature which may with peculiar propriety be denominated POLITICAL, as they relate chiefly to injuries done immediately to the society itself. The prosecution of them, for this reason, will seldom fail to agitate the passions of the whole community, and to divide it into parties more or less friendly or inimical to the accused. In many cases it will connect itself with the pre-existing factions, and will enlist all their animosities, partialities, influence, and interest on one side or on the other; and in such cases there will always be the greatest danger that the decision will be regulated more by the comparative strength of parties, than by the real demonstrations of innocence or guilt.

The delegates to the convention settled on having federal executive officers subjected to the impeachment power and removal from office for "high crimes and misdemeanors," although recent developments have made that phrase seem ambiguous. This inclusion came about from the idea of John Randolph of Virginia, who assigned the initial impeachment trial to the national Supreme Court. In his so-called Ninth Resolution, he explained, "that a National Judiciary be established . . . that the jurisdiction of the inferior tribunals shall be to hear and determine in the first instance, and of the supreme tribunal to hear and determine in the dernier [last] resort . . . impeachments of any National officers, and questions which may involve the national peace and harmony." Gouverneur Morris held that such a trial should take place in the Senate, but be presided over by the chief judge of the national Supreme Court. Once this was agreed to, the exact language regarding the reasons why an officer should be removed was debated. The delegates were proceeding with an offer by Hugh Williamson of North Carolina, whose state constitution allowed for impeachment and removal for "conviction of malpractice and neglect of duty." In August, however, James Madison changed this standard to one involving "treason, bribery, or corruption." Delegate George Mason objected to this standard, declaring, "Why is the provision restrained to Treason and bribery only? Treason as defined in the Constitution will not reach many great and dangerous offences. . . . [I]t is more necessary to extend the power of impeachments." Mason argued that "maladministration" was too vague and insisted that "other high crimes and misdemeanors" besides treason be included. Mason's language was agreed to and became the standard by which all federal executive and judicial officers in the United States are judged if impeached. This so-called impeachment clause, located at Article I, Section 3, Clause 6, reads:

> The Senate shall have the sole Power to try all Impeachments. When sitting for that Purpose, they shall be on Oath or Affirmation. When the President of the United States is tried, the Chief Justice shall preside: And no Person shall be convicted without the Concurrence of two-thirds of the Members present.

Since 1789, federal impeachment proceedings have been initiated more than sixty times; in seventeen of these, impeachment articles were approved by the House, resulting in fourteen trials (three subjects resigned before trial.) Of the fourteen trials in the Senate, there have been seven acquittals; seven of those tried were convicted: John Pickering of the District Court of New Hampshire

(1804); West H. Humphreys, of the District Court of the Eastern, Middle, and Western District of Tennessee (1862); Robert W. Archbald of the Commerce Court (1913); Halsted L. Ritter of the Southern District of Florida (1936); Harry E. Claiborne of the District of Nevada (1986); Alcee L. Hastings, United States District Judge for the Southern District of Florida (1989); and Walter L. Nixon Jr., United States District Judge for the Southern District of Mississippi (1989). (See Appendix Seven for a complete listing.) As time has passed the interpretation of the impeachment statute has grown in importance; that is, what exactly is an impeachable offense? The phrase "high crimes and misdemeanors" leaves this particular offense quite vague and open to wide interpretation. For instance, during the impeachment trial of Judge James Hawkins Peck in 1833, House impeachment manager Representative James Buchanan of Pennsylvania (later president of the United States, 1857–1861), provided his thoughts on what constitutes an impeachable offense:

> What is misbehavior in office? In answer to this question and without pretending to furnish a definition, I freely admit that we are bound to prove that the respondent has violated the Constitution, or some known law of the land. This, I think, is the principle fairly to be deduced from all the arguments on the trial of Judge [Samuel] Chase, and from the votes of the Senate on the Articles of Impeachment against him, in opposition to the principle for which his counsel in the first instance strenuously contended, that in order to render an offence impeachable it must be indictable. But this violation of the law may consist in the abuse, as well as in the usurpation of authority. The abuse of power which has been given may be as criminal as the usurpation of a power which has not been granted.

One subject of impeachment proceedings, Judge George W. English, resigned before an impeachment trial could be held. Another subject, District Judge Albert W. Johnson, resigned in 1946 when it appeared the House would impeach him. When his resignation made the procedure moot, the House committee held that impeachment was not needed, despite the issues involved, because the Senate would have been occupied on such a matter "when that body is engaged in so many issues vital to the welfare of the nation."

The U.S. Constitution gives the Senate the sole power to conduct impeachment trials, and no court can review the results of a trial in that body. Two recent cases, however, have sought to have the power amended. Following the Senate convictions of Judges Walter L. Nixon Jr. and Alcee L. Hastings, both men asked to have the power narrowed because, as Nixon argued, the Senate's failure to give him a full evidentiary hearing before the entire Senate violated its constitutional duty to "try" all impeachments. The District Court for the District of Columbia ruled against him, and the U.S. Court of Appeals for the D.C. Circuit upheld that judgment. Judge Williams, writing for that higher court, held that the U.S. Constitution grants the Senate "the sole Power to try all impeachments" and as well "gives it sole discretion to choose its procedures" to try such impeachments. However, in contrast to *Nixon,* Judge Stanley Sporkin of the U.S. District Court for the District of Columbia held in *Hastings v. United States,* 802 F. Supp. 490 (1992), held that the impeachment power *could* be examined by courts. He wrote, "The key issue in this case is whether a life-tenured Article III judge who has been acquitted of felony charges by a petit jury can thereafter be impeached and tried for essentially the same alleged indiscretion by a committee of the United States Senate consisting of less than the full Senate. This court determines that the answer is no." Sporkin granted Hastings relief by ordering his conviction before the Senate vacated and a new impeachment trial to be held. This was a landmark decision. However, when the U.S. Supreme Court handed down its decision in *Nixon v. United States,* which held that all impeachments before the Senate were beyond any and all judicial review, Sporkin reversed his decision and held against Hastings.

Although the issue of federal impeachment power is more often the subject of study, impeachment power in state constitutions deserves an examination. For instance, since the Constitution was signed in 1787, every state save Oregon has placed this power to remove state officials in their state constitutions. The stipulations of how the power is to be exercised vary from state to state. A few states, such as New York, allow judicial oversight on impeachment trials. For instance, during the impeachment of Governor William Sulzer in 1913, Judge Edgar T. Cullen oversaw the case.

Other states in this category—Missouri and Nebraska, among others—allow for judicial oversight in whole or in part.

Another topic of interest is that in many states the offices that are subject to impeachment are set out. In Alaska, only judges and justices of the state supreme court may be impeached—not the governor, the cabinet, or other state officers. In Alabama, however, impeachment proceedings may be brought against nearly every officeholder in the state. As well, the grounds for impeachment—"treason, bribery, and other high crimes and misdemeanors" in the federal Constitution—vary state by state. Louisiana specifies "incompetence, corruption, favoritism, extortion, or oppression in office, gross misconduct, or habitual drunkenness," while Arizona designates impeachable offenses to include "malfeasance in office." Alabama leaves it to "willful neglect of duty, corruption in office, incompetency, or intemperance in the use of intoxicating liquors or narcotics to such an extent, in view of the dignity of the office and importance of its duties, as to make the officer unfit to discharge such duties, or the commission of any offense, while in office, involving moral turpitude." Utah specifies its impeachment clause with a series of numbered articles, making it one of the longest in the nation. That state sets impeachment for:

(1) personal misconduct, usurpation of power, or habitual disregard for the public interest in the discharge of his official duties;

(2) commission of an indictable criminal offense;

(3) [an] intentional act of omission or commission relating to his official duties involving a substantial breach of trust;

(4) substantial breach of the trust imposed upon the official by the nature of his office, and which conduct is offensive to commonly accepted standards of honesty and morality;

(5) physical or mental disability which affects the person's ability to function properly; or

(6) such other causes as have existed historically and at common law.

Impeachments of state governors include Levi Hubbell of Wisconsin (1853), the aforementioned William Sulzer of New York (1913), James Ferguson of Texas (1917), John C. Walton of Oklahoma (1923), and Evan Mecham of Arizona (1988).

Impeachment differs from the ancient rite of attainder, which is a trial in the English Parliament before the king in which the assembled lords agree to a charge, usually of treason, and discuss a sentence. This was outlawed in the United States by the U.S. Constitution.

See also Hastings, Alcee Lamar; Nixon, Richard Milhous; *Nixon v. United States*

References: *A Collection of Some Memorable and Weighty Transactions in Parliament in the Year 1678, and Afterwards, In Relation to the Impeachment of Thomas Earl of Danby* (London: Privately Published, 1695); Buchanan statement in Peck trial in Hinds, Asher Crosby, *Hinds' Precedents of the House of Representatives of the United States, Including References to Provisions of the Constitution, the Laws, and Decisions of the United States Senate,* 8 vols. (Washington, DC: Government Printing Office, 1907–1908), III:2381; Farrand, Max, *Records from the Federal Convention* (New Haven, CT: Yale University Press, 1911), 550; Hallam, Elizabeth, ed., *Medieval Monarchs* (London: Tiger Books International, 1996), 99; *Hastings v. United States,* 802 F. Supp. 490, at 492 (D.D.C. 1992); Hoffer, Peter C., and N. E. H. Hull, *Impeachment in America, 1635–1805* (New Haven, CT: Yale University Press, 1984); Melton, Buckner F., Jr., *The First Impeachment: The Constitution's Framers and the Case of Senator William Blount* (Macon, GA: Mercer University Press, 1998), 25; *Nixon v. United States,* 506 U.S. 224 (1993); Plucknett, Theodore Frank Thomas, *Studies in English History* (London: Hambledon Press, 1983); Simpson, Alexander, Jr., *A Treatise on Federal Impeachments, With an Appendix Containing, Inter Alia, an Abstract of the Articles of Impeachment in all of the Federal Impeachments in this Country and in England* (Philadelphia: Law Association of Philadelphia, 1916); Staff of the [Presidential] Impeachment Inquiry, *Constitutional Grounds for Presidential Impeachment: Report* (Washington, DC: U.S. Government Printing Office, 1974); Stephen, Sir James Fitz-James, 1st Bart, *A History of the Criminal Law of England,* 3 vols. (London: Macmillan and Company, 1883), I:158.

Income Tax Scandal, Department of Justice (1951–1952)

Scandal that implicated several officials in the Department of Justice in tax-fixing and bribery cases. In 1950, in a growing move to cleanse the Internal Revenue Service (IRS) of potentially scandalous cases, the Truman administration fired, or forced the resignations of, 166 employees of the agency. A congressional subcommittee, investigating allegations of corruption in the Treasury Department, came across the IRS corruption at the same time that Congress was accusing the Department of Justice of stonewalling the investigations. The press got wind of the story and, with Congress, demanded that an independent counsel be appointed by Attorney General J. Howard McGrath. Instead, Truman asked McGrath to investigate the allegations himself, a move loudly criticized both on Capitol Hill and in the media.

McGrath dragged his feet looking into the scandal. When the House Judiciary Committee announced that it would investigate McGrath's investigation, Truman agreed that a special counsel should be named. Instead of allowing McGrath to do the naming, as was customary, Truman himself named a New York Republican, Newbold Morris, to the position. Morris, a protege and former assistant to New York Mayor Fiorello La Guardia, accepted the position when he was assured that Truman would back his entire investigation. Morris told the press on 1 February 1952, after taking office, that he did not need the subpoena power, "because if I want something and can't get it, I can go to the President for it." Morris set out to investigate the corruption with vigor. He decided to send a detailed questionnaire to all Department of Justice employees whose salaries exceeded $10,000 a year. With the questionnaire, Morris wanted to see if the employees were living within their means or had additional income from corruption. On 18 March 1952, Morris distributed 596 questionnaires to Department of Justice employees. McGrath instantly ordered that they not be accepted and that no more questionnaires be sent out. Morris, sensing that McGrath was trying to obstruct his investigation, demanded that he be allowed access to all of McGrath's official and personal records and correspondence. McGrath refused and, on 3 April 1952, fired Morris. The special investigator had been on the job only sixty-three days.

It is unknown what Truman's response was to McGrath's move, but later that day he called McGrath to the White House and fired him, announcing later that Judge James P. McGranery would be the new attorney general. McGranery's first announcement was that the investigation of the Department of Justice and the IRS would be conducted by him and him alone.

Charles S. Murphy, former special counsel to Truman, later said in an oral history interview:

President Truman eventually requested McGrath's resignation as Attorney General. There was a lot of talk, public comment about scandal in the Truman administration. This involved Lamar Caudle, about whom we have spoken sometime earlier, I guess, who was then an Assistant Attorney General. It involved some several collectors of Internal Revenue. Some of whom turned out quite badly. My recollection is, that every one of them was appointed by President Roosevelt, and not one of them by President Truman. However, this rubbed off on him and his administration and there were some other things that were not terribly bad, but on the other hand they were, I think, subject to some adverse criticism. Well, at any rate, this led President Truman to feel that it would be necessary and appropriate to have some independent investigation made of this problem in the executive branch of the Government and to do something about it, find out what needed to be done about it. And he tried, undertook to set up a group, I think a commission to—at any rate, at one point he tried—I know he tried—there was a Federal Judge in New York State named Murphy—still there I think. President Truman asked him to take charge of this activity and Judge Murphy came down to see him about it. And I remember this because he came to see him at the White House and the President had left his office and had gone over to Blair House and I took Judge Murphy over to Blair House to see the President. And at that time Judge Murphy told him he would do it. Then he went back to New York and changed his mind and called up and said he wouldn't do it. My recollection is, and this is not just clear, that he also asked the then Dean of the Harvard Law School to do this. A man who is now the Solicitor General of the United States, what's his name? I think he asked him to do it and he declined. But at any rate, he finally did ask the man from New York City whose name was Newbold Morris, a Republican who had acquired quite a reputation as clean-up man in New York City to come down and work on this and by this time the setup for the project, I think, had changed somewhat from the original concept.

One of McGranery's first announcements was that he would have the investigation done as all investigations were—through regular department processes. Many immediately saw this as a cover-up, mainly because it would be handled by political appointees. Sure enough, when the investigation was completed one minor Department of

Justice official was fired for "unethical conduct," while those who had been initially implicated were entirely cleared. McGranery announced that the investigation was complete, and that was that.

Historians believe that the income tax scandal was one of the worst cover-ups in Washington history—that major Truman administration officials, including T. Lamar Caudle, general counsel to the Bureau of Internal Revenue; Charles Oliphant, the commissioner of internal revenue; former Commissioner of Internal Revenue Josef Nunan; Truman's Appointments Secretary Matthew Connelly (who was nabbed and went to prison on another charge); and several others were heavily involved in embezzlement, and that they all escaped justice due to political considerations and a cover-up by two attorneys general.

References: Abels, Jules, *The Truman Scandals* (Chicago: Regnery, 1956); Dunar, Andrew J., "All Honorable Men: The Truman Scandals and the Politics of Morality," (Ph.D. dissertation, University of Southern California, 1981); "IRS Scandal," in Jay Robert Nash, *Encyclopedia of World Crime: Criminal Justice, Criminology, and Law Enforcement,* 4 vols. (Wilmette, IL: CrimeBooks, Inc., 1989), II:1664; Logan, David A., *Historical Uses of a Special Prosecutor: The Administrations of Presidents Grant, Coolidge, and Truman* (Washington, DC: Congressional Research Service, 1973), 28–29; Oral History interview with Charles S. Murphy, 25 July 1969, Harry S. Truman Presidential Library, Independence, MO; Perry, Anna B., "McGrath, James Howard," in Allen Johnson and Dumas Malone, et al., eds., *Dictionary of American Biography,* X vols. and 10 supplements (New York: Charles Scribner's Sons, 1930–1995), 8:405–406.

Independent Counsel Statute, 28 U.S.C. 1826

Law enacted in 1978 in the wake of the Watergate scandal to solidify in the law the ability of the attorney general to call for a person or persons to investigate certain violations of law by executive branch officers. Prior to the enactment of this law, investigations were carried out by what were called "special prosecutors," usually named by the attorney general.

The United States, despite a myriad of scandals, went without a "special prosecutor" until 1875. It was at that time that the scandals surrounding President Ulysses S. Grant became overwhelming in their scope and public importance. This period

of time, following the end of the Civil War, was racked by massive corruption and profiteering in the American South, especially within the confines of Reconstruction, when many "carpetbagging" officials moved from the North to the defeated Southern states and took advantage of the postwar chaos that permeated that region. As well, there was no civil service system to oversee the hiring of federal officers. Grant blanketed the entire U.S. government with cronies, and one of these was his long-time friend, Orville E. Babcock, who was named his personal secretary. Babcock saw his office not as one of responsibility, but as one to use to enrich himself and his friends. One of these friends was General John McDonald, a Civil War veteran who was named supervisor of revenue for the District of Missouri. McDonald used his office—with the full knowledge of Babcock—to charge local distillers less than the required whiskey tax and ask for a kickback for the privilege. Babcock was himself involved, sending letters in code to McDonald on how to run the operation in St. Louis. Secretary of the Treasury Benjamin Bristow, who oversaw the office that collected whiskey taxes, discovered the scandal and went to Grant with clear and convincing evidence of the "Whiskey Ring" of thieves. Grant, embarrassed by press coverage of the growing scandal, decided to name his own special prosecutor. This man was General John B. Henderson. Henderson, a former U.S. senator from Missouri, went after the Whiskey Ring defendants as he felt he was supposed to do. In the process, his investigation and indictments led him to evidence against General Orville Babcock, Grant's personal secretary. Grant then moved to block Henderson, calling upon a special military court to investigate any charges against Babcock. This court, stacked with Grant cronies, asked Henderson for all evidence against Babcock. Henderson refused and instead presented his case against Babcock to a grand jury, which indicted Babcock in December 1875. The tribunal faced either throwing Henderson off the case, inciting a furor, or backing off. They took the latter action, and Babcock went to trial. However, during the trial of another Whiskey Ring defendant, Henderson slammed Grant's interference with Henderson's investigation as well as that of the secretary of the treasury. When Grant heard of Henderson's accusations, he fired the special counsel. He then

Archibald Cox (center) is sworn in as special Watergate prosecutor during a ceremony at the Justice Department on 25 May 1973. (Bettmann/Corbis)

named another special prosecutor, James Broadhead, who was unfamiliar with the facts of the numerous Whiskey Ring cases. During Babcock's trial, the defense read a lengthy letter from President Grant attesting to Babcock's innocence. This led to an easy acquittal for Babcock and the end of the Whiskey Ring prosecutions.

In 1924 allegations that the secretary of the interior and the secretary of the navy—then an independent cabinet department—had conspired to sell national oil reserves to cronies of the president in return for bribes led Congress to call for a special counsel to investigate what became known as the Teapot Dome scandal. During congressional investigations, President Calvin Coolidge, who had taken over the presidency upon the death of President Warren G. Harding in August 1923, wanted to short-circuit any findings by Congress by naming an "independent counsel." His first picks for this office, Silas Strawn and Thomas Gregory, were both attorneys who had connections with the oil industry, and their confirmation was sorely in doubt. Senator George Pepper (R-PA) offered the name of an outstanding Philadelphia attorney,

Owen Roberts, who had prosecuted espionage cases during World War I. Coolidge decided to name Roberts, a Republican, and Democratic attorney Atlee Pomerene as co-independent counsels. The two men then worked from February 1924 until 1928 ferreting out the truth about the corruption, an investigation that led to Secretary of the Interior Albert Fall going to prison after being convicted of taking a bribe and Attorney General Harry Daugherty resigning in the face of allegations that he had obstructed the investigation. Roberts later was named to the U.S. Supreme Court by President Hoover in 1930, where he became one of the conservative bloc of justices during his fifteen years on that court.

During the administration of President Harry S. Truman, allegations arose that serious corruption was occurring in the Internal Revenue Service and that the Department of Justice was acting slowly in investigating it. A congressional subcommittee, pursuing its own inquiry, demanded that Attorney General J. Howard McGrath name a special counsel or independent counsel to look into the allegations. Instead, President Truman ordered that McGrath do his own internal examination. This move was heavily criticized by Truman's own party, the opposition Republicans, and the press. When it appeared that McGrath, too, was acting slowly on the scandal, calls arose again for the naming of an independent counsel. Seeking to douse the growing political firestorm, President Truman named a New York Republican lawyer, Newbold Morris, to be the special counsel. Morris began his investigation by sending inquiries to all Department of Justice employees remotely close to scandal. When Attorney General McGrath demanded a cessation to Morris's activities, Morris refused and was fired on 3 April 1952, just sixty-three days after being named. Truman, sensing growing frustration on Capitol Hill at McGrath's intransigence, called the flustered attorney general to the White House that same day and fired him, replacing him with Judge James P. McGranery. McGranery, on orders from Truman, conducted his own investigation, cleared all involved except for some low-level workers, and ended the inquiry.

Following a break-in at Democratic Party headquarters in June 1972 at the Watergate Hotel in Washington, D.C., and the capture of several men who were later tied to the Republican National Committee and President Nixon himself, Attorney General Richard Kleindienst resigned, and his replacement, Elliot Richardson, was forced to agree to name a special prosecutor to look into what became known as the Watergate scandal. This man was Harvard Law Professor Archibald Cox. He opened his investigation into Nixon's alleged ties to the break-in by subpoenaing tape recordings allegedly made by Nixon and his aides in the Oval Office. Nixon refused, citing executive privilege. Cox went to court, and a judge ordered Nixon to turn over the tapes. Nixon went around Cox and agreed to a compromise with Senator John C. Stennis (D-MS) to listen to the tapes and report back to the Senate. Cox refused the so-called Stennis Compromise and demanded the tapes. Nixon ordered that Attorney General Richardson fire Cox; Richardson refused and resigned. His deputy, William Ruckelshaus, also refused to fire Cox and also resigned, leaving Solicitor General Robert H. Bork as acting attorney general to fire Cox. This incident, on 20 October 1973, was called the Saturday Night Massacre. The outrage of the press, the public, and Congress forced Nixon to back down, and a new special prosecutor was named by Bork: attorney Leon Jaworski of Texas. Jaworski also subpoenaed the presidential recordings, exposing Nixon's role in the Watergate cover-up and his resignation on 9 August 1974.

In 1978 the U.S. Congress enacted the Ethics in Government Act, establishing a course of action to be followed to name an independent counsel: if allegations of an executive department employee were brought to the attorney general, that attorney general was to apply to a three-judge panel to have an independent counsel investigate the charges. The loophole in the law was that if the attorney general was politically motivated, he or she would cover for the executive branch official, and no independent counsel would ever be named. Allegations of this arose during the administration of President Bill Clinton. When allegations arose that both Clinton and Vice President Albert Gore Jr. had engaged in campaign donation and spending violations, critics of the administration demanded that Attorney General Janet Reno name an independent counsel to investigate the matter. On several occasions, despite overwhelming evidence—as well as support for the naming of a counsel by her own campaign task force leaders—Reno refused, and ultimately only two congressional committees investigated the allegations. During the 1980s, several independent counsels were named to investigate certain Reagan administration officials, as well as the Iran-Contra scandal.

The constitutionality of the Independent Counsel Statute was considered by the U.S. Supreme Court in *Morrison v. Olson,* which found the statute valid. In 1999, amid the anger over the statute, Congress let the law lapse.

See also Henderson, John Brooks; *Morrison v. Olson;* Starr, Kenneth Winston

References: Harriger, Katy Jean, *Independent Justice: The Federal Special Prosecutor in American Politics* (Lawrence: University Press of Kansas, 1992); Morris, Newbold, *Let the Chips Fall: My Battles with Corruption* (New York: Appleton-Century-Crofts, 1955); O'Keefe, Constance, and Peter Safirstein, "Fallen Angels, Separation of Powers, and the Saturday Night Massacre: An Examination of the Practical, Constitutional and Political Tensions in the Special Prosecutor Provisions of the Ethics in Government Act," *Brooklyn Law Review,* 49 (1982), 113; Treanor, William Michael, "Government Lawyering: Independent Counsel and Vigorous

Investigation and Prosecution," *Law & Contemporary Problems,* 61 (1998), 149.

Independent Expenditures

Campaign finance practice, by which organizations independent of a certain candidate air television or print advertisements that support that candidate, thereby being able to get around the spending limits of that particular candidate. The Federal Election Commission (FEC) reports that:

An independent expenditure is an expenditure for a communication which expressly advocates the election or defeat of a clearly identified candidate but which is made independently of any candidate's campaign. Independent expenditures are special because, unlike contributions, they are not subject to any limits. However, an expenditure is "independent" only if it meets certain conditions: It must not be made with the cooperation or consent of, or in consultation with, or at the request or suggestion of, any candidate or any of his or her agents or authorized committees.

For example, during the 1988 presidential election, a group called "Americans for Bush" aired an advertisement on television that showed the face of a convict, Willie Horton, who the Democratic nominee for president, Michael S. Dukakis, had released on furlough from prison while Dukakis was the governor of Massachusetts; Horton, a murderer in jail for life, then went on to rape a woman. Although the Bush campaign never sanctioned the ad, and the ad included a disclaimer that the group was not affiliated with the Bush campaign, the group was allowed to spend monies that could not legally be credited against the Bush campaign itself.

Independent expenditure advertisements, starting in the late 1970s, gave the appearance of political parties trying to subvert the campaign finance laws by producing ads not linked directly to a campaign. Prior to 1985, the FEC banned independent expenditures. Moreover, federal law (26 U.S.C. 9012(f)) made it a criminal offense for an independent "political committee" to expend more than $1,000 to further a candidate's election. However, that year, the Supreme Court held in *Federal Election Commission v. National Conservative PAC,* 470 U.S. 480 (1985), that "Section 9012(f)'s limitation on independent expenditures by political committees is constitutionally infirm, absent any indication that such expenditures have a tendency to corrupt or to give the appearance of corruption."

The Federal Election Commission has formulated rules on independent expenditures: "When making an independent expenditure, you must include a notice stating that you have paid for the communication and that it is not authorized by any candidate's committee. ('Paid for by John Doe and not authorized by any candidate's committee.') Additionally, once you spend more than $250 on independent expenditures during a year, you must file a report with the Federal Election Commission, either FEC Form 5 or a signed statement containing the same information."

See also *Federal Election Commission v. National Conservative Political Action Committee*

References: Federal Election Commission, "Independent Expenditures," in *Campaign Guide for Congressional Candidates and Committees* (Washington, DC: Government Printing Office, 1995); *Federal Election Commission v. National Conservative PAC,* 470 U.S. 480, 480 (1985); Federal Election Commission, "Supporting Federal Candidates: A Guide For Citizens"—An Internet publication of the Federal Election Commission.

Influence Peddling

Criminal conduct, described officially as "the practice of using one's influence with persons in authority to obtain favors or preferential treatment for another, usually in return for payment." Several of the largest scandals in the United States in the last years of the twentieth century had to do with influence peddling: allegations of influence peddling by officers of the Department of Housing and Urban Development during the Reagan administration; the investigation into Secretary of Agriculture Mike Espy in the Clinton administration; the allegations of the use of Chinese money to influence the 1996 Clinton/Gore presidential campaign; the investigation by an independent counsel against Secretary of Labor Alexis Herman; and the U.S. House of Representatives investigation into Representative Bud Shuster (R-PA).

The bar against influence peddling is explicitly written into American law: at 18 U.S.C. § 215, it states, "Whoever solicits or receives, either as a political contribution, or for personal emolument, any money or thing of value, in consideration of the promise of support or use of influence in obtaining for any person any appointive office or place under the United States, shall be fined not more than $1,000 or imprisoned not more than one year, or both." But the line between campaign contributions to a candidate for office and influence peddling is a thin and narrow one, which can be crossed quite easily. Roger Pilon, director of fiscal policy studies at the Center for Constitutional Studies at the Cato Institute said before a Senate hearing on campaign finance reforms:

> But if the egalitarian impetus for public funding is misplaced, that leaves the "corruption" of private money as the main argument for such funding. Set aside the point that no one has stepped forward to declare his own corruption—to say nothing of his colleague's—we all know that money does buy, at least, influence, whether or not that influence leads to quid-pro-quo corruption. But influence was around long before the "reforms" of 1974; it is still around; and it will continue to be around as long as politicians have the power to redistribute and regulate as they do today. Campaign finance "reforms" have done nothing to check that influence. To the contrary, they have only further institutionalized it. For the natural antidote against those who would use their public trust contrary to their oaths of office is a vigorous political campaign to unseat such officials. Yet that, precisely, is what modern "reforms" have made more difficult—if not near impossible, judging from House races—by restricting individual and PAC contributions to artificially low levels.

Influence peddling is considered a high crime and misdemeanor as proscribed by the U.S. Constitution. One man, Judge Robert W. Archbald, was impeached on this very charge and convicted and removed from office in 1912.

But, what is the difference between "lobbying" and "influence peddling"? Where is the fine line drawn when such distinctions mean the difference between complying with the law and breaking it? Writing in *Fortune* magazine in December 1998, journalist Jeffrey Birnbaum called the lobbyists who were in Washington, D.C., "the influence merchants." Each year, lobbyists for a multitude of special interests, both domestic and foreign, lobby Congress and the administration in power, spending tens of millions of dollars (in 1997, that number was nearly $80 million). The only requirement for foreign lobbyists is that they must register with the U.S. government under the 1938 Foreign Agents Registration Act. It seems unlikely that Congress will ever outlaw lobbying, which is seen by many as part of their First Amendment right to be heard on issues.

References: Birnbaum, Jeffrey H., "The Influence Merchants," *Fortune*, 138:11 (7 December 1998), 134–138; Birnbaum, Jeffrey H., *The Lobbyists: How Influence Peddlers Get Their Way in Washington* (New York: Times Books, 1992).

Ingersoll, Robert Green (1833–1899)

American attorney and orator, counsel for those implicated in the Star Route fraud trials (1880). Ingersoll was born in Dresden, New York, on 11 August 1833, the son of the Reverend John Ingersoll, a Congregationalist minister, and Mary (née Livingston) Ingersoll, a member of a famed early American family. (Among her relatives were Edward Livingston, who served as secretary of state, Philip Livingston, a signer of the Declaration of Independence, and Robert R. Livingston, who administered the oath to George Washington as the first president of the United States.) Robert Ingersoll received little education, instead being self-taught, but studied the law, and was admitted to the Illinois bar in 1854, practicing in such cities as Peoria, Illinois; Washington, D.C.; and New York City. For a time he practiced with his brother Ebon Clark Ingersoll, who later went on to serve in the U.S. House of Representatives. When the Civil War began, Ingersoll volunteered for service with the Eleventh Illinois Volunteer Cavalry, being commissioned a colonel. This service ended on 18 December 1862, when Ingersoll was captured by Confederate forces near Lexington, Tennessee. However, the general who captured him, Nathan Bedford Forrest, took such a liking to him that three days later Ingersoll was paroled. He resigned his commission and was honorably discharged on 30 June 1863.

A Republican in politics, Ingersoll moved to Illinois after the war and in 1866 was elected state attorney general, serving from 1867 to 1869. Because of his war activities and commanding voice, he became a noted speaker for several Republican candidates, including Republican presidential candidates Rutherford B. Hayes (1876) and James G. Blaine (1884). In 1876, in nominating Blaine in a losing cause, Ingersoll called the Maine Senator and former House Speaker the "Plumed Knight," and gave Blaine a nickname that stuck with him for the remainder of his life. However, despite his support for the party, Ingersoll's unorthodox religious views prevented his being named to any cabinet or diplomatic post that he clearly desired: Ingersoll was a self-admitted agnostic (one who neither believes nor disbelieves in God), and was called "The Great Agnostic." Questioning Christian beliefs, he explained his views in such works as *The Gods* (1872), *Some Mistakes of Moses* (1879), *Why I Am an Agnostic* (1896) and *Superstition* (1898), the latter penned the year before his death. Despite his views, his public speeches drew tens of thousands of spectators, enhancing his reputation as one of the finest public orators of his day. The Reverend Henry Ward Beecher called him "the most brilliant speaker of the English tongue of all the men on the globe."

It was perhaps for this reason that Ingersoll became caught up in one of the largest governmental scandals of the nineteenth century. Starting in 1880, he defended Thomas J. Brady and Stephen W. Dorsey in the famous Star Route trial. (See the entry on the Star Route frauds for the full story of this scandal.) Dorsey, a former U.S. senator, and Brady, a former assistant postmaster general, were accused of exaggerating the costs of servicing certain rural postal delivery routes—so called Star Routes—to steal from the U.S. government. Besides Dorsey and Brady, there were several other lesser-known Star Route defendants, and Ingersoll became the main counsel for the entire group. Starting on 1 June 1882, Ingersoll claimed that government policy, and not the defendants, were to blame for the alleged frauds.

In his closing address to the jury, Ingersoll said:

Let us understand each other at the very threshold. For one I am as much opposed to official dishonesty as any man in this world. The taxes in this country are paid by labor and by industry, and they should be collected and disbursed by integrity. The man that is untrue to his official oath, the man that is untrue to the position the people have honored him with, ought to be punished. I have not one word to say in defence of any man who I believe has robbed the Treasury of the United States. I want it understood in the first place that we are not defending; that we are not excusing; that we are not endeavoring to palliate in the slightest degree dishonesty in any Government official. I will go still further: I will not defend any citizen who has committed what I believe to be a fraud upon the Treasury of this Government.

One newspaper had this to say about Ingersoll's closing argument:

The most characteristic feature of the trial was the marvelously powerful speech of Colonel Robert G. Ingersoll before the Jury and the Judge. People who knew this gifted gentleman only superficially, had supposed that he was merely superficial as a lawyer. Although acknowledging his remarkable ability as an orator, and his vast accomplishments as a speaker, they doubted the depth of his power. They heard him, and the doubt ceased. It can be said of Ingersoll, as was written of Castelar, that his eloquent utterances are as the finely-fashioned ornamental designs on a Damascus blade, the blade cuts as keenly, and the embellishments beautify without retarding its power.

The jury returned with guilty verdicts for two of the lesser defendants, but there were mistrials for Dorsey and Brady. A second trial in late 1882, which stretched into 1883, led to not guilty verdicts for all. Although there were unsubstantiated allegations of jury-rigging and massive bribery, historians credit Ingersoll for the acquittals.

Ingersoll died of heart failure on 21 July 1899 at Walston, his son-in-law's palatial home in Dobbs Ferry-on-Hudson, New York. He was sixty-five years old. He was buried with military honors in Arlington National Cemetery, in Arlington, Virginia, where his large grave marker can still be seen. His epitaph reads, "Nothing is grander than to break chains from the bodies of men. Nothing is nobler than to destroy the phantoms of the soul."

See also Dorsey, Stephen Wallace; Star Route Frauds
References: Cramer, Clarence Henley, *Royal Bob: The Life of Robert G. Ingersoll* (Indianapolis: Bobbs-Merrill, 1952); Klotsche, J. Martin, "The Star Route Cases," *The Mississippi Valley Historical Review,* XXII:3 (December 1935), 415; Rogers, Cameron, *Colonel Bob Ingersoll: A Biographical Narrative of the Great American Orator and Agnostic* (Garden City, NY: Doubleday, Page, 1927).

Iran-Contra Affair

Scandal, 1986–1993, that implicated high-ranking members of the Reagan administration in selling weapons to Iran to pay for arms to be sent to the anticommunist rebels known as "contras" fighting the Nicaraguan Sandinista government. Following the 1979 Sandinista revolution in Nicaragua, a communist government allied with the Soviet Union came to power in that Central American nation and set about to export revolution to its neighbors, most notably El Salvador and Costa Rica. When Ronald Reagan came into office in 1981, he set about through secret means to undermine the Sandinista government. In the 1980s, several Americans in the Middle East, mostly in Lebanon, were captured by Islamic extremists who held them for ransom and for propaganda. Reagan ordered his National Security Council staff to find ways to secretly bargain for the release of these hostages. Soon, the two foreign policy aims collided. When Congress passed the Boland Amendment, which specifically banned all American aid to a group of anti-Sandinista rebels called the "contras," Reagan set about to use private money to go around the congressional action. However, after he ordered in 1985 that all legal means be used to get the hostages out of Lebanon, national security aide Oliver North, a former Marine officer in Vietnam, approached the Iranian government, a backer of the Islamic extremists. Iran was then in the midst of a horrific war with Iraq and needed all the arms it could to win decisive victories against the Iraqis. North offered them some arms in exchange for their assistance in gaining the release of the Americans held in Lebanon. In a back-door deal, North sold the Iranians 1,000 tube-launched hand-held TOW missiles, with a value of between $6 and $10 million, and the Iranians pushed to have the Americans in Lebanon released. However, North skimmed the money from the Iranian arms deal and sent it directly to the contras to be used for arms, food, and other supplies.

In November 1986 the Lebanese magazine *Al Shiraa* published a story alleging that the U.S. government had been shipping missile parts and Stinger anti-aircraft missiles to Iran in exchange for American hostages held by pro-Iranian terrorists in Lebanon. Because many of the hostages still remained in captivity, the story was not given full credibility. However, as Attorney General Ed Meese investigated, he found not only that the story was true, but that the proceeds from the sale to Iran were used to aid the contras. Thus, the "Iran-Contra Affair" was born. In March 1987 President Reagan admitted that members of his administration had been conducting these deals, but that he did not know of their extent—despite this, he took full responsibility for them. A panel, with Senator John Tower of Texas as chairman and former U.S. Secretary of State Edmund Muskie and foreign policy expert Brent Scowcroft, was named by Reagan to investigate the affair. Their report, called the Tower Commission Report, chastised President Reagan over the lax administration of the National Security Council, where the deals originated, but did not blame Reagan directly for any violations of law. Despite this, the Congress established a select committee to investigate the Iran-Contra Affair. Televised hearings were held, in which North and his secretary, Fawn Hall, became media figures. A special prosecutor, Lawrence Walsh, was named to investigate the affair.

Historian Peter Levey writes, "Ultimately, North, John Marlan Poindexter, McFarlane, and General Richard Secord were indicted, tried, and convicted on charges stemming from the Iran-Contra affair. Many of the convictions were subsequently overturned on technical grounds—namely, that the special prosecutor had relied on information obtained by congressional investigations while under grants of immunity to obtain the convictions." Special prosecutor Walsh indicted former Secretary of Defense Caspar Weinberger just before the 1992 election, but President George Bush pardoned him.

On 18 January 1993, the special prosecutor released his final report. He found that the Reagan and Bush administrations had not committed any criminal offenses, but he did chastise the Reagan administration for misleading Congress and the public.

References: *Final Report of the Independent Counsel for Iran/Contra Matters. Lawrence E. Walsh, Independent Counsel,* 3 vols. (Washington, DC: U.S. Court of Appeals for the District of Columbia Circuit, Division for the Purpose of Appointing Independent Counsel, 1993); Levey, Peter B., *Encyclopedia of the Reagan-Bush Years* (Westport, CT: Greenwood Press, 1996), 207–209; United States House of Representatives,

President Reagan on his knees behind an empty television, presumably announcing the release of hostages in the Middle East, while he hands Ayatollah Khomeini an "arms payoff for hostage release." (Library of Congress)

Select Committee to Investigate Covert Arms Transactions with Iran [with the U.S. Senate Committee on Secret Military Assistance to Iran and the Nicaraguan Opposition], *Report of the* *Congressional Committees Investigating the Iran-Contra Affair, With Supplemental, Minority, and Additional Views,* 3 vols. (Washington, DC: Government Printing Office, 1987), I:3–21.

J

Jackson, Edward Franklin (1873–1954)

Governor of Indiana (1925–1929), implicated and tried for taking a bribe while governor, but acquitted because the statute of limitations had expired. Jackson was also implicated in trying to bribe Governor Warren Terry McCray on behalf of the Ku Klux Klan. Born on his family's farm in Howard County, Indiana, on 27 December 1873, Edward Jackson was the son of Presley Jackson, a millworker, and Mary E. (née Howell) Jackson. He attended the public schools of Howard County, then studied the law and, after being admitted to the state bar, opened a law office in the town of Kennard in nearby Henry County. A Republican, Jackson entered politics when he was elected prosecuting attorney for Henry County, serving from 1901 to 1906. On 13 July 1907, he was appointed a judge of the Henry County Circuit Court to fill a vacancy. He won the seat in his own right in 1908 and served until 1914. In 1916 Jackson was elected Indiana secretary of state. After the United States entered World War I in April 1917, Jackson announced that he would resign as secretary of state to enter the U.S. Army, which he did on 27 November 1917, exactly one year after taking office. Commissioned a captain and later advanced to the rank of major, Jackson was assigned to Lafayette, Indiana, where he served as commandant of the Student Army Training Corps (SATC) at Purdue University. Jackson was discharged from the Army on 11 February 1919. He returned to the practice of law in Lafayette.

On 21 January 1920, Jackson reentered the political field when he was appointed secretary of state of Indiana. William Roach had been named to replace Jackson when Jackson had resigned in 1917, but Roach had died on 18 January 1920 and Jackson, ironically, replaced him. Jackson won election to the secretary of state position in 1920 and served during the administration of Republican Governor Warren Terry McCray. It was during McCray's administration that Jackson became involved in a series of schemes that led to bribery and the near cover-up of a murder. Jackson was a friend of David Curtis Stephenson, who was the Grand Dragon of the Indiana Ku Klux Klan. Under Stephenson, the Klan in Indiana grew to more than a quarter of a million members and was the most powerful single organization in the state. In 1923 Jackson tried to get a Stephenson supporter appointed by the governor to the vacant office of Marion County prosecuting attorney by passing a bribe from Stephenson to McCray. McCray refused to take the bribe, but then became caught up in an unrelated mail-fraud scheme and was forced to resign his office, leaving Lieutenant Governor Emmett F. Branch as governor and Jackson as the second most powerful politician in the state. In 1924 Branch did not run for reelection, and Jackson was named the Republican gubernatorial candidate. He defeated Democrat Carleton McCulloch (who had lost to McCray in 1920). Jackson was backed by the Klan, and their vote helped him to his considerable victory. It was after his election, on 12 January 1925, that Jackson introduced a campaign worker and state government employee, Madge Oberholtzer, to Stephenson, and the two began to date. This action would be Stephenson's, and the Klan's, downfall.

On 15 March 1925, a drunk Stephenson tried to abduct Oberholtzer and take her to Chicago to marry him. On the train to Chicago, Stephenson apparently raped the young woman, and to escape the shame she took poison. She went into a coma and died in an institution one month later, on 14 April 1925. Stephenson was indicted for murder and to avoid prison he threatened to release papers on numerous state officials, mostly Republicans, who had benefited from the political and monetary backing of the Klan. When his threats were ignored, the incriminating papers were given to the press. These included papers on the bribe that he had given Jackson to give to McCray. However, by the time this became public knowledge in 1928, Jackson was in his last year of office, and the statute of limitations on the bribe had run out. He was tried for the crime of bribery, but a conviction was impossible because of this technicality and Jackson walked free. His political career, however, was over.

Jackson returned to his law practice in Indianapolis and in 1937 he moved to his farm near Orleans, Indiana, where he died on 18 November 1954, a month shy of his eighty-first birthday. He is remembered by Indiana historians as one of that state's most crooked governors, despite the fact that he never was actually convicted of a crime.

See also McCray, Warren Terry

References: "Jackson, Edward L.," in Robert Sobel and John Raimo, eds., *Biographical Directory of the Governors of the United States, 1789–1978,* 4 vols. (Westport, CT: Meckler Books, 1978), I:416–417; "Stephenson, David Curtis," in David J. Bodenhamer and Robert G. Barrows, eds., *The Encyclopedia of Indianapolis* (Bloomington: Indiana University Press, 1994), 1296–1297.

Jackson, James (1757–1806)

United States senator from (1793–1795, 1801–1806) and governor of Georgia (1798–1801), responsible for the prosecution of the so-called Yazoo Land frauds. Born in Moreton-Hampstead, in Devonshire, England, on 21 September 1757, Jackson emigrated to the United States when he was fifteen. There he became a ward of one John Wereat, a Savannah, Georgia, attorney. During the American Revolution, Jackson took up arms against his native land and fought for the Georgia militia, seeing action in several battles, including the battle of Savannah (1778) and the battle of Cowpens (1781). In 1782, he was given the rank of lieutenant colonel when General "Mad" Anthony Wayne ordered him to march to Savannah and take the town from the British. Once he accomplished this action, Jackson became an American hero and was awarded by the Georgia legislature a house and a lot.

After the war ended, Jackson studied law with one George Walton and then opened his own practice in Savannah. He served several terms in the Georgia legislature and, still considered a hero, was elected governor of the state in 1788. He declined the honor. However, that same year he was elected to a seat in the U.S. House of Representatives in the First Congress, which opened on 4 March 1789. Jackson held the seat for only one term, after which he was defeated for reelection by his former commander "Mad" Anthony Wayne. Jackson charged that Wayne was wrongly elected, but after the House declared the seat vacant Jackson failed to win it himself. The following year, 1793, the state of Georgia sent Jackson to the U.S. Senate, where he served from 4 March 1793 until his resignation in 1795 because of the Yazoo Land scandal.

The Yazoo Land scandal was perhaps the infant American nation's first major scandal. Land had been sold by the Georgia state government to several land companies at ridiculously cheap prices, and Jackson, despite being in the Senate, then seated in Philadelphia, led the opposition to the sale. After his resignation from the Senate so that he could return to Georgia to concentrate strictly on the matter, Jackson assisted in helping the state rescind the sale on 18 February 1796. During the next two years, during which he was once again elected to the state legislature, Jackson was a leader in fighting the matter in court. For his service to the state, in 1798 both houses of the legislature elected him governor, and he was inaugurated on 12 January 1798. Historians Robert Sobel and John Raimo write:

During his administration, Jackson denounced many of the leading men of Georgia as being culpably involved in the Yazoo fraud. John Berrien, State Treasurer, although impeached for embezzlement because of irregularities in the receipt of payment from some Yazoo purchasers, was not convicted. Governor Jackson recommended that the State Legislature pay Phineas Miller and Eli Whitney only a moderate sum for their patent right to the cotton gin or suppress the right entirely.

Almost as soon as Jackson left the governor's mansion in early 1801, he departed for Washington, D.C., having been elected a second time to the U.S. Senate. This would be the last office he would hold. On 19 March 1806, in the final year of his Senate term, Jackson died in Washington at the age of only forty-eight and was buried in the Congressional Cemetery in Washington. By his work to end the Yazoo Land frauds, Jackson's name is most remembered for his helping to resolve one of the first scandals of the new American nation. Jackson County, Georgia, was named in his honor in 1801.

References: Charlton, Thomas Usher Pulaski, *The Life of Major General James Jackson* (Augusta, GA: Geo. F. Randolph and Co., 1809); Foster, William, *James Jackson: Duelist and Militant Statesman* (Athens: University of Georgia Press, 1960); "Jackson, James," in Robert Sobel and John Raimo, eds., *Biographical Directory of the Governors of the United States, 1789–1978,* 4 vols. (Westport, CT: Meckler Books, 1978), II:282–283; Lamplugh, George R. "'Oh The Colossus! The Colossus!': James Jackson and the Jeffersonian Republican Party in Georgia, 1796–1806," *Journal of the Early Republic,* 9 (Fall 1989), 315–334; Lawrence, Alexander A., "James Jackson: Passionate Patriot," *Georgia Historical Quarterly,* 34 (June 1950), 75–86.

Jenckes, Thomas Allen (1818–1875)

United States representative from Rhode Island (1863–1871), one of the leaders in the United States for civil service reform. Born in Cumberland, Rhode Island, on 2 November 1818, Jenckes attended the public schools of the area, before entering Brown University in Providence, Rhode Island, and graduating from that institution in 1838. He studied the law and was admitted to the Rhode Island bar in 1840, opening a practice in Providence. He supplemented this work by serving as the clerk for the Rhode Island state legislature from 1840 to 1844. In 1842 he served as the secretary for the state constitutional convention. He was a member of the state house of representatives from 1854 to 1857. In 1855 he served as the commissioner of a group appointed to revise the laws of the state.

In 1862 Jenckes ran as a Republican for a seat in the U.S. House of Representatives and was elected, serving in the Thirty-eighth through the Forty-first Congresses, from 4 March 1863 until 3 March 1871. It was during his congressional service that Jenckes became the leader of the movement for civil service reform. In 1866 he was asked by a congressional committee to report on what a program of civil service in the federal government would look like. Two years later he submitted his report, and although it was widely praised, it died a quick death when few people paid attention to it. Many people believed that the spoils system in hiring in government was an entrenched system that could not be rooted out.

Over the years that followed, Jenckes and many other reform-minded individuals came out both with ideas and speeches on behalf of reform. George William Curtis, editor of *Harper's Weekly* magazine, was named by President Ulysses S. Grant to be chairman of a commission to draft rules for a civil service system. When Congress refused to enact appropriations for the continuation of the commission, Curtis angrily helped form the National Civil Service League in 1881. Working with such men as Dorman Eaton, whose own report, *Civil Government in Great Britain* (1880) ranks with Jenckes's report in the annals of civil service reform, and Jenckes, Curtis was able to help with the enactment of civil service reform before the end of the nineteenth century.

After leaving Congress in 1871, Jenckes returned to Rhode Island, where he resumed the practice of law as well as working for civil service reform. He died in Cumberland, Rhode Island, on 4 November 1875, two days after his fifty-seventh birthday. Although largely forgotten today, Jenckes's name is well known among historians who study civil service reform in the United States.

References: *Biographical Directory of the American Congress, 1774–1996* (Alexandria, VA: CQ Staff Directories, Inc., 1996), 1282; Hoogenboom, Ari, "Jenckes, Thomas Allen," in John A. Garraty and Mark C. Carnes, gen. eds., *American National Biography,* 24 vols. (New York: Oxford University Press, 1999), 11:930–931; Hoogenboom, Ari, "Thomas A. Jenckes and Civil Service Reform," *Mississippi Valley Historical Review*, 47 (March 1961), 636–658.

Jenrette, John Wilson, Jr.
See ABSCAM

Jerome, William Travers (1859–1934)

American lawyer and reformer who served as a member of the Lexow Commission in New York that investigated police corruption. Jerome was born in New York City on 18 April 1859, the son of Lawrence Roscoe Jerome and Katherine (née Hall) Jerome. He received his education at the Williston Seminary in Easthampton, Massachusetts, and attended a preparatory school in Switzerland. He spent three years at Amherst College in New Hampshire, but left before earning a degree. He attended the Columbia University School of Law in New York, after which he was admitted to the New York state bar and opened a law practice in New York City.

In 1888 Jerome was named New York district attorney with the backing of Tammany Hall, then the dominant political organization. However, once in office, he sought to distance himself from Tammany at all costs. Just two years in office, in 1890 Jerome backed the People's Municipal League, a reformist group, in their drive for "clean elections" in the city. Because he opposed Tammany Hall in the race, Jerome resigned and returned to private practice. In 1894 state Senator Clarence Lexow of Rockland County, New York, opened an investigation into corruption that was traced directly to Tammany Hall. Jerome became the assistant to John W. Goff, the lead counsel for the Lexow Committee. That same year, he served as a member of the so-called Committee of Seventy, a reformist group that opposed Tammany Hall's power, and he served as the campaign manager for William L. Strong in his campaign for mayor of New York City. As an attorney, Jerome helped to draft legislation that established the court of special sessions in New York. Following Strong's election, the new mayor named Jerome to be the first justice of the new court, where he served from 1895 until 1901. During this time, he changed his party affiliation from Democrat to Republican.

William Travers Jerome, an American lawyer and reformer who served as a member of the Lexow Commission in New York, which investigated police corruption (Library of Congress)

In 1901 Jerome was elected district attorney for a second time, this time without the backing or influence of Tammany Hall. He found that office to have been run as an arm of Tammany, with indictments of Tammany cronies long undelivered. He cracked down on rackets and vice, including the gambling business of one Richard Canfield. However, perhaps his most noted case came when he prosecuted millionaire Harry K. Thaw for the murder of architect Stanford White. He was reelected in 1905 and served until 1909. During his second term, he was criticized for his failure to indict and prosecute the ranking members of the Metropolitan Street Railway after its bankruptcy, and a special counsel, Richard L. Hand, investigated the allegations. Although Hand found the accusations to be unfounded, Jerome was stung by the criticism and retired at the end of his second term. He died in New York City in 1934.

References: Hodder, Alfred, *A Fight for the City* (New York: The Macmillan Company, 1903); O'Connor,

Richard, *Courtroom Warrior: The Combative Career of William Travers Jerome* (Boston: Little, Brown, 1963).

Johnson, Thomas Francis (1909–1988)

United States representative from Maryland (1959–1963), convicted of conspiracy and conflict of interest in 1968 for his attempts to get the Department of Justice to back away from prosecuting a friend of Johnson's who had given him campaign donations. Johnson was born in Worcester County, Maryland, on 26 June 1909, and attended the public schools of that area. He later went to the Staunton (Virginia) Military Academy, graduating in 1926, and to St. John's College in Annapolis (Maryland), the University of Virginia, and the University of Maryland. After studying law, he was admitted to the Maryland bar and opened a practice in the village of Snow Hill. In 1932 Johnson was elected the chairman of the Commercial National Bank of Snow Hill.

In 1934 Johnson began his political career when he was elected the state's attorney; four years later he was elected to a seat in the Maryland state senate and served until 1951. In 1958, after a period of years of out politics during which he became a leader in international law issues, Johnson was elected as a Democrat to a seat in the U.S. House of Representatives, entering the Eighty-sixth Congress on 3 January 1959 and eventually serving until 3 January 1963. In 1962 he was defeated by Republican Rogers C. B. Morton, the scion of a wealthy family (his brother later served as secretary of the interior under Gerald Ford).

In 1963 Johnson was indicted, along with Frank W. Boykin, a former representative from Alabama; J. Kenneth Edlin of Miami, Florida, a savings and loan operator; and William J. Robinson, Edlin's attorney, on charges that he and Boykin had leaned on Attorney General Robert F. Kennedy in 1961 and 1962 to end the Department of Justice's investigation of Edlin on mail fraud charges, and that in exchange Edlin and Robinson had paid both congressmen $17,550 for their work. Johnson was indicted for violating the conflict of interest statute (18 U.S.C. § 281) and for attempting to defraud the government of the United States. At trial in April 1963, Prosecutor Joseph D. Tydings (later a United States senator from Maryland, 1965–1971) told the jury that Boykin and Johnson "personally con-

tacted the Department of Justice an average of once every three days during five months in 1961 in an effort to obtain [a] dismissal of a mail fraud indictment against" Edlin. "The evidence will prove [that] these two Congressmen exerted a veritable drumbeat of pressure on the Department of Justice."

On 13 June 1963, a federal jury in Baltimore convicted Boykin, Johnson, and their two codefendants—Johnson and Boykin on all eight counts of conspiracy and conflict of interest. However, on appeal the U.S. Circuit Court of Appeals for the Fourth Circuit overturned both Johnson's and Boykin's convictions, citing the "Speech and Debate Clause" of the U.S. Constitution. In this clause, Article I, Section 6, the Constitution provides that "for any Speech or Debate in either House, they shall not be questioned in any other place." Johnson was claiming that his work on behalf of Edlin fell under the aegis of his work as a congressman and was protected by this clause. The United States appealed to the United States Supreme Court, and, after arguments were heard on 10 and 15 November 1965, the Court handed down its decision on 24 February 1966. In a landmark ruling, the Court held that the clause prohibited the government from using Johnson's actions on behalf of Edlin in trial, but that a conspiracy charge could still be tried in court. Johnson was reindicted on this charge and in 1967 was tried again, this time with evidence merely that he accepted a $17,550 bribe from Edlin being shown to the jury, and, again, Johnson was convicted. On 30 January 1968, Federal Judge R. Dorsey Watkins sentenced Johnson to six months in prison. His appeals failed, Johnson served his time, after which he returned to private life and his law practice in Berlin, Maryland.

Johnson died in Seaford, Delaware, on 1 February 1988 at the age of seventy-eight.

See also *United States v. Johnson*
References: *Biographical Directory of the American Congress, 1774–1996* (Alexandria, VA: CQ Staff Directories, Inc., 1996), 1296; "Former Lawmaker Gets 6-Month Term," *New York Times,* 31 January 1968, 27; "Intercession is Laid to 2 Ex-Legislators," *New York Times,* 11 April 1963, 43; "Two Ex-Congressmen Are Guilty of Conspiracy with Two Others," *New York Times,* 14 June 1963, 64; "Two Face U.S. Court in 'Influence' Case," *New York Times,* 2 April 1963, 32.

Judicial Conduct and Disability Act of 1980, 28 U.S.C. § 372(c) (1980)

Act of Congress, enacted in 1980, allowing for the investigation and prosecution of federal judges for unethical conduct. Under the act, any person—even one having no connection with the judiciary—may file a complaint in writing alleging ethical misconduct by a judge. The complaint must allege that the judicial officer has been involved in "conduct prejudicial to the effective and expeditious administration of the business of the courts," or that the judicial officer "is unable to discharge all duties of [their] office by reason of mental or physical disability."

(1) Any person alleging that a circuit, district, or bankruptcy judge, or a magistrate, has engaged in conduct prejudicial to the effective and expeditious administration of the business of the courts, or alleging that such a judge or magistrate is unable to discharge all the duties of office by reason of mental or physical disability, may file with the clerk of the court of appeals for the circuit a written complaint containing a brief statement of the facts constituting such conduct. In the interests of the effective and expeditious administration of the business of the courts and on the basis of information available to the chief judge of the circuit, the chief judge may, by written order stating reasons therefor, identify a complaint for purposes of this subsection and thereby dispense with filing of a written complaint.

(2) Upon receipt of a complaint filed under paragraph (1) of this subsection, the clerk shall promptly transmit such complaint to the chief judge of the circuit, or, if the conduct complained of is that of the chief judge, to that circuit judge in regular active service next senior in date of commission (hereafter, for purposes of this subsection only, included in the term "chief judge"). The clerk shall simultaneously transmit a copy of the complaint to the judge or magistrate whose conduct is the subject of the complaint.

(3) After expeditiously reviewing a complaint, the chief judge, by written order stating his reasons, may—

(A) dismiss the complaint, if he finds it to be (i) not in conformity with paragraph (1) of this subsection, (ii) directly related to the merits of a decision or procedural ruling, or (iii) frivolous; or

(B) conclude the proceeding if he finds that appropriate corrective action has been taken or that action on the complaint is no longer necessary because of intervening events. The chief judge shall transmit copies of his written order to the complainant and to the judge or magistrate whose conduct is the subject of the complaint.

Many legal scholars dismiss the effectiveness of the act, mainly because it allows the chief judge of the circuit where the complaint was issued to dismiss the complaint if he or she finds it "directly related to the merits of a decision or procedural ruling, or is frivolous."

Jurney v. MacCracken, 294 U.S. 125 (1935)

United States Supreme Court decision upholding the Court's finding in *McGrain v. Daugherty* that the Congress had the right to subpoena certain papers, that refusal to furnish those papers was contempt of Congress, and that Congress could jail a nonmember for such contempt. William P. MacCracken Jr., along with three other men, was issued a citation on 5 February 1934 to appear before the U.S. Senate "to show cause why they should not be punished for contempt of the Senate, on account of the destruction and removal of certain papers, files, and memorandums from the files of William P. MacCracken, Jr., after a subpoena had been served upon William P. MacCracken, Jr., as shown by the report of the Special Senate Committee Investigating Ocean and Air Mail Contracts." This Senate committee was ordered by the Senate to investigate all mail contracts entered into by the postmaster general for the carriage of air mail and ocean mail. MacCracken, a D.C. attorney with the firm of MacCracken and Lee, was ordered by the court to provide papers regarding some of the clients he represented who held these contracts. MacCracken maintained that some of the papers were privileged communications. When MacCracken appeared but held back some documents, he was arrested on 12 February 1934 and held by Chesley W. Jurney, the sergeant at arms of the Senate. MacCracken sought a writ of habeas corpus in the Supreme Court of the District of Columbia; the writ was issued, and, after the court heard the case, it dismissed MacCracken's writ. On appeal, the U.S. Court of Appeals for the District of Columbia Circuit reversed the judgment and ordered Jurney to release MacCracken. Jurney appealed to the U.S. Supreme Court, which, seeing the importance of the matter, granted certiorari and heard arguments on 7 and 8 January 1935.

As the U.S. Supreme Court stated in its opinion, "It is conceded [by MacCracken] that the Senate was engaged in an inquiry which it had the constitutional power to make; that the committee had authority to require the production of papers as a necessary incident of the power of legislation; and that the Senate had the power to coerce their production by means of arrest." Justice Louis Brandeis wrote for the Court in a unanimous opinion (Justice James McReynolds did not participate) that upheld Jurney's right to detain and arrest Mac-Cracken. Brandeis explained:

> The power to punish a private citizen for a past and completed act was exerted by Congress as early as 1795; and since then it has been exercised on several occasions. It was asserted, before the Revolution, by the colonial assemblies, in imitation of the British House of Commons; and afterwards by the Continental Congress and by state legislative bodies. In *Anderson v. Dunn,* 6 Wheat[on] 204, decided in 1821, it was held that the House had power to punish a private citizen for an attempt to bribe a member. No case has been found in which an exertion of the power to punish for contempt has been successfully challenged on the ground that, before punishment, the offending act had been consummated or that the obstruction suffered was irremediable. The statements in the opinion in *Marshall v. Gordon,* supra, upon which MacCracken relies, must be read in the light of the particular facts. It was there recognized that the only jurisdictional test to be applied by the court is the character of the offense; and that the continuance of the obstruction, or the likelihood of its repetition, are considerations for the discretion of the legislators in meting out the punishment. . . . Here, we are concerned, not with an extension of congressional privilege, but with vindication of the established and essential privilege of requiring the production of evidence. For this purpose, the power to punish for a past contempt is an appropriate means.

See also *McGrain v. Daugherty*

References: *Jurney v. MacCracken,* 294 U.S. 125, 143–152 (1935).

K

Keating Five

Group of five U.S. senators implicated by varying degrees in trying to assist Charles Keating, the head of a failing savings and loan (S & L) bank in avoiding federal regulation in exchange for campaign donations. Starting in the mid-1980s, when Keating's Lincoln Savings and Loan came under the scrutiny of federal investigators, he gave large campaign donations to five particular Senators: Alan Cranston (D-CA), Dennis DeConcini (D-AZ), John Glenn (D-OH), John McCain (R-AZ), and Donald Riegle (D-MI). Later, it was revealed during one of the most massive congressional investigations this century that the five men had received more than $1 million in campaign donations. When Lincoln Savings and Loan collapsed due to fraud and mismanagement, and Keating was indicted, fingers were pointed at the five senators, who had aided Keating in pressuring federal regulators to relax their investigations of Keating and his institution.

In 1987 Charles H. Keating Jr., a real-estate developer, was in deep financial trouble with his Lincoln Savings and Loan, and the federal government seemed ready to take it over. However, over the years, Keating had given tens of thousands of dollars to politicians from both parties (Keating was a Republican, but saw the usefulness of contributing to Democrats as well), and now he used the influence these donations bought. He went to Senator Dennis DeConcini (D-AZ). Keating asked DeConcini if the senator could meet with the federal regulators investigating Lincoln and ask them to back off. DeConcini, looking for political cover, invited his fellow Arizonan, Senator John McCain, a Republican, to join him. McCain was a good friend of Keating, having known him since 1981 when the two men met at a dinner where McCain was the featured speaker. In 1982, when McCain first ran for the U.S. House of Representatives, Keating raised money for him; in 1986, when McCain ran for the U.S. Senate, Keating once again donated to his campaign. By 1987, when DeConcini asked McCain for his help, Keating had given McCain more than $112,000 in donations.

However, McCain was leery of helping Keating. The stories of savings and loans disasters were just hitting the pages of American newspapers, and McCain had only been in the Senate for less than a year. He initially refused to join DeConcini in meeting with the regulators. Keating complained to DeConcini, who told him that McCain was nervous about how the meeting would look. "McCain's a wimp," Keating said. Later that day, Keating met McCain, who promised he would meet the regulators and ask if Keating was being treated fairly. But the "wimp" comment had been told to McCain, and he told Keating off, after which the banker stormed out.

On 2 April 1987, Ed Gray, chairman of the Federal Home Loan Bank Board (FHLBB) was called to DeConcini's Senate office, where he met with

Senator John Glenn confers with his attorney during a break in the proceedings before the Senate Ethics Committee on 15 November 1990. The committee probed the activities of five senators accused of involvement with savings and loan kingpin Charles Keating. (Bettmann/Corbis)

DeConcini, McCain, and two other senators: Alan Cranston (D-CA) and John Glenn (D-OH). The men asked Gray to ease up on his alleged tough treatment of Keating and Lincoln Savings. Gray refused, but he did offer to set up a meeting between the four senators and the actual investigators. This was done on 9 April. The four initial senators were now joined by a fifth—Donald Riegle (D-MI). The investigators at the meeting were William Black, the deputy director of the Federal Savings and Loan Insurance Corporation (FSLIC); James Cirona, the president of the Federal Home Loan Bank of San Francisco; and Michael Patriarca, the director of agency functions at the FSLIC. The five senators told the investigators to either charge Keating with a crime or back off the inquest. DeConcini and McCain, as the senators from Keating's home state of Arizona, told the investigators that they were merely assisting a constituent. Even when the senators were told that Keating was involved in criminal actions and that an indictment was being drawn up by the Department of Justice, they did not back off.

In September 1987, the story emerged about the influence that the five senators used on behalf of Keating. Altogether, the five men had received more than $1.3 million in political donations from Keating. This was the same time that the full scope of the savings and loan financial disaster was hitting home across the United States: billions upon billions of dollars had been imprudently spent, and major financial institutions either went under or were on the brink of bankruptcy. The main focus of the investigation against the five senators was on DeConcini; McCain, as well as the others, claimed that they merely attended the meetings and had done nothing improper. McCain held to this story until 8 October 1989. That day, the *Arizona Republic* reported that McCain and his wife had invested more than $350,000 in a Keating financial property and that Keating had paid for several trips that McCain and his wife had made on Keating's personal jet. McCain had initially denied any financial ties to Keating, calling the allegations lies. Even when faced with evidence of the deal, he claimed that the arrangement did not involve him, but a partnership that had been formed between McCain's wife and her wealthy father. The Senate Ethics Committee, investigating the roles of the senators on behalf of Keating, added McCain to their examination.

In November 1990 the committee held hearings into the conduct of the five senators. By now they were being referred to in the press as the "Keating Five." The committee had hired Robert Bennett, a well known Washington, D.C., attorney who later represented President Bill Clinton during the scandals of Clinton's administration, as lead counsel for the committee. Glenn's counsel was Charles F. C. Ruff, who later served as White House counsel during the Clinton administration and was lead counsel for the president during Clinton's impeachment trial in 1999. In his opening remarks to the committee, he laid into the conduct of DeConcini, Glenn, and Cranston, leaning less on Riegle and even less on McCain. "In the case of Senator McCain, there is very substantial evidence that he thought he had an understanding with Senator DeConcini's office that certain matters would not be gone into at the meeting with Chairman Gray," Bennett said. "Moreover, there is substantial evidence that, as a result of Senator Mc-Cain's refusal to do certain things, he had a fallout with Mr. Keating."

In its final report, the Senate Ethics Committee found that Senators DeConcini, Cranston, and Riegle had interfered with the investigation of Keating, but that McCain and Glenn had not been intimately involved. The committee wrote:

> [A] Senator . . . should make decisions about whether to intervene with the executive branch or independent agencies on behalf of an individual without regard to whether the individual has contributed, or promised to contribute, to the Senator's campaigns or other causes in which he or she has a financial, political or personal interest. Senators should make reasonable efforts to ensure that they and their staff members, including campaign staff, conduct themselves in accordance with this principle.

The committee recommended that Senator Cranston be censured by the full Senate for his conduct, which he was. In 1991 Keating himself was convicted of seventeen counts of securities fraud, but in 1998 this conviction, as well as a 1993 conviction on racketeering and fraud, were overturned by a federal appeals court. Keating served a total of five years in prison.

See also Cranston, Alan MacGregor

References: Binstein, Michael, *Trust Me: Charles Keating and the Missing Billions* (New York: Random House, 1993); Toner, Robin, "Battered DeConcini Fights for His Reputation," *New York Times,* 8 January 1990, A10; United States Congress, Senate, Select Committee on Ethics, *Investigation of Senator Alan Cranston: Report of the Select Committee on Ethics, United States Senate* (Washington, DC: Government Printing Office, 1991); United States Congress, Senate, Select Committee on Ethics, *Preliminary Inquiry into Allegations Regarding Senators Cranston, DeConcini, Glenn, McCain, and Riegle, and Lincoln Savings and Loan: Open Session Hearings before the Select Committee on Ethics, United States Senate, One Hundred First Congress, Second Session, November 15, 1990, through January 16, 1991* (Washington, DC: Government Printing Office, 1991).

Kellogg, William Pitt (1830–1918)

United States senator from Louisiana (1868–1872, 1877–1883), governor of Louisiana (1873–1877), and U.S. representative from Louisiana (1883–1885), impeached as governor but acquitted in 1876, as well the subject of a Senate expulsion hearing in 1884 due to charges of corruption. He was born in Orwell, Vermont, on 8 December 1830, the son of the Reverend Sherman Kellogg, a Congregationalist minister, and Rebecca (née Eaton) Kellogg. He apparently received his primary education at local schools, before attending Norwich University in Vermont, although he never received a degree. In 1848, when he was eighteen, he moved to Peoria, Illinois, where he taught school for several years, studying the law at night. In 1853 he was admitted to the Illinois bar and began a practice at Canton, Illinois.

A Republican, Kellogg served as a presidential elector in Illinois in the 1860 election. On 27 March 1861, Kellogg was appointed to the post of chief justice of the Nebraska Territorial Supreme Court by President Abraham Lincoln. After just a few months on that court, Kellogg resigned when the Civil War began, and he returned home to Illinois to volunteer for service in the Illinois Volunteer Cavalry, although he later resigned because of ill health and never saw any action. Controversy remains as to where Kellogg served from his resignation in the military to his showing up in New

Orleans as collector of the port of New Orleans. Every written biography of Kellogg says that Abraham Lincoln named him to the post in April 1865, despite the fact that Nebraska state historical sources report that Kellogg served on the territorial supreme court for a second term and that he was "granted a leave of absence by President Lincoln to join the 7th Illinois Cavalry. [He] served as a colonel in the regiment from 8 September 1861 to 1 June 1862. Resigned as territorial chief justice in 1865." The questions may arise because Kellogg's nephew, named William Kellogg, was named to that same court in 1865 and served until 1867. Lincoln apparently never named the elder Kellogg to the New Orleans position, having been assassinated on 15 April 1865. It was his successor, Andrew Johnson, who in fact named Kellogg to the collector's position on 15 January 1866. Kellogg would ultimately serve in this position until 1868.

While in Louisiana, Kellogg became a part of the "carpetbag" government of Northerners who controlled post–Civil War Southern states. As a Republican, he had every chance of being promoted, as former Democrats were refused the right to vote until the state was readmitted to the Union after ratifying the Thirteenth and Fourteenth Amendments to the Constitution. In 1868, when this event occurred, Louisiana was eligible to once again send two United States senators to Washington. The legislature chose Kellogg to fill one of these slots. He ultimately served in the Senate from 9 July 1868 until 5 November 1872. In 1872 Kellogg was nominated for governor of Louisiana by the Republicans, and when he was elected he resigned his Senate seat and returned to his new home state, having attained that state's highest elected office. However, controversy arose over whether Kellogg had been truly elected; as well, the state was in the midst of another crisis. Outgoing Governor Henry Clay Warmoth had been impeached, and, despite the fact that no trial was being held, he demanded to remain as governor; at the same time, Lieutenant Governor Pinckney Benton Stewart Pinchback, a black man, was serving as acting governor. Because of the seriousness of the divide between the parties, a riot broke out in the streets of New Orleans, in which former Confederates backing John McEnery, the Democratic Reform candidate, threatened Kellogg to such a degree that he fled the city. In January 1873

both Kellogg and McEnery announced that each had won the election, and both men were sworn into office. In a period of a few days Louisiana had four sitting governors. Two distinct legislatures, each backing the other "governor," held sessions. Finally, in 1874, President Ulysses S. Grant ordered military forces in New Orleans to take control of the state government and deliver it to Kellogg.

In 1874 Democrats, using scare tactics (and the Ku Klux Klan) and the divisions in the Republican Party to their own benefit, were able to cobble together enough votes to take control of the state legislature. These tactics reached a climax on 14 September 1874, when white Democrats, calling themselves the White League, tried to once again remove Kellogg from power. They marched on New Orleans, where an overwhelmed police force could not contain them. Called the Battle of Liberty Place, the ensuing riot led to Kellogg fleeing to the confines of the New Orleans Custom House for protection until the siege could be lifted by federal troops. The election just a few weeks later resulted in a rout by the Democrats. Kellogg refused to allow these Democrats to take power, however. It remained for Representative William Almon Wheeler of New York (later to be elected vice president in the controversial election of 1876) to come to Louisiana to settle the matter. Wheeler, a member of the House Committee on Southern Affairs, came with several other members of the committee to hear evidence from both sides. It was Wheeler who manufactured a compromise, allowing Kellogg to remain as governor and for the committee to examine each legislative seat as to who won. In March 1875 Wheeler's compromise was enacted by the entire U.S. House of Representatives. One of its effects, which came just two years later, was effectively to end Reconstruction in Louisiana and finally all of the Southern states.

The years of division, coupled with the economic panic of 1873, which crippled the nation as a whole, had destroyed Kellogg's chances of governing effectively. In February 1876, as he prepared to step aside to make way for his successor to be elected later in the year, Kellogg was impeached by the Democrat-ruled state house. Few biographies of Kellogg mention this fact, but he remains one of four Louisiana governors to be impeached, making Louisiana the state with more such impeachments than any other. Kellogg's impeachment is so obscure that no records on it exist, and the few historians who do mention it do not specify what crimes were alleged or articles drafted and approved. What is known is that the Republican-controlled state senate never took up the impeachment, and it died a quick death. Kellogg served as governor until the end of his term on 8 January 1877. He left office and headed immediately to Washington, after being elected by the legislature to a seat in the U.S. Senate. Kellogg served a single term there, until 1883. He served as chairman of the Committee on Railroads in the Forty-eighth Congress. Remarkably, in November 1882 he was elected to a seat in the U.S. House of Representatives, and when his Senate term ended he moved to the opposite end of Capitol Hill. The year after taking office in the House, Kellogg was accused of political corruption and was the subject of an expulsion inquiry, but was allowed to serve for the remainder of the two-year term. He left office on 3 March 1885, never to hold elective office again. He served as a delegate to the Republican National Convention in 1884, 1888, 1892, and 1896. Moving to Washington, D.C., from Louisiana, in 1896, he spent his final years there. Kellogg died in Washington on 19 August 1918 at the age of eighty-seven. Because of his military service, he was laid to rest in Arlington National Cemetery in Fort Myer, Virginia.

References: Angle, Paul M., "The Recollections of William Pitt Kellogg," *The Abraham Lincoln Quarterly,* 3 (September 1945), 319–339; "Kellogg, William Pitt," in Robert Sobel and John Raimo, eds., *Biographical Directory of the Governors of the United States, 1789–1978,* 4 vols. (Westport, CT: Meckler Books, 1978), II:573.

Kelly, Richard.
See ABSCAM

Kerner, Otto, Jr. (1908–1976)

Jurist and governor of Illinois (1961–1968), indicted and convicted of bribery, conspiracy, and mail fraud, who served the last years of his life in prison. Kerner led an exemplary life until greed got the better of him. Born on 15 August 1908, Kerner attended local schools before he graduated first from Brown University and then Northwestern Law School. He then married the daughter of

Otto J. Kerner, jurist and governor of Illinois (1961–1968), led an exemplary life until greed got the better of him and he was indicted and convicted of bribery, conspiracy, and mail fraud. (Courtesy of Mark Grossman)

Chicago Mayor Anton Cermak, who had been killed in an assassination attempt on the life of President-elect Franklin Delano Roosevelt in early 1933. Kerner went into private law practice, later serving in the Illinois National Guard and the U.S. Army during World War II. He rose to the rank of major general before leaving the army in 1947.

In 1947 Kerner, a Democrat, was named by President Harry S Truman to be U.S. attorney for the Northern District of Illinois. In 1954 he was elected a county judge for Cook County (Chicago), where he served until 1961. In 1960 the Democrats of Illinois nominated Kerner as their candidate for governor. Running against incumbent William G. Stratton, a Republican, Kerner defeated Stratton by more than half a million votes out of some 4.5 million cast. Kerner was reelected in 1964, defeating Republican Charles Percy. Historians Robert Sobel and John Raimo explain, "While in office Kerner supported an increase and widening of sales tax coverage and an increase in corporate taxes. He supported the passage of a fair employment practices law, consumer credit law, and a new criminal code."

Kerner was seen as a moderating influence in racial problems in America. Ethnic tensions had been rising in the nation for many years, but by the mid-1960s they were on the verge of tearing the country apart. The middle of the decade was marked by riots in black areas in Los Angeles, Newark, and Detroit, among other cities. In August 1967 President Lyndon B. Johnson established a commission to investigate the causes of these riots and explore the area of black-white relations in America. He named Kerner as the commission chairman, and it became known as the Kerner Commission. In March 1968 the commission released its report, a massive 426-page tome that blamed tense race relations on poverty and inequality. On 22 May 1968, Kerner resigned the governorship when Johnson named him to a seat on the U.S. Court of Appeals for the Seventh Circuit, seated in Chicago.

On 15 December 1971, Kerner took a leave of absence from the bench after he was indicted by a federal grand jury on charges of bribery, conspiracy, mail fraud, and income tax evasion. Historian George Kohn wrote, "The prosecution contended, and the jury concurred, that Kerner and Theodore J. Isaacs, the state revenue director of Illinois during Kerner's governorship, had agreed to a lucrative stock offer that netted them more than $400,000 for an investment of $70,000. They bought the stock at a bargain rate in exchange for such favors as helping the racetrack owner to obtain a longer season and giving him permission to expand into harness racing. The two former state officials had declared their profits from the sale of the stock as long-term capital gains, when in fact the money should have been taxed as normal revenue." He was tried and convicted on 19 February 1973 and, on 22 July 1974, after his appeals were exhausted, resigned his seat on the Circuit Court and went to prison. (His resignation came only because of moves in the U.S. House of Representatives to impeach and remove him from office.) With his conviction, Kerner thus became the first sitting federal judge to be found guilty of an imprisonable offense. Sentenced to three years in prison, Kerner soon discovered in jail that he was dying of cancer and was released after only seven months. He died at home on 9 May 1976 at the age of sixty-seven; because of his war service, he was buried in Arlington National Cemetery.

References: Barnhart, Bill, and Gene Schickman, *Kerner: The Conflict of Intangible Rights* (Urbana: University of Illinois Press, 1999); "Kerner, Otto," in Robert Sobel and John Raimo, eds., *Biographical Directory of the Governors of the United States, 1789–1978*, 4 vols. (Westport, CT: Meckler Books, 1978), II:389–390; Messick, Hank, *The Politics of Prosecution: Jim Thompson, Marje Everett, Richard Nixon and the Trial of Otto Kerner* (Ottawa, IL: Caroline House Books, 1978); "Otto Kerner: Convicted Judge," in George C. Kohn, *Encyclopedia of American Scandal: From ABSCAM to the Zenger Case* (New York: Facts on File, 1989), 187–188.

Kilbourn v. Thompson, 103 U.S. 168 (1881)

United States Supreme Court decision that Congress could not hold in contempt those who were not members of Congress, and thus could not imprison such persons. A U.S. House of Representatives committee held a hearing on a real estate pool in which the government held debts, but Hallet Kilbourn, who received a subpoena to testify, refused to appear. Kilbourn was then found in contempt of Congress. Speaker of the House Michael C. Kerr of Indiana ordered John G. Thompson, the sergeant at arms for the House of Representatives, on 4 March 1876 to arrest Kilbourn and place him in prison for thirty-five days for contempt of Congress. Thompson arrested Kilbourn and took him to the Washington, D.C., courthouse, where Kilbourn pled guilty to contempt and served thirty-five days in prison. Thereafter, he sued Thompson and Kerr for false arrest. Kerr died on 19 August 1876 and was thus removed from the lawsuit. The Supreme Court for the District of Columbia ruled against Kilbourn, holding that Congress had a right to hold persons who refused to testify before it in contempt. Kilbourn appealed to the U.S. Supreme Court. In a memorial to Speaker of the House Michael C. Kerr in 1876, Representative William Phillips of Kansas said, "During the heated discussion had on this floor last session over the question of the surrender of Hallet Kilbourn to the District Court, I met Speaker Kerr near the door to the left of his chair and said to him, 'What do you think of the policy of sending Kilbourn to the court and leaving the responsibility of the judgment of the court with the [R]epublican party?' With nervous emphasis he instantly replied, 'It will not do at all. This matter involves one of the important constitutional prerogatives of this House. To yield it would be to place ourselves in the just contempt of the country and to confess our imbecility.'"

On 24 January 1881, the Supreme Court handed down its decision. Justice Samuel Freeman Miller spoke for the Court (there was no dissenting opinion, but no evidence that the opinion was unanimous) in holding that Congress's contempt power was limited to its own members, and thus holding Kilbourn in contempt was an illegal act, as was his jailing. Miller penned:

> The powers of Congress itself, when acting through the concurrence of both branches, are dependent solely on the Constitution. Such as are not conferred by that instrument, either expressly or by fair implication from what is granted, are "reserved to the States respectively, or to the people." Of course, neither branch of Congress, when acting separately, can lawfully exercise more power than is conferred by the Constitution on the whole body, except in the few instances where authority is conferred on either House separately, as in the case of impeachments. No general power of inflicting punishment by the Congress of the United States is found in that instrument. It contains in the provision that no "person shall be deprived of life, liberty, or property, without due process of law," the strongest implication against punishment by order of the legislative body. It has been repeatedly decided by this court, and by others of the highest authority, that this means a trial in which the rights of the party shall be decided by a tribunal appointed by law, which tribunal is to be governed by rules of law previously established. An act of Congress that proposed to adjudge a man guilty of a crime and inflict the punishment, would be conceded by all thinking men to be unauthorized by anything in the Constitution. That instrument, however, is not wholly silent as to the authority of the separate branches of Congress to inflict punishment. It authorizes each House to punish its own members. By the second clause of the fifth section of the first article, "Each House may determine the rules of its proceedings, punish its members for disorderly behavior, and, with the concurrence of two-thirds, expel a member," and by the clause immediately preceding, it "may be authorized to compel the attendance of absent members, in such manner and under such penalties as each House may provide." These provisions are equally instructive in what they authorize and in what they do not authorize. There is no express power in that instrument conferred on either House of Congress to punish for contempts.

This landmark decision held until the Court reversed itself in *McGrain v. Daugherty,* 273 U.S. 135 (1927).

See also McGrain v. Daugherty

References: Guenther, Nancy Anderman, *United States Supreme Court Decisions: An Index to Excerpts, Reprints, and Discussions* (Metuchen, NJ: The Scarecrow Press, 1983), 98; *Kilbourn v. Thompson,* 103 U.S. 168 (1881); Phillips, Rep. William (remarks by) in *Memorial Address of the Life and Character of Michael Crawford Kerr (Speaker of the House of Representatives of the United States,) Delivered in the House of Representatives December 16, 1876, and in the Senate February 27, 1877.* Published by Order of Congress (Washington: Government Printing Office, 1877), 61.

Kim, Jay C. (1939–)

United States Representative from California (1993–1999) who pled guilty in 1997 to raising more than $230,000 in illegal campaign contributions. Kim was born in Seoul, South Korea, on 27 March 1939, but soon immigrated with his family to the United States. He earned his bachelor of science and master of science degrees from the University of Southern California in 1967 and 1973, respectively, and was awarded a second master of science degree from California State University in Los Angeles in 1980. With a civil engineering degree, Kim owned his own engineering firm, called JAYKIM Engineers, and became a successful California businessman. His firm later became one of the top 500 engineering design firms in the United States.

In 1990 Kim ran for a seat on the Diamond Bar, California, city council. Popular with the people, a year later he ran for mayor of that town and was elected. Kim served only one year in this position. In 1992 he ran as a Republican for a seat in the U.S. House of Representatives and, with his election, became the first Korean-born member of that body. Conservative in his positions, he became an outspoken member of the Republican minority.

Starting in 1993, during his first term in office, Kim came under a cloud of suspicion, when FBI and Internal Revenue Service (IRS) investigations showed that he had illegally used some $400,000 of his corporation's money in his campaign for the U.S. House. Then, to make matters worse, Kim dipped into his campaign finance chest to extract $51,755 on legal advice in 1993 and 1994 and in 1995, an additional $46,460. Several Korean companies pled guilty to charges that they contributed illegally to Kim's 1992 congressional campaign, and Kim's campaign treasurer, Seokuk Ma, was convicted of soliciting and receiving illegal contributions. Finally, in 1997, after years of refusing to admit to criminal activity, Kim and his wife, June, pled guilty to five counts of breaking campaign finance laws, admitting to accepting more than $230,000 in illegal campaign contributions. Despite the fact that federal prosecutors demanded that Kim be sent to prison for crimes that they called "substantial, prolonged, deceptive, and serious," Kim was sentenced to only two months' home detention, 200 hours of community service, and a $5,000 fine. In 1998 he ran for his old congressional seat, but did not receive the Republican nomination.

Jay Kim is noted because he admitted to receiving the greatest amount of illegal campaign contributions in American history.

References: *Biographical Directory of the American Congress, 1774–1996* (Alexandria, VA: CQ Staff Directories, Inc., 1996), 1333; Eilperin, Juliet, "Days in the Life of Jay Kim in the U.S. House of Correction," *Washington Post,* 22 May 1998, A23; U.S. Congress, Senate, Committee on Governmental Affairs, *Investigation of Illegal or Improper Activities in Connection with 1996 Federal Election Campaigns—Final Report of the Committee on Governmental Affairs,* 6 vols. Report 105–167, 105th Congress, 2nd Session, 10 March 1998 (Washington, DC: Government Printing Office, 1998), 6:5683–5690.

King, Cecil Rhodes (1898–1974)

United States representative from California (1942–1969), head of the House committee investigation that uncovered the tax fraud scheme that implicated Truman aide T. Lamar Caudle, as well as a well-known influence peddler named Henry Grunewald. King was born in Fort Niagara, New York, on 13 January 1898. In 1908, when he was ten, he moved with his parents to Los Angeles, California, where he attended the public schools. During World War I, he served as a private in the United States Army, although his level of service, and whether he served overseas, is not known.

After he completed his military duty in 1919, he went into private business, working in the public sector until 1942. From 1932 to 1942, he served as a member of the California assembly.

A Democrat, in 1942 King was elected to the U.S. House of Representatives, when a special election was held to fill the vacancy caused by the death of Representative Lee E. Geyer. King was unopposed in his election, which represented the Seventeenth California District. He would serve for fourteen terms, until he refused to run for reelection in 1968.

King was the chairman of the House Ways and Means Subcommittee that had jurisdiction over internal revenue and tax laws. When rumors of misconduct in the Truman administration began to spread in 1950, Senator John J. Williams (R-DE) began an investigation in the Senate. In the House, King's subcommittee launched a similar investigation. The subcommittee called as a witness Abraham Teitelbaum, a Chicago real estate lawyer, who described a scheme in which Bureau of Internal Revenue (BIR, the forerunner of the Internal Revenue Service) agents from Chicago tried to extort $500,000 from Teitelbaum if they dropped his case of income tax evasion. Teitelbaum named Charles A. Oliphant, chief counsel of the BIR; George Schoeneman, former BIR commissioner; Henry W. Grunewald, a Washington, D.C., influence peddler known as "The Dutchman"; and T. Lamar Caudle, head of the Tax Division of the U.S. Department of Justice, as being involved in the scheme. Oliphant, Schoeneman, and Caudle were well known in Washington, but Grunewald was a mysterious figure. South African by birth, he had come to the United States in 1906 and had served for a short time as a prohibition agent before being indicted (and later acquitted) on charges of issuing fraudulent customs permits and removing illegal liquor from government warehouses. Oliphant testified before the King subcommittee that he had accepted loans from Grunewald, who had assisted the BIR with tax cases, but denied the Teitelbaum allegations. Grunewald refused to testify, and he was cited for contempt of Congress by a 332–0 vote in January 1952. He later testified before another House subcommittee, headed by Representative Robert W. Kean (R-NJ), when the Republicans took control of Congress.

The King subcommittee spent all of 1951 and 1952 examining the fraud and chaos in the Bureau of Internal Revenue. King's investigators found that James P. Finnegan, close friend of President Truman and Secretary of the Treasury John W. Snyder, had sent the names of tax evaders to an insurance company that then investigated and split the profits from the tax collections with Finnegan. Pressure from Truman brought his resignation on 14 April 1951. A year later he was indicted, convicted on two counts of bribery, and sent to prison. President Lyndon Johnson pardoned him shortly before his death in 1967.

In its final report to Congress, the King subcommittee reported on the tax scandal:

Two of the nine Collectors separated from service had extorted large sums from delinquent taxpayers. Several evaded personal income taxes while in office and at least one Collector used his authority to prevent [the] audit of his returns. The total confusion which reigned in the office of the two Collectors demonstrated their incompetence as administrators. . . . Field investigations by this subcommittee disclosed that in a number of these offices conditions had been allowed to deteriorate as long as 16 years, because Bureau officials were unwilling to defend the politically appointed Collectors.

The BIR tax scandal inquiry led to the resignation of several Truman aides (including Attorney General James P. McGranery) and the jailing of some of these men. King was widely praised for the judicial manner in which he conducted the hearings.

King left office on 3 January 1969, having not run for reelection in 1968. He resided in Inglewood, California, until his death on 17 March 1974 at the age of seventy-six.

See also Income Tax Scandal, Department of Justice
References: "Bureau of Internal Revenue," in Jeffrey D. Schultz, *Presidential Scandals* (Washington, DC: CQ Press, 2000), 326–328; Dunar, Andrew J., *The Truman Scandals and the Politics of Morality* (Columbia: University of Missouri Press, 1984), 96–134; "Henry Grunewald: Notorious Influence Peddler," in George C. Kohn, *Encyclopedia of American Scandal: From ABSCAM to the Zenger Case* (New York: Facts on File, 1989), 135–137.

King, William Smith (1828–1900)

United States representative from Minnesota (1875–1877), nearly expelled from the House for corruption. Born in Malone, New York, on 16 December 1828, King attended the common schools of the area, later becoming engaged in agricultural pursuits. In 1846 he removed to Otsego County, New York, where he went to work as a solicitor (lawyer) for several mutual insurance companies. Six years later he became the editor of the *Free Democrat* in Cooperstown, New York, and remained in this position for several years. However, by 1858 he had apparently tired of his native state and headed west, settling in Minneapolis, Minnesota, where he was engaged in agricultural pursuits and journalism. He served as a postmaster of the state house of representatives from 1861 to 1865, and again from 1867 to 1873, later serving as the surveyor general of logs and lumber in the Second Congressional District of Minnesota in 1874.

In 1874 King was nominated by the Republicans for a seat in the U.S. House of Representatives and defeated a Democrat (identified only as "Wilson") by 3,000 votes out of some 33,000 cast. King took his seat in the Forty-fourth Congress, which opened on 4 March 1875. Almost from the start of his congressional term, King was tagged with allegations of political corruption. Unfortunately, there is no record as to what corruption was charged to King—only that he faced expulsion.

The House Judiciary Committee, reporting back to the full House on the potential expulsions of King and Democrat John G. Schumaker, both handled at the same time, explained:

Your committee are of the opinion that the House of Representatives has no authority to take jurisdiction of violations of law or offenses committed against a previous Congress. This is purely a legislative body, and entirely unsuited for the trial of crimes. The fifth section of the first article of the Constitution authorizes "each house to determine the rules of its proceedings, punish its members for disorderly behavior, and, with the concurrence of two-thirds, expel a member." This power is evidently given to enable each house to exercise its constitutional function of legislation unobstructed. It cannot vest in Congress a jurisdiction to try a member for an offense committed before his election; for such offense a member, like any other citizen, is amenable to the courts alone.

King did not run for reelection, instead allowing his seat to be filled by someone else. He returned to

Minnesota, where he ran a cattle-raising operation. He died in Minneapolis on 24 February 1900 at the age of seventy-one, and was buried in Lakewood Cemetery in that city.

See also Schumaker, John Godfrey
References: *Biographical Directory of the American Congress, 1774–1996* (Alexandria, VA: CQ Staff Directories, Inc., 1996), 1338; Report on King and Schumaker in House Report No. 815, 44th Congress, 1st Session, 2 (1876).

Kolter, Joseph Paul

See House of Representatives Post Office Scandal

Koreagate

Scandal, 1977–1978, involving allegations that agents of the government of South Korea bribed members of Congress to exert influence over decisions in Congress reflecting on South Korean policy. Although it was alleged that more than 100 congressmen accepted bribes from South Korean agents, only one, Representative Richard Hanna (D-CA), pled guilty and served time in prison. Little is known of the roots of the scandal, except that at the same time that Democrats were denouncing Republicans in the 1974 midterm elections over their ties to Watergate, many high-ranking Democrats were deeply involved in taking money from Korean businessmen and representatives of the South Korean government.

In 1970 President Richard Nixon proposed that many of the 20,000-plus American troops stationed in South Korea since the end of the Korean War in 1953 be removed. South Korean President Park Chung Hee, who had taken power in a coup in 1961 (and who would be assassinated in 1979), opposed the Nixon program and decided to circumvent the administration and influence congressional policy. Utilizing the powers and influence of the Korean Central Intelligence Agency (KCIA), Park decided to lobby influential members of Congress, notably Democrats (who were in control of both houses of Congress), with free

trips, campaign contributions, and other gratuities. Park put one man, Park Tong Sun (no relation) in charge of the operation.

Allegations that Park (under the name of Tongsun Park) had paid senators and representatives some $1 million led the Department of Justice to open an investigation in 1976. Soon it became apparent that a cover-up was being perpetrated. The House Ethics Committee, handling the House investigation, hired attorney Philip A. Lacovara, a former member of the Watergate prosecution team, as the committee's special counsel. However, after only a short time on the job, Lacovara resigned and accused Ethics Committee chairman John J. Flynt (D-GA) of obstructing his investigation. Leon Jaworski, the former Watergate prosecutor, offered to work for the committee for free.

Tongsun Park had fled the United States, and the South Korean government offered to send him back to the United States only if he received immunity from prosecution. This was refused, and Park never testified.

In the end, only two members of Congress were ever charged with crimes stemming from the Koreagate scandal: Representative Richard T. Hanna (D-CA) and Representative Otto E. Passman (D-LA). Passman was not prosecuted due to ill health, and Hanna pled guilty and served a year in prison. The House Ethics Committee recommended that three other congressman—Edward Roybal, Charles H. Wilson, and John J. McFall, all Democrats from California—be reprimanded by the House, although Roybal's punishment was to be censure. None of these three men were ever charged with a crime.

In 1979 the Carter Justice Department dropped all charges against Tongsun Park and closed the Koreagate investigation.

See also Hanna, Richard Thomas
References: Boettcher, Robert B., *Gifts of Deceit: Sun Myung Moon, Tongsun Park, and the Korean Scandal* (New York: Holt, Rinehart and Winston, 1980); "Koreagate," in George C. Kohn, *Encyclopedia of American Scandal: From ABSCAM to the Zenger Case* (New York: Facts on File, 1989), 190–191.

L

Lance, Thomas Bertram "Bert" (1931–)

American banker, director of the Office of Management and Budget (1977), forced to resign over allegations regarding his management of a bank in Georgia. A close friend of James Earl "Jimmy" Carter, who became governor of Georgia and then president of the United States, Lance was born in Young Harris (some sources note Gainesville), Georgia, on 3 June 1931, the youngest of four children of Thomas Jackson Lance and Annie Rose (née Erwin) Lance. One of Bert Lance's older brothers, Robert, was killed during World War II. Bert Lance attended local schools in Calhoun, Georgia, before he went to Emory University in Atlanta for two years and then the University of Georgia, dropping out before he could earn a degree. Despite going to several other colleges and studying for a degree in banking, Lance never formally earned a secondary educational degree. Although he did not graduate, Lance did begin working in a bank as a clerk in Calhoun. In 1958, with a group of investors, Lance purchased control of the bank, the Calhoun First National Bank and was named its vice president. In 1959 he was advanced to executive vice president and in 1963 was named president and chief executive officer (CEO). The partnership purchased other local banks and increased their assets. Lance also helped to build local businesses through investments.

In 1966 Lance met a man who would change his life: James Earl Carter, a local peanut farmer.

The two men met at a regional planning conference, where Carter was shopping around his ideas as he prepared to run for governor of Georgia. Seeing a potential political opportunity, Lance pushed for business support for Carter. But Carter lost the Democratic primary in September 1966. Four years later, when Carter ran again, Lance was there to support him a second time. This time Carter won the Democratic Party nomination and was elected the eightieth governor of Georgia. After Carter took office in January 1971, he named Lance director of the Georgia State Highway Department. Long considered a wasteful agency, the department was turned around by Lance into an efficient government bureau by a series of reforms and expanding services. Because of his work, Carter asked Lance to reorganize all of Georgia state government. Lance worked hard in the few months he was on this job to succeed.

In 1974, as Carter neared the end of his term (he was disallowed by the Georgia state constitution to run for a second term), he threw his support behind Lance's candidacy for the gubernatorial nomination. Lance spent more than $200,000 of his personal funds for the campaign and at the same time funded it with $300,000 in unsecured loans from banks, all of which skirted campaign finance laws. And while Lance was never accused of criminal activity, the revelation that he was worth more than $3 million shattered his image as a "country boy." Lance was defeated in the Democratic primary by former governor Lester Maddox.

Lance returned to banking after his defeat, again joining in a group of investors to purchase the National Bank of Georgia in Atlanta for $7.4 million, and in 1975 was elected the bank's president. As before, Lance's leadership helped the bank to increase its assets and become more successful than before.

In 1976 former Governor Carter ran for the presidency of the United States and was elected, the first Southerner elected to that position since the end of the Civil War. During the contentious campaign, Lance served as one of Carter's closest advisors. Following Carter's election, Lance, along with other economic advisors, went to Carter's home in Plains, Georgia, to discuss the American economy. It was there, on 3 December 1976, that Carter announced his selection of Bert Lance as director of the Office of Management and Budget (OMB), the leading executive branch office that formulates budget and economic policy for the nation. However, with the announcement came allegations that Lance had "bought" the OMB position because he had allowed his bank to give the Carter peanut business loans and credits totaling some $4.9 million. During his confirmation hearings, Lance argued that he had given the loans and credits because he felt that the Carter peanut business was a good business risk. Lance was confirmed by the Senate with only one dissenting vote on 20 January 1977. He took office three days later as the twenty-third director of the OMB.

Lance served as OMB director until August 1977, when additional allegations arose that as head of several banks in Georgia he had engaged in unethical business practices. Responding to the allegations, John Heimann, the comptroller of the currency, an office in the Department of the Treasury, opened an investigation. Heimann discovered that Lance had received several questionable loans, including one for $2.6 million from the Manufacturers Hanover Trust Bank in New York, which was done after the bank created a business relationship with Lance's National Bank of Georgia. However, despite this finding of possible violations of banking law, the investigation was closed. Outrage from the press and Republicans led to Senate investigators looking into Lance's business dealings. These investigators discovered that Lance, when reporting his income and other related matters to the Senate Banking Committee prior to his confirmation hearings, had shielded some assets. Heimann's investigation was criticized and was reopened, along with the Senate Banking Committee inquiry. These explorations discovered that Lance and his wife had borrowed upwards of $3.5 million from Lance's banks over a thirteen-year period and had not paid it back. Robert Bloom, a former comptroller of the currency, admitted to the Senate Banking Committee that he had not informed the panel of Lance's misuse of funds when he supported Lance during the latter's confirmation hearings. On 16 September 1977, clearly under fire, Lance appeared before the Senate committee to explain his position. (His two lawyers for the hearing were former Secretary of Defense Clark Clifford, and Clifford's good friend Robert Altman—both of whom, along with Lance, would later be caught up in the BCCI banking scandal in the 1990s.) Lance claimed that charges of misuse of funds were incorrect and that he had always been ethical in his business dealings with his banks. Despite his denials, the so-called Lancegate scandal continued to dominate the headlines during the month of September, and it slowly began to become a drag on the Carter administration. On 21 September 1977, after several months of intensive investigation, Lance formally sent a letter of resignation to President Carter, claiming that the controversy over his business dealings, and not the actual dealings themselves, were the reasons behind his departure. Carter replaced him with Acting Director James T. McIntyre, who became director at the end of 1977.

Lance's departure from government did not end the investigations against him. In 1978 the Securities and Exchange Commission (SEC), after a lengthy inquiry, filed fraud charges against Lance, after which he agreed not to continue any banking practices that were unethical. A federal grand jury in Atlanta, Georgia, indicted Lance and three of his business associates in May 1979. But after a trial that lasted four months, Lance and was acquitted of some charges, while the jury was hung on the remainder. Lance was never retried on these. In September 1982 Lance was elected chairman of the Georgia Democratic Party, a post he held until July 1985.

References: "Bert Lance: Controversial Banker," in George C. Kohn, *Encyclopedia of American Scandal: From ABSCAM to the Zenger Case* (New York: Facts on File, 1989), 196–197; Harris, Art, and John F. Berry, "Arab Investors Want Lance to Manage Funds," *Washington Post,* 16 December 1977, A1; "Lance, (Thomas) Bert(ram)," in Charles Moritz, ed., *Current Biography 1977* (New York: H. W. Wilson and Co., 1977), 262–264; Lance, Bert, *The Truth of the Matter: My Life In and Out of Politics* (New York: Summit Books, 1991); United States Congress, Senate, Committee on Governmental Affairs, *Matters Relating to T. Bertram Lance: Hearings Before the Committee on Governmental Affairs, United States Senate, Ninety-fifth Congress, First Session, Relating to T. Bertram Lance,* 3 vols. (Washington, DC: Government Printing Office, 1977); United States Congress, Senate, Committee on Governmental Affairs, *Nominations of Thomas B. Lance and James T. McIntyre, Jr.: Hearings Before the Committee on Governmental Affairs, United States Senate, Ninety-fifth Congress, First Session, on Nomination of Thomas B. Lance to be Director of the Office of Management and Budget, January 17 and 18, 1977, and Nomination of James T. McIntyre, Jr., to be Deputy Director of the Office of Management and Budget, March 4, 1977* (Washington, DC: Government Printing Office, 1977).

Langer, William (1886–1959)

Governor of North Dakota (1933–1934, 1937–1939) who was removed from office in 1934 for alleged racketeering, although he was acquitted after three trials. Born on his family's farm in Everest Township, near Casselton, Dakota Territory (now North Dakota), on 20 September 1886, he was the son of Frank Langer, a farmer, and Mary Langer. Langer attended the rural schools of the area, then studied law at the University of North Dakota at Grand Forks and received his law degree in 1906. He then headed east to attend Columbia University in New York City, from which he earned his bachelor of arts degree in 1910. Returning to North Dakota, he was admitted to the bar in 1911 and he began a private practice in the town of Mandan.

In 1914 Langer entered the political field and served as state's attorney for Morton County, North Dakota. He earned the enmity of corporations when he swore out warrants for local liquor dealers and sued the Northern Pacific Railroad for more than $1.2 million in taxes owed to the state. After two years he returned to private law practice. In 1916 he moved to Bismarck and opened a law

practice there. That same year, he was elected attorney general of North Dakota on the Nonpartisan League ticket, serving until 1920. During World War I, he served as the legal advisor for the Council of Defense, a local defense organization formed during the war. After two terms as state attorney general, in 1920 Langer gave up his position to run for governor, but he was unsuccessful. After this loss, he left politics and returned to his law practice.

In 1932 Langer once again ran for governor and, with the backing of the Nonpartisan League, a group of independents, he was able to win the Republican gubernatorial nomination and defeat Democrat Herbert Dupuy by 24,000 votes out of some 245,000 cast. Facing a rising tide of economic misery from the deepening Great Depression, Langer tried to help the state's largest economic sector, farming, by placing moratoriums on the foreclosures of farms deep in debt and embargoes on the sale of wheat to keep the price artificially high.

In 1934 Langer was accused of soliciting funds from state and federal employees for campaign and personal use. After a trial, he was found guilty, sentenced to eighteen months in prison, and fined $18,000. The state supreme court stepped in and, in a rare and highly unusual move, removed Langer from the governorship. His conviction reversed on appeal, Langer was able to clear his name after three trials, and in 1936 he once again ran for governor, this time as an Independent. Amazingly, after being removed from office for alleged ethical violations, Langer was elected over the incumbent, Walter Welford, and Democrat John Moses. Again, as governor, Langer sought to defend farmers from economic pressures. In 1938 Langer ran as an Independent for the U.S. Senate, but lost to Gerald Nye. Two years later, having left the governorship, he ran again for the U.S. Senate, and, winning the Republican nomination, defeated Independent William Lemke and Democrat Charles Vogel. Democrats tried to block him from taking his seat, but after three weeks of debate the Senate voted fifty-two to thirty to allow him to be seated. He was reelected in 1946, 1952, and 1958, ultimately serving from 3 January 1941 until his death. During his service in the Senate, he served as the chairman of the Committee on the Post Office and Civil Service (Eightieth Congress) and as the chairman of the Committee on the Judiciary (Eighty-third Congress).

While still serving in the Senate, Langer died of a heart ailment in Washington, D.C., on 8 November 1959 at the age of seventy-three. He was buried in St. Leo's Catholic Cemetery in Casselton, North Dakota. He was the author of *The Nonpartisan League: Its Birth, Activities and Leaders* (Mandan, ND: Morton County Farmers' Press, 1920).

References: Anhalt, Walter C., and Glenn H. Smith, "He Saved the Farm? Governor Langer and the Mortgage Moratoria," *North Dakota Quarterly*, 44 (Autumn 1976): 5–17; Barber, Charles M., "A Diamond in the Rough: William Langer Reexamined," *North Dakota History*, 64 (Fall 1998), 2–18; Geelan, Agnes, *The Dakota Maverick: The Political Life of William Langer, also Known as 'Wild Bill' Langer* (Fargo, ND: Privately Published, 1975); *Hearings on A Protest to the Seating of William Langer, before the Senate Committee on Privileges and Elections, November 3, 18, 1941*, 77th Congress, 1st Session (1941), 820; Hjalmervik, Gary L., "William Langer's First Administration, 1932–1934" (Master's thesis, University of North Dakota, 1966); Holzworth, John M., *The Fighting Governor: The Story of William Langer and the State of North Dakota* (Chicago: Pointer Press, 1938); Horne, Robert M., "The Controversy over the Seating of William Langer, 1940–1942" (Master's thesis, University of North Dakota, 1964); Johnson, Gordon W., "William Langer's Resurgence to Political Power in 1932" (Master's thesis, University of North Dakota, 1970); "Langer, William," in Robert Sobel and John Raimo, eds., *Biographical Directory of the Governors of the United States, 1789–1978*, 4 vols. (Westport, CT: Meckler Books, 1978), III:1181; Larsen, Lawrence H., "William Langer: A Maverick in the Senate," *Wisconsin Magazine of History*, 44 (Spring 1961), 189–198; Smith, Glenn H., *Langer of North Dakota: A Study in Isolationism, 1940–1959* (New York: Garland Publishing, 1979).

Leche, Richard Webster (1898–1965)

Governor of Louisiana (1936–1939) convicted in 1940 of using the mails to defraud the state government, becoming the first of two governors in Louisiana history to go to prison (Edwin Edwards is the second). Leche was born in New Orleans, Louisiana, on 17 May 1898, the son of Eustace Leche, a schoolteacher and salesman, and Stella Louise (née Richard) Leche. He received a common school education, then attended Tulane University from 1916 to 1917, eventually graduating from Loyola University in New Orleans with a law degree in 1923. He left Tulane in 1917 to volunteer for service in the U.S. Army and was commissioned a second lieutenant of infantry, serving until 1919. It is not known if he served overseas during World War I. After his service, Leche went to Chicago, where for two years he worked as an auto equipment salesman. In 1921 he returned to New Orleans, where he entered Loyola and received his law degree two years later. Admitted to the bar in 1922, he entered into a private law practice with a local attorney, John C. Hollingsworth. Leche eventually established his own practice in 1924.

Leche was involved in politics as a Democrat while he worked as an attorney, working in several campaigns. In 1928 he entered the political realm on his own, running for but losing a seat in the Louisiana state senate. However, his campaign attracted the attention of Huey Pierce Long, known as the "Kingfish," a major force in Louisiana politics, who was serving as governor in 1928. Two years later, when Long ran for a seat in the U.S. Senate, Leche was his campaign manager. At the same time, Leche also managed the congressional campaign of Democrat Paul H. Maloney, who was running for a seat in the U.S. Congress. Both men were successful, and when Long's appointed successor, Oscar K. Allen, became governor, Allen named Leche as his private secretary. For his loyalty to the Long political machine, in 1934 Allen named Leche as a judge of the State Court of Appeals for the Parish of New Orleans. He would serve in this capacity for two years.

On 8 September 1935, Long was the victim of an assassination attempt and succumbed to his injuries two days later. Long's death made Leche the new leader of the Long machine. After the death of Governor Allen on 28 January 1936, Lieutenant Governor James Albert Noe became acting governor. However, he did not wish to remain in that office, so the 1936 Democratic gubernatorial nomination was Leche's for the asking. As the leader of the Long machine he easily won the party nod and, as he was unopposed in the general election, became governor just eight years after entering politics. He took office on 12 May 1936. Historians Robert Sobel and John Raimo wrote:

During his administration, he worked to restore a state torn by political strife [particularly over the assassination of Long], and tried to repair the state's relations with the federal administration. New hospitals were built; roads and bridges were constructed; and schools improved. New industries were given a ten-year tax exemption, resulting in over $500 million in new industrial development; Louisiana's Conservation Law was drafted; and a State Mineral Board was created.

In 1939, right before Leche might be expected to announce a run for reelection, scandal enveloped him. Upon entering office he had stated, "When I took the oath of office, I didn't take any vow of poverty." It now appeared that he had lived up to that. Charges were brought that as governor Leche had conspired with state officials to sell trucks to the Highway Department from cronies, and that he pocketed some $31,000 in kickbacks from the purchase by the state of 233 trucks. Facing indictment, Leche resigned as governor on 26 June 1939 and was succeeded by Lieutenant Governor Earl K. Long, son of Huey Long. In 1940 Leche stood trial for the charges: he was acquitted of bribery, but found guilty of using the mails to help defraud the state in the truck-buying scheme. He was sentenced to ten years in prison, but released on parole in 1943. After leaving prison, Leche operated the Bayou Gardens, a tourist attraction, in Lacombe, Louisiana. In 1953, before leaving office, President Harry S. Truman granted Leche a full pardon, and the former governor was able to return to his law practice three years later. He remained in New Orleans for the remainder of his life.

Richard Leche died in New Orleans on 22 February 1965 at the age of sixty-six.

References: "Leche, Richard Webster," in Robert Sobel and John Raimo, eds., *Biographical Directory of the Governors of the United States, 1789–1978,* 4 vols. (Westport, CT: Meckler Books, 1978), II:585–586; Reeves, Miriam G., *The Governors of Louisiana* (Gretna, LA: Pelican Publishing Company, 1972); "Richard W. Leche Dead at 66; Louisiana Governor in Scandals," *New York Times,* 23 February 1965, 33.

Lobbying Disclosure Act of 1995, Public Law 104-65, 109 Stat. 691, 2 U.S.C. § 1601 (1995)

Congressional enactment, 1 January 1996, that was passed "to provide for the disclosure of lobbying activities to influence the Federal Government,

and for other purposes." Its intent was to close loopholes that had existed in the lobbying law up until that time, the Federal Regulation of Lobbying Act, which allowed certain categories of lobbyists to avoid registering and for ineffective and inconsistent reporting of those who did register.

In the legislation, Congress found that "existing lobbying disclosure statutes have been ineffective because of unclear statutory language, weak administrative and enforcement provisions, and an absence of clear guidance as to who is required to register and what they are required to disclose . . . and the effective public disclosure of the identity and extent of the efforts of paid lobbyists to influence Federal officials in the conduct of Government actions will increase public confidence in the integrity of Government."

The act (also called the LDA) also defined what executive branch and legislative branch officials were covered and which lobbying activities were permissible and which were not.

References: Lobbying Disclosure Act of 1995 (text) 109 Stat. 691, 2 U.S.C. § 1601.

Lorimer, William (1861–1934)

United States senator (1909–1912), expelled from the Senate for bribing a state legislator to help elect him, thus becoming the first sitting senator ever expelled for bribery or charges of political corruption. Despite having this ignominy placed on his name, Lorimer is barely known in American history. He was born in Manchester, England, on 27 April 1861. Five years later he emigrated with his parents to the United States, where the family settled in Michigan. Little is known of his early life, except that he did not receive any formal education. He was apprenticed to a sign painter at the age of ten, later working in several odd jobs, including in the packinghouses. He rose to become a real estate agent, as well as a builder.

A Republican, Lorimer first ran for public office in 1894, winning a seat in the U.S. House of Representatives for the Illinois Second District. He defeated Democrat John Hanahan and a Populist Party candidate, entering the House in the Fifty-fourth Congress on 4 March 1895. He would serve in the House until 3 March 1901. In 1900, after serving three terms, Lorimer lost the election to Democrat John J. Feely. Two years later, however,

Senator William Lorimer was expelled from the Senate for bribing a state legislator. Lorimer became the first sitting senator ever expelled for bribery or associated charges of political corruption. (Library of Congress)

after the state had redrawn the electoral districts, Lorimer ran for the House, this time from Illinois Sixth District, and defeated a Democrat to reenter the Fifty-eighth Congress on 4 March 1903. He would serve until his resignation on 17 June 1909.

In 1908 Lorimer decided to run for the U.S. Senate for the seat filled by Republican Albert J. Hopkins. After a lengthy contest (prior to the rati-

fication of the Seventeenth Amendment to the U.S. Constitution on 8 April 1913, all U.S. senators were elected by state legislatures—thereafter, all were elected by popular vote of the people), Lorimer was elected and took his seat on 18 June 1909. However, whispers soon arose that Lorimer had "bought" his seat through bribery and other means. In 1910 the *Chicago Tribune* ran a series of articles that quoted a former state legislator who claimed he had accepted a bribe to vote for Lorimer for the U.S. Senate. With these allegations, Lorimer rose in the Senate on 28 May 1910 to ask the Senate to investigate the charges. The Senate referred the investigation to the Senate Committee on Privileges and Elections on 1 June 1910. The majority report of the committee reported on 21 December 1910 that Lorimer had not taken any bribes or committed any corrupt practices. However, one of the committee members, Senator Albert Beveridge (R-IN), refused to sign the majority report and held that Lorimer was guilty. Beveridge was joined by three other members of the committee, forcing a floor debate on the committee report. The debate began on the Senate floor on 18 January 1911 and went on for six full weeks. Beveridge was Lorimer's chief accuser and took to the Senate floor to deliver an impassioned speech against his fellow Republican. Despite his remarks, the Senate voted on 1 March 1911 to accept the majority report of the committee and find for Lorimer.

Beveridge left the Senate, but his call for action was taken up by incoming Senator Robert M. La Follette (R-WI), who, acting on national outrage against the Lorimer decision, asked the Senate to again investigate the charges. After further debate, on 7 June 1911 the Senate voted to initiate a second investigation of Lorimer and the 1908 election. On 20 May 1912, after hearing from nearly 200 witnesses and releasing a report that included eight volumes of testimony, the Senate committee again held that there was no evidence that Lorimer had committed any corrupt act. However, the minority in the Senate again argued that several witnesses who claimed to have been bribed had to be believed, and, led by Senator John Worth Kern (who had replaced Beveridge in the Senate) of Indiana, the Senate voted fifty-five to twenty-eight on 13 July 1912 that Lorimer's 1908 election was invalid. Because the Seventeenth Amendment, enacted a year later, took the power to elect senators from state legislators, Lorimer became the last man to be charged with bribing state legislators to be elected to the Senate. When Lorimer asked to be reimbursed some $55,000 in expenses he had incurred in the two investigations, the Senate adjourned, and he was forced to pay the amount out of his own pocket.

Lorimer, who declared his total innocence, returned to private business in Illinois. Despite being tossed out of the Senate due to corruption allegations, he remained a power broker inside the Illinois state Republican Party until his death. Lorimer died in Chicago on 13 September 1934 at the age of seventy-three and was buried in Calvary Cemetery in that city.

References: *Biographical Directory of the American Congress, 1774–1996* (Alexandria, VA: CQ Staff Directories, Inc., 1996), 1413; Butler, Anne M., and Wendy Wolff, *United States Senate Election, Expulsion and Censure Cases, 1793–1990* (Washington, DC: Government Printing Office, 1995), 281–284; Tarr, Joel Arthur, *A Study in Boss Politics: William Lorimer of Chicago* (Urbana: University of Illinois Press, 1971).

Louderback, Harold (1881–1941)

Judge for the Northern District of California (1928–1941), impeached and acquitted on charges of favoritism and conspiracy in the appointment of bankruptcy officers who appeared before him. Louderback was one of only eleven judges to be impeached and tried in the Senate in American history. He was born in San Francisco, California, on 30 January 1881 and received his bachelor's degree from the University of Nevada in 1905 and his law degree from the Harvard Law School three years later. From 1908 until 1917, he was in private law practice in San Francisco. During World War I, he served as a captain in the U.S. Army, returning to his law practice in 1919. From 1921 until 1928, Louderback was a judge for the Superior Court for the City and County of San Francisco.

On 21 March 1928, Louderback was nominated by President Calvin Coolidge for a seat on the U.S. District Court for the Northern District of California, a seat vacated by Judge John S. Partridge. Louderback, a Republican, was confirmed by the Senate on 17 April 1928 and took his seat on that court.

After only five years on that court, allegations that Louderback had used his power to appoint certain bankruptcy receivers—and set their fees from which he got a portion—reached the U.S. House of Representatives, and an investigation was established. Although the House Judiciary Committee found that Louderback had used bad judgment in such appointments, the panel's majority recommended that he be censured rather than impeached.

A minority of the committee, however, urged that the House indeed impeach the Californian. Taking their concerns to the full House, the minority pushed through five articles of impeachment, all charging Louderback with corruptly using his influence as a federal judge to appoint bankruptcy receivers. The full House agreed on these articles on 24 February 1933, making Louderback one of only a handful of federal judges to be impeached in American history. The trial in the U.S. Senate lasted throughout all of May 1933, in the midst of the Congress's legislative attempts to put President Franklin D. Roosevelt's New Deal program into law. Numerous witnesses were called—one was a faith healer who was brought in on a stretcher—all of whom cast doubt on the charges against the judge. On 24 May 1933, only three months after he was impeached by the House, Louderback was acquitted on all charges by the Senate. On only one article, the fifth, did a majority hold against the judge, but this was eight votes shy of the two-thirds necessary for conviction.

Louderback returned to his judge's position, where he served until his death on 11 December 1941, at the age of sixty. His name is now merely a footnote in judicial and impeachment history.

References: "Louderback, Harold," in *The National Cyclopædia of American Biography,* 57 vols. and supplements A–N (New York: James T. White and Company, 1897–1984), B:362; United States House of Representatives, *Conduct of Harold Louderback, United States District Judge, Northern District of California. Hearing Before the Special Committee of the House of Representatives, Seventy-Second Congress, Pursuant to House Resolution 239, September 6 to September 12, 1932,* 3 vols. (Washington, DC: Government Printing Office, 1933); United States House of Representatives, *Conduct of Judge Harold Louderback. Report to Accompany House Resolution 387,* House Report 72–2065, (Washington, DC: Government Printing Office, 1933).

Lyon, Caleb (1822–1875)

United States representative (1853–1855) from New York, implicated, but never tried, on charges that he embezzled some $46,000 from funds intended to assist the Nez Perce Indians. Born in Grieg, New York, on 7 December 1822, Lyon attended a common school in the town of Lyondale, apparently named after his family, as well as a school in Montreal, Canada. He graduated from Norwich University in Northfield, Vermont, in 1841 and in the years following this, traveled around the world, becoming a well-known poet and author. In 1847 he was appointed by President James K. Polk as the United States consul to Shanghai, but instead of taking his office he entrusted it to an associate and went to California, where he settled. He was named secretary of the California constitutional convention and in 1849 designed the seal that was adopted when California became a state.

After being in California for a short time and aiding in that state's formation, Lyon changed his mind about settling there and went back to Lyonsdale, New York. In 1850 he was elected to a seat in the New York state assembly, but he resigned after he opposed state aid in improving the Erie Canal. However, in 1851 he was elected to a seat in the state senate because of his principled stand on the canal matter. He was not connected with any particular party of the time; instead, in 1852 he ran as an Independent for a seat in the U.S. House of Representatives and was elected, taking his seat in the Thirty-third Congress on 4 March 1853. Lyon only served a single term in the House, deciding not to run for reelection in 1854. He moved to Staten Island, near New York City, and remained there for several years.

In 1864 President Abraham Lincoln named Lyon governor of the Idaho Territory, replacing William Wallace, the territory's first governor. Lyon served for two years until 1866. It was during this term that Lyon got into trouble. An audit conducted by the Idaho territorial government discovered that Lyon probably embezzled approximately $46,418 in government funds that were intended for the welfare of Nez Perce Indians. However, a congressional investigation that should have been initiated immediately by Congress was not, and years went by before investigators did look into the matter in 1875. By that time, Lyon had returned to his home, "Lyonsmere," located in Rossville, New York. Lyon died there on 8 September 1875, his name never cleared. All potential investigations were dropped after his death.

References: *Biographical Directory of the American Congress, 1774–1996* (Alexandria, VA: CQ Staff Directories, Inc., 1996), 1425; Brown, Margaret Louise, "Lyon, Caleb," in Allen Johnson and Dumas Malone, et al., eds., *Dictionary of American Biography,* X vols. and 10 supplements (New York: Charles Scribner's Sons, 1930–1995), VI:527–528.

M

Mandel, Marvin (1920–)

Governor of Maryland (1969–1979), convicted in 1977 of charges of mail fraud and racketeering, becoming the second Maryland governor in less than a decade to be convicted of a crime (Spiro Agnew was the other). Mandel, of a Jewish background, was born in Baltimore, Maryland, on 19 April 1920, the son of Harry Mandel and Rebecca (née Cohen) Mandel. He graduated from Baltimore City College in 1937, then attended the University of Maryland and the University of Maryland Law School, receiving his law degree in 1942. That same year, Mandel enlisted in the U.S. Army, and during his two years served as an instructor at the Aberdeen Proving Ground in Maryland, the army's oldest active proving ground for testing arms and other military equipment, and at Texarkana, Texas, before he was discharged in 1944. After returning to Baltimore, he opened a law practice.

Mandel entered the political arena in 1952, when he was appointed by Maryland Governor Theodore R. McKeldin to fill a vacancy in the Maryland state house of delegates. Elected on his own, and eventually reelected eight times, Mandel served as the chairman of the Ways and Means Committee and the Baltimore City delegation, before he was elected as Speaker of the House of Delegates in 1963. He gradually built up power, becoming a kingmaker in 1966; when the Democrats nominated George P. Mahoney for governor, Mandel decided not to back Mahoney and supported the Republican nominee, Spiro T. Agnew. When Agnew was elected, Mandel became the second most powerful politician in the state. And, when Agnew was selected to run for vice president with Richard Nixon in 1968 and was elected, Mandel, on 7 January 1969, was himself selected by the house of delegates to become Maryland's fifty-sixth governor. He was elected to a term on his own in 1970 and reelected in 1974. During his tenure, the state government was organized into twelve separate executive departments, and a system of public defenders to defend the poor was implemented. Historians Robert Sobel and John Raimo add, "Mandel restored persons to the Medicaid rolls who were removed in the Agnew administration; created a Drug Abuse Authority and a State Housing Authority; supported the passage of eight constitutional amendments in 1969; and secured the reorganization of the executive department."

What got Mandel into trouble was his veto in May 1971 of a racing bill that would have increased the number of racing days from the original eighteen to thirty-six allowed by the Marlboro Racing Track, in Prince George's County. As soon as Mandel vetoed the legislation, several friends rushed in to buy the track. These five men were W. Dale Hess, Harry W. Rodgers III, William A. Rodgers, Irvin Kovens, and Ernest N. Cory. They completed the purchase at the end of 1971 and began to secretly pay Mandel off with gifts—gifts that were wholly illegal. By mid-1972 these "gifts" included a $140,000 interest in a security investment company, and a $45,000 share in a land deal. As soon as his friends purchased the track, Mandel supported an extension of the racing days from eighteen to ninety-four, but that legislation was not enacted. However, the State Racing Commission did allow Marlboro to expand races from a half-mile to a full mile, which increased the number of people going to the track.

In 1974 an investigation into the racetrack deal and Mandel's role in it began. In April Harry Rodgers III and W. Dale Hess were notified that they were under investigation by a grand jury. Hess wrote a letter, which he backdated six years, claiming that he owed Mandel fees from a legal matter and that the income from the security investment was to pay back these fees. Mandel was reelected in November 1974 in a landslide, defeating Republican Louise Gore by more than 250,000 votes. In February 1975, after being inaugurated a second time, Mandel held a press conference in which he denied any knowledge of the sale of the Marlboro track. However, that September, he, too, was informed that he was under investigation by the federal grand jury.

On 24 November 1975, Mandel and all five of the Marlboro owners were indicted by the grand jury. Mandel faced counts involving racketeering and mail fraud. The first trial opened on 6 September 1976, but was declared a mistrial by Judge John H. Pratt on 7 December 1976 after a juror came forward with information that two men—later identified as Mafia insiders—had offered the juror a $10,000 bribe if they would hold out for a not guilty verdict. Because Mandel had such influence in Maryland and had named many of the judges who would possibly oversee a second trial, Judge Robert L. Taylor was moved from Tennessee to Baltimore to hear the case. The second trial opened on 31 May 1977, despite the fact that Mandel had suffered a stroke and was hospitalized for numerous illnesses. His own lawyer called him "a broken man." Despite this, on 23 August 1977 Mandel and all five of his codefendants were convicted on eighteen counts of mail fraud and racketeering. The federal grand jury in Baltimore had deliberated for 113 hours—the longest deliberations in history for a federal criminal trial—be-

fore returning with its verdict. Mandel thus became the first sitting governor in more than fifty years to be convicted of a crime. He faced more than 105 years in prison and a fine of $42,000, but Taylor was lenient on him and only gave him a four-year sentence. At sentencing on 7 October 1977, Mandel was suspended as governor and his law license was taken away.

Mandel was broken—physically and financially—by the indictment and two trials. However, on 11 January 1979, a three-judge panel of the U.S. Court of Appeals for the Fourth Circuit struck down Mandel's conviction, citing error by the trial judge. Mandel returned to serve as governor on 15 January for the final forty-five and one-half hours of his term. On appeal by the government to the full court, the court held six to three on 20 July 1979 to reinstate Mandel's conviction. In November, eight judges, with one removed for personal reasons, split four to four on whether to hear Mandel's appeal a second time. Faced with this action, Mandel had to start serving his sentence; in May 1980 he entered the federal prison at Eglin Air Force Base in Florida. He only served nineteen months, being paroled in December 1981 when President Ronald Reagan offered him a full pardon. He was the last of the six defendants to leave prison.

Despite the fact that Mandel had completed his sentence, the courts continued to listen to the matter. In November 1987 federal Judge Frederic N. Smalkin of Baltimore formally entered a judgement of not guilty for all six men, saying in his opinion that the government had "liberally interpreted" the mail fraud and racketeering statutes. The government appealed to the U.S. Supreme Court, but on 19 November 1989 it failed to hear the case, meaning that Mandel's conviction was in essence overturned completely. He then got his law license reinstated and opened a law office in Annapolis. A former aide, Maurice Wyatt, was stripped of his law license in 1982 following a bribery conviction, but after Maryland Governor Donald Schaefer granted him a full pardon, he was reinstated to the bar as well in 1996.

References: Jacobs, Bradford, *Thimbleriggers: The Law v. Governor Marvin Mandel* (Baltimore, MD: Johns Hopkins University Press, 1984); "Mandel, Marvin," in Robert Sobel and John Raimo, eds., *Biographical Directory of the Governors of the United States,*

1789–1978, 4 vols. (Westport, CT: Meckler Books, 1978), II:685; "Marvin Mandel: Governor Convicted in Office," in George C. Kohn, *Encyclopedia of American Scandal: From ABSCAM to the Zenger Case* (New York: Facts on File, 1989), 217; Saperstein, Sandra, "Court Reinstates Conviction of Mandel," *Washington Post,* 21 July 1979, A1; *United States v. Mandel,* 91 F.2d 1347, *vacated en banc,* 602 F.2d 653 (4th Cir. 550 F.2d 1001 [1977]), *second rehearing en banc denied,* 609 F.2d 1076 (4th Cir. 1979), *cert. denied,* 445 U.S. 961 (1980).

Manton, Martin Thomas (1880–1946)

United States judge for the Second Circuit Court of Appeals, convicted of taking bribes and sent to prison. Manton is barely remembered, despite being one of the few sitting federal judges in American history to be convicted of a crime and imprisoned. Born in New York City on 2 August 1880, Manton attended the public schools in that city, then Columbia University Law School, from which he was awarded his law degree in 1901. That year, after being admitted to the New York bar, he opened a law practice in the city, where he remained until 1916. In 1913 he became a law partner of former U.S. Senator W. Bourke Cockran, forming the firm of Cockran and Manton. In 1914 Manton served as counsel for New York City Police Lieutenant Charles Becker, accused of ordering the murder of a criminal. Becker was later convicted and executed in the electric chair.

Following the death of Judge Charles M. Hough of the U.S. District Court for the Southern District of New York, President Woodrow Wilson named Manton, a Democrat, to the vacancy. Confirmed by the Senate on 23 August 1916, Manton took his seat. Just two years later, upon the resignation of Judge Alfred Conkling Coxe of the U.S. Court of Appeals for the Second Circuit, President Wilson elevated Manton to this seat. Confirmed by the Senate on 18 March 1918, Manton stood just one level below the U.S. Supreme Court. By 1939, Manton, as chief judge, was in the position of being a potential Supreme Court nominee.

However, on 28 January 1939, the U.S. Department of Justice announced that it was investigating charges of financial and other misconduct by Manton. The following day, the *New York Times* broke the story that New York District Attorney Thomas E. Dewey had sent a letter to Representative Hatton W. Summers, chairman of the House Judiciary Committee, alleging that Manton had been involved in massive and unethical corruption. In his letter, Dewey wrote, "For the past twelve months my office has been conducting an investigation of Judge Martin T. Manton, senior judge of the United States Court of Appeals for the Second Circuit, with a view to possible criminal prosecution under the income tax laws of the State of New York, among others, arising out of certain acts hereinafter referred to." Dewey charged that Manton had received more than $400,000 from "individuals or concerns acting for parties interested in matters handled by [his] court." The day after the story broke, Manton told reporters that he would issue a statement that would "satisfy the public that there is nothing wrong or immoral" in his business dealings. That statement, issued on 20 January 1939, was a resignation letter to President Franklin D. Roosevelt. The resignation seemed to end matters. When Representative Summers was asked whether Manton should be impeached anyway, he stated, "Why kick at the place where the fellow used to be?" Dewey, however, continued on, specifically on the allegation that Manton had received a $77,000 bribe from the Dictograph Products Corporation to find in their favor against Schick Dry Shaver, Inc., a case before Manton. In April 1939 Manton was indicted on charges of bribery and conspiracy to commit bribery. Tried in May and June of 1939, Manton was convicted only of conspiracy to obstruct justice and sentenced to two years in prison. Because Manton had served on the U.S. Court of Appeals for the Second Circuit, which would normally hear his appeal, a special court consisting of judges who did not know Manton had to be created just to hear his appeal. The appeal was heard but denied, and the U.S. Supreme Court allowed the conviction to stand.

Manton served one year and seven months of his sentence in a federal penitentiary and was released in 1941. He returned home in disgrace, where he died on 18 November 1946 at the age of sixty-six. He was buried in the Immaculate Conception Cemetery in Fayetteville, New York. He remains one of the highest-ranking judges in American history to go to prison for corruption.

See also Miller, Thomas Woodnutt
References: "Dewey Says Judge Manton Got $400,000 from Litigants, Sends Charges to Congress," *New York*

Times, 30 January 1939, 1; "Manton, Martin Thomas," in *Encyclopedia of World Crime: Criminal Justice, Criminology, and Law Enforcement,* edited by Jay Robert Nash, 4 vols. (Wilmette, IL: CrimeBooks, Inc., 1989), 3:2112; "Martin T. Manton," in Joseph Borkin, *The Corrupt Judge: An Inquiry Into Bribery and Other High Crimes and Misdemeanors in the Federal Courts* (New York: Clarkson N. Potter, Inc., 1962), 23–93; "Martin T. Manton Trial: 1939," in Edward W. Knappman, ed., *Great American Trials* (Detroit, MI: Visible Ink Press, 1994), 403–405; "Manton's Conduct Under U.S. Inquiry, He Defers Defense," *New York Times,* 29 January 1939, 1, 2.

Marshall, Humphrey (1760–1841)

United States senator from Kentucky (1795–1801) accused of corruption, whose case helped establish an early congressional rule that illegalities done prior to congressional service would not be dealt with in Congress. Humphrey Marshall's case was one of the first dealing with ethics in the U.S. Senate. Marshall was born in Orlean, Virginia, in 1760. He came from a venerable Virginia family, which included Colonel Thomas Marshall, a friend of George Washington, as well as John Marshall (chief justice of the United States Supreme Court). Marshall pursued what are called "classical studies," which include math, Latin, and Greek. He became a surveyor and served with the forces of Virginia in the Revolutionary War. In 1782 he moved to Kentucky, which at that time was not yet a state (it would be admitted to the Union in 1792), where he studied law and, after being admitted to the bar, opened a practice in Fayette County. He served as a delegate to the so-called Danville Convention, convened in 1787 to decide whether to separate Kentucky from Virginia, which Marshall opposed. That same year, he also served as a delegate to the Virginia convention that ratified the federal Constitution along with such notables as his cousin John Marshall, James Monroe, George Wythe, Bushrod Washington, and Patrick Henry.

Marshall's political career began when he was elected a member of the Kentucky state house of representatives, serving from 1793 to 1794. The year after this service ended, Marshall was elected as a Federalist to a seat in the U.S. Senate, serving a single term from 4 March 1795 to 3 March 1801. Marshall's service is unexemplary, except that in his second year he became embroiled in a controversy that set a precedent in the area of congres-

sional ethics for more than a century. On 26 February 1796, Vice President John Adams, sitting as president pro tem of the Senate, presented to the Senate a letter from the governor of Kentucky, Isaac Shelby, with a letter called a memorial (usually signed by a number of prominent citizens), which made serious allegations against Marshall. Three days later, on 29 February, the letter and memorial were referred to a select committee, consisting of Senators Samuel Livermore of New Hampshire, James Ross of Pennsylvania, Rufus King of New York, John Rutherfurd of New Jersey, and Caleb Strong of Massachusetts, to investigate the allegations. On 17 March the committee reported to the full Senate. This report stated:

> That the representatives of the freemen of Kentucky state in their memorial that in February, 1795, a pamphlet was published by George Muter and Benjamin Sebastian (who were two judges of the court of appeals), in which they say that Humphrey Marshall had a suit in chancery in the said court of appeals, in which it appearing manifest from the oath of the complainant, from disinterested testimony, from records, from documents furnished by himself, and from the contradictions contained in his own answer, that he had committed a gross fraud, the court gave a decree against him; and that in the course of the investigation he was publicly charged with perjury. That Mr. Marshall, in a publication in the *Kentucky Gazette,* called for a specification of the charge; to which the said George Muter and Benjamin Sebastian, in a like publication, replied that he was guilty of perjury in his answer to the bill in chancery exhibited against him by James Wilkinson, and that they would plead justification to any suit brought against them therefor. That no such suit, as the said representatives could learn, had been brought. The said representatives further say that they do not mean to give an opinion on the justice of the said charge, but request that an investigation may immediately take place relative thereto. . . .
>
> Your committee observe that the said suit was tried eighteen months before Mr. Marshall was chosen a Member of the Senate, and that previous to his election mutual accusations had taken place between him and the judges of the said court relating to the same suit. . . .
>
> The representatives of Kentucky have not furnished any copy of Mr. Marshall's answer on oath, nor have they stated any part of the testimony, or produced any of the said records or documents, or

the copy of any paper in the cause, nor have they intimated a design to bring forward those or any other proofs. . . .

Your committee are informed by the other Senator and the two Representatives in Congress from Kentucky that they have not been requested by the legislature of that State to prosecute this inquiry, and that they are not possessed of any evidence in the case, and that they believe no person is authorized to appear on behalf of the legislature. . . .

Mr. Marshall is solicitous that a full investigation of the subject shall take place in the Senate, and urges the principle that consent takes away error, as applying, on this occasion, to give the Senate jurisdiction; but, as no person appears to prosecute, and there is no evidence adduced to the Senate, nor even a specific charge, the committee think any further inquiry by the Senate would be improper. If there were no objections of this sort, the committee would still be of opinion that the memorial could not be sustained. They think that in a case of this kind no person can be held to answer for an infamous crime unless on a presentment or indictment of a grand jury, and that in all such prosecutions the accused ought to be tried by an impartial jury of the State and district wherein the crime shall have been committed. If, in the present case, the party has been guilty in the manner suggested, no reason has been alleged by the memorialists why he has not long since been tried in the State and district where he committed the offense. Until he is legally convicted, the principles of the Constitution and of the common law concur in presuming that he is innocent. And the committee are compelled, by a sense of justice, to declare that in their opinion the presumption in favor of Mr. Marshall is not diminished by the recriminating publications which manifest strong resentment against him.

The members concluded: "[T]hey are also of opinion that as the Constitution does not give jurisdiction to the Senate the consent of the party can not give it; and that therefore the said memorial ought to be dismissed." By this statement, the Senate agreed, when it upheld the report, that if a crime was committed prior to the election of the senator, and the courts had not heard charges against him, the Senate should not and could not try that senator. When the committee urged that the report be transmitted to the governor of Kentucky, with an eye toward a potential prosecution of Marshall, the Senate voted seven to sixteen not to expunge the clause that would refer it to the governor of Kentucky. The committee's decision was also voted on but failed seven votes to seventeen to expunge. The full Senate voted sixteen to eight on 22 March to accept the report. However, no charges appear to have been brought against Marshall, and he concluded his term of office in 1801.

Marshall returned to Kentucky, where he later served a second time as a member of the Kentucky state legislature, from 1807 to 1809. It was during this period that he opposed a proposal by Kentuckian Henry Clay that all Kentucky legislators wear domestic spun cloth instead of British broadcloth; when the two men argued, a duel was called, and both men were wounded but lived. After finishing his political career, Marshall took up agricultural pursuits and authored the comprehensive history of the state up to that time. Marshall died near Lexington, Kentucky, on 3 July 1841 and was buried on his farm, "Glen Willis," in Leestown, Kentucky.

Today, Marshall's name is not remembered for the ignominious precedent he established in the Senate; rather, his famed work, *The History of Kentucky* (1812), has given him the sobriquet "The Historian of Kentucky."

References: *Debates and Other Proceedings of the Convention of Virginia, Convened at Richmond, on Monday the Second of June, 1788, for the Purpose of Deliberating on the Constitution Recommended by the Grand Federal Convention. To Which is Prefixed the Federal Constitution. Taken in Short Hand, by David Robertson of Petersburg,* 3 vols. (Petersburg: Hunter and Prentis, 1788–1789); Hinds, Asher Crosby, *Hinds' Precedents of the House of Representatives of the United States, Including References to Provisions of the Constitution, the Laws, and Decisions of the United States Senate,* 8 vols. (Washington, DC: Government Printing Office, 1907–1908), II:816–817; Quisenberry, Anderson Chenault, *The Life and Times of Hon. Humphrey Marshall: Sometime an Office in the Revolutionary War, Senator in Congress from 1795 to 1801* (Winchester, KY: Sun Publishing Co., 1892).

Matteson, Orsamus Benajah (1805–1889)

United States representative from New York (1853–1857, 1857–1859), accused of corruption in 1857 and 1858, becoming the only representative to face two distinct expulsion hearings in Congress. Matteson was born in Verona, New York, on

28 August 1805. He attended the common schools of the area, after which he studied law in Utica, New York, in the offices of a local attorney, Greene C. Bronson. Admitted to the state bar, he opened a practice in Utica and became a leading attorney in that city. In 1834 and 1836, Matteson served as city attorney of Utica. He later served as a commissioner of the state supreme court.

A follower of the Free Soil movement—which later was folded into the Republican Party—Matteson nonetheless ran as a Whig for a seat in the U.S. House of Representatives in 1846, losing to Democrat Timothy Jenkins. However, two years later, Matteson ran again for the same seat and was elected. He served for a single term during the Thirty-first Congress (1849–1851), losing his bid for reelection. He returned to his law practice. In 1852 he made a comeback, again winning the seat representing New York's Twentieth District as a Whig. Matteson remained in Congress until his resignation on 27 February 1857, serving as chairman of the Committee on the District of Columbia.

In 1857 and again in 1858, Matteson got into trouble, so much that he was the subject of *two* expulsion votes, the only congressman ever to face such disciplinary action. Both times, however, Matteson was censured. The only biography of him reports that "[h]e became conspicuous by being charged with declaring that a large number of the representatives in congress were purchasable, and a resolution to expel him failed to pass." It does appear from the House report, as well as the resolution to censure him, that Matteson was involved in influence peddling—selling his vote for payment. The censure resolution stated:

> Resolved, That Orsamus B. Matteson, a Member of this House from the State of New York, did incite parties deeply interested in the passage of a joint resolution for construing the Des Moines grant to have here and to use a large sum of money and other valuable considerations corruptly for the purpose of procuring the passage of said joint resolution through this House. Resolved, That Orsamus B. Matteson, in declaring that a large number of the Members of this House had associated themselves together and pledged themselves each to the other not to vote for any law or resolution granting money or lands unless they were paid for it, has falsely and willfully assailed and defamed the character of this

House and has proved himself unworthy to be a Member thereof. Resolved, That Orsamus B. Matteson, a Member of this House from the State of New York, be, and is hereby, expelled therefrom. Before the consideration of these resolutions had begun, a communication was presented announcing the resignation of Mr. Matteson from the House.

After serving his final term in Congress, Matteson left Washington on 3 March 1859 and was later involved in a scheme for the construction of the St. Mary's Ship Canal, as well as lumber and iron manufacturing concerns. He also purchased large tracts of land. Matteson died in Utica, New York, on 22 December 1889 at the age of eighty-four and was buried in Utica's Forest Hill Cemetery.

References: *Biographical Directory of the American Congress, 1774–1996* (Alexandria, VA: CQ Staff Directories, Inc., 1996), 1459; "Orsamus Matteson," in Rossiter Johnson, ed., *The Twentieth Century Biographical Dictionary of Notable Americans: Brief Biographies of Authors, Administrators, Clergymen, Commanders, Editors, Engineers, Jurists, Merchants, Officials, Philanthropists, Scientists, Statesman, and Others Who Are Making American History*, 10 vols. (Boston: Biographical Society, 1897–1904), VII; United States Congress, House, Joint Committee on Congressional Operations, *House of Representatives Exclusion, Censure and Expulsion Cases from 1789 to 1973*, 93rd Congress, 1st Session (Washington, DC: Government Printing Office, 1973).

Mavroules, Nicholas James (1929–)

United States representative from Massachusetts (1979–1993) who pled guilty in 1993 to charges of tax fraud and accepting gratuities while in office and was sentenced to fifteen months in prison. Mavroules was born in Peabody, Massachusetts, on 1 November 1929. He attended the schools of Peabody, never attaining a secondary school education. Instead, in 1949, when he was twenty, he went to work for GTE-Sylvania, serving during an eighteen-year career as a supervisor of personnel.

A Democrat, Mavroules was elected in 1958 as a city councilor for Peabody. He did not run for reelection in 1965; however, two years later, he was elected mayor of the town, serving from 1967 until 1978. He was a delegate to the Democratic National Convention in 1976. In 1978 Mavroules ran for a seat in the U.S. House of Representatives, representing the Sixth Massachusetts District. He defeated Republican William Bronson and took his seat in the Ninety-sixth Congress. Mavroules would serve seven terms, until 3 January 1993.

On 27 August 1992, Mavroules was indicted by a federal grand jury in Boston on seventeen counts of racketeering, bribery, and income tax evasion. The indictments were the result of a nine-month investigation of Mavroules by the U.S. attorney's office in Boston. The *Washington Post* stated upon the news of the indictments: "In the factory towns and fishing villages along Boston's north shore, Rep. Nicholas Mavroules (D-Mass.) forged a reputation as a guy who worked his way up from the bottom and never forgot his roots. But federal indictments unsealed today allege that the popular politician used his power to extract money and perquisites from constituents." Mavroules denied the allegations: he said, "In my 30 years as a public official, I never asked for or took a bribe in my life." The embattled congressman spent the time prior to trial fighting a reelection campaign that went from bad to worse. In November 1992 he lost to Republican Peter Torkildsen. He spent some $78,000 of his campaign funds for lawyer's fees. On 15 April 1993, Mavroules pled guilty, admitting that he had accepted seven new automobiles free of charge, falsified financial disclosure statements, and failed to report on his tax returns gifts that he received from 1985 to 1990. He did, however, deny that he had extorted $12,000 from the family of an imprisoned constituent whom Mavroules promised to help get released. On 29 June 1993, he was sentenced to fifteen months in prison and fined $15,000.

References: *Biographical Directory of the American Congress, 1774–1996* (Alexandria, VA: CQ Staff Directories, Inc., 1996), 1461; Hayward, Ed, and Jack Meyers, "Mavroules to Talk About Federalist Corruption Probe," *Boston Herald,* 11 December 1996, A3; "Heavy Hearts for a Favorite Son— Massachusetts Rep. Mavroules Calls Indictments 'A Bunch of Lies,'" *Washington Post,* 29 August 1992, A3; "Indictments Reportedly Name Massachusetts Rep. Mavroules," *Washington Post,* 28 August 1992, A4; "Mavroules Is Sentenced to 15 Months for Gifts," *Washington Post,* 30 June 1993, A2; "Mavroules Pleads Guilty," *Washington Post,* 16 April 1993, A4; *United States v. Mavroules,* 813 F. Supp. 115, 117 (D. Mass. 1993).

May, Andrew Jackson (1875–1959)

United States representative from Kentucky (1931–1947), convicted on charges of accepting bribes for his influence in the award of munitions contracts during World War II, for which he served nine months in prison. Born in Beaver Creek, near Langley, Kentucky, on 24 June 1875, he attended the public schools, after which he taught for five years in the schools of Floyd and Magoffin Counties in Kentucky. May graduated from Southern Normal University Law School (now Union College) in Huntingdon, Tennessee, in 1898. He was admitted to the Kentucky bar that same year and opened a practice in the town of Prestonburg, Kentucky.

Three years after commencing his practice, May was elected county attorney for Floyd County, Kentucky, serving from 1901 to 1909. After he left this position, he returned to private law practice and remained there for the better part of a decade and a half. It was not until 1925 that May reentered the political realm, serving as a special judge of the circuit court of Johnson and Martin Counties, both in Kentucky. During this period, May was also involved in banking and agricultural pursuits.

In 1930 May, a Democrat, ran for a seat in the U.S. House of Representatives, representing the Tenth Kentucky District. He was elected over his Republican opponent, Kathryn Langley, and he took his seat in the House on 4 March 1931. Because May was elected two years before the so-called New Deal Democrats took control of the House, he not only had seniority but also was not beholden to President Franklin D. Roosevelt, upon whose coattails later Democrats were swept into office. During his service in the House in the 1930s, despite his party affiliation, May served as a catalyst for anti-New Deal agitation, voting against many New Deal programs, as well as the Tennessee Valley Authority (TVA). However, after 1940 he was more pro-Roosevelt, voting to increase military preparedness measures.

In 1946 May's career came to a sudden and unexpected halt. In that year the U.S. Senate convened a committee, headed by Senator James M. Mead (D-NY), to investigate war contracts. When allegations arose that May had gone to bat for several constituents in an effort to gain war contracts, the committee called May, but time after time he refused to appear and explain his association with an Illinois munitions company headed by one Henry M. Garsson. The Mead Committee established that during the war May intervened with federal agencies to gain contracts for Garsson worth an estimated $78 million. Finally, the committee subpoenaed May, but on 25 July 1946, he suffered an apparent heart attack. Once he was released from the hospital, instead of returning to Washington, May went home to Kentucky, where he ran for reelection. The charges leveled by the Mead Committee were too much, and May was defeated by Republican Wendell Howes Meade.

Biographer Marian C. McKenna wrote:

Late in 1946 the Mead Committee turned its investigation over to the Justice Department, and on 23 January 1937, May and the Garsson brothers were indicted by a federal grand jury on charges of conspiracy to defraud the government. May pleaded not guilty to this and bribery charges, but testimony during the forty-seven-day trial revealed that he had received more than $53,000 in bribes and that some of the payments were made by the Garsson companies through an affiliate, the Cumberland Land Company in Prestonburg, Kentucky, of which May was an agent. Witnesses at the trial included General Dwight D. Eisenhower, Secretary of State George C. Marshall, and Secretary of War Robert P. Patterson, who testified that May had come to him seeking wartime favors for the Garssons and their friends.

On 3 July 1947, May and the Garsson brothers were convicted on all charges. Despite appeals that went all the way to the U.S. Supreme Court, May's conviction was upheld and in December 1949 he entered the Ashland Federal Correctional Institute in Kentucky to serve a sentence of eight months to two years. Ill health caused him to ask for a reprieve, but this was refused. He was released in September 1950 for good behavior. In June 1952 a Kentucky court of appeals restored May's right to practice law, and he returned to Prestonburg where he remained for the remainder of his life. In December 1952, shortly before leaving office, President Harry S. Truman gave May a full presidential pardon.

May died in Prestonburg on 6 September 1959, reiterating his innocence to the end. He remains one of a handful of congressmen to be convicted of a crime and serve time in a federal prison.

References: *Biographical Directory of the American Congress, 1774–1996* (Alexandria, VA: CQ Staff Directories, Inc., 1996), 1462; McKenna, Marian C., "May, Andrew Jackson," in Allen Johnson and Dumas

Malone, et al., eds., *Dictionary of American Biography*, X vols. and 10 supplements (New York: Charles Scribner's Sons, 1930–1995), 6:436–438.

McCray, Warren Terry (1865–1938)

Governor of Indiana (1921–1924), forced to resign after his conviction for mail fraud related to the collapse of his finances, becoming one of only a handful of American governors to serve time in prison. Warren McCray, the son of Greenberry Ward McCray, a banker, and Martha Jane (née Galey) McCray, was born near Kentland, Indiana, on 3 February 1865. He was educated in the public schools of rural Indiana and from the age of fifteen served as a clerk in his father's bank. When his father died in 1913, McCray became the president of the bank. He used his growing fortune to invest in local business, including a grain elevator and a farm on which he bred Hereford cows. A Republican, McCray was involved in many areas of life in Indiana, including service as the treasurer for Northern Hospital for the Insane from 1904 to 1912 and as a member of the Indiana Board of Agriculture from 1912 to 1916. He worked on agricultural issues during World War I, including serving as chairman of the Food Conservation Committee of Indiana and the Livestock Advisory Board.

In 1920 McCray was nominated by the Republicans for governor, and he defeated Democrat Carleton B. McCulloch by 170,000 votes out of some 1.2 million votes cast, with several minor party candidates getting the remainder of the vote. Historians Robert Sobel and John Raimo wrote, "A number of public buildings were erected during McCray's administration, including the reformatory at Pendleton, which had been moved from Jeffersonville, and several buildings at the Indians State Fairgrounds." During his time as governor, McCray's business affairs suffered and he took a financial blow. He was then indicted by a grand jury for committing mail fraud in an attempt to stave off bankruptcy. McCray was convicted of the charges, and on 29 April 1934 he resigned the governorship. Sentenced to five years in prison, he served three years, after which he was released and returned to his estate, Orchard Lake Farm. In 1930 President Herbert Hoover granted McCray a pardon. Eight years later, on 19 December 1938, Mc-

Cray died at his farm near Kentland, Indiana, at the age of seventy-three. He was buried in Fairhaven Cemetery in Kentland.

See also Jackson, Edward Franklin

References: "McCray, Warren T.," in Robert Sobel and John Raimo, eds., *Biographical Directory of the Governors of the United States, 1789–1978,* 4 vols. (Westport, CT: Meckler Books, 1978), I:415–416; Ruegamer, Lana, *Biographies of the Governors* (Indianapolis: Indiana Historical Society, 1978).

McDade, Joseph Michael (1931–)

United States representative from Pennsylvania (1963–1999), indicted and later convicted of bribery. Although he had been indicted in 1992, McDade held his congressional seat until 1999. Born in Scranton, Pennsylvania, on 29 September 1931, McDade attended local schools before he entered the University of Notre Dame and earned his bachelor's degree in 1953. He later received his law degree from the University of Pennsylvania in 1956. Before he entered the field of law, McDade served as a clerk to federal Judge John W. Murphy of the Middle District of Pennsylvania in 1957. Afterwards, he opened his own law practice. In 1962 McDade was elected the city solicitor for Scranton.

That same year, McDade entered the race for a seat in the U.S. House of Representatives, representing Pennsylvania's Tenth District. A Republican, McDade was elected over Democrat William Combar and took his seat in the Eighty-eighth Congress on 3 January 1963. He would eventually serve seventeen terms. Over the years, he became one of the most powerful leaders in the Republican caucus, rising to become ranking member of the House Appropriations Committee.

On 6 May 1992, McDade was indicted by a federal grand jury in Pennsylvania under allegations that he violated the Racketeer Influenced and Corrupt Organizations (RICO) Act by helping to secure a defense contract for companies that later paid him more than $100,000 in bribes and other gratuities. Despite being under indictment, McDade was serving at the time as the ranking member of the House Appropriations Committee, and on 8 December 1992, he retained his post. This action rubbed Democrats the wrong way; they recalled that when Democratic Representative Dan Rostenkowski, chairman of the House Ways and Means Committee, had been indicted, he was

forced to relinquish control of his committee. Representative Mel Reynolds (D-IL) demanded that Republicans likewise punish McDade. (Ironically, Reynolds was later convicted of bank and wire fraud and served time in prison.) But because McDade was such a powerful congressman, no Republican challenged him, and he remained the ranking member; although when the Republicans took control of the House in 1995, he was denied the chairmanship of the committee. In 1995 McDade challenged his indictment in the U.S. Supreme Court, arguing that under the "Speech and Debate Clause" of the U.S. Constitution, his actions were protected. On 6 March 1995, the Court refused to intervene.

On 1 August 1996, a federal jury acquitted McDade of all charges against him. The blow to Justice Department lawyers who had battled McDade for four years was stunning. However, McDade did not emerge unscathed from the engagement: during the period in which he was under indictment, he developed Parkinson's disease, and by 1996 his hands were noticeably shaking. In November 1996 he was elected to his seventeenth term, but Republicans refused to remove Representative Bob Livingston (R-LA), who had been named as chairman of the House Appropriations Committee in McDade's stead.

In 1998 McDade announced that he would not run for an eighteenth term and departed from the House at the end of his term on 3 January 1999.

References: *Biographical Directory of the American Congress, 1774–1996* (Alexandria, VA: CQ Staff Directories, Inc., 1996), 1478.

McGrain v. Daugherty, 273 U.S. 135 (1927)

United States Supreme Court decision holding that Congress does have the right to compel certain testimony and/or papers from persons who are not members of Congress and that refusal to comply may constitute contempt of Congress, a jailable offense. In 1881 the Supreme Court had held in *Kilbourn v. Thompson* that Congress could not find a nonmember in contempt and could not jail that person; however, the Court had drastically chipped away at *Kilbourn* over the years, especially in its decision in *In re Chapman,* 166 U.S. 66 (1897), in which it gave Congress the green light to compel testimony in matters within constitutional and congressional jurisdiction.

The subject of the *McGrain* case regarded Harry M. Daugherty, attorney general in the Harding and Coolidge administrations from March 1921 until March 1924, when he resigned amid allegations of malfeasance—notably, that he obstructed an investigation into the roles of Secretary of the Interior Albert B. Fall and Secretary of the Navy Edwin Denby in the Teapot Dome scandal. During the congressional investigation into Teapot Dome and Daugherty's role in it, the Senate Committee (established by a resolution) found documents relating to Mally S. Daugherty, the former attorney general's brother and president of the Midland National Bank of Washington Court House, Ohio. The committee issued a subpoena ordering Daugherty to appear, as well as a subpoena *duces tecum* to produce documents relating to certain deposits in his bank since 1 November 1920. Mally Daugherty failed to honor the subpoenas and never appeared before the Senate.

Angered, the Senate committee ordered the sergeant at arms to arrest Mally Daugherty at once. This officer dispatched his deputy, John J. McGrain, to Cincinnati, where he took custody of Daugherty. Immediately, Daugherty petitioned to the federal district court in Cincinnati for a writ of habeas corpus, arguing that his arrest was illegal. The court held that because there was no arrest warrant, Daugherty had to be released. The U.S. Senate, backing McGrain, asked for an immediate appeal to the U.S. Supreme Court, which heard arguments on 5 December 1924. Less than six weeks later, on 17 January 1924, it handed down its ruling.

Justice Willis Van Devanter spoke for a unanimous eight-to-zero Court (Justice Harlan Fiske Stone did not participate) that the Senate's subpoena power gave that body the right to demand persons and/or documents to be delivered, and that avoidance of such subpoenas was a crime. Van Devanter explained:

> We are of opinion that the power of inquiry—with process to enforce it—is an essential and appropriate auxiliary to the legislative function. It was so regarded and employed in American Legislatures before the Constitution was framed and ratified. Both houses of Congress took this view of it early in their history—the House of Representatives with the approving votes of Mr. Madison and other members whose service in the convention that framed the Constitution gives special significance to their action—and both houses have employed the power accordingly up to the present time. The acts of 1798 and 1857, judged by their comprehensive terms, were intended to recognize the existence of this power in both houses and to enable them to employ it "more effectually" than before. So, when their practice in the matter is appraised according to the circumstances in which it was begun and to those in which it has been continued, it falls nothing short of a practical construction, long continued, of the constitutional provisions respecting their powers, and therefore should be taken as fixing the meaning of those provisions, if otherwise doubtful. . . .
>
> We are further of opinion that the provisions are not of doubtful meaning, but, as was held by this court in the cases we have reviewed, are intended to be effectively exercised, and therefore to carry with them such auxiliary powers as are necessary and appropriate to that end. Although the power to exact information in aid of the legislative function was not involved in those cases, the rule of interpretation applied there is applicable here. A legislative body cannot legislate wisely or effectively in the absence of information respecting the conditions that the legislation is intended to affect or change; and where the legislative body does not itself possess the requisite information—which not infrequently is true—recourse must be had to others who do possess it. Experience has taught that mere requests for such information often are unavailing, and also that information which is volunteered is not always accurate or complete; so some means of compulsion are essential to obtain what is needed. All this was true before and when the Constitution was framed and adopted. In that period the power of inquiry, with enforcing process, was regarded and employed as a necessary and appropriate attribute of the power to legislate—indeed, was treated as inhering in it. Thus there is ample warrant for thinking, as we do, that the constitutional provisions which commit the legislative function to the two houses are intended to include this attribute to the end that the function may be effectively exercised.

This landmark case, which is still used as the foundation for congressional investigative power, was upheld by the Supreme Court in *Jurney v. MacCracken* (294 U.S. 125) in 1935.

See also Daugherty, Harry Micajah; *Kilbourn v. Thompson;* Teapot Dome Scandal

References: Giglio, James N., *H. M. Daugherty and the Politics of Expediency* (Kent, OH: Kent State University

Press, 1978); Teapot Dome Resolution in *Congressional Record* (Washington, DC: Government Printing Office, 1925), 68th Congress, 1st Session (1925), 3299, 3409, 3410, 3548, 4126; United States Congress, Senate, Select Committee on Investigation of the Attorney General, *Investigation of Hon. Harry M. Daugherty, Formerly Attorney General of the United States. Hearings before the Select Committee on Investigation of the Attorney General, United States Senate, Sixty-Eighth Congress, First Session, pursuant to S. Res. 157, Directing a Committee to Investigate the Failure of the Attorney General to Prosecute or Defend Certain Criminal and Civil Actions, wherein the Government Is Interested* (Washington, DC: Government Printing Office, 1924).

Mecham, Evan (1924–)

Governor of Arizona (1987–1988), impeached and removed from office for crimes allegedly committed before he took office, for which he was later tried and acquitted. Mecham was born in Duchesne, Utah, on 12 May 1924. He attended Altamont High School in northeastern Utah, before entering Utah State University for a short term. When World War II broke out in 1941, he volunteered for service in the U.S. Army Air Corps. Flying a P-51 Mustang, he was shot down over Germany and spent twenty-two days as a prisoner of war, earning a Purple Heart for his wounds. In 1947 he was discharged from the service and returned to Arizona, where he attended Arizona State University in Tempe, majoring in economics and business management. He never received his degree, instead leaving college in 1950 when he was able to purchase a Pontiac car franchise in Ajo, Arizona. Four years later, he moved the franchise to Glendale, a suburb of Phoenix, and also invested in automobile franchises in California and Washington State. He also served as the publisher of the American Newspaper Group, which owned a number of newspapers across the United States.

In 1960 Mecham, a conservative Republican, entered the political realm when he ran for and won a seat in the Arizona state senate, serving from 1961 to 1963. In 1962 he ran for governor of Arizona, but failed to get his party's nomination. He tried again in 1978 and, although he was the Republican nominee, lost to Acting Governor Bruce Babbitt, who had succeeded to the office following the death of governor Wesley H. Bolin.

In 1986 Babbitt declined to run for reelection, leaving the race open for his successor. Mecham again ran for the office, defeating Representative Burton Barr, majority leader of the state house of representatives in the Republican primary. Mecham was given little chance of winning the general election. However, the favored Democrat, Bill Schulz, left the race for personal reasons; then, after the Democrats had nominated state Schools Superintendent Carolyn Warner, Schulz reentered the race as an Independent. This resulted in the splitting of the Democratic vote. Mecham captured 40 percent of the vote, which, in the three-way race, was enough to win.

Mecham had run on a platform of cutting the state sales tax and ending drug abuse in the state. However, he got into trouble, first with the press and then with the state of Arizona. He canceled the state's observance of the holiday for Dr. Martin Luther King Jr., precipitating a boycott of the state by business and African American groups. Mecham also made comments against homosexuals and blacks and refused to speak to reporters who he felt did not give him proper respect. Four months after he took office, a recall effort was started against him.

The recall effort turned out not to be Mecham's only political problem: a grand jury in Phoenix was investigating a $350,000 loan made to his gubernatorial campaign by Barry Wolfson, a real estate developer. Wolfson had gone to federal investigators in November 1987, claiming that the loan had not been repaid. The loan had not appeared on Mecham's campaign contributions statement to the state. Mecham paid off the loan when the story became public. On 8 January 1988, the grand jury indicted Mecham on six counts, including perjury and filing a false campaign contributions report. At the same time, the grand jury indicted Mecham's brother Willard, who had served as campaign treasurer, on three counts of perjury and one count of filing a false campaign contributions report. On 25 January 1988, Arizona Secretary of State Rose Mofford, a Democrat, announced that a recall petition with some 300,000-plus signatures had been submitted to the state. This was more than the 216,000 needed. Mofford set a date of 17 May 1988 for the recall election. After the grand jury indictment, the Republican-led state house of representatives conducted an impeachment inquiry into

Mecham, the first of a sitting governor in the United States since Alaska's William Sheffield's in 1985. On 5 February 1988, even as some in the state house broke down in tears, the body voted forty-six to fourteen to impeach Mecham on three articles of impeachment: obstruction of justice, delivering false sworn statements relating to official filings made while in office, and misuse of state funds. Mecham had testified before the state house that the charges were all false and that he would be vindicated in the criminal trial. Thus Mecham became the first governor in the history of the United States to be both the subject of a criminal proceeding and impeachment at the same time.

On 29 February 1988, the Senate trial of Mecham began. During the trial, which lasted six weeks, Mecham took the unprecedented move of defending himself. He claimed that he was a political outsider who had been under attack by his political enemies, Majority Leader Burton Barr and state Attorney General Robert Corbin, as well as the press. He opined that he had moved against special interests in getting rid of the King holiday and cutting taxes and had angered many groups with his "naivete." On 30 March 1988, the Senate, voting sixteen to twelve, dismissed the second article, "Delivering False Sworn Statements Relating to Official Filings Made While in Office," so as not to prejudice any part of the pending criminal trial. (If convicted Mecham could have claimed double jeopardy for this offense.) Despite this move, the Senate stood ready to convict Mecham. On 4 April, debating late into the night, the Senate finally voted twenty-one to nine to convict on the first article and twenty-six to four to convict on the third. With that conviction, Mecham became the first state governor since Henry S. Johnston of Oklahoma in 1929 to be convicted in an impeachment trial and removed from office. A vote to prohibit Mecham from ever holding office again in the state fell short of the two-thirds required vote. Secretary of State Mofford was named as acting governor. (Arizona has no lieutenant governor.)

Mecham still faced the criminal trial. His legal counsel branded the prosecutors "guards at Auschwitz" who were toadies of state Attorney General Robert Corbin, widely rumored as wanting to ride a Mecham conviction to the governor's chair, and Corbin's aide, Chief Assistant Attorney General Steve Twist. On 16 June 1988, a Phoenix jury acquitted Mecham and his brother of all charges. Claiming complete vindication, Mecham berated the state officials who had impeached and removed him. He said he wanted to form a group, "Forward Arizona," to elect what he said was "an honest legislature." Ironically, just three years later, many of the legislators who had voted to impeach Mecham were caught up in the "AZSCAM" scandal, when they were videotaped taking payoffs from an alleged underworld figure to promote gambling in the state.

In 1990 Mecham sought the Republican gubernatorial nomination, but lost. In 1992, running as an Independent against Senator John McCain for the U.S. Senate, Mecham got 10 percent of the vote.

References: Jenkins, Sammy S., *Mecham, Arizona's Fighting Governor: A Constitutional Conflict, 'Freedom of the Press' or Political Assassination* (Albuquerque, NM: All States Publishing, 1988); "Mecham, Evan," in John Raimo, ed., *Biographical Directory of the Governors of the United States, 1978–1983* (Westport, CT: Meckler Publishing, 1985), 27–31; Mecham, Evan, *Impeachment: The Arizona Conspiracy* (Glendale, AZ: MP Press, 1988); *Record of Proceedings of the Court of Impeachment: In the Trail of Honorable Evan Mecham, Governor, State of Arizona. Arizona State Senate, Sitting as a Court of Impeachment* (St. Paul, MN: West Publishing Company, 1991).

Miller, Thomas Woodnutt (1886–1973)

United States representative from Delaware (1915–1917), alien property custodian in the administration of Presidents Warren G. Harding and Calvin Coolidge (1921–1925), whose receipt of bribes landed him in prison for one year. Born in Wilmington, Delaware, on 26 June 1886, he attended the prestigious Hotchkiss School, after which he went to Yale University, graduating from that institution in 1908. His fascination with mining led him to go to work soon after leaving Yale as a steel roller for the Bethlehem Steel Company. His employment there was short, however, lasting only two years. In 1910 Miller entered the political arena, going to work as a secretary for U.S. Representative William H. Heald of Delaware until 1912. During this time, Miller studied law in Washington, D.C., and in 1913 was named secretary of state for Delaware. His father, Charles R. Miller, had been elected governor of Delaware the previous year and upon taking office had filled the secretary of state position with his son. The following year, Thomas

Miller was elected to a seat in the U.S. House of Representatives, serving a single term in the Sixty-fourth Congress from 4 March 1915 to 3 March 1917. In 1916 he lost his bid for a second term.

In 1917, after leaving office, Miller volunteered for service in the U.S. Army and in 1918 saw action in the European theater during World War I as a member of the Seventy-ninth Infantry. Wounded in action, he received the Purple Heart. By the end of the war in November 1918, he had risen to the rank of colonel. After his return to the United States, his interest in the welfare of his fellow veterans led him to help form the American Legion, now the leading veterans' rights and interests organization. Miller was joined in this effort by such men as Eric Fisher Woods, George Ared White, William "Wild Bill" Donovan (who later helped form the OSS, the forerunner of the modern CIA), Theodore Roosevelt Jr., and others. Miller served as vice chairman of the Paris caucus, the meeting that helped found the Legion, in March 1919.

In 1920 Miller reentered the political field when he served as a campaign manager for General Leonard Wood in Wood's fight for the Republican presidential nomination. Wood was unsuccessful, but Miller had attracted the attention of the eventual nominee, Senator Warren G. Harding of Ohio, who went on to win the election that year. When Harding took office, he named Miller alien property custodian. In 1917 Congress had established the Office of Alien Property Custodian as part of the Trading with the Enemy Act (40 Stat. 411) to "administer all suits in federal courts and all claims to seizure and vesting of enemy-owned or enemy-controlled property" during World War I. In an oral history interview conducted in 1966, Miller explained:

> The office of Alien Property Custodian was charged with administering the several hundred millions of dollars of property seized under the Trading with the Enemy Act. . . . In addition to the administrative staff of over 300 in the Washington office, there were thousands of others employed to run the various businesses in every state of the Union and overseas. This was the greatest patronage source of any department of the federal government. When the Harding administration took over on March 4, 1921, there were thousands of such jobs and positions held by Democrats under the former Alien Property Custodians, A. Mitchell Palmer, with

whom I had served in Congress before the war, and Francis P. Garvin. This was the situation that confronted the newly-appointed Alien Property Custodian when taking over the operation in the office on March 12, 1921.

Despite Miller eventually getting caught up in the scandals that haunted the Harding administration, his name is barely known to history for this reason. Even his alleged crime is mired in controversy—it is claimed that he took bribes. Miller states:

> While I was abroad in 1925, President Coolidge had dismissed Attorney General Daugherty from his cabinet as a result of an investigation into the operation of his office which had included . . . jurisdiction over the claims allowed by the office of the Alien Property Custodian. There was one such claim allowed for the American Metals Company, which claimed Swiss ownership and was thereby entitled to have returned several million dollars that had been impounded at the start of World War I as enemy property under the Trading with the Enemy Act.
>
> I was indicted by the grand jury in New York early in 1926 together with Mr. Daugherty. The first trial resulted in a hung jury in the fall of 1926. The second trial in the spring of 1927 resulted in a hung jury by one for Mr. Daugherty and a conviction for me.
>
> The charge was "conspiracy to not give my best services to the United States government." The federal conspiracy statute is very broad and all-inclusive. My attorney, former Judge Seabury of investigation fame in connection with the former Mayor Jimmy Walker of New York City, advised me to appeal the conviction to the Circuit Court of Appeals of the Third District, as in his opinion there could not be a one-man conspiracy. Inasmuch as Mr. Daugherty had not been convicted of a similar charge of conspiracy, such a charge could not legally stand against me.
>
> On the United States Circuit Court of Appeals in New York, one of the judges was Martin Manton. To be brief, I was approached by an emissary from Justice Manton who indicated that for the sum of ten thousand dollars, an opinion would be written by Justice Manton quashing the conviction. This I refused to enter into. In due course, my appeal was denied, and a scathing opinion by Justice Manton sent me to Atlanta for one year, May 1928 to May 1929.

Miller was just one of many members of the Harding administration to be involved in graft and corruption: Secretary of the Interior Albert B. Fall went to prison for taking bribes to sell federal oil lands to cronies; Jesse Smith, assistant to Attorney General Harry M. Daugherty, took bribes from bootleggers; Charles R. Forbes, administrator of the Veterans' Bureau, took kickbacks from contractors and stole government property; and Forbes's assistant, Charles Cramer, committed suicide after his own corruption was revealed.

After getting out of prison, Miller moved to Nevada and started his life over. In the nearly four decades following, until his death, Miller became a "spirited" public citizen, serving as a founder of the Nevada state park system and chairman of the Nevada State Park Commission several times in the 1930s, 1950s, and at the time of his death. In 1945 he went to work as a staff field representative of the United States Veterans' Employment Service, serving until 1957. Miller died in Reno, Nevada, on 5 May 1973, at the age of eighty-six. His ashes were interred in the Masonic Memorial Gardens in Reno.

See also Manton, Martin Thomas

References: *Biographical Directory of the American Congress, 1774–1996* (Alexandria, VA: CQ Staff Directories, Inc., 1996); *Memoirs of Thomas Woodnut Miller, a Public Spirited Citizen of Delaware and Nevada. An Oral History Conducted by Mary Ellen Glass* (University of Nevada at Reno Oral History Program, 1966), 109, 127–128.

In the famous "Tidal Basin Incident" (1974), Chairman of the House Ways and Means Committee Wilbur D. Mills was caught with a prostitute. Mills took a leave of absence from Congress. (Library of Congress)

Mills, Wilbur Daigh (1909–1992)

United States representative from Arkansas (1939–1977), caught up in the famous "Tidal Basin" scandal of 1974, in which it was discovered he had hired a prostitute in his House office. Mills was at one time perhaps the most powerful politician in Washington, responsible as chairman of the House Committee on Ways and Means for formulating tax policy. He was born in Kensett, Arkansas, on 24 May 1909 and attended the public schools. He attended Hendrix College in Conway, Arkansas. He also attended the Harvard University Law School and after receiving his law degree returned to Arkansas, where he was admitted to the state bar in 1933. He opened a practice in the town of Searcy, Arkansas.

In 1934, Mills, a Democrat, was elected as a county and probate judge of White County, Arkansas, where he served until 1938. He re-signed his seat to run for a seat in the U.S. House of Representatives. In those days, winning the Democratic primary was akin to winning the election, and Mills easily won the primary and the general election. He entered Congress on 3 January 1939 and remained in that institution for the next twenty-eight years. Mills served for the first eighteen years of his congressional service as a member of the all-important House Ways and Means Committee, where tax policy is debated and written. In 1956 he became the second-ranking Democrat on that committee, under chairman Jere Cooper of Tennessee.

However, on 18 December 1957, Cooper died suddenly, and Mills was promoted to chairman of Ways and Means. Mills would serve as chairman from 1958 until 1974—sixteen years, the longest tenure of one person as chairman of that committee. Mills did not serve as chairman—he was the leader on Capitol Hill of tax legislation. Presidents from Eisenhower to Nixon dealt with Mills to get tax cuts and raises passed. Mills set standards for the committee by limiting membership to twenty-five members, whom he had to approve. He was responsible for numerous tax bills, most notably the

1964 tax cut, the 1965 legislation that established Medicare, and the income tax bill of 1968, and for much of his tenure he was considered a probable successor to John W. McCormack as Speaker of the House.

What did Mills in was an event referred to as "The Tidal Basin Incident." On 7 October 1974, Mills was driving near the Tidal Basin in Washington, D.C., when he was pulled over by police for driving erratically. As the police were giving him a ticket, they noticed that Mills was obviously drunk and was bleeding from cuts on his face. They also noticed a woman slithering away from his car, who then jumped right into the water of the Tidal Basin. This woman was Annabel Battistella, an Argentinian stripper who performed under the name of Fanne Fox; she was also known as the "Argentinian Firecracker." Details soon emerged, not only about Mills's extramarital relationship with Battistella, but also about his alcoholism, which was out of control and impairing his ability to concentrate on his job. Mills took a leave of absence from the chairmanship of the Ways and Means Committee in an attempt to get his life back together. Representative Al Ullman, Democrat of Oregon, stepped in as acting chairman and eventually was made permanent chairman. The scandal, however, was ruinous to Mills's ability to lead. He won reelection in 1974, but never returned as chairman of Ways and Means. In 1976 he did not stand for reelection. Despite his fall from power, he was accepted as a tax consultant with the Washington, D.C., office of the New York law firm Shea, Gould, Climenko and Casey, where he worked on tax policy for several years.

Retiring to his home in Kensett, Arkansas, Mills died in Searcy, Arkansas, on 2 May 1992, three weeks shy of his eighty-third birthday. He was buried in the Kensett Cemetery in Kensett. In 1991 the University of Arkansas established the Wilbur D. Mills Chair in Alcohol and Drug Abuse Prevention.

References: Congressional Biographical Directory; Foxe, Fanne, "Fanne Foxe, by Annabel 'Fanne Foxe' Battistella with Yvonne Dunleavy" (New York: Pinnacle Books, 1975); Green Stephen, and Margot Hornblower, "Mills Admits Being Present during Tidal Basin Scuffle," *Washington Post*, 11 October 1974; Hevesi, Dennis, "Wilbur Mills, Long a Power in Congress, is Dead at 82," *New York Times*, 3 May 1992, 53; Manley, John F., *The Politics of Finance: the House Committee on Ways and Means* (Boston: Little, Brown, 1970); Zelizer, Julian E., *Taxing America: Wilbur D. Mills, Congress, and the State, 1945–1975* (Cambridge, UK: Cambridge University Press, 1999).

Mitchell, John Hipple (1835–1905)

United States senator from Oregon (1873–1879, 1885–1897, 1901–1905), implicated and convicted of various Oregon land frauds but died before he could serve any time in prison. Born John Mitchell Hipple in Washington County, Pennsylvania, on 22 June 1835, he was the son of John Hipple and Jemima (née Mitchell) Hipple, both farmers. In 1837 John Hipple moved with his parents to Butler County, Pennsylvania, where he attended local schools as well as private schools and the Witherspoon Institute. However, there is no record that he received any degree of what is considered secondary education. He taught school for a time, then read the law. In 1857 he was admitted to the Pennsylvania state bar but moved west instead, settling for a time in California before he relocated to Portland, Oregon, in 1860. At that time, he established a law practice in Portland under the name John Hipple Mitchell.

In 1861 Mitchell was elected the corporation attorney for Portland. The following year, he was elected to the Oregon state senate, serving the last two years as president of that body. In 1866 he ran unsuccessfully for a seat in the U.S. Senate, but in 1872 he ran again and won, serving a single six-year term from 4 March 1873 until 3 March 1879. From the start of this tenure, he was plagued by trouble: opponents charged him with bigamy, desertion from the army, and living under an assumed name, and they demanded that he not be allowed to take his seat. However, the Senate committee hearing the charges found them to have no merit and Mitchell served the full term. He left the Senate in 1879 but three years later attempted a comeback to the Senate, which was unsuccessful. In 1885 he ran again and was elected; this time being reelected in 1891 and serving until 1897, when he was defeated for a third term. For a time, it appeared that Mitchell's career was over, and he resumed the practice of law in Portland. However, in 1900 he was elected a third time to the U.S. Senate. It was during this tenure that Mitchell got into the trouble that cost him his reputation and his life.

Land claims in Oregon and other states in the American West were under scrutiny from land offices—and for good reason: many "land grabbers" were using fictitious names and documents to purchase homesteads in areas that the U.S. government was setting aside for wilderness. Thus, such claims, if valid, would be worth a tremendous amount of money. One such "land grabber" was Stephen A. Douglas Puter. When investigated for twelve homesteads he had illegally set up in the Cascade Mountains, Puter went to Mitchell, his U.S. senator, and allegedly paid him $2,000 to ask Commissioner of the General Land Office Binger Hermann to certify the homesteads as valid and end the investigations. Upon Mitchell's recommendation, Hermann did just that, and Puter returned to Oregon, sold the land, and made a quick profit of more than $10,000.

By this time, Secretary of the Interior Ethan Allen Hitchcock, who oversaw the General Land Office, became suspicious of the quick patent approval by Hermann (who was later fired but never charged with any wrongdoing). Bypassing local district attorneys, Allen hired Francis J. Heney (later famed for prosecuting San Francisco Mayor Eugene Schmitz) to convene a grand jury. Puter and his accomplices were indicted, and, on 6 December 1904 were convicted of conspiracy to defraud the government of its public lands. At this time, Puter turned against Mitchell and offered to turn state's evidence, implicating Mitchell in the fraud. Puter testified before a grand jury that he had bribed Mitchell with $2,000 to use his influence to speed the patents on the land in which Puter had invested. Puter was eventually fined and he ultimately served seventeen months in prison before being pardoned by President Theodore Roosevelt in 1907.

On 1 January 1905, Heney obtained an indictment against Mitchell. However, the local U.S. attorney, John H. Hall, was due to prosecute the case; Heney obtained Hall's dismissal, and Heney was appointed to oversee the case. Mitchell, after posting bail, hurried back to Washington, where he took to the floor of the U.S. Senate and denied that he had taken a bribe in exchange for helping Puter. However, Mitchell was also indicted, on 1 February 1905, with receiving $1,750 in fees for helping to expedite seventy claims of one Frederick A. Kribs. William J. Burns, who later helped found the Fed-

eral Bureau of Investigation, traced money from Kribs back to Mitchell's account. After Mitchell's law partner, Judge Albert H. Tanner, admitted to the scheme, Mitchell was finished. Mitchell returned to the Senate after his second indictment, but whereas he had once been warmly received, he was now a pariah. He retained former U.S. Senator John M. Thurston of Nebraska as his counsel.

At trial, Thurston argued that Mitchell had an outstanding record of fighting for Oregon and that the witnesses against him were perjurers and other assorted criminals. In his closing argument, Thurston pointed to the ailing, seventy-year-old Mitchell and said he was "already in the valley, with but a little way for his tottering feet to travel ere he reached the river." On 5 July 1905, Mitchell was convicted on both counts and sentenced to six months in prison and fined $1,000. Friends in the Senate pressured him to resign, but he refused. Before an investigation whether or not to expel him could be undertaken, Mitchell died in Portland on 8 December 1905. The Senate did not pause to remember their deceased colleague, and, in a larger slap, refused to send a delegation to his funeral. Another congressman, John Newton Williamson, was also caught up in the land frauds and convicted, although his role had been far smaller than Mitchell's had been. Mitchell became the first American politician convicted of fraud in the twentieth century.

See also Williamson, John Newton

References: Byrd, Robert C., *The Senate, 1789–1989: Historical Statistics, 1789–1992,* 4 vols. (Washington, DC: Government Printing Office, 1993), IV:667; Cummings, Hilary Anne. "John H. Mitchell, a Man of His Time: Foundations of His Political Career, 1860–1879." (Ph.D. dissertation, University of Oregon, 1985); O'Callaghan, Jerry A. "Senator John H. Mitchell and the Oregon Land Frauds, 1905." *Pacific Historical Review* 21 (August 1952): 255–261; Robbins, William G., "Mitchell, John Hipple," in John A. Garraty and Mark C. Carnes, gen. eds., *American National Biography,* 24 vols. (New York: Oxford University Press, 1999), 15:609–610.

Mitchell, John Newton (1913–1988)

Attorney general of the United States (1969–1973), implicated in his role in the Watergate affair that brought down President Richard Nixon. Mitchell remains an obscure figure, despite his having served in World War II and as Nixon's campaign manager in the 1968 election. Born in Detroit, Michigan, on 15 September 1913, Mitchell grew up on Long Island, New York, attending the Fordham Law School, from which he received a law degree in 1936. That same year, he joined the New York law firm of Caldwell and Raymond as a clerk. After he received his law degree, Mitchell joined the firm as a staff attorney, where he worked on public housing and bond issues. He rose to become a full partner in the firm.

In 1943 Mitchell put his career on hold and joined the U.S. Navy. He became the commander of several squadrons of torpedo boats (PTs), including the PT-109, famed in the story of future U.S. President John F. Kennedy. For bravery during this conflict, Mitchell was awarded the Silver Star, one of the nation's highest military honors. With the conclusion of World War II, Mitchell returned to his position at his old law firm (now Caldwell, Trimble, and Mitchell), focusing his attention on the issue of financing public housing through bonds. His work brought him to the attention of New York state leaders, and beginning in 1960 he worked closely with Governor Nelson Rockefeller on how public housing could be financed.

On 1 January 1967, Mitchell's firm merged with a major firm in California, and this brought Mitchell together with one of that firm's leading partners: former Vice President Richard M. Nixon. This new firm became Nixon, Mudge, Rose, Guthrie, Alexander, and Mitchell. Mitchell and the former vice president became close friends. Nixon, who had lost the 1960 presidential race (ironically to Mitchell's friend John F. Kennedy) had passed up a chance to run again in 1964, but in 1968 he decided to throw his hat into the political ring. Nixon's closeness to Mitchell allowed the former vice president to select Mitchell as his campaign manager. Mitchell had never run a political campaign before—he was basically apolitical—but Nixon's message was particularly attractive to him, and to others who had not voted for a Republican candidate before, because of his sense of law and order, particularly against Vietnam War protestors and black radicals. Nixon won his party's nomination, and that November he was elected over Democrat Hubert Humphrey in one of the closest races in American history.

On 11 December 1968, Nixon held a press conference and announced all of his cabinet selec-

tions—including John Mitchell as attorney general. Mitchell was easily confirmed by the Senate and took office as the sixty-seventh attorney general. In his four years at the Department of Justice, Mitchell used his powers to fight crime and drugs, as well as to use wiretaps to spy on protestors and black radicals. In 1971, Mitchell became embroiled in what became known as the Watergate scandal. A series of leaks of information from the White House and other executive departments led Nixon and his aides to form a secret unit of men called "the Plumbers," who were to investigate these leaks and "plug" them. The head of this group, G. Gordon Liddy, met with Mitchell in his office in the Department of Justice and briefed the attorney general on "Operation Gemstone," a plan to perpetrate a series of break-ins and other illegal acts to find evidence against Nixon's political enemies. Mitchell did not initially agree with this plan, but he did later authorize the payment of some $250,000 to "the Plumbers" directly from Nixon's 1972 election campaign fund. It was the first step in Mitchell's undoing.

On 15 February 1972, in the midst of the activities that would culminate in the Plumbers' break-in of Democratic Party headquarters in the Watergate Hotel in Washington, D.C., Mitchell resigned as attorney general to once again become Nixon's campaign manager for his reelection effort. However, his wife, Martha, a colorful and mercurial figure in Washington social circles, tired of her husband's role in the campaign and demanded he resign. This was done on 1 July 1972 after only four and one-half months on the job.

Just weeks earlier, on 17 June, five men working for Liddy were arrested after breaking into Democratic Party headquarters at the Watergate Hotel, and the scandal that had taken shape first in Mitchell's office in 1971 exploded into full public view. These men were found to have worked for the Committee to Re-Elect the President (CREEP) in 1972, and, by extension, Mitchell. In 1973, as the scandal expanded, the U.S. Senate called many of Nixon's aides in to testify before the Senate Select Committee on Presidential Campaign Activities, known as the Senate Watergate Committee, headed by Senator Samuel J. Ervin (D-NC). These hearings were televised on national television, and millions of people watched as some of the most powerful men in the nation were linked to a massive scandal of untold proportions. On 17 May 1973, White House counsel John W. Dean III testified that Mitchell, along with White House Chief of Staff H. R. "Bob" Haldeman and Presidential Chief Advisor on Domestic Affairs John D. Ehrlichman, were the key men behind Watergate and the myriad of crimes arising from it, and that Nixon himself had approved of the cover-up of the investigation after the Watergate burglars had been arrested. Dean's allegation against Mitchell was backed up by Nixon deputy campaign director Jeb Stuart Magruder, who also fingered Mitchell. Mitchell himself went before the committee, testifying that Magruder's and Dean's allegations were "a palpable, damnable lie."

On 29 September 1972, the *Washington Post* reported that Mitchell, as attorney general, had "personally controlled a secret Republican fund used to gather information about the Democrats." When one of the two reporters on the story, Carl Bernstein, called Mitchell for his comment on the story, he reached the former attorney general at home asleep. Barely awake, Mitchell reportedly said, "All that crap, you're putting it in the paper? It's all been denied. [*Washington Post* publisher] Katie Graham's gonna get her tit caught in a big fat wringer if that's ever published. Good Christ! That's the most sickening thing I ever heard." The story, however, blew open the investigation of Mitchell. A federal grand jury began to look into his role, and in May 1973 he and former Secretary of Commerce Maurice Stans, who had also worked for Nixon's campaign, were indicted on federal charges of obstructing an investigation into illegal contributions made to the campaign. The allegations were not related to Watergate. In April 1974 both men were acquitted by a Washington, D.C., federal jury on these charges. However, a month before this acquittal, Mitchell was once again indicted by a federal grand jury on charges of conspiracy, perjury, and obstruction of justice regarding his role in Watergate. Mitchell was charged with four other Watergate conspirators—Haldeman, Ehrlichman, former Assistant Attorney General Robert C. Mardian, and Kenneth W. Parkinson, an attorney who had worked for the Nixon campaign after the Watergate scandal broke. On 1 January 1975, all but Parkinson were found guilty, and Mitchell was sentenced to two and one-half to eight years in prison. He was sent to a federal prison at Maxwell Air Force Base in Alabama and was released after only nineteen months in confinement. He was paroled on 20 January 1979 and went to work as a private consultant, having been disbarred as an attorney. He was a common figure in his neighborhood in Washington, D.C., walking and smoking his pipe. On 9 November 1988, on one of these walks, Mitchell suffered a fatal heart attack and died in the street. He was seventy-five years old. Despite his conviction, he was laid to rest in Arlington National Cemetery for his service in World War II. His gravestone, a simple block, reads: "United States Attorney General 1969–1972. Lt. J.G. United States Navy."

He is the only attorney general, or former attorney general, to actually serve a prison sentence for crimes committed in office.

See also Nixon, Richard Milhous; Watergate
References: Meyer, Lawrence, "John N. Mitchell: Principal in Watergate, Dies at 75," *Washington Post,* 10 November 1988, A1; "Mitchell, John N(ewton)," in Charles Moritz, ed., *Current Biography 1969* (New York: H. W. Wilson, 1969), 291–293; Oelsner, Lesley, "Watergate Jury Convicts Mitchell, Haldeman, Ehrlichman and Mardian in Cover-up Case; Acquits Parkinson," *New York Times,* 2 January 1975, 1.

Morrison v. Olson, 487 U.S. 654 (1988)

Landmark U.S. Supreme Court decision that upheld the Independent Counsel Act of 1974 as constitutional. In 1982 two subcommittees of the U.S. House of Representatives issued subpoenas to the Environmental Protection Agency (EPA), requesting documents relating to the enforcement of the Superfund, a congressional action that funds the cleanup of hazardous waste sites. President Ronald Reagan received advice from the Department of Justice that the EPA invoke executive privilege (a long-held grant, allowing a president to withhold certain documents he or she deems sensitive from Congress) and not turn over the documents. The EPA administrator, Anne M. Gorsuch Burford, obeyed Reagan's order and refused to turn over the documents. The House subcommittees held Burford in contempt, at which time she and the U.S. government, represented by the Department of Justice, filed suit against the House of Representatives. In March 1983, the suit was settled, with Burford agreeing to allow limited access to some of the documents.

In 1984 the House Judiciary Committee launched an investigation into how the Justice Department handled the entire documents controversy. In 1985 the committee released a report on their findings. Part of the report centered on the testimony of Theodore Olson, who was serving in 1982 as assistant attorney general for the Office of Legal Counsel (OLC) in the Justice Department. Olson had testified before the committee on 10 March 1983, and in their 1985 report the committee concluded that Olson had given "false and misleading testimony" regarding the role of the Justice Department. Two other Justice Department officials were accused of trying to obstruct the committee investigation. The committee sent a report to the attorney general, asking that he seek an independent counsel to look into the charges. Under Title VI of the Ethics in Government Act, 28 U.S.C. § 591–599, an independent counsel can be appointed "to investigate and, if appropriate, prosecute certain high-ranking Government officials for violations of federal criminal laws." The Act requires the attorney general, upon receipt of information that he determines is "sufficient to constitute grounds to investigate whether any person [covered by the Act] may have violated any Federal criminal law." The attorney general directed the Public Integrity Section (PIS) of the Criminal Division of the Department of Justice to see if such a request was warranted. The PIS reported back that an independent counsel should be appointed. The attorney general then asked the three-judge panel in Washington, D.C., to name such a counsel. On 23 April 1986, this panel, called the Special Division, named James C. McKay, to investigate "whether the testimony of Olson . . . violated either 18 U.S.C. § 1505 or § 1001, or any other provision of federal law." McKay did not want the assignment and resigned his office. On 29 May 1986, the Special Division named Alexia Morrison as his replacement. In January 1987 Morrison asked the attorney general to apprise her of the "related matters" regarding the two other Justice Department employees who were investigated by the Judiciary Committee.

Because the Special Division, in their order naming an independent counsel, had specified that only Olson be investigated, the attorney general refused the request and asked the Special Division for a ruling. On 2 April 1987, the Special Division ruled that, because there was no investigation asked of the two other Justice Department employees, there was no authority to demand the requested material. However, the court did rule that the independent counsel could investigate whether Olson had conspired with the other employees named. The independent counsel then convened a grand jury, which served subpoenas *as testificandum* (a subpoena that requires testimony), demanding that all three testify and provide documents. All three men moved to quash the subpoenas, claiming that the Independent Counsel Act was unconstitutional. On 20 July 1987, the federal District Court for the District of Columbia held that the act was constitutional and denied the order to quash. The men then appealed to the U.S. Court of Appeals for the District of Columbia.

Then, on 22 January 1988, a divided court, voting two to one in the case of *In re Sealed Case,* 838 F.2d 476 (1988), held that because the act did not provide for the nomination of the counsel, with the "advice and consent" of the U.S. Senate, the act was unconstitutional. The majority also held that the act violated the "appointments clause" of the U.S. Constitution, Article II, Section 2, Clause 2: "[The President] shall nominate, and by and with the Advice and Consent of the Senate, shall appoint Ambassadors, other public Ministers and Consuls, Judges of the Supreme Court, and all other Officers of the United States, whose Appointments are not herein otherwise provided for, and which shall be established by Law: but the Congress may by Law vest the Appointment of such inferior Officers, as they think proper, in the President alone, in the Courts of Law, or in the Heads of Departments." Morrison, the independent counsel, appealed to the U.S. Supreme Court. That court granted certiorari (the right to hear the case), and heard arguments on 26 April 1988.

On 29 June 1988, the Court reversed the court of appeals and held that the Independent Counsel Act was indeed constitutional. The Court held seven to one (Justice Antonin Scalia delivered a scathing dissent, and Justice Anthony Kennedy did not participate) that the act did not violate the Appointments Clause, or the constitutional right of the president to nominate and the Senate to confirm judges and other "high government officers." The majority opinion, delivered by Chief Justice William H. Rehnquist, upheld the act with cogent arguments. However, it is the dissent by Justice Scalia that came to be quoted later, when independent counsels came under fire for their investigations in the 1990s:

> The notion that every violation of law should be prosecuted, including—indeed, especially—every violation by those in high places, is an attractive one, and it would be risky to argue in an election campaign that that is not an absolutely overriding value. *Fiat justitia, ruat coelum.* Let justice be done, though the heavens may fall. The reality is, however, that it is not an absolutely overriding value, and it was with the hope that we would be able to acknowledge and apply such realities that the Constitution spared us, by life tenure, the necessity of election campaigns. I cannot imagine that there are not many thoughtful men and women in Congress who realize that the benefits of this legislation are far outweighed by its harmful effect upon our system of government, and even upon the nature of justice received by those men and women who agree to serve in the Executive Branch. But it is difficult to vote not to enact, and even more difficult to vote to repeal, a statute called, appropriately enough, the Ethics in Government Act. If Congress is controlled by the party other than the one to which the President belongs, it has little incentive to repeal it; if it is controlled by the same party, it dare not. By its shortsighted action today, I fear the Court has permanently encumbered the Republic with an institution that will do it great harm.

See also Independent Counsel Statute; Starr, Kenneth Winston
References: *In re Sealed Case*, 838 F.2d 476 (1988); *Morrison v. Olson*, 487 U.S. 654 (1988).

Muckrakers

See Political Corruption as Portrayed in Literature.

Mugwumps

Name applied to a group of disaffected members of the Republican Party who bolted from that party in 1884 to support Democrat Grover Cleveland for president. The term allegedly originates from *mugquomp* or *muckquomp,* Algonquin for "chief." It has never been fully explained why this group used this word to delineate their members; but the Mugwumps played a significant role in American history, the first time members of a political party fled in such numbers that they caused the nominee of their party to be defeated. All were civil service reformers who desired to see an end to the "spoils" system of putting cronies into administration and

other positions. Many of these men were key in the passage of the Pendleton Act in 1883. Among them were Edwin L. Godkin, editor of the journal *The Nation;* William Graham Sumner, a professor at Yale University; Henry Adams, a writer and member of the famed Adams family that gave the United States two presidents, and in his own right author of *Democracy: An American Novel;* David Wells, a government worker and statistican; and Carl Schurz, a United States senator from Missouri and former secretary of the interior.

Prior to the 1884 election, these men wrote and spoke out on the leading economic and social issues of the day, taking sides on questions such as tariffs and whether the nation should adopt bimetalism—the use of both gold and silver as a standard for currency—a dispute that came to dominate the last twenty years of the nineteenth century. But their lead issue was civil service reform and, as an extension, clean government. When James G. Blaine, the longtime U.S. senator from Maine who had served as secretary of state and Speaker of the U.S. House of Representatives, won the Republican presidential nomination in 1884, many Mugwumps left the Republican Party, incensed that a man whose political credibility had been questioned (Blaine had been implicated in a railroad bond scandal but had never been prosecuted) had been nominated for the highest office in the land. For instance, Mark Twain wrote:

> The Republican Presidential nomination of James G. Blaine resulted in a political revolt such as the nation had not known. Blaine was immensely popular, but he had many enemies in his own party. There were strong suspicions of his being connected with doubtful financiering—enterprises, more or less sensitive to official influence, and while these scandals had become quieted a very large portion of the Republican constituency refused to believe them unjustified. What might be termed the intellectual element of Republicanism was against Blaine: George William Curtis, Charles Dudley Warner, James Russell Lowell, Henry Ward Beecher, Thomas Nast, the firm of Harper and Brothers, Joseph W. Hawley, Joseph Twichell, Mark Twain—in fact the majority of thinking men who held principle above party in their choice.

Democrats nominated as their standard-bearer New York Governor Stephen Grover Cleveland,

„Mugwumps !!!"

Verschwörer-Terzett: Wer ruft Mugwump?!   Lächerlich!   So was existirt gar nicht! — Zittern?   Fällt uns im Traum nicht ein!

The term "Mugwumps" applied to Republicans who left their party to campaign for Democrat Grover Cleveland—the first time members of a political party fled in such numbers that they caused their party's nominee to be defeated. (Bettmann/Corbis)

noted for his unusual honesty. The Mugwumps decided to side with Cleveland, assisting in his narrow election victory over Blaine. During Cleveland's first administration, 1885–1889, Mugwump influence was never higher.

The defeat of Blaine was the chief goal of the Mugwumps aside from civil service reform. The attainment of these two ideals led to a breakup of the informal group soon after Cleveland left office in 1889.

See also Blaine, James Gillespie
References: Blodgett, Geoffrey T., "The Mind of the Boston Mugwumps," *Mississippi Valley Historical Review,* XLVIII:4 (March 1962), 614–634; McFarland, Gerald W., *Mugwumps, Morals & Politics, 1884–1920* (Amherst: University of Massachusetts Press, 1975); Paine, Albert Bigelow, *Mark Twain: A Biography* (New York: Harper and Brothers, 1912), 778–782; Tucker, David M., *Mugwumps: Public Moralists of the Gilded Age* (Columbia: University of Missouri Press, 1998).

Mulligan Letters
See Blaine, James Gillespie

Myers, Michael Joseph (1943–)
United States representative (1976–1980) from Pennsylvania, expelled from the House in 1980 after being convicted of bribery and conspiracy in the ABSCAM sting by federal agents impersonating

Arab sheikhs to gain political favors from American politicians. Known as "Ozzie" Myers, he was born in Philadelphia, Pennsylvania, on 4 May 1943. He attended the Catholic schools and some public schools in Philadelphia; afterward, he worked as a longshoreman on the docks of Philadelphia from 1961 to 1970. He never received a secondary education. In 1970 Myers was elected to a seat in the Pennsylvania house of representatives, serving until 1976. On 12 April 1976, Representative William Aloysius Barrett (D-PA) died, and Myers announced his candidacy to succeed the late congressman. He was elected and took his seat in the Ninety-fifth Congress on 2 November 1976. Myers was reelected in 1978.

In 1980 Myers and several other congressmen came under scrutiny for taking bribes from supposed Saudi sheikhs—actually FBI agents in disguise—who expressed the desire to gain entry into the United States, a scandal that later became known as ABSCAM, short for "Arab scam." Myers was perhaps one of the most egregious violators nabbed in the investigation. Although many of those implicated had taken bribes from the fake Saudis, Myers was seen on videotape taking the money with glee. In exchange, he simply introduced a bill in Congress to allow the phony sheikhs to emigrate to the United States without the normal immigration procedures. The House Judiciary Committee held hearings on Myers and recommended he be expelled from the House. This is an unusually severe punishment—in the history of the Congress, only a handful of members have faced expulsion, and even fewer have had that punishment imposed on them. Nonetheless, a resolution calling for Myers's expulsion was introduced, and, on 2 October 1980, the House voted 376–30 to expel the Pennsylvania Democrat. Myers thus became the first congressman to be expelled since John B. Clark of Missouri, John W. Reid of Missouri, and Henry C. Burnett of Kentucky were expelled in 1861 for supporting the Confederacy.

Myers had already been convicted by a federal jury of taking a $50,000 bribe in the ABSCAM case. His appeals exhausted, he went to jail. Myers ultimately served twenty and one-half months in prison and was paroled in 1985. For a time after leaving prison, because he was barred from ever running for national political office, he worked in his family's restaurant in Philadelphia. At the time of this writing, he works as a building contractor in New York.

See also ABSCAM

References: *Biographical Directory of the American Congress, 1774–1996* (Alexandria, VA: CQ Staff Directories, Inc., 1996); Tolchin, Martin, "Myers Is Ousted from the House in Abscam Case," *The New York Times*, 3 October 1980, A1, A16; U.S. Congress, House, Committee on Standards of Official Conduct, *In the Matter of Representative Michael J. Myers,* House Report No. 96–1387, 96th Congress, 2nd Session (1980), 5; U.S. Congress, House, Committee on Standards of Official Conduct, *In the Matter of Representative Michael J. Myers: Report of Committee on Standards of Official Conduct (to accompany H. Res. 794)* (Washington, DC: Government Printing Office, 1980).

N

1911 Amendments to the Publicity Act

See Federal Corrupt Practices Act of 1925; Publicity Act of 1910

1940 Amendments to the Hatch Act

See Hatch Act

Newberry v. United States, 256 U.S. 232 (1921)

Supreme Court decision holding that, because the Constitution did not bestow any power on Congress to regulate primary elections, any spending limits set on such elections were invalid. Justice James McReynolds wrote, "The ultimate question for solution here is whether under the grant of power to regulate 'the manner of holding elections' Congress may fix the maximum sum which a candidate therein may spend, or advise or cause to be contributed and spent by others to procure his nomination."

Truman H. Newberry (1864–1945), a Michigan politician who had served in the House of Representatives (1879–1881) and as secretary of the navy (1908–1909), received the Republican nomination for a U.S. Senate seat in a primary held in August 1918 and was elected on 5 November of that same year. After the election, it was alleged that Newberry, in the period from December 1917 until November 1918, "unlawfully and feloniously did conspire, combine, confederate, and agree together to commit the offense on his part of willfully violating the Act of Congress approved June 25, 1910, as amended [the Corrupt Practices Act], by giving, contributing, expending, and using and by causing to be given, contributed, expended and used, in procuring his nomination and election at said primary and general elections, a greater sum than the laws of Michigan permitted and above ten thousand dollars, to wit, $100,000." Newberry and his codefendants (including Henry Ford, his Democratic rival for the U.S. Senate) were convicted on count one of the indictment. Newberry and the others appealed to the United States Supreme Court on the grounds that the Corrupt Practices Act governed acts that were beyond congressional authority. The Supreme Court heard arguments on 7 and 10 January 1921.

On 2 May 1921, Justice McReynolds held for a six-to-three majority (Chief Justice Edward White was joined by Justices John Clarke and Louis Brandeis in dissent) in striking down the convictions and holding that section of the Corrupt Practices Act to be unconstitutional. Justice McReynolds wrote, "Two Senators were allotted to each state and the method was prescribed for determining the number of Representatives. Subject to these important limitations, Congress was empowered by law to regulate the times, places and manner of holding the elections, except as to the places of choosing Senators." Quoting an earlier case, *Kidd v. Pearson*, he continued:

> Many things are prerequisites to elections or may affect their outcome-voters, education, means of transportation, health, public discussion, immigration, private animosities, even the face and figure of the candidate; but authority to regulate the manner of holding them gives no right to control any of these. It is settled, e.g., that the power to regulate interstate and foreign commerce does not reach whatever is essential thereto. Without agriculture, manufacture, mining, etc., commerce could not exist but this fact does not suffice to subject them to the control of Congress. . . . It should not be forgotten that, exercising inherent police power, the state may suppress whatever evils may be incident to primary or convention. As "each house shall be the judge of the elections, qualifications and returns of its own members," and as Congress may by law regulate the times, places and manner of holding elections, the national government is not without power to protect itself against corruption, fraud or other malign influences. The judgment of the court below must be reversed, and the cause remanded for further proceedings in conformity with this opinion.

In 1941, in *United States v. Classic,* 313 U.S. 299 (1941), the Supreme Court held that the Constitution did allow Congress to oversee primary elections, effectively overruling *Newberry.*

See also Federal Corrupt Practices Act of 1925

References: "Convict Newberry, Who Is Sentenced to 2 Years in Jail; Senator Is Also Fined $10,000—Sixteen of His Aids [sic] Also Convicted in Election Plot," *New York Times,* 21 March 1920, 1.

Nixon, Richard Milhous (1913–1994)

Thirty-seventh president of the United States (1969–1974), forced to resign from the presidency for his cover-up of the Watergate affair (1974), the first president in American history to resign his office. Nixon had one of the most illustrious careers in American political history, and despite his ignominious departure from the presidency, he remained a respected statesman until his death. Born in Yorba Linda, California, on 9 January 1913, he was the son of Frank Nixon, who ran a grocery store and gasoline station, and Hannah (née Milhous) Nixon, who was a Quaker and a distant cousin of Herbert Hoover. Richard Nixon attended local schools and worked his way through nearby Whittier College, earning a degree and moving on to Duke University. He graduated third in his class from Duke in 1937 and returned to California, where he went to work for the law firm of Kroop and Bewley. He moved up to become a junior partner in the firm, as well as getting an assistant city attorney position. He met Pat Ryan, a teacher at Whittier High School and the daughter of a truck driver. The two married in 1940.

When the United States entered World War II, Nixon, despite being a Quaker and coming from a pacifistic background, volunteered for service in the U.S. Navy and was given a commission of lieutenant junior grade. He was sent to the South Pacific, seeing limited action before he returned to the United States in 1945. He was discharged the following year with the rank of lieutenant commander. Immediately, he threw his hat into the political ring. Running as a Republican, Nixon challenged veteran U.S. Representative Gerald Voorhis for the seat representing California's Twelfth District. Nixon used his growing political acumen to defeat Voorhis by more than 15,000 votes. Nixon took his place in Congress on 3 January 1947, serving until 4 March 1950. He won reelection in 1948, and it was during this second term in the House that Nixon achieved a national prominence few politicians ever get. As a member of the House Un-American Activities Committee (HUAC), Nixon used a former Communist, Whittaker Chambers, to accuse Alger Hiss, a former State Department official, of being part of a major pro-Soviet Communist spy ring inside the U.S. government. Hiss went before the committee to refute Chambers and Nixon's charges, but he was eventually tried and convicted of perjury. Nixon's role in Hiss's downfall led to national exposure.

In 1950 Nixon decided to forego reelection to the House to seek a seat in the U.S. Senate. His opponent was Representative Helen Gahagan Douglas, a left-wing Democrat who was the wife of motion picture actor Melvyn Douglas. Nixon openly accused Douglas of siding with left-wing and Communist forces in the United States. Nixon was criticized for this tactic but the charge stuck, and he went on to win the election by some 500,000 votes. Nixon would serve only two years of this Senate term. In both the House and the Senate, he became known for his strict conservative views, both on domestic and international matters.

In 1952, at the Republican National Convention in Chicago, when former General Dwight D. Eisenhower received the party's nomination for president, he selected the thirty-nine-year-old Nixon as his running mate. It was a daring selection—Nixon had served only two years of his Senate term and had served only four years in the House. Yet he was considered a heavyweight on international issues, and his nomination seemed sound. During the campaign, however, word leaked that Nixon had illegally accepted some $18,000 in unreported campaign funds from friends in California to pay off his campaign debts. In addition, one of these friends gave Nixon's two daughters a small dog they named "Checkers." The furor over Nixon's alleged corruption forced the Californian to make a prime-time television appearance on 23 September 1952, in which he said that he had done nothing wrong and that his children would keep the dog no matter what. The address, which has come to be known as the "Checkers" speech, is perhaps one of the most important in history—one in which a vice presidential candidate spoke to the nation to avoid being thrown off the ticket. It was later revealed that Eisenhower wanted Nixon to leave the Republican ticket if the press reports did not cease on the funding matter. With the "Checkers" speech, Nixon used his charm and political savvy to his advantage and swayed public opinion in his favor. Eisenhower and Nixon won the 1952 campaign by over 6 million votes, and on 20 January 1953 Nixon, at just forty years old, became vice president of the United States.

As the second most powerful man behind Eisenhower, Nixon was not only a reliable and trusted aide to the president but also a political heavyweight who used his office to build up political capital. On 24 September 1955, Eisenhower suffered a heart attack, but Nixon assured the nation and the world that his service as acting president was in accordance with Eisenhower's wishes. In 1958 Eisenhower sent him to Latin America, despite warnings of rising anti-American feeling. Nixon was attacked by a mob in Caracas, Venezuela, on 13 May 1958, but once again he used the trip to show his political strength. In July 1959 Nixon went to Moscow to attend the American National Exhibition. There, in front of a display of American appliances that were unavailable in the Soviet Union, Nixon argued with Soviet Premier Nikita S. Khrushchev. The contention became known as the "kitchen debate," and once again showed the world that Richard Nixon, despite his young age, was able to take on even the most powerful of world leaders. In 1956 Nixon was renominated for a second term as vice president with Eisenhower, and the two men were easily reelected over their 1952 opponent, Adlai E. Stevenson, who was running for a second time. Nixon stood unopposed for the 1960 Republican presidential nomination. In perhaps one of the most important moments in American political history, Nixon, as the Republican nominee, took on Democrat John F. Kennedy in a nationally televised debate, the first such event between two presidential candidates in American history. Kennedy came off as smooth and cool, while Nixon, suffering from a virus, looked nervous and unsteady, with perspiration on his brow. The debate became the key moment in the campaign, and on election night Kennedy won a narrow victory over Nixon. For the first time since 1947, Nixon was out of office and the political spotlight.

In 1962 Nixon sought and gained the Republican nomination for governor of California. He appeared a shoe-in but lost to newcomer Democrat Edmund G. "Pat" Brown. Angered that reporters were always looking to trip him up, Nixon held a press conference that he called his last. "You won't have Nixon to kick around anymore," he stated. Nixon could have run for president in 1964, but he stuck by his original statement and bowed out of the race.

In 1968, however, Nixon attempted a political comeback. Running in the Republican campaign against such heavy hitters as Governor Nelson Rockefeller of New York, Nixon won early primaries in New Hampshire and Wisconsin. Despite this, polls showed that Nixon would lose if nominated, while Rockefeller would be elected. Governor Ronald Reagan of California threw his hat into the ring for the party nomination but only drew votes away from Rockefeller. In the end, Nixon captured the party's nod and named Maryland Governor Spiro T. Agnew as his running mate. The Democrats nominated Vice President Hubert H. Humphrey, whose nominating convention in Chicago was nearly destroyed by anti-Vietnam War protestors. A

President Richard M. Nixon hangs tangled in a spider's web as recording tapes dangle above him. (Library of Congress)

third candidate, former Governor George C. Wallace of Alabama, also entered the race as an Independent. From the start the race was close, and Nixon avoided an old mistake by refusing to debate Humphrey. On election night, 5 November 1968, Nixon won by a slim 500,000 votes, becoming the nation's thirty-seventh president.

Nixon's first term was mired in issues such as a poor economy and the war in Vietnam. Utilizing international issues to his credit, Nixon went to Communist China in 1972, the first American leader to do so since the 1949 Communist revolution in China. Nixon also established a policy of détente with the Soviet Union and gradually ended American involvement in Vietnam. On domestic matters, he helped to establish the Environmental Protection Agency (EPA), a government bureau responsible for overseeing the environment in the United States. With his renomination for president in 1972, Nixon became one of only two men to get five major nominations from their parties (Franklin Roosevelt is the other).

On 17 June 1972, a group of burglars was caught trying to break in and bug Democratic Party headquarters in the Watergate Hotel in Washington, D.C. Unknown to many, Nixon was made aware the day after the arrests that the burglars were working for Nixon's own 1972 reelection effort. In the Oval Office, Nixon, on audiotape, discussed with his aides how he could use campaign funds to pay off the burglars to keep silent about their ties to the Nixon campaign. At the same time, Nixon ordered the Federal Bureau of Investigation (FBI), the investigative arm of the Department of Justice, not to investigate the men due to national security concerns. Sitting in the chair of the president of the United States, Nixon had committed two crimes, one of which was to end his presidency.

As the Watergate case became bigger and bigger in the national media, the U.S. Senate established the Senate Select Committee on Presidential Campaign Activities, known better as the Senate Watergate Committee. In hearings that were televised on national television, preempting many programs, Nixon's aides went before the committee and either confessed their role in Watergate and other activities that were violations of the law, or, like former Attorney General John N. Mitchell, denied that Watergate was tied to Nixon at all. However, on 17 May 1974, White House counsel John W. Dean III told the committee that he had warned Nixon that "there was a cancer on the presidency" caused by wrongdoing by Nixon and his aides.

Although the White House denied Dean's charges, another witness, Alexander Butterfield, related that Nixon's Oval Office conversations were taped by Nixon himself so that he could keep an oral record of his presidency. A special prosecutor named by the Department of Justice, Archibald Cox, demanded to listen to these tapes. Nixon refused, and Cox took Nixon to court. When Cox demanded further tapes, Nixon ordered Attorney General Elliot Richardson to fire Cox; when Richardson refused, as did his deputy, William Ruckelshaus, it was left to Solicitor General Robert H. Bork, as acting attorney general, to fire Cox. The event, known as the Saturday Night Massacre, led to public outrage against Nixon, and the president was forced to allow for the hiring of a new special prosecutor. This man, Leon A. Jaworski, followed

Cox's lead and demanded to listen to the Oval Office tapes. Nixon stonewalled, claiming that the tapes fell under the aegis of executive privilege, that special right granted to presidents and their aides so that they could formulate policy without political scrutiny. However, Jaworski refused to buy this excuse and took Nixon to court. A federal court, followed by an appeals court and the United States Supreme Court, all ruled against Nixon— the latter case, *United States v. Nixon,* was a landmark decision in demonstrating that even a president could not be shielded from the law. Nixon gave up the tapes.

One tape showed that in the days after the Watergate break-in he ordered the FBI to drop its investigation of the event, bolstering the claim that Nixon had obstructed justice. The House Judiciary Committee, holding hearings on Watergate, passed five articles of impeachment against the president. Nixon saw impeachment as a foregone conclusion but felt he could be victorious in the Senate. On 7 August 1974, however, Senate Republicans visited him at the White House and told him that his chances in the Senate were rapidly fading as the allegations against him were substantiated. The following night, Nixon went on national television and told the nation that he would resign. Vice President Gerald R. Ford—who had come into office when Vice President Spiro Agnew resigned due to his own political corruption— was sworn in as president the following day. A month later, Ford pardoned Nixon for all crimes he may have committed.

In the years following his resignation, Nixon remained at the forefront of national affairs, speaking out on foreign policy matters and writing several important books. His wife's death in 1993 was a cruel blow and may have contributed to Nixon's own death in New York the following year, on 22 April 1994 at the age of eighty-one. He was buried next to his wife at the Richard Nixon Library and Birthplace in Yorba Linda, California.

See also Agnew, Spiro Theodore; Executive Privilege; Mitchell, John Newton; Watergate

References: Costello, William, *The Facts about Nixon: An Unauthorized Biography* (New York: Viking Press, 1960); Mazo, Earl, *Nixon: A Political Portrait* (New York: Harper and Row, 1968); Thompson, Fred Dalton, *At That Point in Time: The Story of the Senate Watergate Committee* (New York: Quadrangle/New York Times Book Co., 1975); White, Theodore H.,

Breach of Faith: The Fall of Richard Nixon (New York: Atheneum Publishers, 1975); Williston, Samuel, "Does a Pardon Blot Out Guilt?," *Harvard Law Review,* 28 (1915), 647–654; U.S. Congress, *Memorial Services in the Congress of the United States and Tributes in Eulogy of Richard M. Nixon, Late a President of the United States* (Washington, DC: U.S. Government Printing Office, 1996), vii–viii, 7–9.

Nixon v. Missouri PAC, 528 U.S. 377 (2000)

United States Supreme Court decision that held that the political contribution limits imposed by the Court in *Buckley v. Valeo* (1976) could withstand constitutional scrutiny. In 1994 the state of Missouri enacted Senate Bill 650, which comprised a series of campaign finance reforms. Under the law, limits were placed on the amount of contributions that could be given to candidates for political office. These specified a maximum of $1,000 to a candidate for statewide office, $500 for a candidate to the state senate, and $250 to a candidate for the state house of representatives. These limits took effect in January 1995, with the state later adjusting these limits for inflation to $1,075, $525, and $275.

In 1998 the Shrink Missouri Government Political Action Committee (PAC) and Zev David Fredman, a candidate for the 1998 Republican nomination for state auditor, filed suit against the state and Jeremiah Nixon, the state attorney general (who was in charge of enforcing the contribution limits), claiming that the limits imposed by Senate Bill 650 infringed on their First and Fourteenth Amendment rights. The Shrink Missouri Government PAC had given Fredman the mandatory $1,025 in 1997 and reported that it wanted to give more but was prohibited by the law, thus infringing on its free speech rights. Fredman alleged that his rights were violated by not being able to raise as much money as he could from contributors. A district court hearing the case denied Fredman's motion to set aside the limits during the hearing and, on 12 May 1998 held that the state limits were constitutional. The Shrink Missouri Government PAC appealed to the United States Court of Appeals for the Eighth Circuit, which issued an injunction against the limits, pending the outcome of the appeal. This court heard arguments on 21 August 1988, and on 20 November held two to one that the limits imposed by the state were unconstitutional, striking them down as "heavy handed." Nixon appealed to the U.S. Supreme Court, which granted certiorari (the right to hear the case) on 25 January 1999. Arguments were heard in the case on 5 October 1999.

On 24 January 2000, the Court overturned the Eighth Circuit ruling and reinstated the political contribution limits. In a strongly worded six-to-three decision written by Justice David Souter (Justices Clarence Thomas, Antonin Scalia, and Anthony Kennedy dissented), the Court held that the limits did not violate the First Amendment right to free speech. Upholding the arguments put forth in *Buckley v. Valeo,* 424 U.S. 1 (1976), Souter held that a state had an interest in setting limits to political contributions. He explained:

> Even without *Buckley,* there would be no serious question about the legitimacy of these interests, which underlie bribery and antigratuity statutes. Rather, respondents take the State to task for failing to justify the invocation of those interests with empirical evidence of actually corrupt practices or of a perception among Missouri voters that unrestricted contributions must have been exerting a covertly corrosive influence. The state statute is not void, however, for want of evidence. The quantum of empirical evidence needed to satisfy heightened judicial scrutiny of legislative judgments will vary up or down with the novelty and plausibility of the justification raised. *Buckley* demonstrates that the dangers of large, corrupt contributions and the suspicion that large contributions are corrupt are neither novel nor implausible.

Souter noted that the evidence presented failed to show that the limits on contributions impaired the ability of candidates to raise as much money as previously. He wrote:

> Here, as in *Buckley* . . . there is no indication that those limits have had any dramatic adverse effect on the funding of campaigns and political associations, and thus there is no showing that the limitations prevented candidates from amassing the resources necessary for effective advocacy. Indeed, the District Court found that since the Missouri limits became effective, candidates for state office have been able to raise funds sufficient to run effective campaigns, and that candidates are still able to

amass impressive campaign war chests. The plausibility of these conclusions is buttressed by petitioners' evidence that in the last election before the contributions became effective, 97.62 percent of all contributors to candidates for state auditor made contributions of $2,000 or less.

See also *Buckley v. Valeo,* 424 U.S. 1

Nixon v. United States, 506 U.S. 224 (1993)

United States Supreme Court decision ruling that a Senate panel, rather than the full Senate, could hear and vote on articles of impeachment. Walter Nixon, a federal district judge in the U.S. District Court for the Southern District of Mississippi, was convicted in that very court in 1986 for committing perjury before a grand jury. Nixon had been called before the grand jury to respond to allegations that he had "accepted a gratuity from a Mississippi businessman in exchange for asking a local district attorney to halt the prosecution of the businessman's son." After he was convicted, Nixon refused to resign from the bench and continued to collect his salary while he served time in prison. The United States then moved in the House of Representatives to impeach him and remove him from office. On 10 May 1989, the U.S. House of Representatives adopted three articles of impeachment for high crimes and misdemeanors against Nixon. The first two articles charges Nixon with making two separate false statements before a grand jury, while the third alleged that he had brought "disrepute" upon the federal judiciary.

After the House delivered the articles of impeachment to the Senate, the Senate voted to implement its own Rule XI, which called for a Senate committee, rather than the whole Senate, to sit and hear evidence in the case. Rule XI reads:

[I]n the trial of any impeachment the Presiding Officer of the Senate, if the Senate so orders, shall appoint a committee of Senators to receive evidence and take testimony at such times and places as the committee may determine, and for such purpose the committee so appointed and the chairman thereof, to be elected by the committee, shall (unless otherwise ordered by the Senate) exercise all the powers and functions conferred upon the Senate and the Presiding Officer of the Senate, respectively, under the rules of procedure and practice in the Senate when sitting on impeachment trials. . . .

Unless otherwise ordered by the Senate, the rules of procedure and practice in the Senate when sitting on impeachment trials shall govern the procedure and practice of the committee so appointed. The committee so appointed shall report to the Senate in writing a certified copy of the transcript of the proceedings and testimony had and given before such committee, and such report shall be received by the Senate and the evidence so received and the testimony so taken shall be considered to all intents and purposes, subject to the right of the Senate to determine competency, relevancy, and materiality, as having been received and taken before the Senate, but nothing herein shall prevent the Senate from sending for any witness and hearing his testimony in open Senate, or by order of the Senate having the entire trial in open Senate.

A committee was established, heard the evidence, and after four days in which ten witnesses, including Nixon, testified, a transcript was delivered to the full Senate and both sides (the impeachment committee and Nixon) were allowed to present their evidence to the full Senate. Nixon himself gave a final argument, and several senators were allowed to question him personally. On 3 November 1989, the Senate voted to convict on the first two articles of impeachment, and the presiding officer then entered a judgment that Nixon was convicted and ordered to be removed from office. Nixon then sued, claiming that under Article 1, Section 3, Clause 6, called the Impeachment Clause, the "entire" Senate had to sit in on the impeachment trial, and not just a committee, and that Rule XI violated his constitutional rights to a fair trial. The U.S. District Court for the District of Columbia held that Nixon's claim was nonjusticiable (meaning that it did not have judicial merit) and, declining to intervene, dismissed the suit. On appeal, the U.S. Court of Appeals for the District of Columbia Circuit upheld the lower court's decision. The United States Supreme Court agreed to hear the case and heard arguments on 14 October 1992.

On 13 January 1993, almost seven years after Nixon was initially convicted, and more than three years after he had been impeached and convicted in the Senate, the Supreme Court held that he had no claim under Rule XI and dismissed his suit, holding that the word "try" in the clause "lacked sufficient precision to afford any judicially manageable standard of review of the Senate's actions, and such word did not provide an identifiable textual limit on the authority which was committed to the Senate," and that "the commonsense meaning of the word 'sole' in the impeachment trial clause was that the Senate alone had the authority to determine whether an individual should be acquitted or convicted." Writing for the unanimous court, Chief Justice William Rehnquist wrote:

> In the case before us, there is no separate provision of the Constitution that could be defeated by allowing the Senate final authority to determine the meaning of the word "try" in the Impeachment Trial Clause. We agree with Nixon that courts possess power to review either legislative or executive action that transgresses identifiable textual limits. As we have made clear, "whether the action of [either the Legislative or Executive Branch] exceeds whatever authority has been committed is itself a delicate exercise in constitutional interpretation, and is a responsibility of this Court as ultimate interpreter of the Constitution." *Baker v. Carr,* [369 U.S. 186] at 211. . . . But we conclude, after exercising that delicate responsibility, that the word "try" in the Impeachment Trial Clause does not provide an identifiable textual limit on the authority which is committed to the Senate.

See also Impeachment
References: *United States v. Nixon,* 816 F.2d (1987), 1022–1031; "Walter Nixon: Perjury on the Federal Bench," in George C. Kohn, *Encyclopedia of American Scandal: From ABSCAM to the Zenger Case* (New York: Facts on File, 1989), 245–246.

Nixon, Walter L.
See Nixon v. United States.

Oakar, Mary Rose

See House of Representatives Post Office Scandal

Obstruction of Justice

Legal term denoting the "impeding or obstruct-t[ion of] those who seek justice in a court, or those who have duties or powers of administering justice therein." The crime of obstructing justice is hard to prove without the testimony of insiders involved in the obstruction. For example, charges against President Richard Nixon for obstruction of justice in the Watergate case were corroborated by his White House Counsel, John W. Dean III, and by tapes recorded by Nixon himself showing that soon after he learned of the break-in at Democratic Headquarters in the Watergate Hotel, he ordered the FBI not to investigate the ties the five burglars captured there might have with Nixon's own 1972 reelection effort. The tape showing Nixon's order was the "smoking gun" proving obstruction of justice.

In a more recent case, President Bill Clinton was accused of obstruction of justice in attempting to shut down an investigation of his conduct with an Arkansas state employee who alleged that he sexually harassed her. Despite an impeachment trial, none of Clinton's cronies would testify against him, and the obstruction charge went unproven.

Although not listed in the Constitution as a "high crime and misdemeanor," Congress has agreed that any official guilty of obstruction of justice has committed an impeachable offense.

References: Nolan, Joseph R., and Jacqueline M. Nolan-Haley, *Black's Law Dictionary: Definitions of the Terms and Phrases of American and English Jurisprudence, Ancient and Modern* (St. Paul, MN: West Publishing Company, 1990), 1077.

Ordway, Nehemiah George (1828–1907)

Territorial governor of Dakota Territory (1880–1884), removed by President Chester A. Arthur amid allegations of rampant corruption. Ordway was born in Warner, New Hampshire, on 10 November 1828. He was a nephew of Sergeant John Ordway, who had been a participant in the famed Lewis and Clark expedition to the American Northwest. Nehemiah Ordway received his common school education in Warner and prospered in the mercantile and banking businesses. At the age of thirty-one, in 1860, he became the chair of the New Hampshire Republican Party and rose slowly through the party hierarchy. Three years after his selection as state party chair, he was named the sergeant at arms for the U.S. House of Representatives, holding the same position in 1865, 1869, and 1871. In 1875, he was elected a member of the New Hampshire state house of representatives, serving until 1878. In that year, he was elected to the state senate from the Ninth New Hampshire District, where he served for a single year.

The obstruction of justice case against President Nixon in the Watergate affair was backed up by his White House Counsel, John W. Dean III. In this photo, Dean testifies to the Senate Watergate Committee against the Nixon administration. (Bettmann/Corbis)

In 1880 President Rutherford B. Hayes named Ordway the seventh territorial governor of the Dakota Territory, replacing William Alanson Howard, who had died in Washington of heart and lung trouble on 10 April 1880. Ordway was inaugurated on 24 June 1880 and took over the territory at a time of tremendous growth. The population of white settlers was growing rapidly, and Ordway made it a point to travel to every settlement in the territory. Seeing potential in further growth (and backed by New Hampshire legislators who owned millions of acres of Western lands), Ordway proposed that the territorial capital be moved from Yankton to Bismarck. The press in the territory did not support moving the capital so Ordway had his own newspaper established and backed it up by founding the Dakota Press Association. The railroads backed Ordway's plan, and when the state legislature met in 1883, it formed a capital commission. Backroom deals and land sales on areas in which Ordway had a financial interest were alleged but never proved. In 1883, acting on these allegations, a grand jury was seated. The following year, the grand jury indicted Ordway on charges of using his influence to buy land in Bismarck and then pushing to have the state capitol moved there to benefit financially. His defense attorneys, however, argued that a territorial governor was immune in territorial courts. Territorial officials wished to have Ordway gone, so they appealed to President Chester A. Arthur to remove Ordway and replace him. Arthur named *Chicago News* editor Gilbert Ashville Pierce, a Civil War veteran, to be the new governor. Pierce was inaugurated on 25 July 1884, and Ordway left the area. He returned to Washington, D.C, where he became a special agent for the Northern Pacific Railway, as head lobbyist in the nation's capital. He never faced any criminal charges.

Ordway died, unknown and unremembered, in Boston, Massachusetts, on 3 July 1907, at the age of seventy-eight. His son, George Ordway, served as Dakota territorial auditor from 1883 to 1885.

References: Jennewein, J. Leonard, and Jane Boorman, eds., *Dakota Panorama* (Bismarck, ND: Dakota Territory Centennial Commission, 1961), 396;

"Ordway, Nehemiah George," in Thomas A. McMullin and David Walker, *Biographical Directory of American Territorial Governors* (Westport, CT: Meckler Publishing, 1984), 87–90; Schell, Herbert S., *History of South Dakota* (Lincoln: University of Nebraska Press, 1975), 203–215.

P

Pardongate

Political scandal, which came in the days before, and the weeks after, President William Jefferson Clinton left the White House at the end of his presidential term in January 2001. Under the law, a pardon is a release from a sentence of guilt, a finding of guilt, or a potential finding of guilt. Although the pardon power is generally given to the chief executive, either of a state or of the nation, legislatures have the right to grant pardons, usually through what is called an act of indemnity, either anticipatory or retrospective, for crimes done in the public interest, which are nonetheless illegal. Under the United States Constitution, the powers granted to the president in the area of pardons are absolute, and it is beyond the scope of Congress or the courts to change it without a constitutional amendment. This power was inserted into the Constitution as part of the famed Virginia Plan by John Rutledge and was supported by Alexander Hamilton, who wrote in *Federalist No. 74* that the president "is also to be authorised 'to grant reprieves and pardons for offences against the United States *except in cases of impeachment* [Hamilton's emphasis].' Humanity and good policy conspire to dictate, that the benign prerogative of pardoning should be as little as possible fettered or embarrassed. The criminal code of every country partakes so much of necessary severity, that without an easy access to exceptions in favor of unfortunate guilt, justice would wear a countenance too sanguinary and cruel."

In 1820 Attorney General William Wirt wrote, "The power of pardon, as given by the constitution, is the power of absolute and entire pardon." The pardon power is situated in Article II, Section II of the Constitution, which reads:

> The President shall be Commander in Chief of the Army and Navy of the United States, and of the Militia of the several States, when called into the actual Service of the United States; he may require the Opinion, in writing, of the principal Officer in each of the executive Departments, upon any Subject relating to the Duties of their respective Offices, and he shall have Power to grant Reprieves and Pardons for Offences against the United States, except in Cases of Impeachment.

The pardon power has been used less and less by recent presidents. Truman issued 1,913 pardons and commutations from 1945 to 1953, while Eisenhower issued 1,110. Nixon issued 863, Carter 534, Reagan 393, and Bush 74. Clinton, in total, issued 395, demonstrating a rise in pardons that was either a sign of a benevolent executive or, as many critics charged, a sign that Clinton sold pardons to cronies and financial friends.

Whatever the reason, as the end of his term neared in January 2001, President Bill Clinton granted numerous pardons and commutations, many to people who, as it later turned out, had contributed vast sums of money either to the Democratic National Committee, to the Clinton Library

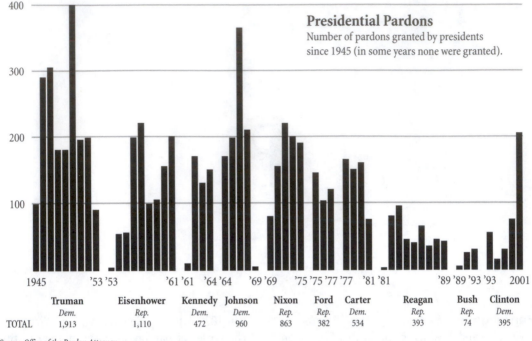

Presidential Pardons

Number of pardons granted by presidents since 1945 (in some years none were granted).

	Truman	Eisenhower	Kennedy	Johnson	Nixon	Ford	Carter	Reagan	Bush	Clinton
	Dem.	Rep.	Dem.	Dem.	Rep.	Rep.	Dem.	Rep.	Rep.	Dem.
TOTAL	1,913	1,110	472	960	863	382	534	393	74	395

Source: Office of the Pardon Attorney

Fund, or to both. The use of the pardon has, in the recent past, been controversial. Richard Nixon's pardon of Teamster boss James R. "Jimmy" Hoffa (1971); the pardon of Nixon himself by his successor, Gerald R. Ford, for any potential crimes Nixon may have committed during the Watergate scandal; the pardon by Ronald Reagan of baseball team owner George Steinbrenner; and the pardon by President George Bush in 1992 of former Secretary of Defense Caspar Weinberger are some examples. However, the 140 pardons and 36 commutations doled out by Clinton in the final days of his administration made for one of the biggest political scandals of 2001.

Normally, a president, when contemplating a pardon or commutation, confers with the appropriate office in the Department of Justice, known as the Office of the Pardon Attorney. This officer investigates the background of the person considered for the pardon or commutation and recommends a course of action to the president. This recommendation is not binding, and the president can choose to ignore it. However, a president should be wary of ignoring the advice of his Department of Justice, either because the pardon could be politically embarrassing or could help a wanted felon or criminal evade justice.

In the days before his administration ended, Clinton issued 140 pardons to a range of criminals and other felons who were either wanted or were serving time for various offenses. Among these were his former secretary of housing and urban development, Henry Cisneros, who lied to the FBI; ex-CIA chief John Deutsch, who faced possible criminal charges for mishandling secret documents; Whitewater figure Susan McDougal, who went to jail on a contempt charge rather than testify against Clinton; Clinton's own brother Roger, who had been convicted of cocaine possession; and heiress Patricia Hearst. But Clinton also pardoned Marc Rich, a man wanted by the United States for tax fraud and conspiring to sell Iranian oil despite an embargo on that country, after his wife, Denise Rich, gave Clinton and his presidential library millions of dollars in donations. Another Clinton pardon went to Carlos Vignali, drug dealer who was serving a fifteen-year sentence for importing 800 pounds of cocaine, after Vignali's father, Horacio, donated thousands of dollars to Democratic politicians, including Representative Xavier Becerra (D-CA), who lost his election for mayor of Los Angeles because of the scandal. Pardons also went to Charles Wilfred Morgan III, an Arkansas man convicted and sentenced to three years in prison in the 1980s for cocaine distribution (his attorney was former Clinton White House counsel William Kennedy III), and Palm Beach attorney Arnold Prosperi, who evaded taxes on $3 million and who donated $45,000 to the White House Historical Association.

Despite the scandalous nature of Clinton's pardons, his power to award them was complete, and none could be overturned. And despite investigations by Congress into those who may have used money and other powers to gain the pardons, no person, as of this writing, has been indicted for any of the pardons.

More than 200 years ago, philosopher Immanuel Kant warned that the pardoning power is the "most slippery of all the rights of the sovereign." As Clinton's pardons, and the scandal surrounding them, prove, Kant was more correct than anyone ever believed.

References: Grunwald, Michael, and Christine Haughney, "4 Pardons Probed for Ties to N.Y. Senate Bid, Felons Were Leaders in Hasidic Community," *Washington Post*, 24 February 2001, A1; Harris, John F., "From Clinton Die-Hards, a Command Performance, Pardons Prompt Podesta, Others to Keep Up Defense," *Washington Post*, 1 March 2001, A2; Moore, Kathleen Dean, *Pardons: Justice, Mercy, and the Public Interest* (New York: Oxford University Press, 1997); Smith, Greg B., "Clinton Library Fundraiser Helped Perjurer Get Pardon," *Daily News* (New York), 4 March 2001, A2.

Patterson, James Willis (1823–1893)

United States representative (1863–1867) and U.S. senator (1867–1873) from New Hampshire, implicated in the Crédit Mobilier scandal and threatened with expulsion from the Senate. Patterson was born in the town of Henniker, New Hampshire, on 2 July 1823 and attended local schools, pursuing what were then called "classical studies" (Greek, Latin, math, etc.). He entered and graduated from Dartmouth College (now Dartmouth University) in Hanover, New Hampshire, in 1848, thereafter working as a principal at the Woodstock Academy in Connecticut for two years. Patterson attended the Theological Seminary in New Haven, Connecticut, after which he studied the law. In 1854 he was hired by Dartmouth as a professor of mathematics, astronomy, and meteorology, and he served there for eleven years, until 1865. In 1863 he served for a single one-year term as a member of the New Hampshire state house of representatives.

A Republican, in 1863 Patterson was elected to a seat in the U.S. House of Representatives (elections for the House were then held in odd years by some states), representing the state's Third District. Patterson served in the Thirty-eighth and Thirty-ninth Congresses (1863–1867). In 1866, prior to the end of his second term, Patterson was elected by the New Hampshire legislature to the United States Senate, and he entered that body on 4 March 1867. In his single six-year term, Patterson served as the chairman of the Committee on Enrolled Bills (Forty-first Congress) and of the Committee on the District of Columbia (Forty-first and Forty-second Congresses).

In 1872 Patterson became mired in the intrigue that became the Crédit Mobilier scandal. He was accused by the newspapers of accepting stock in the railroad concern known as the Crédit Mobilier in exchange for voting for increased appropriations for the company that was overseeing the construction of the Union Pacific Railroad. One of the railroad's chief backers—and a member of the Crédit Mobilier—was Representative Oakes Ames of Massachusetts, who gave Patterson a good number of shares in the company at a cut-rate price. The Poland Committee of the U.S. House of Representatives, so named after its chairman, Representative Luke Poland of Vermont, looked into the charges against Patterson.

Historian Edward Winslow Martin wrote in 1873:

James W. Patterson, Senator from New Hampshire, was one of those charged with purchasing Crédit Mobilier stock. He denied the charge, and declared that he had had no connection with the stock at all. Mr. Ames, upon his examination by the Committee, made oath that he had sold Mr. Patterson thirty shares of the stock of the Crédit Mobilier. Mr. Patterson then stated that he had bought stock of Mr. Ames, but supposed that it was Union Pacific stock. He added, on the 21st of January, in a voluntary statement before the Committee: "I have never received any certificate of stock or other evidence of ownership on the Crédit Mobilier, and am not enough of a lawyer to know how I could draw dividends on what I did not own." In support of his assertion, Mr. Patterson produced a letter written to him by Ames during the late Senatorial contest in New Hampshire [which Patterson had lost]. Mr. E. H. Rollins had assailed Mr. Patterson in this contest for owning Crédit Mobilier stock, and Ames, at Patterson's request, write the latter a letter stating that the books of the Company did not show that he owned any stock.

Mr. Ames, who had listened patiently to Mr. Patterson's statement before the Committee, was then questioned by the Committee as to the accuracy of

Roger Adams (left), pardon attorney of the U.S. Department of Justice, and Eric Holder, former deputy attorney general, testify before the U.S. Senate Judiciary Committee regarding the pardon of Marc Rich. (Bettmann/Corbis)

Patterson's statement. He at once produced his memoranda, and proceeded to read from it, amid a painful stillness, "a connected account of his transaction with Patterson. He invested $3,000 for Patterson in Crédit Mobilier stock, in January 1868; on February 14th he paid him $2,223 in cash, which were the proceeds of the sale of the first bond dividend; $3,000 in Union Pacific first mortgage bonds, less $105 retained for interest, and also thirty shares of Union Pacific stock. On June 19th, 1868, he paid him $1,800 as a sixty per cent, cash dividend. Some time in 1871 he settled the transaction and gave him about seventy shares [of] Union Pacific stock. He supposed that Patterson knew he was buying Crédit Mobilier stock; he talked of nothing else with him. Ames explained his letter by saying that it was literally true although intended to give the wrong impression. His good nature led him to write it at Patterson's opportunity—to help him out of a fix. If Patterson had not gotten the certificate for the thirty shares, then it had been lost. He [Ames] had all the other certificates in his pocket except that. Patterson again denied any knowledge of the fact that Ames had invested his $3,000 in Crédit Mobilier stock."

On 27 February 1873, the committee reported back, and accused Patterson of lying to the committee. In their report, they stated:

The Committee find in the statement of Mr. Patterson before the Committee of the House of Representatives, and his statement before this committee, a contradictory relation of the transaction between him and Mr. Ames; a suppression of material facts, and a denial of other facts which must have been known to him. . . . And further, that being inquired of in relation thereto before committees of both branches of Congress, he gave a false account of the transactions between himself and Mr. Ames, suppressed material facts, and denied the existence of other material facts which must have been well known to him.

The committee have reached a conclusion, after the most attentive consideration and anxious deliberation, which they would fain wish were otherwise, but a sense of duty compels them to declare—they submit the following resolution: *Resolved,* That James W. Patterson be, and is hereby expelled from his seat as a member of the Senate.

Two days later, on 1 March, a caucus of Senate Republicans met and decided that because Patterson would be leaving the Senate on 3 March in any case, such a move to expel him was both unproductive and unnecessary, and no action was taken on the committee's recommendation.

Patterson returned to New Hampshire, where he served as a member of the New Hampshire state house of representatives from 1877 to 1878 and as the state superintendent of instruction from 1881 to 1893. He died in Hanover, New Hampshire, on 4 May 1893, two months shy of his seventieth birthday. He was buried in the Dartmouth Cemetery.

See also Crédit Mobilier Scandal

References: Crawford, J. B., *The Crédit Mobilier of America—Its Origin and History, Its Work of Constructing the Union Pacific Railroad and the Relation of Members of Congress Therewith* (Boston: C. W. Calkins & Co., Publishers, 1880), 148; Martin, Edward Winslow, *Behind the Scenes in Washington. Being a Complete and Graphic Account of the Crédit Mobilier Investigation, the Congressional Rings, Political Intrigues, Workings of the Lobbies, Etc. Giving the Secret History of Our National Government, in All Its Various Branches, and Showing How the Public Money Is Squandered, How Votes Are Obtained, Etc., With Sketches of the Leading Senators, Congressmen, Government Officials, Etc., and an Accurate Description of the Splendid Public Buildings of the Federal Capital* (New York: Continental Publishing Company, 1873), 285–287.

Peck, James Hawkins (1790–1836)

Federal judge, impeached by the United States Senate for his role in removing a lawyer from the practice for criticizing the bench but acquitted. Little is known of Peck, but his case, one of only a handful ever to go before the entire Senate in an impeachment trial, is part of American judicial history. What is known is that Peck was born in Jefferson County, Tennessee, on 12 January 1790. He served in the U.S. Army during the War of 1812 and was in private law practice in Tennessee from 1818 until 1819 and in St. Louis, Missouri, from 1819 until 1822. He was nominated by President James Monroe to a new seat, established by Congress—the U.S. District Court of Missouri—on 29 March 1822 and confirmed by the Senate on 5 April 1822.

In 1830 reports were sent to the U.S. House of Representatives that Peck was abusing his power to hold people in contempt in his court. Although there is no strict holding as to what constitutes an impeachable offense, Peck's alleged behavior was enough for the House Judiciary Committee to recommend he be impeached for this behavior. The full House voted for one article of impeachment

on 24 April 1830. As chairman of the House Judiciary Committee, Representative James Buchanan served as prosecutor in the Senate impeachment trial of Peck; Buchanan later served as U.S. minister to Russia, secretary of state, and as the fifteenth president of the United States. The record of Peck's impeachment, one of the first to be published in the history of the country, is to be found in a work by Arthur J. Stansbury, published in 1833. Peck's alleged crime was held before the Senate to examine, but it was found lacking in criminal intent, and the Senate acquitted Peck on 31 January 1831. Peck remained on the bench until his death on 29 April 1836, almost six years to the day after the House had impeached him. His name passed into history.

In *Green v. United States,* 356 U.S. 165 (1958), the Supreme Court wrote:

The subsequent development of the Federal contempt power lends no support to the Petitioners' position, for the significance of the Act of 1831, 3 Stat. 487, at 488, lies quite in the opposite direction. Sentiment for passage of that act arose out of the impeachment proceedings instituted against Judge James H. Peck because of his conviction and punishment for criminal contempt of a lawyer who had published an article critical of a decision of the judge then on appeal. Although it is true that the act marks the first Congressional step to curtail the contempt powers of the Federal courts, the important thing to note is that the area of curtailment related not to punishment for disobedience of court orders but to punishment for conduct of the kind that had provoked Judge Peck's controversial action. As to such conduct, the 1831 act confined the summary power of punishment to " . . . misbehaviour of any person . . . in the presence of the . . . courts, or so near thereto as to obstruct the administration of justice."

See also Impeachment

References: Bushnell, Eleanore, "The Impeachment and Trial of James H. Peck," *Missouri Historical Review* (January 1980), 137–165; Davis, Charles B., "Judge James Hawkins Peck," *Missouri Historical Review,* XXVII:1 (October 1932), 3–20; "James Hawkins Peck," in Eleanor Bushnell, *Crimes, Follies, and Misfortunes: The Federal Impeachment Trials* (Urbana: University of Illinois Press, 1992), 91–113; "Official Records of the Impeachment of Judge James H. Peck," File 21B-B1, in *Records of Impeachment Proceedings,* 1st–90th Congresses (1789–1968), General Records of the U.S. House of Representatives, 1789–1968, Records Group (RG) 233, National Archives;

Stansbury, Arthur J., "*Report of the Trial of James H. Peck, Judge of the United States District Court for the District of Missouri, Before the Senate of the United States, on an Impeachment Preferred by the House of Representatives Against Him for High Misdemeanors in Office*" (Boston: Hilliard, Gray & Co., 1833).

Pendergast, Thomas Joseph (1872–1945)

American political boss, head of the so-called Pendergast machine that controlled politics and patronage in Kansas City, Missouri. The image of the "political machine" in American history was molded in large part by Pendergast, although his name has faded into history. One of nine children of Irish immigrants, Pendergast apparently attended local schools but never received a secondary education. His older brother James ran a saloon in Kansas City, where the Pendergast machine started among the Irish who voted for Democrats. James Pendergast was elected an alderman in Kansas City in 1892, becoming the only brother to hold political office. Thomas Pendergast took over the growing machine from his brother. When James Pendergast died in 1911, his brother, known as "Big Tom," became one of the most powerful bosses in American political history. Thomas Pendergast was named to a series of low-level appointed offices during World War I, but it appears that elective office was not his interest—though power was. Because Kansas City was not a melting pot of immigrants, unlike New York City and Chicago, for instance, Pendergast built his organization with the help of people from all ethnic groups and backgrounds. And, as historian George Kohn wrote, "In the process, he made himself a great deal of money from kickbacks, payoffs, and illegal settlements."

Following World War I, a young up-and-coming Missouri politician came under the influence of Pendergast; he was a bespeckled veteran of the war named Harry S. Truman. Tying his desire for political office to Pendergast, Truman was elected to a series of offices, rising to be elected to the United States Senate in 1934. The story behind how Truman became the candidate of the Democratic Party is one cloaked in myth; one reports that Truman asked Pendergast for an office that paid at least $25,000 a year, a spectacular sum in those Depression-era days. Pendergast demurred, saying that Truman did not deserve such a highly paid post, instead offering him the Democratic nomination for the United States Senate, an office that at the time paid only $10,000 a year. Another story reports that Pendergast approached Truman to run for the Senate to defeat another Democrat—Senator Bennett Champ Clark of Missouri and son of Champ Clark, a former Speaker of the U.S. House of Representatives. Either way, with Pendergast's backing, Truman easily won the party nod and the election.

The new senator was derided as being from "Tom's Town" and "The Senator from Pendergast." Truman later wrote in a letter, referring to pressure put on him by Pendergast to pad the county payroll with Pendergast-approved people, "I wonder if I did right to put a lot of no account sons of bitches on the payroll and pay other sons of bitches more money for supplies than they were worth." However, while in the Senate, he remained close to Pendergast, confiding with him on ways that Democrats could use the government to edge out Republicans. During the Depression, when Franklin D. Roosevelt's "New Deal" economic program pumped billions of dollars into public works projects across the nation, Pendergast maneuvered himself into controlling first the men who controlled the money, then controlled the money himself via favors and backroom deals. Pendergast even controlled the governor's office—it was dubbed "Uncle Tom's Cabin."

In 1936 Pendergast's health began to fail, and slowly his grip on power slipped. Despite having friends in high places, Pendergast came under investigation by U.S. District Attorney Maurice Milligan and Governor Lloyd Stark of Missouri. For three years, charges of vote rigging and vote fraud were investigated. Finally, in 1939, the Bureau of Internal Revenue, the forerunner of the modern Internal Revenue Service, investigated Pendergast's financial records and discovered more than $1 million in untaxed revenue. Pendergast was indicted on income tax evasion. On 22 May 1939, he was convicted and sentenced to fifteen months in prison. He was released after serving 366 days. In 1940 he was indicted with two others on charges that he had obstructed justice during the investigation of an insurance scam. He was also indicted for contempt of court, but in 1943 the U.S. Supreme Court dismissed this indictment on the grounds that the statute of limitations on such charges had expired.

Nonetheless, Pendergast was too ill to celebrate his victory—he was dying of cancer and had suffered a series of strokes. He died on 26 January 1945 at the age of seventy-four. Ironically, his death came just days after his protege, Truman, was sworn in as vice president of the United States, and just months before Truman became president upon the death of Franklin D. Roosevelt. Truman did not attend the funeral. Pendergast was buried in a simple, nondescript grave at Calvary Cemetery in Kansas City.

References: Larsen, Lawrence H., and Nancy J. Hulston, *Pendergast!* (Columbia: University of Missouri Press, 1997); *Pendergast v. United States,* 317 U.S. 412 (1943); "Tom Pendergast: Boss of Kansas City," in George C. Kohn, *Encyclopedia of American Scandal: From ABSCAM to the Zenger Case* (New York: Facts on File, 1989), 262–263.

Pendleton, George Hunt (1825–1889)

United States representative (1857–1865) and U.S. senator (1879–1885), author of the Pendleton Plan, which established civil service rules in government for the first time. Born in Cincinnati, Ohio, on 19 July 1825, Pendleton was the eldest of the ten children of Nathanael Greene Pendleton (named after the famed American general who served in the American Revolution) and Jane Frances (née Hunt) Pendleton. Nathanael Pendleton was elected to a seat in the U.S. House of Representatives in 1840 but served only one term and retired back to Ohio. His son, George, was to have a far longer political career. He attended local schools and the Cincinnati College. In 1844 he left the United States for Europe, touring numerous countries and attending Heidelberg University in Germany. He eventually left the university, continuing his travels for a time before returning to the United States in 1846. That same year, he married the daughter of Francis Scott Key, who had written the "Star Spangled Banner" in 1814. He studied the law, was admitted to the Ohio bar in 1847 and commenced a practice in Cincinnati with local attorney George E. Pugh.

After being a lawyer for six years, in 1853 Pendleton was nominated by the Democrats of Ohio for a seat in the Ohio state senate. He was easily elected and became the youngest member of that body. The following year, he was nominated for a seat in the U.S. House of Representatives, the same seat his father once held. However, because the controversy over the Kansas-Nebraska Act split the Democrats into pro- and antislavery factions, Pendleton was defeated in a close race by Republican Timothy C. Day, who had received the backing of the American, or "Know Nothing," Party. Two years later, however, the Democrats coalesced, and Pendleton won the seat over token Republican and "Know Nothing" opposition. In the House, Pendleton was a supporter of Senator Stephen A. Douglas of Illinois and denounced the Lecompton constitution, enacted in "bloody" Kansas by a proslavery faction. He maintained a moderate position on other issues of the day and was reelected three more times, serving in the Thirty-fifth through the Thirty-eighth Congresses, until 3 March 1865. He tried to urge conciliation between the sections in the days before the Civil War broke out, urging that the North "grant all their [Southern] reasonable demands. . . . I beg you, in God's name, do it! Do a patriotic duty! Give us peace instead of discord!" During the war, he was one of the group of "Copperheads," Northerners who were critics of the conflict and demanded a quick peace with the South to end the fighting. His tenure in the House was marked by his service as one of the House managers in the impeachment trial of West H. Humphreys, a judge in Tennessee who was removed from office for siding with the Confederacy.

In 1864 Pendleton was nominated for vice president of the United States by the Democrats, meeting in convention in Chicago, Illinois. When the Democrats met, the war was going quite badly for the North, and it appeared that President Abraham Lincoln would need a miracle to be reelected. As the Democrats assembled, they quickly nominated for president one of Lincoln's former generals who had begun to criticize the conduct of the war—General George B. McClellan. Initially, the Democrats sought to nominate James O. Guthrie for vice president, but after two ballots the delegates turned to Pendleton, balancing a military man with a "Peace Democrat." Victory for the Democrats seemed assured, so much so that Lincoln named a "War Democrat," Governor Andrew Johnson of Tennessee, as his running mate to balance his ticket. However, several events occurred between the end of the conventions and the election that led to a surprising electoral victory by Lincoln. On 18 July, the president sent newspaper editor Horace Greeley to Canada to meet with representatives of the Confederate government. Lincoln demanded that the Southern states that had seceded reenter the Union and that slavery be ended at once. Both of these demands were rejected by the Southerners, and the conference broke up. However, Lincoln looked reasonable in trying to end the war quickly, while the Southerners were viewed as intransigent. On 2 September, Union General William Tecumseh Sherman's troops thundered into the state of Georgia and occupied Atlanta, giving a huge boost to Northern morale and cutting the Confederacy in two. Emboldened by Sherman's victory, Lincoln demanded the resignation of his postmaster general, Montgomery Blair, a peace advocate inside his administration. These events led to a turnabout in the election, and on 8 November, Lincoln won by more than 500,000 votes out of some 4.16 million cast, capturing the electoral vote 212 to 21. In the end, the desires of the Democrats to end the war quickly were dashed, and the oratory of Pendleton could not match the aloofness of McClellan, more a military figure than a politician.

Out of politics for the first time in fourteen years, Pendleton ran unsuccessfully in 1866 for a seat in the U.S. House of Representatives. In 1868 he made a desperate but unsuccessful attempt to win the Democratic presidential nomination, losing out to New York Governor Horatio Seymour. The following year, he was nominated by the Democrats for governor, but lost in a close race to Republican Rutherford B. Hayes, who was later elected the nineteenth president of the United States. Pendleton then took a position as president of the Kentucky Central Railroad, which he held until 1879.

In 1878 Pendleton was nominated by the Democrats for a seat in the United States Senate, after Senator Stanley Matthews, who had been named to fill the last two years of the term of Senator John Sherman, decided against running for a full term of his own. Pendleton was easily elected and was named chairman of the Senate Committee on Civil Service. It was here that Pendleton became a giant in the pursuit of government service reform. He embraced a reform measure drafted by reformer Dorman B. Eaton, who called for a system of civil service in federal government hiring. Prior to this time, a new administration rewarded its friends with plum government jobs. Thousands of workers nationwide, from postmasters to tax collectors, were given positions based on their political allegiance. This system allowed for gross mismanagement and corruption, and Eaton, among others, wished to replace it with one in which jobs would be doled out on the basis of ability rather than political connections. Eaton drafted a plan of reform, and Pendleton introduced it in the Senate in 1882. The bill passed both houses of Congress and was signed into law by President Chester A. Arthur on 16 January 1883. The law's impact was wide-ranging, ending the spoils system for a number of plum patronage positions and making sure workers in federal offices were not forced to give contributions to candidates for office in exchange for keeping their jobs.

Despite pushing through the most influential reform bill of the late nineteenth century, in 1884 Pendleton was not renominated by the Democrats in Ohio for the Senate, and he left office in March 1885. President Grover Cleveland, the first Democrat to win election to the White House since 1856, appointed Pendleton envoy extraordinary and minister plenipotentiary to Germany, replacing John A. Kasson. Pendleton served in this position until his death. He was on business in Brussels, Belgium, when he died on 24 November 1889, at the age of sixty-four. His body was returned to the United States and interred at Spring Grove Cemetery in Cincinnati, Ohio.

See also Eaton, Dorman Bridgman; Pendleton Civil Service Act

References: Bing, Julius, "Our Civil Service," *Putnam's Magazine,* New Series II, 8 (August 1868), 233; Bloss, George, *Life and Speeches of George H. Pendleton* (Cincinnati, OH: Miami Printing and Publishing Co., 1868); "Death of G. H. Pendleton. Ex-United States Senate and Ex-Minister to Germany," *The World* (New York), 26 November 1889, 1; Mach, Thomas Stuart, "'Gentleman George' Hunt Pendleton: A Study in Political Continuity" (Ph.D. dissertation, University of Akron, 1996); Mach, Thomas Stuart, "George Hunt Pendleton, The Ohio Idea and Political Continuity in Reconstruction America," *Ohio History,* 108 (Summer-Autumn 1999); 125–144; "New Ministers Selected: The President Fills Four Diplomatic Missions [Pendleton Named to German Mission]," *New York Times,* 24 March 1885, 1.

Pendleton Civil Service Act, 22 Stat. 403 (1883)

Congressional enactment establishing a system of civil service in the hiring and employment of federal workers. Since the early days of the Republic, government ran on the "spoils" system—the ruling administration doled out patronage and favors to the people who supported its policies. Offices from the very top of government to the lowest rungs of the administration were filled by cronies of the president and his party, many of whom were not hired for their skill or experience but because of their largesse or vocal support for the candidate.

In *Putnam's Magazine* in August 1868, Julius Bing wrote of the system prior to the Pendleton Act's passage, "At present there is no organization save that of corruption, no system save that of chaos; no test of integrity save that of partisanship; no test of qualification save that of intrigue." From that time, however, there was no push to end the system in which corruption seemed to permeate at all levels. In 1871 Congress called on the president to decree a certain code of regulations, which led to the establishment of the Civil Service Commission, but that panel collapsed after just a few years. Reformers such as Eaton, Carl Schurz, and George W. Curtis, the latter the editor of *Harper's Weekly* stood for reform. The scandals that enveloped the Grant administration—from the Whiskey Ring to the Star Route frauds—led to an increase in calls for a revival of civil service legislation. In 1877 a New York Civil Service Reform Association was established, and four years later George W. Curtis formed the National Civil Service Reform League.

One of the leading congressional adherents in an effort to pass civil service reform was Representative, then Senator, George Hunt Pendleton of Ohio. Pendleton, who had been the vice presidential candidate of the Democrats in 1868, had for many years fought to get Congress to back a comprehensive civil service reform law, to no avail. The scandals of the administration of Ulysses S. Grant (1869–1877), however, changed all that. When numerous friends of the president were implicated in schemes to profit at public expense from their ties to Grant, congressional, as well as public, support turned toward reform.

George William Curtis, editor of *Harper's Weekly* and a commissioner on the U.S. Civil Service Commission, wrote in 1872, "It is not easy to compute in figures the exact economical difference between a good and bad system of the civil service. It is necessarily a matter of inference and of comparison between the probable operations of a careless and a careful method." Working with the chairman of the commission, Dorman B. Eaton, Pendleton drafted a law in 1883 that passed both houses of Congress and was signed into law by a reluctant Grant. Called the Civil Service Act of 1883, or the Pendleton Act, it established for the first time a schedule to hire government workers not on the basis of party affiliation or amount of donations given to a certain party or candidate, but because of their skill on a government test.

On 12 December 1882, as the civil service bill neared passage in Congress, Pendleton took to the Senate floor and said:

> The necessity of a change in the civil administration of this Government has been so fully discussed in the periodicals and pamphlets and newspapers, and before the people, that I feel indisposed to make any further argument. This subject, in all its ramifications, was submitted to the people of the United States at the fall elections, and they have spoken in low or uncertain tone. . . .
>
> I do not say that the men who are employed in it are all corrupt or inefficient or unworthy. That would do very great injustice to a great number of faithful, honest, and intelligent public servants.

All actions relating to civil service in the U.S. government relate to this enactment. Although there have been reforms of the original law, it remains to this day one of the leading pieces of reformist legislation that lessened to a great degree the influence of parties upon government hiring.

See also Curtis, George William; Eaton, Dorman Bridgman; Pendleton, George Hunt; Whiskey Ring Scandal

References: Bartholomew, Paul C., "Corrupt Practices Acts," in *Dictionary of American History,* 7 vols. (New York: Charles Scribner's Sons, 1976–1978), II:232–233; "George William Curtis" in *Harper's Weekly,* XVI (7 September 1872), 819; Hoogenboom, Ari, *Outlawing the Spoils: A History of the Civil Service Reform Movement, 1865–1883* (Urbana: University of Illinois Press, 1961); Hoogenboom, Ari, "The Pendleton Act and Civil Service," *American Historical Review,* LXIV:2 (January 1959), 301–318; Pendleton's Senate remarks in *Congressional Record,* 12 December 1882, 47th Congress, 2nd Session; Rosenbloom, David

H., ed. (with the assistance of Mark A. Emmert), *Centenary Issues of the Pendleton Act of 1883: The Problematic Legacy of Civil Service Reform* (New York: M. Dekker, 1982); Van Riper, Paul P., *History of the United States Civil Service* (Evanston, IL: Row, Peterson, 1958).

Perkins, Carl Christopher (1954–)

United States representative from Kentucky (1984–1993) who pled guilty to conspiring to defraud the Federal Elections Commission by writing bad checks and filing false personal finance disclosure statements. The son of Congressman Carl Dewey Perkins (1912–1984), Carl Christopher Perkins was born in Washington, D.C., on 6 August 1954. At the time, Carl Dewey Perkins was serving his third term in the U.S. House of Representatives, where he would remain until his death on 3 August 1984. Carl Christopher Perkins attended public schools in Fairfax County, Virginia, near Washington, and then received his bachelor's degree from Davidson College in North Carolina in 1976. He earned his law degree from the University of Louisville in Kentucky in 1978 and that year began practicing law in Kentucky. Elected to a seat in the Kentucky house of representatives in 1980, he remained in that seat until 1984, continuing his law practice through that period.

After Carl Dewey Perkins died in August 1984, Christopher Perkins announced his intention to run for his late father's seat in a special election to fill the vacancy. Perkins was elected and later retained the seat in the regular November election. He would hold it until 1993.

Starting in 1989, Perkins committed a series of acts that would lead to his downfall. In an indictment later handed down, it was alleged that in 1989 and 1990 Perkins filed false statements to the Federal Election Commission (FEC), listing expenses of $45,584 by his campaign committee that had in fact been spent for personal reasons. It was also alleged that Perkins committed bank fraud by involving himself in a check-kiting scheme run by the sergeant at arms of the U.S. House of Representatives. Allegations also were leveled at Perkins for attempting to defraud several banks and other financial institutions in Kentucky by misrepresenting loan information. A third count alleged that Perkins gave false statements on his U.S.

House of Representatives Financial Disclosure Statement (FDS) of $946,135 for 1990. Perkins's secretary, Martha Amburgey, was also charged with conspiring to file false statements with the FEC; she later pled guilty.

In 1992, facing these charges, Perkins did not run for reelection. On 13 December 1994, he pled guilty to all three counts and in 1995 was sentenced to twenty-one months in prison. The same Department of Justice task force looking into Perkins's peccadillos had also nabbed a former sergeant at arms, Jack Russ, as well as Representative Carroll Hubbard Jr. and his wife, Carol Brown Hubbard. After being released from prison, Perkins returned to his home at Hindman, Kentucky.

References: *Biographical Directory of the American Congress, 1774–1996,* (Alexandria, VA: CQ Staff Directories, Inc., 1996), 1649; Perkins plea information from the U.S. Department of Justice, Washington, DC.

Pickering, John (1737?–1805)

Judge for the District of New Hampshire (1795–1804), impeached and convicted by the U.S. Senate for intoxication and using profanity on the bench, expanding the definition of "high crimes and misdemeanors." Pickering himself has become almost a legend, and the facts about his life are few. He was born in New Hampshire about 1737 or 1738 (sources on his impeachment give both dates, with no birthdate) and graduated from Harvard in 1761. He was long remembered for his service to the nation during the American Revolution, his service as a representative in the New Hampshire legislature, as one of the drafters of the New Hampshire state constitution, as a member of his state's convention for ratifying the federal Constitution in 1787, as chief justice of the New Hampshire state supreme court, and, finally, as a federal district judge, placed on the bench by President George Washington in 1795. Pickering was a dedicated Federalist and, at some point in his career on the bench, riled up the anti-Federalist elements in his state.

In 1801 Thomas Jefferson became the first president who was not a Federalist. However, he presided over a government whose judicial branch was filled entirely by Federalists. A congressional ally, Representative William Branch Giles of Virginia, urged Jefferson to use the power of impeachment to remove Federalist judges and replace them with those with Jeffersonian leanings. Giles, in a letter to Jefferson, persuaded him to remove "all of [the judges] . . . indiscriminately." Jefferson and his allies searched the young nation for a plum target, and Pickering came into their sights. By 1803 Pickering was demonstrating behavior on the bench that could only be called eccentric. Many historians believe that Pickering by this time was wholly insane, as well as an alcoholic. Senator William Plumer, Federalist of New Hampshire, realized that Pickering had to be removed, but cautioned against the strong arm of impeachment: "[S]ome of our democrats feel uneasy [about impeaching Pickering]. They do not wish to act either as the accuser of judges or a madman; but one of my brother Senators told me he was resolved *not* to believe Pickering insane; but if the facts alledged [*sic*] in the impeachments were proved to remove him from office. This is the case with several of them. But they still feel embarrassed [and] fear to meet the shaft of ridicule, should the accused attend, the trial would be farcical indeed!"

Jefferson and his allies were set to impeach Pickering for insanity and alcoholism on the bench, when one of his rulings handed them the weapon they needed to finish the job. In 1802 George Wentworth, a surveyor for the district of New Hampshire who had been appointed by Jefferson, seized a ship called the *Eliza* on grounds that it carried goods on which duty had not been paid, a violation of the law. The owner, a Federalist, appealed to Pickering, who ordered the vessel and her cargo released. At a hearing to decide whether the seizure had been legal, Pickering, "in a state of distressing intoxication," held for the owner. Jefferson became aware of how his surveyor had been overruled, and sent to the House on 4 February 1803 criticism on Pickering's conduct in the *Eliza* trial. A select committee was formed to investigate the matter and on 18 February 1803 sent its report to the full House.

On 2 March 1803, the House voted forty-eight to eight to impeach Pickering and established a committee to draw up articles of impeachment. On 27 December 1803, this committee submitted four articles of impeachment, which charged that Pickering (1) had improperly allowed the cargo of the *Eliza* to be released without payment of duty "with the intent to evade federal law"; (2) during the trial refused to hear testimony from witnesses for the United States, "with the intent to defeat the just claims of the United States"; (3) refused to allow an appeal of his ruling, "disregarding the authority of the laws and wickedly meaning and intending to injure the revenues of the United States and thereby impair [*sic*] their public credit"; and (4) during the trial appeared on the bench "in a state of total intoxication, produced by the free and intemperate use of intoxicating liquors," and that "in a most profane and indecent manner [did] invoke the name of the Supreme Being, to the evil example of the good citizens of the United States." On 30 December 1803, the four articles were adopted by the House. Eleven managers, all Jeffersonians, were selected; Representative Joseph Hopper Nicholson of Maryland served as chairman of the group. (Included in the group of managers were several members who would also serve as managers in the impeachment trial of Supreme Court Justice Samuel Chase in 1804: John Boyle of Kentucky, George W. Campbell of Tennessee, Peter Early of Georgia, John Randolph of Virginia, Caesar A. Rodney of Delaware, and Nicholson.)

On 4 January 1804, the Senate trial against Pickering began. Pickering never even bothered to show up. His son, Jacob Pickering, also a judge of the District Court for the District of New Hampshire, answered the charges in a petition, claiming that at the time of the trial "the said John [Pickering] was, and for more than two years before, and ever since has been, and now is, insane, his mind wholly deranged, and altogether incapable of transacting any kind of business which requires the exercise of judgment, or the faculties of reason; and, therefore, that the said John Pickering is incapable of corruption of judgment, no subject of impeachment, or amenable to any tribunal for his action." The Pickering impeachment trial has become the subject of many historical notes and works—the fact that he was impeached for "crimes" not considered jailable is just one reason for argument; the other was that his alleged insanity was used for his defense is another. The Senate quickly voted that the trial's boundaries would be confined as to whether Pickering was guilty or innocent of the charges, and declined to allow argument as to whether the crimes alleged rose to the level of "high crimes and misdemeanors."

However, many side issues were argued. For instance, Senator William Cocke, a Jeffersonian from Tennessee, asked that the words "according to law" be deleted from the oath taken by senators, because, as Cocke saw it, "the judge is deranged—and I know of no law that makes derangement criminal." Cocke's motion was voted down. Senator and future President John Quincy Adams, a Federalist from Massachusetts, called on three senators who had been in the House and had voted for impeachment to be disqualified as judges, but this was voted down as well, twenty to eight. Vice President Aaron Burr was supposed to preside over the trial, but he was campaigning for the governorship of New York and was replaced by Senator Jesse Franklin, a Jeffersonian from North Carolina. Former congressman Robert Goodloe Harper defended Pickering, presenting depositions from doctors and other courtroom observers who testified as to Pickering's mental state. The House managers argued that Pickering was not insane, but drunk, and this was a "high crime and misdemeanor" sufficient for removal. John Samuel Sherburne, the prosecutor in the *Eliza* case, testified that Pickering was consistently drunk. Ironically, days after the Senate trial ended, President Jefferson named Sherburne to the vacancy created by Pickering's removal. It was a conflict of interest no one involved in the case ever broached.

On 12 March 1804, the Senate voted nineteen to seven that Pickering was guilty on all four articles. They then voted twenty to six to remove Pickering office, Senator William H. Wells, a Federalist from Delaware, moving his vote to join the majority. Historian Eleanore Bushnell explains:

> Judge John Pickering goes into the history books as the first United States official on whose conduct the Senate accepted jurisdiction, and the first to be convicted and removed from office under impeachment. His conviction does not provide any constitutional precedent as might have emerged if Congress had faced the question of Pickering's incapacity head-on and decided what could be done if future instances when a judge should not be permitted to stay on the bench and yet had committed no impeachable offense.

William Maxwell Evarts, attorney general and chief counsel for President Andrew Johnson in Johnson's 1868 impeachment, said, "[T]he accusation against Judge Pickering partook of no qualities except of personal delinquency or misfortune, and whose results give us nothing to be proud of, and to Constitutional law give no precedent except that an insane man may be convicted of crime by a party vote."

Pickering did not long survive his removal. He died on 11 April 1805, less than two years after his historic impeachment ended.

References: Hildreth, Richard, *The History of the United States of America, from the Discovery of the Continent to the Organization of Government under the Federal Constitution*, 6 vols. (New York: Harper & Brothers, 1880), II:518; "Impeachment of John Pickering," in Alexander Simpson Jr., *A Treatise on Federal Impeachments, with an Appendix Containing, Inter Alia, an Abstract of the Articles of Impeachment in all of the Federal Impeachments in this Country and in England* (Philadelphia: Law Association of Philadelphia, 1916), 192–194; "John Pickering," in Eleanore Bushnell, *Crimes, Follies, and Misfortunes: The Federal Impeachment Trials* (Urbana: University of Illinois Press, 1992), 43–55; "John Pickering: Loose Morals and Intemperate Habits," in George C. Kohn, *Encyclopedia of American Scandal: From ABSCAM to the Zenger Case* (New York: Facts on File, 1989), 266–267; "Judicial Impeachment: District Judge John Pickering," in Emily Field Van Tassel and Paul Finkelman, *Impeachable Offenses: A Documentary History from 1787 to the Present* (Washington, DC: Congressional Quarterly, Inc., 1999), 91–100; Robinson, William A., "Pickering, John," in Allen Johnson and Dumas Malone, et al., eds., *Dictionary of American Biography,* 10 vols and supplements (New York: Charles Scribner's Sons, 1930–1995), VI:563–564; Turner, Lynn W., "The Impeachment of John Pickering," *American Historical Review*, 54:3 (April 1949), 485–507.

Poindexter, George (1779–1853)

See Swartwout-Hoyt Scandal

Poindexter Commission

See Swartwout-Hoyt Scandal

Political Cartoons and Corruption

It may be that the medium used most effectively to expose political corruption, and with more biting

THE HALL OF HONESTY

H. G. DIOGENES HAS FOUND THE HONEST MAN.

H. G. D. "Whoever says you ain't is 'a vulgar braggart and liar, chattering slander with as little sense of responsibility as a magpie.'"

From its birth, the cartoon has been used to disclose political corruption. This 1871 political cartoon by Thomas Nast lampoons Horace Greeley's opinion of O.K. Hall and the corrupt administration in New York City led by Boss Tweed and the Tammany Society. (Corbis)

satire than either film or the printed word, is the political cartoon.

From early times, the cartoon was used to bring to light the stories of political corruption. The medium got its start in the pages of English journals, such as *Punch, Puck,* and *Judge,* in the early to mid-eighteenth century. The cartoons that appeared in the pages of these magazines exposed not just political corruption in the hierarchy of power in Great Britain but social problems as well. In the United States, these cartoons did play a role in the early formation of American political thought, but the few that did show corruption were unimportant.

This changed in the 1870s, when Thomas Nast, a cartoonist for *Harper's Weekly,* illustrated the "corruption" of Horace Greeley, the Republican-turned-Independent who ran for president in 1872 and whose death is widely believed to have come from the lambasting he took during the campaign, most notable from Nast and his depiction of Greeley. Nast later went after "Boss" William Magear Tweed, head of the Tammany machine in New York City, whose theft of city funds is infamous. Nast used the pages of *Harper's* to publish his portrayal of Tweed as a greedy moneybags—in one famous cartoon, he used a bag with a dollar sign symbol where Tweed's face should have been. Ironically, after Tweed escaped from prison and headed for Europe, he was recognized by someone who had seen one of Nast's cartoons. By the end of the century, Frederick Opper and Homer Davenport were penciling political cartoons for William Randolph Hearst's *New York Evening Journal.*

In the twentieth century, the role of political cartoons waned, and while they are still in use—and are the bane of all politicians, usually ones of national influence—they do not have the power that they did before the advent of radio and television.

References: Croker, Richard, *Political Cartoons, Gathered by Their Target, Richard Croker* (New York: W.P. Mitchell & Sons, 1902?); Hess, Stephen, and Sandy Northrop, *Drawn and Quartered: The History of American Political Cartoons* (Montgomery, AL: Elliott & Clark, Publishers, 1996); West, Richard Samuel, *The Political Cartoons of Joseph Keppler* (Champaign: University of Illinois Press, 1988).

Political Corruption as Portrayed in Films and on Television

Hollywood's zest to use film to portray the citizen or reporter who discovers political corruption in high places and sets out to expose it at any cost has resulted in a number of fine motion pictures since the beginning of the art at the end of the nineteenth century.

The first film to use this motif as its main plot was *The Finger of Justice* (Paul Smith Pictures, 1918). Political boss William Randall (Henry A. Barrows) allows political corruption to flourish in his city to advance his own power. Two citizens, Noel Delaney (Crane Wilbur) and his friend Yvonne (Jane O'Rourke) set out to expose the corruption. The 1919 drama of corruption in the big city, *Beating the Odds,* was based on Irving Ross Allen's 1918 novel *The Money-Maker: The Romance of a Ruthless Man.* In 1915, impeached New York Governor William Sulzer played himself in the drama *The Governor's Boss.* In *Thanks a Million* (1935), Eric Land (Dick Powell) is recruited by a political machine to run for governor and during his campaign exposes the corruption behind the machine.

In 1939 perhaps the greatest film dealing with the issue of American political corruption was released. In *Mr. Smith Goes to Washington,* Jimmy Stewart plays Smith, a politically naive and idealistic man who is elected to the U.S. Senate as a toady to special interests in his state. Yet when Smith arrives in Washington, he sees why he has been sent to the Senate—to help a powerful interest get a dam constructed. He decides to oppose the special interest and in doing so earns the enmity of the powers that elected him, as well as that of other senators. In order to stop the bill he opposes from coming to the floor, Smith launches into a filibuster, lasting more than twenty-four hours. Distraught when the other senators demand he end the tirade, Smith refuses, speaking until he collapses from exhaustion. As he falls, he is covered with the telegrams of people demanding he end the fruitless campaign. Suddenly, the sight of Smith barraged by the telegrams cascading down on his unconscious form forces the senator who had so opposed him to confess his corruption and demands that he, instead of Smith, be expelled from the Senate. Claude Rains plays the corrupt senator, and Jean Arthur plays Smith's loyal secretary. The film did not go down well in Washington: Senate Majority Leader Alben Barkley (D-KY) called it "silly and stupid," and producer Frank Capra later admitted that several senators had tried to purchase the film and have it destroyed before its release.

Orson Welles's masterpiece *Citizen Kane* is the story of a fictional political leader—Charles Foster Kane—who sets out to become the governor of New York, but instead becomes one of the most powerful newspaper magnates in America. Modeled after real-life newspaper owner William Randolph Hearst, the film investigates the life of Kane, who, like Hearst, was accused of political corruption to further both his political and his newspaper's ends. Welles's 1941 work did not focus on corruption, however.

In *Key Largo* (1948), John Rocco (played by Edward G. Robinson says, "I take a nobody, see. Teach them what to say, get his name in the papers. Yes, pay for his campaign expenses. Dish out a lot of groceries and coal, get my boys to bring the voters out, and then count the votes over and over again until they add it up right and he was elected." In *All the King's Men* (1949), Broderick Crawford portrays Willie Stark, who rises from the backwater to the governor's mansion, only to drown in the stench of corruption. The movie won the Best Picture Oscar for 1949, as well as garnering the Best Actor Oscar for Broderick and the Best Supporting Actress Oscar for Mercedes McCambridge. The 1949 film was based on Robert Penn Warren's 1946 Pulitzer Prize-winning work of the same name, which was loosely based on the life of Huey Long (nicknamed "The Kingfish"), who held sway over Louisiana politics because of political corruption. Stark is seen at a picnic telling the people that he is being manipulated to get their vote— and then gets the confidence of the people Stark calls "the hick vote."

The film *On the Waterfront* (1954) is the dramatic award-winning film directed by Elia Kazan that brings to the forefront problems with union corruption, political corruption, and racketeering. Set on the gritty New York docks, it was based on reporter Malcolm Johnson's 1951 twenty-four-part series in the *New York Sun* entitled "Crime on the Waterfront." Marlon Brando plays Terry Malloy, a dockworker; James Westerfield plays Big Mac, the pier boss. In *The Boss* (1956), John Payne plays Matt Brady, a crime boss who rises to the top by paying off politicians. The film did not center squarely on the theme of political corruption, but it was an important part of the backdrop.

On television from 1950 to 1956 was *Big Town*, in which a reporter, Steve Wilson (played by actor Patrick McVey), is the editor of the *Illustrated Press,* a crusading newspaper exposing political corruption in a big city and pushing for reforms in campaigns. The 1950 film *The Reformer and the Redhead* (MGM) has actress June Allyson exposing political corruption with the help of a young attorney (Dick Powell). In *Sharkey's Machine,* a 1981 film starring Burt Reynolds as a brash vice cop, a scheme involving a candidate for governor of Georgia, who has been bought off by a criminal syndicate, is exposed.

Recent films on political corruption have been few and far between. In the last thirty years, only three stand out: *Chinatown* (1974), *Suspect* (1987), and *City Hall* (1996). In *Chinatown,* film noir is used to ably demonstrate the corruption of politicians helping a billionaire (John Huston) buy up land at cheap prices. The film won Best Picture, Best Actor (Jack Nicholson), Best Actress (Faye Dunaway), and Best Director (Roman Polanski) Academy Awards, among many others. In *Suspect,* a federal judge (John Mahoney), in line for a promotion to a higher court seat, murders a clerk who was to expose corruption in his past, after which the judge tries to frame an innocent man for the crime. His exposure, by a juror (Dennis Quaid) in the trial of the innocent man and the innocent man's attorney (Cher), leads to his attempt at another murder. *City Hall* has an up-and-coming mayor of New York City (Al Pacino), potentially destined for the White House, involved in a circle of political corruption. Danny Aiello stars as Frank Anselmo, the head of the Brooklyn political machine who is also mired in the corruption and takes his own life rather than go to prison. Aiello's character is loosely based on the case of Donald Manes, the Queens Borough president who, caught in a ring of corruption, took his own life in 1986. In 1976 *All the President's Men,* based on the bestselling work by *Washington Post* reporters Bob Woodward and Carl Bernstein, portrayed the early years of the Watergate scandal that consumed the administration of President Richard Nixon. Oliver Stone's 1995 film *Nixon* highlights the rise and fall of the thirty-seventh president, brought down by the Watergate scandal. The 1997 film *Primary Colors,* starring John Travolta as a Southern governor running for president who is mired in scandal, closely mirrors the life and 1992 campaign of Bill Clinton, the Arkansas governor who ran for president and won.

References: Gianos, Phillip L., *Politics and Politicians in American Film* (Westport, CT: Praeger, 1999);

Omrcanin, Margaret Stewart, *The Novel and Political Insurgency* (Philadelphia: Dorrance & Company, 1973).

Political Corruption as Portrayed in Literature

The portrayal of political corruption in fictional literature in the United States has been extensive, although nonfiction historical and polemical works have been perhaps more influential.

In *Democracy* (1870), Henry Adams's fictitious character Baron Jacobi rails against political corruption in Washington, D.C.:

> You Americans believe yourselves to be exempted from the operation of general laws. You care not for experience. I have lived seventy-five years, and all that time in the midst of corruption. I am corrupt myself, only I do have the courage to proclaim it, and you others have it not. Rome, Paris, Vienna, Petersburg, London, all are corrupt; only Washington is pure! Well, I declare to you that in all my experiences I have found no society which has had elements of corruption like the United States. The children in the street are corrupt, and know how to cheat me. The citizens are all corrupt, and also the towns and the counties and the States' legislatures and the judges. Everywhere men betray trusts both public and private, steal money, run away with public funds. Only in the Senate men take no money. And you gentlemen in the Senate very well declare that your great United States, which is the head of the civilized world, can never learn anything from the example of corrupt Europe. You are right—quite right! The great United States needs not an example. I do much regret that I have not yet one hundred years to live. If I could then come back to this city, I should find myself very content—much more than now. I am always content where there is much corruption, and ma parole d'honneur!" broke out the old man with fire and gesture, "The United States will then be more corrupt than Rome under Caligula; more corrupt than the Church under Leo X; more corrupt than France under the Regent!

In 1889 the Reverend J. McDowell Leavitt, in his *Capital and Labor in Pictures of Fiction. Being the 'Uncle Tom's Cabin of the Great Labor Problem. An Exciting Story Illustrating by Powerfully Drawn Fiction the Great Battle for Bread*, explained that political corruption and social injustice were plaguing the United States and that the Bible was the only solution. American writer Booth Tarkington's first novel, *The Gentleman from Indiana* (1899), was a fictional expose of political corruption in a small American town.

The first decade of the twentieth century saw a major increase in the number of exposes printed on social ills and political corruption. Stories on alleged abuses by the railroads, monopolies, and trusts began to appear in the pages of such journals as *Collier's*, *McClure's Magazine*, and *Everybody's Magazine*. In 1906, Socialist writer Upton Sinclair used fiction to expose abuses in the meatpacking industry in his famed *The Jungle*.

In his slam against the people who ended slavery and fought the Ku Klux Klan in the Reconstruction period following the American Civil War, writer Thomas Dixon Jr. used the impeached North Carolina Governor William Woods Holden as the model for his character Governor Amos Hogg in his 1902 work *The Leopard's Spots: A Romance of the White Man's Burden, 1865–1900*. Dixon wrote:

> This man, Amos Hogg, was a writer of brilliant and forceful style. Before the war, a virulent Secessionist leader, he had justified and upheld slavery, and had written a volume of poems dedicated to John C. Calhoun. He had led the movement for Secession in the Convention that passed the ordinance. But when he saw his ship was sinking, he turned his back upon the "errors" of the past, professed the most loyal Union sentiments, wormed himself into the confidence of the Federal Government, and actually succeeded in securing the position of Provisional Governor of the state! He loudly professed his loyalty, and with fury and malice demanded that Vance, the great war Governor, his predecessor, who, as a Union man had opposed Secession, should now be hanged, and with him his own former associates in the Secession Convention, whom he had misled with his brilliant pen.

Journalist Lincoln Steffens wrote of political corruption in the big cities in *The Shame of the Cities* (1904). In 1907, John T. McCutcheon "introduced" the world to the corrupt Representative E. Joseph Pumphrey in *Congressman Pumphrey, The People's Friend* (Indianapolis, IN: Bobbs-Merrill, 1907) in a brilliant satire on political corruption in Washington. The movement seemed to be on the verge of cracking the scourge of national political corruption. David Graham Phillips, a writer for *Cosmopolitan* magazine, wrote a series of articles in that journal in 1906, calling attention to the Democratic and Republican parties and accusing both of taking money from large corporations and then legislating the corporate agenda in the Senate. Calling his article "Treason in the Senate," Phillips wrote in March 1906:

> Treason is a strong word, but not too strong, rather too weak, to characterize the situation in which the Senate is the eager, resourceful, indefatigable agent of interests as hostile to the American people as any invading army could be, and vastly more dangerous: interests that manipulate the prosperity produced by all, so that it heaps up riches for the few; interests whose growth and power can only mean the degradation of the people, of the educated into sycophants, of the masses toward serfdom.
>
> The Senators are not elected by the people; they are elected by the interests. A servant obeys him who can punish and dismiss. Except in extreme and rare and negligible instances can the people either elect or dismiss a senator? The senator, in the dilemma which the careless ignorance of the people thrusts upon him, chooses to be comfortable, placed and honoured, and a traitor to oath and people rather than to be true to his oath and poor and ejected into private life.

Phillips accused Senator Nelson W. Aldrich (R-RI) of being the "right arm" of corporate interests and Senator Albert Pue Gorman (D-MD) of being "the left arm." This attack on the political allies of the president brought about a response which was unprepared for by the crusading journalists. President Theodore Roosevelt, despite being a reformer, called these writers, including Ida Tarbell, David Graham Phillips, Steffens, and Ray Stannard Baker, "muckrakers," after the character in John Bunyan's *The Pilgrim's Progress; From This World to That Which Is to Come,* who was, as Bunyan wrote, "the man who could look no way but downward with the muck-rake in his hands; who would neither look up nor regard the crown he was offered, but continued to rake to himself the filth on the floor." Despite this slam, Phillips's articles led to the passage of the Seventeenth Amendment to the Constitution, which provided for direct election of U.S. senators by the people, instead of by

state legislatures (many of which had been bought over the years).

One of the better works of the middle twentieth century was Edwin Greene O'Connor's *The Last Hurrah* (1956), which, while not portraying political corruption, did exemplify the power of machine politics in the big city. Loosely based on the life of Boston politico James Curley, it is the story of Frank Skeffington, the mayor of Boston, who is in the fight of his life in his final campaign for mayor. The work was made into a motion picture in 1958, starring Spencer Tracy as Skeffington.

References: Omrcanin, Margaret Stewart, *The Novel and Political Insurgency* (Philadelphia: Dorrance & Company, 1973); Phillips, David Graham, "The Treason of the Senate," *Cosmopolitan,* XL: 5 (March 1906), 487–502.

Pomeroy, Samuel Clarke (1816–1891)

United States senator (1867–1873) from Kansas, accused, but never convicted, of bribing Kansas state legislators to get himself elected to the Senate. Pomeroy was born in Southampton, Massachusetts, on 3 January 1816, the son of Samuel and Dorcas (née Burt) Pomeroy and a descendent of Eltweed Pomeroy, an immigrant from England to the American colonies in 1630. Samuel Pomeroy apparently attended local schools before he went to Amherst College, leaving in 1838 without a degree. He left Amherst and moved to New York, where he taught school. Four years later, however, he returned to Southampton, where for several years he held various local offices, including serving as a member of the state house of representatives from 1852 to 1853.

While in Massachusetts, Pomeroy served as an organizer and financial agent for the New England Emigrant Aid Company, which assisted people moving into the American West, then mostly unpopulated territory. In 1854 Pomeroy became one of these people himself, pulling up stakes and moving to Kansas. He settled in the town of Lawrence, but later moved to Atchison. In 1858 the people of Atchison elected Pomeroy mayor, an office held until 1859. It was during this period that Kansas became enveloped in a battle between the forces of slavery and abolition, leading to what has been termed by historians "Bloody Kansas." In an attempt to get Kansas entered into the Union as a slave state, slaveowners moved into Kansas in large numbers and established a constitution at the town of Lecompton. Trying to block this move, abolitionists met in convention at Lawrence in 1859 and asked the U.S. Congress not to accept the Lecompton constitution. Congress acceded to these wishes, plunging Kansas into a bloody civil war. When famine struck Kansas in 1860, Pomeroy served on a committee that distributed relief to the beleaguered victims.

On 29 January 1861, Kansas was admitted to the Union as a free state, and the new entity was entitled to send two senators to the United States Senate. Pomeroy, because of his work, was the first of these two officers elected and was sworn in on 4 April 1861. During his time in the Senate, he served as chairman of the Committee on Public Lands. A Republican, he joined the ranks of the Radicals, who opposed any leniency towards the rebellious Southern states that had started the Civil War by seceding to form the Confederate States of America. In 1864 Pomeroy made headlines when he circulated a broadside, known as the "Pomeroy Circular," which claimed that President Lincoln had no chance of being reelected and that the Republican Party should back Secretary of the Treasury Salmon P. Chase for president. When Lincoln was nominated anyway, Pomeroy spoke on the Senate floor that the old political parties were dead and that a new political entity was needed to oppose slavery at all costs and to fight the war until its end. With Lincoln's reelection, and the war slowly turning in favor of the Union by the end of 1864, Pomeroy's call became less and less important.

For his entire first term in the Senate, there were whispers that Pomeroy had purchased his Senate seat with money paid to Kansas legislators; these whispers became outright accusations when Pomeroy was reelected in 1867. The Kansas state legislature convened a committee that investigated allegations of vote buying and unanimously declared that Pomeroy was indeed guilty of the offense. Nonetheless, he was allowed to remain in the Senate. However, in 1872 the Senate began an investigation, a few months before Pomeroy's term ended (he did not run for reelection in 1873). A select committee, headed by Senator Frederick T. Frelinghuysen of New Jersey, was established to investigate the allegations. On 3 March 1873, ironi-

cally Pomeroy's last day in office, the committee's report was released: the committee in essence exonerated Pomeroy and released him from further scrutiny. The report explains, "The committee are unanimously of the opinion that even if the foregoing transactions were made out as cases of bribery, there is no sufficient evidence to connect Senator Pomeroy with any of them." However, Senator Allen Granberry Thurman (D-OH) dissented to a degree, writing a minority report of one page, in which he said:

I cannot agree with the report of the majority of the committee. I think that the testimony proves a corrupt offer by Mr. Pomeroy to [state] Senator Simpson, of the Kansas legislature, to obtain the vote of the latter.

I also believe that the testimony convicts Mr. Pomeroy of having attempted to bribe [state] Senator York, of that legislature, to vote for him; that Pomeroy delivered to York $7,000 is not denied. The only material issue between them is, for what purpose was the money delivered? York says that it was a bribe for his vote. Pomeroy says that it was handed to York to carry it to one [Mr.] Page, whom Pomeroy had promised to assist in starting a national bank. In my judgment, the statements of Mr. Pomeroy on this subject are contradictory, are inconsistent with Page's statements; are so opposed to the usual circumstances attending a business transaction, and are so improbable, especially in view of the circumstances attending the senatorial election, that reliance cannot be placed upon them. Perceiving no good to result from an elaborate statement of the testimony, and reasons that bring me to these conclusions, I refrain from making such statement. Were there time for the Senate to consider the subject fully, I should feel it my duty to give at large the reasons for my convictions. But this is the last day of the session and Mr. Pomeroy's senatorial term. Before the reports can be printed, much less considered, the session will be at an end. I therefore say no more than to repeat the conclusions to which my mind has, reluctantly and painfully, been brought.

Pomeroy, out of office, remained in Washington, D.C. In 1880 he was nominated for vice president by the American Masonic Party, and he ran a nearly nonexistent campaign with John Wolcott Phelps of Vermont for president. The ticket got few votes, and the party went out of existence soon after the election. In 1884 Pomeroy was nominated for president by the American Prohibition Party, but, once again, the ticket got little attention and even fewer votes. After this second attempt at a political comeback, Pomeroy retired to Massachusetts.

Pomeroy died in Whitinsville, Massachusetts, on 27 August 1891, at the age of seventy-five, and was interred in the Forest Hills Cemetery in Boston, Massachusetts.

See also Caldwell, Alexander

References: Butler, Anne M., and Wendy Wolff, *United States Senate Election, Expulsion and Censure Cases, 1793–1990* (Washington, DC: Government Printing Office, 1995), 174–177; "Götterdämmerung in Topeka: The Downfall of Senator Pomeroy," *Kansas Historical Quarterly,* XVIII:3 (Autumn 1950), 243–278; "How Pom Tried to Buy In. And Paid His Money Like a Christian Statesman," *Sun* (New York), 18 February 1873, 1; "S. C. Pomeroy and Alexander Caldwell," in George S. Taft, *Compilation of Senate Election Cases from 1789 to 1885* (Washington, DC: Government Printing Office, 1885), 368–385; Stephenson, Wendell H., "Pomeroy, Samuel Clarke," in Allen Johnson and Dumas Malone, et al., eds., *Dictionary of American Biography,* 10 vols. and supplements (New York: Charles Scribner's Sons, 1930–1995), VIII:55–56; U.S. Senate, "Report [of] the Committee Appointed to investigate the Charges of Bribery in the Recent Senatorial Election of Kansas, Preferred against Senator Pomeroy by A. M. York and B. F. Simpson," Senate Report No. 523, 42nd Congress, 3rd Session (1873) (Thurman's statement appears on the final, unpaginated page of the report), 266.

Powell, Adam Clayton, Jr. (1908–1972)

United States representative from New York (1945–1967, 1970–1971), the subject of a famed Supreme Court decision that forced the U.S. House of Representatives to seat him, despite that body having voted to strip him of his seat. Powell was born in New Haven, Connecticut, on 29 November 1908, the son of the famed black minister Adam Clayton Powell Sr. When the junior Powell was only six months old, his family moved to New York City, where the senior Powell became the head of the Abyssinian Baptist Church and turned it into one of the most influential black churches in the nation. The junior Powell attended the public schools of New York City. He entered Colgate University in Hamilton, New York, and graduated with a bachelor's degree in 1930. He then attended Columbia University in New York City, graduating from that institution in 1932 with a master's degree in religious education. Powell completed his education by receiving a theological degree from Shaw University in Raleigh, North Carolina, in 1934. Taking time off, he headed for Europe, North Africa, and Asia Minor for four months. Having been ordained in 1931, he returned to the United States and picked up his duties as a minister.

During the Depression, Powell was one of a growing number of voices in the black community calling for civil rights. Powell served as a member of the New York City Council in 1941, before he left to become the editor and publisher of the *People's Voice,* a weekly newspaper for the African American community from 1941 to 1945. In 1942 he was named a member of the New York State Office of Price Administration, a New Deal program, and served until 1944. He also served as part of the Manhattan Civil Defense until 1945. In 1944 Powell was elected to a seat in the U.S. House of Representatives, representing the Twenty-second New York District, which later became the Eighteenth District. Powell served from 3 January 1945 until 1 March 1967. He sat as a member of the committees on Indian Affairs, Invalid Pensions, Labor, and, when the latter committee was reorganized, on the Education and Labor Committee. Powell was best known during his time in Washington for challenging long-held policies in which even black congressmen ate in separate dining facilities in the Capitol. He was a leading author of antipoll tax and antilynching legislation that he introduced in every Congress, only to see these bills go down to defeat. In 1961 he became the chairman of the House Committee on Education and Labor and oversaw a period of legislative initiatives that included school lunches funded by the government, vocational training, minimum wage increases, student loans, and vocational schooling.

In 1965 and 1966 Powell became the target of a series of investigations into allegations that he misused travel funds and his authority to hire clerks and pay them with public funds. These allegations were based on a series of events that went back to the early 1950s. At that time, several Powell aides were convicted of income tax evasion, and there were reports that Powell had received some of their income via kickbacks. Powell was indicted for tax evasion in 1958, but a hung jury resulted and the Department of Justice did not retry him.

In 1960 Powell accused a constituent of transporting payoffs to the police. This constituent sued Powell in New York for libel and won a large judgment against the congressman, who refused to honor the court's finding. Powell spent an incredible amount of time in the early 1960s trying to avoid paying the fine, before he agreed to settle.

But it was the allegation that Powell had placed his wife on the Education and Labor Committee's payroll and took his wife on vacations to Europe and the Bahamas on committee funds that led to the investigation against him. A special subcommittee of the Committee on House Administration investigated these allegations and found them to have merit. Because there was no House Ethics Committee at that time, the subcommittee submitted their findings to the House Democratic Caucus. On 9 January 1967, the caucus stripped Powell of his chairmanship of the Education and Labor Committee. The full House then voted to refuse Powell his seat until the Judiciary Committee could complete a fuller investigation. On 28 February 1967, the Judiciary Committee recommended that Powell be censured, fined, and deprived of seniority in the House. However, on 1 March, the full House voted 307 to 116 to exclude Powell completely from the House, despite his having won re-election in November 1966.

A special election to fill the seat was ordered on 11 April 1967. Remarkably, Powell was elected to the vacancy, but once again the House voted to refuse him his seat. Powell stood for reelection in November 1968, but despite once again winning this seat, he was refused entry when the Ninety-first Congress assembled in January 1969. Powell sued to the U.S. Supreme Court to have himself reinstated to the House and, on 16 June 1969, the Supreme Court voted eight to one that Powell's exclusion was illegal. (See *Powell v. McCormack* for the issues before the Court in the case.) Because of the court action, Powell was allowed to take his seat in the Ninety-first Congress, but without the twenty-two years of seniority he had previously accrued. Powell by this time was spent from his years of litigation, and when he stood for reelection in 1970, Democrats chose a newcomer, Charles Rangel. Powell tried to get on the ballot as an Independent, but failed.

Finished with politics, Powell retired to become a minister at his father's church, the Abyssinian Baptist Church in New York. On 4 April 1972, while in Miami, Florida, Powell suffered a heart attack and died at the age of sixty-three. His remains were cremated and the ashes scattered over South Bimini in the Bahamas.

Powell's case ultimately led to a major step in ethics investigations: on 13 April 1967, the House of Representatives established the Committee of Standards and Ethics in response to the Powell case and named Representative Melvin Price (D-IL) its chairman. Today all ethics investigations in the House are referred to that committee.

See also *Powell v. McCormack*
References: "Adam Clayton Powell, Jr.: Fallen Congressman," in George C. Kohn, *Encyclopedia of American Scandal: From ABSCAM to the Zenger Case* (New York: Facts on File, 1989), 272–273; *Biographical Directory of the American Congress, 1774–1996* (Alexandria, VA: CQ Staff Directories, Inc., 1996), 1682–1683; Hamilton, Charles V., *Adam Clayton Powell, Jr.: The Political Biography of An American Dilemma* (New York: Atheneum, 1991); Powell, Adam Clayton, *Adam by Adam* (New York: The Dial Press, 1971).

Powell v. McCormack, 395 U.S. 486 (1969)

Supreme Court decision that Congress could not formally remove a sitting member for any cause without actually expelling that person. The case dealt with whether Congress could institute "requirements" for a member to take his or her seat other than those specified in the Constitution—age, citizenship, and residence. Adam Clayton Powell Jr. was elected to the U.S. House of Representatives in 1944 from New York's Twenty-second Congressional District, later reorganized as the Eighteenth District. A leading spokesman for civil rights in that body, he rose to become chairman of the Committee on Education and Labor in 1961, even though in 1958 he had been acquitted of tax evasion. However, during the Eighty-ninth Congress (1965–1967), Powell was accused of financial irregularities in the management of the committee. A Special Subcommittee of the Committee on House Administration commenced an investigation, which showed that Powell and some of his staff had submitted false statements as to travel expenses and that Powell had illegally paid his wife a salary when she did not work. No action was taken during the Eighty-ninth Congress, and Powell was re-elected in 1966. However, at the start of the Nineti-eth Congress in January 1967, the Democratic Cau-cus, meeting in session, decided to strip Powell of his chairmanship, and pursuant to a House resolu-tion, he was not allowed to take his seat. On 1 March 1967, the report of the subcommittee was officially released, and a resolution was offered that Powell be excluded from the House. On that date, the House voted 307 to 116 to exclude Powell and directed the Speaker, John McCormack of Massachusetts, to no-tify the governor of New York that the seat which Powell had held was vacant.

At this point, Powell and thirteen supporters in his district sued in federal district court, claiming that the House could exclude him only if he failed to meet those requirements specified in the Con-stitution—namely age, citizenship, or residence. The district court dismissed the suit "for want of jurisdiction," and the U.S. Court of Appeals for the District of Columbia Circuit upheld the dismissal. The U.S. Supreme Court granted certiorari and heard arguments in the case on 21 April 1969.

Less than two months later, on 16 June 1969, the Court held eight to one that Powell could not be excluded from Congress except for failure to meet the qualifications for election as prescribed in the Constitution. Chief Justice Earl Warren de-livered the opinion of the Court, holding that while the Court could not decide on cases of expulsion, Powell could not be "excluded" on the basis of the allegations made against him. The chief justice ex-plained:

> Analysis of the "textual commitment" under Article I, section 5, has demonstrated that in judging the qualifications of its members Congress is limited to the standing qualifications prescribed in the Con-stitution. Respondents concede that Powell met these. Thus, there is no need to remand this case to determine whether he was entitled to be seated in the 90th Congress. Therefore, we hold that, since Adam Clayton Powell, Jr., was duly elected by the voters of the 18th Congressional District of New York and was not ineligible to serve under any pro-vision of the Constitution, the House was without power to exclude him from its membership.

Adam Clayton Powell had been reelected to his seat in 1968, but at that time Congress refused to seat him, and he sat out the entire term. After the Court reversed his exclusion, he returned to the House, albeit without his seniority or chairman-ship. In June 1970 he was defeated in the Demo-cratic primary and failed to get on the ballot as an Independent. He retired to become the minister of the Abyssinian Baptist Church in New York City, where his father had preached. Clayton died in Miami on 4 April 1972.

See also Powell, Adam Clayton, Jr.
References: Dionisopoulos, P. Allan, *Rebellion, Racism and Representation: The Adam Clayton Powell Case and Its Antecedents* (DeKalb: Northern Illinois University Press, 1970); Ragsdale, Bruce A., and Joel D. Treese, *Black Americans in Congress, 1870–1989* (Washington, DC: Government Printing Office, 1990), 113–115; Weeks, Kent M., *Adam Clayton Powell and the Supreme Court* (New York: Dunellen, 1971).

Publicity Act of 1910, 36 Stat. 822

Act of Congress, enacted 25 June 1910, also called the Federal Corrupt Practices Act of 1910, which sought to revise the Tillman Act of 1907, at the same time requiring the disclosure of campaign contributions and spending.

This legislation was pushed by the National Publicity Law Association (NPLA), a reformist or-ganization set up in the wake of the allegations that President Theodore Roosevelt took massive corporate contributions in his 1904 campaign for president. The 1907 Tillman Act covered campaign contributions by banks and corporations. In 1910 Congress sought to cover reports of election con-tributions and spending not only by campaigns for the House (Senate campaigns were not re-quired until the passage of the Seventeenth Amendment, which made election of senators di-rectly by the people), but by the national parties.

Excerpts from the law read:

> *An Act providing for publicity of contributions made for the purpose of influencing elections at which Rep-resentatives in Congress are elected.*
>
> *Be it enacted,* That the term "political commit-tee" under the provisions of this Act shall include the national committees of all political parties and the national congressional campaign committees of all political parties and all committees, associa-tions, or organizations which shall in two or more States influence the result or attempt to influence the result of an election at which Representatives in Congress are to be elected.

Sec[tion] 2. That every political committee as defined in this Act shall have a chairman and a treasurer. It shall be the duty of the treasurer to keep a detailed and exact account of all money or its equivalent received by or promised to such committee or any member thereof, or by or to any person acting under its authority or in its behalf, and the name of every person, firm, association, or committee from whom received, and of all expenditures, disbursements, and promises of payment or disbursement made by the committee or any member thereof, or by any person acting under its authority or in its behalf, and to whom paid, distributed, or disbursed. No officer or member of such committee, or other person acting under its authority or in its behalf, shall receive any money or its equivalent, or expend or promise to expend any money on behalf of such committee, until after a chairman and treasurer of such committee shall have been chosen.

Sec[tion] 3. That every payment or disbursement made by a political committee exceeding ten dollars in amount be evidenced by a receipted bill stating the particulars of expense, and every such record, voucher, receipt, or account shall be preserved for fifteen months after the election to which it relates.

Sec[tion] 4. That whoever, acting under the authority or in behalf of such political committee, whether as a member thereof or otherwise, receives any contribution, payment, loan, gift, advance, deposit, or promise of money or its equivalent shall, on demand, and in any event within five days after the receipt of such contribution, payment, loan, gift, advance, deposit, or promise, render to the treasurer of such political committee a detailed account of the same, together with the name and address from whom received, and said treasurer shall forthwith enter the same in a ledger or record to be kept by him for that purpose.

Sec[tion] 5. That the treasurer of every such political committee shall, within thirty days after the election at which Representatives in Congress were chosen in two or more States, file with the Clerk of the House of Representatives at Washington, District of Columbia, an itemized, detailed statement, sworn to by said treasurer and conforming to the requirements of the following section of this Act. The statement so filed with the Clerk of the House of Representatives shall be preserved by him for fifteen months, and shall be a part of the public records of his office, and shall be open to public inspection.

In 1911, Congress desired to add amendments to the 1910 law and enacted these in a law on 19

August 1911 (37 Stat. 25). These amendments expanded the rules covering the financial disclosure of campaign spending and expenditures and set limits for campaign spending by House candidates at for $5,000 and by Senate candidates at $25,000. Disclosure was extended to primary, general election, and postelection expenditures, the first time such rules were established.

Excerpts from the amendments read:

> *An Act to amend an act entitled "An act providing for publicity of contributions made for the purpose of influencing elections at which Representatives in Congress are elected" and extending the same to candidates for nomination and election to the offices of Representative and Senator in the Congress of the United States and limiting the amount of campaign expenses.*
>
> *Be it enacted,* That sections five, six, and eight of an Act entitled "An Act providing for publicity of contributions made for the purpose of influencing elections at which Representatives in Congress are elected," . . . be amended to read as follows:
>
> Sec[tion] 5. That the treasurer of every such political committee shall, not more than fifteen days and not less than ten days next before an election at which Representatives in Congress are to be elected in two or more States, file in the office of the Clerk of the House of Representatives at Washington, District of Columbia, with said Clerk, an itemized detailed statement; and on each sixth day thereafter until such election said treasurer shall file with said Clerk a supplemental itemized detailed statement. Each of said statements shall conform to the requirements of the following section of this Act, except that the supplemental statement herein required need not contain any item of which publicity is given in a previous statement. Each of said statements shall be full and complete, and shall be signed and sworn to by said treasurer.
>
> It shall also be the duty of said treasurer to file a similar statement with said Clerk within thirty days after such election, such final statement also to be signed and sworn to by said treasurer and to conform to the requirements of the following section of this Act. The statements so filed with the Clerk of the House shall be preserved by him for fifteen months and shall be a part of the public records of his office and shall be open to public inspection.
>
> Sec[tion] 8. The word "candidate" as used in this section shall include all persons whose names are presented for nomination for Representative or Senator in the Congress of the United States at any

primary election or nominating convention, or for indorsement [*sic*] or election at any general or special election held in connection with the nomination or election of a person to fill such office, whether or not such persons are actually nominated, indorsed, or elected.

In 1921 the U.S. Supreme Court in *Newberry v. United States* held that the provisions of the 1911 act that covered primary elections were unconstitutional and struck them down. The Congress then voided this action with the passage of the Federal Corrupt Practices Act of 1925. However, in *United States v. Classic* in 1941 the Court reversed itself and held that Congress could oversee spending limits for primaries and other preelection activities.

See also Federal Corrupt Practices Act of 1925; *Newberry v. United States,* 256 U.S. 232; Tillman Act of 1907

References: "Federal Corrupt Practices Act of 1910 and 1911," in William C. Binning, Larry Esterly, and Paul A. Sracic, *Encyclopedia of American Parties, Campaigns, and Elections* (Westport, CT: Greenwood Press, 1999), 169.

R

Rebuke

See Censure

Recall

Mechanism utilized to "recall" a politician by removing him or her from office via a special election prior to the end of that politician's set term. Now a popular plan of action against politicians involved in corruption—but also against those politicians who defy the will of their constituents—recall as a measure was introduced into the American political system only in the twentieth century.

The recall, like its counterparts, the referendum and the initiative, was first used in California. The Los Angeles city charter, drafted in 1903, provided for recall. As the tax revolt of the 1970s swept the country, so did the use of the recall, mostly to check local officials who were accused of corrupt activities. Oregon was the first state to use it for state officials (1908), with California adopting it in 1911. Arizona, which became a state in 1912, made the right of recall a part of its state constitution. (When President William Howard Taft was to sign the Arizona constitution, he objected to this single provision and vetoed the measure, but Congress overrode his veto.) Kansas's recall measure was extended to appointed, as well as elected, officials. Several states, including Washington, disallow the use of recall of judges as a check to ensure an independent judiciary.

President William Howard Taft. When Taft went to sign the Arizona constitution, he objected to the recall provision and vetoed the measure, but the Congress overrode his veto. Recall is now considered a popular plan of action used against politicians involved in corruption. (Library of Congress)

Under a recall initiative, citizens opposing an incumbent politician collect signatures on a petition to force a special election. A certain number of signatures from registered voters in the targeted politician's district must be collected and verified to have such an election. Once this barrier is passed, an election date is set, and the targeted politician must mount a campaign to convince voters that he or she has been wrongfully accused and is worthy of retention in office. An opposition candidate may enter the race to challenge the subject of the recall. The election is conducted like any other regular election. If there is no candidate opposing the target of the recall, the governor may appoint a person to fill the vacant seat if the recall is successful. If it is not successful, the politician continues to serve the remainder of his or her term until the next scheduled election.

References: Munro, William Bennett, *The Initiative, Referendum and Recall* (New York: Appleton, 1912); Taft's veto in House Exec Doc 106, 62nd Congress, 1st Session (1912).

Reed, Harrison (1813–1899)

Governor of Florida (1868–1873), the subject of three separate impeachment inquiries (and acquitted in trial once) on various charges, becoming the only state executive in American history to be the subject of such numerous investigations in the same term. None of the charges of political corruption against Reed were ever proved, but the fact that he was nearly impeached three different times makes his story an interesting one and illustrative of how the procedure is used. Reed was born in Littleton, Massachusetts, on 26 August 1813, the son of Serb Harrison Reed and Rhode (née Finney) Reed. He moved with his parents to Wisconsin when he was twenty-three. In Wisconsin he served as editor of the *Milwaukee Sentinel* before leaving that paper to found the town of Neenah, located on the Fox River. He got into a land dispute with some of the partners with whom he had founded Neenah, and eventually he moved to found another town, Menasha, nearby. He then became the editor of the *Neenah-Menasha Observator* and, in 1857, became the editor of the *Wisconsin State Journal,* headquartered in Madison.

A Whig in politics, Reed was an early member of the Wisconsin Republican Party, founded on a platform of opposition to slavery. In 1861 he moved to Washington, D.C., where he became an employee in the Department of the Treasury. In 1863 President Abraham Lincoln appointed him the direct tax commissioner for the state of Florida, which was in the Confederacy and at war with the United States. He remained in Washington until the Union army occupied the city of Fernandina, Florida, after which time he set up his offices there. When the Civil War ended, Reed was named the federal postal agent for the state of Florida by President Andrew Johnson.

After the state of Florida drafted a new constitution in 1868, Reed was nominated by the Republican Party there for governor. He had been one of the party's founders in 1867, and despite his being considered a "carpetbagger" his moderate tone helped him win election over two other candidates. Taking office on 8 June 1868 as Florida's ninth governor, Reed struggled from the start to reestablish law and order and make the state government work again. The Republican Party in Florida was at the time made up of numerous factions, and some demanded that Reed move faster to bring full rights to former slaves. Before Reed had completed a year in office, an impeachment inquiry began, initiated by these disaffected Republicans. Emboldened by the impeachment attempt earlier that year against President Andrew Johnson, Reed's accusers advanced charges of various nefarious schemes and crimes against him. Historian William Watson Davis, writing in 1913 on the Reed case, gave this account:

At the beginning of the afternoon session of the [state] house, Horatio Jenkins, Jr., a member of the senate, presented charges, as "a private citizen," against Governor Reed. He accused him of "falsehood and lying" in transacting business with the legislature; of "incompetency" in appointing state and county officials; of lawlessness in declaring seats in the legislature vacant; of "embezzling" state securities; of corruption in the disposal of state offices. For these "high crimes and misdemeanors" Jenkins demanded the impeachment of the governor at the hands of the house. . . . Reed, in the meantime, was little inclined to be passive or compromising. The last two charges made by Jenkins were grave and concrete enough to put the governor in the state penitentiary if they could be substantiated with reasonably good proof. As a matter of fact no good evidence was ever forthcoming substantiating any of the charges. The state accounts up to that time did not yield proof of executive embezzlement. If Reed traded in local offices he kept the proof of such transactions profoundly to himself. If the appointees were bad or incompetent, the senate were equally guilty with the governor—it had ratified his choice[s].

Despite the charges by Jenkins, the legislature adjourned on 7 November 1868 without bringing forth articles of impeachment. However, that same day Lieutenant Governor William H. Gleason declared that he was the new governor. When he was barred from the official governor's office by Reed supporters and state officials, Gleason established his own office and began to sign documents as though he were the state's chief executive. Reed penned him a short and stern letter: "Sir: I am, under the Constitution and laws of this State, the rightful Governor thereof, and shall continue to exercise the power and authority, and discharge all of the duties belonging to the office of the executive Department until the Judicial tribunals of the State shall determine otherwise.—To the determination of the Judiciary I will, like any other good citizen, yield peaceful and immediate obedience." On 24 November, the Florida Supreme Court ruled that because Reed had never been impeached, much less convicted and removed from office, he remained governor and Gleason was a usurper. Reed then had Gleason removed from office. Reed never faced an impeachment vote and remained in office despite his difficulties with the legislature.

In 1870 the Republicans in the state legislature again moved to impeach Reed. They accused him of attempting to bribe all the members of the legislature in 1869, of illegally receiving a payoff of $7,500 from a lobbyist for a railroad and of embezzling enormous sums from state coffers. However, the state house adopted the minority report, which cleared Reed of any such charges.

Finally, in January 1872, when the legislature again convened, yet another impeachment inquiry was brought against Reed. This time, working with Democrats, Republicans were able to pass (in the middle of the night) sixteen separate articles of impeachment, charging Reed with everything from illegally issuing state bonds to embezzlement to bribing legislators to bribing a justice of the state supreme court. The state senate convened as a court of impeachment on 10 February, but when Reed asked for a quick trial the senate adjourned. Reed was caught in a trap: the state constitution specifically stated that "any officer when impeached by the assembly shall be deemed under arrest and shall be disqualified from performing any duties of his office until acquittal by the Senate." This placed Reed in official limbo. However, Reed continued to act as governor, even taking with him to his home in Jacksonville the state seal. President of the senate pro tem, Samuel T. Day, who was acting as lieutenant governor, proclaimed himself the new chief executive and proceeded to name a new cabinet and offer appointments to supporters.

Finally, on 2 May, the trial opened in the state senate. Reed's attorneys demanded that the body dismiss all charges and allow Reed to continue as governor. The vote was ten to seven in agreement, and Reed escaped being convicted for the third time. Despite this vindication, Reed was *persona non grata* to the Republicans in Florida, and when they met in convention they nominated former slaveowner and state supervisor of elections Ossian Bingley Hart, who went on to win the election that November. Reed left office exonerated of all charges leveled against him, but he was broken by the campaign that had been waged against him. He settled down on a farm along the St. Johns River in Florida. He remained a staunch Republican, speaking out on issues ranging from economic development to agriculture. From 1875 to 1878 he served as the editor of the Jacksonville journal the *Semi-Tropical*, a magazine devoted to agricultural issues related to the American South. From 1889 to 1893 he served as postmaster for Jacksonville. Reed died in Jacksonville on 25 May 1899 at the age of eighty-five.

References: Brown, Canter, Jr., "Carpetbagger Intrigues, Black Leadership, and a Southern Loyalist Triumph: Florida's Gubernatorial Election of 1872," *Florida Historical Quarterly,* 72:3 (1994), 275–301; "The Carpetbagger as Conservative: Harrison Reed," in Richard N. Current, *Three Carpetbag Governors* (Baton Rouge: Louisiana State University Press, 1967), 3–35; Davis, William Watson, *The Civil War and Reconstruction in Florida* (New York: Columbia University, 1913), 547; "Reed, Harrison," in Robert Sobel and John Raimo, eds., *Biographical Directory of the Governors of the United States, 1789–1978,* 4 vols. (Westport, CT: Meckler Books, 1978), I:256; "Reed to William H. Gleason, 7 November 1868, Governor, State Governors' Incoming Correspondence, 1857–1888," Series 577, Florida Department of State, Division of Library & Information Services, Bureau of Archives & Records Management, Tallahassee, Florida; Shofner, Jerrell H., *Nor Is It Over Yet: Florida in the Era of Reconstruction, 1863–1877* (Gainesville: The University Presses of Florida, 1974).

Reeder, Andrew Horatio (1807–1864)

Governor of Kansas Territory (1854–1855), implicated, but never charged or convicted, in illegal land speculation while in office. Born in the village of Easton, Pennsylvania, on 12 July 1807, he was the son of Absalom Reeder and Christiana (née Smith) Reeder. He was educated at a local school run by a minister and then at a private school in Lawrenceville, New Jersey. He then studied the law in the office of a New Jersey attorney and was admitted to that state's bar in 1828. He married and became a leading Democrat in Pennsylvania, although he did not run for a local or state office.

In May 1854 the Kansas Territory had been established as part of the Kansas-Nebraska Act, dividing that huge area into two smaller entities. On 29 June 1854, President Franklin Pierce, a Northerner who supported slavery, appointed Reeder as the first territorial governor of Kansas. Reeder was set to uphold the right of popular sovereignty, the idea that the people of Nebraska and Kansas would decide themselves whether these territories would allow slavery or outlaw it. Reeder arrived in Leavenworth in October 1854, called for the election of a congressional delegate to represent the territory in Washington, conducted a census, and authorized a session of the territorial legislature. Senator David Rice Atchison of Missouri, seeing an opportunity to help make Kansas a slave state, and thinking Reeder was proslavery as well, called on Missourians to head into Kansas to vote for a legislative slate to help shape the territory's politics. When these migrants helped elect John Wilkins Whitfield as the territorial delegate, Reeder threatened to declare the election null and void because outsiders decided the contest. When his life was threatened by proslavery forces, he backed down. In fact, Reeder was sympathetic to slavery—but he had warned President Pierce that outsiders invading Kansas would cause more trouble and asked for federal intervention.

What got Reeder into trouble, and led to what many historians claim was the real reason for his dismissal by Pierce, was the allegation that he spent much of his time as territorial governor purchasing land illegally. In January 1855 he and two federal judges purchased four large tracts of land illegally from the Shawnee Indians in the area. As such purchases had to be cleared through the Department of Interior, which oversaw Indian affairs,

the transaction was disallowed. The commissioner of Indian affairs, George W. Many Penny, alerted President Pierce of the matter.

Early in 1855 Reeder went to Washington to present evidence that the 1854 election had been rife with proslavery fraud. Pierce, already alerted to Reeder's land dealings, asked him for evidence of antislavery fraud. Reeder informed him that there had been none—only fraud from the proslavery side. Pierce asked about Reeder's land purchases, and, after having the deal explained, was wholly satisfied. But Pierce, bowing to his proslavery supporters, asked for Reeder's resignation anyway. Reeder refused, left Washington, and returned to Kansas. There, he faced the legislature that had been illegally elected, spending his time vetoing laws that made even the speaking against slavery a criminal offense. He called for a new legislature to meet at Pawnee City, where, ironically, he had purchased several large tracts of land and wished to establish the state capital when the territory entered the Union. Pawnee City, however, was more than 100 miles from the Missouri border, where many of the proslavery activists hid. Instead, they assembled at Shawnee Mission, on the Missouri-Kansas border. Assembling there, they called on President Pierce to remove Reeder from power. When Reeder protested the workings of this "legislature" directly to Pierce, the president removed him on 28 July 1855. In retaliation, the antislavery supporters set up a rival government in Topeka. This was the start of the struggles that gave the territory the epithet "Bloody Kansas." Territorial Secretary Daniel Woodson, a slavery sympathizer from Virginia, replaced Reeder until Wilson Shannon, a former representative in the U.S. Congress, could arrive as the new territorial governor. It is not known what happened to Reeder's land speculation, as he never returned to the area.

Reeder was made the scapegoat by Pierce for all that happened in Kansas. In his 1856 state of the Union speech, Pierce blamed Reeder outright. However, Democrats were upset that one of their own had pointed out the failings of the popular sovereignty program in Kansas. At the 1856 Democratic National Convention, they withheld enough delegates from Pierce and instead nominated former Secretary of State James Buchanan for president. Many historians blame Pierce's attacks on Reeder for his failure to be nominated for a second term, among other issues. In 1856 Reeder backed the first nominee of the new Republican Party, John C. Fremont. At the 1860 Republican National Convention, Reeder chaired the Pennsylvania delegation and received several votes for vice president. At the outbreak of the Civil War, President Abraham Lincoln offered Reeder an appointment as a brigadier general in the Union Army, but Reeder, at fifty-four, turned down the honor.

Reeder retired to his home in Easton, Pennsylvania. He died there on 5 July 1864, a week shy of his fifty-seventh birthday. He was buried in the Easton Cemetery in that town.

References: "Reeder, Andrew," in Thomas A. McMullin and David Walker, *Biographical Directory of American Territorial Governors* (Westport, CT: Meckler Publishing, 1984), 161–162; Schultz, Jeffrey D., *Presidential Scandals* (Washington, DC: CQ Press, 2000), 98–100.

Reynolds, Melvin Jay (1952–)

United States representative (1993–1994) from Illinois, convicted (1997) of fifteen counts of bank fraud, wire fraud, and lying to the Federal Electoral Commission. Reynolds was born in Mound Bayou, Mississippi, on 8 January 1952. He attended local schools before earning an associate of arts degree from Chicago City College in 1972, a bachelor's degree from the University of Illinois in 1974, and a law degree from Oxford University in 1979. A master's degree from Oxford in 1981 led to a professorial position in political science at Roosevelt University in Chicago, Illinois. For several years, Reynolds was interested in world hunger issues, and to this end he founded and served as president of the group called American Scholars against World Hunger and as executive director of the Community Economic Development Education Foundation.

In 1988 Reynolds, a Democrat, ran for a seat in the U.S. House of Representatives from Illinois, but was unsuccessful. He also lost a second race in 1990. However, in 1992 he ran a third time and was elected, entering the 103rd Congress. He was reelected in 1994, ultimately serving until his resignation on 1 October 1995.

In 1994, in the midst of his reelection effort, Reynolds was accused of sexual assault on an underage girl as well as possessing child pornography. He won reelection despite these allegations;

however, soon after winning his second term, more serious allegations arose when Reynolds was indicted by a federal grand jury on charges that he obstructed justice. In 1995 a grand jury indicted him on charges of criminal sexual assault and possessing child pornography. Forced to leave Congress, he was sentenced to five years in prison. On 8 November 1996, Reynolds was indicted with his wife by a federal grand jury in Washington on sixteen separate charges of defrauding several banks, misusing campaign funds, and making false statements to the Federal Election Commission. On 16 April 1997, Reynolds was convicted on all charges, sentenced to an additional six and one-half years in prison. His wife turned state's evidence and testified for the prosecution.

On 20 January 2001, in his last day in office, President Bill Clinton commuted Reynolds's sentence, and he was released from prison.

References: *Biographical Directory of the American Congress, 1774–1996* (Alexandria, VA: CQ Staff Directories, Inc., 1996), 1723; Ordonez, Jennifer, "Jury Finds Former Rep. Reynolds Guilty of Fraud," *Washington Post,* 17 April 1997, A3; "Reynolds Gets 6 More Years for Bank Fraud Conviction; Ex-Lawmaker Already in Prison in Sex Case," *Washington Post,* 16 July 1997, A7; Walsh, Edward, "U.S. Indicts Illinois Ex-Rep. Reynolds and Wife," *Washington Post,* 8 November 1996, A12.

Richmond, Frederick William (1923–)

United States representative from New York (1975–1982), convicted in 1982 and sent to prison for tax evasion and improper payments to a federal employee. Born in Boston, Massachusetts, on 15 November 1923, he attended local schools in Mattapan and Roxbury, Massachusetts, and earned his bachelor's degree from Boston University in 1945. From 1943 to 1945, Richmond served in the U.S. Navy. He returned at the end of World War II and entered private business. He helped to found the Walco National Corporation and in 1969 merged it with the National Casket Company. This company was later to figure in massive corrupt activities by Richmond.

In 1958, Richmond, a Democrat, served as deputy finance chairman for the Democratic National Committee. Later, from 1965 to 1975, he served as budget director for the New York State Council on the Arts. He also served as human rights commissioner (1964–1970), commissioner of the New York City Taxi and Limousine Service (1970–1972), and a New York City councilman (1973–1974). In 1974 Richmond was elected to a seat in the U.S. House of Representatives. His career was undistinguished in that body, and he did not introduce any major pieces of legislation.

For many years, whispers of business and other corruption against Richmond went unproved. However, in 1978, he was arrested for soliciting sex from a boy in Washington, D.C. Despite this, he was reelected that same year to a third term. In 1982 the Department of Justice opened an investigation into allegations of drug use and corruption inside his congressional office. The investigation uncovered proof that Richmond had ordered his staff to purchase, and then he used in his office, marijuana and cocaine; that he had paid a kickback to an employee of the U.S. Navy for a ship-repairing business established in Richmond's congressional district; and that he had accepted a pension of $100,000 from Walco, which was found to be illegal. Further, Richmond had helped an escaped convict named Earl Randolph to obtain a job in the House of Representatives mailroom. Richmond decided to make a deal with the Justice Department, pleading guilty to three minor charges regarding tax evasion, possession of marijuana, and improper payments to a federal employee. He was sentenced to a year and a day in prison, but ultimately only served nine months, being released on 6 September 1983.

References: *Biographical Directory of the American Congress, 1774–1996*, (Alexandria, VA: CQ Staff Directories, Inc., 1996), 1730; "Frederick Richmond: Crooked Congressman," in George C. Kohn, *Encyclopedia of American Scandal: From ABSCAM to the Zenger Case* (New York: Facts on File, 1989), 282–283.

Ritter, Halsted Lockwood (1868–1951)

United States judge for the Southern District of Florida (1929–1936), impeached by the U.S. House and convicted by the U.S. Senate in 1936 for accepting fees regarding cases he was adjudicating. Born in Indianapolis, Indiana, on 14 July 1868, he was the son of Eli Foster Ritter, an attorney, and Narcissa (née Lockwood) Ritter. Halsted Ritter earned his Ph.B. degree from Depauw University in Indiana in 1891; he subsequently received his law degree (1892) and master's degree (1893) from the same institution. Admitted to the Indiana bar in 1892, he entered into a practice with his father that same year in Indianapolis. However, three years later, he moved to Denver, Colorado, and began a law practice there that he continued until 1925. While in Denver, he served as the assistant prosecuting attorney for Arapahoe County in 1897 and as city attorney for Denver from 1900 to 1903.

In 1925 Ritter moved to West Palm Beach, Florida, and became a senior partner in the firm of Ritter & Rankin. He remained a partner in that firm until 1929, when President Calvin Coolidge named Ritter, a Republican, to a seat on the U.S. District Court for the Southern District of Florida, seated in Miami. Serving on this court until 1936, Ritter got himself into trouble regarding real estate deals he had overseen while an attorney. In Denver Ritter had been a corporation attorney; in Florida, he specialized in real estate. Even after he became a judge and was required to remove himself from the cases he was handling, he did not do so and solicited and accepted fees for this work. He also did not pay income taxes on the income derived from this work in 1929 after he became a judge; this income was estimated later by the U.S. House to be $12,000. Additional unreported income in 1930 equaled $5,300.

But what got Ritter into deeper trouble was his cozy relationship with his former law partner. In 1929, for instance, he conspired with his former law partner to place a hotel into receivership and then have the hearing on the receivership held before Ritter's own court. When the parties involved in the receivership objected, Ritter dismissed their motion and appointed his former law partner as a receiver. In July 1930 Ritter appointed his former law partner as the receiver for another piece of property; after a fixed sum for the receivership was set at $15,000, Ritter increased it to $75,000 and was paid $4,500 from this.

In 1936 the U.S. House investigated Ritter's dealings and issued seven articles of impeachment, all of which passed the House on 2 March 1936. On 30 March, the House amended Article 5 to make it more inclusive of several of the charges. The Senate held a trial and, on 17 April 1936, acquitted Ritter of six of the seven charges. The seventh article alleged that "[t]he reasonable and probable consequences of Ritter's actions was 'to bring his court into scandal and disrepute,' to the prejudice of the court and public confidence in the administration of justice therein. Specifically, in addition to the conduct alleged in Articles 1–6, when one of his decisions came under public criticism, Ritter agreed to recuse himself from the case if the city commissioners of Miami passed a resolution expressing confidence in his integrity. Ritter thereby bartered his judicial authority for a vote of confidence." On this charge the Senate convicted Ritter by a vote of fifty-six to twenty-eight, and Ritter was removed from office, although the Senate did not vote to disallow him from holding public office again. Ritter became one of only seven people ever convicted by the Senate for impeachable offenses, and the last until Judge Harry Claiborne in 1986.

Ritter never did hold public office again. He apparently spent the remaining years of his life in the law. He died in Laurel, Mississippi, on 15 October 1951 at the age of eighty-three.

References: "Halsted Ritter: 'Scandal and Disrepute,'" in George C. Kohn, *Encyclopedia of American Scandal: From ABSCAM to the Zenger Case* (New York: Facts on File, 1989), 283; "Ritter, Halsted Lockwood," in *The National Cyclopædia of American Biography*, 57 vols. and supplements A-N (New York: James T. White & Company, 1897–1984), XLIII:549–550.

Roach, William Nathaniel (1840–1902)

United States senator from North Dakota (1893–1899), accused of embezzlement and threatened with expulsion from the U.S. Senate, although he did in the end serve out his term. Born in Washington, D.C., the son of Edward Neale Roach and Ann (née Manning) Roach, both English emigrants, on 25 September 1840, he attended the public schools of Washington. He then attended Gonzaga College, Holy Cross College, and Georgetown College (now Georgetown University), although he never earned his degree. In 1859 he left college to work as a clerk and deputy to his father, the registrar of wills and a clerk of the orphan's court in Washington, until the elder Roach's death in 1861. William Roach served as a clerk in the Quartermaster's Department of the Department of War during the Civil War. After the conflict ended, he entered the mercantile trade, which earned him a small fortune. In 1879 he moved west to the Dakota Territory and settled in the burgeoning town of Grand Forks. There, he opened a mail route from Grand Forks to Fort Totten. Later, he purchased large tracts of land and was one of the founders of the town of Larimore.

A Democrat, Roach entered the political realm in the territory by running for a seat in the territorial house of representatives and winning, serving in 1885. When the territory broke into the states of North Dakota and South Dakota, Roach was approached to run for governor of the new northern state. He captured the gubernatorial nomination, but lost to Republican and Farmer's Alliance leader John Miller. Two years later, Roach was once again the Democratic nominee, but again he was defeated, this time by Republican banker Andrew H. Burke.

In 1892 Roach was the leading nominee of the Democrats for election to the United States Senate. In 1889, with the admission of North Dakota to the Union, Republican Lyman Rufus Casey had been elected to the U.S. Senate, but only for a four-year term, so in 1892 his term was ready to expire. The legislature, which elected senators until the passage of the Seventeenth Amendment to the U.S. Constitution, was composed of fifty-three Republicans, twenty-three Democrats, and seventeen Independents, so it appeared that Senator Casey would easily be reelected. However, Casey was considered a "machine Republican," and many of the Republicans in the legislature refused to vote for him. This group, allied with populists sitting in the Independent camp and the Democrats, helped elect Roach after fifty-three separate votes, making Roach the first Democrat in Congress from North Dakota.

Almost as soon as Roach journeyed east to take his seat, allegations began swirling around him that nearly led to his expulsion from the Senate. A charge of embezzlement from 1880 was resurrected and brought forward against Roach, and the Senate decided to inquire. Asher Crosby Hinds, editor of the *Rules, Manual, and Digest of the House of Representatives* in 1899, reported in his *Precedents:*

On the 28th day of March, 1893, Mr. Hoar submitted a resolution providing for an investigation of certain allegations charging Mr. Roach with the offense of criminal embezzlement. On the 10th day of April,

1893 a substitute for this resolution was introduced by Mr. Hoar, and on the 14th day of April, 1893, a substitute for the resolutions then pending in said matter was introduced by Mr. Gorman. The resolution and the substitutes were the subject of debate in the Senate, but no action was had or taken thereon. It appears from the debates that the case presented the question as to the right of the Senate to take cognizance of an accusation against a Senator of an offense committed before his election to the Senate.

After extensive deliberations and discussion, the Senate agreed that it lacked jurisdiction to hold a member accountable for an action committed before the member's election to the Senate.

Roach completed his single six-year term without any further difficulties. He served as the chairman of the Select Committee to Investigate Trespasses upon Indian Lands and was a member of the Committees on Agriculture and Forestry, Indian Affairs, Irrigation, and the Five Civilized Tribes of Indians. He attempted to run for reelection in 1898, but by then the coalition that had served to elect him had faded, and the Republicans, now in complete control of the legislature, elected Porter J. McCumber to the seat.

Roach retired to Washington, D.C., after his election loss. He was in New York City on business on 7 September 1902 when he suddenly died, two weeks shy of his sixty-second birthday. His body was returned to Washington and buried in the Congressional Cemetery in that city.

References: "Roach, William Nathaniel," in *Biographical Directory of the United States Congress, 1774–1989: The Continental Congress, September 5, 1774, to October 21, 1788, and the Congress of the United States, from the First through the One Hundredth Congresses, March 4, 1789, to January 3, 1989, Inclusive* (Washington, DC: Government Printing Office, 1989), 1737; "Roach, William Nathaniel," in *The National Cyclopædia of American Biography,* 57 vols. and supplements A-N (New York: James T. White & Company, 1897–1984), V:263; Schlup, Leonard C., "William N. Roach: North Dakota Isolationist and Gilded Age Senator," *North Dakota History,* 57 (Fall 1990), 2–11.

Roberts, Owen Josephus (1875–1955)

Attorney who served as special counsel in the Teapot Dome investigation and later as an associate justice on the United States Supreme Court. He was born in Germantown, Pennsylvania, on 2 May 1875. He attended local schools, including the prestigious Germantown Academy, before graduating at the top of his class from the University of Pennsylvania in 1895. He then earned a law degree from the University of Pennsylvania law school. He opened a private law practice in Philadelphia, at which he worked from 1898 until 1903. He served as a professor of law at the University of Pennsylvania School of Law from 1898 to 1919 and served as first district attorney for the city of Philadelphia from 1906 to 1930. Roberts became one of Philadelphia's most respected attorneys, with his practice heavily involved in corporate law. In 1912 he formed a law partnership with two local attorneys, William W. Montgomery Jr. and Charles L. McKeehan, who later served on the U.S. District Court for the Eastern District of Pennsylvania. In 1918 Roberts was named by Attorney General A. Mitchell Palmer as his special assistant to prosecute cases involving the 1917 Espionage Act in Pennsylvania. Roberts obtained several convictions.

In 1923 after Congress began to investigate the so-called Teapot Dome scandal, in which Secretary of the Interior Albert B. Fall had taken bribes from oil men to lease government reserves in California and Wyoming to their companies, Congress became suspicious that Attorney General Harry M. Daugherty was dragging his feet in the department's own inquiry. Congress began to draft a law to name a special prosecutor on Teapot Dome. However, before Congress could act, President Calvin Coolidge, who had become president upon President Warren G. Harding's death in August 1923, announced he would name his own special prosecutor "of high rank drawn from both political parties to enforce the law." Coolidge asked that Congress pass legislation allowing for *two* special prosecutors—one Republican, one Democrat. These two men would have the full backing of the president and the Congress "to prosecute all illegal acts that occurred in connection with the granting of the [oil] leases."

On 16 February 1924 Coolidge named Roberts and Atlee Pomerene, a Democrat and former U.S. senator from Ohio, to the two positions. When the Senate confirmed them, it became the first and only time in history that a special prosecutor's position was confirmed with the advice and consent of the U.S. Senate. As the American Bar Associa-

Owen J. Roberts, special counsel in the Teapot Dome investigation. In 1930, President Herbert Hoover rewarded Roberts for his work for the nation by naming him to a seat on the U.S. Supreme Court. (Library of Congress)

tion *Journal* pronounced in 1955 upon Roberts's death, "Six years were spent by the two counsel in this litigation, resulting in a restoration to the Navy of all lands which had been leased, and later in the conviction of Secretary of the Interior Albert B. Fall, and the holding in senatorial and judicial contempt of Harry F. Sinclair." Roberts and Pomerene proved that Fall had received some $300,000 in bribes, and Fall was sentenced to prison. Harry F. Sinclair and Edward Doheny, the oilmen who had bribed Fall, ironically were found not guilty of making the bribes.

On 2 June 1930, President Herbert Hoover rewarded Roberts for his work for the nation by naming him to a seat on the U.S. Supreme Court. He was confirmed without delay by the U.S. Senate and took his seat on the high court, serving until his resignation on 5 July 1945. He was a moderate

voice on that court, swinging between conservative and liberal positions. He retired to his farm in Pennsylvania, where he died on 17 May 1955, just two weeks after his eightieth birthday.

See also: Teapot Dome Scandal

References: District of Columbia, Supreme Court, *Title United States v. Harry F. Sinclair and Albert B. Fall. Indictment: Violation Section 37, Penal Code, Conspiracy to Defraud the United States. (Presented May 27, 1925.) Atlee Pomerene, Owen J. Roberts, Special Counsel of the United States* (Washington, DC: Government Printing Office, 1925); District of Columbia, Supreme Court, *United States v. Edward L. Doheny and Albert B. Fall. Indictment: Violation Section 37, Penal Code. Conspiracy to Defraud the United States (presented May 27, 1925). Atlee Pomerene, Owen J. Roberts, Special Counsel of the United States* (Washington, DC: Government Printing Office, 1925); "Owen J. Roberts, 1875–1955," *ABA Journal*, 41:7 (July 1955), 616–617; "Roberts Confirmed for Oil Counsel,

Philadelphian Is Accepted by the Senate by a Vote of 68 to 8," *New York Times*, 19 February 1924, 2.

Robinson, Charles (1818–1894)

Governor of Kansas (1861–1863), impeached but acquitted of charges that he sold state bonds at a price less than their actual value. Charles Robinson was born in Hardwick, Massachusetts, on 21 July 1818, the son of Jonathan Robinson, a farmer, and Huldah (née Woodward) Robinson. Robinson attended a series of academies in the area, as well as the Berkshire Medical School, graduating with a medical degree in 1843. He opened a medical practice serving the Springfield and Belchertown areas and also taught school. In 1849 he decided to throw his lot in with a wagon train headed to the California gold fields, and he settled down near Sacramento, opening a restaurant and editing a newspaper for gold field squatters. He became the president of the association that defended squatters' rights and during a squatters' riot was severely wounded. Despite his wounds, Robinson won a seat in the California state house of representatives, where he served from 1850 to 1851. When he finished his term in the California house, Robinson returned to Massachusetts and took up the editing of a newspaper in the town of Fitchburg.

When the Kansas Territory opened up on 30 May 1854, Robinson was chosen by a group of Massachusetts citizens to go to Kansas and become the leader of a colony of Massachusetts settlers there. Instead of practicing medicine in Kansas, Robinson instead became a gentleman farmer, buying and selling land in the new territory. He was one of the founders of the territory's Free Soil Party (an offshoot of the Whig Party, whose main goal was the ending of slavery in the territories) and served as a delegate to the constitutional convention held in Topeka in 1855. When the Free Soilers at this convention formed a new "state" of Kansas, they elected Robinson governor, but the founding was invalid and Robinson never actually served in any official function. Yet Robinson was the leader of the antislavery movement in Kansas.

In 1859, after another constitutional convention, Robinson was nominated by the Republicans (a party which had grown out of the Free Soil movement) for governor. Robinson had been one of the organizers of the Republican Party and was quite popular for his stand against slavery. On 1 December 1859, while Kansas was still a territory, Robinson was elected governor over the incumbent territorial governor, Samuel Medary, the Democratic candidate, by 2,400 votes out of some 13,000 cast. However, because Robinson was to become the first state governor (Medary was to be the last territorial governor), Robinson could not take office until Congress passed an enabling act making Kansas a state. Medary was proslavery, and he was able to delay passage of the act in Congress throughout all of 1860. Following the election of Republican Abraham Lincoln to the presidency in November 1860, Medary realized that statehood was inevitable, and he resigned the following month. On 9 February 1861, Robinson was sworn in as the first state governor of Kansas. His job was immediate and intense: he needed to form a state government (the territorial government had been quite limited) and, when the Civil War exploded, to hold the state together and remain in the Union. The new state was also on the verge of bankruptcy, and Robinson needed to sell bonds to build railroads and finance other pieces of the infrastructure. But Robinson was also in a deadly game with his arch-rival in the Republican Party, Senator James H. Lane.

The downfall of Robinson began when the state legislature approved the sale of $150,000 in bonds. Robinson helped to sell the bonds but came under harsh criticism and was accused of selling the bonds at a rate lower than that established by the legislature. On 14 January 1862 the legislature met and appointed a committee to investigate these charges. Two weeks later, on 30 January, this committee submitted its report. It stated:

> With regard to bonds issued by the state during the year 1861, under the acts referred to, your committee would state that the total issue of bonds, of every description, amounted to $189,400. Of these $40,000 were ten per cent. bonds, issued under the act of May 7th, and known as war bonds. Thirty-one thousand dollars of these ten per cent. bonds have been sold by the treasurer to R. S. Stevens, for forty cents on the dollar; the balance are in the treasurer's hands. It appears, on evidence before us, that a large portion of these bonds ($26,000) were sold by Mr. Stevens to the Interior Department at Wash-

ington for ninety-five cents on the dollar. Of the seven per cent. bonds, $62,200 were used in taking up state scrip, and $87,200 were delivered to R. S. Stevens, for which sixty cents on the dollar was to be accounted for by him to the state. It appears, from evidence before us, that these bonds were sold to the Interior Department at Washington for eighty-five cents on the dollar. The evidence before your committee regarding the sale of the bonds is quite lengthy and will be placed before your body in printed form.

The conclusions arrived at by your committee are such as to warrant them in the belief that this House will take decisive measures, and deeming a fair and full examination of all the evidence proper in the premises, would commend it to the attention of the House.

Of the $40,000 issued under the act of May 7th, your committee are clearly of the opinion that $20,000 are illegal, and the House should take some action regarding them.

Your committee also are clearly of the opinion that the treasurer had no authority to sell any of the ten per cent. bonds at less than par, and is liable to the state for the face of all ten per cent. bonds sold, and of which $12,400 have been paid into the treasury, leaving a deficiency on bonds sold, to be accounted for, of $18,600.

The committee recommended that Robinson and some of his cabinet be impeached. The Speaker of the state house appointed one Preston B. Plumb (later a United States senator from Kansas) to head a committee to draw up impeachment articles; on 20 February 1862, this panel submitted eight articles of impeachment against John W. Robinson (no relation), the secretary of state; on the 26th, it approved seven articles against George S. Hillyer, the auditor of the state; and, on that same day, it reported five articles against Robinson, making Robinson the first state governor in the nation's history to be impeached. The trial of the three men began on 2 June 1862. Hillyer testified that he had hired one R. S. Stevens as state agent to sell the bonds and that he, not Governor Robinson, was solely responsible for the sale. Because Stevens had worked with Hillyer and John W. Robinson, both men were convicted and removed from office. Governor Robinson was acquitted of all charges, but politically he was ruined. On 17 September the Republicans met in convention in Topeka and nominated Thomas W.

Carney, a Leavenworth dry-goods entrepreneur, for governor. After Carney's election, Robinson left office on 12 January 1863.

Robinson remained in Kansas and took sides in many political questions of the day, including standing for black and women's suffrage and against the prohibition of alcohol. He became a supporter of the Kansas Union Party and, in 1872, was elected to the Kansas state senate, serving until 1881. The following year he was nominated by the National Labor Greenback Party for governor and got more than 20,000 votes in a losing cause. He then became a Democrat and was nominated by that party for seats in the state senate, U.S. House of Representatives, and for governor, but he was defeated each time. In 1886 President Grover Cleveland named him the superintendent of the Haskell Indian Institute in Kansas, and he served there from 1887 until 1889. Robinson died at his home, "Oak Ridge," near Lawrence, Kansas, on 17 August 1894, and was buried in the Oak Hill Cemetery. The town of Robinson, Kansas, is named in his honor.

References: Blackmar, Frank Wilson, *The Life of Charles Robinson, the First State Governor of Kansas* (Topeka, KS: Crane & Company, Printers, 1901); Ewing, Cortez A. M., "Early Kansas Impeachments," *Kansas Historical Quarterly,* I:4 (August 1932), 307–325; *Proceedings in the Cases of the Impeachment of Charles Robinson, Governor, John W. Robinson, Secretary of State, George S. Hillyer, Auditor of State, of Kansas* (Lawrence: Kansas State Journal Steam Press, 1862); "Robinson, Charles," in Robert Sobel and John Raimo, eds., *Biographical Directory of the Governors of the United States, 1789–1978,* 4 vols. (Westport, CT: Meckler Books, 1978), II:459–460.

Ross, Robert Tripp (1903–1981)

United States representative from New York (1952–1953), deputy assistant secretary of defense for legislative affairs (1954–1956), and deputy assistant secretary of defense for legislative and public affairs (1956–1957), accused of a conflict of interest in the awarding of a defense contract for which he was forced from his position. Ross was born in Washington, North Carolina, on 4 June 1903 and attended the public schools there. In 1929, when he was twenty-six, he moved to New York and went to work as a druggist. Later he was employed by a large pharmaceutical firm in New York, where he rose to managerial positions and remained with the company until 1947.

In 1946 Ross entered the political arena, running for a seat in the U.S. House of Representatives from New York's Fifth District and defeating Democrat James A. Phillips. Ross ultimately served a single term, losing in 1948 to Democrat Thomas Vincent Quinn. He then reentered private business, working on the manufacture and sale of clothing and athletic equipment. In 1950, in another attempt to recapture his House seat, he was defeated by Quinn. However, when Quinn resigned on 30 December 1951 to become the district attorney for Queens County, New York, a special election was held, and Ross defeated Quinn's son Hugh. Ross served from 19 February 1952 until 3 January 1953. The Fifth District seat he held was moved to the Sixth District, and Ross was defeated by Democrat Lester Holtzman in the 1952 election.

Again out of Congress, Ross returned to private business. In March 1954 President Dwight D. Eisenhower named Ross as deputy assistant secretary of defense for legislative affairs, a position that coordinated Department of Defense policy with legislators on Capitol Hill. In March 1956 this position was renamed deputy assistant secretary of defense for legislative and public affairs.

While in this position, Ross was instrumental in getting the Department of Defense to award a contract to a company called Wynn Enterprises, which provided army trousers. The contract totaled $835,135. What Ross did not report was that his wife was president of Wynn and that he had once served as the vice president of the company and its affiliate, Southern Athletic Company. Both companies were owned by Herman Wynn, the brother of Ross's second wife, Claire. In 1957 the U.S. Senate Permanent Subcommittee on Investigations came across the contract, saw its potential conflict of interest, and the chairman, Senator John L. McClellan of Arkansas, called Ross in for questioning before the subcommittee.

Appearing for two hours on 13 February 1957, Ross said under oath that he had severed all contacts with the companies in 1952 and that he had not been responsible for the contract for trousers that had gone to the company. However, he had taken a leave of absence from his position when the questions first arose. When Ross admitted that he had arranged for a marine to meet with his brother-in-law, the handwriting was on the wall:

on 14 February, just a day after giving testimony to the Senate subcommittee, Ross resigned his office. In his letter to President Eisenhower, Ross wrote that "nothing was brought to my attention to indicate that the subcommittee had found any evidence of any wrongdoing, impropriety, or conflict of interest on my part," but he conceded that his position had been "impaired by the serious implications contained in the numerous press stories. . . . I feel it would be unfair to the Department of Defense for me to continue."

Ross returned to New York, where he went to work as assistant borough works commissioner for Queens County, from March 1957 until January 1958. He then went to work as vice president of the Merchandising Apparel Company, serving until 1968. Thereafter he retired to Jackson Heights, New York, until his death there on 1 October 1981 at the age of seventy-eight. He was buried in Oakdale Cemetery in Washington, North Carolina.

References: *Biographical Directory of the American Congress, 1774–1996* (Alexandria, VA: CQ Staff Directories, Inc., 1996), 1758; "Robert Ross: Questionable Awarding of Defense Contracts," in George C. Kohn, *Encyclopedia of American Scandal: From ABSCAM to the Zenger Case* (New York: Facts on File, 1989), 289–290.

Rostenkowski, Daniel David (1928–)

United States representative from Illinois (1959–1995), powerful chairman of the House of Representatives Committee on Ways and Means, implicated in the House Post Office scandal, for which he served 451 days in prison. Born in Chicago, Illinois, on 2 January 1928, Rostenkowski attended local schools and graduated from St. John's Military Academy before attending Loyola University in Chicago for a short time. He left Loyola when he volunteered for duty in the U.S. Army and was sent to Korea, where he was stationed from 1946 to 1948.

Rostenkowski was elected to a seat in the Illinois state house of representatives, where he served in the Sixty-eighth General Assembly in 1952. A Democrat, he was elected to a single term in the Illinois state senate, from 1954 to 1956. In 1958 Rostenkowski was elected to a seat in the U.S. House of Representatives, entering the Eighty-sixth Congress on 3 January 1959 and serving through the next seventeen congresses until he left on 3 January 1995. A member of the House Committee on Ways and Means, he rose to become chairman of the committee in 1981 rather than become the Majority Whip for the Democrats in the House and was without a doubt one of the most powerful members of Congress. Presidents had to deal with him to get any legislation requiring appropriations passed in the House. His reelection campaigns were against either token opposition or none at all.

On 31 May 1994, a District of Columbia grand jury returned indictments against Rostenkowski, alleging that he and others had "devised . . . a scheme" to "defraud the United States of its money, its property, and its right" to what the jury called Rostenkowski's "fair and honest services." Seventeen counts of malfeasance, including six counts of devising a scheme to defraud, two counts involving a "Payroll Scheme," two counts on a "House Stationery Store Scheme," and additional counts alleging that he defrauded the House Post Office and appropriated vehicles which did not belong to him, were returned. Rostenkowski then asked the Court of Appeals for the District of Columbia Circuit to quash the indictment, claiming that all of the actions for which he was indicted were covered by the Speech or Debate Clause of the Constitution, Article I, Section 6, which holds that "for any Speech or Debate in either House, [a Member of Congress] shall not be questioned in any other place," and which has been held by the Supreme Court to protect members of Congress from prosecution for legislative actions. In a second motion, Rostenkowski sought an in-camera review by the justices of all evidence presented to the grand jury. In *United States v. Rostenkowski*, 59 F.3d 1291 (D.C. Cir. 1995), argued on 17 March 1995 and decided on 18 July 1995, Judge Douglas Ginsburg, holding for the circuit court, dismissed both of Rostenkowski's arguments. Judge Ginsburg explained:

> There is no reason on the face of the indictment to suggest that any Speech or Debate material was presented to the grand jury. Moreover, Rostenkowski offers virtually no specific reason to believe that such material was presented to the grand jury. Instead, he gives us only the general warning that "courts should be wary of accepting prosecutorial assurances that constitutional violations have not occurred" before the grand jury. Although Rostenkowski obviously cannot be expected to know

exactly what transpired before the grand jury or what was presented to that body, he must be able to provide, either from the allegations of the indictment or from some other source, at least some reason to believe that protected information was used to procure his indictment. To give him a right to in-camera review without any particular reason apart from his status as a Member of Congress and therefore a person protected by the Speech or Debate Clause would completely disregard the "long-established policy" in favor of grand jury secrecy . . . and would fail to strike an appropriate (indeed any) balance between the grand jury's "functional independence from the Judicial Branch" . . . and a Congressman's right to be free from prosecution for his legislative acts. Lacking any reason to think that prohibited material was submitted to the grand jury, we have no reason to believe that the district court's denial of his motion was in error, and we affirm that decision.

Because of the criminal indictment hanging over his head, in November 1994 Rostenkowski lost his reelection effort to an unknown Republican, Michael P. Flanagan. Having stepped aside earlier as chairman of the Ways and Means Committee—Democrat Sam Gibbons (D-FL) served as acting chairman for the remainder of the 103rd Congress—Rostenkowski held steadfast that he was innocent of any and all crimes. However, on 9 April 1996, he pled guilty to two counts of mail fraud and was sentenced to seventeen months in prison and fined $100,000. He served his prison sentence in a minimum-security prison in Wisconsin.

Richard Cohen, a journalist and biographer of Rostenkowski, wrote in the *National Journal* in 1999:

> Rostenkowski was convicted on charges that were picayune compared with those of the indictment. Although prosecutors indicted him on 17 counts for allegedly misusing hundreds of thousands of dollars in official funds, he pleaded guilty to only two counts. He admitted that he illegally purchased assorted china from the House stationary store, including $200 crystal sculptures of the U.S. Capitol that were inscribed with his friends' names—which he sent as gifts. The second charge he admitted in court dealt with the "padding" of his payroll with employees who did little or no work, aside from routine tasks for Rostenkowski and his family.

He steadfastly maintained his innocence on the broader and more publicized abuses at the House post office, including the claim that he traded official stamps for personal cash, which was the linchpin for the criminal focus. . . .

Perhaps the greatest personal tragedy was that the Chicago pol who had risen to such national influence was brought down by the type of penny-ante abuse that ensnared two-bit local politicians. "Certain of his activities made sense from a Chicago perspective," said former Rep. Ed Derwinski, the Illinois Republican. "If you understand the relationship of ward committeemen, you can understand the mind-set of giving the gifts . . . and maintaining the principle of loyalty."

See also: House of Representatives Post Office Scandal

References: *Biographical Directory of the American Congress, 1774–1996* (Alexandria, VA: CQ Staff Directories, Inc., 1996), 1758–1759; Cohen, Richard E., *Rostenkowski: The Pursuit of Power and the End of the Old Politics* (Chicago, IL: Ivan R. Dee, 1999); Cohen, Richard E., "Rosty Revisited," *National Journal,* 31:42 (16 October 1999), 2956–2965; Merriner, James L., *Mr. Chairman: Power in Dan Rostenkowski's America* (Carbondale: Southern Illinois University Press, 1999); *United States v. Rostenkowski,* 59 Federal 3d 1291.

S

Schenck, Robert Cumming (1809–1890)

United States representative from Ohio (1843–1851, 1863–1871), U.S. minister to Great Britain (1870–1876), accused, but later cleared, of using his office in London for financial gain. Born in Franklin, Ohio, on 4 October 1809, he attended rural schools before graduating from Miami University in Oxford, Ohio, in 1827. He served as a professor at the university for two years, after which he studied the law and was admitted to the state bar in 1833. He opened a practice in the town of Dayton, Ohio.

Schenck, a Whig, entered the Ohio state house of representatives in 1839 and served until 1843. In 1842 he was elected as a Whig to a seat in the U.S. House of Representatives, entering the Twenty-eighth Congress on 4 March 1843 and serving through the Thirty-first Congress. He served as chairman of the Committee on Roads and Canals. When David Tod, U.S. minister to Brazil, was recalled in early 1851, President Millard Fillmore named Schenck to succeed him. At the same time, Schenck was also accredited as the minister to Uruguay, to the Argentine Confederation, and to Paraguay. On 8 October 1853, after his successor, William Trousdale, had been selected, Schenck stated that he had been recalled, and he sailed for home.

When the Civil War broke out in early 1861, Schenck volunteered for service, entering the U.S. Army on 17 May 1861. He was given the rank of brigadier general of volunteers, eventually being promoted to major general, the rank he held until he resigned his commission on 3 December 1863. At that time, having again been elected to a seat in the U.S. House of Representatives, he left the field of battle to enter the political realm. This time, however, he was elected as a Republican, and he took his seat in the Thirty-eighth Congress, serving from 4 March 1863 until his resignation on 5 January 1871. He eventually served as chairman of the Committee on Ways and Means and chairman of the Committee on Military Affairs. As the chairman of the House Committee on Ways and Means, he earned the nickname "Poker Bob" because of his card playing.

In 1870 Schenck was defeated for reelection, and to award him for his service to the Republican Party President Ulysses S. Grant named Schenck to the post of minister to Great Britain. Grant had first named U.S. Senator Frederick T. Frelinghuysen of New Jersey, and then U.S. Senator Oliver T. Morton of Indiana to the position, but both men had declined. Schenck accepted and sailed to London, where he presented his credentials on 23 June 1871. While in London, Schenck picked up his card playing, achieving some notoriety when he penned a letter to an English duchess on how to play poker.

What got Schenck into trouble was his investment in the Emma Silver mine in Nevada. He decided to make money on the deal before the mine went broke, selling near worthless stock to unsuspecting British investors at the same time that he was supposed to be carrying out his official duties. It was later ascertained that Schenck had been paid more than £10,000 for the mine to use his name in its English advertisements. When the mine did indeed go bankrupt, the investors complained, and a congressional investigation, initiated by Representative Abram S. Hewitt (D-NY), was begun to look into the matter. Historian George Kohn writes, "Ultimately, Schenck was cleared of fraud charges, but his reputation had been badly stained. Both British and Americans accused him of using his dignified public position for personal gain. His dealings caused a British court to issue a writ against him, which he dodged by pleading diplomatic immunity. In May 1876, Schenck resigned and came home in shame, to be replaced as minister to Great Britain by Edwards Pierrepont, who had been Attorney General of the United States."

Schenck settled in Washington, D.C., where he practiced law for the remainder of his life. In 1880 he penned a book on card playing, entitled *Draw Poker*. He died in Washington on 23 March 1890, two weeks shy of his eighty-first birthday. He was buried in Woodland Cemetery in Dayton, Ohio.

References: Joyner, Fred B., "Robert Cumming Schenck, First Citizen and Statesman of the Miami Valley," *Ohio State Archaeological and Historical Quarterly*, 58 (July 1949), 286–297; "Robert C. Schenck: Humiliated Diplomat," in George C. Kohn, *Encyclopedia of American Scandal: From ABSCAM to the Zenger Case* (New York: Facts on File, 1989), 294–295; "Schenck, Robert Cumming," in Allen Johnson and Dumas Malone, et al., eds., *Dictionary of American Biography*, 10 vols. and 10 supplements (New York: Charles Scribner's Sons, 1930–1995), VIII, 427–428.

Schmitz, Eugene Edward (1864–1928)

Mayor of San Francisco (1902–1907), convicted of numerous counts of graft and bribery in his operations of the city before and during the San Francisco earthquake of 1906. Schmitz remains somewhat obscure, despite being one of the most corrupt mayors in American history. Perhaps this corruption arises from the fact that little is known of his life before he assumed the mayorship. He was born in San Francisco on 22 August 1864, the son of pioneer parents. What little education he re-

ceived has been lost to history, except that he apparently took up music at an early age; he became a drummer boy working in the Standard Theater in San Francisco. He rose to become president of the city Musicians' Union and became the bandleader of the Columbia Theater orchestra in 1900.

Somehow, Schmitz's musical talent caught the eye of Abraham Ruef, political boss of the city, and Ruef pushed Schmitz to run for mayor in 1901. The city was looking for a change. Despite many years of clean government under Mayor James Duval Phelan, mayor since 1897, a series of labor disputes had become violent. When Phelan used the police to crush a strike by the City Front Federation of Waterfront Workers against the Employers' Association, the unions formed the Union Labor Party to gain political power. Ruef, head of the city's Republican Party, moved to become head of the Union Labor group, and enlisted bandleader—and musical union member— Schmitz as the Union Labor candidate for mayor. Schmitz won easily over Phelan, becoming the first labor-backed candidate to win a major office in the United States. Historian Peter D'A. Jones writes,

> "Handsome Gene" Schmitz was good-looking, and well-liked, and, although not "the smallest man mentally and meanest man morally" ever to be mayor, as one opponent claimed, he was easily ruled by Ruef. With each passing day, the links between the city administration and the underworld ramified, especially after the large electoral victory of 1905, after which the city began taking "tributes" from respectable businessmen.

By 1905 Schmitz and his administration were openly accused by several people of corruption, including taking kickbacks and bribery. Attorney Francis J. Heney, who had been named by President Theodore Roosevelt to prosecute land frauds in Oregon (and had netted U.S. Senator John H. Mitchell), held a rally in San Francisco and denounced Schmitz and Ruef as corrupt. Despite this, Schmitz was easily reelected in 1905 over attorney John S. Partridge, the candidate of the Democrats and Republicans. Ruef, with Schmitz's backing, was given control of every department in the San Francisco municipal government.

At this point, former mayor Phelan joined with local business leader Rudolph Spreckels and Fremont Older, editor of the San Francisco *Evening Bulletin,* to call on Heney in December 1905 to open an investigation into the alleged corruption. Heney employed William J. Burns, founder of the U.S. Secret Service (which guards the president), to investigate. Heney and Burns worked in conjunction with San Francisco District Attorney William H. Langdon. Then the Great San Francisco Earthquake, striking on 18 April 1906, derailed the investigation. During the crisis Schmitz rose to the occasion, displaying great leadership to a torn and destroyed city. As soon as the emergency passed, however, Schmitz resumed his parade of graft, shaking down builders for a piece of the action to reconstruct the city. On 24 October 1906, D. A. Langdon announced that Heney would become deputy district attorney to investigate alleged graft and corruption in city government. Ruef and the Union Labor Party decried the selection; at a mass rally on 31 October, Ruef denounced Heney as "the Benedict Arnold of San Francisco," while other speakers called Schmitz "the peerless champion of the people's rights" and Ruef "the Mayor's loyal, able and intrepid friend." Schmitz, on a business trip in Europe, was replaced for a time by Supervisor James L. Gallagher as acting mayor. Gallagher, working with Ruef and Schmitz, decided to forestall the investigation, and on 25 October removed D. A. Langdon and Heney from office and appointed Ruef to investigate the alleged graft. The *San Francisco Call* printed, under a picture of Ruef, the words "This Man's Hand Grips the Throat of San Francisco."

Ruef moved to put an end to a grand jury, which had been empaneled to hear the charges. Ruef could not stop it, however, and Heney presented the evidence. On 7 November Schmitz and Ruef were indicted on charges of extorting kickbacks from brothels; members of the board of supervisors, testifying under grants of immunity, confessed to being in on the massive corruption scheme. During Schmitz's trial, the heads of the United Railroads (a labor union) were implicated in payoffs. Editor Older was kidnapped to shut him up, but was later released, and an ex-felon was paid to murder Heney in open court, shooting the prosecutor but merely wounding him in the jaw. (Heney was replaced for a time by a young attorney named Hiram W. Johnson, who rose to become governor of California and a U.S. senator.)

Schmitz was convicted of several counts and sentenced to five years in prison. His conviction was ultimately reversed by an appellate court and by the state supreme court, and he ultimately never served any prison time, unlike Ruef. In 1915 and 1919 Schmitz ran again for mayor, losing both races. In 1916 he was elected to a seat on the city Board of Supervisors, where he served until 1925. Thereafter he was engaged in private business. Schmitz died of heart disease in San Francisco on 20 November 1928 at the age of sixty-four.

Historian Barnaby Conrad explained:

> San Francisco cleared away not only the ruins of the fallen City Hall but the human rubble that had been in it, for the graft and corruption had reached heroic—if that's the word—proportions. Rudolph Spreckels financed an investigation of the appalling conditions to the tune of $100,000, and was aided by his friend James Phelen and Fremont Older, editor of the *Call Bulletin,* who dedicated his newspaper to a crusade against the underworld. The rodents to be fumigated turned out to be Mayor Schmitz himself and his sly cohort, Abe Ruef. Prosecution was difficult because of lack of witnesses, who quite rightly feared for their lives if they testified. The trials were the most explosive ever held in San Francisco, with the house of the chief witness being dynamited, prosecuting attorney Francis J. Heney was shot in the jaw, and Fremont Older himself was kidnapped. The upshot was that in 1907 Schmitz was sentenced to San Quentin for five years, and in 1908 Ruef was convicted on 129 counts of civic graft and sentenced to a fourteen-year term.

Perhaps Schmitz has been "lucky" in his obscurity, mainly because his graft did not occur in New York or Chicago. Books on city bosses do not list him; even works on the history of graft and corruption in municipal situations do not even mention him.

References: Conrad, Barnaby, *San Francisco: A Profile With Pictures* (New York: Bramhall House, 1959); Hansen, Gladys, *San Francisco Almanac: Everything You Want to Know About the City* (San Francisco: Chronicle Books, 1975), 85–86; Hichborn, Franklin, *"The System" as Uncovered by the San Francisco Graft Prosecution* (San Francisco: Press of the James H. Barry Company, 1915), 18–21, 74–89, 370–373; "Indicted Mayor Gets Himself Into Japanese Controversy; Schmitz Advises School Board in Matter," *San Francisco Chronicle,* 1 February 1907, 1;

Jones, Peter d'A., "Schmitz, Eugene E.," in Melvin G. Holli and Peter d'A. Jones, *Biographical Dictionary of American Mayors, 1820–1980: Big City Mayors* (Westport, CT: Greenwood Press, 1981), 320–321; San Francisco [Municipal Government], "Report on the Causes of Municipal Corruption in San Francisco, as Disclosed by the Investigations of the Oliver Grand Jury, and the Prosecution of Certain Persons for Bribery and other Offenses against the State; Schmitz Advises School Board in Matter," *San Francisco Chronicle*, 1 February 1907, 1; "William Denman, Chairman. Committee appointed by the Mayor, October 12, 1908. Reprinted with a Preface and Index of Names and Subjects by the California Weekly." (San Francisco: Rincon Publishing Co., 1910).

Schumaker, John Godfrey (1826–1905)

United States representative from New York (1869–1871, 1873–1877), the subject of expulsion proceedings in the House in 1875 on allegations of corruption. He was born in the town of Claverack, New York, on 27 June 1826 and completed preparatory studies at the Lenox Academy (Massachusetts). He studied law and was admitted to the New York bar in 1847. That year he opened a practice. In 1853 he relocated to Brooklyn, New York, and continued his law practice. In 1856 he was named district attorney for Kings County (Brooklyn), serving until 1859 and in 1862 as corporation counsel for the city of Brooklyn (it became part of New York City in 1898), serving until 1864. In 1862 (and later 1867 and 1894) he served as a member of the New York state constitutional convention.

In 1868 Schumaker defeated Republican Henry S. Bellows to win a seat in the U.S. House of Representatives, representing New York's Second Congressional District. In 1870 he did not run for reelection. Although he had served as a Democrat, Schumaker jumped on board the liberal Republican movement and ran under that banner in 1872, defeating a Republican only identified as "Perry" to win another term to the House. He won reelection in 1874.

Although the cause has been lost to history, Schumaker was investigated for allegations of political corruption. (An examination of congressional records from the period does not turn up the charge or allegation.) At the same time, another representative, William Smith King (R-Minnesota), was also investigated. Some light can be derived by the report of the committee, which held that:

Your committee are of opinion that the House of Representatives has no authority to take jurisdiction of violations of law or offenses committed against a previous Congress. This is purely a legislative body, and entirely unsuited for the trial of crimes. The fifth section of the first article of the Constitution authorizes "each house to determine the rules of its proceedings, punish its members for disorderly behavior, and, with the concurrence of two-thirds, expel a member." This power is evidently given to enable each house to exercise its constitutional function of legislation unobstructed. It cannot vest in Congress a jurisdiction to try a member for an offense committed before his election; for such offense a member, like any other citizen, is amenable to the courts alone.

Schumaker did not run for reelection in 1876 and returned to private life. He died in 1905, having slipped into obscurity.

See also King, William Smith

References: *Biographical Directory of the American Congress, 1774–1996* (Alexandria, VA: CQ Staff Directories, Inc., 1996); Schumaker and King report in House Report No. 815, 44th Congress, 1st Session (Washington, DC: Government Printing Office, 1876), 2.

Seabury, Samuel (1873?–1958)

Noted jurist, head of the Seabury Commission that investigated and helped to bring down Mayor James J. "Jimmy" Walker of New York City. Born in New York City possibly in 1873, he was the great-grandson of the famed clergyman Samuel Seabury (1729–1796) and was named after him. Seabury was educated at the New York Law School and received his law degree from that institution. In 1906 he was elected as a justice to the New York Supreme Court and served until 1914, when he resigned to take a seat on the New York Court of Appeals. In 1916 he resigned that post to run as the Democratic candidate for governor of New York, but he was defeated by Governor Charles S. Whitman.

Ironically, Seabury had sat on the second trial in a case that had made Whitman governor—that of Charles Becker. Becker, a police sergeant, had been accused of participating in the murder-for-hire of gangster Herman "Beansie" Rosenthal in 1912. After Becker's first trial, in which he was convicted but the conviction was struck down on appeal, Seabury was named as the judge to oversee the second trial. Whitman was the prosecutor and obtained a second conviction before Seabury. Becker eventually died in the electric chair in 1916. After losing to Whitman in the election in 1916, Seabury then entered into a private law practice for the next two decades.

In 1930 New York Governor Franklin D. Roosevelt, faced with a growing scandal involving allegations of corruption in the magistrate courts of New York City, appointed Seabury as a special counsel to investigate. His inquiry, while not headline-grabbing, did result in the removal of two magistrates, three magistrates resigning, and a sixth running from the law. Impressed by his investigative skill, Roosevelt named Seabury in 1931 to be the special counsel for a state legislative committee "to investigate the affairs of New York City." After a period of investigation, Seabury, as counsel, called his first witness: New York Mayor Jimmy Walker. The *New York Times* later commented, "Seabury was a patient, shrewd and tenacious cross-examiner in connection with financial advantages that had accrued to the Mayor." In fact, in an unprecedented move, Governor Roosevelt presided over the hearings. Walker, known as the "Debonair Mayor," tried to use glib expressions and humor to overcome the evidence that Seabury had collected; instead, the charm offensive backfired, and Seabury's relentless questioning drove Walker to crack on the stand. On 1 August 1932, Walker returned to New York City and resigned, afterwards heading off to Europe. In early 1932, the play *Face the Music* debuted on Broadway. The play, composed by playwright Moss Hart and lyricist Irving Berlin, was aimed directly at the Walker administration and the Seabury investigation.

But Seabury was not finished: instead, he turned his sights on corruption in the operation of Tammany Hall, the leading political organization in New York City, one that controlled all patronage and other facets of city government. Starting with lower Tammany employees and working up to the more important ones, Seabury exposed the Tammany operation. Thomas A. Farley, sheriff of New York City, admitted on the stand that $100,000 that he had deposited in his account in 1928 "came out of a wonderful tin box." James A. McQuade, register of King's County, could only say that he "borrowed" more than $510,000 in six years, but couldn't say

from whom. Seabury's extensive investigation cast light on massive corruption that had been going on for years, unchallenged, in Tammany politics. Because of the investigation, an "anti-Tammany" candidate for mayor was named. Seabury himself vetoed Robert Moses and Major General John F. O'Ryan, selecting instead Fiorello La Guardia, who went on to victory in the 1933 election. La Guardia went on to serve as mayor from 1934 to 1945.

After the corruption investigation, Seabury was elected president of the New York Law Institute. The author of *New Federation* (1950), Seabury died in New York City on 7 May 1958. Although he was one of the leading investigators into corruption in New York state in the twentieth century, he is almost wholly forgotten.

See also Tammany Hall; Walker, James John

References: Dewey, John, ed., *New York and the Seabury Investigation: A Digest and Interpretation of the Reports by Samuel Seabury Concerning the Government of New York City, Prepared by a Committee of Educators and Civic Workers under the Chairmanship of John Dewey* (New York: The City Affairs Committee of New York, 1933); Mitgang, Herbert, *The Man Who Rode the Tiger: The Life of Judge Samuel Seabury and the Story of the Greatest Investigation of City Corruption in This Century* (New York: Norton, 1979); Mitgang, Herbert. *Once Upon a Time in New York: Jimmy Walker, Franklin Roosevelt, and the Last Great Battle of the Jazz Age* (New York: Free Press, 2000); New York State Supreme Court, Appellate Division, *The Investigation of the Magistrates Courts in the First Judicial Department and the Magistrates Thereof, and of Attorneys-at-Law Practicing in Said Courts: Final Report of Samuel Seabury, Referee* (New York: The City Club of New York, 1932); Northrop, William Bacot, *The Insolence of Office: The Story of the Seabury Investigations* (New York and London: G. P. Putnam's Sons, 1932); "Seabury Declares Walker Is Not Worthy of Belief, Scores Legal Quibbling," *New York Times,* 4 August 1932, 1.

Select Committee on U.S. National Security and Military/Commercial Concerns with the People's Republic of China.

See Cox Report

Senate Finance Committee Hearings 1997 (Thompson Committee)

Congressional investigation that examined campaign finance irregularities by the Democratic

Party in the 1996 presidential campaign. During that election campaign, allegations of improper fundraising were advanced against the Democratic Party and its candidates for president and vice president, Bill Clinton and Albert Gore. These allegations reached a fever pitch that October, when it was alleged that foreign donors, prohibited by law from giving to American election campaigns, were nonetheless pumping funds into the Clinton/Gore campaign as well as the Democratic National Committee (DNC). On 14 October, the DNC acknowledged receiving more than $450,000 from an Indonesian couple, Arief Wiriadinata and his wife, both partners of a wealthy friend of Clinton, James Riady, head of the Lippo Group, an Indonesian banking concern with a branch in Arkansas, where Clinton was governor. Allegations also arose that a Buddhist temple with ties to Taiwan had raised funds during a visit by Gore the past April. Gore explained that he did not know the event was a fundraiser, even though he was warned by his staff in memos that funds would be raised, a violation of law. On 28 October, the DNC refused to release a preelection spending report showing the donors to their party; after an outcry, they relented two days later and released a partial list of donors. Clinton was reelected overwhelmingly on 7 November, but the controversy did not end there.

During his first postelection new conference, a reelected Clinton declared that alleged contributions from Indonesia had "absolutely not" influenced his policies toward Asia, and, at the same time, he called for congressional passage of the so-called McCain-Feingold campaign finance bill, introduced by Senator John McCain (R-Arizona) and Senator Russ Feingold (D-Wisconsin). The following day, DNC cochairman Don Fowler held his own press conference, in which he stated that "never has there been any desire, plan or intent to evade requirements of applicable laws and regulations. . . . In fact, we have tried to comply strictly with all relevant requirements." On 13 November, the Justice Department refused to honor a request from McCain for the appointment of an independent counsel to investigate DNC donations. By January, allegations of further wrongdoing by the Clinton campaign and the DNC prompted further calls from congressional Republicans for either the appointment of an independent counsel or a congressional investigation. When stories of "coffees," or

meetings in the White House that were attended by Clinton and Gore in which fundraising calls were issued, a violation of law, became public, the potential scandal reached a fever pitch. In February, Clinton acknowledged that he had rewarded top donors to the DNC and his campaign with overnight stays in the Lincoln Bedroom in the White House.

On 11 March 1997, the U.S. Senate voted unanimously to authorize the Governmental Affairs Committee, headed by Senator Fred D. Thompson of Tennessee, to conduct "an investigation of illegal or improper activities in connection with 1996 Federal election campaigns"—a deadline of 31 December 1997 was imposed as a condition that the hearings not get out of hand. Starting in July and lasting through October, in 33 total days of testimony, the committee heard direct testimony from more than 70 witnesses, with an additional 200 witnesses interviewed; 418 subpoenas were issued for testimony and documents, and more than 1.5 million documents were reviewed.

On the first day of the hearings, 8 July 1997, Senator Thompson gave an opening statement that outlined what he saw coming out of the hearings:

> On March 11 1997, the United States Senate voted 99–0 to authorize an investigation of illegal or improper activities in connection with the 1996 federal election campaigns. . . . Article One of our Constitution grants Congress its legislative powers. Implied within those powers is the right of Congress to conduct investigations with regard to matters that are of concern to this nation. Therefore, from time to time throughout our history when problems arise that raise grave questions about our government, Congress has carried out such investigations through congressional hearings such as the ones we begin today.
>
> These hearings serve two purposes. One purpose is to make determinations as to whether or not our laws should be changed or whether additional legislation is needed. The second purpose of hearings is to inform the American people as to how their government is operating—to pull back the curtain and give the American people an unfiltered review as to how their system is working.
>
> Within this broad outline, I believe it is important for us to remember what these hearings are and what they are not. First of all, they are not trials where people are prosecuted. They are not soap operas, designed to titillate. They are not athletic events where we keep a running score. Rather, these hearings are

serious looks at how our system is working with a view toward making our system better.

A lot of facts are already out on the public record. In fact, there has been an outpouring of information and allegations in the media for the last several months. There has been so much troubling information that it is easy for the average citizen to get lost in the maze of competing stories. Therefore, we are tempted to look for one key witness or one document which will explain it all. However, the truth seldom emerges that way. Our obligation in these hearings is to take this virtual blizzard of information, add new facts, provide some depth and context, and pull the material together and present it in a comprehensible form. And at the end of the day, I'm convinced that the true picture will emerge.

The allegations before us are serious. They include illegal foreign contributions and other illegal foreign involvement in our political process, money laundering, influence peddling, violations of the Hatch Act—which prevents fundraising on government time or government property—violations of the Ethics in Government Act, violations of the conflict of interest laws, the improper use of the White House in fundraising activities and questions of whether our government's domestic and foreign policy was affected by political contributions.

These matters go to the basic integrity of our government and our electoral process and will constitute the first phase of our hearings.

There apparently was a systematic influx of illegal money in our presidential race last year. We will be wanting to know: Who knew about it? Who should have known about it? And was there an attempt to cover it up?

It has been pointed out that certain witnesses have fled the country or taken the Fifth Amendment. It has also been noted that we have a cutoff date of December 31. However, it should be remembered that we have much evidence available to us. And if anyone should unlawfully impede or misinform this Committee, there are criminal sanctions available.

Valuable information can be obtained in various ways. It seems that due to the fact these hearings are about to start, the White House has decided to release certain information before this Committee discloses it. Since information is being disclosed that the American people have long since been entitled to, we welcome being preempted. We expect that those under investigation will have cause to preempt us many times in the future.

When the first phase of our hearings is complete, we will begin the second phase, in which we will address the broader issues concerning our electoral process, including the role of soft money and the role of independent groups.

While most of the activities examined in the second phase are presumably legal, I believe that common practices in these areas by both parties are a far cry from the intent of Congress when it drafted our campaign finance laws after Watergate. I personally believe we can do much better than the campaign finance system we have today. However, we cannot move forward unless we have accountability for the past. We cannot let calls for campaign finance reform be used as a shield to prevent examination of the violations of existing law. Otherwise, calls for reform will be viewed as merely partisan and the cause of reform will be harmed, not enhanced.

These hearings come at a time of economic prosperity, but at a time of increasing public cynicism about government. We now have less than half our people voting. I believe that part of this is due to what has happened to our political process, as evidenced by the matters before us. The American people see their leaders go to greater and more extreme lengths to raise unprecedented amounts of money for their political campaigns.

During its hearings, the committee was faced with several delays and obstructions. Despite the fact that the vote to authorize the hearings was bipartisan, the Democrats on the panel, led by Senator John Glenn (D-OH), orchestrated a campaign to denounce the hearings as one-sided and partisan, refusing at times to vote to issue subpoenas or to cooperate at all. In addition, twenty-three witnesses called before the committee asserted their Fifth Amendment rights against self-incrimination and refused to testify; nine additional witnesses refused to testify until the committee had granted them immunity from prosecution. Ten other witnesses, included Yah Lin "Charlie" Trie, a close friend of Clinton, Ted Sioeng, and Pauline Kanchanalak, fled the United States and refused to return or be interviewed. Another dozen foreign witnesses, including James Riady, also refused to be interviewed.

On 5 March 1998, the Senate Governmental Affairs Committee released its final report, a 1,100-page tome, on the campaign finance scandal. Writing in the report, the majority explained;

In mid-1995, the President and his strategists decided that they needed to raise and spend many millions of dollars over and above the permissible limits of the Presidential campaign funding law if the President were going to be reelected. They devised a legal theory to support their needs and proceeded to raise and spend $44 million in excess of the Presidential campaign spending limits.

The lengths to which the Clinton/Gore campaign and the White House-controlled Democratic National Committee were willing to go in order to raise this amount of money is essentially the story of the 1996 Presidential campaign scandal. The President and his aides demeaned the offices of the President and Vice President, took advantage of minority groups, pulled down all the barriers that would normally be in place to keep out illegal contributions, pressured policy makers, and left themselves open to strong suspicion that they were selling not only access to high-ranking officials, but policy as well. Millions of dollars were raised in illegal contributions, much of it from foreign sources. When these abuses were uncovered, the result was numerous Fifth Amendment claims, flights from the country, and stonewalling from the White House.

See also Campaign Finance Scandal 1996; Clinton, William Jefferson; Gore, Albert Arnold, Jr.

References: Baker, Peter, "White House Seeks to Protect Gore in Temple Inquiry," *Washington Post,* 3 September 1997, A1; Baker, Peter, and Susan Schmidt, "President Had Big Role in Setting Donor Perks," *Washington Post,* 26 February 1997, A1; *Final Report of the Investigation of Illegal or Improper Activities in Connection With 1996 Federal Election Campaigns, together with Additional and Minority Views* (Report of the Senate Governmental Affairs Committee, 105th Congress, 2nd Session, 1998), i; Gugliotta, Guy, "For Tamraz, Pursuit of Presidential Access Was Also Pursuit of American Dream," *Washington Post,* 19 September 1997, A7; Gugliotta, Guy. "Senate Campaign Probers Release Findings," *Washington Post,* 6 March 1998, A6; "'92 Democratic Fund-Raisers May Have Kept Cash: Almost $160,000 Went to Firms of Couple Guilty in Separate Scheme," *Washington Post,* 17 December 1997, A6; Suro, Roberto, "Reno Decides Against Independent Counsel to Probe Clinton, Gore," *Washington Post,* 3 December 1997, A1; "White House, in Its Thirst For Money, Took Control," *Washington Post,* 10 February 1998, A6; Woodward, Bob, "Gore Donors' Funds Used as 'Hard Money', Federal Restrictions Apply to Such Gifts," *Washington Post,* 3 September 1997, A1.

Senate Select Committee on Ethics

United States Senate panel, established to oversee ethics in that legislative branch body. Under Article I, Section 5 of the U.S. Constitution, each house of Congress "may determine the Rules of its Proceedings, punish its Members for disorderly Behaviour, and, with the Concurrence of two thirds, expel a Member." However, the Senate and House did not establish formal rules for members to follow, or to discipline members, until the 1960s.

The move to establish these rules started in the 1950s, during hearings in the Senate into alleged corruption in the Reconstruction Finance Corporation, a government aid program created by President Herbert Hoover in 1930. Chaired by Senator J. William Fulbright of Arkansas, the conclusion of the hearings called for ethics rules to be incorporated into the Senate. Fulbright said on the Senate floor, "What should be done about men who do not directly and blatantly sell the favors of their offices for money and so place themselves within the penalties of the law? How do we deal with those who, under the guise of friendship, accept favors which offend the spirit of the law but do not violate its letter?" Fulbright offered a resolution calling for hearings into the creation of a code of ethics. Before a special subcommittee of the Senate Committee on Labor and Public Welfare, chaired by Senator Paul H. Douglas of Illinois, rules that had been advocated since 1951 by Representative Charles Edward Bennett of Florida, calling for "all Government employees, including officeholders" to adhere to a congressional ethics code, were presented for consideration. Douglas later said, "When is it proper to offer [gifts to] public officials and what is it proper for them to receive? A cigar, a box of candy, a modest lunch . . .? Is any one of these improper? It is difficult to believe so. They are usually a courteous gesture, an expression of good will, or a simple convenience, symbolic rather than intrinsically significant. Normally they are not taken seriously by the giver nor do they mean very much to the receiver. At the point at which they do begin to mean something, however, do they not become improper? Even small gratuities can be significant if they are repeated and come to be expected." Formal rules were established in 1958.

On 24 July 1964, following the famed case of Robert Gene "Bobby" Baker, who was the secretary to the Senate majority leader, the Senate adopted Resolution 338, which established the Senate Select Committee on Standards and Conduct with

Senator Tom Dodd, standing at right, attends a 1967 Senate hearing that is investigating his alleged financial wrongdoings. (Wally McNamee/CORBIS)

the power to "receive complaints and investigate allegations of improper conduct which may reflect upon the Senate, violations of law, and violations of rules and regulations of the Senate." As the new committee assembled to draft provisions for ethics rules, the Senate was forced to deal with ethics charges against Senator Thomas J. Dodd (D-CT). After Dodd was censured by the Senate for financial impropriety, the committee released new rules on 15 March 1968. On 1 March 1977, Congress enacted the Official Conduct Amendments of 1977, which revised and expanded not only the 1968 set of rules, but the jurisdiction and authority of the select committee. At the same time, in 1977, the Senate Select Committee on Standards and Conduct was changed into the modern Senate Select Committee on Ethics.

This committee, the first to deal with the ethics issue, was charged with the responsibility to:

> Receive complaints and investigate allegations of improper conduct which may reflect upon the Senate, violations of law, violations of the Senate Code of Official Conduct, and violations of rules and reg-

ulations of the Senate, relating to the conduct of individuals in the performance of their duties as Members of the Senate, or as officers of employees of the Senate, and to make appropriate findings of fact and conclusions with respect thereto;

> Recommend, when appropriate, disciplinary action against Members and staff;

> Recommend rules or regulations necessary to insure appropriate Senate standards of conduct;

> Report violations of any law to the proper Federal and State authorities;

> Regulate the use of the franking privilege in the Senate;

> Investigate unauthorized disclosures of intelligence information;

> Implement the Senate public financial disclosure requirements of the Ethics in Government Act;

> Regulate the receipt and disposition of gifts from foreign governments received by Members, officers, and employees of the Senate;

> Render advisory opinions on the application of Senate rules and laws to Members, officers, and employees . . .

The committee's rules have been expanded, most recently in 1995, with the enactment of the

Gifts Rule, which restricts the acceptance by members of gifts. In 2000 a new set of rules established by the committee included those covering the Internet.

According to the standing rules of the U.S. Senate, the committee "investigates alleged misconduct of Senate members and employees, and also keeps senators and staff abreast of new rules and regulations of conduct."

See also Dodd, Thomas Joseph
References: Amer, Mildred, *The Senate Selection Committee on Ethics: A Brief History of Its Evolution and Jurisdiction* (Washington, DC: Congressional Research Service, 1993); "Ethical Standards in Government," *Report of the Special Subcommittee on the Establishment of a Commission on Ethics in Government,* Senate Committee on Labor and Public Welfare, 82nd Congress, 1st Session (1951), 23; "Study of Reconstruction Finance Corporation: Hearings Before a Subcommittee of the Senate Comm. on Banking and Currency" (81st Congress, 2nd Session, and 82nd Congress, 1st Session (1950–1951)); United States Senate, Select Committee on Ethics, *Senate Ethics Manual* (Washington, DC: Government Printing Office, 2000).

Senate Select Committee on Standards of Conduct

See Senate Select Committee on Ethics

Shepherd, Alexander Robey (1835–1902)

Territorial governor of the District of Columbia (1873–1874), known as "Boss" Shepherd for numerous acts of corruption of which he was accused but never found guilty. Shepherd remains a highly obscure figure. He was born in Washington, D.C., on 31 January 1835 and attended the schools of that city. Following his father's death, Shepherd left school and worked in odd jobs, most notably as a clerk, a carpenter's apprentice, and as a plumber's assistant. He eventually opened his own plumbing business and became a wealthy man. At the same time, he was involved in numerous real estate deals.

A Republican, Shepherd volunteered for service when the Civil War broke out and served in the military for three months before being elected to the Washington, D.C., Common Council. He served for three years, rising to the presidency of the council in 1862. Because Washington, D.C., at that time was a run-down and dirty city with unpaved roads, Shepherd took on the task of advocating a program of construction and modernization. In 1871 Shepherd was instrumental in establishing a territorial form of government for the district. Two years later, Shepherd was named governor of the territory by President Ulysses S. Grant, replacing Henry D. Cooke. Historian Lowell Ragatz wrote:

He quickly overshadowed his colleagues and won the name "Boss Shepherd" by assuming complete control. Imbued with the callous philosophy of a notoriously corrupt era and carried away by his enthusiasm, he spent millions beyond the legally authorized expenditures and hopelessly involved District finances. His custom of awarding contracts to friends in casual fashion without competitive bidding led to accusations that he was sharing in the spoils. . . . His recklessness and unscrupulous methods led to congressional investigation and the passage of the act of June 20, 1874, which replaced territorial government by commission rule. Grant thereupon named him commissioner, but the Senate refused to confirm the appointment, although he had been found innocent of dishonesty.

Hurt by the accusations made against him and the Senate's refusal to confirm him, Shepherd left Washington and moved to Mexico, where he went to work at a silver mine in Batopilas, Chihuahua. He died there of appendicitis on 12 September 1902 at the age of sixty-seven.

References: Ragatz, Lowell Joseph, "Shepherd, Alexander Robey," in Allen Johnson and Dumas Malone, et al., eds., *Dictionary of American Biography,* X vols. and 10 supplements (New York: Charles Scribner's Sons, 1930–1995), IX:77–78; "Shepherd, Alexander Robey," in *The National Cyclopædia of American Biography,* 57 vols. and supplements A-N (New York: James T. White & Company, 1897–1984), XIII:80–81; "Shepherd, Alexander Robey," in Rossiter Johnson, ed., *The Twentieth Century Biographical Dictionary of Notable Americans: Brief Biographies of Authors, Administrators, Clergymen, Commanders, Editors, Engineers, Jurists, Merchants, Officials, Philanthropists, Scientists, Statesman, and Others Who Are Making American History,* 10 vols. (Boston: Biographical Society, 1897–1904), IX.

Shuster, Elmer Greinert "Bud" (1932–)

United States representative from Pennsylvania (1973–2001), rebuked by the House Ethics Committee for allegedly accepting improper gifts and

HARPER'S WEEKLY.

A JOURNAL OF CIVILIZATION

Vol. XVIII.—No. 916.]   NEW YORK, SATURDAY, JULY 18, 1874.   [WITH A SUPPLEMENT. PRICE TEN CENTS.

Entered according to Act of Congress, in the Year 1874, by Harper & Brothers, in the Office of the Librarian of Congress, at Washington.

"DON'T LET US HAVE ANY MORE OF THIS NONSENSE. IT IS A GOOD TRAIT TO STAND BY ONE'S FRIENDS; BUT—"

A woman symbolizing justice talks to Ulysses S. Grant, who is reaching for a paper that reads "Shepherd rejected by the Senate. . . ." The Senate refused to confirm Shepherd's appointment as commissioner, although he had been found innocent of dishonesty. (Library of Congress)

favoring a lobbyist. Born in Glassport, Pennsylvania, on 23 January 1932, Shuster attended the public schools of Glassport before attending the University of Pittsburgh, from which he was awarded a bachelor of science degree in 1954, and Duquesne University in Pittsburgh, where he earned a master of business degree in 1960. He completed his education by earning a Ph.D. in economics and management from American University in Washington, D.C., in 1967. After receiving his degree from the University of Pittsburgh, Shuster entered the U.S. Army and served in the infantry and as a counterintelligence agent from 1954 to 1956. When he finished his duty, Shuster returned to Pennsylvania and became involved in the then-infant computer industry, becoming vice president of RCA's Electronic Computer Division. Involved in the early installation of the UNIVAC, the world's first computer system, he left RCA to found his own computer software company.

A conservative Republican in politics, Shuster ran for a seat in the U.S. House of Representatives in 1972. Defeating Democrat Earl D. Collins, Shuster entered the House on 3 January 1973, representing the Ninth Pennsylvania District. Shuster would eventually serve fourteen terms, from the 93rd through the 106th Congress. A member of the House Transportation Committee, he would eventually become known as "The King of Asphalt" for helping to send millions of dollars to his home state to pave roads, one of which was named in his honor. During his tenure in Congress, Shuster became one of the leading authors of much of the transportation-related legislation in Congress, including the Surface Transportation Act of 1982, the Surface Transportation and Uniform Relocation Assistance Act of 1987, and the Intermodal Surface Transportation Efficiency Act of 1991 (ISTEA). This latter action completed the Interstate Highway System begun under the administration of President Dwight D. Eisenhower. In 1995, when Republicans took control of the House, Shuster became chairman of his committee, renamed the Committee on Transportation and Infrastructure. Three years later, Shuster introduced the Transportation Equity Act for the 21st Century, known as TEA-21. This legislation directed that funds collected for highway construction nationwide be dedicated specifically for that purpose.

Shuster got into ethical trouble starting in 1996. On 6 March of that year, Common Cause, a well-known political watchdog group, sent a letter to the chair of the House Committee on Standards of Conduct (known as the House Ethics Committee), asking for investigation into Shuster's dealings with Ann Eppard, a former Shuster chief of staff who left his employ to go to work as a lobbyist for some of the companies doing business before Shuster's committee. Eppard was also in criminal difficulty—on 9 April 1998 she was indicted by a grand jury in Boston for embezzling $27,500 from Shuster's campaign at the same time that she accepted $230,000 in illegal payments while working for Shuster to help in the passage of the "Big Dig" construction project in Boston. On 9 November 1997, the chairman of the committee, Representative Lamar Smith, a Republican, and ranking minority member, Representative Howard Berman, a Democrat, formed an investigative subcommittee to look into the allegations. Representatives Joel Hefley, a Republican, and Zoe Lofgren, a Democrat, were named to head the subcommittee.

On 1 November 1999, Eppard pled guilty in Boston to accepting illegal compensation from a lobbyist. On 26 July 2000, the investigative subcommittee of the House Committee on Standards of Conduct concluded that Shuster had violated House ethics rules and adopted a Statement of Alleged Violation. Presented with this statement and a pending report, Shuster accepted the committee's findings. This 147-page report was released on 5 October 2000. In it, the committee explained that Shuster brought "discredit to the House of Representatives." In its letter to Shuster, the Committee explained:

> By a unanimous vote on October 4, 2000, the Committee on Standards of Official Conduct, acting on behalf of the House of Representatives, voted to issue to you this Letter of Reproval. The Committee unanimously voted to adopt the Report of the Investigative Subcommittee concerning its investigation of the numerous allegations of misconduct lodged against you.
>
> By your actions you have brought discredit to the House of Representatives.
>
> On November 14, 1997, the Chairman and Ranking Minority Member of the Committee on Standards of Official Conduct established an Inves-

tigative Subcommittee pursuant to Committee Rule 17(c)(2) in the matter of Representative Bud Shuster. The Investigative Subcommittee's inquiry focused on the allegations in a complaint filed by the Congressional Accountability Project and expanded to include an examination of whether your campaign committee violated House Rules and/or federal laws between 1993 and 1998. During the course of its inquiry the Investigative Subcommittee thoroughly investigated the allegations against you. The Investigative Subcommittee issued over 150 subpoenas, counsel interviewed approximately 75 witnesses and the Investigative Subcommittee deposed 33 witnesses. At the conclusion of the inquiry, the Investigative Subcommittee found substantial reason to believe that you had committed violations of House Rules within the Committee's jurisdiction. On July 26, 2000, the Investigative Subcommittee unanimously adopted a Statement of Alleged Violation finding that you engaged in a pattern of conduct that did not reflect creditably on the House of Representatives in violation of former Rule 43, clause 1, of the House of Representatives. As part of a negotiated settlement you admitted, under penalty of perjury, to the Statement of Alleged Violation. By voluntarily admitting to the Statement of Alleged Violation, you agreed that your conduct did not reflect creditably on the House of Representatives through five areas of conduct.

The Statement of Alleged Violation to which you admitted provides that your conduct did not reflect creditably on the House of Representatives in the following manner:

You engaged in a pattern and practice of knowingly allowing your former chief of staff to appear before or communicate with you in your official capacity, during the 12-month period following her resignation from your staff, in a manner that created the appearance that your official decisions might have been improperly affected.

You violated House Gift Rules by accepting expenses from two sources related to a trip to Puerto Rico with your family in December 1995 and January 1996.

You violated former House Rule 45 by authorizing and/or accepting the scheduling and advisory services of your former chief of staff on matters that were official in nature for approximately 18 months after she resigned from your congressional office.

While under your supervision and control, employees in your congressional office worked for your campaign committee to the apparent detriment of the time they were required to spend in your con-

gressional office. While under your supervision and control employees of your congressional office performed services for your campaign in your congressional office.

Expenditures for "political meetings" and expenditures for transportation on chartered aircraft by your campaign committee combined with inadequate record-keeping practices to verify the legitimate campaign purposes of these expenditures, created the appearance that between 1993 and 1998 certain expenditures of your campaign committee may not have been attributable to bona fide campaign or political purposes.

Common Cause President Scott Harshbarger stated, "The sanction imposed today by the House Committee on Standards of Official Conduct upon Representative Bud Shuster (R-PA) makes crystal clear that he brought discredit to the House of Representatives by engaging in a staggeringly wide array of ethical violations. These include a problematic relationship with his former Chief of Staff, flagrant violations of the House Gift Rules, blurring of the lines between official staff and campaign staff, and misuse of campaign funds for apparent personal benefit. . . . The Letter of Reproval issued by the Committee also shows that Representative Shuster has displayed a cavalier and arrogant attitude toward these serious charges—a tone, according to the letter, of 'blame-shifting and trivializing of misconduct.' But the Committee's report also shows that Shuster escaped punishment for potentially more serious allegations involving special favors and possible quid-pro-quos."

Despite this action, Shuster was overwhelmingly reelected in November 2000 to another term. However, health concerns and a feeling by Shuster that he had "reached the pinnacle of my congressional career," led the fourteen-term congressman to announce on 4 January 2001 that he would resign from the House on 31 January. In May 2001, Shuster's son, William "Bill" Shuster, won a special election to fill his father's seat.

References: *Biographical Directory of the American Congress, 1774–1996* (Alexandria, VA: CQ Staff Directories, Inc., 1996); Pianin, Eric, "Veteran Lawmaker Shuster to Retire—'King of Asphalt' Cites Health Reasons," *Washington Post,* 5 January 2001, A4; Plungis, Jeff, "The Driving Force of Bud Shuster," *CQ Weekly,* 7 August 1999, 1914–1919; U.S. House of Representatives, Committee on Standards of Official

Conduct, *In the Matter of Representative E. G. 'Bud' Shuster: Report* (Washington, DC: Government Printing Office, 2000).

Sikes, Robert Lee Fulton (1906–1994)

United States representative from Florida (1941–1944, 1945–1979), reprimanded by the U.S. House of Representatives for financial misconduct, for which he eventually lost his seat. Sikes was born in the village of Isabella, near the town of Sylvester, Georgia, on 3 June 1906, the son of Benjamin Fulton Sikes and Clara (née Ford) Sikes. Robert Sikes attended the public schools of the area before he entered the University of Georgia at Athens, which awarded him a bachelor of science degree in 1927. He later earned a master of science degree from the University of Florida at Gainesville in 1929, after which he entered the publishing business in Crestview, Florida. Through this business—and the running of two local newspapers, in Crestview and Valparaiso—Sikes gained important contacts and status in the community.

Sikes's political career began in Florida in 1935, when he was elected to that state's house of representatives, serving from 1936 until 1940. In 1940 he ran for a seat in the U.S. House of Representatives as a Democrat from the Third District of Florida. That seat had been held by Representative Millard Caldwell, who had retired. Sikes, being unopposed, was elected to the first of two terms. He would have been reelected in 1944, but on 19 October 1944 he resigned his seat to serve in the U.S. Army during World War II. He was allowed to run for his seat in the 1944 elections, however, and once again he was elected. He would hold the seat until his resignation in 1979.

Sikes became an important leader for the district he represented; one constituent referred to him as a "He Coon," a metaphor for the revered leader of a tribe of racoons, which were in abundance in West Florida when the first British and Spanish settlers arrived. It was a name that stuck, and his followers were called "He Coons." It also became the name of Sikes's autobiography. Sikes's praise was due mainly because of his leadership in bringing dollars to the area he represented for defense. Sikes was also a leader in helping to build the Apalachicola-Chattahoochee-Flint River system, which brought water to areas of Florida,

Georgia, and Alabama. For this work he was popular among his constituents and his colleagues in Congress. But at the same time, Sikes was involved in financial dealings that would ultimately cause his downfall. As chairman of the House Military Construction Appropriations Subcommittee, Sikes had the power to push or resist lucrative military construction projects. On 28 April 1976, the House Committee on Standards of Official Conduct began an inquiry into conflict of interest allegations lodged against Sikes by Common Cause, the citizens' lobbying group that called for strict ethics rules in Congress. Common Cause alleged that Sikes, as chairman of the House subcommittee, had not reported the ownership of stock in Fairchild Industries Inc., a military contractor doing business before the subcommittee, as well as stock in the First Navy Bank at the Pensacola Naval Air Station in Pensacola, Florida, in violation of Rule 44 of the House Ethics rules. The group also charged that Sikes had sponsored legislation in the House in 1961 that removed restrictions on parcels of land in Florida for use in construction, despite the fact that Sikes had a financial interest in this land. On 12 May 1976, the panel voted nine to zero to initiate a "factual investigation" into the charges. Committee chairman John J. Flynt Jr. (D-GA) told reporters that "as far as he knew" it was the first such intensive investigation by the House committee charged with upholding ethics.

Following a comprehensive investigation, the committee voted ten to two on 21 July 1976 to approve a report prepared by investigators that recommended that the full House reprimand Sikes for financial misconduct only, despite the overwhelming evidence of violations of conflict-of-interest laws. All three charges made by Common Cause were proved; however, the panel held that Sikes's failure to report the Fairchild stock did not appear to be "an effort to conceal" ownership, but deserved a reprimand nonetheless. The charges involving the land deals were cited as a conflict of interest, but no further action was called for. A fourth charge, alleging that Sikes voted for a fiscal 1975 military appropriations bill, which included $73 million for an aircraft contract with Fairchild, did not violate House rules because he had only a limited number of shares in the company, and such ownership did not disqualify him from voting on the matter.

On 29 July 1976, the House voted 381 to 3 to reprimand Sikes, the first time a sitting member had been so punished since Representative Adam Clayton Powell in 1969. Despite this punishment, Sikes won reelection in 1976. However, on 27 May 1978, he announced he would not be a candidate for reelection in that year's election. He left office on 3 January 1979. He retired to Crestview, Florida, where he remained until his death from pneumonia on 28 September 1994 at the age of eighty-eight.

References: "[The Case of] Robert L. F. Sikes," in *Congressional Ethics* (Washington, DC: Congressional Quarterly, 1980), 22; Sikes, Bob, *He-Coon: The Bob Sikes Story* (Pensacola, FL: Perdido Bay Press, 1984); United States Congress, *Biographical Directory of the United States Congress, 1774–1989: The Continental Congress, September 5, 1774, to October 21, 1788, and the Congress of the United States, from the First through the One Hundredth Congresses, March 4, 1789, to January 3, 1989, Inclusive* (Washington, DC: Government Printing Office, 1989).

Simmons, James Fowler (1795–1864)

Rhode Island industrialist and U.S. senator (1841–1847, 1857–1862), who resigned his seat because of corruption. Born on his family's farm near the town of Little Compton, Rhode Island, on 10 September 1795, Simmons attended a private school in Newport, Rhode Island. In 1812 he moved to Providence, Rhode Island, and worked in various manufacturing concerns in both Rhode Island and Massachusetts. In 1822 he again moved, this time to a small town in New Hampshire that he renamed Simmonsville, and there he opened a yarn factory. Five years later, he relocated the factory to Johnston, Rhode Island.

In 1827 Simmons was elected to the New Hampshire state house of representatives, where he served until 1841. A Whig, Simmons was elected to the U.S. Senate, where he initially served from 4 March 1841 until 3 March 1847.

On 2 July 1862, Senator Joseph A. Wright, Unionist of Indiana, submitted a resolution calling for Simmons's expulsion. Wright claimed that Secretary of War Edwin M. Stanton had reported to him that Simmons had used his influence as a U.S. senator to try to obtain a war contract for two Rhode Island companies that had contributed to Simmons's election efforts—allegedly two $10,000 promissory notes, as well as a promise of some $500,000 in profits from the company if they got the contract. The matter was referred to the Senate Judiciary Committee—there was no Ethics Committee as of yet—which reported back to the Senate within a week. Historians Anne Butler and Wendy Wolff explain:

The committee ascertained that an agent of a Rhode Island business firm approached Simmons and requested aid in procuring a government contract for the manufacture of 50,000 breech-loading rifles. Simmons corroborated the testimony of the agent, C. D. Schubarth, but insisted that the manufacturers' payments to him were not tied to a guarantee of government contracts. Simmons detailed the transactions with great frankness, expressing his complete astonishment at the charges and contending that he acted for the benefit of both his constituents and his government. Simmons cited the recent Union draft of 500,000 men, for whom the government had but 200,000 weapons. With such a critical shortage, Simmons assumed that the prompt delivery from a responsible firm could only aid the war effort. The unabashed senator made no move to deny that he still held the promissory notes or that he expected them to be paid in full.

In its July 14 report, the committee set forth Simmons's case in the most deferential terms, citing his age and honorable life, but ultimately found the senator's behavior entirely inexcusable.

However, because the Senate session was nearly ended, no action was taken on Simmons's case. Simmons was warned that once the Senate reconvened, he would be the subject of an expulsion resolution. Facing this, he resigned his seat on 15 August 1862, one of only a handful of senators to take such a step because of political corruption.

Simmons returned to Rhode Island and his manufacturing pursuits. He lived only two years after leaving the Senate, dying in Johnston, Rhode Island, on 10 July 1864 at the age of sixty-eight. His name, and his case, have slipped into obscurity.

References: *Biographical Directory of the American Congress, 1774–1996* (Alexandria, VA: CQ Staff Directories, Inc., 1996); Butler, Anne M., and Wendy Wolff, *United States Senate Election, Expulsion and Censure Cases, 1793–1990* (Washington, DC: Government Printing Office, 1995), 115–116.

Small, Lennington "Len" (1862–1936)

Governor of Illinois (1921–1929), implicated in massive corruption in that state but acquitted by a jury. Born near Kankakee, Illinois, on 16 June

1862, Lennington Small, known as "Len," was the son of a doctor. He attended public schools and Northern Indiana Normal School. Little is known about his early life. A Republican, in 1901 Small was elected to a seat in the Illinois state senate, serving until 1905. He was elected state treasurer in 1904 and served until 1908. From 1908 until 1912 he served as assistant treasurer in charge of the United States Subtreasury in Chicago. In 1916 he was again elected Illinois state treasurer, serving from 1917 until 1921.

In 1920 Small captured the Republican nomination for governor and went on to defeat Democrat James H. Lewis by more than half a million votes out of 2 million cast. Assuming office on 10 January 1921, Small won a second term in 1924.

Almost from the start of his administration, Small was beset by allegations of massive corruption from his days as state treasurer from 1917 to 1921. It was during this period that Small worked with William "Big Bill" Thompson, mayor of Chicago and himself a corrupt politician. Small aided Thompson in keeping Chicago in the grips of the corrupt powers that had elected Thompson as mayor. Historian Jay Robert Nash explained, "Not long after taking office for the first time in 1921, [Small] was indicted for embezzling $600,000 during his previous term as state treasurer. Small was charged with depositing millions of dollars of state funds in a bank controlled by his friend, State Senator E. C. Curtis, and profited by the interest in 1917 when he was serving as state treasurer." Historian George Kohn adds, "The experience of undergoing judicial arraignment did not, however, deter Small. He found a way to circumvent the authority of the court. He teamed up with a notorious gunman, a lawyer turned crook, and a dishonorable union official to bribe and threaten members of the jury and their families. He was, in due course, acquitted."

Small was now free from embezzlement charges, but instead of remaining clean he decided to use the governor's office to sell pardons to the highest bidder. From the time of his acquittal until he left office, Small sold some 8,000 pardons—making him one of the most corrupt governors in American history. Working closely with Thompson in Chicago and Robert E. Crowe, the state's attorney for Cook County, Small would find convicts, have a third party approach them with the offer of a pardon, and then grant it for a fixed sum. Small would then split the fees with Crowe. One such parolee was Ignatz Potz, sentenced to death for killing a police officer. Small commuted his sentence in 1922 to life and in 1926 granted him a full pardon that released Potz from prison altogether. Small became known as "The Pardoning Governor of Illinois."

In 1928 Small actually tried to run for a third term. In what was called the "Pineapple Primary" (in which extremists from both sides set off bombs, nicknamed "pineapples," to force the other parties' voters away from the polls), Small and Crowe were defeated, despite having the financial and political backing of Mafia boss Al Capone. Small lost the Republican primary to Louis L. Emmerson, the Illinois secretary of state. Small ran for governor again in 1932, but lost to Democrat Henry Horner; he also ran in 1936, but lost the Republican nomination to C. Wayland Brooks. Shortly after the 1936 primary, Small died on his farm near Kankakee on 17 May 1936. He was buried in Kankakee. Although it is obvious that Small was indeed one of the most corrupt, if not the most corrupt, governor in American history, his name is almost wholly forgotten.

See also Thompson, William Hale
References: "Len Small," in Jay Robert Nash, *Encyclopedia of World Crime: Criminal Justice, Criminology, and Law Enforcement,* 4 vols. (Wilmette, IL: CrimeBooks, Inc, 1989), IV:2780; "Len Small: Pardoning Governor," in George C. Kohn, *Encyclopedia of American Scandal: From ABSCAM to the Zenger Case* (New York: Facts on File, 1989), 302; "Small, Lennington," in Robert Sobel and John Raimo, eds., *Biographical Directory of the Governors of the United States, 1789–1978,* 4 vols. (Westport, CT: Meckler Books, 1978), II:384–385.

Smith, Frank Leslie (1867–1950)

United States representative (1919–1921) and senator-elect (1926–1928) from Illinois, refused his seat in the U.S. Senate because of allegations of fraud and corruption in his campaign. Born in the village of Dwight, Illinois, on 24 November 1867, Frank Smith attended local public schools and for a time taught in local schools, although it does not appear that he ever received any secondary education or a degree. Branching out into private business pursuits, he entered the fields of insurance, real estate, banking, and agriculture. In 1894 he served as the village clerk for Dwight, apparently his first political position.

In 1904 Smith was nominated by the Republicans for the office of lieutenant governor of Illinois. However, although the Republican gubernatorial nominee, Charles S. Deneen, was elected easily, Smith was defeated by Democrat Lawrence Yates Sherman (1858–1939), former Speaker of the Illinois House of Representatives. Smith did serve, from 1905 to 1909, as the internal revenue collector for Illinois. Smith left office in 1909 and returned to private business, but ten years later was elected to a seat in U.S. House of Representatives, serving in the Sixty-sixth Congress from 4 March 1919 to 3 March 1921. In 1920 he gave up his seat to try for the Republican nomination for the U.S. Senate, but lost to William Brown McKinley. Again, he returned to his business pursuits. In 1921 Illinois Governor Lennington "Len" Small named Smith chairman of the Illinois Commerce Commission, where he served until 1926. In 1926 Smith ran for the U.S. Senate seat held by McKinley—who was seriously ill—and defeated Democrat George E. Brennan. On 7 December 1926, Senator McKinley died, and Governor Small named Smith to the vacancy, which expired on 3 March 1927.

Smith went to Washington, both as the appointed senator and as the senator-elect in his own right. As soon as he presented his credentials, protests were made to his taking his seat. These protests alleged that Smith had used "fraud and corruption" in his 1926 campaign for the U.S. Senate, and the case was sent to the Senate Committee on Privileges and Elections (now the Committee on Rules and Administration). After a lengthy inquiry into the 1926 contest, on 17 January 1928, the committee held that Smith not be allowed to take his seat because of corruption perpetrated by him and his supporters. On 19 January the Senate adopted this resolution, and the seat was declared vacant. Despite the fact that he had never served a single day in the U.S. Senate, Smith "resigned" on 9 February 1928. Otis F. Glenn, a Republican, was elected to take the vacant seat and he began his service on 3 December 1928.

Tarred by the scandal that cost him a seat in the U.S. Senate, Smith ran for a seat in the U.S. House of Representatives in 1930, but was unsuccessful.

He served as a member of the Republican National Committee in 1932, then left politics altogether to return to his business pursuits, including serving as chairman of the board of directors of the First National Bank of Dwight, Illinois. Smith died in Dwight on 30 August 1950 at the age of eighty-two and was buried in Oak Lawn Cemetery in that city.

References: Wooddy, Carroll Hill, *The Case of Frank L. Smith: A Study in Representative Government* (Chicago: The University of Chicago Press, 1931).

Smith, John (1735?–1824)

U.S. senator from Ohio (1803–1808), nearly expelled (and later resigned) from the Senate for his role in the conspiracy of Vice President Aaron Burr to separate several western states from the Union and create a new nation. Little is known of his early life: he was born in either Virginia or Ohio about 1735. He prepared for the ministry and for much of his life served as a pastor in various Baptist congregations in Ohio and Virginia. In 1790 he was serving in a Baptist church on the forks of the Cheat River in what is now West Virginia. In 1791 he moved to Columbia, Ohio, later a part of the city of Cincinnati, where he became a preacher and merchant. His gifts of public speaking brought him great notice, and in 1798 he was elected to the first of four terms in the Northwest Territorial legislature that ended in 1803.

When Ohio was admitted as a state into the Union in 1803, the new state legislature moved to elect two men to the United States Senate. One of these men was John Smith, most likely to reward him for his actions in pushing statehood. While in the Senate, from 1 April 1803 until 25 April 1808, he apparently made only one speech, spending most of his time engaged in private pursuits. These caused his downfall in 1808. Rumors of his ties with Vice President Aaron Burr's attempts to get several western states to secede from the Union, as well as the obvious neglect of his senatorial duties, led to his being called by a grand jury in Frankfort, Kentucky, which was investigating Burr's actions. Fearing that he would be called before the panel, Smith fled to West Florida, where he waited until Burr was tried and acquitted. When he arrived back in Washington in January 1807, the U.S. Senate took up a call to investigate Smith's actions. Senator John Quincy Adams, a Federalist from Massachusetts, chaired the committee that investigated whether to expel or censure Smith. In its report, released 31 December 1807, the committee stated, "When a man whom his fellow citizens have honored with their confidence on the pledge of a spotless reputation has degraded himself by the commission of infamous crimes, which become suddenly and unexpectedly revealed to the world, defective, indeed, would be that institution which should be impotent to discard from its bosom the contagion of such a member." Smith's counsel was Francis Scott Key, who later wrote the "Star Spangled Banner." On 9 April 1808, the Senate voted nineteen to ten to expel Smith, but, lacking a two-thirds vote, Smith was saved from expulsion. Sixteen days later, Smith resigned his seat.

In 1844 Representative Edward Junius Black of Georgia went before the House and spoke about the right of either house to expel certain members, citing specifically the Smith case. He said:

In 1807, when John Smith was the unhappy culprit, Mr. [John Quincy] Adams, as chairman of the committee to whom the case was referred, believed that the Senate might well entertain even the higher and more important question of expulsion, without "depriving him of rights secured by the constitution of the United States." Hear him—for nothing can so fully illustrate his position in 1842, and his deliberate opinions in 1807, as to place them in contrast by quoting his own words. How curses will come home! Smith represented himself "as solitary, friendless, and unskilled"; and intimated that his rights were about to be denied him by senators "liable, so long as they held their offices, to have his case made their own." The chairman, in his "pride of place," not dreaming that his own words were prophetic of his own future condition, replied: "The committee are not unaware that, in the vicissitudes of human events, no member of this body can be sure that his conduct will never be made a subject of inquiry and decision before the assembly to which he belongs. They are aware that, in the course of proceeding which the Senate may sanction, its members are marking out a precedent which may hereafter apply to themselves. They are sensible that the principles upon which they have acted ought to have the same operation upon their own claims to privilege as upon those of Mr. Smith; the same relation to the rights of their constituents which they have to those of the legislature which he represents."

What John Smith did with the remainder of his life remains unknown; what is known is that he moved in 1812 to West Florida (now Louisiana), settling for a time in Pensacola and later in St. Francisville, now in Louisiana. He died in St. Francisville on 30 July 1824.

References: Cox, Isaac J., "Smith, John," in Allen Johnson and Dumas Malone, et al., eds., *Dictionary of American Biography*, X vols. and 10 supplements (New York: Charles Scribner's Sons, 1930–1995), IX:296–297; Pitcher, M. Avis, "John Smith, First Senator from Ohio and his Connections with Aaron Burr," *Archaeological and Historical Society Quarterly*, 45 (1936), 68–75; *Speech of Mr. Black, of Georgia, on the Right of Members to Their Seats in the House of Representatives. Delivered in the House of Representatives, February 12, 1844* (Washington, DC: Printed at the Globe Office, 1844), 11; Wilhelmy, Robert W., "Senator John Smith and the Aaron Burr Conspiracy," *Cincinnati Historical Society Bulletin*, 28 (Spring 1970), 39–60.

Special Prosecutor (Federal)

See Independent Counsel Statute

Speech or Debate Clause of the U.S. Constitution

Section of the United States Constitution providing that legislators cannot he held criminally liable for words spoken on the floor of the U.S. House or U.S. Senate, which the Supreme Court has interpreted to protect "against inquiry into acts that occur in the regular course of the legislative process and into the motivation for those acts." Located in Article 1, Section 1, Clause 6, the clause reads, "They shall in all cases, except treason, felony and breach of the peace, be privileged from arrest during their attendance at the session of their respective Houses, and in going to and returning from the same; and for any speech or debate in either House, they shall not be questioned in any other place." Legislators under potential corruption charges have used this clause to shield themselves from inquiries into activities that involve their official duties.

The immunity for lawmakers from prosecution for speech pursuant to their legislative duties has its origins in the fight between the English Parliament and the king over control of the nation. During the reign of Richard II (1396–1397), one member of Parliament, Thomas Haxey, was thrown into prison and condemned to death for introducing a bill calling for the reduction of royal household expenditures. Richard was murdered before Haxey could be put to death, and his successor, Henry IV, set aside the judgment. When Henry VII threw Richard Strode, another member of Parliament, into prison in 1512 for trying to regulate the English tin industry, Parliament enacted a law annulling the judgment against Strode, releasing him from prison and declaring null and void all future attempts by English monarchs to regulate the speech of members of Parliament. This law was followed by the monarchy until Charles I, in 1632, imprisoned Sir John Elliot and William and Valentine Strode (no known relation to the aforementioned Richard Strode) for speaking against the Crown in Parliament. Elliot died in the Tower of London, and it was not until 1643 that the Strodes were released because Parliament had raised an army to fight the king. In 1689, as part of the English Bill of Rights, Parliament declared "that the Freedom of Speech, and Debates or Proceedings in Parliament, ought not to be impeached or questioned in any Court or Place out of Parliament."

The drafters of the Articles of Confederation were so concerned about this freedom that they incorporated into that document as Article V, "Freedom of speech and debate in Congress shall not be impeached or questioned in any court or place out of Congress." The Speech or Debate Clause was inserted into the Constitution without debate or dissent—James Wilson, one of the signers of the Constitution, penned, "In order to enable and encourage a representative of the public to discharge his public trust with firmness and success, it is indispensably necessary, that he should enjoy the fullest liberty of speech, and that he should be protected from the resentment of every one, however powerful, to whom the exercise of that liberty may occasion offence." James Madison, one of the framers of the Constitution, wrote in *Federalist No. 48*:

It is agreed on all sides, that the powers properly belonging to one of the departments, ought not to be directly and completely administered by either of the other departments. It is equally evident, that neither of them ought to possess directly or indirectly, an overruling influence over the others in the administration of their respective powers. It will not be denied, that power is of an encroaching nature, and that it ought to be effectually restrained from passing the limits assigned to it. After discriminating therefore in theory, the several classes of power, as they may in their nature be legislative, executive, or judiciary; the next and most difficult task, is to provide some practical security for each against the invasion of the others. What this security ought to be, is the great problem to be solved.

This right is considered one of the most fundamental to the system of checks and balances, which is a major component of the American system of government. The clause has been used both by those claiming heroic causes and those who eventually fell in ignominy. The Speech or Debate Clause slowed an investigation into a committee that entered the Pentagon Papers into a hearing report and also delayed a probe into wrongdoing by former House Ways and Means Chairman Dan Rostenkowski (D-IL). The Supreme Court has visited the issue of the use of the clause in five separate cases: *Kilbourn v. Thompson,* 103 U.S. 168 (1881); *Tenney v. Brandhove,* 341 U.S. 367 (1951); *United States v. Johnson,* 383 U.S. 169 (1966); *Dombrowsky v. Eastland,* 387 U.S. 82 (1967); and *Powell v. McCormack,* 395 U.S. 486 (1969). Justice Sandra Day O'Connor wrote in *Flanagan v. United States,* 465 U.S. 259 (1984), "Similarly, the right guaranteed by the Speech or Debate Clause is more than the right not to be convicted for certain legislative activities: it is the right not to 'be questioned' about them—that is, not to be tried for them." In *United States v. Helstoski,* 422 U.S. 477 (1971), Chief Justice Burger wrote that the clause's intent is "to preserve the constitutional structure of separate, coequal, and independent branches of government. The English and American history of the privilege suggests that any lesser standard would risk intrusion by the Executive and the Judiciary into the sphere of protected legislative activities." The right of the Senate to use its investigative powers under the clause, which fall under the power of a "legitimate legislative sphere," is absolute—so said the Court in *Eastland v. United States Servicemen's Fund,* 421 U.S. 491 (1975). However, in an earlier case, *United States v. Brewster,* 408 U.S. 501 (1972), the same Court held that the sole exception to the clause was an inquiry into alleged criminal conduct by a congressman or senator aside from his or her actions as a member of Congress.

See also *United States v. Brewster*

References: Andrews, James De Witt, ed., *The Works of James Wilson: Associate Justice of the Supreme Court of the United States and Professor of Law in the College of Philadelphia, Being his Public Discourses Upon Jurisprudence and the Political Science, Including Lectures and Professor of Law, 1790–1792,* 2 vols. (Chicago: Callaghan & Co., 1896), II:38; Elliot, Jonathan, ed., *The Debates in the Several State Conventions on the Adoption of the Federal Constitution, as Recommended by the General Convention at Philadelphia in 1787. Together with the Journal of the Federal Convention, Luther Martin's letter, Yates's Minutes, Congressional Opinions, Virginia and Kentucky Resolutions of '98–'99, and other Illustrations of the Constitution. Collected and Revised from Contemporary Publications, by Jonathan Elliott. Published under the Sanction of Congress,* Printed for the editor, 5 vols. (Washington, DC: Printed for the editor, 1836–1845), V:406; Farrand, Max, ed., *The Records of the Federal Convention of 1787,* 3 vols. (New Haven, CT: Yale University Press, 1911), II:246; *Flanagan v. United States,* 465 U.S. 259, 266 (1984); Great Britain, Public Record Office, *Calendar of State Papers: Domestic Series, of the Reign of William and Mary. Preserved in the Public Record Office. Edited by William John Hardy,* 5 vols. (London, Printed for His Majesty's Stationery Office by Eyre and Spottiswoode, 1895–1906), session 2, chapter 2; *Helstoski v. United States,* 442 U.S. 477, 491 (1979); "History of the Foundations of the Speech and Debate Clause," in Trevelyan, George Macaulay, *History of England* (New York: Longmans, Green, 1927), 335–336, *Tenney v. Brandhove,* 341 U.S. 367, 371 n.2, (1951); Jefferson, Thomas, *The Writings of Thomas Jefferson: Collected and Edited by Paul Leicester Ford,* 10 vols., Paul Leicester Ford, ed. (New York: G. P. Putnam's Sons, 1892–1899), VIII:322; Lederkramer, David M., "A Statutory Proposal for Case-by-Case Congressional Waiver of the Speech or Debate Privilege in Bribery Cases," *Cardozo Law Review,* 3:3 (Spring 1982), 465–518.

Star Route Frauds

Scandal in which bribes were given to postal officials in exchange for plum routes of mail sending and delivery. In the nineteenth century mail was delivered in the western and southern United States via the sale of postal routes to locals who could deliver the mail to rural areas at the lowest cost possible. Called "Star Routes" because an asterisk appeared next to them on official post office department documents, this program allowed for mail delivery to some of the most remote areas of the western United States. Mail was delivered by horse, buggy, and cart. Historian J. Martin Klotsche wrote that after the Civil War these routes sprang up. "In time," he explained, "the large unoccupied regions between the Pacific Coast and the 'jumping-off place' were filled in and by the [1870s] weekly, semi-weekly, and daily mails were being carried to what at one time had been considered inaccessible regions. So important had the 'star service' become that by 1880 the total annual transportation amounted to over 75 million miles."

In 1880 James A. Garfield, a member of the U.S. House of Representatives from Ohio, was elected president. As soon as he took office the following March, he discovered that the Star Route program was rife with massive fraud and corruption—a circle of officials, mostly in Garfield's own Republican Party, had used the Star Route program to line their own pockets at the same time that services were either cut or nonexistent. It is estimated by some that approximately $4 million dollars was stolen from government coffers. He also discovered that the former postmaster general, John A. J. Creswell, had investigated these frauds in 1869 and 1870, but had dismissed all claims of corruption. A House committee investigation in 1872 looked into the matter, but no charges were brought forward.

Upon taking office and discovering the fraud, Garfield ordered Postmaster General Thomas Lemuel James to investigate the corruption. Garfield allegedly told James "Go ahead [and investigate]. Regardless of where or whom you hit, I direct you to probe this ulcer to the bottom and then to cut it out." He added that "the proposed investigation must be aimed at a system, and not at men . . . that if the inquiry should disclose the fact that any person or persons had been guilty of corruption or fraud, that person or those persons must be handed over to the Department of Justice." Garfield also named William Cook, a criminal attorney, to aid James with any criminal prosecutions. In his own internal inquiry inside the Post Office Department, James discovered that the second assistant postmaster general, Thomas J. Brady, was involved, and forced Brady's resignation. Brady had aided to increase compensation to

Star Route contractors, many of whom were his friends. With Brady's ouster, the investigation centered on one of the contractors, former U.S. Senator Stephen W. Dorsey. Dorsey, who served in the U.S. Senate from Arkansas (1873–1879), also served as chairman of the Republican National Committee during the 1880 election and had been instrumental in Garfield's election. Letters later turned up showed that when Garfield was composing his cabinet, Dorsey expressed his dissatisfaction with several reformist members being named, most notably Thomas L. James in the Post Office Department. When Brady was forced out, Dorsey threatened in a letter to *The World* of New York that if he were targeted for prosecution he would name those officers of the party who were involved in the fraud, corruption that he said helped to carry Indiana for the Republicans in 1880.

On 2 July 1881, Garfield was shot by a crazed mental patient, and while he lingered over the summer the Star Route investigation slowly faded from the public. In 19 September 1881 Garfield succumbed to his wounds, and Vice President Chester Alan Arthur was sworn in as his successor. Dorsey, seeing Arthur as more pliable than Garfield, asked to meet with the new president, but was refused. In fact, Arthur's message to Congress in December called attention not only to the investigations but also to his push for reforms in the department.

On 4 March 1882, a federal grand jury in Washington, D.C., indicted seven men, including Brady and Dorsey, on charges of defrauding the government. The trial for the two men began on 1 June 1882. From the start, the prosecution was hampered by several factors—one was in the choice of one of the prosecutors, A. M. Gibson, who, it was later proved, had been paid $2,500 by one Star Route contractor. He was eventually removed from the case. Another factor was that the Star Route defense all pointed to a government conspiracy as the true cause of the prosecutions. The prosecution at trial presented 115 witnesses and more than 3,600 exhibits. When the jury returned with verdicts, two lower defendants were acquitted, two were found guilty, and for the rest there was a hung jury. The judge set aside the guilty verdicts, calling them "unreasonable." The men, including Dorsey and Brady, were retried in late 1882 and 1883, but all

were found not guilty. Other cases around the country of lesser figures in the scandal also led to not guilty verdicts. To recover some of the funds stolen by those targeted, the government instituted numerous civil lawsuits, but local judges who sympathized with the defendants dismissed all of them—one as late as 1922. When the government attempted to prosecute alleged acts of bribery of jurors, only one went to a jury trial, and that case was dismissed by Grover Cleveland's postmaster general, William F. Vilas. In total, of all the Star Route trials, only two lesser figures, Thomas McDevitt and Christian Price, were convicted on charges of defrauding the government and sent to prison. When the Democrats retook control of the House of Representatives in 1883, they opened an investigation into the frauds, but this investigation ended with no further prosecutions.

The Star Route frauds were a turning point in government corruption, leading to the passage of civil service reform. It also led to the wholesale repudiation of Republican rule in the 1884 elections.

See also Dorsey, Stephen Wallace; Ingersoll, Robert Green
References: Klotsche, J. Martin, "The Star Route Cases," *Mississippi Valley Historical Review*, XXII:3 (December 1935), 407–418; "Star Route Frauds," in George C. Kohn, *Encyclopedia of American Scandal: From ABSCAM to the Zenger Case* (New York: Facts on File, 1989), 307; *Star Route Transportation of Mails,* House Report 1701, 47th Congress, 1st Session (1882), 1–6; *Testimony Relating to Expenditures in the Department of Justice. The Star-Route Cases,* House Miscellaneous Doc. 38 (Part 2), 48th Congress, 1st Session (1884), 1–9.

Starr, Kenneth Winston (1946–)

Solicitor General of the United States (1989–1993), independent counsel in the Whitewater and Monica Lewinsky investigations (1994–2000), the first independent counsel to bring impeachment charges against the focus of his investigation, President William Jefferson "Bill" Clinton. Starr was born in Vernon, Texas, on 21 July 1946, the son of a Baptist minister. He received his education in Texas, then earned a bachelor's degree from George Washington University in 1968, his master's degree in political science from Brown University in Rhode Island in 1969, and law degree from Duke University in 1973. Because of his family's poverty, Starr sold Bibles door to door to pay for his college education. After he received his law

Ken Starr reading from the U.S. Constitution during the Clinton impeachment inquiry of the House Judiciary Committee on November 19, 1998. Starr was also the independent counsel in the Whitewater and Monica Lewinsky investigations (1994–2000). (Reuters NewMedia Inc./CORBIS)

court with Starr were Antonin Scalia, who would one day sit on the U.S. Supreme Court, and Robert H. Bork, a former solicitor general who was named to the court by Reagan in 1987 but defeated in the Senate. Starr's conservative philosophy shone through in his decisions—including striking down an affirmative action plan for the District of Columbia—but his honesty and integrity earned him respect even among judges who disagreed with him.

In 1988 Reagan's vice president, George H. W. Bush, was elected president. He invited Starr to serve as his solicitor general, the chief government officer who argues the cases of the United States before the U.S. Supreme Court. Starr enjoyed his work on the Court of Appeals—often a stepping stone to a Supreme Court appointment—so he waited several days before accepting the offer. As solicitor general (1989–1993), Starr argued several important cases before the Supreme Court, most notably arguing that burning an American flag was an activity not protected by the First Amendment; as well, he penned briefs with a conservative outlook on such issues as abortion. Following the election of Bill Clinton in 1992, Starr left office and became a partner in the Washington office of the Chicago law firm Kirkland and Ellis. His clientele included numerous business interests.

On 5 August 1994, Starr came back into the public eye when a three-judge panel in Washington named him the new independent counsel to succeed Robert B. Fiske Jr. in investigating the Whitewater affair, a complicated land deal in Arkansas in which President Bill Clinton and his wife, Hillary, had been involved. Fiske was delving through allegations that the Clintons had used shady means to finance the land deal when the court decided that Starr should replace him. The decision sent shockwaves through the media: who was this man Starr, and why did the three-judge panel decide Fiske needed to be replaced? It became known that several Republican senators, most notably Lauch Faircloth of North Carolina, had written to the court complaining about Fiske's dilatory approach to the investigation. Starr took up his duties.

Starr first went to Arkansas to investigate Whitewater. (See the entry on Whitewater for the full information on this scandal.) He was later

license, Starr went to work as a clerk for Judge David W. Dyer of the U.S. Court of Appeals for the District of Columbia Circuit. Two years later, Starr joined the Los Angeles, California, law firm of Gibson, Dunn & Crutcher. In 1977 he became an associate partner in the firm.

In 1975 Starr was appointed a law clerk to Supreme Court Chief Justice Warren E. Burger, a position he held for two years. He left his law firm to serve Burger, but, after leaving the Court, rejoined the firm as an associate partner. One of the partners of the firm was William French Smith, a close friend and confidante of former California Governor Ronald Reagan. In 1980 Reagan was elected president and named Smith his attorney general. Starr, a conservative Republican, was named a counselor at the Department of Justice.

After only three years in Washington, Starr was named by Reagan to a seat on the U.S. Court of Appeals for the District of Columbia Circuit, one level below the U.S. Supreme Court. Sitting on that

asked to look into such issues as the suicide of White House counsel Vincent W. Foster Jr. in 1993, and the 1993 firing of White House Travel Office employees. Starr got several convictions relating to Whitewater, most notably Arkansas Governor Jim Guy Tucker and the Clintons' Whitewater business partners Jim and Susan McDougal.

In January 1998 a former White House employee, Linda R. Tripp, brought to Starr several audiotapes. On these tapes, a former aide to Clinton, Monica Lewinsky, bragged that she had had a long-running affair with Clinton. The president was in the midst of a lawsuit brought by a former Arkansas worker, Paula Corbin Jones, in which it was alleged that Clinton asked for sexual favors from Jones and then retaliated against her when she resisted by hindering her career advancement. The U.S. Supreme Court had allowed her lawsuit to continue while Clinton was in office, and in January 1998 Clinton was deposed. Tripp's tapes implied that Lewinsky, asked by Jones's attorneys for information, was going to lie under oath in a deposition—and that Clinton had asked her to do it. Further, Lewinsky told of the destruction of evidence, again ordered by Clinton. Lewinsky said that she was being rewarded for her silence with a high-paying job arranged by Clinton's friend, civil rights advocate Vernon E. Jordan Jr. In investigating Whitewater, Starr had suspected that Jordan was the middleman between Clinton and Webster Hubbell, a former assistant attorney general and law partner of Hillary Clinton, when Hubbell was allegedly paid off to keep silent about Whitewater.

When the allegations of Clinton's affair with Lewinsky and his role in trying to buy her silence were uncovered, it exploded across the nation. Clinton denied all of the allegations in an angry speech, his wife went on national television and alleged that the whole scandal was part of some "right-wing conspiracy" to attack Clinton, and his political allies openly declared "war" on Starr. As the months of investigation followed, Starr doggedly followed uncovered evidence that Lewinsky did indeed have an affair with Clinton and that the president had lied under oath before a grand jury. Starr, as part of his duties as an independent counsel, sent a referral report to the U.S. House of Representatives, demonstrating several crimes by Clinton that could lead to impeachment. Starr's re-port, laden with talk of sex and crimes by Clinton, was a national scandal in itself.

In December 1998 the U.S. House of Representatives impeached Clinton on three articles dealing with lying under oath and obstruction of justice. Starr thus became the first—and only—independent counsel to send a referral report to the House that led to impeachment articles being adopted. Clinton was tried in the Senate and acquitted on 12 February 1999, and Starr was seen as an overzealous prosecutor. He left the independent counsel's office in 2000 and returned to his law practice.

References: Labaton, Stephen, "Judges Appoint New Prosecutor for Whitewater; Ruling Is Surprise," *New York Times,* 6 August 1994, A1; Lacayo, Richard, and Adam Cohen, "Inside Starr and His Operation, *Time,* 9 February 1998, 42–48; Manegold, Catherine S., "Kenneth Winston Starr: A Prosecutor Overnight," *New York Times,* 6 August 1994, 12; "Starr, Kenneth W.," in Clifford Thompson, ed., *Current Biography 1998* (New York: H. W. Wilson Company, 1998), 50–54.

Sullivan, Timothy Daniel (1862–1913)

New York political boss, known as "Big Tim" and "The Big Feller," whose death in a strange accident left his place in history obscured. Sullivan was in fact two men: one who worked for the needy of New York and one who profited from his own corruption. Born in the rough Five Points section of New York City on 23 July 1862, he was the son of Daniel Sullivan, an Irish laborer, and Catherine Connelly. Daniel Sullivan had emigrated, as did his wife, from Ireland during the Potato Famine of the 1840s, and their son was born in a tenement in the Lower East Side of Manhattan. Timothy grew up in poverty, exacerbated when his father died in 1867, leaving his mother to care for four small children. When Catherine Sullivan remarried, her family's circumstances changed little as they moved to another ghetto. She did laundry, and one of Timothy Sullivan's sisters worked in a sweatshop. Sullivan himself started working at the age of seven, selling newspapers on corners. Four years later, when he finished grammar school, he left school and survived on the little education he had received. He earned a reputation as a hard fighter who defended the poorer newsboys.

In 1882, when Sullivan was twenty, he had saved enough money to purchase a saloon. As a member of the Whyos, one of the city's most notorious street gangs, Sullivan made his saloon a meeting place for the gang. However, Sullivan saw advancement in politics instead of street robbery, so in 1886 he ran for a seat in the state assembly, representing the Five Points area. As he had when he was younger, he made his name in politics by standing up for the rights of the poor and downtrodden. However, rumors surrounded Sullivan that he was knee deep—if not deeper—in massive corruption, including taking proceeds from prostitutes working the seedy streets of New York City. Daniel Czitrom wrote on Sullivan's defense to these charges:

> On April 17, 1889, members of the New York State Assembly crowded around an obscure young colleague as he angrily and tearfully defended himself that he was the boon companion of thieves, burglars, and murderers. Timothy Sullivan had first been elected to represent the Five Points slum district of New York City in 1886, at the age of 23. His accuser was the formidable Thomas E. Byrnes, chief inspector of the New York police department, hero of a popular series of mystery novels, and the most famous detective in the nation. Sullivan had angered the inspector by opposing a bill that would have given the city police the power to jail on sight any person who had ever been arrested. After learning that his two saloons had been suddenly "pulled" for excise law violations and after reading Byrnes's denunciations of him in the New York press, Sullivan disregarded the advice of friends, rose on the assembly floor, and made what everyone agreed was an extraordinary response. "The speech," reported the New York Herald, "was given in the peculiar tone and language of a genuine Fourth Warder, and while was interesting in that respect to the countrymen, its tone was so manly that Tim gained much sympathy. If the Inspector's bill had come up today it would have been beaten out of sight."

As a member of the state assembly, Sullivan made a name for himself—one that lasts to this day—when he introduced a bill to make it a crime to carry a concealed weapon in the state. Still on the books, it is known as Sullivan's Law. One of the women who lobbied him for increased protection for female laborers was future Secretary of Labor Frances Perkins. Sullivan was an early advocate of the suffrage for women.

Despite his protestations of innocence, Sullivan was widely involved in a number of crooked schemes that netted his gang and Tammany Hall, whose backing he had, money and influence in the city wards they controlled. Historian Jay Robert Nash explained Sullivan's connections this way:

> For most of the nineteenth century, the political fortunes of New York City were in the hands of a puissant ethnic-Irish cabal that came to be known as Tammany Hall. Through the usual blend of charity and patronage dispensed through the wards by the district leaders, the Tammany "Democracy," as corrupt and venal as it was, became an invincible political machine. It reached the height of its power around 1901, when "Big" Tim Sullivan, the swaggering boss of the Lower East Side, installed Tom Foley as the Tammany leader of the rebellious second district. To ensure the victory of this saloon keeper against the respected incumbent Paddy Divver, Sullivan brought in members of Paul Kelly's Five Points Gang to form a human chain around the polling places. Kelly's gang was composed mostly of Italians. The Irish residents of the Fourth Ward organized their own gang to do battle, but the heavily armed Italians drove them away from the polls, while Police Chief William Dovery and his men passively stood by. Devery was Sullivan's erstwhile "business" partner, who regulated (as opposed to suppressing) gambling and vice in the city.

Sullivan also involved himself in legitimate enterprises, such as theaters and vaudeville houses. However, he earned the name "the King of the Underworld."

His time in Albany done, in 1902 Sullivan ran as a Democrat for a seat in the U.S. House of Representatives. Elected, he served in the Fifty-eighth and Fifty-ninth Congresses (4 March 1903–27 July 1906), resigning before his second term was over because he was bored. He returned to the state senate in 1908 and 1910; in 1912 he was elected again to a seat in the U.S. House of Representatives, but never took it. It was at that time that he descended into madness, possibly brought on by syphilis. In January 1913 he was declared insane and committed to a sanitarium in Yonkers, New York, on 10 January 1913. However, he was later moved to his brother's home in East Chester, New York.

On 31 August 1913, Sullivan escaped from his brother's home. Meandering along the railroad tracks near what is today the Pelham Parkway in New York City, Sullivan wandered into the path of a train and was struck and killed. The train so disfigured him that he remained unidentified for days in the morgue before a policeman recognized him just before he was to be shipped to a potter's field. After a huge funeral attended by thousands of his supporters, Sullivan was buried in Calvary Cemetery in Long Island City, New York.

References: Baldwin, Peter C., "Sullivan, Timothy Daniel," in John A. Garraty and Mark C. Carnes, gen. eds., *American National Biography*, 24 vols. (New York: Oxford University Press 1999), 21:126–127; Czitrom, Daniel, "Underworlds and Underdogs: Big Time Sullivan and Metropolitan Politics in New York, 1889–1913," *Journal of American History*, 78:2 (September 1991), 536–558; "Sullivan, Timothy," in Jay Robert Nash, *Encyclopedia of World Crime: Criminal Justice, Criminology, and Law Enforcement*, 4 vols. (Wilmette, IL: CrimeBooks, Inc, 1989), IV:2876.

Sulzer, William (1863–1941)

United States representative from New York (1895–1912), governor of New York (1913), impeached and removed from office because of numerous financial and other improprieties. Born on his father's farm near Elizabeth, New Jersey, on 18 March 1863, he was the second son of seven children of Thomas Sulzer, a German immigrant, and Lydia (née Jelleme) Sulzer. Of his siblings, two brothers eventually died in the Spanish-American War, and a third brother, Charles Augustus Sulzer (1879–1919), served as a territorial delegate from Alaska (1919). William Sulzer attended a country school near his home and when still young went to work on a ship sailing to South America. In 1877 his family moved to the Lower East Side of New York City, and Sulzer worked while he attended classes first at the Cooper Union and then at Columbia University. He studied law and in 1844 was admitted to the New York bar. He opened a practice in that city. He also went to work for the Tammany organization, the powerful political association that controlled jobs, patronage, and all other political services in New York City.

Five years after beginning his practice, Sulzer entered the political arena, running for and winning a seat in the New York state assembly, representing the Lower East Side. He served in this post for five years, rising to serve as speaker in 1893. In 1894 he gave up his assembly seat to run for a seat in the U.S. House of Representatives. Elected to the Fifty-fourth Congress, he sat as chairman of the Committee on Foreign Affairs and was a supporter of progressive causes, including the passage of a graduated income tax. He was reelected eight times, serving until 1 January 1913.

In 1912 Sulzer was nominated by the Democratic Party of New York as their candidate for governor. He ran in a crowded field that included Job E. Hedges, the Republican, and Oscar S. Straus (a former secretary of commerce and labor), on the Independence League ticket. Despite his once having worked for the Tammany organization, Sulzer was considered a reformer, and the head of Tammany, Charles F. Murphy, backed him only reluctantly. Sulzer campaigned as "The People's Governor." On 5 November 1912, Sulzer was elected governor. Immediately, he angered Tammany by denying that organization patronage in Albany and ordering investigations into scandals in state government offices that were run by Tammany-backed appointees. An investigation into the Highway Department led to Sulzer's dismissal of the Democratic superintendent, C. Gordon Reel. However, Sulzer was bipartisan in his attacks on state government—he demanded that the Republican warden of Auburn prison be replaced with a Democrat. When the state prison superintendent, Joseph F. Scott, refused, Sulzer fired Scott for being "inefficient, incompetent, derelict and neglectful of duty." When the state legislature refused to confirm several of Sulzer's appointees to state positions, he initiated what some legislators called "a reign of terror" on the state. One assemblyman, Anthony Griffin, wrote that "until we destroy the Constitution, I will not take the dictation of one man as to what I shall do as a legislator. . . . [Sulzer is trying] to usurp legislative functions." Griffin denounced the governor as "Sulzer the First."

To fight Sulzer, the state legislature established a committee under the direction of state Senator James J. Frawley, a friend of Tammany, to investigate how state government was running. Historian Robert Wesser wrote:

> Begun as a means of showing Sulzer "in his true light to the voters," the Frawley inquiry accomplished much more. First in private investigations, then in public hearings in July and August, the legislative

snoopers unraveled a web of wrongdoing and chicanery that made a mockery of the governor's charges against the "crooks" and "grafters" of Tammany and its allies. They discovered that his widely publicized scrutiny of the prison department was a farce and a fraud. They heard testimony that he indirectly bargained with legislators for their support of his primary bill. They found that after the campaign of 1912 Sulzer had failed to report thousands of dollars as political contributions in violation of state law. Where had the money gone? The investigators learned that some of it went into Sulzer's personal account with the Farmers' Loan and Trust Company. Some of it also made it way into a secret investment account held by the New York brokerage firm of Fuller and Gray. Known as "number 100" on the company books, this account was used to purchase nearly $12,000 of stocks in a mid-western railroad. The stocks were delivered to Sulzer by a "bagman." The committee then heard testimony about the existence of a second investment account, this one with Harris and Fuller, and designated "number 63." Sulzer had utilized this account, kept open until July 15, 1913, to speculate in the market at the very time that he was sponsoring Wall Street reform legislation. Even the committee members who thought the worst of Sulzer were shocked by these disclosures.

In the end, the Frawley Committee found evidence of massive and gross fraud perpetrated by Sulzer. Jacob Friedman, one of those who wrote on Sulzer's impeachment, explained, "The man who had traveled from one end of the state to the other, calling his opponents crooks and grafters, had himself been caught in dishonorable dealings." On 8 August 1913 the Frawley Committee hearings ended, with the chairman declaring that the evidence already heard had proved Sulzer had violated the New York Corrupt Practices Act. Sulzer denied all—and also added that he could not be removed from office for any crime committed prior to his taking office on 1 January 1913. Immediately word leaked that a resolution of impeachment would be introduced in the lower house of the legislature. On 12 August, seventy-two Democrats and seven Republicans voted to impeach, while twenty-six Democrats, sixteen Republicans, and three Progressives voted against it. A last-ditch confession by his wife that it was she who forged her husband's names on stocks and bank statements did not halt the action. With his impeachment, Sulzer was effectively removed as governor, but he refused to relinquish power to Lieutenant Governor Martin H. Glynn.

Sulzer's impeachment trial opened on 18 September 1913 in front of the New York state senate, presided over by Judge Edgar T. Cullen. There were few "new" revelations—much of the evidence presented was the same that had been examined by the Frawley Committee. Representing Sulzer was criminal attorney Louis Marshall, while the prosecution was presented on behalf of the impeachment managers by Judge Alton B. Parker, who had been the Democrat's presidential candidate in 1904 and was himself a former chief justice of the New York State Court of Appeals. Sulzer's attorneys first argued that because the impeachment vote had been passed during a special session, when only legislation proposed by the governor could be heard, the vote was unconstitutional. When that failed, the defense maintained that the acts alleged occurred before Sulzer took office and were outside the scope of the legislature's authority. One of Sulzer's counsel said, "Was the proceeding instituted because of a desire to accomplish a public good, or was it for the purpose of getting rid of a public official who was performing his duty?" The evidence against Sulzer was damning, and many (including the newspapers, which reported every minute of the trial) speculated he would take the stand in his own defense. Sulzer even said that "amazing revelations" would come from his testimony. In the end, he did not testify, perhaps because his attorneys knew that he could be cross-examined on the bank accounts that damned his case. On 15 October 1913, the Senate voted forty to seventeen to convict Sulzer on three of the eight counts against him, count one being his filing of a false campaign statement, count two that he committed perjury in swearing to that statement's truthfulness, and count four that Sulzer suppressed evidence by threatening witnesses who were to appear before the Frawley Committee. Cullen voted against conviction, but said of Sulzer that his crimes were of "such moral turpitude and delinquency that if they had been committed during the respondent's incumbency of office I think they would require his removal." The following day, the Senate voted forty-three to twelve to remove Sulzer from office, and at that time Lieutenant Governor Glynn was sworn in as the new governor.

Despite becoming the first (and, of this writing, the only) New York governor to be impeached and removed from office, Sulzer was not barred from further public office and in November 1913, just a month after he was convicted, he was elected as an Independent to a seat in the state assembly. The following year he was nominated by both the American Party and the Prohibition Party for governor of New York. Governor Glynn, his successor, was defeated by Charles S. Whitman, a former prosecutor. In 1916 Sulzer refused a nomination for president by the American Party. Sulzer left office and returned to the practice of law, in which he remained until his death. In 1928 he came out against the election of Governor Al Smith for president, and letters from the time show Sulzer to have hated Smith for Roman Catholicism and lack of support for Prohibition.

On 16 September 1941, Sulzer collapsed at his law office and died in bed on 6 November 1941 at the age of seventy-eight. His obituary was relegated to the back pages of the New York state newspapers.

References: Friedman, Jacob Alexis, *The Impeachment of Governor William Sulzer* (New York: Columbia University Press, 1939), 147; "Gov. Sulzer Denies Everything After an All Night Conference, Boldly Declares He Did Not Speculate in Wall Street," *New York Times*, 11 August 1913, 1; Morganthau, Henry, "All in a Life-Time—Chapters from an Autobiography. II. What I Learned From Sulzer and Tammany," *The World's Work*, XLII:5 (September 1921), 465–479; New York State, Court for Trial of Impeachment, *Proceedings of the Court for the Trial of Impeachments. The People of the State of New York, by the Assembly thereof, against William Sulzer as Governor. Held at the Capital in the City of Albany, New York, September 18, 1913, to October 17, 1913* (Albany: J. B. Lyon Company, Printers, 1913); "Sulzer, Guilty on Three Counts, to Be Ousted from Office To-Day, Acquitted of Bribery Charge," *New York Times*, 17 October 1913, 1; "Sulzer, William," in Robert Sobel and John Raimo, eds., *Biographical Directory of the Governors of the United States, 1789–1978*, 4 vols. (Westport, CT: Meckler Books, 1978), III:1097; Weiss, Nancy J., "Sulzer, William," in Allen Johnson and Dumas Malone, et al., eds., *Dictionary of American Biography*, X vols. and 10 supplements (New York: Charles Scribner's Sons, 1930–1995), 3:751–752; Wesser, Robert F., "The Impeachment of a Governor: William Sulzer and the Politics of Excess," *New York History*, LX:4 (October 1979), 407–438; "William Sulzer, Ex-Governor, 78," *New York Times*, 7 November 1941, 23.

Swartwout-Hoyt Scandal

Nefarious doings in the Port of New York Collectors' Office, exposed in 1841 by President John Tyler. In 1829 President Andrew Jackson appointed Samuel Swartwout as collector for the Port of New York. During his nine years in that position, Swartwout stole millions of dollars and, in 1838, when President Martin Van Buren did not retain him, Swartwout sailed to Europe carrying the money from nine years of corruption. Van Buren ordered an audit of the office, which showed that Swartwout had stolen nearly $2.25 million. Van Buren named an old friend, Jesse D. Hoyt, as collector of New York to oversee correcting the problems that allowed Swartwout to get away with such a degree of theft. What Van Buren did not know is that Hoyt saw his own opportunity and began to steal from the office as well.

Rumors of Hoyt's fraud began to surface in 1841, after President John Tyler had taken office following the death of President William Henry Harrison after only a month in office. In May 1841, only a month in office himself, Tyler, without the approval of Congress, established a three-man committee, headed by Senator George Poindexter of Mississippi, to investigate the problems and fraud in the New York Collectors' Office. In addition to Poindexter, Tyler named two Boston manufacturers, Samuel Lawrence and William W. Stone, as private members of the panel. The commission discovered the Hoyt, in addition to Swartwout, had embezzled government funds.

The Whig-dominated House, despite hearing of fraud from two Democratic administrations, felt more slighted that Tyler had named a commission without their authority and had named two private citizens, to be paid with government funds, to the panel. On 29 April 1842, when Poindexter delivered the report to Tyler, the House demanded to see it. Tyler assented and presented a copy the following day. Again, despite the findings of massive fraud, the House passed a resolution asserting that a president had "no rightful authority" to name a commission to investigate fraud or other corruption and that the president could not name private citizens to a commission to be compensated "at public expense." The resolution was tabled at the request of Representative John Quincy Adams, the former president, but the final provision of the resolution, that private citizens were not to be paid with public funds to sit on commissions, was added to an appropriations bill enacted in August of that same year.

References: *Review of the Communications of Samuel Lawrence and William W. Stone, Manufacturers of Boston: To the Speaker of the House of Representatives, on the Subject of the Investigation at the New York Custom-House, in Two Letters. From the Hon. Geo. Poindexter* (Washington, DC: National Intelligence Office, 1842); Schultz, Jeffrey D., "Presidential Scandals" (Washington, DC: CQ Press, 2000), 71–72, 77; United States Congress, House, Select Committee to Inquire into the Causes and Extent of the Late Defalcations of the Custom-House at New York and Other Places, *Report of the Minority of the Select Committee of the House of Representatives, Appointed on the Seventeenth of January, 1839, to Inquire into the Causes and Extent of the Late Defalcations of the Custom-House at New York and Other Places* (Washington, DC: Blair and Rives, 1839).

Swayne, Charles Henry (1842–1907)

Judge for the Northern District of Florida (1890–1907), impeached but acquitted in the U.S. Senate in 1905 on charges of corruption, which may have been politically motivated. Little is known about Swayne. He was born in Newcastle County, Delaware, on 10 August 1842, the son of Henry and Ann (née Parry) Swayne, and the grandson of Joel Swayne, a Society of Friends (Quaker) missionary to the Seneca Indians at Allegheny, New York. Henry Swayne served as a member of the Delaware legislature (1846–1847, 1880–1881). His son Charles grew up on his family's farm and received his education in public schools and at an academy in Wilmington. Brought up in the Quaker religion, he served as a principal of a Society of Friend's scientific and mathematical school in West Chester, Pennsylvania. In 1869 he moved to Philadelphia, where he studied law under a local attorney, Joseph B. Townsend, and at the University of Pennsylvania, from which he earned a law degree in 1871. He was admitted to the Pennsylvania bar that same year and practiced in that state until he moved to Florida in 1884. In May 1889 President Benjamin Harrison named him a judge of the District Court for the Northern District of Florida.

The state election of 1888 in Florida occasioned many allegations of fraud and corruption, and many of these charges, mainly against Democrats, went before Judge Swayne, a lifelong Republican. Bitterness arose over his alleged handling of the cases, and Democrats swore to avenge his sentencing of Democrats to prison. Starting in 1890, Florida Democrats sent memorials to the U.S. Congress, asking that Swayne be impeached. On 10 December 1903, Representative William Bailey Lamar (D-FL) presented a memorial from the Florida legislature asking for Swayne's impeachment. Lamar asked for an investigation, and the resolution was referred to the House Judiciary Committee. Despite the committee's recommendation of impeachment, Representative Henry Wilbur Palmer of Pennsylvania asked for a delay so that the charges could be further investigated. On 9 December 1904, the Judiciary Committee again submitted a report recommending impeachment. The House adopted the report on 13 December and asked a select committee to draw up impeachment articles. Twelve articles were drawn up, and on 18 January 1905, Swayne was impeached by the U.S. House of Representatives.

On 24 January 1905, only six days later, the first full impeachment trial in the U.S. Senate since that of President Andrew Johnson in 1868 opened. (In 1876 the Senate considered the impeachment of former Secretary of War William Worth Belknap, but did not hold a trial because Belknap had resigned his office.) Representative Palmer served as one of the House managers, along with James Breck Perkins of New York, Henry De Lamar Clayton of Alabama (who was later to serve as a House manager in the impeachment trial of Judge Robert W. Archbald in 1912), David Albaugh De Armond of Missouri, and David Highbaugh Smith of Kentucky. The charges against Swayne were small: Article I, for instance, charged that as a judge he submitted an expense report for travel in which he charged $230, which the House alleged was false; Article VIII claimed that Swayne "did knowingly and unlawfully" hold an attorney in contempt. In total, he was accused of filing false travel vouchers, improperly traveling on rail cars, and for living outside his district while he looked for a home inside of it. Swayne's attorneys admitted their client was guilty of the offenses, but called each one "inadvertent." The Senate, on 27 February 1905, acquitted Swayne of all charges, holding that none of the crimes advanced to the level of "high crimes and misdemeanors," the standard set for conviction of impeachment. It was decided during the Swayne trial that if an impeachment trial would be held, it should be before a small, established group of Senators sitting as a jury, with their recommendation going to the full Senate. Senator George F. Hoar of Massachusetts recommended the change, and his suggestion is now embodied in Rule XI of the Senate rules.

Swayne returned to the bench, but it appears from all historical evidence that he was physically broken by the impeachment. He died two years later, his name barely known if at all.

References: Johnson, Rossiter, ed., *The Twentieth Century Biographical Dictionary of Notable Americans,* 10 vols. (Boston: The Biographical Society, 1904), X; United States Congress, House, *Proceedings in the House of Representatives, Fifty-Eighth Congress, Concerning the Impeachment of Charles Swayne, Judge of the Northern District of Florida* (Washington, DC: Government Printing Office, 1905).

Symington, John Fife, III (1945–)

Governor of Arizona (1991–1997) who was convicted of fraud and resigned from office, but was later cleared by a federal court and pardoned by President Clinton in 2001. The scion of a famous family, John Fife Symington III was born in New York City on 12 August 1945, a great-grandson of the industrialist and steel magnate Henry Clay Frick and a cousin of William (Stuart) Symington, a powerful senator from Missouri who nearly became John F. Kennedy's running mate in 1960. He attended the prestigious Gillman Country Day School and earned a bachelor's degree from Harvard University in 1968. While in Harvard, he became politically active and was a supporter of Arizona Senator Barry Goldwater's presidential run in 1964. After his graduation, Symington went to Arizona, where he was assigned to Luke Air Force Base near Tucson as a U.S. Air Force second lieutenant. He was eventually moved to the 621st Tactical Air Command in Thailand, overseeing air flights over Vietnam. For his service, which ended in 1971, Symington was awarded the Bronze Star for meritorious service.

After returning from Vietnam, Symington settled in Phoenix, Arizona, then a small metropolis with huge potential for growth. He invested in numerous properties, using his name and his reputation to accumulate a small fortune. By 1990

Symington decided to run for governor. Symington ran against Phoenix Mayor Terry Goddard, a Democrat, and defeated him in the November 1990 election, but because neither man had more than 50 percent of the vote a runoff was held. On 26 February 1991, Symington defeated Goddard to become the eighth Republican governor of Arizona since statehood in 1912. He pushed new education reforms, the cleanup of waste from incineration, and tried to put an end to Indian gambling on reservations in Arizona. He was reelected in 1994, easily defeating supermarket magnate Eddie Basha.

Although Symington was never accused of dishonesty in office, his business dealings prior to becoming governor resulted in his undoing. On 13 June 1996, Symington was indicted by an Arizona grand jury on twenty-three counts of making false financial statements, bankruptcy fraud, and wire fraud. The indictment charged that in the 1980s Symington had exaggerated his net worth to obtain bank loans for properties he wanted to buy and that properties he had purchased had declared bankruptcy. Symington went on trial in 1997, during which he charged that the allegations were politically motivated by a Democratic U.S. attorney and that any irregularities in his financial statements were due to his tax advisors and not him. Despite this, Symington was convicted on 3 September 1997 on seven counts, and one hour later he resigned as governor, making Jane Dee Hull the second female governor in Arizona history. Symington was sentenced to two and one-half years in prison, five years probation, and a $60,000 fine, all of which were stayed pending appeal.

However, it appeared Symington's conviction was in trouble. A juror had been dismissed prior to the verdict; she claimed that she had been removed because the jurors had made up their minds about Symington's guilt and wanted her removed because she stood for an acquittal. Almost immediately, it became apparent that the dismissal of the single juror was potential reversible error. And on appeal to the U.S. Court of Appeals for the Ninth Circuit, this was one of Symington's motions. On 22 June 1999, that court agreed that the juror should not have been removed and vacated Symington's conviction. Until late 2000, prosecutors were still looking at how they could retry the former governor.

Then, on 20 January 2001, his last day in office, President Bill Clinton gave Symington a full pardon. The reasons behind why a Democratic president would pardon a Republican governor are shadowy, but they are appear to be this: Thomas Caplan, a Baltimore novelist who went to school with Clinton at Georgetown University, was also a friend of Symington's and asked the president to pardon the embattled former governor. What Caplan, nor anyone else, didn't know was that in college Symington had rescued Clinton from drowning, and Clinton had never forgotten the favor. Whatever the reason, Symington, now a chef at a trendy Scottsdale, Arizona, restaurant, was ecstatic at the prospect that he was freed from future criminal charges. "I'm humbled and gratified," he said in an interview after word of the pardon came out. "I thank the president, and I praise God."

References: Flannery, Pat, "Clinton Pardons Symington," *Arizona Republic*, 21 January 2001, A1; "J. Fife Symington III," in Marie Marmo Mullaney, *Biographical Directory of the Governors of the United States, 1988–1994* (Westport, CT: Greenwood Press, 1994), 27–31; Kelly, Charles, and Jerry Kammer, "Symington Conviction Overturned, Court Voids 1997 Verdict," *Arizona Republic*, 23 June 1999, A1; United States Congress, House, Committee on Banking, Finance, and Urban Affairs, Subcommittee on General Oversight and Investigations, *Relationship of Arizona Governor J. Fife Symington III with Southwest Savings and Loan Association: Hearing before the Subcommittee on Oversight and Investigations of the Committee on Banking, Finance, and Urban Affairs, House of Representatives, One Hundred Second Congress, Second Session, February 20, 1992* (Washington, DC: Government Printing Office, 1992).

T

Talmadge, Herman Eugene (1913–2002)
Governor of Georgia (1947, 1948–1953) and a U.S. senator from that state (1957–1981), who was denounced by the Senate in 1979 for financial misconduct. Born on his family's farm near McRae, Georgia, on 9 August 1913, he is the son of Eugene Talmadge, a long-time Georgia politician who served as governor from 1933–1937, and from 1941–1943. He studied at local schools in McRae and then went to the University of Georgia at Athens, where he studied law and earned his law degree in 1936. When his father decided to run for governor in 1932, Herman Talmadge left school for a period of time to serve as his father's campaign manager. After earning his law degree, Talmadge was admitted to the state bar in 1936 and commenced the practice of law in Atlanta. In 1941, when World War II broke out, he volunteered for service in the U.S. Navy and saw major action in the Pacific theater of operations and, by the end of the conflict, when he was discharged, he had attained the rank of lieutenant commander.

It was at this time that Talmadge got caught up in one of the most interesting moments in American political history. Eugene Talmadge, Herman's father, had served two separate terms as governor before leaving office in 1943. In 1946 the elder Talmadge, called the "Wild Man from Sugar Creek," decided to take on Governor Ellis Arnall for another term. But unknown to many, Talmadge was in declining health. Word spread among his supporters to write in his son's name in the Democratic primary, which Eugene Talmadge won, with his son, just home from the war, coming in second. Then Eugene Talmadge suffered a burst blood vessel in his stomach. His health slipped, and on 21 December 1946, after he had been elected governor, Eugene Talmadge died. Governor Arnall announced that he could remain governor for Talmadge's term, but instead would turn the office over to Melvin E. Thompson, the newly elected lieutenant governor. Talmadge supporters, now led by Herman Talmadge, demanded that the legislature choose the governor from the candidates in the election. On 15 January, the legislature chose Talmadge, and he was sworn into office. When Talmadge went to take over the office, he found Arnall there, refusing to budge and calling the new governor a "pretender." The next day, armed with a gun, Talmadge went to the governor's offices, changed the locks, and named several state officers. Arnall set up a governor's office in downtown Atlanta. On 18 January, Lieutenant Governor Thompson was sworn in as governor and Arnall "resigned." The two rival governors then took the case to the state supreme court, which held on 19 March that Thompson was the actual governor. Talmadge had served for sixty-seven days. A year later, Talmadge was elected governor in a special election mandated by his father's death and was reelected in 1950, serving until January 1955. He was a popular governor, but stood for segregation of Georgia and Southern society.

In 1956 Senator Walter F. George (D-GA) decided not to run for reelection in the midst of failing health. (He would die on 4 August 1957.) Talmadge, having the year before left the governorship and become a farmer, threw his hat into the ring for the Democratic nomination. In those years the primary *was* the general election, with the Democrat winning the general election with ease. Talmadge won the primary and was elected without opposition. He took his seat in the Senate on 3 January 1957 and would serve until 3 January 1981. During his tenure, Talmadge voted the conservative Southern line, voting against civil rights measures. As the chair of the Agriculture Committee for many years, he worked for farm subsidies for Georgia farmers. He remained chairman when the committee was renamed the Committee on Agriculture and Forestry. He was a member of the Ervin Committee, which heard charges on the Watergate affair in 1973 and 1974.

In August 1978 Talmadge's administrative assistant, Daniel Minchew, told the *Washington Star* that in 1973 and 1974 he had withdrawn, at Talmadge's request, expense money from his congressional expense fund totaling nearly $13,000, for the senator's private use. Secretly, a federal grand jury was assembled to hear the charges, and the Senate Select Committee on Ethics was investigating. In December 1978 the Senate committee issued a report calling for a full-blown investigation, claiming that there was "substantial and credible evidence" of financial misconduct by Talmadge. By a four to one vote, taken on 18 December, the committee decided to enter formal adjudicatory proceedings. On 20 April 1979, Talmadge appeared before the committee, denouncing his accuser (Minchew), calling the charges "petty," and claiming they were either untrue or the result of unintended negligence. When the panel questioned Minchew's credibility, Talmadge's ex-wife, Betty, came forward to substantiate the allegations. During a second hearing, Ethics Committee chairman Senator Adlai Stevenson of Illinois noted that Talmadge had never expressed regret for "this whole sordid episode," and asked him if he had any regret now. "I am human," Talmadge answered. "I have made errors, and I am confident I will make errors in the future. I have never used my office for profit and I never will."

On 15 September 1979, after fifteen months of investigation, the Senate Select Committee on Ethics unanimously voted to denounce Talmadge, calling his conduct "reprehensible." The committee distinctly chose not to use the term "censure," despite the fact that most congressional historians equate a senatorial or House "denouncement" with "censure." So stated the committee, "there is no finding of intentional wrongdoing. There is no recommendation of censure." On 11 October 1979, the full Senate voted eighty-one to fifteen to uphold the denouncement of Talmadge. After the vote, Talmadge called it a "victory." "I stand before you firmly criticized," he said on the Senate floor. "But I am not found guilty of intentional, wrongful, unlawful conduct. There is no recommendation of censure."

In 1980, in the midst of the so-called "Reagan landslide," Talmadge won the Democratic primary but lost his seat to Republican Mack Mattingly. Ironically, in the primary he had defeated an up-and-coming politician, Zell Miller, who later served as governor of Georgia and in the U.S. Senate.

Herman Talmadge died at his home in Hampton, Georgia, on 21 March 2002 at the age of eighty-eight.

References: Ayres, B. Drummond, Jr., "Senate Denounces Talmadge, 81 to 15, Over His Finances," *New York Times,* 12 October 1979, A1, D12; *Congressional Ethics* (Washington, DC: Congressional Quarterly, 1980), 30–31; Hackbart-Dean, Pamela, "Herman E. Talmadge: From Civil Rights to Watergate," *Georgia Historical Quarterly,* 77 (Spring 1993), 145–157; Talmadge, Herman E., with Mark Royden Winchell, *Talmadge: A Political Legacy, A Politician's Life: A Memoir* (Atlanta: Peachtree Publishers, Ltd., 1987).

Tammany Hall

Political organization, famed for its control of New York City machine politics and led by a number of politicians either imprisoned or accused of corrupt activities. Also known as the Columbian Order, the Tammany Society was founded in New York City in 1789 by William Mooney, a veteran of the Revolutionary War, whose strident anti-Federalist thinking led him to form a political society with the expressed intent of opposing all Federalist candidates and policies. Mooney chose the name "Tammany" after the Indian chief who al-

Tammany Hall and 14th Street West in 1914. Tammany Hall was the headquarters of the Tammany Society, a major Democratic political machine in New York City from the mid-nineteenth to mid-twentieth centuries. (Library of Congress)

legedly sold the land now known as Pennsylvania to William Penn. Mooney created thirteen "tribes" within Tammany, with one tribe representing each of the thirteen original United States; as well, each of the organization's officers were given Indian denominations—leaders were endowed with the names "sagamore" and "sachem." But Tammany did not become a national organization like the Federalist Party. Instead, the party organizations outside of New York City slowly died off, until only the New York City office remained open. It was this group, which became known as "Tammany Hall" or the "Tammany machine," that earned respect for its mobilization of voters in New York City, but also scorn for its incredible amount of corruption that drained untold millions of dollars from city coffers through payoffs and bribes and shoddy bookkeeping. At the same time the organization handled the patronage that kept the city moving.

Although Tammany was involved in several political battles in the first half of the nineteenth century—most notably in the fight between Andrew Jackson and the Congress over the Bank of the United States—it did not achieve any political power until one of its officers, Fernando Wood, was elected mayor of New York City in 1855. Wood utilized the office of mayor to his and Tammany's advantage, doling out patronage and, as many historians suspect, using the city's money for projects that aided Tammany cronies. Following Wood, the machine was commanded by William Magear Tweed, Grand Sachem of Tammany, whose political control of the city was nearly absolute by 1868. Corruption in New York City reached its pinnacle under Tweed, as he and his cronies stole in excess of some $200 million. Tweed was later prosecuted and (after escaping and being caught) later died in prison, but the rest of the "Tweed Ring" escaped harsh punishment.

Tweed's successor, John Kelly, saw the need for reform within Tammany and was able to convince such reformers as Samuel Tilden and Horatio Seymour, leading New York Democrats, to join. However, Kelly, followed by Richard Croker and Charles

F. Murphy, failed to reign in massive corruption. Murphy was investigated by Mayor John P. Mitchel in 1906, but was cleared of wrongdoing.

Following Murphy's death in 1924, Judge George W. Olivany, a district leader for the Democrats, became the titular head of Tammany Hall and, with the assistance of New York Governor Alfred E. Smith, planned a revolution in Tammany to clean it up once and for all. However, the old forces of corruption went to work, and, in March 1929, after only five years in power, Olivany was tossed from the machine in favor of John F. Curry, a student of Croker and Murphy. When the Seabury investigation showed massive corruption in the administration of Mayor James J. Walker, a Tammany protege, Curry was thrown into disfavor, but it took several electoral defeats to dislodge him from control of Tammany. In July 1934 he was succeeded by James H. Dooling. Dooling's reign was marked mostly by the administration of Mayor Fiorello H. LaGuardia, a reformist who distanced himself from Tammany, leaving the organization for the first time not in control of the mayor's office. At the same time, the rise in influence of leaders from the Bronx and Brooklyn also diminished Tammany's power base. Battered by changing times, the Tammany society sold the building where its headquarters had been maintained.

Tammany was not dead yet, however. In the 1945 citywide elections, William O'Dwyer, a Tammany-backed candidate, was elected mayor of New York and dismissed Brooklyn Democratic Party leader Edward Loughlin, replacing him with Tammany crony Frank J. Sampson. Sampson was later ousted by Hugo Rogers, who himself was replaced by Carmine G. De Sapio. De Sapio may have been the most powerful Tammany leader since Tweed, but he could not stem the flow of reform, aimed specifically at Tammany Hall. Robert F. Wagner Jr., son of the former senator and a reformist in his own right, became the head of an "anti-Tammany" group of politicians. Wagner was elected mayor of New York in 1953 and began an anticorruption campaign that targeted Tammany. Despite De Sapio becoming a Democratic national committeeman, as well as secretary of state for New York, Tammany's days as a power force were numbered. De Sapio was ousted from power in 1961. Later attempts by De Sapio to regain power and to revive Tammany failed. Under the leadership of Mayor John V. Lindsay (1966–1973), New York was able to rid itself at last of the taint of Tammany. With its power gone, the Tammany machine faded from existence.

See also Croker, Richard; Seabury, Samuel; Tweed, William Magear

References: Allen, Oliver E., *The Tiger: The Rise and Fall of Tammany Hall* (Reading, MA: Addison-Wesley, 1993); Myers, Gustavus, *The History of Tammany Hall* (New York: Boni & Liveright, Inc., 1917); Riordon, William L., *Plunkitt of Tammany Hall: A Series of Very Plain Talks on Very Practical Politics, Delivered by Ex-Senator George Washington Plunkitt, the Tammany Philosopher, from his Rostrum—the New York County Court-House Bootblack Stand—and Recorded by William L. Riordon* (New York: McClure, Phillips, 1905); Werner, Morris Robert, *Tammany Hall* (Garden City, NY: Doubleday, Doran & Co., 1928).

Tate, James Williams (1831–?)

Kentucky state treasurer (1867–1888), known as "Honest Dick" Tate, impeached in absentia after absconding with the entire state treasury—some $247,000. He disappeared from the state and his whereabouts thereafter remained unknown. The grandson of a Revolutionary War soldier, Tate was born near the Forks of Elkhorn, Kentucky, on 2 January 1831. Nothing is known of his early life or education. What is known is that he was heavily involved in property speculation and accumulated a tremendous amount of wealth. In 1854 Governor Lazarus M. Powell named Tate assistant secretary of state, and Governor Beriah Magoffin reappointed Tate to that office in 1859. In 1865 Tate became the assistant clerk of the state house of representatives and, two years later, was named state treasurer. He held this office through a series of reelection victories, due mostly in fact to his alleged honesty, earning him the nickname "Honest Dick" Tate. Historian John J. McAfee wrote in 1886 of Tate, "The secret of this ardent esteem may be traced to the fact that, beyond most men, he adheres strictly to principle in all his dealings with his fellowmen. . . . In his boyhood he was taught that honesty was the best policy, and he grew up in that belief."

In 1888 questions began to be raised over Tate's oversight of the state treasury. This happened after Tate vanished. On 14 March, he told coworkers that he was going on a trip to Louisville. After staying in Louisville, he took a train to Cincinnati—where he vanished into history. Officials looking into his affairs discovered that Tate had taken in total $247,000 in state funds in gold, silver, and cash with him. Tate was not a poor man—his land investments had kept him in good stead for many years, and he was well paid by the state—so his absconding with these funds surprised everyone. Governor Simon Bolivar Buckner announced that Tate had fled the state with the embezzled state funds. An investigation later showed that for many years Tate had been forging official records to cover up a rampant pattern of fraud. Immediately, a chorus rose to impeach Tate in absentia. He was charged with six offenses: among them abandoning his office, absenting himself without providing for proper administration, "misapplying and perverting, taking and converting" the sum of $197,000—this number representing an initial estimate of how much Tate had stolen. The state house impeached on all six charges quickly, and Tate's trial in the state senate began on 29 March 1888—just two weeks after he vanished. The trial lasted for three days, and Tate was found guilty on four of the six charges. He was removed from office and disqualified from ever holding a state office again.

Of Tate thereafter nothing is known, although some rumors had him in Bremen, Germany, or Toronto, Canada. In 1893, it was reported that he was under arrest in Arizona Territory, but this proved false. In 1897 his daughter came forward to have him declared dead, although she had letters from him from places as far away as China. He was never declared dead, but his date of death, and place of burial, remain a mystery.

Because of the Tate case, Kentucky changed its laws allowing state officials to serve two terms in succession. That did not change until 2000, when several state officials were allowed to run for reelection.

References: The author would like to thank Joe Horton, reference librarian at the Department for Libraries and Archives, Frankfort, Kentucky, for his assistance in gathering the information on "Honest Dick" Tate. Bryant, Ron D., "'Honest Dick' Tate," *Kentucky Gazette*, 4 November 1997, 15; Klotter, James C., "Tate, James W.," in John E. Kleber, ed., *Kentucky Encyclopedia* (Lexington, KY: University Press of Kentucky, 1992), 867–868; McAfee, John J., *Kentucky Politicians—Sketches of Representatives* (Louisville, KY: The Courier Job Printing Company, 1886), 148; Mittlebeeler, Emmet V., "The Great Kentucky Absconsion," *Filson Club History Quarterly*, XXVII (1953), 335–352; "Tate Captured Again. Kentucky's Defaulting Treasurer Said to Have Been Seen on a Cotton Belt Train," *Louisville Courier-Journal*, 26 October 1893, 1.

Teapot Dome Scandal

Federal scandal (1923–1929) that forced Attorney General Harry Daugherty from office, led to the indictment and conviction of Secretary of the Interior Albert B. Fall, and nearly cost Attorney General Harlan Fiske Stone a seat on the United States Supreme Court. The scandal, in effect, started in 1915, when the administration of President Woodrow Wilson set aside several areas in the nation to be used as strategic oil reserve centers in case of a national emergency. Among these places were Naval Reserve Number One at Elk Hills, California, and Naval Reserve Number Three, located at Salt Creek, Wyoming, but better known as Teapot Dome because of the resemblance of the shape of the land to the top of a teapot. (The third reserve, listed as number two, was located at Buena Vista, California.)

In 1920 Senator Warren G. Harding won the presidency and named U.S. Senator Albert Bacon Fall of New Mexico to be his secretary of the interior. He also named former Representative Edwin Denby of Michigan to be his secretary of the navy. Unknown to Harding, Fall was close friends with two oil men, Harry F. Sinclair, president of the Mammoth Oil Company, and Edward L. Doheny, president of the Pan-American Petroleum and Transport Company. Once in office, Fall persuaded President Harding to transfer control of the reserves from the secretary of the navy to the Interior Department. Denby, convinced on his own by Fall's arguments, supported Fall's move. Harding then signed an executive order on 31 May 1921, which transferred authority.

Fall then secretly leased Teapot Dome to Sinclair and Elk Hills to Doheny—apparently in exchange for bribes. In November 1921 Doheny made what was later characterized as a "loan" of $100,000 to Fall. In exchange for rights to the oil, Doheny was supposed to erect a refinery in California and construct a pipeline from the reserve to the refinery. For Teapot Dome, Sinclair paid Fall in fourteen animals, including a thoroughbred horse and a bull. On 7 April 1922, Fall, Denby, and Sinclair signed a secret deal allowing full access to Sinclair's company to the Teapot Dome reserves. Historians Morris R. Werner and John Starr wrote, "By the time he was finished leasing the Navy's reserves, Fall had given his two benefactors reserves which each of them estimated roughly to be worth $100 million dollars, and he had collected from them $409,000 in cash and bonds."

Before long, however, the "secret" deal behind the oil reserve leases began to leak out. Oilmen in California and Wyoming began to get suspicious that Doheny was obtaining oil from a government oil lease. Fall was seen to be purchasing new lands around his ranch in New Mexico, as well as showing off the horse and bulls and cows that he received as part of the deal. Soon, newspapermen were hunting for clues. On 14 April 1922, the *Wall Street Journal* reported that Fall, in a secret deal, had illegally leased Teapot Dome to Sinclair. The following day, amid angry voices in the U.S. Senate, that body passed Resolution 277, demanding that the secretary of the navy and the secretary of the interior inform the Senate of any deals involving the leasing of the oil reserves to anyone and whether there was competitive bidding regarding these leases. The resolution, submitted by Senator John Benjamin Kendrick (D-WY) read:

Whereas, there have recently appeared in the public press statements purporting to have been authorized by the Department of the Interior, to the effect that the Secretary of the Interior and the Secretary of the Navy are negotiating with private parties for the operation of lands included in Naval Petroleum Reserve Number 3, Wyoming number 1, withdrawn by Executive order of the President, dated April 30, 1915, known as the Teapot Dome; therefore it is Resolved that the Secretary of the Interior and the Secretary of the Navy are requested to inform the Senate, if not incompatible with the public interests, whether such negotiations are pending, and if so the names of all parties, the terms and conditions of all proposed operating agreements, and whether opportunity will be given the public for competitive bidding for the operation of these lands, or whether it is proposed to award a lease or other operating contract or agreement for the entire area to one person, corporation or association.

Acting Secretary of the Interior Edward Finney, in control of the department while Fall was out of Washington, gave the Senate a copy of the leases on 29 April 1922. Finney also told the Senate that the deals were done in the name of national security, in that the oil in the reserves could not be used in ships and needed to be refined into fuel. This explanation was unacceptable to the Senate, and that body that same day enacted Resolution 282, which established an investigation of the leases in the Committee of Public Lands and Surveys. Senator Miles Poindexter (R-WA) said: "I think Congress ought to know, and that the country ought to know, whether or not the interests of the public are being protected by the terms of the contract or lease which has been made for the extraction of the oil from the Government reserve, and that will be ascertained, I assume, by this investigation."

President Harding stood up for Fall and Denby, telling the Senate in an official letter that he was involved in all of the negotiations regarding the leases. "The policy which has been adopted by the Secretary of the Navy and the Secretary of the Interior in dealing with these matters was submitted to me prior to the adoption thereof, and the policy decided upon and the subsequent acts have at all times had my entire approval," Harding wrote. Senator Reed Smoot (R-UT) was the chairman of the committee, but it included several Republican insurgents who differed with the administration, as well as Senator Thomas J. Walsh (D-MT), who desired to make the hearings part of his attack on the Harding administration.

Walsh's plans changed on 2 August 1923 when Harding, while on a trip to Alaska and California, died in San Francisco. He was succeeded by his vice president, Calvin Coolidge. Hearings on the scandal now known as Teapot Dome opened in the Committee on Public Lands and Surveys on 15 October 1923. Within a week, witnesses started to testify, starting with Secretary of the Interior Fall. Former Secretary Fall, under pressure from the new president, had resigned his office on 4 March 1923. Following Fall was Secretary of the Navy Denby. Walsh dominated the hearings, releasing tidbits of information to reporters behind the scenes and then announcing the stories the following day as important information for the committee to investigate. Fall told the committee that he had borrowed $100,000 in cash from Edward B. McLean, publisher of the *Washington Post*. McLean initially refused to testify, but finally denied that he had ever given Fall any

Who Says a Watched Pot Never Boils?

This 1924 cartoon shows the U.S. Capitol as a boiling and overflowing teapot. Teapot Dome remains one of the most extensive scandals implicating executive branch members of outright bribery and the selling of government assets for bribes. (Library of Congress)

funds. Edward Doheny later admitted that he was the source of the payment, having paid it to Fall via Doheny's own son in "a little black bag."

As new allegations appeared on the oil deals, political damage mounted for President Coolidge despite his having no ties to any of part of the scandal. To clear his own administration of any taint, Coolidge decided to name a special prosecutor to investigate the affair. When it appeared that Coolidge was prepared to name the prosecutor to investigate Teapot Dome, Attorney General Harry M. Daugherty wrote him an impassioned letter, in which he explained:

> May I again urge the desirability that you immediately appoint two outstanding lawyers who as such shall at once take up all phases of the oil leases under investigation of the Senate or others and advise you as to the facts and law justifying legal proceedings of any kind. As you know, I do not desire to evade any responsibility in this or other matters; but considering that Mr. Fall and I served in the Cabinet together, this would be fair to you, to Mr. Fall, and the American people, as well as to the Attorney General, the Department of Justice, and my associates and assistants therein. I do not desire to be consulted as to whom you shall appoint. The only suggestion I have to make in that regard is that those appointed shall be lawyers whom the public will at once recognize as worthy of confidence and who will command the respect of the people by not practicing politics or permitting others to do so in connection with this important public business.

Coolidge disagreed. He wrote:

> It is not for the President to determine criminal guilt or render judgment in civil causes. That is the function of the courts. It is not for him to prejudge. I shall do neither; but when facts are revealed to me that require action for the purpose of insuring the enforcement of either civil or criminal liability, such action will be taken. That is the province of the Executive.
>
> Acting under my direction the Department of Justice has been observing the course of the evidence which has been revealed at the hearings conducted by the senatorial committee investigating certain oil leases made on naval reserves, which I believe warrants action for the purpose of enforcing the law and protecting the rights of the public. This is confirmed by reports made to me from the committee. If there has been any crime, it must be pros-

ecuted. If there has been any property of the United States illegally transferred or leased, it must be recovered.

> I feel the public is entitled to know that in the conduct of such action no one is shielded for any party, political or other reason. As I understand, men are involved who belong to both political parties, and having been advised by the Department of Justice that it is in accord with the former precedents, I propose to employ special counsel of high rank drawn from both political parties to bring such action for the enforcement of the law. Counsel will be instructed to prosecute these cases in the courts so that if there is any guilt it will be punished; if there is civil liability it will be enforced; if there is any fraud it will be revealed; and if there are any contracts which are illegal they will be canceled.

Coolidge picked two lawyers—Republican Silas Strawn and Democrat Thomas Gregory (the latter having served as attorney general in the Woodrow Wilson administration)—but because both had ties to the oil industry, they faced a storm on Capitol Hill. Coolidge withdrew their names when it appeared that neither would be confirmed. On a referral from Senator George Pepper (R-PA), Coolidge selected Philadelphia attorney Owen J. Roberts, a Republican, and attorney Atlee Pomerene, a Democrat and former U.S. senator. Pomerene was confirmed by the Senate by a vote of fifty-nine to thirteen on 16 February 1924, and Roberts was confirmed by a vote of sixty-eight to eight two days later. On the day Roberts was confirmed, 18 February 1924, Secretary of the Navy Edwin Denby handed in his resignation.

Only a month into their inquiry, Roberts and Pomerene indicted Fall, Doheny, and Sinclair. Fall was later convicted of accepting a bribe, although Sinclair and Doheny were acquitted of giving the bribe, a strange and ironic twist. Fall went to prison, the first of two cabinet members ever to be sentenced to a prison term. (The other was Attorney General John Newton Mitchell, implicated in Watergate.) Attorney General Daugherty resigned on 28 March 1924, but he was never tried on any charges relating to Teapot Dome. In all, Roberts and Pomerene indicted eight people, resulting in six criminal trials and two civil trials. Sinclair was later sent to prison for contempt of Congress, and the oil reserves were restored to the control of the

U.S. government. Roberts remained on the investigation until President Herbert Hoover elevated him to a seat on the United States Supreme Court in 1930. Pomerene stayed with the prosecution until he closed it, using his power to exact compensation from Sinclair's and Doheny's oil companies for the oil they stole. Hoover named Pomerene, a Democrat, to head the Reconstruction Finance Corporation in 1932, where he served until Hoover left office the following year.

Teapot Dome remains perhaps one of the most extensive scandals implicating executive branch members and outright bribery and the selling of government assets for bribes. At the time of the scandal Senator Gerald Nye (R-ND) said:

The investigation has uncovered the slimiest of slimy trails beaten by privilege. The investigation has shown, let us hope, privilege at its worst. The trail is one of dishonesty, greed, violation of law, secrecy, concealment, evasion, falsehood, and cunning. It is a trail of betrayals by trusted and presumably honorable men—betrayals of a government, of certain business interests and the people who trusted and honored them; it is a trail showing a flagrant degree of the exercise of political power and influence, and the power and influence of great wealth upon individuals and political parties; it is the trail of despoilers and schemers, far more dangerous to the well-being of our Nation and our democracy than all those who have been deported from our shores in all time as undesirable citizens. And in the end the story of one of the crushing of brilliant careers when finally the light was played upon those who schemed those unhealthy schemes born in darkness.

See also Denby, Edwin; Fall, Albert Bacon
References: Busch, Francis X., *Enemies of the State: An Account of the Trials of the Mary Eugenia Surratt Case, the Teapot Dome Cases, the Alphonse Capone Case, the Rosenberg Case* (Indianapolis, IN: Bobbs-Merrill, 1954); Ferrell, Robert H., "Teapot Dome," in Donald C. Bacon, Roger H. Davidson, and Morton Keller, eds., *Encyclopedia of the United States Congress,* 4 vols. (New York: Simon & Schuster, 1995), IV:1935–1937; Noggle, Burl. *Teapot Dome: Oil and Politics in the 1920s* (New York: Norton, 1962); "Normalcy," in David Loth, *Public Plunder: A History of Graft in America* (New York: Carrick & Evans, Inc., 1938), 312–323; Nye, Gerald, senator, comments in United States Senate, *Leases Upon Naval Oil Reserves and Activities of the Continental Trading Co. (Ltd.) of Canada,* Senate Report 1326, 70th Congress, 1st Session (1928), II:2–3; Poindexter, Miles, senator, comments in *Congressional Record—Proceedings and Debates of the 67th Congress, 2nd Session* (Washington, DC: Government Printing Office, 1922), 6048; Werner, Morris Robert, and John Starr, *Teapot Dome* (New York: Viking Press, 1959), 86.

Thomas, John Parnell (1895–1970)

United States representative from New Jersey (1937–1950), convicted of fraud and sent to prison for nine months. Thomas was one of the most powerful lawmakers of the late 1940s in his role as chairman of the Committee on Un-American Activities (HUAC). Thomas's fall from grace was perhaps one of the farthest of any politician in American history, although his name is little remembered today. Born in Jersey City, New Jersey, on 16 January 1895, Thomas attended local schools before studying at the University of Pennsylvania. When World War I began, he volunteered for service and served as a second lieutenant in Company B of the 306th Infantry, rising to the rank of first lieutenant and then captain in the Headquarters Regimental Staff of the 50th Infantry. He was discharged in 1919 with the rank of captain. For several years he worked in securities investments and later in the insurance business in New York City.

In 1925, Thomas, a Republican, was elected a member of the borough council of Allendale, New Jersey, and a year later mayor of Allendale. He served in that capacity until 1930. In 1935 he was elected to a seat in the New Jersey House of Assembly, where he served until 1937. In 1936 he ran for a seat in the U.S. House of Representatives, representing the seventh New Jersey district. He defeated Democrat Harold J. P. Hoffmann and took his seat in the Seventy-fifth Congress on 3 January 1937. Because of his conservative views, he harshly opposed President Franklin Delano Roosevelt's "New Deal" program of government relief, calling it a threat to the capitalist system. His greatest barbs were aimed at the Federal Theater and Writers Project, a New Deal program that gave stipends to writers and performers. Many of the plays and works that had been created during the program were of a left-wing nature, and conservatives like Thomas objected both to their content and to the donation of government funds to advance them.

Thomas stated, "Practically every play presented under the auspices of the project is sheer propaganda for Communism or the New Deal." Despite his stands against the popular Roosevelt, Thomas was reelected in 1938, 1940, 1942, 1944, 1946, and 1948.

In 1947 Thomas was named chairman of the House Committee on Un-American Activities, designed to investigate alleged Communist influences in the United States. Under Thomas, the committee began an investigation into the role of Communists in the motion picture industry. Calling numerous witnesses before the committee, including leading players in motion pictures, several people in the industry were accused of being present or former Communists. Ten men—including writers Dalton Trumbo and Ring Lardner Jr. and directors Herbert Biberman, Edward Dmytryk, John Howard Lawson, and Lester Cole—refused to answer any of the committee's questions and were cited for contempt of Congress. These men became known as "The Hollywood Ten."

Rising anger about Thomas's command over the committee's hearings led to secret investigations of the New Jersey congressman's personal dealings. Unfortunately for Thomas, scandal was ripe for the finding. Soon reports that Thomas had submitted billing statements to Congress for allegedly nonexistent employees and then pocketed the excess payments, brought a grand jury investigation. Appearing before that panel, Thomas ironically took the Fifth Amendment—the same tactic used by witnesses before his own committee. Thomas was indicted for conspiracy to defraud the United States government. He was convicted on all charges and resigned his House seat on 2 January 1950. He was sentenced to prison, serving only nine before he was paroled. Ironically, he served in the same prison with Lester Cole and Ring Lardner Jr., who were still serving out their contempt of Congress citations.

After being released from prison, Thomas worked as the editor and publisher of three daily newspapers in Bergen County, New Jersey; later, he worked as a real estate solicitor and investment adviser. He ran for a U.S. House seat in 1954, but was defeated for the Republican nomination. Thomas moved to St. Petersburg, Florida, where he died on 19 November 1970 at the age of seventy-five.

References: *Biographical Directory of the American Congress, 1774–1996* (Alexandria, VA: CQ Staff Directories, Inc., 1996).

Thompson, Fred Dalton (1942–)

Actor and politician, United States Senator (1995–2002), chairman of the Senate Governmental Affairs Committee's hearings into campaign finance irregularities by the Democratic Party. Born in Sheffield, Alabama, on 19 August 1942, Thompson grew up in Lawrenceburg, Tennessee. He received his undergraduate degree in philosophy from Memphis State University (now the University of Memphis) in 1964 and his law degree from Vanderbilt University in 1967, while working his way through school. Two years after law school, Thompson was named an assistant U.S. attorney and at the age of thirty was appointed minority counsel to the Senate Watergate Committee, where he served from 1973 to 1974. It was Thompson who asked witness Alexander Butterfield whether the Oval Office had any recording devices, exposing the existence of tapes of the Watergate conspirators admitting to covering up criminal activities and heralding the beginning of the end for the Nixon administration. In 1975 Thompson wrote *At That Point in Time: The Story of the Senate Watergate Committee.*

After leaving Washington in 1974, Thompson defended the chairman of the Tennessee Parole Board after she had been suspiciously fired. Thompson's work helped to expose a cash-for-clemency scheme that ultimately toppled the governor. The scandal became the subject of a best-selling book and later a film, *Marie,* starring Sissy Spacek, in which Thompson played himself. The role exposed the dynamic Thompson to movie audiences, and he began to get more acting opportunities. He went on to act in eighteen motion pictures, including *In the Line of Fire* (1993), *Die Hard II* (1990), and *The Hunt for Red October* (1990).

In 1994 Thompson ran for the remaining two years left in the vacant U.S. Senate seat from Tennessee once held by Vice President Al Gore. Facing Representative Jim Cooper, an establishment Democrat with strong credentials and a large monetary war chest, Thompson portrayed himself as an outsider and won a bitter contest with 61 percent of the vote to Cooper's 39 percent in his first campaign for office. Once in Congress, Thompson quickly established himself as a force for change, making historic progress on the reform of Congress and the balanced budget, working for campaign finance reform, and calling for a smaller federal government. He was returned for a full term by the voters in 1996, winning his second election in two years, each by more than 20 percentage points. In his reelection victory, Senator Thompson received more votes than any candidate for any office in Tennessee history. Presently, Senator Thompson serves as a member of the Senate Judiciary Committee, and in 1997 was elected chairman of the Governmental Affairs Committee, making him the first senator since World War II to serve as chairman of a major Senate committee after only two years of service.

After the 1996 election, reports of large irregularities in Democratic party fundraising, particularly by the Clinton administration, came to light. On 11 March 1997, the Senate voted ninety-nine to zero to direct the Governmental Affairs Committee to investigate illegal or improper activities in connection with the 1996 federal election campaigns, giving Thompson a national spotlight. Thompson's political career seemed on the rise, even though the Republicans were forced into the minority in the Senate in 2001. In 2002, however, Thompson decided not to seek a third term, instead returning to his first love: acting. As of this writing, he works as the Manhattan district attorney in the popular NBC crime drama, *Law and Order.*

See also Senate Finance Committee Hearings

References: Duncan, Philip D., and Christine C. Lawrence, *Congressional Quarterly's Politics in America 1996: The 104th Congress* (Washington, DC: Congressional Quarterly Inc., 1995), 1213–1214; Thompson, Fred D., *At That Point in Time: The Inside Story of the Senate Watergate Committee* (New York: Quadrangle/New York Times Book Co., 1975).

Thompson, William Hale (1867–1944)

Mayor of Chicago (1915–1923, 1927–1931), investigated but never convicted for fraud, which forced him to leave the mayorship in 1923, but his support of the sale of liquor and his backing of known gangsters led to his reelection in 1927. Despite the lack of a conviction, Thompson is figured by historians to have been one of the most corrupt mayors

to ever serve in American history. Soon after he was born on 14 May 1867, in Boston, Massachusetts, the son of Colonel William Hale Thompson, a Civil War veteran, he and his family moved to the growing metropolis of Chicago. Colonel Thompson was a member of an affluent New England family—he had served in the New Hampshire state legislature in the late 1870s—and he passed on his wealth to his son William. The younger Thompson attended the prestigious Charles Fessenden Preparatory School in Chicago, after which he decided to head west. His father bought him a 3,800 acre ranch in Nebraska in 1888, but Thompson returned to Chicago in 1891 following his father's death.

In 1899 Thompson entered the political realm after one of his friends told him about an empty aldermanic seat. Thompson ran and won the seat, representing Chicago's Second Ward. Although his record was undistinguished, he was noticed by Republican Party boss William Lorimer (later a United States senator), who pushed Thompson to run for a seat on the Cook County (Chicago) Board of Supervisors in 1902. He was elected, but after another two undistinguished years in this position, he felt he had had enough of politics and returned to private life. This would be a short-term move, however.

In 1915 Thompson was again convinced to enter politics, this time with the backing of Lorimer's crony Fred Lundin, and run for mayor of Chicago. With Lundin's backing, he defeated two Republicans in the February 1915 primary, then overcame a massive field of several candidates—including Socialist Seymour Stedman, who would serve as the Socialist vice presidential candidate with Eugene V. Debs in the 1920 election—to be elected Chicago's thirty-third mayor. Although he had never been involved in corruption, Thompson's entire tenure as mayor was marked by massive influence peddling and wholesale bribery. The police department was left in the hands of the criminals who paid for protection; a race riot in July 1919 was ignored as many died; and organized crime figures were allowed to run their illegal businesses, usually involving liquor, as Thompson either didn't care or was actively involved in their crimes. During World War I, he openly espoused the German cause and denounced the British. (He later threatened to punch the king of England in the face if the king ever appeared in Chicago.) The *Chicago Tribune* accused Thompson of stealing $2 million from the city. In 1923, after eight years in office, Thompson backed off running for a third term in exchange for not being prosecuted. (Prior to the election, Fred Lundin and his associates were indicted for stealing more than $1 million from the city's education fund, but Lundin was acquitted, thanks to the tactics of his attorney, Clarence Darrow.) In the 1923 election, a reformer, Democrat William Dever, was elected and began a massive cleanup of the neglect and corruption that had reigned for eight years of "Big Bill" Thompson's tenure. He cracked down on the huge number of speakeasies (illegal bars) that had sprouted up in the city and began wholesale arrests of organized crime figures, including Chicago's Johnny Torrio, and he harassed Alphonse Capone, the leader of Chicago's mafia. He forced prohibition on the city, and threatened police with arrest if liquor was sold in their districts.

After four years, organized crime and the liquor distributors were fed up with Dever's success and sought to toss him out of office. William Thompson was recruited to get his old job back on behalf of these criminal elements. Using strong-arm tactics, Capone initiated a citywide campaign of terror to force people to vote for Thompson, or he used his muscle for massive vote fraud. Thompson also promised an end to prohibition, and a populace more interested in drink than corruption listened intensely. Thompson "defeated" Dever by more than 80,000 votes, and as soon as Thompson took office for his third term, the police crackdown of Capone and organized crime ended. This time, however, Thompson allowed wholesale corruption to reign freely. Historian Jay Robert Nash explained: "Chicago careened out of control between 1927 and 1931 when Thompson left office for the final time. The city was in the hands of the gangsters, and all the civil works projects the mayor had introduced did little to compensate for the sorry record of the city police and the administration which controlled them."

In 1931 Thompson ran for a fourth term, but voters, disgusted with the wholesale corruption, voted in another reformer, Democrat Anton Cermak, who ran on a platform of cleaning up the police and reigning in organized crime. (Cermak was killed in an assassination attempt on the life of President-elect Franklin D. Roosevelt in 1933.) Undaunted, Thompson ran for governor of Illinois in 1936 and 1939, but was defeated both times. He died from heart disease at the Hotel Blackstone in Chicago on 19 March 1944 at the age of seventy-six. Many historians consider him to be the most crooked mayor in American history.

See also Small, Lennington "Len"

References: Prinz, Andrew K., "Thompson, William Hale," in Melvin G. Holli and Peter d'A. Jones, *Biographical Dictionary of American Mayors, 1820–1980: Big City Mayors* (Westport, CT: Greenwood Press, 1981), 362; "Thompson, William Hale," in Jay Robert Nash, *Encyclopedia of World Crime: Criminal Justice, Criminology, and Law Enforcement,* 4 vols. (Wilmette, IL: CrimeBooks, Inc., 1989), IV:2936–2937; Wendt, Lloyd, and Herman Kogan, *Big Bill of Chicago* (Indianapolis, IN: Bobbs-Merrill Company, 1953).

Tillman Act of 1907, 34 Stat. 864 (1907)

Act of Congress, enacted 26 January 1907, which attempted for the first time to limit campaign finance spending.

Sponsored by Senator Ben "Pitchfork" Tillman of South Carolina, this legislation for the first time set out to limit the campaign spending contributions from corporations and banking concerns. It banned corporate gifts to campaigns, a prohibition that has remained in effect, despite the proliferation of "soft money" spending.

The act reads:

An Act to prohibit corporations from making money contributions in connection with political elections.

Be it enacted, That it shall be unlawful for any national bank, or any corporation organized by authority of any laws of Congress, to make a money contribution in connection with any election to any political office. It shall also be unlawful for any corporation whatever to make a money contribution in connection with any election at which Presidential and Vice Presidential electors or a Representative in Congress is to be voted for or any election by any State legislature of a United States Senator. Every corporation which shall make any contribution in violation of the foregoing provisions shall be subject to a fine not exceeding five thousand dollars, and every officer or director of any corporation who shall consent to any contribution by the corporation in violation of the foregoing provisions shall upon conviction be punished by a fine of not exceeding one thousand and not less than two hundred and fifty dollars, or by imprisonment for a term of not more than one year, or both such fine and imprisonment in the discretion of the court.

Despite the fact that the Tillman Act was revolutionary for its time, it was loaded with loopholes, and within three years Congress saw fit to revise it. In 1925, as part of the sweeping law known as the Federal Corrupt Practices Act, the Tillman Act was repealed.

See also Federal Corrupt Practices Act of 1925; Publicity Act of 1910

References: Simkins, Francis Butler, *Pitchfork Ben Tillman: South Carolinian* (Baton Rouge, LA: Louisiana State University Press, 1944).

Torricelli, Robert Guy (1951–)

United States representative (1983–1997) and U.S. senator (1997–2002) from New Jersey, reprimanded by the Senate Ethics Committee for taking illegal gifts and aiding a donor with his influence in obtaining contracts with foreign governments. Torricelli was born in Paterson, New Jersey, on 27 August 1951. He attended local schools in New York, particularly Storm King School in Cornwall-on-the-Hudson, New York, from which he graduated in 1970. He attended Rutgers University in New Brunswick, New Jersey, from which he earned a bachelor's degree in 1974, and Harvard University's Kennedy School of Government, which awarded him a masters in public administration degree in 1980. In 1973 Torricelli went to work on the campaign of Democrat Brendan Byrne, running for governor of New Jersey. Following Byrne's election, Torricelli went to work as his deputy legislative counsel, serving until 1977. Torricelli was admitted to the New Jersey bar in 1978. That same year, Vice President Walter Mondale named Torricelli as his counsel, a post he held until 1980. Torricelli left the White House to earn his degree from Harvard.

In 1982 Torricelli ran for a seat in the U.S. House of Representatives from New Jersey's Ninth Congressional District. Defeating Republican Harold Hollenbeck, he entered the House on 3 January 1983 and served in the 98th–104th Congresses. In 1996, when Senator Bill Bradley of New Jersey retired, Torricelli announced his candidacy for that seat. He defeated Republican Representative Dick Zimmer and entered the Senate on 2 January 1997.

Torricelli, known as "the Torch" for his antagonistic style, was linked for many years with shady dealings. However, it was not until late in his first term that the Department of Justice looked into these allegations. It was discovered that one of Torricelli's campaign donors, David Chang, a businessman, had given Torricelli improper campaign contributions as well as gifts that violated the gift ban established by the Senate. Chang was arrested and sent to prison; Torricelli, however, decried the charges and maintained his innocence. On 3 January 2002, the Department of Justice announced that it did not have clear and convincing evidence of wrongdoing by Torricelli, but it did hand over all of its materials to the Senate Ethics Committee and asked the panel to make its own findings.

On 30 July 2002, the committee released its report on the Torricelli/Chang investigation. Finding many of Chang's charges to be in fact true, the committee recommended that Torricelli be admonished by the full Senate rather than censured or expelled. In their letter to Torricelli, the committee wrote:

> Your acceptance of a television and stereo CD player upon payment to David Chang of an amount you understood to be the cost to Mr. Chang, rather than fair market retail value, evidenced poor judgment, displayed a lack of due regard for Senate rules. . . .
>
> Your acceptance on loan from Mr. Chang of bronze statues . . . for display in your Senate office under your office's policy of accepting the loan of home state artwork was not consistent with Senate rules governing such loans, evidenced poor judgment, displayed a lack of due regard for Senate rules . . .
>
> Your failure to act to prevent the acceptance of or to pay for gifts of earrings from Mr. Chang to individuals (your sister, an employee, and a friend) in your home at Christmas on the mistaken belief that such items were of little value or were not gifts to you . . . evidenced poor judgment, displayed a lack of due regard for Senate rules . . .
>
> Continuation of a personal and official relationship with Mr. Chang under circumstances where you knew that he was attempting to ingratiate himself, in part through a pattern of attempts to provide you and those around you with gifts over a period of several years when you and your Senate office were taking official actions of benefit to Mr. Chang . . . evidenced poor judgment.

After evaluating the extensive body of evidence before it and your testimony, the committee is troubled by incongruities, inconsistencies, and conflicts, particularly concerning actions taken by you which were or could have been of potential benefit to Mr. Chang.

The Senate Select Committee on Ethics . . . expresses its determination that your actions and failure to act led to violations of Senate rules (and related statutes) and created at least the appearance of impropriety, and you are hereby severely admonished.

You must pay Mr. Chang an amount sufficient to bring the total to fair market retail value of the TV and CD player, as well as the fair market retail value of the earrings given to the three individuals at your home, with appropriate interest. The committee understands that you have previously delivered the bronze statues to the Department of Justice, from whence they should be returned to Mr. Chang.

Torricelli, shocked by the findings and punishment by his Senate colleagues, appeared on the Senate floor late that same night and apologized both to his fellow Senators and to the people of New Jersey. "I want my colleagues in the Senate to know I agree with the committee's conclusions, fully accept their findings and take full personal responsibility," he said. "I want to apologize to the people of New Jersey for having placed the seat in the United States Senate they have allowed me to occupy to be placed in this position. . . . I never stopped fighting for things I believed, I never compromised the struggle to make the lives of the people I love better."

Torricelli was deep in the middle of a tough reelection bid before the Ethics Committee admonished the New Jersey Senator; his work only became harder with this ethics violation on his record just a few months before voters went to the polls. On 26 September 2002, a federal appeals court in Philadelphia held that legal documents regarding Torricelli's case, including a memo produced by investigators in his case, must be released immediately. Polls taken that same week showed that Torricelli's campaign took a large hit from the fresh allegations in the memo—as well as an interview with a local New York television station with Chang—and, on 30 September 2002, just thirty-six days before the election, Torricelli announced his resignation from the race, but not

his Senate seat. He was replaced on the ballot by former Senator Frank Lautenberg, who had retired from the U.S. Senate in 2000. Lautenberg won Torricelli's seat on 5 November 2002.

References: *Biographical Directory of the American Congress, 1774–1996* (Alexandria, VA: CQ Staff Directories, Inc., 1996), 1956; Schmidt, Susan, and James V. Grimaldi, "Torricelli and the Money Man: N.J. Senator Had Symbiotic Relationship with Executive," *Washington Post,* 13 May 2001, A1; VandeHei, Jim, and Helen Dewar, "Senate Ethics Panel Rebukes Torricelli; Reprimand over Gifts Could Have Political Consequences for N.J. Democrat," *Washington Post,* 31 July 2002, A1.

Traficant, James A., Jr. (1941–)

United States representative from Ohio (1985–2002), convicted in April 2002 of bribery, racketeering, and fraud, and expelled from the House of Representatives, the second such action by the House of Representatives since the end of the Civil War. He was later sentenced to eight years in prison. A colorful and mercurial politician who bucked his party to support ideas he felt deserved backing, many of which were not positions of the Democratic Party, Traficant was born in Youngstown, Ohio, on 8 May 1941. He attended local schools in Youngstown before going to the University of Pittsburgh in Pennsylvania, where he earned a bachelor of science degree in 1963 and in 1973 a master of science degree from the same university. From 1971 to 1981, Traficant served as the executive director of the Mahoning County (Ohio) Drug Program. In 1980 he was elected sheriff of Mahoning County and he earned a reputation as a strong law-and-order officer with a short fuse. In 1983 he was tried on charges relating to taking bribes, but he was acquitted.

In 1984, disgusted with what he felt was a malaise with the national Democratic Party, Traficant ran as a Democrat for a seat in the U.S. House of Representatives, representing Ohio's Seventeenth District. Elected, he would serve until he was expelled by a vote of Congress on 24 July 2002. During his tenure, he fought his party on tax increases and stood for stronger national security. Always a bane to the party's leaders in Congress, he was nonetheless popular with his blue-collar district where Ronald Reagan earned many votes. In 2000, after he was reelected to his ninth term, he voted to seat Republican Dennis Hastert as Speaker of the House, angering his Democratic colleagues, which led to his being removed from all committee assignments. Appearing on numerous talk shows, he used colorful language to describe his views on important topics. He also used the same language during his speeches on the House floor—one of his favorite phrases was "Beam me up, Scotty!"

On 3 May 2001, Traficant was indicted on ten counts of bribery and conspiracy. Federal prosecutors alleged in the multicount indictment that Traficant had received free labor and materials from construction businesses in Youngstown, Ohio, which was in his district, in exchange for his intervention on behalf of the construction businesses before federal regulators; that he ordered one of his staff to turn over $2,500 from his monthly paycheck; that he tried to get his staff to destroy evidence as well as provide false testimony; that he ordered his staff to do free work on his farm and boat; that he filed false tax returns; and that he committed bribery and mail fraud. Traficant condemned the indictment and the prosecutors and said he would act as his own attorney (known as a *pro se* appearance). Two of his associates, former Chief of Staff Henry DiBlasio and contractor Bernard Bucheit were also indicted on federal charges of bribing Traficant and lying to a federal grand jury.

Traficant's trial began on 13 February 2002. Traficant, acting as his own attorney, claimed that he was the victim of prosecutorial misconduct and that the witnesses called against him were either intimidated or bribed. These witnesses testified that Traficant had received unknown amounts of cash from unknown sources and that his staff was charged with putting the cash into Traficant's bank accounts. Despite Traficant's protestations about a "vendetta" against him, on 11 April 2002 the jury convicted him of all ten charges after just four days of deliberations. Minutes after the guilty verdicts were announced, leaders of the House of Representatives began an ethics investigation. Representative Richard A. Gephardt (D-MO), the Minority Leader, called on Traficant to resign.

On 23 July 2002, the House Ethics Committee released its report on the Traficant matter—it recommended that the Ohio congressman be expelled if he did not resign his seat. Traficant refused to resign, forcing an expulsion vote for the first time since 1980. On 25 July, following a three-hour debate on the House floor, the House voted 410–1 to expel him—the only vote against expulsion was by Representative Gary Condit (D-CA), who was entangled in his own ethical troubles and had lost in the Democratic primary earlier in the year. Representative Joel Hefley (R-CO), the chairman of the Committee on Standards of Conduct and floor manager of the expulsion proceedings, told the House that there were "1,000 pages" of evidence against Traficant and that he had to be expelled. "Many of us are very fond of Representative Traficant but at times like this we are required to set aside those feelings," Hefley told a stunned House.

On 30 July 2002, Traficant was sentenced to eight years in federal prison by Judge Lesley Brooks Wells. He maintained his innocence and ran a 2002 congressional campaign from his prison cell that garnered few votes.

References: *Biographical Directory of the American Congress, 1774–1996* (Alexandria, VA: CQ Staff Directories, Inc., 1996), 1960; Eilperin, Juliet, "Ethics Panel Weighs Traficant Expulsion; Convicted Lawmaker Won't Go Quietly," *Washington Post*, 16 July 2002, A4; Eilperin, Juliet, "House Votes 410 to 1 to Expel Traficant," *Washington Post*, 25 July 2002, A1; Pierre, Robert E., and Juliet Eilperin, "Traficant Is Found Guilty; Ohio Congressman Could Face House Sanctions," *Washington Post*, 12 April 2002, A1.

Tucker, James Guy, Jr. (1943–)

Governor of Arkansas (1992–1996), implicated along with his predecessor, President Bill Clinton, in the Whitewater affair, for which Tucker was found guilty of bank fraud. Although he rose to serve in some of the highest offices in Arkansas, Tucker was born in Oklahoma City, Oklahoma, on 13 June 1943. However, he moved with his family to Little Rock, Arkansas, as a youngster and attended the public schools of that city. He earned his bachelor's degree from Harvard University in 1964 and his law degree from the University of Arkansas at Fayetteville four years later. In 1964 Tucker volunteered for service in the U.S. Marine Corps Reserve and served for two tours (1965, 1967) as a free-lance reporter in Vietnam. After finishing these stints, Tucker returned to Little Rock, where in 1968 he was admitted to the Arkansas bar. He opened a practice in Little Rock.

Two years after opening his practice, Tucker left to run for the office of prosecuting attorney of the Sixth Judicial District of Arkansas, which he served in from 1971 to 1972. He left that office to run for Arkansas state attorney general. Elected, he served a single term (1973–1977). At that same time, he served as a member of the Arkansas Criminal Code Revision Commission.

In 1976 Tucker was elected to a seat in the U.S. House of Representatives. He only served a single two-year term, declining to run for reelection in 1978, to run instead for a seat in the U.S. Senate. Unsuccessful in that race, he found himself out of politics for the first time in nearly a decade and returned to his law practice. Tucker remained in Little Rock for the entire decade of the 1980s. In 1990 he was selected by the Democrats as their candidate for lieutenant governor. Lieutenant Governor Winston Bryant was stepping down from his position to become a candidate for state attorney general. Bryant had served in the state's second executive position since 1981 under two different governors—William Jefferson "Bill" Clinton, and Frank D. White. Tucker was elected because of the popularity of Clinton, the longest-serving governor of the state. Tucker's two years as lieutenant governor were undistinguished. In 1993, after Clinton left Arkansas to serve as the forty-second president of the United States, Tucker was elevated to become the forty-fifth governor of Arkansas. A special election was held to select Tucker's successor as lieutenant governor, and Republican Mike Huckabee won, making him the highest-ranking Republican in the state.

Tucker would have remained the governor of a small state, barely noticed on the national stage, but for his association with Clinton, whose national administration was racked from its start with scandal and allegations of scandal. The first large affair that struck the administration was Whitewater, a land scheme gone wrong in Arkansas that was financed with money from failing savings and loan institutions. Prosecutors in the Whitewater scandal later accused Tucker of meeting in 1985 with Clinton friend James McDougal, head of the Madison Guaranty Savings & Loan, and David Hale, head of the Arkansas Small Business Administration (SBA), and scheming to defraud the U.S. government of $3 million through an illegal loan that was procured

from the SBA for Susan McDougal, some of which ended up in the Whitewater land deal (which was run by McDougal and his wife, Susan, and Bill and Hillary Clinton), some in Tucker's pocket, and some in Clinton's reelection campaign. In 1993 federal investigators looking into why McDougal's savings and loan bank failed discovered the illegal loan and charged Hale. He plea-bargained a lesser sentence in exchange for testifying against Tucker, the McDougals, and Clinton (who was never charged) and implicated the president and Tucker in illegalities. On 17 August 1995, Tucker and both McDougals were indicted by a Little Rock grand jury on numerous counts alleging that they conspired to defraud the savings and loan, and thus the government. The conspiracy charge against Susan McDougal was later dismissed. Their trial began in Little Rock on 4 March 1996. Hale testified against the three defendants, and President Clinton likewise testified, via videotaped statement, for the defendants. On 28 May 1996, all three were convicted, Tucker being found guilty on all counts. On 15 July 1996, following the refusal of the judge overseeing the case to set aside the verdict, Tucker resigned as governor, and Lieutenant Governor Mike Huckabee became governor of Arkansas. At the time, Tucker pleaded to have his sentencing put off, as he was diagnosed with liver failure and said he needed a transplant. This operation occurred later in 1996. Because of his medical condition, Tucker was eventually sentenced to eighteen months' home detention. However, when prosecutors pushed in 1998 to have him sentenced to prison, Tucker agreed on 20 February 1998 to plead guilty to charges of defrauding the government. In exchange for not having to go to prison, he appeared before the Whitewater grand jury and cooperated in the investigation against Clinton. Because Clinton was never formally charged with Whitewater crimes, Tucker became the highest-ranking public official to be tried in the scandal.

See also Clinton, William Jefferson; Whitewater
References: Haddigan, Michael, "Tucker Sentenced to 4 Years' Probation," *Washington Post,* 20 August 1996, A1; "James Guy Tucker, Jr.," in Timothy P. Donovan, Willard B. Gatewood, Jr., and Jeannie M. Whayne, eds., *The Governors of Arkansas: Essays in Political Biography* (Fayetteville, AR: University of Arkansas Press, 1995), 284–287.

Tweed, William Magear (1823–1878)

New York alderman and powerful politician, indicted and sent to prison (where he died) for massive corruption. Born in New York City on 23 April 1823, he was the son of Richard Tweed and Eliza (née Magear) Tweed. Many historians have cited Tweed's middle name as "Marcy," apparently after William Learned Marcy, a Jacksonian Democrat who was elected governor of New York in 1830. But Marcy was unknown when William Tweed was born, and it is biographer Leo Hershkowitz who writes that Tweed's middle name is in fact Magear, his mother's maiden name. He was born at his family's residence of 1 Cherry Street, which has since been demolished to make way for the entrance to the Brooklyn Bridge. Tweed did not attend school for long—he left at age eleven to go to work for his father learning the chair-making trade. Later, he was apprenticed to a saddler and for a time studied bookkeeping and served as a clerk in a mercantile office in New York City. He also became a fireman, joining a volunteer company, Engine Company No. 12, when he was invited by the local assemblyman, John J. Reilly, to firm a new company, No. 6, in 1848. Tweed became the foreman of the company the following year, and it was through this association that he became involved in local municipal politics.

In 1852 Tweed, while running his father's chair-making company, ran for the post of New York City alderman. He was elected and served until 1853. In 1852, as well, he ran as a Democrat for a seat in the U.S. House of Representatives, winning the election and taking his seat in the Thirty-third Congress. However, when he stood for reelection, Tweed was defeated. In 1856 he was appointed to the Board of Education, serving as schools commissioner from 1856 to 1857; that same year, he was elected to the board of supervisors for New York County. By 1858 he had become one of the leading politicians in New York City. Despite this, he was defeated as a candidate for sheriff in 1861.

Starting in 1861, Tweed began to hold a series of positions that took him to the pinnacle of power in the city. Elected deputy street commissioner, serving until 1870, he garnered power by attracting the votes of Catholics and immigrants in his ward. Although he had never studied the law, Tweed was certified by a friend as an attorney and opened a law office at 95 Duane Street in 1860. He was named chairman of the Democratic General Committee of New York County, and, on 1 January 1864 was selected to lead Tammany Hall, the Democratic political machine in the city. When he was named as grand sachem, or leader, of Tammany, that April, he earned the nickname "Boss" Tweed.

Over the next decade, Tweed used his position to build a power base that was a first in American politics. Having been influenced by the dictatorial control of New York City Mayor Fernando Wood, Tweed assembled a group of men in control to rob the city of its wealth. Using the power of Mayor Abraham Oakey Hall, Comptroller Richard B. Connolly, and chief of the Department of Public Works Peter B. Sweeny, Tweed was able to siphon millions of dollars from city coffers. Tweed also controlled the votes of six Democrats on the Board of Supervisors and paid one of the six opposing Republicans, Peter Voorhis, to stay away from the meetings so he could have a majority of the votes. Judges were bought: one, Albert Cardozo, was the father of future Supreme Court Justice Benjamin Cardozo. Another, George G. Bernard, was a former pimp who slept through the trials he was hearing. (Barnard was later the subject of impeachment inquiries in New York State.)

Tweed used every avenue to bleed the city's budget. Historian Jay Robert Nash explained:

> To control the elections of the late 1860s, Tweed and his fellows took over the naturalization of immigrants who made up almost half of New York's population. Tammany members sold naturalization papers to those who would vote the Tammany ticket. These papers were genuine and issued by Tweed's controlled courts. A man named Rosenberg sold thousands of these papers to immigrants before being arrested by U.S. Marshal Robert Murray, who posed as a foreigner without papers. Said Rosenberg before he was promptly set free by Tweed's hirelings: "Mr. Murray, every certificate that you have purchased from me is genuine, and came out of the courtroom. I am at work for the democratic [sic] party, and paid for this thing[;] I get but very little of the $2 that is paid for these certificates."

The corruption reached new levels in the 1870s. After being named by Tammany to be the commissioner of public works, Tweed pushed for the building of City Hall Park and was paid

A GROUP OF VULTURES WAITING FOR THE STORM TO "BLOW OVER."—"LET US *PREY*."

William "Boss" Tweed and members of his ring, Peter B. Sweeny, Richard B. Connolly, and A. Oakley Hall, weather a violent storm on a ledge, while the picked-over remains of New York City lie below. (Library of Congress)

through back channels; he also purchased benches for $5 each and resold them to the city for $600 each. Tweed controlled all aspects of New York City life for the better part of a decade. It was not until *Harper's Weekly* and the *New York Times* started investigating the city's finances that the massive corruption was uncovered, albeit slowly. On 21 July 1870, the *New York Times* reported on its front page that cronies of Tweed's were being paid massive sums to do ordinary work—for instance, one George Miller, a carpenter with ties to Tweed, was paid more than $360,000 a month for his labor. The governor of New York, Samuel Tilden, and the state attorney general, Charles Fairchild, opened up investigations. Fairchild, figuring Tweed to be a low man on the totem pole, called him in and offered him freedom in exchange for his testimony. Tweed told Fairchild the whole story, but implicated himself as the leader of the crooked gang. Fairchild then backed off his deal and instead charged Tweed, using the evidence Tweed himself had supplied to indict him. Tweed was arrested and his bail set at $6 million, an incredible sum in those days. Using backdoor accounts, Tweed sent his entire family into exile in Europe.

Day after day, Tweed was pilloried in the press—noted journalist/artist Thomas Nast drew Tweed in his popular cartoon as a buffoon and even drew him with a moneybag for a face. Tweed knew the impact these pictures would have on his case. He told the editor of *Harper's*, "I don't care a straw for your newspaper articles, my constituents don't know how to read, but they can't help seeing them damned pictures." Tweed approached Nast and offered him a bribe of $500,000—far more than his $5,000 annual salary—to stop drawing his cartoons, but Nast refused.

In 1874 Tweed was put on trial and convicted of embezzlement, although the prosecutors did not fully divulge to the jury the vulgar amounts that were stolen. Tweed was sentenced to eight years in prison and served his time in the New York City prison called "The Tombs." However, in December 1875, he managed to bribe a guard and escaped, catching a ship to Spain. He would have made good his flight, but he was recognized in Europe due to Nast's cartoons. Captured, he was sent back on a U.S. man-of-war and again confined in the Ludlow Street jail. Less than a year and a half after he was returned to America,

Tweed, in rapidly declining health, died in prison on 12 April 1878, eleven days shy of his fifty-fifth birthday.

In the years since his death, Tweed has become known as perhaps the greatest single instance of political corruption in American history. Few positive assessments, if any could be found, have ever been published on his reign of financial terror over New York City. Because of his pudgy and scraggly appearance, the cartoons of Thomas Nast, and his seeming lack of remorse for his thievery, Tweed continues to earn popular derision more than a century after his death. Historians even continue to get his middle name wrong.

References: Allen, Oliver E., *The Tiger: The Rise and Fall of Tammany Hall* (Reading, MA: Addison-Wesley, 1993); Hershkowitz, Leo, *Tweed's New York: Another Look* (Garden City, NY: Anchor Press-Doubleday, 1977), 5; Lynch, Denis Tilden, *'Boss' Tweed: The Story of a Grim Generation*" (New York: Boni and Liveright, 1927); Roger A. Fischer, *Them Damned Pictures: Explorations in American Cartoon Art* (North Haven, CT: Archon Books, 1996); Share, Allen J., "Tweed, William M(agear) 'Boss,'" Brown, Mary Elizabeth, "Tweed Courthouse," and Mushkat, Jerome, "Tweed Ring," in Kenneth T. Jackson, ed., *The Encyclopedia of New York City* (New Haven: Yale University Press, 1995), 1205–1207; "Tweed, William Marcy," in Jay Robert Nash, *Encyclopedia of World Crime: Criminal Justice, Criminology, and Law Enforcement*, 4 vols. (Wilmette, IL: CrimeBooks, Inc., 1989), IV:3007–3009; "Tweed, William Marcy," in *The National Cyclopædia of American Biography*, 57 vols. and supplements A–N (New York: James T. White & Company, 1897–1984), III:389.

Tyner, James Noble (1826–1904)

United States representative (1869–1875), postmaster general in the administration of Ulysses S. Grant (1876–1877), charged but acquitted of massive corruption in the Post Office Department. Tyner was born in the town of Brookville, Indiana, on 17 January 1826 (although the date had been also reported as 7 January 1826), the son of Richard Tyner, a merchant and dry goods store owner. James Tyner studied at local academies before graduating from the Brookville Academy in 1844. He entered private business, working for his father and spending ten years accumulating some wealth, before he studied law and was admitted to the Indiana bar in 1857. He opened a practice in the town of Peru, Indiana.

While studying for the bar, Tyner ran for a seat as a representative in the Indiana General Assembly, representing Miami County, but he was defeated. However, soon after he was admitted to the bar, he was elected secretary of the Indiana state senate, where he served until 1861. He left that position to become a special agent for the United States Post Office Department, starting a career in that government department that would last for most of his life. Five years after starting work there he resigned to return to the practice of law. However, his law practice period was short. In 1868, Tyner decided to reenter the political field. Republican Daniel D. Pratt had been elected to a seat in the U.S. House of Representatives, but when a U.S. Senate seat had opened he was advanced to that position, opening the House seat. Tyner ran as a Republican to fill the vacancy and was elected in early 1869, taking his seat in the Forty-first Congress. In the House from 4 March 1869 to 3 March 1875, Tyner, as a former member of the U.S. Post Office Department, served as a member of the House Committee on Post Offices and Post Roads. In the Forty-third Congress, the committee's chairman, Representative James A. Garfield, selected Tyner to oversee all congressional activity relating to the appropriations for the Post Office Department. In February 1875 President Ulysses S. Grant named Tyner second assistant postmaster general, making the Indiana Republican the third most powerful man inside the Post Office Department. During his tenure in that office, from 26 February 1875 until 12 July 1876, Tyner was put in charge of the department's contract system with local postmasters.

On 11 July 1876, President Grant fired Postmaster General Marshall Jewell—historians believe that Jewell's investigations into massive corruption by Republican postmasters nationwide caused pressure on Grant to remove him. The following day, Tyner was named as Jewell's replacement. Despite having served under Grant and being named to the department's top position by Grant, Tyner was a close political ally of Ohio Governor Rutherford B. Hayes, who was being pushed by many in his party to challenge Grant's attempts at a third presidential nomination in 1876. Numerous scandals during the eight years of Grant's presidency, including the Whiskey Ring frauds, the Indian Ring frauds, the Sanborn Contract scandal, among

others, led many Republicans to become disillusioned with Grant. Tyner secretly worked behind the scenes to aid Hayes and was rewarded when the Ohioan received the presidential nomination of the party and was elected in a close election. Despite being demoted by Hayes to first assistant postmaster general to make way for a Democrat, David M. Key, Tyner was given control of the day-to-day activities of the department. Many historians believe that it was during this period that Tyner abetted corruption and may have even been involved in it.

In October 1881, when the massive corruption of the Star Route frauds came to light, Tyner claimed that he had informed Postmaster General Keys in 1878, and then Postmaster General Thomas L. James in 1879, but was ignored. This half-baked story was believed by no one, and the constant press attention forced Tyner to resign. The *New York Times* dubbed his story "Mr. Tyner's Lame Defense," and editorialized, "Mr. Tyner, by his report of August 1879, shows that he was cognizant of the fraudulent methods being practiced in connection with the postal service, and yet, in February 1880, when the frauds were being exposed in Congress, Mr. Tyner was daily on the floor of the House exerting his influence, to shield [those accused in the frauds] and to secure the passage of a deficiency appropriation of nearly $2,000,000 to continue to perpetuate frauds. It is singular that Mr. Tyner did not produce his report at that time, and thus save the Treasury from further plunder."

Despite this accusation, Tyner was never charged with a crime. And having helped Hayes gain the nomination in 1876, he remained a powerful force in Republican politics. In 1888, when Senator Benjamin Harrison of Indiana was elected president, Tyner was rewarded once again, being named assistant attorney general for the Post Office Department. Again, Tyner allegedly set out and used his position to collect bribes and to look away while corruption went on unabated. He remained in the administration until Harrison left office in 1893. However, in 1896, when Republican William McKinley was elected president, again Tyner was rewarded with the assistant attorney general position and he spend five more years profiting from his position. Finally, in 1902, after years and years of corruption, allegations arose as to his deeds. President Theodore Roosevelt named Fourth Assistant Postmaster General Joseph L. Bristow to investigate. Bristow concluded that Tyner had been taking bribes and kickbacks for much of his tenure. When word leaked what Bristow had concluded as to Tyner's guilt, the seventy-six-year-old Tyner sent his wife and sister-in-law to his Post Office Department office to retrieve and destroy vital documents and other papers. Tyner was indicted nonetheless, but without the key evidence he was acquitted. He then quietly resigned, his three-decade career of graft and corruption put to an end.

Just two years after he was acquitted, on 5 December 1904, Tyner died in Washington, D.C., at the age of seventy-eight, and was buried in that city's Oak Hill Cemetery. Despite his lengthy career of corruption, one of the longest in American history, his name remains unknown today.

References: Fowler, Dorothy Ganfield, *The Cabinet Politician: The Postmasters General, 1829–1909* (New York: Columbia University Press, 1943), 156; "James N. Tyner Dead. Was a Member of President Grant's Cabinet. Years in the Service. Was Recently Before the Court on Charges and Was Acquitted by Jury," *Evening Star* (Washington, DC), 5 December 1904, 8; "Mr. Tyner's Lame Defense. His Unavailing Efforts to Retain Office," *New York Times,* 24 October 1881, 1; "Mr. Tyner's Pet Star Route. Costly Postal Service for his Personal Benefit," *New York Times,* 25 October 1881, 1; "Tyner, James Noble," in *The National Cyclopædia of American Biography,* 57 vols. and supplements A-N (New York: James T. White & Company, 1897–1984), IV:20; Tyner to Chandler, 1 November 1876, in file "Correspondence 1876," *Zachariah Chandler Papers,* Library of Congress.

U

United States v. Bramblett, 348 U.S. 503 (1955)

United States Supreme Court decision that "the Disbursing Office of the House of Representatives is a 'department or agency' of the United States within the meaning of 18 U.S.C. 1001, which forbids the willful falsification of a material fact 'in any matter within the jurisdiction of any department or agency of the United States.'" Bramblett, a former Congressman, was found guilty after telling the House Disbursing Office, which pays salaries of House workers, that a particular person known to Bramblett was serving as his clerk, when in fact the person had no official duties in the House. Bramblett was convicted of violating 18 U.S.C. § 1001, which states that "Whoever, in any matter within the jurisdiction of any department or agency of the United States knowingly and willfully falsifies, conceals or covers up by any trick, scheme, or device a material fact, or makes any false, fictitious or fraudulent statements or representations, or makes or uses any false writing or document knowing the same to contain any false, fictitious or fraudulent statement or entry, shall be fined not more than $10,000 or imprisoned not more than five years, or both." Of the eighteen original charges against Bramblett, a trial judgment of acquittal was entered in counts eight to eighteen, and the jury returned with guilty verdicts on the remaining seven counts. The court then granted the defendant's motion that the verdict be arrested, because he claimed that he had not falsified a material fact "within the jurisdiction of any department or agency of the United States," and that the Disbursing Office was not such an office within the meaning of the statute. The United States appealed, and the U.S. Supreme Court granted certiorari (the right to hear the case). Arguments were heard on 7 February 1955.

On 4 April of that same year, Justice Stanley Reed spoke for a six-to-zero majority (Chief Justice Earl Warren and Associate Justices Harold Burton and John Marshall Harlan did not participate) in holding that the Disbursing Office of the House *was* a "department or agency" of the United States government within the meaning of the relevant statute, 18 U.S.C. § 1001. As Justice Reed explained:

> It might be argued that the matter here involved was within the jurisdiction of the Treasury Department, as the appellee's misstatements would require the payment of funds from the United States Treasury. Or, viewing this as a matter within the jurisdiction of the Disbursing Office, it might be argued, as the Government does, that that body is an "authority" within the definition of "agency." We do not rest our decision on either of those interpretations. The context in which this language is used calls for an unrestricted interpretation. This is enforced by its legislative history. It would do violence to the purpose of Congress to limit the section to falsifications made to the executive departments. Congress

could not have intended to leave frauds such as this without penalty. The development, scope and purpose of the section shows that "department," as used in this context, was meant to describe the executive, legislative and judicial branches of the Government.

In 1995 the U.S. Supreme Court overruled *Bramblett,* holding it to be a "seriously flawed decision," in the case *Hubbard v. United States.*

References: *Hubbard v. United States,* 514 U.S. 695, 115 S. Ct. 1754 [1995]).

United States v. Brewster, 408 U.S. 501 (1972)

United States Supreme Court decision holding that the Speech or Debate Clause of the U.S. Constitution does not preclude an inquiry into the alleged conduct of a congressman or a senator apart from his or her actions as a member of Congress. Senator Daniel Brewster (D-MD) was charged with the solicitation and acceptance of bribes in violation of 18 U.S.C. §§ 201(c)(1) and 201(g) (the latter now 18 U.S.C. § 201(c)(1)(B)), which read:

> (c) Whoever (1) otherwise than as provided by law for the proper discharge of official duty (A) directly or indirectly gives, offers, or promises anything of value to any public official, former public official, or person selected to be a public official, for or because of any official act performed or to be performed by such public official, former public official, or person selected to be a public official; or (B) being a public official, former public official, or person selected to be a public official, otherwise than as provided by law for the proper discharge of official duty, directly or indirectly demands, seeks, receives, accepts, or agrees to receive or accept anything of value personally for or because of any official act performed or to be performed by such official or person shall be fined or imprisoned for not more than two years.

Brewster lost his reelection bid in 1968 and in 1969 was indicted on ten counts alleging that, while sitting as a member of the Senate Committee on Post Office and Civil Service, he "directly and indirectly, corruptly asked, solicited, sought, accepted, received and agreed to receive [sums] . . . in return for being influenced in his performance of official acts in respect to his action, vote, and decision on postage rate legislation which might at any time be pending before him in his official capacity." When the case got to trial, the district court judge threw out five of the counts, holding that they related to the acceptance of bribes in connection with the performance of a legislative function by a senator of the United States, which was protected under the Speech and Debate Clause of the U.S. Constitution. The prosecutor appealed directly to the U.S. Supreme Court; the Court agreed to hear the case, and it was argued—first on 18 October 1971, and again on 20 March 1972.

On 29 June 1972, the Court held six to three that the inquiry into taking bribes in contravention of the law was not protected by the Speech and Debate Clause and reinstated the five counts that had been dismissed. Holding for the majority, Chief Justice Warren Burger (Justices William O. Douglas, Byron White, and William Brennan dissented) held that bribes were not part of the "performance of a legislative function," and thus inquiry into them were not shielded by the Speech and Debate Clause. Chief Justice Burger explained:

> The question is whether it is necessary to inquire into how appellee spoke, how he debated, how he voted, or anything he did in the chamber or in committee in order to make out a violation of this statute. The illegal conduct is taking or agreeing to take money for a promise to act in a certain way. There is no need for the Government to show that appellee fulfilled the alleged illegal bargain; acceptance of the bribe is the violation of the statute, not performance of the illegal promise. . . .
>
> Taking a bribe is, obviously, no part of the legislative process or function; it is not a legislative act. It is not, by any conceivable interpretation, an act performed as a part of or even incidental to the role of a legislator. It is not an "act resulting from the nature, and in the execution, of the office." Nor is it a "thing said or done by him, as a representative, in the exercise of the functions of that office," . . . . Nor is inquiry into a legislative act or the motivation for a legislative act necessary to a prosecution under this statute or this indictment. When a bribe is taken, it does not matter whether the promise for which the bribe was given was for the performance of a legislative act as here or, as in *Johnson,* for use of a Congressman's influence with the Executive Branch. And an inquiry into the purpose of a bribe "does not draw in question the legislative acts of the defendant member of Congress or his motives for performing them. . . .

Nor does it matter if the Member defaults on his illegal bargain. To make a prima facie case under this indictment, the Government need not show any act of appellee subsequent to the corrupt promise for payment, for it is taking the bribe, not performance of the illicit compact, that is a criminal act. If, for example, there were undisputed evidence that a Member took a bribe in exchange for an agreement to vote for a given bill and if there were also undisputed evidence that he, in fact, voted against the bill, can it be thought that this alters the nature of the bribery or removes it from the area of wrongdoing the Congress sought to make a crime?

With these counts restored, and, having been convicted of the other five counts (which had been reversed), in 1975 Brewster pled guilty to a charge of accepting an illegal gratuity while a United States senator and served a short prison term.

See also Speech or Debate Clause of the U.S. Constitution

References: "Former Senator Brewster Charged with Bribery," *News and Observer* (Raleigh, NC), 2 December 1969, 1.

United States v. Gillock, 445 U.S. 360 (1980)

United States Supreme Court decision that upheld the right of a court to allow the introduction of evidence involving a legislator's legislative career in cases dealing with political corruption. Although not a corruption case per se, the determination nevertheless allowed a widening of latitude in such cases.

Tennessee State Senator Edgar H. Gillock was indicted on 12 August 1976 in the federal District Court for the Western District of Tennessee on five counts of "obtaining money under the color of official right . . . one count of using an interstate facility to distribute a bribe . . . and one count of participating in an enterprise through a pattern of racketeering activity." The indictment charged Gillock, who was also a practicing attorney, "with accepting money as a fee for using his public office to block the extradition of a defendant from Tennessee to Illinois, and for agreeing to introduce in the State General Assembly legislation which would enable four persons to obtain master electricians' licenses they had been unable to obtain by way of existing examination processes." Before the

trial, Gillock asked that the court suppress all evidence relating to his legislative activities under a privilege granted by Rule 501 of the Federal Rules of Evidence, which prohibits courts from allowing the introduction of evidence of one's legislative acts or "underlying motivations." The district court, in granting the motion, held that the ban on such evidence was necessary "to protect the integrity of the [state's] legislative process by insuring the independence of individual legislators" and "to preserve the constitutional relation between our federal and state governments in our federal system." The prosecution appealed, and the ruling was struck down the by United States Court of Appeals for the Sixth Circuit, which vacated the order and remanded back to the district court for additional consideration. (See 559 F.2d 1222 (1977).) In a hearing before the district court judge, the government explained that it intended to use evidence of Gillock's legislative activities to prove that he had violated his office to obtain a bribe and fees for introducing certain legislation. After the hearing, the district court again suppressed this evidence. Again, the government appealed to the Court of Appeals for the Sixth Circuit. In a divided decision, the court upheld the suppression, holding that "the long history and the felt need for protection of legislative speech or debate and the repeated and strong recognition of that history in the cases . . . from the Supreme Court, fully justify our affirming [the District Court] in [its] protection of the privilege in this case." (See 587 F.2d 284, 290 (1978).) The government then appealed to the U.S. Supreme Court, which granted certiorari (the right to hear the case). As Chief Justice Warren Burger wrote, "We granted certiorari [in this case] to resolve a conflict in the Circuits over whether the federal courts in a federal criminal prosecution . . . should recognize a legislative privilege barring the introduction of evidence of the legislative acts of a state legislator charged with taking bribes or otherwise obtaining money unlawfully through exploitation of his official position."

Arguments were heard on 4 December 1979.

On 19 March 1980 the Court handed down its decision. Speaking for a seven-to-two majority, Chief Justice Burger held that "in the absence of a constitutional limitation on the power of Congress to make state officials, like all other persons, subject to federal criminal sanctions, we discern no basis in these circumstances for a judicially created limitation that handicaps proof of the relevant facts." Finding on the grounds that Congress did not intend for such legislative immunity to be extended to state officials, the Court ordered that evidence of Gillock's legislative activities may be allowed. "We conclude, therefore, that although principles of comity command careful consideration, our cases disclose that where important federal interests are at stake, as in the enforcement of federal criminal statutes, comity yields," Burger went on:

> We recognize that denial of a privilege to a state legislator may have some minimal impact on the exercise of his legislative function; however, similar arguments made to support a claim of executive privilege were found wanting in *United States v. Nixon,* 418 U.S. 683 (1974), when balanced against the need of enforcing federal criminal statutes. There, the genuine risk of inhibiting candor in the internal exchanges at the highest levels of the Executive Branch was held insufficient to justify denying judicial power to secure all relevant evidence in a criminal proceeding. See also *United States v. Burr,* 25 F. Cas. 187 (No. 14,694). Here, we believe that recognition of an evidentiary privilege for state legislators for their legislative acts would impair the legitimate interest of the Federal Government in enforcing its criminal statutes with only speculative benefit to the state legislative process.

References: Text of *United States v. Gillock,* 445 U.S. 360 (1980).

United States v. Helstoski, 442 U.S. 477 (1979)

United States Supreme Court decision holding that the legislative actions of a congressperson that are evidence of political corruption are inadmissible in a court of law. Representative Henry Helstoski (1925–1999) served in the U.S. House of Representatives (1965–1977) as a representative from New Jersey. In 1974 the Department of Justice began investigating reports of political corruption involving Helstoski, including allegations that aliens had paid him for the introduction and processing of private bills that would suspend the application of the immigration laws so as to allow them to remain in the United States. In June 1976 a grand jury returned a twelve-count indictment charging Helstoski and others with numerous criminal acts, including "accepting money in return for Helstoski's 'being influenced in the performance of official acts, to wit: the introduction of private bills in the United States House of Representatives.'" During the grand jury proceedings, Helstoski refused to produce documents that dealt with the controversy, citing the so-called Speech or Debate Clause of the U.S. Constitution. This provision, in Article 1, Section 6, says that "for any Speech or Debate in either House, they [the Senators and Representatives] shall not be questioned in any other Place." On this subject, the trial court held that "The United States may not, during the presentation of its case-in-chief at the trial of [this] Indictment, introduce evidence of the performance of a past legislative act on the part of the defendant, Henry Helstoski, derived from any source and for any purpose." The prosecution appealed to the United States Court of Appeals for the Third Circuit, which rejected both of the government's arguments: (a) that legislative acts could be introduced to show motive; and (b) that legislative acts could be introduced because Helstoski had waived his privilege by testifying before the grand juries. The court relied on *United States v. Brewster,* 408 U.S. 501 (1972), which prohibited "the introduction of evidence as to how a Congressman acted on, voted on, or resolved a legislative issue," reasoning that "to permit evidence of such acts under the guise of showing motive would negate the protection afforded by the Speech or Debate Clause." The government appealed to the United States Supreme Court. Helstoski also sued Judge Meanor, the district judge, for refusing to allow him to quash the indictment with a writ of mandamus. The U.S. Supreme Court heard arguments in both of Helstoski's suits on the same day, 27 March 1979.

The Court handed down its decision on 18 June 1979. In *Helstoski v. Meanor,* the court held that a writ of mandamus was an improper way to get a court to throw evidence out. In *United States v. Helstoski,* Chief Justice Burger spoke for a seven-to-one majority (Justice William Brennan dissented, and Justice Lewis Powell did not participate) in refusing to allow the government to introduce evidence of Helstoski's legislative actions. "The Speech or Debate Clause was designed to preclude prosecution of Members for legislative acts," the Chief Justice wrote. "The Clause protects 'against inquiry into acts that occur in the regular course of the legislative process and into the motivation for those acts' . . . It 'precludes any showing of how [a legislator] acted, voted, or decided.'" Chief Justice Burger further explained:

> The Clause does not simply state, "No proof of a legislative act shall be offered"; the prohibition of the Clause is far broader. It provides that Members "shall not be questioned in any other Place." Indeed, as MR. JUSTICE STEVENS recognizes, the admission of evidence of legislative acts "may reveal [to the jury] some information about the performance of legislative acts and the legislator's motivation in conducting official duties.". . . Revealing information as to a legislative act—speaking or debating—to a jury would subject a Member to being "questioned," in a place other than the House or Senate, thereby violating the explicit prohibition of the Speech or Debate Clause.

See also *United States v. Brewster; United States v. Johnson*
References: *Helstoski v. Meanor*, 442 U.S. 500 (1979), 489.

United States v. Johnson, 383 U.S. 169 (1966)

United States Supreme Court decision that representatives could not be convicted of political corruption on evidence arising from their legislative activities.

Thomas Francis Johnson, a former United States representative from the state of Maryland, was indicted and convicted on seven counts of violating the federal conflict-of-interest statute (18 U.S.C. § 281) and on one count of conspiring to defraud the United States (18 U.S.C. § 371). On appeal, the United States Court of Appeals for the Fourth Circuit set aside Johnson's conviction on the single conspiracy count, holding that the government's allegation that Johnson had conspired to make a speech for compensation on the floor of the House of Representatives was barred by the so-called Speech or Debate Clause of the U.S. Constitution, which says that "for any Speech or Debate in either House, they [Senators and Representatives] shall not be questioned in any other Place." The court then ordered a new trial on the remaining counts, holding that the evidence

brought forth to prove conspiracy had "infected the entire prosecution." The United States appealed this ruling to the United States Supreme Court. Arguments were heard on 10 and 15 November 1965.

On 24 February 1965, Justice John Marshall Harlan spoke for a seven-to-zero majority (Justices Hugo Black and Byron White did not participate) in affirming the lower court's decision. Justice Harlan found, in giving a history of the Speech or Debate clause, that it was a fundamental right of representatives to be free from the "intrusions" of other branches, namely the judicial branch, when discussing their legislative activities, particularly their speeches. He wrote,

> [T]he Government contends that the Speech or Debate Clause was not violated because the gravamen of the count was the alleged conspiracy, not the speech, and because the defendant, not the prosecution, introduced the speech itself. Whatever room the Constitution may allow for such factors in the context of a different kind of prosecution, we conclude that they cannot serve to save the Government's case under this conspiracy count. It was undisputed that Johnson delivered the speech; it was likewise undisputed that Johnson received the funds; controversy centered upon questions of who first decided that a speech was desirable, who prepared it, and what Johnson's motives were for making it.

See also Johnson, Thomas Francis; Speech or Debate Clause of the U.S. Constitution; *United States v. Brewster; United States v. Helstoski*

United States v. National Treasury Employees Union
See Honoraria

United States v. Shirey, 359 U.S. 255 (1959)

Supreme Court decision holding that a law that prohibits an "offer or promise . . . of money or thing of value, to any person, firm or corporation in consideration of the use or promise to use any influence to procure any appointive office or place under the United States for any person" includes political parties as well as people not in a legislative seat under the definition of "person." George Donald Shirey was charged with violating this federal law (18 U.S.C. § 214), when he told Congressman S. Walter Stauffer (R-PA) that he would "donate $1,000 a year to the Republican Party to be used as they see fit" in return for Stauffer's help in getting Shirey appointed postmaster of York, Pennsylvania. Stauffer told the authorities, and Shirey was arrested. In federal district court, Shirey asked that the indictment be quashed on the grounds that he was not a "person" covered by the statute, and that offering $1,000 a year to the Republican Party was not offering a bribe to a "person." The district court agreed, and the U.S. government appealed directly to the United States Supreme Court, which agreed to hear the case. Justice Felix Frankfurter wrote, "One sensible reading is to say that even though the Republican Party was to be the ultimate recipient of the money, this was a promise to Stauffer of money (which it plainly was) in consideration of his use of influence." Arguments were heard on 19 January 1959.

Almost exactly three months later, on 20 April 1959, Justice Frankfurter spoke for a unanimous court in reversing the district court's decision and holding that Shirey and the Republican Party could be considered "persons" under the meaning of 18 U.S.C. § 214. Justice Frankfurter explained:

> Applying these generalities to the immediate occasion, it is clear that the terms, the history, and the manifest purpose of 18 U.S.C. 214 coalesce in a construction of that statute which validates the information against Shirey. The evil which Congress sought to check and the mischief wrought by what it proscribed are the same when the transaction is triangular as when only two parties are involved. It is incredible to suppose that Congress meant to prohibit Shirey from giving $1,000 to Stauffer, to be passed on by the latter to the Party fund, but that Shirey was outside the congressional prohibition for securing the same influence by a promise to deposit $1,000 directly in the Party's fund. That is not the kind of finessing by which this Court has heretofore allowed penal legislation to be construed. . . . the judgment is reversed.

United States v. Worrall, 2 U.S. (2 Dall.) 384 (1798)

Important Pennsylvania district case, one of the first to be heard in the United States regarding bribery of federal and state officials and how such a crime could be charged under the common law. In 1792, Alexander Hamilton, the secretary of the treasury, appointed Tench Coxe commissioner of revenue, a position in which he collected the taxes and tariffs accrued in the nation as a whole.

In 1794 Congress enacted a law calling for the construction of a lighthouse at Cape Hatteras, North Carolina. Coxe, in his position as commissioner of revenue, was put in charge of soliciting proposals for the project and settling on a builder. On 28 September 1797, he received a letter from one Robert Worrall, who was interested in obtaining the contract to build the lighthouse. In his letter, Worrall wrote that he was the right man for the job and, in his closing line, stated:

> If I should be so happy in your recommendation of this work, I should think myself very ungrateful, if I did not offer you one half of the profits as above stated, and would deposit in your hand at receiving the first payment £ 350, and the other £ 350 at the last payment, when the work is finished and completed [*sic*]. I hope you will not think me troublesome in asking for a line on the business by your next return and will call for it at the Post-Office, or in Third Street. In the mean time I shall subscribe myself to be, your obedient and very humble servt. [*sic*] to command.

Worrall was promising Coxe a bribe of some £700 pounds, or $1,866.67 at the time. Although Coxe was in dire financial straits when the letter was received, he presented it to authorities, who arrested Worrall and charged him with trying to bribe a federal officer. Worrall was tried and found guilty of both counts. He appealed to the Circuit Court of Pennsylvania's Third Circuit—sitting as judges were Samuel Chase of the U.S. Supreme Court (on circuit duty) and Judge Richard Peters. Two issues were presented: 1) whether a federal common law of crimes existed that prohibited Worrall's conduct, and 2) whether Congress had lawfully passed a statute making it illegal for a federal officer to accept a bribe. Chase argued that under the Tenth Amendment, the federal government could not assume a power not specifically granted to it by the Constitution. Moreover, even if Congress was permitted to enact the law outlawing bribery to certain named federal officials, the commissioner of revenue was not included, so any bribe to him was not covered by the statute. Peters, however, claimed that political corruption went to the heart of a democracy's well-being. He wrote:

> Whenever a government has been established, I have always supposed, that a power to preserve itself, was a necessary, and an inseparable, concomitant. But the existence of the Federal government would be precarious, it could no longer be called an independent government, if, for the punishment of offences of this nature, tending to obstruct and pervert the administration of its affairs, an appeal must be made to the State tribunals, or the offenders must escape with absolute impunity. The power to punish misdemeanors, is originally and strictly a common law power; of which, I think, the United States are constitutionally possessed. It might have been exercised by Congress in the form of a Legislative act; but, it may, also, in my opinion be enforced in a course of Judicial proceeding. Whenever an offence aims at the subversion of any Federal institution, or at the corruption of its public officers, it is an offence against the well-being of the United States; from its very nature, it is cognizable under their authority; and, consequently, it is within the jurisdiction of this Court, by virtue of the 11th section of the Judicial act.

Because the court was split, Worrall's conviction was upheld, and, after the two judges consulted with the other Supreme Court justices sitting in Philadelphia, they sentenced Worrall to three month's imprisonment and a fine of $200.

Although little studied today, *United States v. Worrall* was the first case dealing with the impact of political corruption on society and politics and whether or not it could be punished or should be punished.

References: Kawashima, Yasuhide, "Congress Should First Define the Offenses and Apportion the Punishment: Federal Common Law Crimes [*United States v. Worrall*]," in John W. Johnson, ed., *Historic U.S. Court Cases, 1690–1990: An Encyclopedia* (New York: Garland Publishing, 1992), 19–22; "Trial of Robert Worrall, For Attempting to Bribe a Commissioner of the Revenue, In the Circuit Court of the United States for the Pennsylvania District, Philadelphia, 1798," in Francis Wharton, ed., *State Trials of the United States During the Administrations of Washington and Adams, With References Historical and Professional and Preliminary Notes on the Politics of the Times* (Philadelphia: Carey & Hart, 1849), 189–199.

V

Vare, William Scott (1867–1934)

United States representative (1912–1923, 1923–1927) and U.S. senator-elect (1927–1929), denied his seat because of allegations of fraud in his senatorial election, the legality of which denial was determined in a landmark Supreme Court decision. Vare was born in Philadelphia, Pennsylvania, on 24 December 1867. He attended public schools in Philadelphia, but quit his formal education at the age of fifteen to enter the mercantile business in that city. By 1893 Vare was a successful contractor in the city. In 1898 he entered the political realm, running for and winning a seat on the select council of Philadelphia, where he served until 1901. From 1902 to 1912, he served as the recorder of deeds for the city of Philadelphia and in 1912 was elected to a seat in the Pennsylvania state senate. With his brothers George and Edward, he came to control the political machine in Pennsylvania once run by Simon Cameron and his son James Donald Cameron. Vare later succeeded Senator Boies Penrose as the political "boss" in the state.

Vare did not hold his state senate seat long; following the death of Representative Henry Harrison Bingham on 22 March 1912, a special election was held and Vare won the vacant seat. Vare would ultimately serve in the U.S. House from 24 April 1912 until 2 January 1923, when he resigned. Vare returned to Pennsylvania after his resignation and served for a short time as a member of the state senate. Elected back to the U.S. House of Represen-

tatives, he served in the Sixty-eighth and Sixty-ninth Congresses (4 March 1923–3 March 1927).

In 1926 Vare was elected to the United States Senate. At least, at first glance, it *appeared* that he had been elected. Nominated by the Republicans, Vare easily defeated the Democrat and Labor candidate, William B. Wilson (the former secretary of labor (1913–1921) under Woodrow Wilson), by more than 180,000 votes out of some 1.4 million cast. When the new Congress began its session, Vare went to Washington to present his credentials. But Wilson, the defeated candidate, filed an appeal with the Senate, charging massive corruption by Vare during both the Republican primary and the general election. In his petition before Congress, Wilson alleged that Vare and his supporters used padded registration lists, misused campaign expenditures, counted votes for Vare from persons who were dead or never existed, and engaged in intimidation and discouragement of prospective voters. The Senate then voted to refuse Vare his seat until an investigation could be concluded. The Senate Committee on Privileges and Elections began to examine the election controversy. However, they were blocked: Senator David A. Reed (R-PA) filibustered, forcing the investigation to continue into the Seventieth Congress, which convened in December 1927. The Senate's refusal to act left the committee with no jurisdiction for nine full months, until the end of 1927. The Senate had passed, on 11 January 1927,

Resolution 324, which empowered the Senate committee to "take . . . and preserve all ballot boxes, . . . ballots, return sheets . . . and other records, books, and documents used in said Senate election." The committee appointed investigator Jerry South to go to Pennsylvania to take control of the materials specified. However, when South went to the commissioners of Delaware County, who had custody of the ballots, they refused to hand them over. Reed, as a member of the Senate committee, demanded the boxes, and when the commissioners refused, he sued in federal court. The case reached the U.S. Supreme Court in 1928. In *Reed v. County Commissioners of Delaware County,* 277 U.S. 376 (1928), the Court held that Reed and the Senate committee did not have standing to sue. The Court held that since the Senate resolution did not allow for senators to sue, they could not even if the Senate Committee was blocked in its investigation. When the Seventieth Congress convened on 5 December 1927, Vare presented his credentials, but was again refused his seat. The Senate committee then began its investigation. Vare and Wilson were able to get the records, and they were presented to the committee for inspection. The Philadelphia district attorney testified that Vare supporters had been involved in election fraud and that they had been obstructing his own investigation into systematic campaign fraud in the city. In examining the ballots from Philadelphia and Pittsburgh, the committee found that "the fraud pervading the actual count by the division election officers is appalling." Vare was asked for additional testimony before the committee, but he suffered a cerebral hemorrhage, delaying the committee's report. On 22 February 1929, the committee reported unanimously that because of the corruption, neither Vare nor Wilson was entitled to the seat. On 6 December 1929, the Senate voted by fifty-eight to twenty-two that Vare could not be seated, and by sixty-six to fifteen that Wilson was equally ineligible. On 12 December 1929, the Senate seated Joseph R. Grundy, who had been appointed to the vacancy by Pennsylvania Governor John S. Fisher.

Vare was politically ruined by his failure to capture the Senate seat and returned home to Pennsylvania, where he resumed his business activities. His health declined soon after, and on 7 August 1934, while on a business trip to Atlantic City, New Jersey, he died at the age of sixty-six. He was buried in West Laurel Hill Cemetery in Philadelphia.

Although the name of William Vare is forgotten today, his case ranks as one of the longest contested Senate campaigns in American history. Allegations of excessive campaign expenditures and voter fraud were as big a problem then as they are today.

See also *Barry v. United States ex rel. Cunningham*

References: Astorino, Samuel J., "The Contested Senate Election of William Scott Vare," *Pennsylvania History,* 28 (April 1961), 187–201; Salter, John T., *The People's Choice: Philadelphia's William S. Vare* (New York: Exposition Press, 1971); Vare, William S., *My Forty Years in Politics* (Philadelphia: Roland Swain Co., 1933); "William B. Wilson v. William S. Vare," in Anne M. Butler and Wendy Wolff, *United States Senate Election, Expulsion and Censure Cases, 1793–1990* (Washington, DC: Government Printing Office, 1995), 323–329.

Vermont Right to Life Committee v. Sorrell, 19 F. Supp. 2d 204 (1998), 216 F. 3d 264 (2000)

Federal court of appeals decision holding that federal or state governments may regulate only those political communications that expressly advocate the election, or the defeat, of a clearly identified candidate. In 1997 the state of Vermont enacted a law to reform its campaign financing system. The law, Act No. 64, specifically stated that it was "a response to rising costs of running for state office, the influence of those who make large campaign contributions, and the effect of large campaign expenditures on what the Vermont General Assembly called the '[r]obust debate of issues, candidate interaction with the electorate, and public involvement and confidence in the electoral process.'" The act changed the way Vermont campaigns were financed. It provided for the "public financing of campaigns for the offices of governor and lieutenant governor, limited campaign contributions and expenditures, amended the reporting requirements for candidates and contributors, and imposed disclosure and reporting requirements on, respectively, all 'political advertisements' and 'mass media activities.'" However, in this case, only the political advertising and the mass media activities provisions were at issue. The plaintiff, the Vermont Right to Life Committee (VRLC), charged that the statute was an unconstitutional abridgement on its ability to advertise during an election. The VRLC sued William H. Sorrell, the state attorney general, as well as numerous states' attorneys, to stop the enforcement of three of the provisions of the statute, namely the ones that required that all "political advertisements" disclose the identity of the person or persons or entity paying for the ad, as well as the candidate, party, or political committee on whose behalf it was being aired, and that expenditures for "mass media activities" that were made within thirty days of an election be reported to the state twenty-four hours after they were given.

The VRLC claimed that its activities potentially violated two sections of the act, namely, those regarding "political advertisements" and their definitions, and those requiring the name of a candidate to be clearly given on each ad. The U.S. District Court for the District of Vermont gave a summary judgment to the state and to several "intervenor" organizations, among them Common Cause of Vermont, and the League of Women Voters of Vermont. The VRLC appealed to the U.S. Court of Appeals for the Second Circuit.

On 15 June 2000, the court of appeals reversed the district court ruling. Basing its decision on the U.S. Supreme Court decision in *Buckley v. Valeo,* 424 U.S. 1 (1976), the court of appeals held that in order for a state or the federal government to regulate a "communication"—be it an ad in a paper, on television, or on a billboard—"that communication must actually advocate the election, or the defeat, of a clearly identified candidate." Judge Robert D. Sack, appointed to the court of appeals by President Bill Clinton in 1998, spoke for the two-to-one majority (Judge Milton Shadur, a district judge replacing another judge on the Second Circuit, dissented) in holding that issue advocacy was protected by the First Amendment and that the provisions regulating issue advocacy, as well as the disclosure requirements, which infringed on the privacy of association, were unconstitutional. Judge Sack explained:

There is, meanwhile, reason to think that when the Vermont legislature said "expenditures . . . for mass media activities" it meant all "expenditures," not only "funds used for communications that expressly advocate the election or defeat of a clearly identified

candidate" under *Buckley.* We have seen in the course of our analysis of [the provisions in question] that the General Assembly was willing to attempt to regulate advertising that "implicitly advocates the success or defeat of a candidate" despite *Buckley*'s clear mandate to the contrary. There is therefore no reason for us to think that when the General Assembly came to consider [that provision], it then intended to follow, rather than test or ignore, principles established by *Buckley,* through the use of the word "expenditure" to exclude expenditures for issue advocacy.

In discussing the law's provision that "communications" such as ads in papers, on television, or on billboards had to clearly show the name of a candidate whom the ad was either supporting or opposing for election, Judge Sack explained:

In *Virginia Soc'y for Human Life,* 152 F.3d 268 (4th Cir. 1998), the Fourth Circuit considered a Virginia statute that required certain people or organizations that spent money "for the purpose of influencing the outcome of any election," . . . to . . . report their expenditures. . . . The plain language of the statute suggested that it applied to issue advocacy contrary to *Buckley.* . . . The court of appeals disapproved the district court's narrowing construction of the words "for the purpose of influencing the outcome of any election" to exclude issue advocacy in an effort to conform the statute to the *Buckley* requirements. . . . The reviewing court reached that conclusion in part because of the limited nature of such a review of a state statute by a federal court— only if such a reading was readily apparent would it survive. But also, "[i]n fact, a de novo review of the text, structure and history of the election laws at issue suggested to [the court] that they did apply to issue advocacy" contrary to *Buckley.* . . . We likewise find that in light of the text, structure and history of Vermont's [provision in question], the narrowing reading of the provision given to it by the district court was unwarranted. . . . We conclude that the district court erred in granting summary judgment for the defendants and in failing to enter an injunction forbidding the enforcement by the defendants of the provisions of [the statute].

There is no word as of this writing on whether Vermont will appeal this decision to the U.S. Supreme Court.

References: *Vermont Right to Life Committee v. Sorrell,* 216 F.3d 264 (2000), 270–272.

W

Walker, James John (1881–1946)

Mayor of New York City (1925–1932), implicated in, but never formally charged with, massive political corruption. Even though corrupt, Walker was the personification of the "dapper" politician, whose flamboyance was a key to his popularity. The second of nine children, he was born in the Greenwich Village section of New York City on 19 June 1881, the son of an Irish immigrant father and an Irish woman born in America. He attended Catholic schools in New York City, but dropped out. He was allowed to attend the New York Law School, from which he earned a law degree in 1904. Walker did not enter politics immediately. His real calling was songwriting, and he began a career in what was called "The Great White Way." He wrote several songs that became popular and in 1912 married a singer. That same year, he was admitted to the New York state bar.

Walker's father, William Henry Walker, who died in 1916, was a longtime New York City politician who worked under the aegis of Tammany Hall, the preeminent political organization. With the recommendation of his father and an up-and-coming politician named Alfred Emanuel Smith (who would one day serve as governor of New York and the Democrat's presidential candidate in 1928), the younger Walker was allowed to join Tammany Hall and in 1909 was elected to a seat in the New York state assembly. In 1914 he was elected to a seat in the New York state senate.

Hewing to the Democratic Party line, he worked closely with Smith and Tammany to enact progressive legislation. As such he remained in Tammany's good graces, and in 1925 Tammany nominated Walker for mayor of New York City. In New York City in the 1920s, Tammany ruled the Democratic Party machinery, and once Walker won the party's nomination he was a shoe-in to be elected. In his first term, he helped to create a Department of Sanitation, created parks for children, and pushed the Board of Transportation to establish a citywide train and bus system. In 1929 Walker was overwhelmingly reelected to a second term, defeating the fusion candidate, Fiorello H. La Guardia. His dapper and freewheeling style endeared him to the people of New York City and made him a popular national figure. Walker was so popular that when he marched in a street fair in Philadelphia in November 1926, people cried out that he be the next president of the United States. It seemed that nothing could go wrong for Jimmy Walker.

Within two years of his second electoral victory, however, Walker was under increasing scrutiny for alleged political corruption. In 1931 the New York state legislature established the Hofstadter Committee to investigate allegations of rampant corruption in the Walker administration. The counsel for the committee, Judge Samuel Seabury, was allowed by Governor Franklin Delano Roosevelt complete investigatory powers to find corruption in New York City and root it out. Historian Jay Robert Nash wrote:

> Judge Samuel Seabury . . . called on Walker to explain his connection with Russell T. Sherwood, a low-ranking accountant who mysteriously accumulated a fortune of $700,225 and then disappeared. Seabury accused Sherwood of "fronting" for Walker, a charge vigorously denied by the mayor. But it was conclusively shown that on the eve of a cruise Walker took to Europe, Sherwood withdrew $263,838 from the bank for his boss.

Seabury called Walker before the committee and placed him on the stand for lengthy cross-examination. On the stand, Walker admitted that he had put a tremendous amount of money—upwards of nearly half a million dollars—in his own personal bank account, although he said it was from stock speculation on Wall Street. Walker derided Seabury's investigation; he said openly that "Little Boy Blue is going to blow his horn—or his top." Historian Paul Sann noted:

> [Walker] couldn't explain—at least not with any conviction—how he happened to make $26,535.51 in oil stock deals with taxicab impresario J. A. Sisto without having to invest a dime of his own. Nor why J. Allan Smith, contact man for a bus company, staked him to a European jaunt in 1927 with a $10,000 letter of credit and an extra $3,000 to cover an overdraft. Or how he happened to pick up an extra $246,000 bonanza in a joint stock account with Paul Block, Brooklyn financier and publisher.

As the allegations of corruption rose, Governor Roosevelt became more concerned for his party and the appearance of Walker's dishonesty. Roosevelt demanded that Walker resign before Roosevelt, slated to run for President in 1932, was himself tarnished. On 1 September 1932, as Seabury was getting closer to Walker's cronies, Walker resigned as mayor and set sail on a cruise to Europe. No charges were ever brought against him despite the breadth and depth of the corruption tied to him.

Walker returned to New York in 1935 and in 1937 was named assistant counsel to the New York State Transit Commission. Three years later, his successor as mayor, Fiorello La Guardia, named him municipal arbiter of the New York City gar-

ment industry. From 1945 until his death, Walker served as the president of Majestic Records in New York. Walker died of a cerebral hemorrhage—a blood clot in the brain—in Doctor's Hospital in New York City on 18 November 1946 at the age of sixty-five. He was buried in the Gate of Heaven Cemetery in Westchester County, New York.

Despite the allegations of corruption against him and the cowardice shown in his forced resignation, Walker remains a popular figure. In 1957 Bob Hope played Walker in the film *Beau James*.

See also Seabury, Samuel

References: Biles, W. Roger, "Walker, James John," in Melvin G. Holli and Peter d'A. Jones, *Biographical Dictionary of American Mayors, 1820–1980: Big City Mayors* (Westport, CT: Greenwood Press, 1981), 380; "[Editorial:] James J. Walker," *New York Times,* 19 November 1946, 30; "Ex-Mayor Walker Succumbs at 65 to Clot on Brain, City Chief for Seven Years Kept Popularity After Resigning Under Seabury Charges," *New York Times,* 19 November 1946, 1; "Hail Mayor Walker as 'Next President'; Philadelphians Line Streets as He Leads New Yorkers' March to Fair Grounds," *New York Times,* 13 November 1926, 1; "Jimmy Walker: The Destruction of 'Beau James'," in George C. Kohn, *Encyclopedia of American Scandal: From ABSCAM to the Zenger Case* (New York: Facts on File, 1989), 346–347; "The Night Mayor of New York," in Paul Sann, *The Lawless Decade: A Pictorial History of a Great American Transition: From the World War I Armistice and Prohibition to Repeal and the New Deal* (New York: Bonanza Books, 1977), 216; "Walker, James John," in Jay Robert Nash, *Encyclopedia of World Crime: Criminal Justice, Criminology, and Law Enforcement,* 4 vols. (Wilmette, IL: CrimeBooks, Inc., 1989), IV:3076–3077.

Walsh, Thomas James (1859–1933)

United States senator from Montana (1913–1933), the lead Senate investigator in the Teapot Dome scandal, for which he was considered for the post of U.S. attorney general before his untimely death. He was born in the village of Two Rivers, Wisconsin, on 12 June 1859 and attended the public schools, although he never earned a degree. He taught school for a time and then studied the law. In 1884 he earned a law degree from the University of Wisconsin at Madison and was admitted to the state bar that same year. He immediately left the state and settled in Redfield, in the Dakota Territory, where he commenced a law practice. Six years later, he relocated again, this time to Helena, Montana, where again he opened a law office. He would be identified with the state of Montana for the remainder of his life.

In 1906 Walsh, a Democrat, ran for a seat in the U.S. House of Representatives, but was unsuccessful. Four years later, he tried for a U.S. Senate seat, but again was defeated, this time by Democrat Henry L. Myers. In 1912, however, when Republican Senator Thomas Henry Carter did not run for reelection, Walsh threw his hat into the ring. Prior to the passage of the Seventeenth Amendment, which allowed for the direct election of senators by the people, legislatures chose senators, and Walsh was able to win because of the Democratic control of the Montana state legislature. He entered the U.S. Senate on 4 March 1913 and remained in that body until his death. He served as the chairman of the Committee on Mines and Mining (Sixty-third to Sixty-fifth Congresses), the Committee on Pensions (Sixty-fifth Congress), and the Committee on the Disposition of Useless Executive Papers (Sixty-fifth Congress).

Early in 1923, rumors surfaced that at least two members of President Warren G. Harding's cabinet were involved in potentially illegal activities, including his attorney general, Harry M. Daugherty. Then Harding died suddenly in San Francisco on 2 August 1923, leaving Vice President Calvin Coolidge as the new president. Congress soon discovered that Harding's secretary of the interior, Albert B. Fall, had leased oil reserves owned by the government in Wyoming and California to two of his cronies. The Senate formed a special committee to investigate the leases and whether any illegalities were involved—Walsh was named chairman of the committee. Using the power of the Senate, Walsh was able to uncover bribes paid to Fall and helped drive both the interior secretary and Attorney General Daugherty from office. He also helped to expose illegal payments to William Gibbs McAdoo, former secretary of the treasury under Woodrow Wilson and a leading Democrat, lending a bipartisan flavor to the scandal. Walsh's skilled oratory and demeanor during the hearings earned him wide praise.

In an article that appeared in *The Forum* in July 1924, Walsh explained:

An all too general view prevails that corruption in high places in the government is not uncommon, but that the operators are ordinarily so clever as to defy detection, or that upon one consideration or another, perhaps in anticipation of reciprocal toleration, even political opponents in a situation to do so refrain from making public official misdeeds or delinquencies. Notwithstanding the startling revelations of the committees inquiring during the recent session of Congress into the conduct of the executive departments, I believe that "crookedness" in Washington is rare, and I am convinced that the notion that it is ever condoned by those who might profit politically by the exposure of it, either through hope or fear, is wholly false. It should be added that I refer to instances in which conduct would be universally, at least generally, condemned as contrary to good morals or plainly involving turpitude. It would seem as though there could be no such thing as degrees of dishonesty, and yet of many acts of public officials varying views are held as to whether they are culpable or as to the degree of culpability which should attach to those concerned in them.

Walsh won considerable praise, both for his handling of the committee hearings and for his steadfast ability to reach across party lines in a fair manner to get to the truth behind the scandal.

In 1932, when New York Governor Franklin D. Roosevelt won the presidency, he turned to Walsh and named the Montana senator his selection for attorney general. Despite his age—Walsh was seventy-two when named—his appointment was hailed. It appeared his confirmation would face no opposition. After the New Year, Walsh and his new wife traveled south for a vacation. He made the train trip back to Washington on 2 March to attend Roosevelt's inauguration, to be held on the fourth. However, as the train neared Wilson, North Carolina, Walsh suffered a fatal heart attack and died before he could be revived. His death stunned Washington, and his funeral was held in the chamber of the U.S. Senate, the body he had served in for nearly twenty years. Walsh's body was taken back to Montana, and he was laid to rest in Resurrection Cemetery in Helena. Today his name is forgotten, but his work in exposing the Teapot Dome frauds shaped the way successful investigations of government corruption are conducted.

See also Teapot Dome Scandal
References: *Biographical Directory of the American Congress, 1774–1996* (Alexandria, VA: CQ Staff Directories, Inc., 1996); Walsh, Thomas J., "The True

Story of Teapot Dome," *The Forum*, LXXII:1 (July 1924), 1–12.

Walton, John Callaway (1881–1949)

Governor of Oklahoma (1923), impeached and removed from office for suspending the writ of habeas corpus to combat the violence of the Ku Klux Klan. Walton is one of only a handful of governors ever to be impeached and removed from office, but he remains the only one who was accused of violating a state's constitution to combat racial violence. He was born near Indianapolis, Indiana, on 6 March 1881, the son of Louis Walton, a farmer, and Callaway (also spelled Calloway) Walton. In 1885 the family moved to Nebraska, but just four years after that relocated to Arkansas. John Walton was educated in the public schools, completing his secondary education at Fort Smith Commercial College in Fort Smith, Arkansas, in 1898. He volunteered for service in the U.S. Army's field artillery unit during the Spanish-American War, after which he returned to the United States and studied engineering in Mexico. In 1903 he settled in Oklahoma City, Oklahoma. He served in the Engineering Corps of the U.S. Army during World War I with the rank of colonel.

A Democrat, Walton entered the political realm in 1916, when he was elected commissioner of public works for Oklahoma City. Two years later, he ran for and was elected mayor of Oklahoma City, a position he held for four years. Considered honest and reliable (he was nicknamed "Our Jack"), in August 1922 he was nominated for governor by the Democrats and in November 1922 was elected over Republican John Fields by more than 50,000 votes out of some 510,000 cast. Almost from the start of his administration, Walton became unpopular with the members of the state legislature. The early 1920s had seen a revival of the power of the Ku Klux Klan, and many legislative members were either backed by the Klan or were Klan members themselves. Thus when Walton placed Tulsa County under martial law and suspended the writ of habeas corpus, the legislature was up in arms. To stymie the legislature's opposition, Walton used the power of the state National Guard to prevent it from being convened. However, members of the legislature circulated a petition among the state's citizens demanding that a special session of the legislature be convened on the matter. Walton had no choice but to call the legislature into special session. Immediately, the members set about an impeachment inquiry and, on 23 October 1923, impeachment articles were passed. Walton was suspended from office pending the impeachment trial, and Lieutenant Governor Martin Edwin Trapp became acting governor. Walton's critics contended that it was not his opposition to the Klan that was his downfall, but his lavish spending in the state budget and his attacks on the regents of the University of Oklahoma and Oklahoma A&M, whom he removed and replaced with cronies. These university presidents resigned in protest, and there were street protests against Walton's administration. The legislature then met to discuss this situation; however, once they assembled, Walton's conduct was the main focus and he was immediately impeached. Quickly, the state senate voted to convict Walton, and, just ten months after entering office, he was removed. Lieutenant Governor Martin Trapp finished Walton's term.

Walton remained in Oklahoma, but lived the rest of his life in disgrace. He died in Oklahoma City on 25 November 1949 at the age of sixty-eight and was buried in Rose Hill Cemetery in that city.

References: Neuringer, Sheldon, "War on the Ku Klux Klan," *Chronicles of Oklahoma*, XLV:2 (Summer 1967); "Walton, John C.," in Robert Sobel and John Raimo, eds., *Biographical Directory of the Governors of the United States, 1789–1978*, 4 vols. (Westport, CT: Meckler Books, 1978), III:1244–1245.

Warmoth, Henry Clay (1842–1931)

Governor of Louisiana (1868–1872), impeached but not removed (his term ended before a trial could take place) on charges of massive corruption of which many historians believe him to have been guilty. Warmoth was born in McLeansboro, Illinois, on 9 May 1842, the son of Isaac Sounders Warmoth, a postmaster who worked in New Orleans, and Eleanor (née Lane) Warmoth. The Warmoths apparently named their son after the famous U.S. senator and former secretary of state, Henry Clay, although this fact cannot be completely substantiated. His paternal grandfather, Henry Warmoth, had been an early settler in the American Midwest, settling near Albion, Illinois, in the early 1800s. Eleanor Lane Warmoth was the daughter of an Illinois state senator, Levin Lane. She died around 1853, when her son Henry was eleven, and he moved with his father to Fairfield, Illinois, spending some time with friends of the family. He received his education in the public schools of Fairfield and Salem and, after completing his primary education, worked in the offices of the *Springfield (Illinois) Journal* while he studied the law. In 1861 he was admitted to practice the law in Lebanon, Missouri. The following year, in the midst of the American Civil War, Warmoth was appointed district attorney for the Eighteenth Judicial District of Missouri, but he soon resigned this office to volunteer for service in the Thirty-second Missouri Infantry, where he was given the rank of lieutenant colonel. He assisted in the capture of Arkansas Post, after which he was assigned to the staff of Major General John A. McClernand, and saw action at Vicksburg, Mississippi, where he was terribly wounded. In a personal battle for power between McClernand and General Ulysses S. Grant, Warmoth was discharged. However, after a personal appeal to President Abraham Lincoln, he was reinstated to his previous rank and position.

In June 1864 Lincoln assigned Warmoth to the post of judge of the Provost Court for the Gulf of Mexico, with its seat in Louisiana. When the war ended, Warmoth remained in Louisiana, opening a law office in New Orleans. In November 1865 he was elected by a coalition of pro-Unionists in Louisiana to a seat as a "territorial delegate" to Congress (because Louisiana had not be readmitted to the Union, it was not allowed to have congressional representation), but he was denied his seat due not to his own war stance but the state he was representing. In 1868, when the Republicans in Louisiana met in convention to nominate a gubernatorial candidate, Warmoth was the overwhelming choice for governor, but because he was only twenty-six years of age, the convention passed a resolution ending the limitation on age (it was thirty at the time) for one to hold the governor's office. On his ticket was Oscar J. Dunn, a black man, nominated for lieutenant governor, the first black in the history of the United States to be nominated for such a high post. Because most whites in Louisiana had their voting rights taken away, no Democrat was nominated for governor,

and Warmoth easily defeated Independent James Taliaferro by nearly 30,000 votes out of slightly more than 100,000 votes cast. Joshua Baker had been serving as governor, with General Winfield Scott Hancock serving as district military commander over the state. On 27 June 1868, Hancock was removed from power by President Andrew Johnson, and Johnson named Warmoth to serve as military governor of Louisiana until the state was readmitted to the Union. This occurred on 13 July 1868, and Warmoth was inaugurated as the twenty-third governor of Louisiana. His tenure lasted until 13 January 1873.

From the beginning, Warmoth fought against the Democrats, who did not want civil rights for blacks, and wings of his own party, which wanted more civil rights for blacks. Warmoth explained the hostility against his administration in his 1930 memoir, *War, Politics and Reconstruction: Stormy Days in Louisiana:*

> But, of course, my administration was exceedingly obnoxious to the colored Lieutenant-Governor, Oscar J. Dunn, to the *New York Orleans Tribune,* to United States Marshall Packard, to Senator [William Pitt] Kellogg and the 'Pure Radical' Federal officials, who looked only to negro voters to support the Republican Party. They claimed that in my appointment of conservative white men to office, I was guilty of treason to the negro people.

But Warmoth also gradually dug his own political grave by speculating in railroad and treasury bonds, holding a partnership in the newspaper printing company that was also the state printer, and establishing a State Returning Board, which was instilled with the power to throw out ballots thought to be questionable. Warmoth used this board to have votes from Democrats routinely cast aside, allowing him and his party to keep a firm reign on power. Historians Robert Sobel and John Raimo wrote, "His gubernatorial term was characterized by turbulence, discontent, a wild orgy of speculation in state-aided railroads, a depleted treasury, and bitter strife over the question of black suffrage. He signed the bill which opened the restaurants, railroad coaches, and schools to blacks, but later vetoed a more radical measure." Warmoth's administration saw the state's bond debt rise from $6 million to over $100 million.

After Dunn's death early in Warmoth's term, he was replaced by the senate president pro tempore, Pinckney Benton Stewart Pinchback, also a black man.

In 1872, as his term came to an end, Warmoth was passed over for renomination by his party, which then proceeded to break up into three different factions, each nominating different gubernatorial tickets. Democrats and a Reform Party also nominated tickets for governor. After the election, in which there was a dispute over the winner, Warmoth on 4 November 1872 called for an extra session of the state legislature to start on 9 December. The Republicans, in control of the legislature, instead took control over all of state government, impeached Warmoth, and installed Lieutenant Governor Pinckney Benton Stewart Pinchback as acting governor. He was inaugurated on 8 December as the new governor. Warmoth, in the midst of an impeachment inquiry, nonetheless sued to the Louisiana Supreme Court, which held that Pinchback was indeed the true governor. Pinchback then proceeded to sign ten bills into law and make several appointments. Warmoth was not allowed to serve the last thirty-five days of his term. In the meantime Senator William Pitt Kellogg, a Republican but a political nemesis of Warmoth's, had been declared the winner of the 1872 election, and he took office on 13 January 1873 before an impeachment trial could be held on the charges against Warmoth. Historians do believe that the allegations of widespread corruption, both by Warmoth and his allies, were valid and could have led to his conviction and removal from office. Because he was out of office, Warmoth was considered beyond the reaches of the impeachment inquiry, and it was dropped.

Despite the turbulence of his last days in office, Warmoth remained in Louisiana and in 1876 was elected to a seat in the lower house of the state legislature, serving for one two-year term. In 1879 he served as a delegate to the state constitutional convention and in 1888 ran for governor, but was defeated badly by Democrat Francis Redding Tillou Nicholls by over 80,000 votes out of nearly 200,000 cast. His last office held was as collector of customs for New Orleans from 1890 to 1893.

In the last years of the nineteenth century and the first years of the twentieth, Warmoth spent his time on his sugar plantation, "Magnolia," south of New Orleans. He outlived all of his contemporaries and lived long enough to publish his memoirs in 1930. Warmoth died in New Orleans on 30 September 1931 at the age of eighty-nine.

References: "The Carpetbagger as Corruptionist: Henry Clay Warmoth," in Richard N. Current, *Three Carpetbag Governors* (Baton Rouge: Louisiana State University Press, 1967), 35–66; "Warmoth, Henry Clay," in Robert Sobel and John Raimo, eds., *Biographical Directory of the Governors of the United States, 1789–1978*, 4 vols. (Westport, CT: Meckler Books, 1978), II:571–572; Warmoth, Henry Clay, *War, Politics and Reconstruction: Stormy Days in Louisiana* (New York: The Macmillan Company, 1930), 165, 199.

Watergate

American political scandal that drove President Richard Nixon from office before he could be impeached for obstructing justice. Although no one in power profited financially from the matter, Watergate nonetheless is perhaps the most egregious example of political corruption because of the effect it had in subverting the political process. "Watergate," as the entire affair was called, did not start, as many believe today, with the burglary by five men from the Committee to Reelect the President (ironically called CREEP) at Democratic Committee Headquarters located in the Watergate Hotel Complex in Washington, D.C., in the morning hours of 17 June 1972. From the start of his presidency, faced with growing protests nationwide over the Vietnam War, Richard Nixon initialed the start of a massive use of illegal wiretapping and information gathering to seek out his enemies, political and otherwise, with the approval of his attorney general, John N. Mitchell. This gathered steam on 23 July 1970 when Nixon secretly ordered expanded domestic intelligence gathering by the Federal Bureau of Investigation (FBI), the Central Intelligence Agency (CIA), and other federal government agencies. This approval was rescinded a few days later, but the die had been struck: plans were then undertaken to stem a series of leaks of government plans on the handling of the Vietnam War.

The publication, starting on 13 June 1971, by *New York Times* (and, within a week, *Washington Post*) of the classified Pentagon report later known as "The Pentagon Papers," which was commissioned by President Lyndon Johnson's secretary of defense, Robert McNamara, and detailed the history of how the United States became involved in Vietnam, enraged the administration. Nixon and his administration were determined to find how the report was leaked. A plan, called "Operation Gemstone," was conceived in Attorney General Mitchell's office sometime in 1971, in which a covert White House unit, aptly called "The Plumbers" (in order to "plug" security leaks), was ordered to use any means, including burglary, to find and contain leaks of government secrets on administration policy on Vietnam, and was funded with $250,000 directly from the account of the committee established to aid in Nixon's reelection efforts in 1972. When it was discovered that a former Pentagon worker, Daniel Ellsberg, was responsible for the release of the "Pentagon Papers," the Plumbers, led by attorney George Gordon Liddy, broke into Ellsberg's psychiatrist's office in Los Angeles, California, on 3 September 1971 seeking incriminating material on Ellsberg to destroy his reputation. None was found, but the action set the stage for grander and more dangerous schemes in the future. One of these was an aborted effort to start a fire at the Brookings Institution, a think tank in Washington, D.C., where Plumbers members suspected files on Vietnam War policies were housed.

Sometime in 1972, the Plumbers, backed by men who worked directly for President Nixon, including White House Chief of Staff Harry Robbins ("H.R.") Haldeman and Assistant to the President for Domestic Affairs John Ehrlichman, wanted information on the movement of Democrats running for president in that election year. Ehrlichman was the mastermind behind the Plumbers, and approved of their actions in the Ellsberg break-in. To get information on the Democrats, both Haldeman and Ehrlichman ordered that wiretaps be established on the phone of Larry O'Brien, a former postmaster general and the present chairman of the Democratic National Committee, whose offices were located in the Watergate Hotel Complex in Washington, D.C. Sometime in June 1972 members of the Plumbers broke in and tapped the phones, but some of the taps did not work and much of the material that was collected was inadequate. A return visit was ordered. In the early morning hours of 17 June 1972, five men, among them James McCord, a security official for

the Committee to Reelect the President, and E. Howard Hunt, a former CIA official who was the author of several spy novels, broke into O'Brien's office. Unknown to the men, a Watergate security officer found masking tape across a door lock so that it would not close, and began to search for intruders. The men were arrested, and the affair known as Watergate began.

When the men were arraigned the following day, two things were clear: the alleged burglars were connected to the CIA in some way, as well as to Nixon's reelection efforts. In response, the White House called the break-in "a third-rate burglary." On 19 June, *Washington Post* reported McCord's connection with CREEP; former Attorney General Mitchell, who had resigned to head up Nixon's reelection campaign, denied any link between CREEP and the break-in. Two *Post* reporters, Carl Bernstein and Bob Woodward, were placed on the story, and soon traced a cashier's check for $25,000 directly from CREEP accounts into the bank accounts of one of the Watergate burglars. On 29 September, the *Post* reported that John Mitchell, while serving as attorney general, controlled a secret fund from CREEP coffers that was used "to finance widespread intelligence-gathering operations against the Democrats," which included staging phony events, trailing candidates, and inventing material that was used to destroy the candidacies of Senator Edmund Muskie and former Vice President Hubert Humphrey. By October, just before the 1972 election, the FBI had discovered that Watergate was just a part of "a massive campaign of political spying and sabotage conducted on behalf of the Nixon reelection effort." The next month, even with these allegations swirling, Nixon was reelected over South Dakota Senator George McGovern with over 60 percent of the vote in one of the largest landslides in American political history.

Even after President Nixon was inaugurated for a second term on 20 January 1973, investigators were homing in on officials of his administration. Ten days later, the five Watergate burglars were convicted in a District of Columbia court of conspiracy, burglary, and eavesdropping. After being sentenced, James McCord sent a letter to Judge John J. Sirica, who presided over the trials, alleging that he had taken his orders from high-ranking officers of the Republican Party, including former Attorney

General John N. Mitchell (who served as the chairman of CREEP in the 1972 election), and that had they were involved in the cover-up. As a result of McCord's letter, federal investigators in the Department of Justice and Federal Bureau of Investigation opened up an investigation into Nixon's aides. Federal grand juries were empaneled, and the U.S. Senate established the Select Committee on Presidential Campaign Activities, better known as the Senate Watergate Committee. Named to chair this panel was Senator Samuel J. Ervin Jr. (D-NC). In hearings that opened on 18 May 1973, held before television cameras and riveting the nation, Ervin's homespun demeanor made him one of the most important persons in the investigation. The *Washington Post* later said of the senator, "With his arching eyebrows and flapping jowls that signaled his moral indignation at much of the testimony before his committee, his half-country, half-courtly demeanor and his predilection for making points by quoting the Bible and Shakespeare and telling folksy stories, Ervin quickly became a hero to many." Numerous witnesses were brought before the committee, including White House counsel John W. Dean III, who told the committee that he had warned Nixon that "a cancer" was on the presidency regarding the cover-up of the Watergate break-in. Dean implicated most of the men around the president and said that Nixon had ordered the payoff of the Watergate burglars to buy their silence. Dean told Nixon that the cost of buying the men off would be $1 million. Dean quoted Nixon as saying, "You could get the money. . . . You could get a million dollars. And you could get it in cash. I know where it could be gotten."

Allegations that had surfaced prior to the committee hearings led to the resignations of White House Chief of Staff H. R. "Bob" Haldeman, Presidential Adviser on Domestic Affairs John Ehrlichman, and Attorney General Richard Kleindienst on 30 April 1973. White House counsel Dean was fired. To replace Kleindienst, Nixon tapped former cabinet Secretary Eliott Richardson. At the same time that the Senate was investigating the scandal, a special prosecutor, Archibald Cox, who had ties to Senator Edward Kennedy (and had been Richardson's law professor at Harvard), was empowered by the Department of Justice and Attorney General Eliott Richardson to look into any part of the scandal.

On 13 July 1973, Alexander P. Butterfield, the former appointments secretary for President Nixon, told the Senate Watergate Committee that Nixon had been audiotaping Oval Office conversations for several years and that a taped record of these conversations had been archived. At once, Special Prosecutor Cox demanded access to the White House tapes; the Senate Watergate Committee followed suit. Five days later, according to several sources, Nixon ordered that the Oval office taping system be disconnected. On 23 July, Nixon announced that he would refuse to turn over any taped conversation based upon the president's right to executive privilege. Cox, undeterred, went to court to get a subpoena to force Nixon to turn over the tapes. When Nixon ordered Cox to stop his quest for a subpoena and Cox refused Nixon ordered Attorney General Richardson to fire the special prosecutor. Richardson refused and resigned. Nixon then ordered Richardson's assistant, Deputy Attorney General William D. Ruckelshaus, to fire Cox—but Ruckelshaus also refused and likewise resigned. It was left to the number three in the Department of Justice, Solicitor General Robert H. Bork, to assume the office of acting attorney general and fire Cox. This action, on 20 October 1973, became known as the "Saturday Night Massacre." Anger at Nixon exploded—politicians across the political spectrum condemned the firing and demanded that Nixon retract it. Among some, talk of impeachment arose.

To placate the critics, Nixon named a new special prosecutor, attorney Leon Jaworski. Jaworski, armed with confidence in his office that was backed by Congress and the American people, took up Cox's crusade and went to court to get a subpoena to force Nixon to hand over his taped conversations. Jaworski then got indictments against Haldeman, Ehrlichman, White House lawyer Charles Colson, and others for conspiracy, perjury, obstruction of justice, and other crimes. He also revealed that when the five Watergate burglars had been indicted, Nixon had been named as an unindicted coconspirator.

Facing a revolt in Congress, Nixon offered to release transcripts of the taped conversations that Jaworski wanted. Despite Nixon's appearing to deliver some of the tapes, Jaworski was unimpressed and fought to have the actual tapes heard. While preparing the transcript of one tape, presidential

President Nixon clings to his desk as the Watergate tidal wave crashes into the oval office. (Library of Congress)

secretary Rosemary Woods accidentally "erased" part of it—leaving a gap of eighteen and one-half minutes. Many historians believe that Woods erased evidence showing crimes committed by Nixon, but this has never been proved. On 30 April 1974, Nixon released 1,200 pages of edited transcripts, turning them over to Jaworski and the House Judiciary Committee, now investigating potential impeachment charges against the president. The committee replied that this was not satisfactory, and Jaworski got a subpoena for the tapes. Nixon fought this decision to the U.S. Supreme Court, which held unanimously on 24 July 1974, in *United States v. Nixon*, that the president could not use executive privilege as the basis for withholding the tapes from scrutiny. Three days later, the House Judiciary Committee passed an article of impeachment, charging Nixon with obstruction of justice. Two other articles followed, alleging abuse of power and defiance of congressional subpoenas. Nixon felt that while he would be impeached in the House, he could win the battle in the Senate. However, after he listened to the tapes that would soon be released, he found one, from 23 June 1972, in which he told Chief of Staff Haldeman that he ordered the Federal Bureau of Investigation to stop investigating the Watergate scandal and any ties to the White House. This tape was clear evidence of Nixon's obstruction of justice. It was "the smoking gun." Several senators came to the president and told him that he would be convicted in the Senate and removed from office. On 7 August 1974, Nixon told the American people in a televised speech that he would resign the presidency the following day. Vice President Gerald R. Ford—who had replaced Vice President Spiro T. Agnew when he resigned due to political corruption—was sworn in as the thirty-eighth president on 8 August.

In the end, as many historians and commentators explain, it was not the crime, but the cover-up, that destroyed Richard Nixon. Watergate's effects led to laws increasing the accountability of campaign finance laws and limiting the presidential power of executive privilege. Judge John Sirica, noted for his independence in forcing President Nixon to release the tapes that doomed his presidency, wrote of the scandal in his 1979 work, *To Set the Record Straight: The Break-In, the Tapes, the Conspirators, the Pardon.* He retired from the bench in 1986 and died on 14 August 1992 at the age of eighty-eight. Former White House counsel John W. Dean III, who literally brought down the president, was charged with obstruction of justice and spent four months in prison for his role in the Watergate cover-up. After serving his sentence, he penned the autobiographical *Blind Ambition* (1976), which became a national best-seller. His wife, Maureen, known as "Mo," also wrote a Watergate book—*Mo: A Woman's View of Watergate* (1975). John Ehrlichman was convicted of conspiracy to obstruct justice and perjury in Watergate, and of conspiracy in the Ellsberg break-in, and served eighteen months in jail. He wrote *Witness to Power: The Nixon Years* (1982). Senator Sam Ervin retired from the Senate in December 1974, just four months after Nixon resigned, and returned to his home in North Carolina; he wrote, among other works, *The Whole Truth: The Watergate Conspiracy* (1980). Ervin died on 23 April 1985 at the age of eighty-eight. H. R. 'Bob' Haldeman, Nixon's chief of staff, spent eighteen months in prison after he was convicted of conspiracy and obstruction of justice in 1974. After leaving prison, he wrote *The Ends of Power* in 1978. In his later years, Haldeman became a real estate developer in California and an investor in restaurants. He died of cancer in California on 12 November 1993 at the age of sixty-seven. Six months later, *The Haldeman Diaries,* about the initial days of the Watergate crisis, was published. G. Gordon Liddy, the former FBI agent, who was the brains behind the Watergate break-in and was convicted for his role in that, as well as for conspiracy and contempt of court, spent four and one-half years in prison. When he emerged, unrepentant, he penned *Will* (1980), his explanation of the scandal. Today, he is a conservative radio talk-show host in Virginia and has assumed an air of respectability more than a quarter century after the break-in.

Watergate and its effects have lasted far longer, and cast a much broader shadow, across the political spectrum of today. Charles Ruff, the fourth and final Watergate special counsel, later served as chief counsel of the White House during the darkest days of the Clinton administration. Earl Silbert, the U.S. attorney for the District of Columbia in the 1970s who prosecuted many of the Watergate figures, was hired in 1997 as counsel for James Riady, the Indonesia businessman and friend of

President Bill Clinton who was implicated in the campaign finance scandal that rocked the Clinton/Gore 1996 reelection campaign. But it is the word "Watergate" that haunts American politics. Today, political scandals routinely append the word "gate" to their names—Travelgate, Irangate, and so on. The limits put on presidential power by the U.S. Supreme Court in *United States v. Nixon* had consequences for the Clinton impeachment in 1998–1999. The use of presidential immunity to shield the testimony of friends and cronies has been given new boundaries. But perhaps Watergate's most lasting effect has been a loss of innocence for the American public as they came to view their government with distrust.

See also Federal Election Commission; Mitchell, John Newton; Nixon, Richard Milhaus; Thompson, Fred Dalton

References: Dickinson, William B., Jr., *Watergate: Chronology of a Crisis,* 2 vols. (Washington, DC: Congressional Quarterly, 1974); *The Fall of a President* (New York: Dell Publishing Company, 1974); Mankiewicz, Frank, *United States v. Richard Nixon: The Final Crisis* (New York: Quadrangle/New York Times Book Company, 1975); Meyer, Lawrence, "John N. Mitchell, Principal in Watergate, Dies at 75," *Washington Post,* 10 November 1988, A1; Rosenberg, Kenyon C., and Judith K. Rosenberg, *Watergate: An Annotated Bibliography* (Littleton, CO: Libraries Unlimited, 1975); Saffell, David C., *Watergate: Its Effects on the American Political System* (Cambridge, MA: Winthrop Publishers, 1974); Smith, J. Y., "H.R. Haldeman Dies, Was Nixon Chief of Staff, Watergate Role Led to 18 Months in Prison," *Washington Post,* 13 November 1993, A12; "Watergate," in George C. Kohn, *Encyclopedia of American Scandal: From ABSCAM to the Zenger Case* (New York: Facts on File, 1989), 349–350; Weil, Martin, and Eleanor Randolph, "Richard M. Nixon, 37th President, Dies, Funeral Scheduled for Wednesday for Only Chief Executive Forced From Office," *Washington Post,* 23 April 1994, A1.

Welch, William Wickham (1818–1892)

United States representative from Connecticut (1855–1857), accused of corruption and the subject of an expulsion hearing in the House in 1857. Welch was a noted physician who happened to run for a seat in Congress and win; little else is known about him. He was born in Norfolk, Connecticut, on 10 December 1818, the son of Benjamin Welch and Louisa (née Guiteau) Welch. Benjamin Welch, one of thirteen children, had studied medicine under a local Norfolk doctor, Ephraim Guiteau, and married his daughter. William Welch was one of ten children, of whom all five sons became physicians. He studied medicine under his father (nothing is noted of his primary school education), graduated from the Yale Medical School in 1839, and began the practice of medicine in Norfolk with his father. He apparently entered the political realm when he ran for and won a seat in the Connecticut state house of representatives, serving from 1848 to 1850. He then won a seat in the state senate, serving in that body in 1851 and 1852. Welch was a member of the American, or "Know Nothing," Party, so named because its platform of excluding Catholics and immigrants was so controversial that its members claimed to "know nothing" if asked about it. In 1855 he ran for a seat in the U.S. House of Representatives under the American Party banner and defeated a Democrat named Noble (no first name has been found) to win the seat representing the Fourth Connecticut District. Welch's time in Washington was limited to one term. Few sources note what occurred, but he was under consideration first for expulsion and/or censure by the House. However, after a thorough investigation by "a committee, consisting of 5 Members, to be appointed by the Speaker, with power to send for persons and papers, to investigate said charges; and that said committee report the evidence taken, and what action, in their judgment, is necessary on the part of the House, without any unnecessary delay," it was held that Welch was not proved guilty and released from further action.

Despite this, Welch did not run for a second term. He resumed the practice of medicine, although he later served as a member of the Connecticut state house in 1869 and 1881. He also served as president of the Norfolk Leather Company and was one of the incorporators of the Connecticut-Western Railroad and the Norfolk Savings Bank. His biography in the *Dictionary of American Biography* highlights his work as a doctor rather than his congressional career. Welch died in Norfolk on 30 July 1892 at the age of seventy-three and was buried in Center Cemetery in that city.

References: Hinds, Asher Crosby, *Hinds' Precedents of the House of Representatives of the United States, Including References to Provisions of the Constitution, the Laws, and Decisions of the United States Senate,* 8 vols. (Washington, DC: Government Printing Office, 1907–1908), V:834–836; MacCullum, William G., "Welch, William Wickham," in Allen Johnson and Dumas Malone, et al., eds., *Dictionary of American Biography,*10 vols. and 10 supplements (New York: Charles Scribner's Sons, 1930–1995), X:624–625; United States Congress, House, Joint Committee on Congressional Operations, *House of Representatives Exclusion, Censure and Expulsion Cases from 1789 to 1973,* 93rd Congress, 1st Session (Washington, DC: Government Printing Office, 1973).

Whiskey Ring Scandal

National scandal, in which government agents in St. Louis, Missouri, were caught siphoning off tax revenues intended to go into the national treasury from the sale of whiskey. The scandal was exposed in 1875 through the efforts of Secretary of the Treasury Benjamin H. Bristow. Evidence showed that for some years prior to 1875, the United States government had lost at least $1.2 million of tax revenue it should have received from whiskey sales in St. Louis, Missouri, alone. Yet special agents of the Treasury Department sent to investigate from time to time had failed to do more than cause an occasional flurry among the thieves.

The Whiskey Ring was organized in St. Louis when the Liberal Republican Party in that city achieved its first electoral success. Soon after their electoral achievement, it occurred to certain politicians to have revenue officers raise a campaign fund among the many liquor distillers in the city. This idea the officers later modified, raising money in the same way for themselves and conniving at the grossest thievery. As it became necessary to hide the frauds, newspapers and higher officials were hushed with payoffs, until the ring assumed national dimensions, diverting untold millions from federal coffers. Its headquarters were at St. Louis, but it had branches in Milwaukee, Chicago, Peoria, Cincinnati, and New Orleans and even had an agent in Washington, D.C. A huge ill-gotten fund was distributed among storekeepers, collectors, and other officials, according to a fixed schedule of prices.

Following an investigation—conducted in secret by Secretary of the Treasury Benjamin Bristow to avoid alerting any of those being targeted—federal agents under the control of Bristow, working without the knowledge of the attorney general or the president, moved on the ring on 10 May 1875 and arrested more than 350 men in raids across the United States. Indictments were handed down by federal grand juries against 152 liquor sellers, as well as 86 persons in the government, including the chief clerk of Bristow's own Treasury Department.

Bristow was widely cheered for his actions, though not by everyone inside the administration. Grant had named Bristow to the Treasury in June 1874 after criticism from reformers, both Republican and otherwise, who saw widespread political corruption as the Achilles' heel of the party for the 1874 midterm elections. Yet Bristow's actions were considered unhelpful by Grant's cronies as exposing the failings of friends of the administration.

Initially, Grant backed Bristow's efforts. However, as the continuing investigation uncovered massive graft and corruption by men tied directly to Grant and the Republican Party, he became less and less interested in getting to the bottom of the scandal. But still bowing to reformers and embarrassed by press reports regarding the affair, he decided to name a special prosecutor to oversee all of the indictments and trials. This man was General John B. Henderson, a former United States senator from Missouri, who decided that his role required him to prosecute these cases to the fullest extent of the law. As he began trials of Whiskey Ring defendants, evidence was discovered that implicated President Grant's personal secretary, General Orville E. Babcock. The evidence linking Babcock to the graft came from the prosecution of John McDonald, a revenue supervisor in St. Louis, who later wrote a book, *Secrets of the Whiskey Ring; and Eighteen Months in the Penitentiary* (1880), exposing some of the frauds. Letters in code written from Babcock to McDonald were found, with instructions on how to siphon Whiskey Ring funds. When Henderson indicted Babcock, Grant intervened, arguing that as a military officer Babcock must be tried by a military court. This court, with its members named by Grant, asked Henderson for copies of all of his evidence against Babcock. Henderson refused to allow a civilian court to give way to a military one. Grant backed down, and Babcock went on trial in the civilian court. However, when Henderson decried Grant's interference in the Babcock prosecution, Grant fired Henderson—a move mirrored 100 years later when President Richard Nixon fired Special Prosecutor

Archibald Cox, a move called "The Saturday Night Massacre." In 1875, though, few took notice of Grant's action, and Henderson left quietly. Grant replaced him with James Broadhead, an attorney with little experience in criminal prosecutions who was unfamiliar with the facts behind the Whiskey Ring trials. In another move to block the trials, Grant wrote a two-page letter on behalf of Babcock, in which the president declared his secretary's innocence. Babcock was acquitted, and the Whiskey Ring trials ended on a low note. Only a few defendants were ever found guilty, none tying the frauds to Grant or his administration.

Although many historians consider the Whiskey Ring frauds to be one of the worst governmental scandals in American history, few people are familiar with it today, and historical works barely cover it. In October 1876 a lengthy article appeared under the byline of one H. V. Boynton in regards to the Whiskey Ring frauds. Summing up the complexity of the frauds, Boynton explained:

> Congressional investigations and the press have made known, though in somewhat disjointed form, the chief features of the late war upon [the] whiskey thieves and their abettors. . . . While this movement of Secretary Bristow for the suppression of whiskey frauds was a clearly defined campaign, having a definite beginning, sharp outlines, and a sudden ending, it is yet too early for any one to attempt its full history. Much of it cannot be known, unless the Secretary himself discloses it. The secret machinations by which a formidable array continually excited the President against his Secretary as yet partially appear. For each of the cities where the blow [of prosecution] fell, there is a local history full of interest and illustrative of the political power wielded by the ring, which was not fully known in Washington. Some further developments yet await the ongoing chariot of justice, the wheels of which drag heavily just now.

To this day, the entire story of the Whiskey Ring frauds, their cover-up, and the role of members of the Grant administration in the affair, has yet to be fully told.

See also Henderson, John Brooks

References: Boynton, H. V., "The Whiskey Ring," *North American Review*, CCLII (October 1876), 280–281; Logan, David A., *Historical Uses of a Special Prosecutor: The Administrations of Presidents Grant, Coolidge, and Truman* (Washington, DC:

Congressional Research Service, 1973), 13; McDonald, John, *Secrets of the Great Whiskey Ring, Containing a Complete Exposure of the Illicit Whiskey Frauds Culminating in 1875, and the Connection of Grant, Babcock, Douglas, Chester H. Krum, and Other Administration Officers, Established by Positive and Unequivocal Documentary Proofs, Comprising Facsimiles of Confidential Letters and Telegrams Emanating From the White House, Directing the Management of the Ring. Also Photographs of Grant, Babcock, Bristow, Garfield and the Famous Sylph. To Which Is Added the Missing Links in the Chain of Evidence of James A. Garfield's Implication with the District of Columbia Ring and Crédit Mobilier Bribery* (Chicago: Belford, Clarke & Co., 1880); Rives, Timothy, "Grant, Babcock, and the Whiskey Ring," *Prologue: Quarterly of the National Archives and Records Administration*, 32:3 (Fall 2000); Seemätter, Mary E., "The St. Louis Whiskey Ring," *Gateway Heritage* (Spring 1988), 32–42; "The Whiskey Fraud Trials: General Henderson's Dismissal," *New York Times*, 11 December 1875, 1; "Whisky Trust Bribery," *New York Times*, 9 February 1893, 9.

Whitewater

Scandal, 1993–2001, that in many ways encapsulated the history of scandal in the administration of President Bill Clinton. The scandal has it roots in land fraud, Southern politics, a rising politician in a small Southern state, and stolen U.S. government funds in the wake of the savings and loan scandal of the 1980s. The scandal started in 1978, when an Arkansas land broker, James McDougal, and his wife, Susan, formed a fifty-fifty land partnership with a young up-and-coming Arkansas politician, Bill Clinton, and his wife, Hillary. This land deal encompassed a huge area of forty-two lots of land along the White River in Arkansas. The two couples named the real estate concern the Whitewater Development Corporation, with the intention of selling the land for homes. Clinton and McDougal had become acquainted in 1968, when both men worked for the reelection of Senator William Fulbright of Arkansas. McDougal himself had never entered the political realm, instead becoming the owner of the Madison Guaranty Savings and Loan in Arkansas. He secretly used funds from the S&L to finance the Whitewater land deal. Although it appeared on paper that both the Clintons and the McDougals lost money in the venture, many allegations later appeared that money was indeed earned and hidden from the state and federal government. The attorney for the land deal was Vincent Foster, an Arkansas attorney who was a boyhood friend of Bill Clinton and later served with Hillary Clinton as a member of the Rose Law Firm, one of the most prestigious law firms in Arkansas and the United States. In 1980 Clinton was elected governor of Arkansas, and, although he lost the office in 1982, he won it back in 1984 and held it until 1992. During this period, there were allegations that McDougal used funds from his S&L to finance parts of Clinton's gubernatorial campaigns.

For many years, the McDougals offered the Clintons a buyout of their share of Whitewater, but the Clintons refused until Clinton decided in 1991 to run for president of the United States. After Clinton was elected president, he named Vincent Foster deputy White House counsel. However, during the 1992 campaign, the allegations of financial and other shenanigans involving Whitewater bubbled to the surface, and reporters headed down to Arkansas to look into them. After Clinton took office, demands rose in Washington, D.C., that the land deal be investigated for possible illegalities. The voices rose to a crescendo when Foster was found dead in a Washington park on 20 July 1993—an alleged suicide. Suspicion focused on the White House when White House counsel Bernard Nussbaum ordered that confidential papers, many possibly dealing with Whitewater, be removed from Foster's office after word came that he was found dead. On 12 January 1994, Clinton himself asked that an independent counsel be named, and, on 20 January 1994, Attorney General Janet Reno named New York lawyer and former U.S. attorney Robert B. Fiske Jr., circumventing a court that, under the Independent Counsel Statute, is required to get a recommendation for the naming of an independent counsel and name one of their choosing. Fiske immediately launched an investigation of Foster's death and what he knew of the details of the Whitewater land deal. By August 1994 Fiske had concluded that Foster's death was indeed a suicide and that the Clintons did not impede an investigation by the Resolution Trust Corporation (RTC), a federal government agency established to investigate potential savings and loans criminality. It appeared that the Clintons were cleared and that the controversy would die down.

However, on 5 August 1994, when Fiske went to the special three-member judicial panel that had authority to name independent counsels, so that he could close parts of the investigation and get jurisdiction into other areas, the panel instead shocked Washington by removing Fiske from his post, explaining that he had not been properly named by the court initially. Instead, the court named Kenneth Winston Starr Jr., a former federal appeals judge and a former solicitor general under President George H. W. Bush. Immediately, Starr issued subpoenas for documents, such as the Rose Law Firm billing records relating to the land dealings. These records were missing from the firm and they did not turn up for two years, when they were found lying on a table in the White House—eliciting even more suspicion of the Clintons. These records showed that, despite earlier statements that she had done little if any work on behalf of the Whitewater project, Mrs. Clinton in fact had done sixty hours of work on Whitewater. In January 1996 Mrs. Clinton was summoned by Starr before a Washington grand jury to elaborate on the records issue.

The independent counsel's investigation also looked into the role of the Clintons in the collapse of the Madison Guaranty Savings and Loan. After the S&L went under in the mid-1980s, the U.S. government bailed it out at the expense of some $68 million. In 1989 James McDougal was indicted on state charges of bank fraud, but he was acquitted in 1990. However, Starr looked into whether Madison funds were used prior to the bank's demise to bolster the Whitewater land deal. Starr was able to track a 1985 fundraiser by McDougal that assisted in retiring campaign debt from Clinton's 1984 gubernatorial race. The fundraiser raised some $30,000, but $12,000 was traced to checks drawn from Madison. While Starr was investigating, both houses of the U.S. Congress opened investigations. The House Banking Committee, chaired by Representative Jim Leach (R-IA) held hearings, which concluded on 10 August 1995, with the finding that no illegalities occurred in Whitewater. The Senate, however, formed the Senate Special Whitewater Committee, chaired by Senator Alfonse D'Amato (R-NY). This latter committee became bogged down in politics between Republicans and Democrats on the panel.

In all, Starr, and his successor, Robert Ray, who closed the Whitewater investigation in 2001, spent some $52 million under the Independent Counsel Statute, which was not renewed by Congress in 1999. Starr officially ended the Whitewater investigation on 19 November 1998, reporting to the three-member court that while he believed that Clinton himself lied under oath regarding Whitewater, he could not prove the case beyond a reasonable doubt. In 2000 Starr resigned his position and was succeeded by Ray, who issued a report in 2001 that while there were suspicions that the Clintons were involved in illegalities, "this office determined that the evidence was insufficient to prove to a jury beyond a reasonable doubt that either President or Mrs. Clinton knowingly participated in any criminal conduct." The final Whitewater report, issued by Ray's office on 20 March 2002, specifically stated that while there was insufficient evidence to indict either of the Clintons, both had been involved in illegal activity.

James McDougal holds a Whitewater deed. McDougal was convicted of 18 felony counts but received a reduced sentence, from 84 years to 3, after he testified against his ex-wife, Susan, and Arkansas Governor Jim Tucker. McDougal died in prison on 7 March 1998. (Reuters NewMedia Inc./CORBIS)

See also Clinton, William Jefferson, Tucker, James Guy, Jr.

References: Thompson, Marilyn W., "Whitewater Probe's Insufficient Evidence," *Washington Post,* 20 November 1998, A32; United States Congress, Senate, Special Committee to Investigate Whitewater Development Corporation and Related Matters, *Investigation of Whitewater Development Corporation and Related Matters: Final Report of the Special Committee to Investigate Whitewater Development Corporation and Related Matters, Together with Additional and Minority Views* (Washington: Government Printing Office, 1996).

On 17 August 1995, a grand jury in Little Rock, Arkansas, indicted James and Susan McDougal, as well as Arkansas Governor Jim Guy Tucker on charges of bank fraud relating to loans to Whitewater. On 28 May 1996, all three were convicted, despite Clinton testifying for the defense via videotape, the first time a president had testified in a criminal trial. James McDougal made a deal to turn states' evidence against his ex-wife, Susan, and Jim Tucker. When Susan McDougal was offered a similar deal for her testimony, she refused, and after being held in contempt of court she was sent to prison for two years. She never testified against the Clintons.

In another trial in which Starr brought charges, Arkansas bankers Robert Hill and Herby Branscum Jr., political supporters of Clinton in Arkansas, were tried on charges of using deposits from their Arkansas banks to reimburse themselves for contributions to Clinton's 1990 gubernatorial campaign. However, on 1 August 1996, an Arkansas jury acquitted the two men on four charges and deadlocked on the others.

Whittemore, Benjamin Franklin (1824–1894)

United States representative from South Carolina (1868–1870), resigned his seat because of allegations that he sold appointments to the U.S. military and naval academies. Born in Malden, Massachusetts, on 18 May 1824, Whittemore attended public schools in nearby Worcester and finished his education at Amherst. (However, Amherst does not have a record of his having attended or graduating). He then entered private business, engaging in a mercantile concern until 1859, when he studied theology and became a minister in the Methodist Episcopal Church in the New England Conference in 1859. It appeared that he would make the church his life's work.

When the Civil War exploded in 1861, instead of serving as a soldier, Whittemore served the Union Army as a chaplain for the Fifty-third Regiment of the Massachusetts Volunteers, and later with the Thirtieth Regiment of the Veteran Volunteers. There is no record of what kind of action Whittemore may have seen during the war. When the conflict ended, he settled in Darlington, South Carolina, serving as a delegate to the state constitution convention in 1867. Elected president of the Republican state Executive Board that same year, he founded the newspaper the *New Era* in Darlington. In 1868 he served as a member of the South Carolina state senate. When South Carolina was readmitted to the Union under Reconstruction, Whittemore was elected to a seat in the U.S. House of Representatives as a Republican, serving in the Fortieth and Forty-first Congresses from 18 July 1868 to 24 February 1870.

Whittemore apparently got into ethical trouble for selling appointments to West Point and Annapolis for either political favors or cash—which one is not specified. Following a House investigation, it was recommended that Whittemore face expulsion from the House—a sanction not sought since the Civil War. *Hinds' Precedents,* which are the proceedings of Congress, reported:

On February 21, 1870, Mr. John A. Logan, of Illinois, from the Committee on Military Affairs, who were instructed to inquire into the alleged sale of appointments to the Military and Naval Academies by Members of Congress, submitted a report, in writing, accompanied by the following resolution, viz:

"Resolved, That B. F. Whittemore, a Representative in Congress from the First Congressional district of South Carolina, be, and is hereby, expelled from his seat as a Member of the House of Representatives in the Forty-first Congress."

On February 23 the Speaker ruled that Mr. Whittemore might, under the resolution, be heard either orally or in writing. So his affidavit was presented and read, in denial of the charge. After it had been read, Mr. Benjamin F. Butler, of Massachusetts, desired to be heard in behalf of the accused Member, having been deputed by him to make his defense.... On February 24, as the House was considering the resolution of expulsion, the Speaker laid before the House a communication from B. F. Whittemore, informing the House that he had transmitted to the governor of South Carolina his resignation of his seat in Congress. The same having been read,

Mr. Whittemore was about to address the House, when the Speaker decided that, in view of the communication just read to the House, he could not recognize him as any longer a Member of the House or entitled to address the same. Mr. Whittemore's notice to the Speaker that he had resigned did not reach the desk until after the speech had begun. The Speaker, as soon as he read the notice of resignation, caused Mr. Whittemore to suspend his remarks, and ruled that it was not within the power of the Chair to recognize anyone not a Member of the House. Therefore he ruled that Mr. Whittemore might proceed only by unanimous consent of the House.

After speaking, Whittemore left the House in disgrace. However, no legal or criminal action was ever taken against him. His constituents, angered by his forced resignation, reelected him to fill the vacancy caused by his resignation, but when Whittemore went to present the credentials of the election to the House, he was rebuffed, and the House declined to seat him. Whittemore returned to South Carolina. He later served as a member of the South Carolina state senate in 1877, but after this term, left the state and returned to Massachusetts, where he became the publisher of a small newspaper. Whittemore died in Montvale, Massachusetts, on 25 January 1894 at the age of sixty-nine and was buried in the Salem Street Cemetery in Woburn, Massachusetts.

References: *Biographical Directory of the American Congress, 1774–1996* (Alexandria, VA: CQ Staff Directories, Inc., 1996), 2050; Hinds, Asher Crosby, *Hinds' Precedents of the House of Representatives of the United States, Including References to Provisions of the Constitution, the Laws, and Decisions of the United States Senate,* 8 vols. (Washington, DC: Government Printing Office, 1907–1908), V:829–832; Whittemore Amherst information in Robert Fletcher, ed., *Amherst College: Biographical Record of the Graduates and Non-Graduates. Centennial Edition, 1821–1921* (Amherst, MA: Published by the College, 1927).

Willett, William Forte, Jr. (1869–1938)

United States representative from New York (1907–1911), indicted and convicted for bribery and conspiracy in his attempts to secure a seat on the Queens County (New York) Supreme Court, for which he served more than a year in prison. Willett remains an obscure figure despite being one of only a handful of U.S. representatives to serve time in prison. Born in Brooklyn, New York, on 27 November 1869, he attended the public schools of that city before he received a law degree from New York University in 1895. He was admitted to the bar the following year and opened a law practice in New York City.

Willett was elected as a Democrat to the U.S. House of Representatives in 1906, taking his seat in the Sixtieth Congress on 4 March 1907. He was reelected in 1908, but was not a candidate for re-election in 1910. Historians who have studied his congressional career note that he is known for doing only two things: delivering a speech on the House floor on 18 January 1909 in which he called outgoing President Theodore Roosevelt "a grinning gargoyle," and the House vote on 27 January 1909 of 126 to 78 expunging that speech from the congressional record. After leaving Congress, Willett returned to New York, where he entered into the business of selling real estate.

In October 1911, according to his indictment, Willett bribed Queens Democratic leader "Curley Joe" Cassidy in the amount of $10,000 in order to get a nomination for a seat on the Queens County Supreme Court. The scheme, however, somehow became public: on 1 November 1911, New York City District Attorney Charles Whitman reported that he had proof that Willett paid $37,000 in total bribes to get the Democratic nomination. Tammany Hall leader Charles Murphy told reporters that Tammany Hall did not get any of the money. Whitman went to court and presented evidence against Willett; L. T. Walters Jr., who nominated Willett; Cassidy; and Kings County Democratic Chairman J. H. McCooey on charges of conspiracy and corrupt practices, including bribery. On 2 November, a Long Island bank where Willett banked revealed that Willett had borrowed $10,000 "for campaign purposes." McCooey denied that he had been involved with Willett or his attempts to get on the ballot. On 20 November, Willett, Walters, and Cassidy were arrested; all three pled not guilty and posted bail. Although a Queens County grand jury refused to indict the men, a grand jury in Kings County opened an investigation and indicted Walters and Willett on 20 June 1912.

In 1913 all three men went on trial and were convicted on all charges. His appeals exhausted, in 1914 Willett entered Sing Sing prison in upstate New York state. He served fourteen months there, being paroled in 1915. While in prison, Willett be-

came unpopular for enforcing discipline and was beaten up severely.

After leaving prison, Willett quietly worked in real estate ventures, never again surfacing in the political realm. He died in New York City on 12 February 1938 at the age of sixty-eight and was buried in the Cemetery of the Evergreens in Kings County, New York.

References: *Biographical Directory of the American Congress, 1774–1996* (Alexandria, VA: CQ Staff Directories, Inc., 1996), 2058.

Williams, Harrison Arlington, Jr. (1919–2001)

United States representative (1953–1957) and senator (1959–1982) from New Jersey, the only senator implicated in the ABSCAM scandal, resigned his seat and was convicted of his involvement in the scandal. Born in Plainfield, New Jersey, on 10 December 1919, Williams attended the public schools of New Jersey before attending Oberlin College in Ohio and graduating from that institution in 1941. He then moved to Washington, D.C., where he went to work as a cub reporter for the *Washington Post*. He attended the Georgetown University Foreign Service School until he was called to active duty as a seaman in the United States Naval Reserve. He entered that service as a naval aviator, although it is unknown if he saw any action. When he was discharged in 1945, Williams held the rank of lieutenant, junior grade.

Following the war, Williams went to work in private business in the steel industry. However, he decided to get his law license. He entered Columbia Law School in New York and graduated with a law degree in 1948. He was admitted to the New York bar, but went to New Hampshire for a short time where he opened a law practice. He returned to New Jersey, settled in the town of Plainfield, and opened a law practice there. A Democrat, he entered the political realm in 1951, unsuccessfully running for a seat in the New Jersey House of Assembly. He ran a campaign for the Plainfield city council early the following year, but also lost that race. In late 1952, when Republican Clifford Case left his House seat to run for the U.S. Senate, Williams ran for Case's seat in the U.S. House, representing the sixth district. Elected, he entered the Eighty-third Congress on 3 November 1953 and served in that body until 3 January 1957. He was reelected in 1954, but defeated in 1956. In 1957 he campaigned for the reelection of New Jersey Governor Robert B. Meyner, a Democrat. Meyner, returning the favor, pushed Williams to run in 1958 for the U.S. Senate against Senator Robert W. Kean, a Republican.

In 1958 Williams defeated Kean and held his Senate seat until his resignation on 11 March 1982. A liberal, he supported Social Security, conservation, and civil rights legislation. He rose to become chairman of the Senate Committee on Labor and Human Resources, losing the chairmanship when the Republicans took control in 1981. He was reelected three times to the Senate.

In the late 1970s, the Federal Bureau of Investigation, acting on rumors that some congressmen and senators were willing to take bribes to aid foreigners to gain citizenship, set up Operation Arab Scam—better known as ABSCAM. An agent of the bureau was dressed as an Arab sheikh, and congressmen and senators who took the bait were invited to speak to the phony sheikh, who offered them bribes in exchange for getting the sheikh and his friends American citizenship. The only senator who decided to take the money and work for the sheikh was Harrison Williams. Videotapes later released showed Williams asking for a loan of $100 million, which he said was to provide for his and his family's security after he left the Senate. The Senate Ethics Committee later called these tapes not just a "smoking gun," but a "smoking machine gun." Williams was indicted on 30 October 1980, and his trial began in Brooklyn, New York, on 1 April 1981. The videotapes were the piece of evidence that nailed Williams. As the *New York Times* stated:

> The prosecutors sought to show that Mr. Williams and [his codefendant, Alexander] Feinberg were "predisposed" to commit illegal acts in the immigration and titanium-mining matters. The prosecutors did this by introducing evidence of the defendants' behavior in situations involving an Atlantic City gambling casino and an unsuccessful venture to build a New Jersey garbage-recycling facility—situations that were not part of the charges in the trial.
>
> In the casino matter, the prosecutors played a videotape of a 1979 meeting in which the Senator told the Abscam agents that he had interceded with

a New Jersey official to help gain a decision from the state's Casino Control Commission that would have saved a casino-development group $30 million, had its proposed project been carried out. The casino had been proposed by a company in which the controlling interest was held by a second company that employed the Senator's wife as a consultant. . . .

The key prosecution evidence in the titanium-mining and immigration matters were videotapes of two meetings the Senator had with the bogus sheik, played by F.B.I. agent Richard Farhart.

In the first tape, made at a meeting held in an Arlington, Virginia, motel in June 1979, Senator Williams says that there would be "no problem" in using his relationships with the nation's top officials—including President Jimmy Carter—in trying to get the government contract for the mine. In the second tape, made at the Plaza Hotel in January 1980, the Senator gave the phony sheik assurances of help in seeking permanent residency in the United States.

On 1 May 1981, Williams was found guilty of bribery and conspiracy charges. He refused to resign from the Senate, and the Senate Ethics Committee opened an investigation into whether or not Williams should be expelled. Williams continued to assert his innocence, instead decrying FBI tactics in snaring him. Robert S. Bennett, the Washington, D.C., attorney who defended President Bill Clinton, served as special counsel for the Senate Ethics Committee in the Williams investigation. However, the stunning evidence of Williams on tape shaking down the fake Arab sheikhs was his undoing. The Ethics committee recommended on 24 August 1981 that Williams be expelled for his crimes. Debate in the Senate regarding the recommendation began on 3 March 1982. Senator after senator took to the floor to discuss Senate Resolution 204—the expulsion of Harrison Williams. "The unfortunate but unavoidable task of considering Senate Resolution 204 is an arduous responsibility; a disturbing responsibility for every senator, a weighty responsibility for the institution itself," Senator Howard Baker (R-TN), the first speaker, stated. Senator Howell Heflin (D-AL) said, "At any point during this drawn-out, sordid affair, Senator Williams could have said, 'Wait a minute. What you're proposing is wrong. This is not what I had in mind. I can't be involved in this.' But he didn't. . . . He stayed; he discussed; he agreed; he promised; he pledged to abuse his office, his public trust, for which, now he must be expelled." Senator Daniel Inouye (D-HI) was one of the few voices to speak for Williams. The senator was guilty of nothing "so dastardly, so sinister," but instead had been entrapped "by the FBI, an agency of the executive branch of government. . . . Who among us has not touted our importance to our constituents? We are here because our egos are immense." Williams spoke to his colleagues for four hours, imploring them not to vote to expel. "It is not only Pete Williams that stands accused or indicted. It is all of us, the entire Senate, that stands accused and intimidated by another branch of government. . . . The chairman of the Select Committee on Ethics [then-Sen. Malcolm Wallop (R-WY)] . . . shelters the FBI and its malcontents from criticism in his prosecution of me. In so doing, I believe he makes the next Abscam easier and more legitimate."

Williams's arguments fell on deaf ears—even his own fellow New Jerseyan, Senator Bill Bradley, supported his expulsion. A move by some Democrats only to censure Williams failed, and, facing an inevitable vote to expel him, the New Jersey senator resigned on 11 March 1982. Williams told his supporters, "I announce my intention to resign. Time, history and Almighty God will vindicate me and the principles for which I fought here in the Senate. I will be vindicated before the people in our land." Williams was sentenced to three years in prison, entering the federal correction facility in Allenwood, Pennsylvania, in 1983, becoming the first senator in eighty years to go to prison. He was paroled in 1986, and returned home to Bedminster, New Jersey.

In his final years, Williams sought the vindication he argued for, asking President Bill Clinton for a pardon in 2000, but Clinton refused. Williams, suffering from cancer and other ailments, died on 20 November 2001, one month shy of his eighty-second birthday.

References: Bernstein, Adam, "Harrison A. Williams Jr. Dies, Abscam Ousted N.J. Senator," *Washington Post,* 20 November 2001, B7; *Biographical Directory of the American Congress, 1774–1996* (Alexandria, VA: CQ Staff Directories, Inc., 1996), 2061; Byrd, Robert C., *The Senate, 1789–1989: Historical Statistics, 1789–1992* (Washington, DC: Government Printing Office, four volumes, 1993), IV:668; Fried, Joseph P., "Senate Ethics Unit to Consider Action on Williams Verdict," *New York Times,* 3 May 1981, A1; Fried, Joseph P., "Williams Is Guilty on All Nine Counts in Abscam Inquiry, Vows Not to Resign," *New York Times,* 2 May 1981, A1; Sullivan, Joseph F., "Senate Opens Debate on Williams, 'Did Nothing Criminal,' He Insists," *New York Times,* 4 March 1982, A1; Sullivan, Joseph F., "Williams Pleads with Colleagues in 4-Hour Speech on Senate Floor," *New York Times,* 5 March 1982, A1; Sullivan, Joseph F., "Williams Quits Senate Seat as Vote to Expel Him Nears, Still Asserts He Is Innocent," *New York Times,* 12 March 1982, A1.

Williams, John James (1904–1988)

United States senator (1947–1970) from Delaware, instrumental in numerous investigations into corruption, including the Bobby Baker affair (1964). Born in Bayard, Delaware, on 17 May 1904, the ninth of eleven children of a farming family, he attended local schools before he borrowed some money and established the Millsboro Feed Company in Millsboro, Delaware, with his brother Preston. This enterprise grew to include the Williams Hatchery, where chickens and turkeys were raised, as well as 2,000 acres of farms and other lands. In 1946 he served in the Millsboro town council.

In late 1946, with little political experience under his belt, Williams decided to run for the United States Senate against Democratic incumbent James M. Tunnell, a popular supporter of President Harry S. Truman. Williams, a Republican who railed against what he perceived to be the slide of the Democratic Party toward socialism and who decried Truman's economic and social policies, was given little if any chance to upset the popular Tunnell. Williams easily won the Republican nomination and, during the campaign, portrayed himself as a small businessman fighting against big government. Tunnell, though only in his first term, was nearly seventy, while Williams was in his early forties. The contrast, and the arguments of Williams, swayed the electorate, and on election day Williams was elected with a nearly 12,000-vote advantage out of 113,500 votes cast.

Williams began his career in the Senate by speaking out against the price supports of the administration, which he felt helped large corporations over the small farmer, the policies of the New Deal Office of Price Administration, and called for a cut in income taxes. In 1947 he was seated on the Committee to Investigate the National Defense, which investigated contracts handed out during World War II to see if there was fraud or waste in any of them. For his work, in 1949 he was named to the prestigious Finance Committee. He eventually rose to become the ranking minority leader on that panel. As a member of the committee, he became skilled in taxation and budgetary issues. A critic of overspending in both Democratic and Republican administrations, in the early 1950s he alleged bookkeeping errors that cost some $350 million at the Commodities Credit Corporation (CCC). As a member of the Agriculture Committee, he worked to expose costly farm programs that he felt benefited a few corporations and not the family farmers the programs were intended to help. For this work, in 1967 he was awarded the American Farm Bureau's highest award for his work on agricultural issues.

Yet Williams's greatest role was in the investigation into Robert G. "Bobby" Baker, the secretary to the former Senate Majority Leader and later Vice President Lyndon Johnson. Starting in 1963, before Johnson became president upon the assassination of John F. Kennedy, Williams was tipped off that Baker had been involved in shady business dealings and called upon the Senate Rules Committee to open a formal investigation. When the Rules Committee seemed to hesitate to investigate one of their own (the issue could serve to embarrass Johnson, running for a full term on his own in 1964), Williams went public with his accusations. Because of this, in 1964 Johnson spearheaded an effort to defeat him in Delaware, but Williams won, despite the contest being the narrowest of his four victories. Williams was not shy in pointing out corruption within his own party—in 1959 he was one of the first senators to call upon President Eisenhower to fire his chief of staff, Sherman Adams.

In 1960 Williams had been named to the Foreign Relations Committee and when he retired in 1970, he became the last man to serve on both the Senate Finance and Foreign Relations Committees. (A Senate rule passed during Williams's tenure prohibited joint service on two of the "big five" committees, which included Finance and Foreign Relations.) He criticized the misuse of funds from the Agency for International Development (AID), and by the mid-1960s, was a major critic of the war in Vietnam. He opposed continuing the war during both the Johnson and subsequent Nixon administrations. He was, however, considered a leading authority on the issue of honesty in

the Senate, and in 1952 and 1968 was considered a leading candidate for vice president, but he refused both times. In 1973, when Vice President Spiro Agnew was forced to resign, Williams's name was floated as a possible replacement. Had he accepted, Williams would have become the thirty-eighth president in 1974.

Starting in 1969, Williams announced that he would retire at the age of sixty-five and not run for a fifth term in 1970. Representative William Roth won the seat that year and has held it ever since. Williams retired with his wife to Millsboro, where he worked in real estate. He died there on 11 January 1988 at the age of eighty-three.

Williams is considered by many historians to have been one of the most honest men ever to serve in the Senate. He was called "The Lonewolf Investigator," "Watchdog of the Treasury," "Honest John," "Mr. Integrity," and "the Conscience of the Senate" by his peers, the press, and his constituents. In 1963 Senator Sam Ervin said of him, he is "the gadfly of the Senate . . . on many occasions he has stung the Congress and the executive agencies into righteous conduct."

See also Baker, Robert Gene

References: *Biographical Directory of the American Congress, 1774–1996* (Alexandria, VA: CQ Staff Directories, Inc., 1996), 2063.

Williamson, John Newton (1855–1943)

United States representative from Oregon (1903–1907), convicted, with Senator John Hipple Mitchell, of land fraud and forced to leave Congress before he could be stripped of his seat. Because Mitchell was the leading character in that episode, Williamson's name and deeds were largely ignored by the media at the time, and he has slipped into obscurity. Little is known of his life—he was born near Junction City, Oregon, on 8 November 1855, and he attended country schools. He did attend Willamette University in Salem, Oregon, but he apparently never obtained any degree from that institution. Sometime after leaving school, Williamson went into business raising livestock.

A Republican, Williamson was elected sheriff of Cook County, Oregon, in 1886, and served for two years. At the end of that term of office, he was elected to a seat in the Oregon state house of representatives, where he served until 1898. From 1893 until 1896, he owned and edited the *Prineville Review*. In 1900 Williamson was elected to a seat in the state senate, where he served until 1902. In that year Williamson was elected to the U.S. House of Representatives, representing Oregon's Second District. He served in the Fifty-eighth and Fifty-ninth Congresses, from 4 March 1903 until 3 March 1907.

In his time before and during his congressional tenure, Williamson became involved in purchasing land in Oregon. Working closely with Senator John H. Mitchell of Oregon, he bought up homesteads fraudulently from the U.S. government by using fake names and fake documents. Williamson was convicted of the same charges as Mitchell: conspiracy to defraud the United States government. However, a study of Williamson's biography shows no prison term, so the disposition of his case remains unknown. He did not stand for reelection in 1906 and returned to Oregon.

Williamson spent the remainder of his life in Oregon, working on a ranch and engaging in agricultural pursuits; he served as postmaster of Prineville, Oregon, from 1922 until 1934. He died in Prineville on 29 August 1943 and was buried in the Masonic Cemetery in that town.

See also Mitchell, John Hipple
References: *Biographical Directory of the American Congress, 1774–1996* (Alexandria, VA: CQ Staff Directories, Inc., 1996); Cummings, Hilary Anne, "John H. Mitchell, a Man of His Time: Foundations of His Political Career, 1860–1879," (Ph.D. dissertation, University of Oregon, 1985); O'Callaghan, Jerry A., "Senator John H. Mitchell and the Oregon Land Frauds, 1905." *Pacific Historical Review* 21 (August 1952): 255–261.

Wilson, Charles Herbert (1917–1984)

United States representative from California (1963–1981), censured by the U.S. House of Representatives in 1980 for financial misconduct, one of only twenty-two House members ever to receive that punishment. Wilson was born in Magna, Utah, on 15 February 1917, but moved with his parents to Los Angeles, California, in 1922. He attended the public schools there and in the nearby town of Inglewood, after which he went to work in a bank starting in 1935. In 1942 he was enlisted in the U.S. Army, and, with the rank of staff sergeant, served from June 1942 to December 1945, seeing limited action in the European theater of operations before he was discharged. Returning to the United States, Wilson established an insurance agency in Los Angeles.

In 1953 Wilson entered the political arena and ran as a Democrat for a seat in the California state legislature. Elected, he served from 1954 to 1962 as an assemblyman from the Sixty-sixth California District. In 1962 he gave up this post to run for a seat in the U.S. House of Representatives, representing the Thirty-first California District. Defeating Republican Gordon Kahn, Wilson took his seat in Congress and ultimately served from 3 January 1963 until 3 January 1981, from the Eighty-eighth through the Ninety-sixth Congresses.

During the 1970s, Wilson was at the forefront of a secret campaign inside the House to advance the influence of the Korean government—and he took gifts and other remuneration from the Korean government for his support. In 1980 the House investigated the role of Wilson in the so-called Koreagate scandal and found that he had accepted improper gifts, as well as used "ghost" employees in his office (so he could collect additional paychecks) and improperly used campaign funds. However, the House Ethics Committee recommended that Wilson be censured instead of being the subject of an expulsion vote. Wilson was censured by the full House on 6 June 1980. Wilson lost in the Democratic primary in 1980 and left Congress on 3 January 1981.

In his final years, Wilson lived in Tantallon, Maryland, until his death in Clinton, Maryland, on 21 July 1984 at the age of sixty-seven. He was buried in Inglewood, California.

References: *Biographical Directory of the American Congress, 1774–1996* (Alexandria, VA: CQ Staff Directories, Inc., 1996).

Worrall, Robert.

See United States v. Worrall.

Wright, James Claude, Jr. (1922–)

United States representative from Texas (1954–1989) and Speaker of the House (1986–1989), forced to step down from the speakership and his seat after he was accused of violating House rules on financial improprieties and limits on outside earned income. Born in Fort Worth, Texas, on 22 December 1922, James Wright Jr. attended the public schools of Fort Worth and Dallas, before he went to Weatherford College in Texas from 1939 to 1940 and the University of Texas from 1940 to 1941. After the Japanese attack on Pearl Harbor and the entry of the United States into World War II, Wright enlisted in the U.S. Army Air Force. Commissioned in 1942, he was posted to the Pacific theater of operations and flew combat missions in the South Pacific, for which he was awarded the Distinguished Service Cross. After the war, Wright returned home and entered the Texas political arena. He was elected to the Texas state house of representatives in 1946, but was defeated after serving a single term. He then moved to Weatherford, Texas, where he had gone to college, and ran for mayor. He was elected and served from 1950 to 1954. In that latter year, he ran unopposed for a seat in the U.S. House of Representatives, representing Texas's Twelfth District. Wright would be reelected seventeen times. (He ran unsuccessfully for a U.S. Senate seat in 1961.) In 1977, when Majority Leader Thomas P. "Tip" O'Neill was elevated to the Speakership, Wright was named as his replacement for the majority leader position. Wright served in this capacity from the Ninety-fifth through the Ninety-ninth Congresses. When O'Neill retired from the Speakership and the House in 1985, Wright was elected by the Democrats, then in the majority, to be the Forty-ninth Speaker of the House. Wright would serve as Speaker through the 100th and the 101st Congresses.

Jim Wright got into ethical trouble just as he was becoming one of the most powerful politicians in America. He rented a condominium in Fort Worth from a close friend, real estate developer George Mallick, and paid Mallick for the use of the condo—Mallick's gift of the condo use was in violation of a ban on more than $100 in gifts from any one person. He intervened with federal regulators on behalf of three Texans—a real estate developer, and two executives from a Fort Worth Savings & Loan—in dealings with the Federal Home Loan Bank Board. However, the worst allegation came regarding his memoirs. Wright had penned *Reflections of a Public Man* in 1984; it was a 117-page trifle that was sold in bulk by lobbyists. It had been published by Carlos Moore, whose printing firm had worked for Wright's campaigns for many years. Finally, Wright had gotten 55 percent in royalties from the sales of the book, when normally authors get 10 to 15 percent. In May 1988 Common Cause, a public citizens' action group, called for a congressional inquiry into these allegations. Within days of Common Cause's complaint, Representative Newt Gingrich of Georgia, a firebrand member of the Republican minority in the House, sent a letter, cosigned by seventy-two of his Republican colleagues, to the House Committee on Standards of Official Conduct, the panel which oversees ethics in the House, asking for an investigation of the charges. The Democrat-led committee voted unanimously on 9 June 1988 to conduct a preliminary inquiry; later, a full-blown investigation was ordered, and a special outside counsel, Chicago attorney Richard J. Phelan, was retained. Wright testified for more than five hours before the committee, and on 22 February 1989, Phelan gave his 279-page report to the committee. It alleged that on sixty-nine separate occasions, Wright had broken congressional rules—specifically regarding the cozy book deal from which he had profited and taking more than $145,000 in gifts from his friend George Mallick. An allegation that Wright was illegally involved in an oil-well deal that resulted in huge profits for him was never investigated, and, in the end, the House committee dropped more than half of the allegations Phelan disclosed. Wright's attorneys claimed that the committee and Phelan were "misinterpreting" House rules so as to make Wright look guilty and asked for the Speaker to be exonerated. He was not.

On 31 May 1989, Wright took to the floor of the House to deliver his resignation speech and direct a stinging rebuke at the "mindless cannibalism" of ethics investigations. As his voice quivered with emotion, Wright said, "Let me give you back this job you gave to me as a propitiation for all of this season of bad will that has grown up among us. . . . I don't want to be a party to tearing up this institution. I love it." Wright thus became the first sitting Speaker of the House to resign his post because of scandal. Less than a month later, on 30 June 1989, Wright resigned from the House altogether, ending a forty-four-year congressional career. He and his wife returned to Texas, where he still lives.

Dennis F. Thompson, writing on institutional corruption in American politics, explained in 1995, "The charges against Wright combine in the same case the individual and institutional corruption found, respectively, in the cases of [Senator David] Durenberger and the Keating Five. . . . The presence of both kinds of corruption in the same case offer an opportunity for a direct comparison. Confronted with a case of both kinds of corruption, the House ethics committee took seriously only the allegations of individual corruption, even though they were arguably less serious than those of institutional corruption."

References: Barry, John M., *The Ambition and the Power* (New York: Viking, 1989); *Congressional Ethics* (Washington, DC: Congressional Quarterly, 1980), 20–21; "Impassioned Wright Quits, Speaker Asks End to Rancor," *Miami Herald,* 1 June 1989, A1; Thompson, Dennis F., *Ethics in Congress: From Individual to Institutional Corruption* (Washington, DC: The Brookings Institution, 1995), 43–44; Toner, Robin, "Wright Resigning As Speaker, Defends His Ethics and Urges End of 'Mindless Cannibalism,'" *New York Times,* 1 June 1989, A1, D21; "Transcript of Wright's Address to House of Representatives," *New York Times,* 1 June 1989, D22–23; United States Congress, *Biographical Directory of the United States Congress, 1774–1989: The Continental Congress, September 5, 1774, to October 21, 1788, and the Congress of the United States, from the First through the One Hundredth Congresses, March 4, 1789, to January 3, 1989, Inclusive* (Washington, DC: Government Printing Office, 1989); United States Congress, House, Committee on Standards of Official Conduct, *Report of the Special Outside Counsel in the Matter of Speaker James C. Wright, Jr. Committee on Standards of Official Conduct, U.S. House of Representatives, One Hundred First Congress* (Washington, DC: Government Printing Office, 1989).

Z

Zenger, John Peter (1697–1746)

Journalist and writer, whose trial for exposing the corruption of the British governor of New York set the stage for the enunciation of the free speech principle in the colonies and later the United States. And although his name belongs to history for his role in standing for free speech, few know of the details of his life or his infamous trial. Zenger was born in what was called the Upper Palatinate (now Bavaria, Germany) sometime in the year 1697 and around 1710 emigrated with his family to New York, then a prosperous English colony. The elder Zenger died en route to the New World, leaving his widow, Johanna, to care for Peter and his two siblings. The year after he came to the colonies, Zenger went to work as an apprentice for William Bradford, the famed printer who was the royal printer for the New York colony. This apprenticeship ended in 1719, but, six years later, Bradford invited Zenger to become his partner. In 1726 Zenger struck out on his own, starting his own printing establishment. His printing was little noticed except for several theological tracts, but in 1730 he published the first arithmetic book in the colonies.

In 1733 Zenger founded the *New York Weekly Journal,* which would become, in its short history, one of the most important newspapers in American history. The first issue appeared on 5 November 1733. Zenger's enterprise was backed financially by the Popular Party, a group of men in New York colony who opposed the administration of William Cosby, the governor of the colony. One of the leaders of the Popular Party, James Alexander, served as the paper's editor in chief. With each new issue, new editorials and stories called attention to the corruption of Cosby. In these days before any such thing as the First Amendment existed, Zenger and his friends pushed an envelope that really was never opened.

The *New York Weekly Journal* explained in its 25 February 1733 edition:

A Lible [*sic*] is not the less a Libel for being true, this may seem a Contradiction; but it is neither one in Law, or in common Scope. There are some Truths not fit to be told; where, for Example, the Discovery of a small Fault may do mischief; or where the Discovery of a great fault can do no good, there ought to be no discovery at all, and to make faults where there are none is still worse. . . . But this Doctrine only holds true as to private and personal failings; and it is quite otherwise when the crimes of Men come to Affect the Publick. Nothing ought to be so dear to us as our Country, and nothing ought to come in Competition with its Interests. Every crime against the Publick, is a great crime, tho there be some greater than others. Ignorance and Folly may be pleaded in Alleviation of private Offenses; but when they come to be publick Offenses, they lose all Benefit of such a Plea; we are no longer to then consider, to what Causes they are owing, but what Evils they may produce, and here we shall readily find, that Folly has overturned States, and private Interest been the parent of Publick Confusion.

The 1734 trial of Peter Zenger in New York. Defended by Andrew Hamilton, Zenger was acquitted of libel; the Court's decision established freedom of the press in the United States. (Bettmann/Corbis)

Cosby and his friends, angered at the newspaper's growing popularity, established a grand jury that found the editorials to be libelous and seditious, and ordered Zenger's arrest and for the paper to be closed down. On 17 November 1734, Zenger was arrested and imprisoned in Manhattan. Two of the paper's writers, James Alexander and William Smith, condemned the move. They questioned the authority of the Crown to arrest Zenger and condemned the high bail set for him. They wrote a stinging letter to the colonial assembly: "Instead of consulting our law books, and doing what we think consistent therewith, for the benefit of our clients . . . [attorneys] must study in great men's causes, and only what will please the judges, and what will most flatter men is power."

Initially finding a lawyer who would oppose the Crown proved difficult (all of those who had acted on behalf of Zenger were disbarred by the colonial authorities), but Scottish attorney Andrew Hamilton (1676?–1741), a leading lawyer in the Pennsylvania colony, stepped forward to defend Zenger on principle despite his sympathy for the royal forces. The trial, taking place in 1735, dealt with whether Zenger's editorials libeled Cosby. Hamilton argued to the jury that the editorials were factually true,

and thus could not be libelous. In his classic statement before the jury, Hamilton told them that men had a right "to complain when they are hurt . . . publicly to remonstrate the abuses of power in the strongest forms . . . and to assert with courage the sense they have of the blessing of liberty, the value they put upon it, and their reputation at all hazards to preserve it." Although the judge instructed the jury that Zenger must be found guilty whether or not his editorials were true, the jury returned with a not guilty verdict, accepting Hamilton's stand that truth is a defense to libel. It was also the first known case of jury nullification. The verdict set the standard for freedom of the press—so much so, that this case was used by the Founding Fathers forty years later as the basis for the First Amendment to the U.S. Constitution.

Zenger was released, but never made an impact in the printing world again. He worked, ironically, as the public printer for the colony of New York in 1737 and in the same position for the colony of New Jersey in 1738. He died quietly in 1746.

References: *New-York Weekly Journal, Containing the Frequent Advices, Foreign, and Domestick* (Editorial), 25 February 1733, 1; Morris, Richard B., "Zenger, John Peter," in Allen Johnson and Dumas

Malone, et al., eds., *Dictionary of American Biography,* 10 vols. and 10 supplements (New York: Charles Scribner's Sons, 1930–1995), X:648–650; Rutherfurd, Livingston, *John Peter Zenger, His Press, His Trial and a Bibliography of Zenger Imprints, by Livingston Rutherfurd. Also a Reprint of the First Edition of the Trial* (New York: Dodd, Mead, 1904);"Trial of John Peter Zenger Before the Supreme Court of New York, For Two Libels on the Government, New York, 1735," in Peleg W. Chandler, *American Criminal Trials,* 2 vols. (Boston: Charles C. Little and James Brown, 841–844), I:154–209; *The Trial of John Peter Zenger, of New York, Printer: Who was Charged with Having Printed and Published a LIBEL against the Government, and Acquitted. With a Narrative of His Case* (London: Printed for J. Almon, Opposite Burlington-House, Piccadilly, 1735).

APPENDIX ONE

Cases of Expulsion, Censure, and Condemnation in the U.S. House of Representatives and U.S. Senate, 1798–Present

Under Article I, Section 5 of the United States Constitution, each house of Congress may determine the rules of its proceedings and set the rules for punishing members as it sees fit—and whether to reprimand, condemn, censure, or, in the most egregious examples, expel a member. Since 1789 the House has expelled only four men (three of these for supporting the Confederacy), and the Senate has expelled fifteen men, fourteen of whom were charged with supporting the Confederacy. Thus, despite a history of many members being accused of corrupt acts, only two have been formally removed because of political corruption: Representatives Michael J. "Ozzie" Myers (D-PA), implicated in the famed ABSCAM scandal, and James A. Traficant (D-OH), who was convicted of several crimes relating to corruption. In the Senate, only four members in total have been convicted in a courtroom of criminal acts: Republicans Joseph R. Burton (1905), John H. Mitchell (1905), and Truman H. Newberry (1920), and Democrat Harrison Williams (1981). Newberry resigned, but his conviction was later overturned; Mitchell died before he could be expelled from the Senate, and Burton and Williams resigned before they, too, could be expelled.

Cases of Expulsion in the House

Year	Member	Grounds	Disposition
1798	Matthew Lyons (AF–Vermont)	Assault on another representative	Not expelled
1798	Roger Griswold (F–Connecticut)	Assault on another representative	Not expelled
1799	Matthew Lyon (AF–Vermont)	Sedition	Not expelled
1838	William J. Graves (W–Kentucky)	Killing of another representative in a duel	Not expelled
1839	Alexander Duncan (W–Ohio)	Offensive publication	Not expelled
1856	Preston S. Brooks (SRD–S.C.)	Assault on U.S. senator[1]	Not expelled
1857	Orsamus B. Matteson (W–New York)	Corruption	Not expelled
1857	William A. Gilbert (W–New York)	Corruption	Not expelled
1857	William W. Welch (Am–Connecticut)	Corruption	Not expelled
1857	Francis S. Edwards (Am–New York)	Corruption	Not expelled
1858	Orsamus B. Matteson (W–New York)	Corruption	Not expelled
1861	John B. Clark (D–Missouri)	Support of rebellion	Expelled
1861	Henry C. Burnett (D–Kentucky)	Support of rebellion	Expelled
1861	John W. Reid (D–Missouri)	Support of rebellion	Expelled
1864	Alexander Long (D–Ohio)	Treasonable utterance	Not expelled[2]
1864	Benjamin G. Harris (D–Maryland)	Treasonable utterance	Not expelled[2]
1866	Lovell H. Rousseau (R–Kentucky)	Assault on another representative	Not expelled[2]
1870	Benjamin F. Whittemore (R–South Carolina)	Corruption	Not expelled[2]
	Roderick R. Butler (R–Tennessee)	Corruption	Not expelled[2]
1873	Oakes Ames (R–Massachusetts)	Corruption	Not expelled[2]
1873	James Brooks (D–New York)	Corruption	Not expelled[2]

(continues)

Cases of Expulsion in the House *(continued)*

Year	Member	Grounds	Disposition
1875	John Y. Brown (D–Kentucky)	Insult to representative	Not expelled[2]
1875	William S. King (R–Minnesota)	Corruption	Not expelled
1875	John G. Schumaker (D–New York)	Corruption	Not expelled
1884	William P. Kellogg (R–Louisiana)	Corruption	Not expelled
1921	Thomas R. Blanton (D–Texas)	Abuse of Leave to Print	Not expelled[2]
1979	Charles C. Diggs, Jr. (D–Michigan)	Misuse of clerk funds	Not expelled[2]
1980	Michael J. Myers (D–Pennsylvania)	Corruption	Expelled
1988	Mario Biaggi (D–New York)	Corruption	Not expelled[3]
1990	Barney Frank (D–Massachusetts)	Discrediting House	Not expelled[4]

Cases of Expulsion in the Senate

Year	Member	Grounds	Disposition
1797	William Blount (R–Tennessee)	Anti–Spanish conspiracy	Expelled
1808	John Smith (R–Ohio)[5]	Disloyalty/Treason	Not expelled
1858	Henry M. Rice (D–Minnesota)	Corruption	Not expelled
1861	James M. Mason (D–Virginia)	Support of rebellion	Expelled
1861	Robert M. T. Hunter (D–Virginia)	Support of rebellion	Expelled
1861	Thomas L. Clingman (D–N.C.)	Support of rebellion	Expelled
1861	Thomas Bragg (D–N.C.)	Support of rebellion	Expelled
1861	James Chesnut Jr. (D–S.C.)	Support of rebellion	Expelled
1861	Alfred O. P. Nicholson (D–TN)	Support of rebellion	Expelled
1861	William K. Sebastion (D–AR)[6]	Support of rebellion	Expelled
1861	Charles B. Mitchel (D–AR)	Support of rebellion	Expelled
1861	John Hemphill (D–TX)	Support of rebellion	Expelled
1861	Louis T. Wigfall (D–TX)[7]	Support of rebellion	Expelled
1861	John C. Breckinridge (D–KY)	Support of rebellion	Expelled
1862	Lazarus W. Powell (D–KY)	Support of rebellion	Not expelled
1862	Trusten Polk (D–MO)	Support of rebellion	Expelled
1862	Jesse D. Bright (D–IN)	Support of rebellion	Expelled
1862	Waldo P. Johnson (D–MO)	Support of rebellion	Expelled
1862	James F. Simmons (R–RI)[8]	Corruption	Resigned
1873	James W. Patterson (R–NH)[9]	Corruption	Term Expired
1893	William N. Roach (D–ND)[10]	Embezzlement	Not expelled
1905	John H. Mitchell (R–OR)[11]	Corruption	Not expelled
1906	Joseph R. Burton (R–KS)[12]	Corruption	Resigned
1907	Reed Smoot (R–UT)[13]	Mormonism	Not expelled
1919	Robert M. LaFollette (R–WI)[14]	Disloyalty	Not expelled
1922	Truman H. Newberry (R–MI)[15]	Election fraud	Resigned
1924	Burton K. Wheeler (D–MT)[16]	Conflict of interest	Not expelled
1934	John H. Overton (D–LA)[17]	Election fraud	No Senate action
	Huey P. Long (D–LA)[18]	Election fraud	No Senate action
1942	William Langer (R–ND)[19]	Corruption	Not expelled
1982	Harrison A. Williams, Jr. (D–NJ)[20]	Corruption	Resigned
1995	Robert W. Packwood (D–OR)[21]	Misconduct	Resigned

Cases of Censure in the House

Year	Member	Grounds	Disposition
1798	Matthew Lyons (AF–Vermont)	Assault on another representative	Not censured
1798	Roger Griswold (F–Connecticut)	Assault on another representative	Not censured
1832	William Stanbery (JD–Ohio)	Insult to speaker	Censured
1836	Sherrod Williams (W–Kentucky)	Insult to speaker	Not censured
1838	Henry A. Wise (TD–Virginia)	Acted as Second in Duel	Not censured
1839	Alexander Duncan (W–Ohio)	Offensive Publication	Not censured
1842	John Quincy Adams (W–Mass.)	Treasonable Petition	Not censured
	Joshua R. Giddings (W–Ohio)	Offensive Paper	Censured
1856	Henry A. Edmundson (D–Virginia)	Complicity in Assault on a U.S. senator	Not censured
	Laurence M. Keitt (D–S.C.)[1]	Complicity in Assault on a U.S. senator	Censured
1860	George S. Houston (D–Alabama)	Insult to representative	Not censured
1864	Alexander Long (D–Ohio)	Treasonable utterance	Censured
	Benjamin G. Harris (D–Maryland)	Treasonable utterance	Censured
1866	John W. Chanler (D–New York)	Insult to House	Censured
	Lovell H. Rousseau (R–Kentucky)	Assault on another representative	Censured
1867	John W. Hunter (I–New York)	Insult to representative	Censured
1868	Fernando Wood (D–New York)	Offensive utterance	Censured
	E. D. Holbrook (D–Idaho)[22]	Offensive utterance	Censured
1870	Benjamin F. Whittemore (R–S.C.)	Corruption	Censured
	Roderick R. Butler (R–Tennessee)	Corruption	Censured
	John T. Deweese (D–North Carolina)	Corruption	Censured
1873	Oakes Ames (R–Massachusetts)	Corruption	Censured
	James Brooks (D–New York)	Corruption	Censured
1875	John Y. Brown (D–Kentucky)	Insult to representative	Censured[23]
1876	James G. Blaine (R–Maine)	Corruption	Not censured
1882	William D. Kelley (R–Pennsylvania)	Offensive utterance	Not censured
	John D. White (R–Kentucky)	Offensive utterance	Not censured
1882	John Van Voorhis (R–New York)	Offensive utterance	Not censured
1890	William D. Bynum (D–Indiana)	Offensive utterance	Censured
1921	Thomas L. Blanton (D–Texas)	Abuse of leave to print	Censured
1978	Edward R. Roybal (D–California)	Lying to House committee	Not censured[24]
1979	Charles C. Diggs, Jr. (D–Michigan)	Misuse of clerk funds	Censured
1980	Charles H. Wilson (D–California)	Financial misconduct	Censured
1983	Gerry E. Studds (D–Massachusetts)	Sexual misconduct	Censured
	Daniel B. Crane (R–Illinois)	Sexual misconduct	Censured
1990	Barney Frank (D–Massachusetts)	Discrediting house	Not censured[4]

Cases of Censure in the Senate

Year	Member	Grounds	Disposition
1811	Timothy Pickering (F–Massachusetts)	Reading confidential documents; "breach of confidence"	Censured
1844	Benjamin Tappan (D–Ohio)	Releasing confidential documents; "breach of confidence"	Censured
1850	Thomas H. Benton (D–Missouri)	Disorderly conduct	Not censured
	Henry S. Foote (U–Mississippi)	Disorderly conduct	Not censured
1902	Benjamin R. Tillman (D–S.C.)	Fighting in Senate chamber	Censured
	John L. McLaurin (D–S.C.)	Fighting in Senate chamber	Censured

(continues)

Cases of Censure in the Senate *(continued)*

Year	Member	Grounds	Disposition
1929	Hiram Bingham (R–Connecticut)	"Bringing Senate into Disrepute"	Condemned[25]
1954	Joseph R. McCarthy (R–Wisconsin)	Obstruction of legislative process	Condemned[25]
1967	Thomas J. Dodd (D–Connecticut)	Financial misconduct; Corruption	Censured
1979	Herman E. Talmadge (D–Georgia)	Financial misconduct	Denounced[26]
1990	David F. Durenberger (R–Minnesota)	Financial misconduct	Denounced[26]
1991	Alan Cranston (D–California)	Improper conduct	Reprimanded[27]

Key to Party Affiliation:
AF = Anti-Federalist
Am = American
F = Federalist
I = Independent
JD = Jacksonian Democrat
R = Republican
S = Socialist
SRD = States' Rights Democrat
TD = Tyler Democrat
U = Unionist
W = Whig

Notes

1. Brooks was threatened with expulsion for physically attacking Senator Charles Sumner (R-MA), who had made a speech attacking Brooks's cousin, Senator Andrew Pickens Butter (SC). Representatives Henry A. Edmundson (D-VA) and Laurence M. Keitt (D-SC) were threatened with censure proceedings because of their complicity in Brooks's attack. Keitt was censured, Edmundson was not.

2. Censured after expulsion move failed or was withdrawn.

3. Facing probable expulsion, Biaggi resigned from Congress on 8 August 1988.

4. Reprimanded after expulsion and censure moves failed.

5. Expulsion failed on a vote of nineteen to ten, less than the necessary two-thirds majority. At the request of the Ohio legislature, Smith resigned two weeks after the vote. (His counsel was Francis Scott Key.)

6. On 3 March 1877, the Senate reversed its decision to expel Sebastian. Because Sebastian had died in 1865, his children were paid an amount equal to his Senate salary between the time of his expulsion and the date of his death.

7. In March 1861, the Senate took no action on an initial resolution expelling Wigfall because he represented a state that had seceded from the Union. Three months later, on 10 July 1861, he was expelled for supporting the Confederacy.

8. On 14 July 1862, the Judiciary Committee reported that the charges against Simmons were essentially correct. The Senate adjourned three days later, and Simmons resigned on 15 August before the Senate could take action.

9. A Senate select committee recommended expulsion on 27 February. On 1 March, a Republican caucus decided that there was insufficient time remaining in the session to deliberate the matter. Patterson's term expired 3 March, and no further action was taken.

10. After extensive deliberation, the Senate took no action, assuming that it lacked jurisdiction over members' behavior before their election to the Senate. The alleged embezzlement had occurred thirteen years earlier.

11. Mitchell was indicted on 1 January 1905 and convicted on 5 July of that same year, during a Senate recess. Mitchell died on 8 December while his case was still on appeal and before the Senate, which had convened on 4 December, could take any action against him.

12. Burton was indicted and convicted of receiving compensation for intervening with a federal agency. When the Supreme Court upheld his conviction, he resigned rather than face expulsion.

13. After an investigation spanning two years, the Committee on Privileges and Elections reported that Smoot was not entitled to his seat because he was a leader in a religion that advocated polygamy and a union of church and state, contrary to the U.S. Constitution. By a vote of twenty-seven to forty-three, however, the Senate failed to expel him, finding that he satisfied the constitutional requirements for serving as a senator.

14. The Committee on Privileges and Elections recommended that the Senate take no action as the speech in question (a 1917 speech opposing U.S. entry into World War I) did not warrant it. The Senate agreed fifty to twenty-one.

15. On 20 March 1920, Newberry was convicted on charges of spending $3,750 to secure his Senate election. The U.S. Supreme Court overturned this decision (2 May 1921) on the grounds that the U.S. Senate exceeded its powers in attempting to regulate primary elections. By a vote of forty-six to forty-one (12 January 1922), the Senate declared Newberry to have been duly elected in 1918. On 18 November, two days before the start of the third session of the Sixty-seventh Congress, Newberry resigned as certain members resumed their efforts to unseat him.

16. Wheeler was indicted for serving while a senator in matters in which the United States was a party. A Senate committee, however, found that his dealings related to litigation before state courts and that he received no compensation for any service before federal departments. The Senate exonerated him by a vote of fifty-six to five.

17. The Committee on Privileges and Elections concluded that the charges and evidence were insufficient to warrant further consideration.

18. The Privileges and Elections Committee considered this case in conjunction with that against Senator Overton (see footnote 17) and reached the same conclusion.

19. Recommending that this case was properly one of exclusion, not expulsion, the Committee on Privileges and Elections declared Langer guilty of moral turpitude and voted, thirteen to two, to deny him his seat. The Senate disagreed, fifty-two to thirty, arguing that the evidence was hearsay and inconclusive. Langer retained his seat.

20. The Committee on Ethics recommended that Williams be expelled because of his ethically repugnant conduct in the ABSCAM scandal, for which he was convicted of conspiracy, bribery, and conflict of interest. Prior to a Senate vote on his expulsion, Williams resigned on 11 March 1982.

21. The Committee on Ethics recommended that Packwood be expelled for abuse of his power as a senator by repeatedly committing sexual misconduct and by engaging in a deliberate plan to enhance his personal financial position by seeking favors from persons who had a particular interest in legislation or issues that he could influence, as well as for seeking to obstruct and impede the committee's inquiries by withholding, altering, and destroying relevant evidence. On 7 September 1995, the day after the committee issued its recommendation, Packwood announced his resignation without specifying an effective date. On 8 September he indicated that he would resign effective 1 October 1995.

22. Holbrook was a territorial delegate, not a representative.

23. The House later rescinded part of the censure resolution against Brown.

24. Roybal was reprimanded after the censure motion failed and was withdrawn.

25. In the cases of Bingham and McCarthy, "condemned" carries the same weight as "censured."

26. In the cases of Talmadge and Durenberger, "denounced" carries the same weight as "censured."

27. The Senate Ethics Committee reprimanded Cranston on behalf of the full Senate, after determining that it lacked the authority to issue a censure order in the same manner. The reprimand was delivered on the floor of the U.S. Senate by committee leaders, but there was not vote or formal action by the full Senate. It is the first use of the punishment of "reprimand" in the U.S. Senate's history.

References: U.S. Congress, Senate, Committee on Rules and Administration, *Senate Election, Expulsion and Censure Cases from 1793 to 1972,* Senate Document No. 92-7, 92nd Congress, 1st Session, 1972; *Congress A to Z: CQ's Encyclopedia of American Government* (Washington, DC: Congressional Quarterly, 1993), 462–465.

APPENDIX TWO

Senate Cases Involving Qualifications for Membership

According to the rules of the U.S. House and Senate, the members themselves may establish regulations for who may sit in those bodies. Over the 200-year history of the U.S. Congress, several members have had their qualifications for membership questioned and investigated. The following lists these members, with the grounds for potential disqualification, and the disposition of their cases.

Congress	Year	Member-elect	Grounds	Disposition
3rd	1793	Albert Gallatin (D-Penn.)	Questioned Citizenship	Excluded
11th	1809	Stanley Griswold (D-Ohio)	Questioned Residence	Admitted
28th	1844	John M. Niles (D-Conn.)	Sanity	Admitted
31st	1849	James Shields (D-Illinois)	Citizenship	Excluded
37th	1861	Benjamin Stark (D-Oregon)	Loyalty	Admitted
40th	1867	Philip F. Thomas (D-Maryland)	Loyalty	Excluded
41st	1870	Hiram R. Revels (D-Mississippi)	Citizenship	Admitted
41st	1870	Adelbert Ames (R-Mississippi)	Residence	Admitted
59th	1907	Reed Smoot (R-Utah)	Mormonism	Admitted[1]
69th	1926	Arthur R. Gould (R-Maine)	Character	Admitted
74th	1935	Rush D. Holt (D-West Virginia)	Age	Admitted
75th	1937	George L. Berry (D-Tennessee)	Character	Admitted
77th	1942	William Langer (R-North Dakota)	Character	Admitted
80th	1947	Theodore G. Bilbo (D-Miss.)	Character	None[2]

Footnotes:
1. The Senate decided that a two-thirds majority, as in expulsion cases, would be required to exclude a senator from being seated in this case.
2. Bilbo died before the Senate could act.

References: U.S. Congress, Senate, Committee on Rules and Administration, Subcommittee on Privileges and Elections, *Senate Election, Expulsion and Censure Cases from 1793 to 1972* (Washington, DC: Government Printing Office, 1972); Congressional Quarterly, *Congressional Ethics* (Washington, D.C.: Congressional Quarterly, 1980), 152.

APPENDIX THREE

Independent Counsel Investigations, 1979–1999

Independent Counsel	Subject(s)	Result(s)	Cost
Arthur H. Christy (29 November 1979)	Hamilton Jordan	No charges	$182,000
Gerard J. Gallinghouse (9 September 1980)	Timothy Kraft	No charges	$3,300
Leon Silverman (29 December 1981)	Raymond Donovan	No charges	$326,000
Jacob A. Stein (2 April 1984)	Edwin Meese III	No charges	$312,000
James C. McKay (23 April 1986) Alexia Morrison (29 May 1986)	Theodore B. Olson	No charges	$2.1 million
Whitney N. Seymour, Jr. (29 May 1986)	Michael K. Deaver	1 Guilty plea	$1.6 million
Lawrence E. Walsh (19 December 1986)—(Iran Contra Scandal)	Elliott Abrams, Carl Channell, Alan Fiers, Albert Hakim, Robert McFarlane, Richard Miller, Richard Secord, Thomas Clines, John Poindexter, Oliver North, Clair George, Duane Clarridge, Joseph Fernandez, Caspar Weinberger	7 Guilty pleas, 4 Convictions (2 Overturned on Appeal), 6 Presidential Pardons	$47.4 million
James C. McKay (2 February 1987)	Lyn Nofziger, Edwin Meese III	1 Conviction (Overturned on appeal), 1 Acquittal	$2.8 million
Carl Rauh (19 December 1986) James R. Harper (17 August 1987)	Investigated finances of former Assistant Attorney General W. Lawrence Wallace	No charges	$50,000
Sealed (31 May 1989)	Confidential	Confidential	$15,000
Arlin M. Adams (1 March 1990)—(HUD Scandal) Larry D. Thompson (3 July 1995)	Samuel Pierce, Deborah Dean, Tom Demery, Phillip Winn, S. DeBartolomeis, Lance	7 Guilty pleas, 11 Convictions, 1 Acquittal	$27.1 million

(continues)

Independent Counsel	Subject(s)	Result(s)	Cost
	Wilson, Carlos Figueroa, J. Queenan, Ronald Mahon, Catalina Villapando, Robert Olson, Len Briscoe, Maurice Steier, Elaine Richardson, Sam Singletary, Victor Cruise		
Sealed (19 April 1991)	Confidential	Confidential	$93,000
Joseph diGenova (14 December 1992) Michael F. Zeldin (11 January 1996)	Janet Mullins, Margaret Tutwiler	No charges	$3.2 million
Robert B. Fiske, Jr. (21 January 1994)	William Clinton et al.	3 Guilty pleas	$6.1 million
Kenneth W. Starr (5 August 1994) Robert Ray	William Clinton et al.	6 Guilty pleas, 3 Conviction, 2 Acquittals, Impeachment Report sent to Congress	$52 million
Donald C. Smaltz (9 September 1994)	Michael Espy	1 Guilty plea, 2 Convictions, 2 Acquittals	$11.9 million
David M. Barrett (24 May 1995)	Henry G. Cisneros et al.	Presidential pardon	$3.8 million
Daniel S. Pearson (6 July 1995)	Ronald H. Brown	Terminated (subject deceased)	$3.2 million
Sealed (27 November 1996)	Confidential	Confidential	$48,784
Carol Elder Bruce (19 March 1998)	Bruce Babbitt	No charges	Unknown or Not Released
Ralph I. Lancaster, Jr. (1998)	Alexis Herman	No charges	Not Released
John C. Danforth (9 September 1999)*	Government Assault on Branch Davidian Compound in Waco, Texas	No charges	Not Released

Footnote:
*Because the Independent Counsel Act had expired, Attorney General Janet Reno herself named Danforth "special counsel," and not an independent counsel.

References: Office of the Independent Counsel, Washington, D.C.; "Clinton Probes Cost $60 Million; Total Counsel Costs for Administration Top $110 Million," *Washington Post,* 31 March 2001, A10.

APPENDIX FOUR

House Cases Involving Qualifications for Membership

Just like the Senate, the House of Representatives has had many cases in which members' qualifications to hold their seats have been challenged. The following table highlights these cases, with the year, the member, the grounds, and what happened to that member's case.

Congress	Year	Member–elect	Grounds	Disposition
1st	1789	William L. Smith (Fed.–S.C.)	Questionable citizenship	Admitted
10th	1807	Philip B. Key (Fed.–Maryland)	Questionable residence	Admitted
10th	1807	William McCreery (R–Md.)	Questionable residence	Admitted
18th	1823	Gabriel Richard (I–Mich. Terr.)	Questionable citizenship	Admitted
18th	1823	John Bailey (I–Massachusetts)	Questionable residence	Excluded
18th	1823	John Forsyth (D–Georgia)	Questionable residence	Admitted
27th	1841	David Y. Levy (R–Fla. Terr.)	Questionable citizenship	Admitted
36th	1857	John Y. Brown (D–Kentucky)	Age	Admitted
40th	1867	William H. Hooper (D–Utah Terr.)	Mormonism	Admitted
40th	1867	Lawrence S. Trimble (D–Kentucky)	Loyalty	Admitted
40th	1867	John Y. Brown (D–Kentucky)	Loyalty	Excluded
40th	1867	John D. Young (D–Kentucky)	Loyalty	Excluded
40th	1867	Roderick R. Butler (R–Tennessee)	Loyalty	Admitted
40th	1867	John A. Wimpy (I–Georgia)	Loyalty	Excluded
40th	1867	W.D. Simpson (I–S.C.)	Loyalty	Excluded
41st	1869	John M. Rice (D–Kentucky)	Loyalty	Admitted
41st	1870	Lewis McKenzie (U–Virginia)	Loyalty	Admitted
41st	1870	George W. Booker (C–Virginia)	Loyalty	Admitted
41st	1870	Benjamin F. Whittemore (R–S.C.)	Malfeasance	Excluded
41st	1870	John C. Conner (D–Texas)	Misconduct	Admitted
43rd	1873	George Q. Cannon (R–Utah Terr.)	Mormonism	Admitted
43rd	1873	George Q. Cannon (R–Utah Terr.)	Polygamy	Admitted
47th	1881	John S. Barbour (D–Virginia)	Questionable residence	Admitted
47th	1881	George Q. Cannon (R–Utah Terr.)	Polygamy	Seat Vacated[1]
50th	1887	James B. White (R–Indiana)	Questionable citizenship	Admitted
56th	1899	Robert W. Wilcox (I–Hawaii Terr.)	Bigamy, Treason	Admitted
56th	1900	Brigham H. Roberts (D–Utah)	Polygamy	Excluded
59th	1905	Anthony Michalek (R–Illinois)	Questionable citizenship	Admitted
66th	1919	Victor L. Berger (Soc.–Wisconsin)	Sedition	Excluded
66th	1919	Victor L. Berger (Soc.–Wisconsin)	Sedition	Excluded
69th	1926	John W. Langley (R–Kentucky)	Criminal misconduct	Resigned

(continues)

Congress	Year	Member–elect	Grounds	Disposition
70th	1927	James M. Beck (R–Pennsylvania)	Questionable residence	Admitted
70th	1929	Ruth B. Owen (D–Florida)	Questionable residence	Admitted
90th	1967	Adam Clayton Powell, Jr. (D–N.Y.)	Misconduct	Excluded[2]
96th	1979	Richard A. Tonry (D–Louisiana)	Vote fraud	Resigned

Footnotes

1. Discussions on Mormonism and polygamy led to a debate and to a declaration that Cannon's seat was vacant.
2. The U.S. Supreme Court held in *Powell v. McCormack* that the House had improperly excluded Powell and ordered his reinstatement.

References: Hinds, Asher Crosby, *Hinds' Precedents of the House of Representatives of the United States, Including References to Provisions of the Constitution, the Laws, and Decisions of the United States Senate,* 8 vols. (Washington, DC: Government Printing Office, 1907); *Congressional Ethics* (Washington, DC: Congressional Quarterly, 1980), 18–19.

APPENDIX FIVE

United States Senators Tried and Convicted and Tried and Acquitted, 1806–1981

The following listing examines the cases of those U.S. Senators who were tried in criminal courts for crimes, some relating to corruption, others not. The table shows the name of the member, the date of conviction or acquittal, and the resolution of his case.

Senator	Date Acquitted	Date Convicted	Resolution of Case
John Smith (D–Ohio)	1806		Later subject of Senate Expulsion action, which failed. Resigned seat on 25 April 1808.
Charles H. Dietrich (R–Nebraska)	1904[1]		Left the Senate 3 March 1905 at end of term.
John H. Mitchell (R–Oregon)		1905	Died 8 December 1905, pending appeal.
Joseph R. Burton (R–Kansas)		1905	Resigned seat in June 1906 after the U.S. Supreme Court upheld his conviction.
Truman Newberry (R–Michigan)		1920	U.S. Supreme Court reversed conviction, May 1921, but Newberry resigned from Senate November 1922.
Burton K. Wheeler (D–Montana)	1924		Acquitted of bribery charge. Returned to Senate seat.
Edward J. Gurney (R–Florida)	1975/76[2]		Had resigned seat 31 December 1974.
Harrison A. Williams (D–New Jersey)		1981	Resigned his seat, 11 March 1982, after it appeared that he would be expelled.

Footnotes:

1. Charges were dropped on a technicality.

2. Gurney was indicted in April 1974 for election law violations. This indictment was dismissed in May 1974. He was indicted in July 1974 on charges of bribery and perjury, and Gurney resigned his Senate seat. He was acquitted of the bribery solicitation charge in August 1975, and on the perjury charge in October 1976.

Reference: Congressional Ethics (Washington, DC: Congressional Quarterly, 1980), 18–19.

APPENDIX SIX

United States Governors in Ethical Trouble—
Impeachments, Crimes, and Convictions, 1851–Present

Governors have also had a long record of criminal mischief no different from their counterparts in the U.S. Congress. Although previous appendices examined only those members of Congress who were actually tried for their crimes, this specific appendix broadly examines all sitting or former governors who were merely accused of criminal activity. It includes the state they served, whether they were impeached, whether they were criminally charged in a court of law, and the disposition of their cases.

Governor	State	Year	State Action	Criminally Charged?	Outcome
John A. Quitman	Mississippi	1851	None	Yes	Resigned[1]
Charles Robinson	Kansas	1862	Impeached	No	Acquitted
Harrison Reed	Florida	1868	Impeached	No	Acquitted
William W. Holden	North Carolina	1870	Impeached	No	Convicted and removed
Powell Clayton	Arkansas	1871	Impeached	No	Acquitted
David C. Butler	Nebraska	1871	Impeached	No	Convicted and removed
Henry C. Warmoth	Louisiana	1872	Impeached	No	Term Ended
Harrison Reed	Florida	1872	Impeached	No	Acquitted
Adelbert Ames	Mississippi	1876	Impeached	No	Resigned
Alexander Davis	Mississippi	1876	Impeached	No	Convicted and removed
William P. Kellogg	Louisiana	1876	Impeached	No	Acquitted
William Sulzer	New York	1913	Impeached	No	Convicted and removed
James Ferguson	Texas	1917	Impeached	No	Convicted and Resigned
Lynn J. Frazier	North Dakota	1921	Not impeached	No	Recalled by voters
John C. Walton	Oklahoma	1923	Impeached	No	Convicted and removed
Warren T. McCray	Indiana	1924	Not impeached	Yes	Resigned[2]
Edward F. Jackson	Indiana	1928	Not impeached	Yes	Finished term[3]
Henry S. Johnston	Oklahoma	1928	Impeached	No	Acquitted
Henry S. Johnston	Oklahoma	1929	Impeached	No	Convicted and removed
Huey P. Long	Louisiana	1929	Impeached	No	Acquitted
Henry Horton	Tennessee	1931	Impeached	No	Acquitted
William L. Langer	North Dakota	1934	Not impeached	Yes	Removed from office[4]
Thomas L. Moodie	North Dakota	1935	Not impeached	No	Removed from office[5]
Richard Leche	Louisiana	1939	Not impeached	No	Resigned[6]
J. Howard Pyle	Arizona	1955	Not impeached	No	Term ended[7]
Arch A. Moore, Jr.	West Virginia	1975	Not impeached	Yes	Acquitted[8]
Marvin Mandel	Maryland	1979	Not impeached	Yes	Removed from office[9]
Edwin Edwards	Louisiana	1985	Not impeached	Yes	

(continues)

Governor	State	Year	State Action	Criminally Charged?	Outcome
Evan Mecham	Arizona	1988	Impeached	Yes	Convicted and removed[10]
Guy Hunt	Alabama	1992	Not impeached	Yes	Resigned[11]
David Walters	Oklahoma	1993	Not impeached	Yes	
J. Fife Symington	Arizona	1997	Not impeached	Yes	Resigned[12]
Edwin Edwards	Louisiana	2000	Not impeached[13]	Yes	Out of office[14]

Footnotes:

1. Quitman resigned on 3 February 1851 after he was indicted on charges of violating U.S. neutrality laws by collaborating with a Cuban insurrection against Spain. He was later acquitted of all charges.

2. McCray resigned following his conviction for mail fraud.

3. Jackson was tried after leaving office on charges of conspiracy to bribe an official, but was cleared only because the statute of limitations had expired.

4. Langer was removed from office by the North Dakota state supreme court after he was indicted for various crimes, including soliciting funds from federal employees which he then used for his personal spending. He was tried four times with three hung juries before being acquitted on all charges in 1936. He later ran again for governor in 1936 as an Independent and was elected.

5. Moodie was found to have been a citizen of another state when he ran for governor of North Dakota. He was removed from office by the North Dakota state supreme court after serving just thirteen months in office.

6. Leche was threatened with impeachment, forcing his resignation.

7. A recall petition against Pyle was certified, but Pyle's term expired before a recall election could be held.

8. Moore was indicted in 1975 on charges of extortion, but acquitted in 1976. He pled guilty in 1990 to federal corruption charges.

9. Mandel was removed after he was tried and convicted on charges of federal mail fraud and bribery.

10. Mecham was impeached on charges that he accepted a loan for his business, charges unrelated to his term in office, but he was convicted and removed. He stood trial in 1988 and, with his brother Willard, was acquitted on all charges.

11. Indicted on 28 December 1992, on charges of taking more than $200,000 from his 1987 inaugural fund for personal uses, Hunt was convicted in April 1993. He then resigned his office.

12. Symington was convicted in 1997 on charges that prior to becoming governor he had used his influence to get loans that he should have been denied. He resigned the same day of his conviction. An appeals court later overturned his conviction, and in January 2001 Symington was pardoned by President Bill Clinton.

13. Edwards had already left office when he was indicted and tried.

14. Edwards was convicted of nine charges relating to kickbacks on 9 May 2000, and sentenced to ten years in prison.

APPENDIX SEVEN

Impeachments of Federal Officials, 1799–1999

The Senate has sat as a court of impeachment in the following cases:

William Blount, senator from Tennessee; charges dismissed for want of jurisdiction, 14 January 1799.

John Pickering, judge of the U.S. District Court for New Hampshire; removed from office 12 March 1804.

Samuel Chase, associate justice of the Supreme Court; acquitted 1 March 1805.

James H. Peck, judge of the U.S. District Court for Missouri; acquitted 31 January 1831.

West H. Humphreys, judge of the U.S. District Court for the Middle, Eastern, and Western Districts of Tennessee; removed from office 26 June 1862.

Andrew Johnson, president of the United States; acquitted 26 May 1868.

William W. Belknap, secretary of war; acquitted 1 August 1876.

Charles Swayne, judge of the U.S. District Court for the Northern District of Florida; acquitted 27 February 1905.

Robert W. Archbald, associate judge of the U.S. Commerce Court; removed 13 January 1913.

George W. English, judge of the U.S. District Court for the Eastern District of Illinois; resigned 4 November 1926, proceedings dismissed.

Harold Louderback, judge of the U.S. District Court for the Northern District of California; acquitted 24 May 1933.

Halsted L. Ritter, judge of the U.S. District Court for the Southern District of Florida; removed from office 17 April 1936.

Harry E. Claiborne, judge of the U.S. District Court for the District of Nevada; removed from office 9 October 1986.

Alcee L. Hastings, judge of the U.S. District Court for the Southern District of Florida; removed from office 20 October 1989.

Walter L. Nixon, Judge of the U.S. District Court for Mississippi; removed from office 3 November 1989.

William Jefferson Clinton, president of the United States; acquitted 12 February 1999.

Footnote:
The procedure for the impeachment of Federal officials is detailed in Article I, Section 3, of the Constitution.

APPENDIX EIGHT

Rules of Procedure and Practice in the Senate when Sitting on Impeachment Trials

[Revised pursuant to Senate Resolution 479, 99–2, 16 August 1986.]

I. Whensoever the Senate shall receive notice from the House of Representatives that managers are appointed on their part to conduct an impeachment against any person and are directed to carry articles of impeachment to the Senate, the Secretary of the Senate shall immediately inform the House of Representatives that the Senate is ready to receive the managers for the purpose of exhibiting such articles of impeachment, agreeably to such notice.

II. When the managers of an impeachment shall be introduced at the bar of the Senate and shall signify that they are ready to exhibit articles of impeachment against any person, the Presiding Officer of the Senate shall direct the Sergeant at Arms to make proclamation, who shall, after making proclamation, repeat the following words, viz: "All persons are commanded to keep silence, on pain of imprisonment, while the House of Representatives is exhibiting to the Senate of the United States articles of impeachment against_____"; after which the articles shall be exhibited, and then the Presiding Officer of the Senate shall inform the managers that the Senate will take proper order on the subject of the impeachment, of which due notice shall be given to the House of Representatives.

III. Upon such articles being presented to the Senate, the Senate shall, at 1 o'clock afternoon of the day (Sunday excepted) following such presentation, or sooner if ordered by the Senate, proceed to the consideration of such articles and shall continue in session from day to day (Sundays excepted) after the trial shall commence (unless otherwise ordered by the Senate) until final judgment shall be rendered, and so much longer as may, in its judgment, be needful. Before proceeding to the consideration of the articles of impeachment, the Presiding Officer shall administer the oath hereinafter provided to the members of the Senate then present and to the other members of the Senate as they shall appear, whose duty it shall be to take the same.

IV. When the President of the United States or the Vice President of the United States, upon whom the powers and duties of the Office of President shall have devolved, shall be impeached, the Chief Justice of the United States shall preside; and in a case requiring the said Chief Justice to preside notice shall be given to him by the Presiding Officer of the Senate of the time and place fixed for the consideration of the articles of impeachment, as aforesaid, with a request to attend; and the said Chief Justice shall be administered the oath by the Presiding Officer of the Senate and shall preside over the Senate during the consideration of said articles and upon the trial of the person impeached therein.

V. The Presiding Officer shall have power to make and issue, by himself or by the Secretary of the Senate, all orders, mandates, writs, and precepts authorized by these rules or by the Senate, and to make and enforce such other regulations and orders in the premises as the Senate may authorize or provide.

VI. The Senate shall have power to compel the attendance of witnesses, to enforce obedience to its orders, mandates, writs, precepts, and judgments, to preserve order, and to punish in a summary way contempts of, and disobedience to, its authority, orders, mandates, writs, precepts, or judgments, and to make all lawful orders, rules, and regulations which it may deem essential or conducive to the ends of justice. And the Sergeant at Arms, under the direction of the Senate, may employ such aid and assistance as may be necessary to enforce, execute, and carry into effect the lawful orders, mandates, writs, and precepts of the Senate.

VII. The Presiding Officer of the Senate shall direct all necessary preparations in the Senate Chamber, and the Presiding Officer on the trial shall direct all the forms of proceedings while the Senate is sitting for the purpose of trying an impeachment, and all forms during the trial not otherwise specially provided for. And the Presiding Officer on the trial may rule on all questions of evidence including, but not limited to, questions of relevancy, materiality, and redundancy of evidence and incidental questions, which ruling shall stand as the judgment of the Senate, unless some Member of the Senate shall ask that a formal vote be taken thereon, in which case it shall be submitted to the Senate for decision without debate; or he may at his option, in the first instance, submit any such question to a vote of the Members of the Senate. Upon all such questions the vote shall be taken in accordance with the Standing Rules of the Senate.

VIII.Upon the presentation of articles of impeachment and the organization of the Senate as hereinbefore provided, a writ of summons shall issue to the person impeached, reciting said articles, and notifying him to appear before the Senate upon a day and at a place to be fixed by the Senate and named in such writ, and file his answer to said articles of impeachment, and to stand to and abide the orders and judgments of the Senate thereon; which writ shall be served by such officer or person as shall be named in the precept thereof, such number of days prior to the day fixed for such appearance as shall be named in such precept, either by the delivery of an attested copy thereof to the person impeached, or if that can not conveniently be done, by leaving such copy at the last known place of abode of such person, or at his usual place of business in some conspicuous place therein; or if such service shall be, in the judgment of the Senate, impracticable, notice to the person impeached to appear shall be given in such other manner, by publication or otherwise, as shall be deemed just; and if the writ aforesaid shall fail of service in the manner aforesaid, the proceedings shall not thereby abate, but further service may be made in such manner as the Senate shall direct. If the person impeached, after service, shall fail to appear, either in person or by attorney, on the day so fixed therefor as aforesaid, or, appearing, shall fail to file his answer to such articles of impeachment, the trial shall proceed, nevertheless, as upon a plea of not guilty. If a plea of guilty shall be entered, judgment may be entered thereon without further proceedings.

IX.At 12:30 o'clock afternoon of the day appointed for the return of the summons against the person impeached, the legislative and executive business of the Senate shall be suspended, and the Secretary of the Senate shall administer an oath to the returning officer in the form following, viz:

"I,_____, do solemnly swear that the return made by me upon the process issued on the___day of___, by the Senate of the United States, against_____, is truly made, and that I have performed such service as therein described: So help me God." Which oath shall be entered at large on the records.

X.The person impeached shall then be called to appear and answer the articles of impeachment against him. If he appears, or any person for him, the appearance shall be recorded, stating particularly if by himself, or by agent or attorney, naming the person appearing and the capacity in which he appears. If he does not appear, either personally or by agent or attorney, the same shall be recorded.

XI.That in the trial of any impeachment the Presiding Officer of the Senate, if the Senate so orders, shall appoint a committee of Senators to receive evidence and take testimony at such times and places as the committee may determine, and for such purpose the committee so appointed and the chairman thereof, to be elected by the committee, shall unless otherwise ordered by the Senate, exercise all the powers and functions conferred upon the Senate and the Presiding Officer of the Senate, respectively, under the rules of procedure and practice in the Senate when sitting on impeachment trials. Unless otherwise ordered by the Senate, the rules of procedure and practice in the Senate when sitting on impeachment trials shall govern the procedure and practice of the committee so appointed. The committee so appointed shall report to the Senate in writing a certified copy of the transcript of the proceedings and testimony had and given before such committee, and such report shall be received by the Senate and the evidence so received and the testimony so taken shall be considered to all intents and purposes, subject to the right of the Senate to determine competency, relevancy, and materiality, as having been received and taken before the Senate, but nothing herein shall prevent the Senate from sending for any witness and hearing his testimony in open Senate, or by order of the Senate having the entire trial in open Senate.

XII.At 12:30 o'clock afternoon, or at such other hour as the Senate may order, of the day appointed for the trial of an impeachment, the legislative and executive business of the Senate shall be suspended, and the Secretary shall give notice to the House of Representatives that the Senate is ready to proceed upon the impeachment of_____, in the Senate Chamber.

XIII.The hour of the day at which the Senate shall sit upon the trial of an impeachment shall be (unless otherwise ordered) 12 o'clock m.; and when the hour shall arrive, the Presiding Officer upon such trial shall cause proclamation to be made, and the business of the trial shall proceed. The adjournment of the Senate sitting in said trial shall not operate as an adjournment of the Senate; but on such adjournment the Senate shall resume the consideration of its legislative and executive business.

XIV.The Secretary of the Senate shall record the proceedings in cases of impeachment as in the case of legislative proceedings, and the same shall be reported in the same manner as the legislative proceedings of the Senate.

XV.Counsel for the parties shall be admitted to appear and be heard upon an impeachment.

XVI.All motions, objections, requests, or applications whether relating to the procedure of the Senate or relating immediately to the trial (including questions with respect to admission of evidence or other questions arising during the trial) made by the parties or their counsel shall be addressed to the Presiding Officer only, and if he, or any Senator, shall require it, they shall be committed to writing, and read at the Secretary's table.

XVII.Witnesses shall be examined by one person on behalf of the party producing them, and then cross-examined by one person on the other side.

XVIII.If a Senator is called as a witness, he shall be sworn, and give his testimony standing in his place.

XIX.If a Senator wishes a question to be put to a witness, or to a manager, or to counsel of the person impeached, or to offer a motion or order (except a motion to adjourn), it shall be reduced to writing, and put by the Presiding Officer. The parties or their counsel may interpose objections to witnesses answering questions propounded at the request of any Senator and the merits of any such objection may be argued by the parties or their counsel. Ruling on any such objection shall be made as provided in Rule VII. It shall not be in order for any Senator to engage in colloquy.

XX.At all times while the Senate is sitting upon the trial of an impeachment the doors of the Senate shall be kept open, unless the Senate shall direct the doors to be closed while deliberating upon its decisions. A motion to close the doors may be acted upon without objection, or, if objection is heard, the motion shall be voted on without debate by the yeas and nays, which shall be entered on the record.

XXI.All preliminary or interlocutory questions, and all motions, shall be argued for not exceeding one hour (unless the Senate otherwise orders) on each side.

XXII. The case, on each side, shall be opened by one person. The final argument on the merits may be made by two persons on each side (unless otherwise ordered by the Senate upon application for that purpose), and the argument shall be opened and closed on the part of the House of Representatives.

XXIII. An article of impeachment shall not be divisible for the purpose of voting thereon at any time during the trial. Once voting has commenced on an article of impeachment, voting shall be continued until voting has been completed on all articles of impeachment unless the Senate adjourns for a period not to exceed one day or adjourns sine die. On the final question whether the impeachment is sustained, the yeas and nays shall be taken on each article of impeachment separately; and if the impeachment shall not, upon any of the articles presented, be sustained by the votes of two-thirds of the Members present, a judgment of acquittal shall be entered; but if the person impeached shall be convicted upon any such article by the votes of two-thirds of the Members present, the Senate shall proceed to the consideration of such other matters as may be determined to be appropriate prior to pronouncing judgment. Upon pronouncing judgment, a certified copy of such judgment shall be deposited in the office of the Secretary of State. A motion to reconsider the vote by which any article of impeachment is sustained or rejected shall not be in order.

FORM OF PUTTING THE QUESTION ON EACH ARTICLE OF IMPEACHMENT.

The Presiding Officer shall first state the question; thereafter each Senator, as his name is called, shall rise in his place and answer: guilty or not guilty.

XXIV. All the orders and decisions may be acted upon without objection, or, if objection is heard, the orders and decisions shall be voted on without debate by yeas and nays, which shall be entered on the record, subject, however, to the operation of Rule VII, except when the doors shall be closed for deliberation, and in that case no member shall speak more than once on one question, and for not more than ten minutes on an interlocutory question, and for not more than fifteen minutes on the final question, unless by consent of the Senate, to be had without debate; but a motion to adjourn may be decided without the yeas and nays, unless they be demanded by one-fifth of the members present. The fifteen minutes herein allowed shall be for the whole deliberation on the final question, and not on the final question on each article of impeachment.

XXV.Witnesses shall be sworn in the following form, viz: "You,_____, do swear (or affirm, as the case may be) that the evidence you shall give in the case now pending between the United States and_____, shall be the truth, the whole truth, and nothing but the truth: So help you God." Which oath shall be administered by the Secretary, or any other duly authorized person.

FORM OF A SUBPOENA BE ISSUED ON THE APPLICATION OF THE MANAGERS OF THE IMPEACHMENT, OR OF THE PARTY IMPEACHED, OR OF HIS COUNSEL.

To_____, greeting:

You and each of you are hereby commanded to appear before the Senate of the United States, on the___day of___, at the Senate Chamber in the city of Washington, then and there to testify your knowledge in the cause which is before the Senate in which the House of Representatives have impeached_____.

Fail not.

Witness_____, and Presiding Officer of the Senate, at the city of Washington, this___day of___, in the year of our Lord_____, and of the Independence of the United States the_____.

_____,[signed]

Presiding Officer of the Senate.

FORM OF DIRECTION FOR THE SERVICE OF SAID SUBPOENA

The Senate of the United States to_____, greeting: You are hereby commanded to serve and return the within subpoena according to law.

Dated at Washington, this___day of___, in the year of our Lord___, and of the Independence of the United States the_____.

_____,[signed]

Secretary of the Senate.

FORM OF OATH TO BE ADMINISTERED TO THE MEMBERS OF THE SENATE AND THE PRESIDING OFFICER SITTING IN THE TRIAL OF IMPEACHMENTS

"I solemnly swear (or affirm, as the case may be) that in all things appertaining to the trial of the impeachment of_____, now pending, I will do impartial justice according to the Constitution and laws: So help me God."

FORM OF SUMMONS TO BE ISSUED AND SERVED UPON THE PERSON IMPEACHED

The United States of America, ss:

The Senate of the United States to_____, greeting:

Whereas the House of Representatives of the United States of America did, on the___day of___, exhibit to the Senate articles of impeachment against you, the said_____, in the words following:

[Here insert the articles]

And demand that you, the said_____, should be put to answer the accusations as set forth in said articles, and that such proceedings, examinations, trials, and judgments might be thereupon had as are agreeable to law and justice. You, the said_____, are therefore hereby summoned to be and appear before the Senate of the United States of America, at their Chamber in the city of Washington, on the___day of___, at___o'clock___, then and there to answer to the said articles of impeachment, and then and there to abide by, obey, and perform such orders, directions, and judgments as the Senate of the United States shall make in the premises according to the Constitution and laws of the United States.

Hereof you are not to fail.

Witness_____, and Presiding Officer of the said Senate, at the city of Washington, this___day of___, in the year of our Lord____, and of the Independence of the United States the____.

_____,[signed]

Presiding Officer of the Senate.

FORM OF PRECEPT TO BE INDORSED ON SAID WRIT OF SUMMONS

The United States of America, ss:

The Senate of the United States to_____, greeting:

You are hereby commanded to deliver to and leave with_____, if conveniently to be found, or if not, to leave at his usual place of abode, or at his usual place of business in some conspicuous place, a true and attested copy of the within writ of summons, together with a like copy of this precept; and in whichsoever way you perform the service, let it be done at least___days before the appearance day mentioned in the said writ of summons.

Fail not, and make return of this writ of summons and precept, with your proceedings thereon indorsed, on or before the appearance day mentioned in the said writ of summons.

Witness_____, and Presiding Officer of the Senate, at the city of Washington, this___day of___, in the year of our Lord____, and of the Independence of the United States the____.

_____,[signed]

Presiding Officer of the Senate.

All process shall be served by the Sergeant at Arms of the Senate, unless otherwise ordered by the Senate.

XXVI. If the Senate shall at any time fail to sit for the consideration of articles of impeachment on the day or hour fixed therefor, the Senate may, by an order to be adopted without debate, fix a day and hour for resuming such consideration.

CHRONOLOGY

1635

April   The first impeachment in the English colonies occurs. Governor John Harvey of Virginia is informed by the House of Burgesses that he is being impeached according to provisions established by Parliament in London for his Indian, land-grant, and trade policies. No corruption is alleged, but this "petition of grievances" leads to Harvey's departure from the colony and return to London in disgrace. No impeachment trial is ever held.

1649

22 May   The first fraudulent campaign law in the British colonies is passed. The General Court in Warwick, Rhode Island, enacts the law, which provides that "no one should bring into any votes that he did not receive from the voter's own hands, and that all votes should be filed by the Recorder in the presence of the Assembly."

1685

Nicolas More, chief justice of Philadelphia, is impeached by the Pennsylvania Assembly on ten charges, among them "assuming himself an unlimited and arbitrary power in office." He is convicted and removed from office on 2 June 1685, but the council in London overseeing the colony refuses to sanction the proceedings or the removal.

1757

During his race for a seat in the Virginia House of Burgesses, George Washington is questioned about the spending of money by his campaign. Washington reportedly bought wine and spirits for the few hundred constituents in his district.

1795

28 December   Robert Randall and Charles Whitney are taken into custody for attempting to bribe several congressmen. Whitney would be discharged on 7 January 1796, before he could stand trial; however, on 6 January, Randall is tried in Congress and found guilty of contempt and breach of the privileges of Congress, reprimanded by the Speaker of the House, Jonathan Dayton of New Jersey, and committed to the custody of the sergeant at arms. On 13 January his petition to be discharged is granted, after he pays a fine.

1795–1796

The U.S. House of Representatives is asked to investigate Judge George Turner of St. Clair, in the Ohio Territory, for unspecified crimes.

1797

The House committee investigating Judge George Turner recommends further proceedings, but Turner resigns. A new judge, Jonathan Return Meigs, is named to his vacant post on 12 February 1798.

July   President John Adams sends a message to the U.S. Senate, describing in detail alleged charges against Senator William Blount of Tennessee. Based on Adams's letter, the Senate votes to expel Blount by a vote of twenty-five to one.

1798

29 January   Former U.S. Senator William Blount of Tennessee is impeached by the U.S. House of Representatives for assisting in a "military expedition against Spanish Florida and [the] Louisiana Territories, [and] interference with [an] Indian agent," among other crimes.

1799

11 January   The U.S. Senate votes fourteen to eleven that U.S. Senator William Blount of Tennessee is not a civil officer of the government subject to the

impeachment power and dismisses all charges against him.

1800
The U.S. House of Representatives debates a measure of censure against President John Adams, criticizing him for communicating with a judge, which is found to be a "dangerous interference of the Executive with Judicial decisions," but the censure motion is not passed.

1803
30 December   The U.S. House of Representatives votes to impeach John Pickering, judge for the federal district of New Hampshire, for tyrannical conduct and drunkenness.

1804
The U.S. House of Representatives investigates whether to bring impeachment articles against Judge Richard Peters for misconduct in the so-called Sedition Trials. In the end, the House finds that such articles are not warranted.

12 March   The U.S. Senate votes nineteen to seven to convict Judge John Pickering of all four impeachment articles against him and then votes twenty to six to remove him from office. Pickering becomes the first federal judge in the United States to be impeached and removed from office.

4 December   The U.S. House of Representatives votes to impeach Samuel Chase, associate justice of the Supreme Court of the United States, for "conduct[ing] himself in a manner highly arbitrary, oppressive, and unjust" during a trial he sat on, and for other crimes, totaling eight articles.

1805
1 March   The U.S. Senate fails to reach a two-thirds vote on any of the impeachment articles against Associate Justice Samuel Chase, leading to Chase's acquittal.

1807–1808
The U.S. House of Representatives investigates whether Judge Harry Innis plotted with Spain "to seduce Kentucky from the Union," but absolves Innis of all charges.

1808
11 April   A resolution of the U.S. House of Representatives orders Delegate George Poindexter, from the Mississippi Territory, to investigate allegations against Judge Peter B. Bruin, presiding judge of the territory.

1809
7 March   The investigation against Judge Peter B. Bruin ends when Francis Xavier Martin is named to replace Bruin on the bench. No explanation is found in the records whether Bruin died or resigned.

1811
16 December   The Speaker of the Mississippi House of Representatives, Cowles Mead, sends a letter to the U.S. House, asking for Judge Harry Toulmin, judge of the superior court for the Washington District of Mississippi, to be impeached and removed from office, after a grand jury in Mississippi brings an indictment against Toulmin for alleged malfeasance in office. Delegate George Poindexter, from the Mississippi Territory, is asked to head up a panel to look into potential impeachment proceedings.

1812
21 May   The panel headed up by Delegate George Poindexter finds no impeachable offenses committed by Judge Harry Toulmin and asks that the House investigation into the judge be closed.

1818
The U.S. House of Representatives opens an inquiry into the conduct of Judges William P. Van Ness and Mathias B. Tallmadge of the district court of New York and William Stephens, judge of the district court of Georgia. Under pressure, Stephens resigns, and he is dismissed from any further proceedings. Representative John C. Spencer of New York is ordered to make an inquiry into potential impeachable offenses. Immediately, Spencer finds that the complaints against Van Ness relate to his judicial opinions, and it is agreed that any inquiry into his case should be dismissed immediately.

1819
17 February   Representative John C. Spencer of New York reports that while Judge Mathias B. Tallmadge of New York had not held court on the dates he was instructed to by law, this was not an impeachable offense, and asks for and end to the inquiry against Tallmadge.

1822–1823
The U.S. House of Representatives investigates charges of improper court conduct against Judge Charles Tait. Tait is ultimately exonerated.

1825

The U.S. House is asked to investigate the conduct of Judge Buckner Thurston, associate judge of the Circuit Court of the United States for the District of Columbia. Representative William Plumer Jr. of the House Judiciary Committee finds no reason for an inquiry, and the case is closed.

1825–1826

The U.S. House opens a series of three inquiries into Judge Joseph L. Smith, judge of the Supreme Court of the Territory of Florida, calling attention to alleged "dictatorial powers" he wielded in court. All inquiries are ended with no impeachment proceedings.

1829–1830

The U.S. House of Representatives investigates potential impeachment charges against Judge Alfred Conkling for "unjudicial conduct, malice, and partiality," but tables the investigation.

1830

The "citizens of East Florida" send a memorial to the U.S. House of Representatives asking for Judge Joseph L. Smith to be removed because of "tyrannical and oppressive conduct," but a motion to open an impeachment inquiry is tabled.

1 May   The U.S. House of Representatives votes to impeach James H. Peck, judge of the District of Missouri, for a "misuse of powers."

1831

21 January   The U.S. Senate acquits Judge James H. Peck by a vote of twenty-one to twenty-two.

1833

In United States v. Wilson, 32 U.S. (7 Pet.) 150, at 160, Chief Justice Marshall of the U.S. Supreme Court defines a presidential pardon as "an act of grace, proceeding from the power intrusted [sic] with the execution of the laws, which exempts the individual, on whom it is bestowed, from the punishment the law inflicts for a crime he has committed." The U.S. House of Representatives investigates potential impeachment charges against Judge Benjamin Johnson for "favoritism and drunkenness." The investigation is ultimately tabled.

1837

31 January   The House is asked to investigate Judge Buckner Thurston, associate judge of the District Court for the District of Columbia, for the second time (the first was in 1825). Evidence is eventually taken, including that from Judge Thurston. There is no record relating to the case, but the House later chooses not to impeach the judge. He remains on the court until his death in 1845.

1839

The U.S. House of Representatives investigates potential impeachment charges against Judge Philip K. Lawrence for "abuse of power and drunkenness." The investigation is tabled when Judge Lawrence resigns.

1841

Charles Franklin Mitchell, a U.S. Representative from New York (1837–1841) is sent to prison for forgery.

1845

22 September   After it is revealed that he gave a speech that had been plagiarized from one delivered by former Vice President Aaron Burr, former representative and Speaker of the House of Representatives John White takes his own life.

1849

The U.S. House of Representatives investigates, for the second time (the first was in 1829), charges against Judge Alfred Conkling. Again, the investigation is tabled.

1852–1853

A major investigation by the U.S. House of Representatives into charges against Judge John C. Watrous begins. He is accused of validating fraudulent land certificates. The investigation will ultimately last eight years. Initially, it is tabled.

1857

The investigation by the U.S. House of Representatives into Judge John C. Watrous reaches a higher stage when the House Judiciary Committee recommends against impeachment.

1859

The U.S. House of Representatives investigates potential impeachment charges against Judge Thomas Irwin; the investigation concludes when Irwin resigns his seat.

1860

The U.S. House of Representatives adopts a resolution of "reproof," similar to that of censure or a rebuke, by a vote of 106 to 61, against President James Buchanan and Secretary of the Navy Isaac Toucey, accusing the two men of "receiving and considering the party relations of bidders for contracts with the United States, and the effect of awarding contracts upon pending elections" which was "dangerous to the public safety."

1860–1861

The House Judiciary Committee, investigating the case against Judge John C. Watrous for the third time in eight years, recommends that impeachment charges be brought, but reverses the action when Watrous resigns his seat.

1862

The U.S. House of Representatives debates, and then tables, a resolution of censure against former President James Buchanan for not taking proper actions to prevent the secession of the Southern states from the Union.

19 May   The U.S. House of Representatives votes to impeach West H. Humphreys, judge for the District of Tennessee, for siding with the Confederate revolt.

26 June   The U.S. Senate votes to convict Judge West H. Humphreys of six of the seven articles of impeachment against him and then votes thirty-eight to zero to remove him from office and thirty-six to zero to disqualify him from holding any future office under the United States.

15 August   Senator James Fowler Simmons of Rhode Island resigns his seat rather than face expulsion for helping a contractor from his home state gain a federal contract in exchange for a payoff of $50,000.

1866

26 March   Governor Frederick Low of California signs into law the first state fraudulent election law. Entitled "an Act to protect the elections of voluntary political associations, and to punish frauds therein," it becomes a landmark in state election law.

11 July   Senator James Henry Lane (R–KS) takes his own life after being implicated in the sale of illegal contracts that provide services to Indian reservations.

1867

Congress enacts, as part of the Naval Appropriations Bill, the first congressional attempt to regulate campaign finance spending. An impeachment investigation against Charles Francis Adams, U.S. minister to Great Britain, for "neglect of American citizens in England and Ireland," is initiated, but no action is taken. A second impeachment investigation is begun against William West, American consul in Ireland, for "failure to aid American prisoners in Ireland." No action is ever taken on the charges.

1868

An impeachment investigation begins in the U.S. House of Representatives regarding Henry A. Smythe, the collector of customs in New York, for "maladministration of New York Custom House receipts and other charges." No action is taken on the charges.

2 March   The U.S. House of Representatives votes to impeach President Andrew Johnson for violating the Tenure of Office Act.

16 May   The U.S. Senate votes thirty-five to nineteen to sustain Article 11 of the impeachment charges against President Johnson, falling short of conviction by one vote. The Senate then adjourns.

26 May   The U.S. Senate reconvenes then votes thirty-five to nineteen to convict President Johnson on Articles 2 and 3, again falling one vote shy of the two-thirds needed to convict. The Senate then votes to adjourn the impeachment trial, and Chief Justice Salmon P. Chase, sitting as the trial judge, announces Johnson's acquittal.

1869–1877

During the eight years of the administration of President Ulysses S. Grant, Congress undertakes thirty-seven separate inquiries into maladministration in the executive and legislative branches—a record.

1871

22 March   Governor William Woods Holden of North Carolina becomes the first state governor to be impeached and removed from office. Charged in 1870 with eight separate articles, he is convicted of six.

1872

2 December   The U.S. House of Representatives appoints a select committee, headed by Representative Luke P. Poland (R–VT), to investigate the allegations involved in the Crédit Mobilier scandal.

1873

The Judiciary Committee of the U.S. House of Representatives recommends that Judge Mark H. Delahay be impeached for "intoxication and other corrupt dealings," but Delahay resigns before an impeachment vote can be taken. Vice President Schuyler Colfax is investigated for his role in the Crédit Mobilier railroad scandal, but because he has left office as of 4 March, no action is taken. The House investigates charges of alleged influence peddling by Judge Charles T. Sherman, but before it can vote on potential impeachment charges Sherman resigns his seat.

6 January   The U.S. House of Representatives forms a second select committee to investigate the Crédit Mobilier affair, this time to investigate the financial relationship between the company and the Union Pacific Railroad. This committee is headed by Representative Jeremiah M. Wilson (R–IN).

4 February   The U.S. Senate establishes its own select committee to investigate the Crédit Mobilier affair, headed by Senator Lot M. Morrill (R–ME).

18 February   The Poland Committee files its report with the House, clearing Speaker of the House James G. Blaine of complicity in the Crédit Mobilier scandal, but recommending that Representatives Oakes Ames and James Brooks be expelled.

27 February   The U.S. House of Representatives condemns Representatives James Brooks and Oakes Ames for their roles in the Crédit Mobilier railroad scandal, passing over a chance to expel them.

1 March   The Morrill Committee releases its report, saying that of all the senators alleged to have been involved, Senator James W. Patterson (R–NH) was found to be liable, and asked for his expulsion from the Senate. Due to Patterson having lost his reelection attempt in November 1872 and his leaving the Senate on 3 March, the Senate holds off action and allows Patterson to simply retire.

3 March   The Wilson Committee releases its report, saying that the financial relationship between the Crédit Mobilier and the Union Pacific Railroad was too cozy, and that some officers of both companies had held bonds illegally. Court action is recommended.

24 March   Senator Alexander Caldwell of Kansas resigns his seat to avoid being expelled after he is accused of using bribes to get elected to the Senate.

1874

The U.S. House of Representatives investigates charges of irregularities in court funds lodged against Judge William F. Story. The House decides to pass on impeaching Story, instead passing the evidence on to the attorney general, who closes the case with no further proceedings ordered. Kansas State Treasurer Josiah Hayes is impeached for financial irregularities; however, when his trial opens in Topeka on 12 May, his resignation is announced, and the impeachment is abandoned.

1875

The Judiciary Committee of the U.S. House of Representatives recommends that Judge Richard Busteed be impeached for "non-residence, failure to hold court, and [the] improper use of [his] official position," but the vote is tabled when Busteed resigns his seat. The House also investigates Judge Edward H. Durell for drunkenness and improper business transactions. The inquiry ends when Durell resigns his seat.

1876

The U.S. House of Representatives investigates charges of court administration irregularities against Judge Andrew Wylie of the Supreme Court of the District of Columbia. The inquiry ends when Wylie resigns his seat.

2 March   Secretary of War William Worth Belknap resigns his office amid allegations of massive financial misconduct.

3 April   Despite Belknap's resignation, the U.S. House of Representatives impeaches him on five articles accusing him of taking bribes.

1 August   Belknap appears at his Senate trial, but refuses to enter a plea, saying that as a private citizen he could not be impeached. The Senate agrees, voting on this date by a vote of thirty-seven to twenty-five to find Belknap guilty, but short of the two-thirds necessary to convict. Twenty-two of the senators who voted to acquit, as well as two who voted to convict, later report that they agreed that the Senate lacked jurisdiction over the case.

1878

The U.S. House of Representatives investigates Consul-General Oliver B. Bradford on charges of corruption, but no action is taken after the matter is referred to the Judiciary Committee.

1879

The U.S. House of Representatives investigates Consul-General George F. Seward on charges of "corruptly receiv[ing] monies in the settlement of estates, and appropriat[ing] U.S. funds for [his] own use." No further action is ever taken on the ensuing investigation. Judge Henry W. Blodgett is also investigated by the House for allegedly "defrauding creditors, enriching friends in bankruptcy proceedings, and exceeding jurisdiction" in cases, but the investigation is tabled for lack of evidence.

1880

The United States Supreme Court, in *Kilbourn v. Thompson,* 103 U.S. 168, holds that the Congress may not hold persons outside of members of Congress in contempt and thus may not jail them for such contempt.

1883

Congress enacts the Pendleton Act, which outlaws the collection of campaign contributions on federal property. This ends the practice of forcing government workers to contribute money to campaigns to keep their jobs.

1884

The U.S. House of Representatives investigates Judge James W. Locke on charges of interfering in elections, but exonerates him. Judge Samuel B. Axtell is also investigated on charges of incompetence and misconduct while in office, but a House committee finds that the charges do not merit an impeachment vote.

23 May   Speaker of the U.S. House of Representatives John G. Carlisle tells the House that no member of that body should ever be punished for any offense alleged to have been committed previous to their congressional service and adds that "that has been so frequently decided by the House that it is no longer a matter of dispute."

1890

Maryland state Treasurer Stevenson Archer is charged with embezzlement after an investigation finds some $132,000 in state funds under his control missing. He pleads guilty to the charge, telling the court that he spent the money and had only $1 of it left. Sentenced to five years in prison, by 1894 he is in failing health and is pardoned by Governor Frank Brown. He dies in August 1898, having never divulged where he spent the money.

1892

Judge Aleck Boardman is investigated by the U.S. House of Representatives on charges of the misuse of court funds and is censured by the subcommittee hearing the evidence rather than face an impeachment trial.

1894

May   Responding to published charges that senators had taken bribes to support tariff schedules favorable to the sugar industry, the U.S. Senate establishes the Special Investigative Committee. Uncertain as to the scope of its investigative powers, the Senate in August orders a comprehensive survey of all other congressional investigations. The resulting thousand-page compilation, "Decisions and Precedents of the Senate and House of Representatives Relating to Their Powers and Privileges Respecting Their Members and Officers," usefully documents Congress's institutional development throughout its first century.

1895

Delegate Robert William Wilcox from Hawaii is tried by a jury for his role in the Hawaiian Rebellion of 1895 and sentenced to death; his sentenced is commuted to thirty-five years in prison, and he is pardoned by the Hawaiian president in 1898. He dies in 1903.

1901

Eugene Schmitz, a bandleader, is elected Mayor of San Francisco, California, and begins an era rife with graft and corruption.

1903

20 September   In San Francisco, a deputy U.S. marshal takes his own life, and three deputy sheriffs from the city are arrested on charges of taking bribes to allow Chinese immigrants into the country in violation of the Exclusion Act, which placed a barrier on immigration.

1904

Theodore Roosevelt campaigns for a full term as president on a platform of campaign reform and control of the so-called trusts despite the fact that many of these same trusts are funding his campaign. Democratic presidential candidate Judge Alton B. Parker alleges that corporations are funding Roosevelt's campaign. Roosevelt initially denies this, only to admit to the charge after the election. Representative William Bourke Cochran of New York calls for federal financing of elections. *San Francisco Bulletin* publisher R. A.

Crothers is mugged by an unknown assailant, after the *Bulletin* charges the administration of Mayor Eugene Schmitz and Schmitz's political leader Abe Ruef with graft and corruption.

1905
In his annual message, President Theodore Roosevelt calls for campaign finance reform. This move, building on a second call in his 1906 annual message, leads to the establishment of the National Publicity Law Organization (NPLO), which lobbies for national campaign finance reform.

1906
24 October   San Francisco District Attorney William H. Langdon names Francis J. Heney, the special counsel in the Oregon land frauds cases, to assist him in prosecuting fraud and corruption in San Francisco. Heney is appointed assistant district attorney.

25 October   Acting Mayor James L. Gallagher of San Francisco suspends District Attorney William H. Langdon for "neglect of duty" and appoints political boss Abe Ruef in his place. Assistant District Attorney Francis J. Heney says that he does not recognize Ruef as district attorney.

26 October   A local San Francisco judge signs a temporary restraining order barring Ruef from becoming district attorney. District Attorney Langdon has guards protect his office from Ruef or his cronies to prevent them from taking control.

31 October   A demonstration held in San Francisco by Ruef protests graft inquiries against the Schmitz administration.

15 November   A grand jury empaneled by District Attorney Langdon hands down indictments against Mayor Eugene Schmitz, "Boss" Abe Ruef, and Police Chief Jeremiah Dinan.

1907
26 January   Congress enacts the Tillman Act, which bans direct contributions from corporations to individuals, but leaves a loophole allowing the heads of corporations to continue to contribute unlimited amounts of money.

4 March   "Boss" Abraham Ruef surrenders and is arraigned. He posts bond, then vanishes.

8 March   The judge overseeing the Ruef prosecution orders his arrest and names William J. Biggy to find him. Two hours later, Ruef is found at the Trocadero House, a hotel in Stern Grove, California, near San Francisco. Biggy is later named to replace Jeremiah Dinan as chief of police.

13 June   Mayor Eugene Schmitz is convicted by a San Francisco jury of extortion.

1908
16 November   Assistant District Attorney Francis J. Heney is shot in court by Morris Haas, whose criminal activity had been revealed by Heney some months earlier. Heney survives, but must be replaced by Hiram W. Johnson. Haas is a bagman for "Boss" Ruef. He is later found dead in his jail cell, a potential suicide from a smuggled gun. In the aftermath of the shooting of Heney and the death of Haas, Chief of Police Biggy is suspected of being in the pay of "Boss" Ruef.

1 December   Police Chief Biggy disappears off a police boat in San Francisco Bay.

10 December   "Boss" Ruef is found guilty of bribing a supervisor to vote to build the United Railroad and is sentenced to fourteen years in prison.

15 December   The body of Police Chief Biggy is found near Angel Island in San Francisco Bay. The coroner rules that his was an accidental death. The circumstances of his death are never revealed, and the case goes unsolved.

1909
After Theodore Roosevelt leaves the White House, it is discovered that his 1904 campaign was funded by railroads, oil companies, and other businesses on which he was cracking down at the time as monopolies. For instance, J. P. Morgan alone gave $150,000.

1910
25 June   Congress enacts the Federal Corrupt Practices Act (also called the Publicity Act), requiring all U.S. House candidates—and, later, all U.S. Senate candidates when such candidates are directly elected by the people—to fully disclose all campaign contributions and spending.

1911
11 August   Congress enacts amendments to the Publicity Act of 1910, which established firm spending

limits for federal campaigns. The amendments are designed to improve disclosure requirements.

1912
13 July   The U.S. Senate declares the election of William Lorimer (R–IL) to be invalid after it hears allegations that he won the seat in the Illinois legislature through bribery.

1913
Colonel Martin M. Mulhall, a lobbyist for the National Association of Manufacturers (NAM), implicates Representative James T. McDermott (D–IL) in bribe taking. Mulhall states that he had paid McDermott approximately $2,000 for "legislative favors." A congressional investigation leads to disciplinary charges against McDermott by the full House, but he is not expelled or censured. McDermott resigns his seat in 1914, but is reelected in November to his old seat.

1921
Senator Truman H. Newberry (R–MI) is indicted by a grand jury and later convicted of violating campaign spending limits in his 1918 Senate race against Democrat Henry Ford. The U.S. Supreme Court, in Newberry v. United States, 256 U.S. 232, holds that congressional authority to regulate elections does not extend to party primaries and election activities and strikes down the spending limits Newberry had been convicted of violating.

1922
Secretary of the Interior Albert B. Fall leases the Teapot Dome oil reserves in Wyoming to cronies to pay them back for the campaign contributions they gave to President Warren G. Harding in his 1920 presidential campaign.

1923
22 October   The first hearing on the Teapot Dome allegations takes place.

1925
28 February   Congress revises the 1910 Federal Corrupt Practices Act, putting a cap on spending for senatorial campaigns at $25,000 and congressional campaigns at $5,000. Passed in response to the burgeoning Teapot Dome scandal, the law does not cover primary campaigns. Despite flagrant violations of this law and its revisions, only two men, Republicans William S. Vare of Pennsylvania and Frank L. Smith of

Virginia, are ever prosecuted for violating it. They are excluded from Congress.

1926
District of Columbia Commissioner Frederick A. Fenning is impeached for "acting as an attorney while commissioner, champerty [a sharing in the proceeds of a lawsuit by an outside party who has promoted the litigation], exorbitant remuneration for guardianship of lunatics, among other charges." Fenning is later censured and forced to resign under pressure from President Calvin Coolidge.

12 April   In a stunning move, the U.S. Senate votes along party lines, forty-five to forty-one, to seat Democrat Daniel Steck over Republican Smith Brookhart, after Steck alleges voting irregularities.

1928
Representative Edgar Howard (D–NE) proposes a bill that would mandate a prison sentence for any former member of Congress who remains in Washington after his term of office to lobby his former colleagues.

1929
Representative Frederick N. Zihlman (R–MD) offers not to run for reelection and resigns as chairman of the House Committee on the District of Columbia, after he is indicted on charges of corruption.

1934
Two members of the "Anti-Smith Committee of Virginia," James Cannon Jr. and Ada L. Burroughs, are acquitted of using campaign funds to defeat former Governor Al Smith of New York in violation of the Federal Corrupt Practices Act.

1936
President Franklin Delano Roosevelt receives a $250,000 contribution from the head of the Congress of Industrial Organizations (CIO), the first major donation from a union to a political candidate.

Donn M. Roberts, mayor of Terre Haute, Indiana, who had been convicted in 1915 of bribery and served three and one-half years in prison, is convicted of embezzlement and sentenced to prison a second time; however, following a heart attack, he is released from prison and dies on 3 August 1936.

1939
Responding to allegations that the administration of President Franklin Delano Roosevelt has forced

federal government workers to donate to his presidential campaign, Congress enacts the Hatch Act, which prohibits federal employees from contributing to, or participating in, federal campaigns.

25 June   Roy E. Brownmiller, Pennsylvania secretary of highways, is convicted of using state payroll funds to finance the 1938 election campaign of Governor George Howard Earle III, who lost. Brownmiller eventually serves prison time, but is released after one year due to declining health.

1940

19 July   Congress enacts amendments to the Hatch Act, imposing a limit of $5,000 a year on individual contributions to federal candidates or national party committees.

1941

In *United States v. Classic,* 31 U.S. 299, the U.S. Supreme Court reverses its 1921 ruling in *Newberry v. United States* and holds that Congress does have the authority to regulate spending limits for primaries and election activities.

1943

Congress enacts, over President Franklin Delano Roosevelt's veto, the Smith-Connally Anti-Strike Act (also known as the War Labor Disputes Act) to prevent labor unions from making political contributions. It is passed as a war measure only and expires six months after the end of the war in 1945.

16 September   A federal grand jury indicts Representative James M. Curley (D–MA) on charges of using the mails to defraud companies.

1 November   A federal court voids the indictment against Representative James Curley, stating that the grand jury was "illegally summoned."

1944

18 January   Another federal grand jury in Washington, D.C., indicts Representative James M. Curley.

1946

18 January   Representative James M. Curley is convicted by a federal jury in Washington of using the mails to defraud companies of mail contracts during the Second World War.

1947

13 January   The U.S. Court of Appeals for the D.C. Circuit upholds the conviction of Representative James M. Curley.

23 January   A federal grand jury in Washington, D.C., indicts Representative Andrew J. May (D–KY) for accepting funds to influence war contracts during the Second World War.

18 February   Representative James M. Curley is sentenced to six to eighteen months in prison and fined $1,000 for mail fraud.

2 June   The U.S. Supreme Court upholds Curley's conviction.

23 June   Congress reenacts the provisions against campaign spending by labor unions as part of the Labor Management Relations Act of 1947, also called the Taft-Hartley Act.

26 June   Representative James M. Curley enters a prison to begin serving his sentence.

3 July   Representative Andrew J. May is convicted on charges of bribery and conspiracy.

26 November   President Harry S. Truman commutes the remainder of Curley's jail sentence.

1948

8 November   Representative J. Parnell Thomas (R–NJ) is indicted on charges of defrauding the government by padding his congressional payroll and taking kickbacks from his staff.

1949

14 November   The U.S. Supreme Court refuses to review the conviction of Representative Andrew J. May (D–KY).

30 November   Representative J. Parnell Thomas pleads no contest to charges that he took illicit payoffs from his staff.

5 December   Representative Andrew J. May begins serving his prison sentence.

9 December   Representative J. Parnell Thomas is sentenced to six to eighteen months in prison and fined $10,000.

1950

10 September   Representative J. Parnell Thomas is paroled from prison after serving eight and one-half months in prison.

18 September   Representative Andrew J. May is paroled after serving nine months of his prison sentence.

20 December   Representative Walter E. Brehm (R–OH) is indicted for accepting contributions from his congressional staff.

24 December   President Harry S. Truman pardons Representative Andrew J. May.

1951

In the wake of charges that supporters of Taiwan's Nationalist Party (called "The China Lobby") have been trying to influence Congress, Senator Wayne Morse (R–OR) calls for an investigation into lobbying by foreign governments to influence U.S. foreign policy. Representative Charles Bennett (D–FL) introduces a resolution calling on "all Government employees, including officeholders" to adhere to a congressional ethics code.

30 April   Representative Walter E. Brehm is convicted of accepting campaign contributions from one of his employees.

8 June   Representative Theodore Leonard Irving (D–MO) is indicted by a federal grand jury in Washington, D.C., for violating the Corrupt Practices Act and the Taft-Hartley Act for misusing funds when he served as the head of a labor union during his 1948 campaign for Congress.

11 June   Representative Walter E. Brehm is sentenced to five to fifteen months in prison and fined $5,000. His sentence is summarily suspended by the judge, and Brehm never serves any time in prison.

28 December   Representative Theodore Leonard Irving is acquitted by a federal jury of all charges.

1953

14 January   Representative John L. McMillan (D–SC) is indicted for violating a law barring members of Congress from making contracts with the government when he leased oil and gas properties in Utah from the Department of the Interior.

16 May   Representative John L. McMillan is acquitted of all charges.

17 June   Representative Ernest K. Bramblett (R–CA) is indicted for making false statements in connection with a kickback investigation involving congressional aides and staff.

1954

9 February   Representative Ernest K. Bramblett is convicted of charges that he lied during a House kickback investigation.

14 April   Bramblett's sentencing is stayed pending an appeal to the United States Supreme Court.

1955

4 April   The U.S. Supreme Court upholds the conviction of Representative Ernest K. Bramblett.

15 June   Bramblett is sentenced to four to twelve months in prison and fined $5,000. The judge suspends the sentence, and Bramblett does not serve any jail time.

1956

5 March   Representative Thomas J. Lane (D–MA) is indicted for federal income tax evasion for the years 1949–1951.

20 April   Representative Lane pleads guilty to income tax evasion and is sentenced to four months in prison and fined $10,000.

14 December   Representative William J. Green (D–PA) is indicted with six others for conspiracy to defraud the government when he accepted business for his personal company in exchange for working to gain a contract with the U.S. Army Signal Corps for a contributor.

1958

8 May   Representative Adam Clayton Powell (D–NY) is indicted for federal income tax evasion.

1959

27 February   Representative William J. Green is acquitted of all charges.

1960

5 and 7 April   A federal judge dismisses two of the three charges against Representative Adam Clayton Powell.

22 April   Representative Adam Clayton Powell's trial on a single charge of income tax evasion is declared a mistrial due to a hung jury.

23 May   The judge overseeing the trial of Representative Adam Clayton Powell refuses to dismiss the indictment against him.

1961

13 April   The U.S. attorney overseeing the trial of Representative Adam Clayton Powell asks to have the single charge still against him dismissed.

1962

16 October   Representative Thomas F. Johnson (D–MD) is indicted with Representative Frank W. Boykin (D–AL) and two others for conspiracy to defraud the government by trying to influence a Department of Justice inquiry into fraud at a Maryland savings and loan bank.

1963

13 June   Representative Thomas F. Johnson is convicted on all charges relating to his attempt to end an investigation of a Maryland savings and loan bank. Also convicted is Representative Frank Boykin on charges of conflict of interest and conspiracy to defraud the government.

7 October   Representative Frank Boykin is sentenced to probation for six months and fined $40,000.

1964

24 July   The U.S. Senate Committee on Rules and Administration rules on the Bobby Baker case, holding that the Senate aide had used his office for personal gain. However, he is not charged with any crime.

16 September   The U.S. Court of Appeals for the Fourth Circuit strikes down the conviction of Representative Thomas F. Johnson on the grounds that the conviction arose from a speech he gave on behalf of a Maryland savings and loan bank; the court holds that such speech is protected by the Speech or Debate clause of the U.S. Constitution. The court does order a new trial on other charges relating to a conflict of interest.

1965

9 July   A year after it was established, the first members of the Senate Committee on Standards and Conduct are named. John Stennis (D–MS) is named chairman.

17 December   President Lyndon Baines Johnson pardons Representative Frank Boykin of Alabama.

1966

24 February   The U.S. Supreme Court affirms the striking down of the conviction of Representative Thomas F. Johnson, sustaining the Speech or Debate clause of the U.S. Constitution.

1967

29 January   Former Senate Majority Leader Secretary Bobby Baker is convicted on seven counts of income tax invasion, theft, and conspiracy to defraud the government. On 7 April he is sentenced to at least one year in prison.

23 June   Senator Thomas J. Dodd (D–CT) is censured by the Senate for using campaign funds for personal use, setting off a new wave of campaign finance reform efforts.

A former congressman, W. Pat Jennings, becomes the first clerk of the House to actually collect campaign finance reports and to report violators to the Department of Justice, as directed by the 1925 Federal Corrupt Practices Act. The United States Senate opens an investigation into the dealings of Senator Edward V. Long (D–MO) for allegedly accepting legal fees from a lawyer representing James R. Hoffa, the head of the Teamsters union, at the same time that Long was conducting a Senate investigation of government wiretapping and electronic eavesdropping of officials under FBI investigation, which included Hoffa. The Senate later clears Long of any wrongdoing.

1968

26 January   Representative Thomas F. Johnson is convicted of conflict of interest charges relating to his work to hinder the investigation of a Maryland savings and loan bank.

30 January   Representative Thomas F. Johnson is sentenced to six months in prison.

4 October   President Lyndon B. Johnson withdraws the name of Justice Abe Fortas for the position of chief

justice after allegations of corruption against him are aired.

1969
18 December   Representative Hugh J. Addonizio (D–NJ) is indicted on charges of extortion, conspiracy, and income tax evasion relating to crimes he allegedly committed while serving as mayor of Newark, New Jersey.

1970
31 March   Representative John V. Dowdy (D–TX) is indicted on charges of bribery, conspiracy, and perjury relating to his receipt of money from a Maryland company under investigation for fraud.

22 July   Representative Hugh J. Addonizio is convicted of sixty-four counts of extortion, conspiracy, and income tax evasion.

23 July   President Nixon secretly approves a plan to expand domestic wiretapping and other intelligence gathering activities by the FBI, the CIA, and other federal agencies. A few days later, after having second thoughts, he rescinds the order. Former Secretary of Health, Education, and Welfare John Gardner founds Common Cause, a citizen lobbying and reform group.

22 September   Representative Hugh J. Addonizio is sentenced to ten years in prison and fined $25,000.

16 December   Representative Martin B. McKneally (R–NY) is indicted for failure to file federal income taxes for the years 1964–1967.

1971
Speaker of the House of Representatives John McCormack (D–MA) retires after one of his top aides, Martin Sweig, is accused of using the Speaker's office and name for dishonest purposes.

3 September   A unit is formed inside the White House to plug leaks inside administration offices. The group is called "The Plumbers."

18 October   Representative Martin B. McKneally pleads guilty to federal income tax evasion.

20 December   Representative McKneally is sentenced to one year in prison and one year on probation and fined $5,000. The judge suspends the prison sentence, and McKneally does not serve any jail time.

30 December   Representative John Dowdy is convicted of all charges relating to bribery and perjury.

1972
7 February   President Nixon signs the Federal Election Campaign Act, establishing spending limits on both presidential and congressional candidates and requiring the reporting of campaign contributions.

15 February   Attorney General John N. Mitchell resigns from his post to serve as the chairman of President Nixon's 1972 reelection campaign.

23 February   Representative John Dowdy is sentenced to eighteen months in prison and fined $25,000.

7 April   Representative Cornelius Gallagher (D–NJ) is indicted for federal income tax evasion for the years 1966–1967, perjury, and conspiracy for his work in assisting two other people to evade income tax payment.

28 May   Unknown to all but the small group called "The Plumbers," electronic surveillance equipment is installed at Democratic National Committee headquarters in the Watergate building in Washington, D.C.

17 June   Five men break into the office of the Democratic National Committee in the Watergate Hotel in Washington, D.C., in an attempt to fix a broken bug that has been installed a few weeks earlier. All five are arrested.

19 June   The *Washington Post* reports that a Republican security aide, James W. McCord Jr., is one of the Watergate burglars.

1 August   The *Washington Post* reports that a $25,000 check, made out to the Nixon 1972 campaign reelection committee, wound up in the bank account of one of the Watergate burglars.

30 August   President Nixon reports that an investigation of potential White House involvement in the Watergate break-in, conducted by White House counsel John Dean, shows no White House involvement.

15 September   E. Howard Hunt, G. Gordon Liddy, and the five Watergate burglars, Bernard Barker, Virgilio Gonzalez, Eugenio Martinez, James W. McCord Jr., and

Frank Sturgis are indicted by a federal grand jury in the burgeoning Watergate scandal.

29 September   The *Washington Post* reports that while serving as attorney general, John Mitchell controlled a secret slush fund that he used to finance secret bugging and other intelligence-gathering activities, much of which was illegal.

10 October   The *Washington Post* reports that the FBI has concluded that the Watergate break-in was part of a massive campaign of political spying and espionage by the Nixon reelection committee.

21 December   Representative Cornelius Gallagher pleads guilty to income tax evasion.

1973
8 January   The trial of the Watergate defendants begins.

11 January   Watergate defendant E. Howard Hunt pleads guilty.

15 January   Watergate defendants Barker, Gonzalez, Martinez, and Sturgis plead guilty.

30 January   G. Gordon Liddy and James W. McCord Jr. are convicted of conspiracy, burglary, and wiretapping for their roles in the Watergate break-in.

7 February   Amid growing questions over the role of high Nixon administration officials in the Watergate break-in, the U.S. Senate establishes the Select Committee on Presidential Campaign Activities, also known as the Senate Watergate Committee. Senator Sam Ervin (D–NC) is named the committee's chairman, while Senator Howard H. Baker (R–TN) is named vice chairman.

13 March   The U.S. Court of Appeals for the Fourth Circuit strikes down the bribery and conspiracy convictions of Representative John V. Dowdy; however, the court does uphold the perjury conviction.

19 March   Convicted Watergate defendant James W. McCord Jr. writes a letter to Judge John Sirica, overseeing the Watergate trials, and tells him that the five Watergate defendants who pled guilty shortly before the start of their trial were pressured into doing so, that perjury was committed in the trial, and that other people were involved in the break-in.

29 March   The *Los Angeles Times* and the *Washington Post* both report that James McCord told Samuel Dash, chief counsel to the Senate Watergate Committee, that former Nixon aide Jeb Stuart Magruder and White House counsel John Dean knew of the plan to break in to Democratic headquarters and bug the phones. The *Post* states that Liddy had told McCord that the operation had the backing and approval of former Attorney General John Mitchell and Charles Colson, former special counsel to Nixon.

6 April   White House counsel John Dean begins to cooperate with Watergate investigators.

30 April   Nixon aides H. R. Haldeman and John Ehrlichman, as well as Attorney General Richard Kleindienst, resign in the midst of the growing Watergate scandal. President Nixon fires White House counsel John Dean.

18 May   The Senate Watergate Committee begins televised hearings, capturing the nation's attention. Attorney General-designate Elliot Richardson names former Solicitor General Archibald Cox as the Department of Justice special prosecutor on Watergate.

3 June   The *Washington Post* reports that John Dean told Watergate investigators that he discussed the Watergate scandal with President Nixon at least thirty-five times.

13 June   Watergate investigators discover a memo addressed to former Nixon aide John Ehrlichman outlining a plan to burglarize the office of the psychiatrist of former Department of Defense official Daniel Ellsberg, who had released the so-called Pentagon Papers.

15 June   Representative Cornelius Gallagher is sentenced to two years in prison and fined $10,000.

25 June   In televised hearings before the Senate Watergate Committee, former White House counsel John Dean tells the committee under oath that the White House had a major plan for domestic espionage of the president's political enemies and that Nixon planned the cover-up of the Watergate burglary within days of the occurrence of the break-in.

7 July   President Nixon tells the Senate Watergate Committee that he will not appear in person before the committee or grant the committee access to any presidential papers.

13 July   Former presidential appointments secretary Alexander Butterfield tells the Senate Watergate Committee that President Nixon had been taping all White House conversations since 1971. The committee concludes that the Nixon campaign was involved in domestic spying, abuse of campaign funds, favors for the milk industry in return for campaign contributions, and that President Nixon had hampered the investigation, although no charge of obstruction of justice was put forward.

23 July   Following a request from the Senate Watergate Committee and Special Watergate Prosecutor Archibald Cox for any and all tapes regarding Oval Office conversations, President Nixon refuses to turn over any tapes, citing executive privilege.

25 July   Nixon refuses to comply with a subpoena from Cox.

26 July   The Senate Watergate Committee votes to subpoena the Nixon tapes.

2 August   Vice President Spiro Agnew is notified that he is under investigation by the U.S. Attorney's Office in Baltimore, Maryland, for his role in a milk bribery scheme while he served as governor of that state.

9 August   The Senate Watergate Committee sues President Nixon for access to the White House tapes.

29 August   Judge John Sirica orders President Nixon to deliver nine Oval Office tapes for the judge to privately review.

26 September   Vice President Spiro Agnew's request for a congressional investigation in his alleged role in a milk bribery scheme while he served as governor of Maryland is refused by Speaker of the U.S. House of Representatives Carl Albert (D–OK).

27 September   A federal grand jury in Baltimore begins to hear evidence in the bribery investigation of Vice President Spiro Agnew.

9 October   The U.S. Supreme Court upholds the perjury conviction of Representative John V. Dowdy.

10 October   Vice President Spiro Agnew resigns, becoming the second vice president to resign his office, the first being John Calhoun, who resigned in 1832 over political differences with President Andrew Jackson.

19 October   President Nixon tries to broker a deal over the White House tapes with Senator John Stennis (D–MS), under which Stennis would be allowed to hear the actual tapes while Nixon would provide a detailed summary to special prosecutor Cox.

20 October   Special prosecutor Cox refuses to accept the Stennis compromise and demands additional tapes from Nixon. President Nixon then orders Attorney General Elliot Richardson to fire Cox. Richardson refuses and resigns. Deputy Attorney General William D. Ruckelshaus also refuses and also resigns. It is left up to Solicitor General Robert H. Bork to fire Cox. The event is known as the Saturday Night Massacre.

23 October   Nixon agrees to comply with a subpoena to hand over certain White House taped conversations.

1 November   Under increasing pressure in Congress, President Nixon names attorney Leon Jaworski as the new Watergate special prosecutor.

12 November   Nixon decides to hand over several unsubpoenaed recordings and portions of his diary for inspection.

17 November   In a press conference, Nixon tells reporters that he is innocent of any crimes in the Watergate scandal. "I am not a crook," Nixon says with fervor.

7 December   Officials of the Nixon administration cannot explain why there is a gap of eighteen and one-half minutes on one of the subpoenaed Watergate tapes.

1974
28 January   Representative John V. Dowdy enters prison to serve a six-month sentence after the U.S. Supreme Court upholds his perjury conviction.

6 February   The U.S. House of Representatives votes to authorize the House Judiciary Committee to hold hearings on possible impeachment charges being brought against President Nixon.

1 March   Seven former aides of President Nixon are indicted for various offenses relating to Watergate; Nixon is named as an unindicted coconspirator.

6 April   Senator Edward J. Gurney (R–FL) is indicted by a Florida grand jury on charges that he violated state campaign finance laws.

16 April   Watergate special prosecutor Leon Jaworski demands access to sixty-four White House tapes.

30 April   The White House releases 1,200 pages of transcripts edited from Oval Office tapes, but the Senate Watergate Committee continues to demand the tapes themselves.

9 May   The House Judiciary Committee begins hearings on possible impeachment charges against President Nixon.

17 May   The indictment against Senator Edward J. Gurney is dismissed.

10 July   A federal grand jury indicts Senator Edward J. Gurney and six other defendants for conspiracy, perjury, and soliciting bribes in the form of campaign contributions from Florida construction concerns.

23 July   Representative Lawrence Hogan (R–MD) becomes the first Republican in the Congress to call for President Nixon's resignation.

24 July   The U.S. Supreme Court, in *Nixon v. United States,* 418 U.S. 683, holds that Nixon must turn over tapes from sixty-four White House conversations and that these conversations are not protected by executive privilege.

27 July   The House Judiciary Committee votes for an article of impeachment, charging President Nixon with obstruction of justice.

29 July   The House Judiciary Committee votes a second article of impeachment, charging President Nixon with misuse of presidential powers and violation of his oath of office.

30 July   The House Judiciary Committee adopts a third article of impeachment, charging President Nixon with a failure to comply with House subpoenas for White House tapes.

5 August   Nixon releases the transcript of a conversation with H. R. Haldeman from 23 June 1972, six days after the Watergate break-in, in which Nixon orders the Federal Bureau of Investigation to abandon its inquiry into the burglary. This tape is considered the "smoking gun" implicating Nixon in obstruction of justice.

7 August   Republican leaders meet with Nixon, telling him that impeachment was assured in the House and that he was quickly losing support in the Senate to forestall conviction.

8 August   Nixon tells the nation in a televised address that he will resign the following day.

9 August   Nixon resigns, becoming the first American president to do so. Vice President Gerald R. Ford becomes the thirty-eighth president of the United States.

8 September   One month after becoming president, Gerald Ford pardons former President Richard Nixon for any and all crimes he may have committee during his presidency.

1975
The Senate resolves one of the most corrupt elections in American history. Senator Henry Bellmon (R–OK) was challenged by Democrat Ed Edmondson. In a close race, Bellmon won, but Edmondson challenged the result. After a Senate investigation, which held that Oklahoma election rules were violated, but that it was unable to determine which side would have won the election if the violations had not occurred, the full Senate voted forty-seven to forty-six that Bellmon would be seated and Edmonson's challenge be thrown out.

26 June   Jack L. Chestnut, a former aide to Senator and former Vice President Hubert H. Humphrey, is sentenced to four months in prison and fined $5,000 for accepting an illegal campaign contribution during Humphrey's 1970 U.S. Senate campaign.

6 August   Senator Edward J. Gurney is acquitted of the bribery charge, but the jury fails to reach a verdict on the other counts.

1976
26 January   Representative Andrew Jackson Hinshaw (R–CA) is convicted by a jury in California on two

counts of bribery stemming from his first run for Congress in 1972.

29 January   Representative James R. Jones (D–OK) pleads guilty to a misdemeanor on the allegation that he failed to report a cash contribution in 1972 from the Gulf Oil Corporation.

24 February   Representative Andrew Jackson Hinshaw is sentenced to concurrent one-to-fourteen-year prison sentences.

2 June   Representative Henry Helstoski (D–NJ) is indicted by a federal grand jury in New Jersey on charges that he solicited and accepted bribes from Chilean and Argentinean immigrants in exchange for introducing bills in Congress designed to block their extradition from the United States. Helstoski, along with three aides, were charged with bribery, conspiracy, obstruction of justice, and lying to a federal grand jury.

21 September   Former Representative James F. Hastings (R–NY), who had served in the House from 1965 to 1975, is indicted by a federal grand jury in Washington, D.C., on charges that he operated a kickback scheme out of his congressional office with members of his congressional staff. Despite pleading not guilty to the charges, Hastings is convicted on twenty-eight counts on 17 December and sentenced to serve twenty months to five years in federal prison.

24 October   The *Washington Post* breaks the "Koreagate" story, leading to the largest congressional scandal in decades.

27 October   The Justice Department announces that it is dropping its civil suit against Representative William "Bill" Clay (D–MO), after Clay agrees to reimburse the U.S. government $1,754 he overcharged on travel expenses. Senator Edward J. Gurney (R–FL) is acquitted by a federal jury of lying to a federal grand jury.

1977
April   Former Representative Hugh J. Addonizio is released from prison after serving five years of a ten-year sentence.

11 April   William Cahn, district attorney of Nassau County, New York, is convicted of forty-five counts of mail fraud arising from the embezzlement of travel expenses. A first trial in February 1976 had ended with a hung jury.

1978
20 January   Judge Herbert Allen Fogel of the Eastern District of Pennsylvania writes to President Jimmy Carter that he will resign from the bench, effective 1 May, after the Department of Justice threatens to prosecute him for numerous offenses.

October   Representative Charles C. Diggs Jr. (D–MI) is convicted by a jury for illegally diverting more than $60,000 of his employees' salaries for his personal use. On 20 November, he is sentenced to three years in prison.

21 November   James Y. Carter, the Chicago taxi commissioner since 1960, is convicted of nine counts of extortion, racketeering, and income tax evasion.

1979
Congress amends the Federal Election Campaign Act so that "soft money" is exempt from 1971 limitations. This allows the explosion of "soft money" advertising and spending that is to dominate elections over the next twenty years.

January   House leaders convince Representative Charles C. Diggs Jr. to resign as chairman of the House Foreign Affairs Subcommittee on Africa after he is convicted of financial misconduct.

18 July   Cleveland City Council President George L. Forbes, the city's top black leader, is acquitted by a jury of eleven counts of bribery, theft in office, and extortion, all tied to an alleged gambling kickback scheme.

31 July   The U.S. House of Representatives censures Representative Charles C. Diggs Jr., by a vote of 414–0, for the misuse of his clerk-hire funds. This is only the second time in the twentieth century that a sitting member has been censured. (The first, Representative Thomas L. Blanton (D–TX), was censured for using objectionable language that was printed in *The Congressional Record.*)

1980
29 May   The House Democratic Caucus passes a rule to automatically remove a committee or subcommittee chairmanship from any party member who is censured by the House or indicted or convicted

of a felony with a sentence lasting more than two years.

1981
24 August   The Senate Ethics Committee votes unanimously to expel Senator Harrison Williams for his role in the ABSCAM scandal.

1982
3 March   The Senate begins debate on the punishment for Senator Harrison Williams of New Jersey.

11 March   Senator Harrison Williams resigns after it appears he will be expelled from the Senate for his conviction in the ABSCAM case.

1984
2 April   Representative George Hanson (R–ID) becomes the first person convicted of violating the Ethics in Government Act of 1978, when he is found guilty by a federal jury in Washington, D.C., of four counts of filing incorrect financial statements. On 25 June, Hansen is sentenced to five to fifteen months in prison and fined $40,000. On 31 July, the U.S. House of Representatives votes 354–42 to reprimand Hansen. Hansen loses his seat in the election in November.

1986
10 January   Queens (New York) Borough President Donald R. Manes is discovered by police driving erratically; upon closer examination, he is found with his wrists slashed in a failed suicide attempt. It is soon discovered that Manes is in the middle of a vast financial scandal.

11 February   Queens Borough President Donald R. Manes resigns his office.

13 March   Donald R. Manes commits suicide by shoving a knife into his heart.

25 November   Bronx Democratic Party Chairman Stanley M. Friedman is convicted by a federal jury of racketeering, conspiracy, and mail fraud. The U.S. attorney, Rudolph W. Guiliani, calls the scheme that Friedman was involved in an "enterprise for illegal plunder."

19 December   A court in Washington, D.C., names attorney Lawrence Walsh to investigate potential violations of law in the Iran-Contra Affair.

1987
January   William Sterling Anderson, a former Speaker of the South Carolina House of Representatives pro tem, is sentenced to fourteen months in prison for falsifying the customer credit records of his mobile home business.

21 January   The U.S. Parole Commission votes eight to zero against an appeal for early release by impeached Judge Harry E. Claiborne, convicted of tax fraud. The commission states that Claiborne had "seriously breached the public's trust."

22 January   At a news conference prior to his sentencing for taking a $300,000 kickback, former Pennsylvania Treasurer R. Budd Dwyer shoots himself in the mouth with a pistol in front of the television cameras in Harrisburg, Pennsylvania.

1988
18 May   The public affairs group Common Cause calls for an investigation of House Speaker Jim Wright, alleging that Wright may have broken the law in his financial arrangement surrounding the publication of his book, *Reflections of a Public Man,* and that Wright intervened with federal bank regulators regarding a Texas savings and loan bank.

26 May   Representative Newt Gingrich of Georgia, backed by seventy-two Republican members of the U.S. House of Representatives, files a complaint with the House Committee on Standards of Official Conduct regarding Speaker of the House Jim Wright.

9 June   The House Committee on Standards of Official Conduct votes unanimously to conduct an inquiry into the Wright matter, including other allegations of wrongdoing.

26 July   The House Committee on Standards of Official Conduct hires attorney Richard J. Phelan of Chicago as special outside counsel to investigate House Speaker Jim Wright.

4 August   Representative Mario Biaggi (D–NY) resigns from the House when he faces an almost certain expulsion vote for his role in the Wedtech scandal.

14 September   Speaker Jim Wright testifies before the House Committee on Standards of Official Conduct for five hours.

21 November   Representative Robert Garcia (D–NY) is indicted on charges of influence peddling in the Wedtech case.

1989
22 February   Richard Phelan, special outside counsel to the House Committee on Standards of Official Conduct, submits a 279-page report on the Jim Wright investigation.

13 April   Speaker Wright goes before television cameras to call for fairness, as word leaks out that special outside counsel Phelan has found evidence of serious crimes committed by Wright. The Speaker is emotional as he tries to rebut the accusations lodged against him.

17 April   The House Committee on Standards of Official Conduct releases its report on Wright, detailing that it has "reason to believe" that the Speaker has violated the rules of congressional conduct sixty-nine separate times. These sixty-nine charges fall into two categories that Wright conspired to use the sales of his book to hide income from House-imposed limits and that he accepted $145,000 in improper gifts from George Mallick, a Fort Worth developer and real estate businessman who was a friend of Wright's.

23 May   Lawyers for Speaker Wright appear before the House Committee on Standards of Official Conduct and claim that the panel has misinterpreted House rules and ask that the charges against Wright be thrown out.

31 May   Taking to the floor of the U.S. House, Speaker Jim Wright tells the members that he will resign as Speaker and offers to vacate his House seat as well.

30 June   Former Speaker Jim Wright resigns his House seat.

20 October   Representative Robert Garcia (D–NY) and his wife are convicted on charges of extortion and influence peddling in the Wedtech scandal.

1990
7 January   Representative Robert Garcia resigns from the House. Twelve days later he is sentenced to three years in prison for his role in the Wedtech case.

29 June   The convictions of former Representative Robert Garcia and his wife in the Wedtech scandal are struck down by a federal appeals court.

1992
24 December   In a controversial move, President George H. W. Bush, in his last days in office, pardons former Secretary of Defense Caspar Weinberger and five others—Elliott Abrams, a former assistant secretary of state for inter-American affairs; former National Security Adviser Robert McFarlane; and Duane Clarridge, Alan Fiers, and Clair George, all former employees of the Central Intelligence Agency—for their roles in the Iran-Contra scandal. Weinberger had been indicted shortly before the 1992 election and was scheduled to go on trial 5 January 1993.

1993
19 May   Several longtime employees of the White House Travel Office are fired. Controversy erupts when it is discovered that several of President Clinton's friends—including a cousin, Catherine Cornelius—were behind the firings, allegedly so that they could get the business.

25 May   Following a wave of protest and anger, five workers from the White House Travel Office who were fired on 19 May are reinstated.

19 July   Senator Robert J. Dole (R–KS) calls for the appointment of a special counsel to investigate the White House Travel Office firings.

1994
9 January   Senator Daniel Patrick Moynihan (D–NY) calls for the appointment of a special counsel to investigate the allegations against President Clinton and his wife regarding the Whitewater land deal in Arkansas.

12 January   Amid calls from other Democrats, President Clinton agrees to ask the attorney general to name an independent counsel to investigate the Whitewater land deal.

February   Jay Stephens, a Republican attorney, is named to investigate the Resolution Trust Corporation's investigation of the Clinton's ties to the failure of Little Rock-based Madison Guaranty Bank.

14 March   Following allegations that he was involved in misconduct at his law firm in Arkansas, Associate Attorney General Webster Hubbell resigns.

26 July   The U.S. House of Representatives opens hearings on the Whitewater allegations.

5 August   A panel of three federal judges names former Solicitor General Kenneth W. Starr to be the independent counsel overseeing the Whitewater investigation, replacing Robert B. Fiske, who had been on the job since January 1994.

3 October   Secretary of Agriculture Mike Espy resigns after he is implicated in accepting gifts from companies over which his department had jurisdiction.

15 December   Former Associate Attorney General Webster Hubbell, a former law partner of First Lady Hillary Rodham Clinton, pleads guilty in Arkansas to charges of mail fraud and tax evasion and is sentenced to twenty-one months in prison.

1995
3 January   The Senate Banking Committee holding hearings on the Whitewater land deal finds that no laws were broken and closes the investigation.

17 May   The U.S. Senate votes ninety-six to three to establish the Special Committee to Investigate Whitewater Development Corporation and Related Matters, also known as the Senate Whitewater Committee, chaired by Senator Alfonse D'Amato (R–NY).

9 June   The U.S. Court of Appeals for the Seventh Circuit upholds the conviction of Judge Adam Stillo Sr., who had been convicted, along with his nephew, of conspiracy to commit extortion under the color of official right, in violation of the Hobbs Act.

10 August   The House Banking Committee closes hearings on the Madison Guaranty Bank allegations, finding no illegalities.

17 August   A grand jury in Little Rock, Arkansas, indicts Governor Jim Guy Tucker and James and Susan McDougal on charges of bank fraud related to the Whitewater land scheme.

26 October   The Senate Whitewater Committee issues forty-nine subpoenas to the White House and other agencies for documents.

19 December   Congress enacts the Lobbying Disclosure Act of 1995, which requires the semiannual disclosure of the hiring of lobbyists, the areas of legislation they specialize in, and whether a certain

lobbyist has worked for the government in the past year.

1996
4 January   First Lady Hillary Rodham Clinton's billing records from the Rose law firm in Little Rock are found on a table in the White House residence book room; it is unknown how they got there, two years after being subpoenaed.

22 January   Independent Counsel Kenneth Starr subpoenas Hillary Rodham Clinton to appear before a federal grand jury on the Rose law firm billing records.

26 January   First Lady Hillary Rodham Clinton appears before a Washington, D.C., federal grand jury, the first such case in the American history.

22 April   David Hale, a former chief of a government lending agency, testifies at the trial of Governor Jim Guy Tucker that then-Governor Bill Clinton pressured him to make a fraudulent $300,000 loan to Susan McDougal.

26 April   Vice President Al Gore attends a fundraising event at the Hsi Lai Buddhist temple in Los Angeles. Initially billed as "community outreach," it is later discovered that money was raised from the monks for the Clinton/Gore 1996 campaign in violation of campaign finance laws.

29 May   A jury convicts Whitewater defendants James and Susan McDougal. James is convicted of eighteen counts, while his wife is convicted of four.

14 June   The FBI issues a report on the "Filegate" scandal stating that the White House had requested specific files.

17 June   White House security chief Craig Livingston is questioned by the House Committee on Government Reform and Oversight on the "Filegate" scandal.

20 June   Attorney General Janet Reno asks Independent Counsel Kenneth Starr to take over the "Filegate" investigation.

15 July   Arkansas Governor Jim Guy Tucker resigns after he is threatened with impeachment by Lieutenant Governor Mike Huckabee. Tucker resigns and Huckabee is sworn in as governor.

20 August   Facing ten years' imprisonment for his Whitewater crimes, former Arkansas Governor Jim Guy Tucker, suffering from a failing liver, receives mercy and is given four-years' probation.

17 October   The *Wall Street Journal* reports that monks from the Hsi Lai Buddhist temple visited by Vice President Al Gore in April had contributed some $50,000 to the Democratic National Committee.

18 October   Following the story on the Hsi Lai Buddhist temple in the *Wall Street Journal,* the Democratic National Committee announces it will reimburse the temple $15,000 for Gore's fundraiser.

28 October   The Democratic National Committee, stung by reports of alleged massive campaign finance law violations, announces that it will not file a preelection spending report with the Federal Election Commission.

30 October   After forty-eight hours of denunciations, the Democratic National Committee reverses course and releases a partial list of DNC donors. John Huang, an agent of the People's Republic of China, is shown to have visited the White House seventy-eight times in the year before.

8 November   In his first postelection news conference, Clinton says contributions from Indonesian sources had "absolutely not" influenced his foreign policy. The president calls for campaign finance reform and endorses the so-called McCain-Feingold campaign finance bill.

13 November   Attorney General Janet Reno turns down a request from Senator John McCain (R–AZ) to appoint an independent counsel to investigate President Clinton and Vice President Gore and their 1996 campaign fundraising activities.

15 November   The Democratic National Committee announces that it will investigate tens of thousands of dollars in contributions made to the party by Thai businesswoman Pauline Kanchanalak and her American company, Ben Chang International.

23 November   The Democratic National Committee announces that it will return a $450,000 donation from Arief and Soraya Wiriadinata, former U.S. residents who had ties to the Lippo Group. This is the largest donation returned by the Democratic

National Committee in the burgeoning financial scandal.

17 December   The legal defense fund founded to aid President and Mrs. Clinton during their legal difficulties while in office divulges that some $640,000 in questionable donations had been returned; much of these funds had come from Clinton's friend Yah Lin "Charlie" Trie, an Arkansas businessman. An additional $122,000 is later returned to Trie.

19 December   The Department of Justice announces that its investigation into Democratic National Committee fundraising is being expanded to examine the Clintons' legal defense fund. Department attorneys issue subpoenas to the Presidential Legal Expense Trust demanding documents on the funds returned to Yah Lin "Charlie" Trie.

20 December   The White House admits that Yah Lin "Charlie" Trie had helped Wang Jun, a Chinese arms dealer with connections to the Communist government in Beijing, get into the White House for a reception in which Wang met with President Clinton. White House Press Secretary Mike McCurry says that Clinton had no idea who Wang was when he met him.

28 December   The Democratic National Committee releases documents showing that the party put together a program called the National Asia Pacific American Campaign Plan, established to raise some $7 million from Asians and Asian Americans. The documents show that John Huang, aided by Doris Matsui, a deputy assistant to President Clinton, put together the plan with officials from the Democratic National Committee and the Clinton/Gore 1996 campaign.

1997
January   The White House releases documents showing that the Democratic National Committee sponsored thirty-one "coffees" at the White House, with an unknown number attended personally by President Clinton and Vice President Gore.

24 January   Documents released by the White House show that approximately 100 "coffees," arranged by the Democratic National Committee, were held at the White House, with President Clinton at most of them and Vice President Al Gore at several. In an interview, Gore admits to "mistakes" in raising contributions, especially the controversial 29 April 1996 Buddhist

Temple event, of which Gore says, "I knew it was a political event and I knew there were finance people who were going to be present."

28 January   In his first press conference since being inaugurated, President Clinton admits that "mistakes were made" in his 1996 fundraising effort but denies that any policies were made because of the donations.

29 January   Senator Fred Thompson (R–TN), in a speech on the U.S. Senate floor, calls for an investigation of the burgeoning White House fundraising scandal with a staff of some eighty people and a budget of $6.5 million.

12 February   Allegations surface that the Democratic National Committee has accepted contributions from the Chinese government in Beijing.

13 February   In a press conference, President Clinton calls for a "vigorous" and "thorough" investigation into allegations that people from the government of the People's Republic of China used contributions to the Democratic National Committee to influence American foreign policy.

14 February   The White House releases documents showing that the National Security Council warned the Clinton administration that Democratic National Committee fundraising trips to Asia could endanger American policy there. The documents focused on DNC official Johnny Chung, who gave some $366,000 to the party in exchange for influence and contacts. The documents from the National Security Council called Chung a "hustler" and denounced his trips to China, where he was flouting his ties to the White House, as "very troubling".

16 February   Representative Dan Burton (R–IN), chairman of the House Government Reform and Oversight Committee issues twenty subpoenas in the growing DNC fundraising scandal and tells reporters he plans to interview some 500 people before the committee.

20 February   News reports show that several Asian American businessmen told investigators that John Huang pressured them to provide some $250,000 in donations to the Democratic National Committee and the Clinton/Gore campaign and asked that the money be masked to show it came from their lobbying group. Huang denies the charge.

21 February   John Huang and former Assistant Attorney General Webster Hubbell both take the Fifth Amendment and refuse to provide congressional investigators with documents relating to the Democratic National Committee fundraising scandal. Huang reportedly demands partial immunity in exchange for the documents. Democratic National Committee chairman Roy Romer admits that an additional $1 million in donations to the party would have to be returned due to questionable circumstances.

26 February   In a press conference, President Clinton admits that large donors to the Democratic National Committee were rewarded with overnight stays in the Lincoln Bedroom. Figures later reveal that these donors gave the Clinton/Gore campaign and/or the Democratic National Committee some $5.4 million.

28 February   The Democratic National Committee discloses that it will return an additional $1.5 million in improper donations that it received from seventy-seven donors in the 1996 election year. Documents released by the White House show that former Deputy Chief of Staff Harold Ickes planned a program to reward large donors with "better coordination on appointments to boards and commissions."

2 March   The *Washington Post* reports that Vice President Al Gore made numerous fundraising calls from his White House office in violation of the law.

3 March   Former Clinton advisor George Stephanopoulos tells reporters that Vice President Al Gore did make fundraising calls from his office in the White House in violation of campaign donation law. Gore, in a press conference, says his calls were within the law and that he had used a Democratic National Committee credit card to make the calls. It is later revealed that Gore had used a Clinton/Gore 1996 credit card.

7 March   The Senate Rules Committee approves funding of $4.3 million to probe the White House/Democratic National Committee fundraising scandal, specifying that the investigation must end by 31 December 1997 and a report turned in by January 1998.

9 March   The *Washington Post* reports that the FBI warned six unnamed members of Congress that the Communist Chinese government was using Asian donors to buy influence in Congress and the

administration. In a press conference, President Clinton says that he had never received this warning.

10 March   Senator Dianne Feinstein (D–CA) reports that she will return some $12,000 in donations from the Lippo Group.

11 March   The U.S. Senate votes unanimously to authorize the Senate Governmental Affairs Committee to conduct "an investigation of illegal and improper activities in connection with 1996 Federal election campaigns" in an effort to get to the bottom of the Democrats' potential illegal fundraising.

12 March   The Democratic National Committee reports that it will return a donation of $107,000 from an American Indian tribe after it is reported that the tribe may have taken the funds from a tribal welfare account.

13 March   White House Press Secretary Mike McCurry reports that no further White House coffees will be held.

17 March   Clinton Central Intelligence Agency nominee Anthony Lake withdraws his nomination in the face of allegations over his finances and his contacts with controversial Democratic National Committee donors.

18 March   U.S. House of Representatives Minority Leader Richard Gephardt (D–MO) reports that he will return donations totaling $22,000 given by the Lippo Group.

23 March   White House documents released show that White House coffees were estimated to raise $400,000 each time they were held, despite earlier White House statements that their main reason to was discuss policy and government issues.

25 April   The *Washington Post* reports that Department of Justice and other investigators have discovered a Communist Chinese plan to spend up to $2 million to buy influence in the Clinton administration and Congress.

29 April   Visiting Washington, Chinese foreign minister Qian Qichen denies the report on the Chinese government plan to use money to buy influence in the U.S. government.

8 May   The Republican National Committee reports that it has found donations of more than $110,000 from Asian sources it could not properly identify.

9 May   Chinese President Jiang Zemin denies that the Chinese government contributed to American politicians to gain influence in the United States.

30 May   The Federal Election Commission fines the Clinton/Gore 1992 campaign $15,000 for illegal loans.

9 June   Documents released by the Republican National Committee show that the party raised some $1.6 million from Asian donors in Hong Kong.

8 July   Hearings begin before Senator Fred Thompson's committee. In his introduction, Thompson reports that he has discovered links between the Chinese government and the attempts to influence the 1996 U.S. election.

13 July   The Justice Department tells reporters that Senator Thompson's assertion that the Chinese government was behind the fundraising scandal has not been proved.

15 July   Senator Joseph I. Lieberman (D–CT) backs Senator Thompson's claim that the Chinese government was behind the fundraising scandal.

24 July   The first Republican to testify before the Thompson Committee, former Republican National Committee chairman Haley Barbour, testifies that the repayment of a loan from Asian sources was "legal and proper." He says that the money was not used for the 1994 elections and that he did not discover it came from foreign sources until the 1996 election.

25 July   Lobbyist Richard Richards disputes Barbour's testimony, claiming that the Asian loan was in fact to elect new congressmen in 1994 and that Barbour was told in mid-1994 of the loan's source.

5 August   President Clinton tells reporters that he is "sick at heart" that the Democratic National Committee may have accepted foreign donations. He calls for an end to soft money in American elections.

11 August   Representative Jay Kim (R–CA) pleads guilty to charges that he accepted illegal foreign donations to his congressional campaigns.

20 August   NBC News airs an interview with Johnny Huang in which he says that he funneled a $25,000 donation from the Chinese government to the Democratic National Committee to obtain a meeting between a Chinese chemical official and then-Secretary of Energy Hazel O'Leary.

24 October   The *Washington Post* reports that the Republicans gave some $1 million to independent groups for the 1996 election.

11 December   Former Secretary of Housing and Urban Development Henry Cisneros is indicted by a federal grand jury in Washington, D.C., on charges that he lied to the FBI regarding hush payments to a mistress.

1998
18 March   Ronald Blackley, the former chief of staff to former Secretary of Agriculture Mike Espy, is sentenced to twenty-seven months in prison for lying to federal investigators in the Espy investigation.

19 March   A three-judge panel names Washington, D.C., attorney Carol Elder Bruce as the independent counsel to investigate Secretary of the Interior Bruce Babbitt and his potential ties to illegal fundraising from Native Americans.

8 October   The U.S. House of Representatives votes to start an impeachment investigation of President Bill Clinton on charges of perjury and obstruction of justice stemming from his testimony in a lawsuit brought by former Arkansas government employee Paula Jones who alleged that Clinton sexually harassed her when he was governor of the state. Clinton's denials that he had a sexual relationship with White House intern Monica Lewinsky when he testified in the Jones case were found to be untrue and are the basis of the impeachment charges.

19 December   The U.S. House of Representatives votes to impeach President Clinton.

1999
12 February   The U.S. Senate acquits Clinton of both impeachment articles.

7 September   Former Secretary of Housing and Urban Development Henry Cisneros pleads guilty to a

misdemeanor after a four-year, $9 million probe into charges he lied about payments to a former mistress.

2000
20 September   Independent Counsel Robert Ray clears both Clintons of criminal wrongdoing in the Whitewater land deal.

28 December   President Clinton ends a five-year ban on the lobbying of government appointees after they have left government.

2001
20 January   In the final hours of his presidency, President Bill Clinton offers 140 pardons and 36 clemencies and commutations, many to controversial figures, including Marc Rich, a fugitive from American justice for 18 years; Carlos Vignali, a convicted drug dealer; Glenn Braswell, convicted of selling vitamins as a cure for diseases in the 1980s; and John Hemmingson, convicted in 1996 of laundering money to cover a campaign loan for the brother of former Agriculture Secretary Mike Espy.

15 June   A federal judge sentences former Mayor Milton Milan of Camden, New Jersey, to seven years, three months in prison for his convictions on fourteen counts of bribery, racketeering, and money laundering, linked to his acceptance of bribes from undercover world figures. The judge tells Milan that he made his city "a laughingstock."

21 June   The House Ethics Committee unanimously rebukes Representative Earl Hilliard (D–AL) for numerous campaign finance violations, but gives him the mildest punishment because Hilliard admits to the wrongdoing and asks for leniency from the committee.

2002
11 April   Representative James A. Traficant Jr. (D–OH) is convicted in a federal court in Cleveland of ten counts of racketeering, bribery, and fraud.

27 September   Former Representative Edward Mezvinsky (D–IA) pleads guilty to thirty-one counts of fraud after admitting to bilking investors in one of his companies of more than $10 million.

7 November   The U.S. government files a lawsuit for Medicare and Medicaid fraud against Dr. Steve Henry, the lieutenant governor of Kentucky, claiming that he

was involved in fraud while running for office in 1995 and even while serving as lieutenant governor of the state.

2003

6 March   A federal grand jury in Austin, Texas, indicts former state Attorney General Dan Morales on charges of misusing state tobacco fund money and campaign funds. Morales, who had once been the Democratic candidate for governor of Texas, was also charged with mail fraud, conspiracy, filing a false tax return, and making false statements on a loan application.

References: "Congressional Ethics: History, Facts, and Controversy" (Washington, D.C.: Congressional Quarterly, 1992); Hoffer, Peter C., and N. E. H. Hull, "The First American Impeachments," The William and Mary Quarterly, Third Series, XXXV:4 (October 1978), 653–667; *The New York Times; The Washington Post.*

BIBLIOGRAPHY

Books

Abbott, Richard H., "The Republican Party Press in Reconstruction Georgia, 1867–1874," *Journal of Southern History* 61, 4 (November 1995), 725–760.

Abels, Jules, *The Truman Scandals* (Chicago: Regnery, 1956).

Abernathy, Thomas Perkins, *The Burr Conspiracy* (New York: Oxford University Press, 1954).

An Account of the Impeachment and Trial of the Late Francis Hopkinson, Esquire, Judge of the Court of Admiralty for the Commonwealth of Pennsylvania (Philadelphia: Printed by Francis Bailey, at Yorick's Head, 1795).

Adams, George Burton, and H. Morse Stephens, eds., *Select Documents of English Constitutional History* (New York: Macmillan, 1927).

Adams, Samuel Hopkins, *Incredible Era: The Life and Times of Warren Gamaliel Harding* (Boston: Houghton Mifflin, 1939).

Adams, Sherman, *Firsthand Report: The Story of the Eisenhower Administration* (New York: Harper, 1961).

Agnew, Spiro T., *Go Quietly . . . Or Else* (New York: Morrow, 1980).

Albright, Joseph, *What Makes Spiro Run: The Life and Times of Spiro Agnew* (New York: Dodd, Mead, 1972).

Allen, Oliver E., *The Tiger: The Rise and Fall of Tammany Hall* (Reading, MA: Addison-Wesley, 1993).

Amer, Mildred, *The Senate Select Committee on Ethics: A Brief History of Its Evolution and Jurisdiction* (Washington, DC: Congressional Research Service, 1993).

Ames, Blanche Ames, *Adelbert Ames, 1835–1933: General, Senator, Governor* (New York: Argosy-Antiquarian, 1964).

Amick, George, *The American Way of Graft: A Study of Corruption in State and Local Government, How It Happens, and What Can Be Done About It* (Princeton, NJ: Center for Analysis of Public Issues, 1976).

Andrews, James De Witt, ed., *The Works of James Wilson: Associate Justice of the Supreme Court of the United States and Professor of Law in the College of Philadelphia, Being His Public Discourses upon Jurisprudence and the Political Science, Including Lectures and Professor of Law, 1790–1792*, 2 vols. (Chicago: Callaghan, 1896).

Angle, Paul M., "The Recollections of William Pitt Kellogg," *Abraham Lincoln Quarterly* 3 (September 1945), 319–339.

Anhalt, Walter C., and Glenn H. Smith, "He Saved the Farm? Governor Langer and the Mortgage Moratoria," *North Dakota Quarterly* 44 (Autumn 1976), 5–17.

Anyon, Jean, *Ghetto Schooling: A Political Economy of Urban Educational Reform* (New York: Teachers College Press, 1997).

Astorino, Samuel J., "The Contested Senate Election of William Scott Vare," *Pennsylvania History* 28 (April 1961), 187–201.

Bacon, Donald C., Roger H. Davidson, and Morton Keller, eds., *The Encyclopedia of the United States Congress*, 3 vols. (New York: Simon and Schuster, 1995).

Baker, Bobby, with Larry King, *Wheeling and Dealing: Confessions of a Capitol Hill Operator* (New York: W. W. Norton, 1978).

Baker, Peter, *The Breach: Inside the Impeachment and Trial of William Jefferson Clinton* (New York: Scribner, 2000).

Baker, Ross K., *The New Fat Cats: Members of Congress as Political Benefactors* (New York: Priority Press, 1989).

Balch, William Ralston, *The Life of James Abram Garfield, Late President of the United States. The Record of a Wonderful Career* (New York: William H. Shepard, 1881).

Baltimore Reform League, *Special Report of the Executive Committee of Baltimore Reform League as to the Statements of Candidates and Others, Filed under Provisions of the Corrupt Practices Act Subsequently to the Primary Election for Representatives in Congress, Held August 30, 1910* (Baltimore, MD: The League, 1910).

Barber, Charles M., "A Diamond in the Rough: William Langer Reexamined," *North Dakota History* 64 (Fall 1998), 2–18.

Barnhart, Bill, and Gene Schickman, *Kerner: The Conflict of Intangible Rights* (Urbana: University of Illinois Press, 1999).

Barry, John M., *The Ambition and the Power* (New York: Viking, 1989).

Barth, Alan, *Government by Investigation* (New York: Viking, 1955).

Bates, J. Leonard, "Walsh of Montana in Dakota Territory: Political Beginnings, 1884–90," *Pacific Northwest Quarterly* 56 (July 1965), 114–124.

———, "Politics and Ideology: Thomas J. Walsh and the Rise of Populism," *Pacific Northwest Quarterly* 65 (April 1974), 49–56.

———, *Senator Thomas J. Walsh of Montana: Law and Public Affairs, from TR to FDR* (Urbana: University of Illinois Press, 1999).

Bean, Walton, *Boss Ruef's San Francisco: The Story of the Union Labor Party, Big Business, and the Graft Prosecution* (Berkeley: University of California Press, 1952).

Beatty, Jack, *The Rascal King: The Life and Times of James Michael Curley* (Reading, MA: Addison-Wesley, 1993).

Bell, William Gardner, *Secretaries of War and Secretaries of the Army: Portraits and Biographical Sketches* (Washington, DC: United States Army Center of Military History, 1982).

Benson, George Charles Sumner, *Political Corruption in America* (Lexington, MA: Lexington Books, 1978).

Berg, Larry L., *Corruption in the American Political System* (Morristown, NJ: General Learning Press, 1976).

Berger, Raoul, *Impeachment: The Constitutional Problems* (Cambridge, MA: Harvard University Press, 1973).

———, *Executive Privilege: A Constitutional Myth* (Cambridge, MA: Harvard University Press, 1974).

Bernard, George S., *Civil Service Reform versus the Spoils System. The Merit Plan for the Filling of Public Offices Advocated in a Series of Articles Originally Published in a Virginia Journal* (New York: J. B. Alden, 1885).

Bingham, Alfred M., "Raiders of the Lost City," *American Heritage* 38 (July/August 1987), 54–64.

———, *Portrait of an Explorer: Hiram Bingham, Discover of Machu Picchu* (Ames: Iowa State University Press, 1989).

Bingham, Hiram, *An Explorer in the Air Service* (New Haven, CT: Yale University Press, 1920).

Bingham, Woodbridge, *Hiram Bingham: A Personal History* (Boulder, CO: Bin Lan Zhen, 1989).

Binning, William C., Larry Esterly, and Paul A. Sracic, *Encyclopedia of American Parties, Campaigns, and Elections* (Westport, CT: Greenwood Press, 1999).

Binstein, Michael, *Trust Me: Charles Keating and the Missing Billions* (New York: Random House, 1993).

Biographical Directory of the American Congress, 1774–1996 (Alexandria, VA: CQ Staff Directories, 1996).

Birnbaum, Jeffrey H. *The Lobbyists: How Influence Peddlers Get Their Way in Washington* (New York: Times Books, 1992).

———, "The Influence Merchants," *Fortune* 138, 11 (7 December 1998), 134–138.

Black, Charles L., Jr., *Impeachment: A Handbook* (New Haven, CT: Yale University Press, 1974).

Blackmar, Frank Wilson, *The Life of Charles Robinson, the First State Governor of Kansas* (Topeka, KS: Crane & Company, 1901).

Black's Law Dictionary, 6th ed. (St. Paul, MN: West, 1990).

Blodgett, Geoffrey T., "The Mind of the Boston Mugwumps," *Mississippi Valley Historical Review* 48, 4 (March 1962), 614–634.

Bloss, George, *Life and Speeches of George H. Pendleton* (Cincinnati, OH: Miami Printing and Publishing Co., 1868).

Bodenhamer, David J., and Robert G. Barrows, eds., *The Encyclopedia of Indianapolis* (Bloomington: Indiana University Press, 1994).

Boettcher, Robert, *Gifts of Deceit: Sun Myung Moon, Tongsun Park, and the Korean Scandal* (New York: Holt, Rinehart and Winston, 1980).

Bollens, John Constantinus, *Political Corruption: Power, Money, and Sex* (Pacific Palisades, CA: Palisades Publishers, 1979).

Boomhower, Ray, *Jacob Piatt Dunn, Jr.: A Life in History and Politics* (Indianapolis: Indiana University Press, 1998).

Borkin, Joseph, *The Corrupt Judge: An Inquiry into Bribery and Other High Crimes and Misdemeanors in the Federal Courts* (New York: Clarkson N. Potter, 1962).

Bouvier, John, *A Law Dictionary, Adapted to the Constitution and Laws of the United States of America, and of the Several States of the American Union: with References to the Civil and other Systems of Foreign Law,* Daniel Angell Gleason, ed. (Philadelphia: G. W. Childs, Printer, 1868).

Boynton, H. V., "The Whiskey Ring," *North American Review* 252 (October 1876), 280–327.

Bridges, Tyler, *Bad Bet on the Bayou: The Rise of Gambling in Louisiana and the Fall of Governor Edwin Edwards* (New York: Farrar, Straus & Giroux, 2001).

Brown, Canter, Jr., "Carpetbagger Intrigues, Black Leadership, and a Southern Loyalist Triumph: Florida's Gubernatorial Election of 1872," *Florida Historical Quarterly* 72, 3 (1994), 275–301.

Buice, S. David, "The Military Career of Adelbert Ames," *Southern Quarterly* 2 (April 1964), 236–246.

Burnham, David, *Above the Law: Secret Deals, Political Fixes and Other Misadventures of the U.S. Department of Justice* (New York: Charles Scribner's Sons, 1996).

Busch, Francis X., *Enemies of the State: An Account of the Trials of the Mary Eugenia Surratt Case, the Teapot Dome Cases, the Alphonse Capone Case, the Rosenberg Case* (Indianapolis, IN: Bobbs-Merrill, 1954).

Bushnell, Eleanore, "The Impeachment and Trial of James H. Peck," *Missouri Historical Review* 74 (January 1980), 137–165.

———, "One of Twelve: The Nevada Impeachment Connection," *Nevada Historical Society Quarterly* 26, 4 (Winter 1983), 2–12.

———, "Judge Harry E. Claiborne and the Federal Impeachment Process," *Nevada Historical Society Quarterly* XXXII:32, 4 (Winter 1989), 3–12.

———, *Crimes, Follies, and Misfortunes: The Federal Impeachment Trials* (Urbana and Chicago: University of Illinois Press, 1992).

Butler, Anne M., *United States Senate Election, Expulsion, and Censure Cases, 1793–1990* (Washington, DC: Government Printing Office, 1995).

Butler, Anne M., and Wendy Wolff, *United States Senate Election, Expulsion and Censure Cases, 1793–1990* (Washington, DC: Government Printing Office, 1995).

Byrd, Robert C., *The Senate, 1789–1989: Historical Statistics, 1789–1992,* 4 vols. (Washington, DC: Government Printing Office, 1993).

Calendar of State Papers: Domestic Series, of the Reign of William and Mary, 5 vols. William John Hardy, ed. (London: Printed for His Majesty's Stationery Office by Eyre and Spottiswoode, 1895–1906).

Calkins, Hiram, and Dewitt Van Buren, *Biographical Sketches of John T. Hoffman and Allen C. Beach: The Democratic Nominees for Governor and Lieutenant-Governor of the State of New York. Also, a Record of the Events in the Lives of Oliver Bascom, David B. McNeil, and Edwin O. Perrin, the Other Candidates on the Same Ticket* (New York: New York Printing Company, 1868).

Caperton, Thomas J., *Rogue! Being an Account of the Life and High Times of Stephen W. Dorsey, United States Senator and New Mexico Cattle Baron* (Santa Fe, NM: Museum of New Mexico Press, 1978).

Caplan, Lincoln, *The Tenth Justice: The Solicitor General and the Rule of Law* (New York: Alfred A. Knopf, 1987).

Cary, Edward, *George William Curtis* (Boston: Houghton, Mifflin, 1894).

Chandler, Peleg W., *American Criminal Trials,* 2 vols. (Boston: Charles C. Little and James Brown, 1841–1844).

Charlton, Thomas Usher Pulaski, *The Life of Major General James Jackson* (Augusta, GA: Geo. F. Randolph & Co., 1809).

Chase, Harold, et al., comps., *Biographical Dictionary of the Federal Judiciary* (Detroit, MI: Gale Research Company, 1976).

Chester, Edward W., "The Impact of the Covode Congressional Investigation," *Western Pennsylvania Historical Magazine* 42 (December 1959), 343–350.

Clark, John G., "Mark W. Delahay: Peripatetic Politician," *Kansas Historical Quarterly* 25, 3 (Autumn 1959), 301–312.

Clarke, Mary Patterson, *Parliamentary Privilege in the American Colonies: Essays in Colonial History Presented to Charles McLean Andrews* (New Haven, CT: Yale University Press, 1943).

Clayton, Powell, *The Aftermath of the Civil War, in Arkansas* (New York: Neale Publishing, 1915).

Clinton, Henry Lauren, *Celebrated Trials* (New York: Harper & Brothers, 1897).

Clopton, John, *Mr. Clopton's Motion Proposing an Amendment to the Constitution of the United States* (Washington, DC: A. & G. Way, 1808).

Cockburn, Alexander, *Al Gore: A User's Manual* (London: Verso, 2000).

Cohen, Richard E., *Rostenkowski: The Pursuit of Power and the End of the Old Politics* (Chicago: Ivan R. Dee, 1999).

———, "Rosty Revisited," *National Journal* 31, 42 (16 October 1999), 2956–2965.

Cohen, Richard M., and Jules Witcover, *A Heartbeat Away: The Investigation and Resignation of Vice President Spiro T. Agnew* (New York: Viking, 1974).

Cohen, William S., and George J. Mitchell, *Men of Zeal: A Candid Inside Story of the Iran-Contra Hearings* (New York: Viking, 1988).

A Collection of Some Memorable and Weighty Transactions in Parliament; in the Year 1678, and Afterwards; In Relation to the Impeachment of Thomas Earl of Danby (London: Privately Published, 1695).

Congressional Ethics (Washington, DC: Congressional Quarterly, 1980).

Congressional Ethics: History, Facts, and Controversy (Washington, DC: Congressional Quarterly, 1992).

Connally, John B., with Mickey Herskowitz, *In History's Shadow: An American Odyssey* (New York: Hyperion, 1993).

Conrad, Barnaby, *San Francisco: A Profile with Pictures* (New York: Bramhall House, 1959).

Cook, James F., *The Governors of Georgia, 1754–1995* (Macon, GA: Mercer University Press, 1995).

Costello, William, *The Facts about Nixon: An Unauthorized Biography* (New York: Viking, 1960).

Cramer, Clarence Henley, *Royal Bob: The Life of Robert G. Ingersoll* (Indianapolis, IN: Bobbs-Merrill, 1952).

Crawford, Jay Boyd, *The Crédit Mobilier of America–Its Origin and History, Its Work of Constructing the Union Pacific Railroad and the Relation of Members of Congress Therewith* (Boston: C. W. Calkins & Co., 1880).

Croker, Richard, "Tammany Hall and the Democracy," *North American Review* 154, 423 (February 1892), 225–230.

Cumming, Hiram, *Secret History of the Perfidies, Intrigues, and Corruptions of the Tyler Dynasty, with the Mysteries of Washington City, Connected with that Vile Administration, in a Series of Letters to the Ex-acting President, by One Most Familiar with the Subject* (Washington and New York: [Published by] The Author, 1845).

Curley, James Michael, *I'd Do It Again: A Record of All My Uproarious Years* (Englewood Cliffs, NJ: Prentice-Hall, 1957).

Current, Richard N., *Three Carpetbag Governors* (Baton Rouge: Louisiana State University Press, 1967).

Curtis, George William, *Orations and Addresses of George William Curtis,* Charles Eliot Norton, ed. (New York: Harper & Brothers, 1894).

Czitrom, Daniel, "Underworlds and Underdogs: Big Time Sullivan and Metropolitan Politics in New York, 1889–1913," *Journal of American History* 78, 2 (September 1991), 536–558.

Daugherty, Harry M., and Thomas Dixon, *The Inside Story of the Harding Tragedy* (New York: Churchill Company, 1932).

Davidson, Roger H., and Walter J. Oleszek, *Congress and Its Members* (Washington, DC: CQ Press, 1994).

Davis, Charles B., "Judge James Hawkins Peck," *Missouri Historical Review* 27, 1 (October 1932), 3–20.

Davis, Joseph Stancliffe, *Essays in the Earlier History of American Corporations* (Cambridge, MA: Harvard University Press, 1917).

Davis, William Watson, *The Civil War and Reconstruction in Florida* (New York: Columbia University, 1913).

DeShields, James T., *They Sat in High Places: The Presidents and Governors of Texas* (San Antonio: Naylor Company, 1940).

Dewey, John, ed., *New York and the Seabury Investigation: A Digest and Interpretation of the Reports by Samuel Seabury Concerning the Government of New York City, Prepared by a Committee of Educators and Civic Workers under the Chairmanship of John Dewey* (New York: City Affairs Committee of New York, 1933).

Dewey, Thomas E., *Twenty against the Underworld* (New York: Doubleday, 1974).

Dickinson, William B., Jr., comp., *Watergate: Chronology of a Crisis* (Washington, DC: Congressional Quarterly, 1973).

Dictionary of American History, 7 vols. (New York: Charles Scribner's Sons, 1976–1978).

Dimock, Marshall Edward, *Congressional Investigating Committees* (Baltimore, MD: Johns Hopkins University Press, 1929).

Dinneen, Joseph F., *The Purple Shamrock: The Honorable James Michael Curley of Boston* (New York: W. W. Norton, 1949).

Dionisopoulos, P. Allan, *Rebellion, Racism and Representation: The Adam Clayton Powell Case and Its Antecedents* (DeKalb: Northern Illinois University Press, 1970).

Dionne, E. J., and William Kristol, eds., *Bush v. Gore: The Court Cases and the Commentary* (Washington, DC: Brookings Institution Press, 2001).

Donovan, Timothy P., Willard B. Gatewood Jr., and Jeannie M. Whayne, eds., *The Governors of Arkansas: Essays in Political Biography* (Fayetteville: University of Arkansas Press, 1995).

Dorman B. Eaton: 1823–1899 (New York: Privately Published, 1900).

Draper, Robert, "Elegy for Edwin Edwards, Man of the People," *GQ* (July 2000), 160–167, 184–186.

Driggs, Orval Truman, Jr., "The Issues of the Powell Clayton Regime, 1868–1871," *Arkansas Historical Quarterly* 8 (Spring 1949), 1–75.

Duker, William F., "The Presidential Power to Pardon: A Constitutional History," *William and Mary Law Review* 18 (1977), 475–538.

Dunar, Andrew J., *The Truman Scandals and the Politics of Morality* (Columbia: University of Missouri Press, 1984).

Duncan, Philip D., and Christine C. Lawrence, *Congressional Quarterly's Politics in America 1996: The 104th Congress* (Washington, DC: Congressional Quarterly, 1995).

Duran, Tobias, "Francisco Chalvez, Thomas B. Catron, and Organized Political Violence in Santa Fe in the 1890s," *New Mexico Historical Review* 59 (July 1984), 291–310.

Dwight, Theodore, "Trial by Impeachment," *American Law Register* (University of Pennsylvania Law Review) 6 (November 1866–November 1867), 257–283.

Easby-Smith, J. S., *The Department of Justice: Its History and Functions* (Washington, DC: W. H. Lowdermilk & Co., 1904).

Eberling, Ernest J., *Congressional Investigation: A Study of the Origin and Development of the Power of Congress to Investigate and Punish for Contempt* (New York: Columbia University Press, 1928).

Elkin, Steven L., "Contempt of Congress: The Iran-Contra Affair and the American Constitution," *Congress and the Presidency* 18, 1 (Spring 1991), 1–16.

Elliot, Jonathan, ed., *The Debates in the Several State Conventions on the Adoption of the Federal Constitution, as Recommended by the General Convention at Philadelphia in 1787. Together with the Journal of the Federal Convention, Luther Martin's letter, Yates's Minutes, Congressional Opinions, Virginia and Kentucky Resolutions of '98–'99, and other Illustrations of the Constitution. Collected and Revised from Contemporary Publications, by Jonathan Elliott. Published under the Sanction of Congress,* 5 vols. (Washington, DC: Printed for the editor, 1836–1845).

Essays in the History of New York City: A Memorial to Sidney Pomerantz (Port Washington, NY: Kennikat Press, 1978).

Evans, C. Lawrence, *Leadership in Committee: A Comparative Analysis of Leadership Behavior in the U.S. Senate* (Ann Arbor: University of Michigan Press, 1991).

Ewing, Cortez A. M., "Early Kansas Impeachments," *Kansas Historical Quarterly* 1, 4 (August 1932), 307–325.

———, "Two Reconstruction Impeachments," *North Carolina Historical Review* 15, 3 (July 1938), 204–225.

———, "Notes on Two Kansas Impeachments," *Kansas Historical Quarterly* 23, 3 (Autumn 1957), 281–297.

The Fall of a President by the Staff of the Washington Post (New York: Dell, 1974).

Farrand, Max, *Records from the Federal Convention* (New Haven, CT: Yale University Press, 1911).

Faust, Patricia L., ed., *Historical Times Illustrated Encyclopedia of the Civil War* (New York: Harper & Row, 1986).

Federal Election Commission, *Campaign Guide for Congressional Candidates and Committees* (Washington, DC: Government Printing Office, 1995).

Feerick, John, "Impeaching Federal Judges: A Study of the Constitutional Provisions," *Fordham Law Review* 39 (1970–1971), 1–58.

Fischer, Roger A., *Them Damned Pictures: Explorations in American Cartoon Art* (North Haven, CT: Archon Books, 1996).

Fisher, Louis, *Constitutional Conflicts Between Congress and the President* (Lawrence: University Press of Kansas, 1997).

Fletcher, Robert, ed., *Amherst College: Biographical Record of the Graduates and Non-Graduates. Centennial Edition, 1821–1921* (Amherst, MA: Published by the College, 1927).

Foley, Michael, *The New Senate: Liberal Influence on a Conservative Institution, 1959–1972* (New Haven, CT: Yale University Press, 1980).

Forward, Ross, *Political Reform. An Exposition of the Causes Which Have Produced Political Corruption in the United States, and a Presentation of the Only Reform Now Adequate to Save Our Present Form of Government* (Cincinnati, OH: Printed by James Barclay, 1886).

Foster, William, *James Jackson: Duelist and Militant Statesman* (Athens: University of Georgia Press, 1960).

Fowle, Eleanor, *Cranston, the Senator from California* (San Rafael, CA: Presidio Press, 1980).

Fowler, Dorothy Ganfield, *The Cabinet Politician: The Postmasters General, 1829–1909* (New York: Columbia University Press, 1943).

———, "Precursors of the Hatch Act," *Mississippi Valley Historical Review* 47, 2 (September 1960), 247–262.

Foxe, Fanne, *Fanne Foxe, by Annabel "Fanne Foxe" Battistella with Yvonne Dunleavy* (New York: Pinnacle Books, 1975).

Frankfurter, Felix, and James Landis, *The Business of the Supreme Court: A Study in the Federal Judicial System* (New York: Macmillan, 1928).

Friedman, Jacob Alexis, *The Impeachment of Governor William Sulzer* (New York: Columbia University Press, 1939).

Fuller, Hubert Bruce, *The Speakers of the House* (Boston: Little, Brown, 1909).

Galloway, George Barnes, *History of the House of Representatives* (New York: Crowell, 1962).

Garment, Suzanne, *Scandal: The Crisis of Mistrust in American Politics* (New York: Times Books, 1991).

Garraty, John A., and Mark C. Carnes, gen. eds., *American National Biography,* 24 vols. (New York: Oxford University Press, 1999).

Geelan, Agnes, *The Dakota Maverick: The Political Life of William Langer, also Known as "Wild Bill" Langer* (Fargo, ND: Privately Published, 1975).

Gertz, Bill, *Betrayal: How the Clinton Administration Undermined American Security* (Washington, DC: Regnery Publishing, 1999).

Gianos, Phillip L., *Politics and Politicians in American Film* (Westport, CT: Praeger, 1999).

Giglio, James N., *H. M. Daugherty and the Politics of Expediency* (Kent, OH: Kent State University Press, 1978).

Goehlert, Robert, *Political Corruption: A Selected Bibliography* (Monticello, IL: Vance Bibliographies, 1985).

Golden, David A., "The Ethics Reform Act of 1987: Why the Taxman Can't Be a Paperback Writer," *Brigham Young University Law Review* 1991 (1991), 1025–1051.

Goodpasture, Albert V., "William Blount and the Southwest Territory," *American Historical Magazine and Tennessee Historical Society Quarterly* 8 (January 1903), 1–13.

"Götterdämmerung in Topeka: The Downfall of Senator Pomeroy," *Kansas Historical Quarterly* 18, 3 (Autumn 1950), 243–278.

Grabow, John C., *Congressional Investigations: Law and Practice* (Clifton, NJ: Prentice Hall Law & Business, 1988).

Grant, Marilyn, "Judge Levi Hubbell: A Man Impeached," *Wisconsin Magazine of History* 64, 1 (Autumn 1980), 28–39.

Griffin, Appleton Prentiss Clark, *Selected List of References on Impeachment* (Washington, DC: Government Printing Office, 1905).

Grossman, Mark, *The ABC-CLIO Companion to the Native American Rights Movement* (Santa Barbara, CA: ABC-CLIO, 1996).

———, *Encyclopedia of the United States Cabinet,* 3 vols. (Santa Barbara, CA: ABC-CLIO, 2000).

Guenther, Nancy Anderman, *United States Supreme Court Decisions: An Index to Excerpts, Reprints, and Discussions* (Metuchen, NJ: Scarecrow Press, 1983).

Hackbart-Dean, Pamela, "Herman E. Talmadge: From Civil Rights to Watergate," *Georgia Historical Quarterly* 77 (Spring 1993), 145–157.

Hall, Kermit L., "West H. Humphreys and the Crisis of the Union," *Tennessee Historical Quarterly* 34, 1 (Spring 1975), 48–69.

Hallam, Elizabeth, ed., *Medieval Monarchs* (London: Tiger Books International, 1996).

Hamilton, Charles V., *Adam Clayton Powell, Jr.: The Political Biography of an American Dilemma* (New York: Atheneum, 1991).

Hamilton, James, *The Power to Probe: A Study of Congressional Investigations* (New York: Random House, 1976).

Hansen, Gladys, *San Francisco Almanac: Everything You Want to Know about the City* (San Francisco: Chronicle Books, 1975).

Harriger, Katy Jean, *Independent Justice: The Federal Special Prosecutor in American Politics* (Lawrence: University Press of Kansas, 1992).

Hazard, Rowland, "The Crédit Mobilier of America: A Paper Read Before the Rhode Island Historical Society, Tuesday Evening, February 22, 1881, by Rowland Hazard" (Providence, RI: S. S. Rider, 1881).

Heidenheimer, Arnold, Michael Johnston, and Victor LeVine, eds., *Political Corruption: A Handbook* (New Brunswick, NJ: Transaction Publishers, 1990).

Herbert, Edward, *The Impeachment of Sir Edward Harbert, Knight, His Maiesties Attourney Generall, by the Commons Assembled in Parliament* (London: Printed for Iohn Burroughes, and Iohn Franke, 1641).

Hershkowitz, Leo, *Tweed's New York: Another Look* (Garden City, NY: Anchor Press/Doubleday, 1977).

Hichborn, Franklin, *"The System" as Uncovered by the San Francisco Graft Prosecution* (San Francisco: Press of the James H. Barry Company, 1915).

Hildreth, Richard, *The History of the United States of America, from the Discovery of the Continent to the Organization of Government under the Federal Constitution,* 6 vols. (New York: Harper & Brothers, 1880).

Hillin, Hank, *FBI Codename TENNPAR: Tennessee's Ray Blanton Years* (Nashville, TN: Pine Hall Press, 1985).

Hinds, Asher Crosby, *Hinds' Precedents of the House of Representatives of the United States, Including References to Provisions of the Constitution, the Laws, and Decisions of the United States Senate,* 8 vols. (Washington, DC: Government Printing Office, 1907–1908).

Hodder, Alfred, *A Fight for the City* (New York: Macmillan, 1903).

Hoffer, Peter C., and N. E. H. Hull, "The First American Impeachments," *William and Mary Quarterly,* 3d Series, 35, 4 (October 1978), 653–667.

———, *Impeachment in America, 1635–1805* (New Haven, CT: Yale University Press, 1984).

Hoffman, John Thompson, *Law and Order* (New York: United States Publishing Company, 1876).

Holden, William Woods, *Memoirs of W. W. Holden* (Durham, NC: Seeman Printery, 1911).

Holli, Melvin G., and Peter d'A. Jones, eds., *Biographical Dictionary of American Mayors, 1820–1980* (Westport, CT: Greenwood Press, 1981).

Holzworth, John M., *The Fighting Governor: The Story of William Langer and the State of North Dakota* (Chicago: Pointer Press, 1938).

Hoogenboom, Ari, "The Pendleton Act and Civil Service," *American Historical Review* 64, 2 (January 1959), 301–318.

———, "Thomas A. Jenckes and Civil Service Reform," *Mississippi Valley Historical Review* 47 (March 1961), 636–658.

———, *Outlawing the Spoils: A History of the Civil Service Reform Movement, 1865–1883* (Urbana: University of Illinois Press, 1961).

Hoogenboom, Ari, and Olive Hoogenboom, *A History of the ICC: From Panacea to Palliative* (New York: W. W. Norton, 1976).

Howard, Thomas W., "Peter G. Van Winkle's Vote in the Impeachment of President Andrew Johnson: A West Virginian as a Profile in Courage," *West Virginia History* 35, 4 (1974), 290–295.

Humbert, W. H., *The Pardoning Power of the President* (Washington, DC: American Council on Public Affairs, 1941).

"Impeachment of the President," *Law Reporter* 7 (August 1844), 161–169.

Impeachment Trial of David Butler, Governor of Nebraska, at Lincoln. Messrs. Bell, Hall and Brown, Official Reporters (Omaha, NE: Tribune Steam Book and Job Printing House, 1871).

Ingersoll, Lurton D., *A History of the War Department of the United States, with Biographical Sketches of the Secretaries* (Washington, DC: Francis B. Mohun, 1879).

Jackley, John L., *Below the Beltway: Money, Power, and Sex in Bill Clinton's Washington* (Washington, DC: Regnery Publishing, 1996).

Jackson, Brooks, *Honest Graft: Big Money and the American Political Process* (Washington, DC: Farragut Publishing, 1990).

Jackson, Kenneth T., ed., *The Encyclopedia of New York City* (New Haven, CT: Yale University Press, 1995).

Jacobs, Bradford, *Thimbleriggers: The Law v. Governor Marvin Mandel* (Baltimore, MD: Johns Hopkins University Press, 1984).

Jacobsen, Joel K. "An Excess of Law in Lincoln County: Thomas Catron, Samuel Axtell, and the Lincoln County War," *New Mexico Historical Review* 68 (April 1993), 133–151.

Jefferson, Thomas, *The Writings of Thomas Jefferson,* 10 vols. Collected and edited by Paul Leicester Ford (New York: G. P. Putnam's Sons, 1892–1899).

Jenkins, Sammy S., *Mecham, Arizona's Fighting Governor: A Constitutional Conflict, "Freedom of the Press" or Political Assassination* (Albuquerque, NM: All States Publishing, 1988).

Jennewein, J. Leonard, and Jane Boorman, eds., *Dakota Panorama* (Bismarck: Dakota Territory Centennial Commission, 1961).

Johnson, Allen, and Dumas Malone, et al., eds., *Dictionary of American Biography,* X vols. and 10 supplements (New York: Charles Scribner's Sons, 1930–1995).

Johnson, John W., ed., *Historic U.S. Court Cases, 1690–1990: An Encyclopedia* (New York: Garland, 1992), 19–22.

Johnson, Loch K., Erna Gelles, and John C. Kuzenski, "The Study of Congressional Investigations: Research Strategies," *Congress and the Presidency* 19, 2 (Autumn 1992), 137–156.

Johnson, Rossiter, ed., *The Twentieth Century Biographical Dictionary of Notable Americans: Brief*

Biographies of Authors, Administrators, Clergymen, Commanders, Editors, Engineers, Jurists, Merchants, Officials, Philanthropists, Scientists, Statesman, and Others Who Are Making American History, 10 vols. (Boston: Biographical Society, 1897–1904).

Jones, Robert F., "William Duer and the Business of Government in the Era of the American Revolution," *William and Mary Quarterly* 32, 3 (July 1975), 393–416.

Joyner, Fred B., "Robert Cumming Schenck, First Citizen and Statesman of the Miami Valley," *Ohio State Archaeological and Historical Quarterly* 58 (July 1949), 286–297.

Kleber, John E., ed., *The Kentucky Encyclopedia* (Lexington: University Press of Kentucky, 1992).

Klotsche, J. Martin, "The Star Route Cases," *Mississippi Valley Historical Review* 22, 3 (December 1935), 405–418.

Klotter, James C., *William Goebel: The Politics of Wrath* (Lexington: University Press of Kentucky, 1977).

Knapperman, Edward W., ed., *Great American Trials* (Detroit, MI: Visible Ink Press, 1994).

Kohn, George C., *Encyclopedia of American Scandal: From ABSCAM to the Zenger Case* (New York: Facts on File, 1989).

Kvasnicka, Robert M., and Herman J. Viola, *The Commissioners of Indian Affairs, 1824–1977* (Lincoln: University of Nebraska Press, 1979).

Lacayo, Richard, and Adam Cohen, "Inside Starr and His Operation," *Time,* 9 February 1998, 42–48.

LaForte, Robert S., "Gilded Age Senator: The Election, Investigation, and Resignation of Alexander Caldwell, 1871–1873," *Kansas History* 21, 4 (Winter 1998–1999), 234–255.

Lamplugh, George R. "'Oh The Colossus! The Colossus!': James Jackson and the Jeffersonian Republican Party in Georgia, 1796–1806," *Journal of the Early Republic* 9 (Fall 1989), 315–334.

Lance, Bert, *The Truth of the Matter: My Life in and out of Politics* (New York: Summit Books, 1991).

Larsen, Lawrence H., "William Langer: A Maverick in the Senate," *Wisconsin Magazine of History* 44 (Spring 1961), 189–198.

Larsen, Lawrence H., and Nancy J. Hulston, *Pendergast!* (Columbia: University of Missouri Press, 1997).

Lawrence, Alexander A., "James Jackson: Passionate Patriot," *Georgia Historical Quarterly* 34 (June 1950), 75–86.

Lawrence, William, "The Law of Impeachment," *American Law Register* 6 (1867), 641–680.

Lederkramer, David M., "A Statutory Proposal for Case-by-Case Congressional Waiver of the Speech or Debate Privilege in Bribery Cases," *Cardozo Law Review* 3, 3 (Spring 1982), 465–518.

Lee, David D. "The Attempt to Impeach Governor Horton," *Tennessee Historical Quarterly,* XXXIV:2 (Summer 1975), 188–201.

Levey, Peter B., *Encyclopedia of the Reagan-Bush Years* (Westport, CT: Greenwood Press, 1996).

Lewis, Alfred Henry, *Richard Croker* (New York: Life Publishing, 1901).

Littlefield, Charles E., "The Impeachment of Judge Swayne," *Green Bag* 17 (April 1905), 193–207.

Logan, David A., *Historical Uses of a Special Prosecutor: The Administrations of Presidents Grant, Coolidge, and Truman* (Washington, DC: Congressional Research Service, 1973).

Lord, Stuart B., "Adelbert Ames, Soldier Politician: A Reevaluation," *Maine Historical Society Quarterly* 13 (Fall 1973), 81–97.

Loth, David, *Public Plunder: A History of Graft in America* (New York: Carrick & Evans, 1938).

Lowry, Sharon K., "Mirrors and Blue Smoke: Stephen Dorsey and the Santa Fe Ring in the 1880s," *New Mexico Historical Review* 59 (October 1984), 395–409.

Lucas, Jim Griffing, *Agnew: Profile in Conflict* (New York: Award Books, 1970).

Lynch, Denis Tilden, *"Boss" Tweed: The Story of a Grim Generation* (New York: Boni and Liveright, 1927).

Mach, Thomas Stuart, "George Hunt Pendleton, The Ohio Idea and Political Continuity in Reconstruction America," *Ohio History* 108 (Summer–Autumn 1999), 125–144.

Makinson, Larry, and Joshua Goldstein, *Open Secrets: The Encyclopedia of Congressional Money and Politics* (Washington, DC: Congressional Quarterly, 1992).

Malone, Michael P., "Midas of the West: The Incredible Career of William Andrews Clark," *Montana: Magazine of Western History* 33 (Autumn 1983), 2–17.

Mankiewicz, Frank, *U.S. v. Richard Nixon: The Final Crisis* (New York: Quadrangle/New York Times Book Company, 1975).

Manley, John F., *The Politics of Finance: the House Committee on Ways and Means* (Boston: Little, Brown, 1970).

Marsh, Robert, *Agnew: The Unexamined Man—A Political Profile* (New York: M. Evans, 1971).

Marshall, James V., *The United States Manual of Biography and History* (Philadelphia: James B. Smith & Co., 1856).

Marshall, Prince J. *The Impeachment of Warren Hastings* (London: Oxford University Press, 1965).

Martin, Edward Sandford, *The Life of Joseph Hodges Choate, As Gathered Chiefly from His Letters,* 2 vols. (New York: Charles Scribner's Sons, 1920).

Martin, Edward Winslow, *The Life and Public Services of Schuyler Colfax, Together with His Most Important Speeches* (New York: United States Publishing Company, 1868).

May, Thomas Erskine, Lord Farnborough, *A Treatise on the Law, Privileges, Proceedings and Usage of Parliament* (London: Butterworths, 1873).

Mazo, Earl, *Nixon: A Political Portrait* (New York: Harper & Row, 1968).

McAfee, John J., *Kentucky Politicians—Sketches of Representatives* (Louisville, KY: Courier Job Printing Company, 1886).

McDonald, John, *Secrets of the Great Whiskey Ring, Containing a Complete Exposure of the Illicit Whiskey Frauds Culminating in 1875, and the Connection of Grant, Babcock, Douglas, Chester H. Krum, and Other Administration Officers, Established by Positive and Unequivocal Documentary Proofs, Comprising Facsimiles of Confidential Letters and Telegrams Emanating From the White House, Directing the Management of the Ring. Also Photographs of Grant, Babcock, Bristow, Garfield and the Famous Sylph. To Which Is Added the Missing Links in the Chain of Evidence of James A. Garfield's Implication with the District of Columbia Ring and Crédit Mobilier Bribery* (Chicago: Belford, Clarke & Co., 1880).

McFarland, Gerald W., *Mugwumps, Morals & Politics, 1884–1920* (Amherst: University of Massachusetts Press, 1975).

McGeary, Nelson, *The Developments of Congressional Investigative Power* (New York: Columbia University Press, 1940).

McGinnis, Patrick J., "A Case of Judicial Misconduct: The Impeachment and Trial of Robert W. Archbald," *Pennsylvania Magazine of History and Biography* 101 (1977), 506–520.

McMullin, Thomas A., and David Walker, *Biographical Directory of American Territorial Governors* (Westport, CT: Meckler Publishing, 1984).

McMurray, Carl D., *The Impeachment of Circuit Judge Richard Kelly* (Tallahassee: Florida State University, 1964).

Mecham, Evan, *Impeachment: The Arizona Conspiracy* (Glendale, AZ: MP Press, 1988).

Melton, Buckner F., Jr., *The First Impeachment: The Constitution's Framers and the Case of Senator William Blount* (Macon, GA: Mercer University Press, 1998).

Merriner, James L., *Mr. Chairman: Power in Dan Rostenkowski's America* (Carbondale: Southern Illinois University Press, 1999).

Messick, Hank, *The Politics of Prosecution: Jim Thompson, Marje Everett, Richard Nixon and the Trial of Otto Kerner* (Ottawa, IL: Caroline House Books, 1978).

Miller, Lillian B., et al., *"If Elected . . .": Unsuccessful Candidates for the Presidency, 1796–1968* (Washington, DC: Smithsonian Institution Press, 1972).

Milne, Gordon, *George William Curtis and the Genteel Tradition* (Bloomington: Indiana University Press, 1956).

Mitchell, Jack, *Executive Privilege: Two Centuries of White House Scandals* (New York: Hippocrene Books, 1992).

Mitgang, Herbert, *The Man Who Rode the Tiger: The Life of Judge Samuel Seabury and the Story of the Greatest Investigation of City Corruption in this Century* (New York: W. W. Norton, 1979).

———, *Once Upon a Time in New York: Jimmy Walker, Franklin Roosevelt, and the Last Great Battle of the Jazz Age* (New York: Free Press, 2000).

Mittlebeeler, Emmet V., "The Great Kentucky Absconsion," *Filson Club History Quarterly* 27 (1953), 335–352.

Moore, Kathleen Dean, *Pardons: Justice, Mercy, and the Public Interest* (New York: Oxford University Press, 1997).

Morgan, Chester, *Redneck Liberal: Theodore G. Bilbo and the New Deal* (Baton Rouge: Louisiana State University Press, 1985).

Morgenthau, Henry, "All in a Life-Time—Chapters from an Autobiography. II. What I Learned From Sulzer and Tammany," *World's Work* 42, 5 (September 1921), 465–479.

Moritz, Charles, ed., *Current Biography 1977* (New York: H. W. Wilson & Co., 1977).

Morris, Newbold, *Let the Chips Fall: My Battles with Corruption* (New York: Appleton-Century-Crofts, 1955).

Mullaney, Marie Marmo, *Biographical Directory of the Governors of the United States, 1983–1988* (Westport, CT: Greenwood Press, 1988).

———, *Biographical Directory of the Governors of the United States, 1988–1994* (Westport, CT: Greenwood Press, 1994).

Munro, William Bennett, *The Initiative, Referendum and Recall* (New York: Appleton, 1912).

Muzzey, David Saville, *James G. Blaine: A Political Idol of Other Days* (New York: Dodd, Mead, 1935).

Myers, Gustavus, *The History of Tammany Hall* (New York: Boni and Liveright, 1917).

Nalle, Ouida Ferguson, *The Fergusons of Texas; Or, "Two Governors for the Price of One": A Biography of James Edward Ferguson and His Wife, Miriam Amanda Ferguson, ex-Governors of the State of Texas* (San Antonio, TX: Naylor Company, 1946).

Nash, Jay Robert, *Encyclopedia of World Crime: Criminal Justice, Criminology, and Law Enforcement,* 4 vols. (Wilmette, IL: CrimeBooks, 1989).

The National Cyclopædia of American Biography, 57 vols. and supplements A-N (New York: James T. White & Company, 1897–1984).

Noggle, Burl, *Teapot Dome: Oil and Politics in the 1920s* (Baton Rouge: Louisiana State University Press, 1962).

Northrop, William Bacot, *The Insolence of Office: The Story of the Seabury Investigations* (New York and London: G. P. Putnam's Sons, 1932).

O'Callaghan, Jerry A. "Senator John H. Mitchell and the Oregon Land Frauds, 1905," *Pacific Historical Review* 21 (August 1952): 255–261.

O'Connor, Richard, *Courtroom Warrior: The Combative Career of William Travers Jerome* (Boston: Little, Brown, 1963).

Omrcanin, Margaret Stewart, *The Novel and Political Insurgency* (Philadelphia: Dorrance & Company, 1973).

Paine, Albert Bigelow, *Mark Twain: A Biography* (New York: Harper & Brothers, 1912).

Peskin, Allan, *Garfield: A Biography* (Kent, OH: Kent State University Press, 1999).

Phillips, Cabell B. H., *The Truman Presidency: The History of a Triumphant Succession* (New York: Macmillan, 1962).

Phillips, David Graham, "The Treason of the Senate," *Cosmopolitan* 40, 5 (March 1906), 487–502.

Pink, Louis Heaton, *Gaynor, the Tammany Mayor Who Swallowed the Tiger: Lawyer, Judge, Philosopher* (New York: International Press, 1931).

Pitcher, M. Avis, "John Smith, First Senator from Ohio and His Connections with Aaron Burr," *Archaeological and Historical Society Quarterly* 45 (1936), 68–75.

Plucknett, Theodore Frank Thomas, *Studies in English History* (London: Hambledon Press, 1983).

Plummer, Mark A., "Profile in Courage? Edmund G. Ross and the Impeachment Trial," *Midwest Quarterly,* 27 (1985), 30–48.

Plungis, Jeff, "The Driving Force of Bud Shuster," *CQ Weekly,* 7 August 1999, 1914–1919.

Pollock, Sir Frederick, Bart., and Frederic William Maitland, *The History of English Law Before the Time of Edward I,* 2 vols. (Cambridge, UK: Cambridge University Press, 1899).

Porter, David, "Senator Carl Hatch and the Hatch Act of 1939," *New Mexico Historical Review,* 48 (April 1973), 151–161.

Posner, Richard A., *An Affair of State: The Investigation, Impeachment, and Trial of President Clinton* (Cambridge, MA: Harvard University Press, 1999).

Powell, Adam Clayton, *Adam by Adam* (New York: Dial Press, 1971).

Powers, Caleb, *My Own Story: An Account of the Conditions in Kentucky Leading to the Assassination of William Goebel, Who Was Declared Governor of the State, and My Indictment and Conviction on the Charge of Complicity in His Murder, by Caleb Powers* (Indianapolis, IN: Bobbs-Merrill, 1905).

Prickett, Robert C., "The Malfeasance of William Worth Belknap, Secretary of War, October 13, 1869 to March 2, 1876," *North Dakota History,* 17:1 (January 1950), 5–51, and 17:2 (April 1950), 97–134.

Priest, Loring B., *Uncle Sam's Stepchildren* (New Brunswick, NJ: Rutgers University Press, 1975).

Proceeding in the Second Trial of the Case of the United States v. John W. Dorsey, John R. Miner, John M. Peck, Stephen W. Dorsey, Harvey M. Vaile, Montfort C. Rerdell, and Thomas J. Brady, for Conspiracy, 4 vols. (Washington, DC: Government Printing Office, 1883).

Quisenberry, Anderson Chenault, *The Life and Times of Hon. Humphrey Marshall: Sometime an Officer in the Revolutionary War, Senator in Congress from 1795 to 1801* (Winchester, KY: Sun Publishing, 1892).

Ragsdale, Bruce A., and Joel D. Treese, *Black Americans in Congress, 1870–1989* (Washington, DC: Government Printing Office, 1990).

Reams, Bernard D., Jr., and Carol J. Gray, *The Congressional Impeachment Process and the Judiciary: Documents and Materials on the Removal of Federal District Judge Harry E. Claiborne* (Buffalo, NY: W. S. Hein, 1987).

Record of the Proceedings of the High Court of Impeachment on the Trial of Calvin Pease: Consisting of the Senate of the State of Ohio as Is Provided by the Constitution and in Pursuance of a Resolution of the Senate (Chillicothe, OH: Nashee & Denny for Collins, 1809).

Reeves, Miriam G., *The Governors of Louisiana* (Gretna, LA: Pelican Publishing, 1972).

Remarks on the Trial of John Peter Zenger, Printer of the New-York Weekly Journal, who was Lately Try'd and Acquitted for Printing and Publishing Two Libels against the Government of That Province (London: Printed by J. Roberts, 1738).

Report of the Trial of the Hon. Samuel Chase: One of the Associate Justices of the Supreme Court of the United States, before the High Court of Impeachment, Composed of the Senate of the United States, for Charges Exhibited against Him by the House of Representatives, in the Name of Themselves and of all the People of the United States, for High Crimes and Misdemeanors Supposed to Have Been by Him Committed, with the Necessary Documents and Official Papers from His Impeachment to Final Acquittal . . . Taken in Short Hand by Charles Evans, and the Arguments of Counsel Revised by Them from His Manuscript (Baltimore, MD: Printed for Samuel Butler and George Keatinge, 1805).

Reston, James, *The Lone Star: The Life of John Connally* (New York: Harper & Row, 1989).

Review of the Communications of Samuel Lawrence and William W. Stone, Manufacturers of Boston: To the Speaker of the House of Representatives, on the Subject of the Investigation at the New York Custom-House, in Two Letters. From the Hon. Geo. Poindexter (Washington, DC: Printed at the National Intelligence Office, 1842).

Richardson, James D., ed., *A Compilation of the Messages and Papers of the Presidents, 1789–1907*, 9 vols. and 1 appendix (Washington, DC: Government Printing Office, 1896–1900).

Riordon, William L., *Plunkitt of Tammany Hall: A Series of Very Plain Talks on Very Practical Politics, Delivered by Ex-Senator George Washington Plunkitt, the Tammany Philosopher, from His Rostrum—the New York County Court-House Bootblack Stand—and Recorded by William L. Riordon* (New York: McClure, Phillips, 1905).

Rogers, Cameron, *Colonel Bob Ingersoll: A Biographical Narrative of the Great American Orator and Agnostic* (Garden City, NY: Doubleday, Page, 1927).

Rosenberg, Kenyon C., and Judith K. Rosenberg, *Watergate: An Annotated Bibliography* (Littleton, CO: Libraries Unlimited, 1975).

Rosenbloom, David H., ed. (with the assistance of Mark A. Emmert), *Centenary Issues of the Pendleton Act of 1883: The Problematic Legacy of Civil Service Reform* (New York: M. Dekker, 1982).

Roske, Ralph J. "The Seven Martyrs?" *American Historical Review*, 64 (January 1959), 323–330.

Rozell, Mark J., *In Contempt of Congress: Postwar Press Coverage on Capitol Hill* (Westport, CT: Praeger, 1996).

Rudnick, Sharon A., "Speech or Debate Clause Immunity for Congressional Hiring Practices: Its Necessity and Its Implications," *UCLA Law Review* 28, 2 (December 1980), 217–251.

Ruegamer, Lana, *Biographies of the Governors* (Indianapolis, IN: Indiana Historical Society, 1978).

Russell, Francis, *The Shadow of Blooming Grove: Warren G. Harding in His Times* (New York: McGraw-Hill, 1968).

Rutherford, Bruce, *The Impeachment of Jim Ferguson* (Austin, TX: Eakin Press, 1983).

Rutherfurd, Livingston, *John Peter Zenger, His Press, His Trial and a Bibliography of Zenger Imprints, by Livingston Rutherfurd. Also a Reprint of the First Edition of the Trial* (New York: Dodd, Mead, 1904).

Saffell, David C., *Watergate: Its Effects on the American Political System* (Cambridge, MA: Winthrop Publishers, 1974).

Salokar, Rebecca Mae, *The Solicitor General: The Politics of Law* (Philadelphia: Temple University Press, 1992).

Salter, John T., *The People's Choice: Philadelphia's William S. Vare* (New York: Exposition Press, 1971).

Sann, Paul, *The Lawless Decade: A Pictorial History of a Great American Transition: From the World War I Armistice and Prohibition to Repeal and the New Deal* (New York: Bonanza Books, 1977).

Schell, Herbert S., *History of South Dakota* (Lincoln: University of Nebraska Press, 1975).

Schlup, Leonard C., "William N. Roach: North Dakota Isolationist and Gilded Age Senator," *North Dakota History* 57 (Fall 1990), 2–11.

Schmidt, John R., *The Mayor Who Cleaned Up Chicago: A Political Biography of William E. Dever* (DeKalb: Northern Illinois University Press, 1989).

Schultz, Jeffrey D., *Presidential Scandals* (Washington, DC: CQ Press, 2000).

Sears, Edward I., "The Impeachment Trial and Its Results," *National Quarterly Review* 17 (June 1868), 144–156.

Seghetti, Michael R., "Speech or Debate Immunity: Preserving Legislative Independence while Cutting Costs of Congressional Immunity," *Notre Dame Law Review* 60, 3 (1985), 589–602.

Shapansky, Jay R., "Congress' Contempt Power," Congressional Research Service Report No. 86–83A, 28 February 1986.

Shofner, Jerrell H., *Nor Is It Over Yet: Florida in the Era of Reconstruction, 1863–1877* (Gainesville: University Presses of Florida, 1974).

Short, Jim, *Caleb Powers and the Mountain Army: The Story of a Statesman from Eastern Kentucky* (Olive Hill, KY: Jessica Publications, 1997).

Sikes, Bob, *He-Coon: The Bob Sikes Story* (Pensacola, FL: Perdido Bay Press, 1984).

Simkins, Francis Butler, *Pitchfork Ben Tillman: South Carolinian* (Baton Rouge: Louisiana State University Press, 1944).

Simpson, Alexander, Jr., *A Treatise on Federal Impeachments, With an Appendix Containing, Inter Alia, an Abstract of the Articles of Impeachment in all of the Federal Impeachments in this Country and in England* (Philadelphia: Law Association of Philadelphia, 1916).

Smith, Gaddis, *Impeachment: What Are Its Origins, History and the Process by Which It Is Carried Out?* (Washington, DC: Center for Information on America, 1973).

Smith, Glenn H., *Langer of North Dakota: A Study in Isolationism, 1940–1959* (New York: Garland, 1979.)

Smith, Mortimer Brewster, *William Jay Gaynor, Mayor of New York* (Chicago: H. Regnery Co. 1951).

Smith, Steven S., and Christopher J. Deering, *Committees in Congress* (Washington, DC: CQ Press, 1990).

Smith, W. Calvin, "The Reconstruction 'Triumph' of Rufus B. Bullock," *Georgia Historical Quarterly* 52, 4 (December 1968), 414–425.

Sobel, Robert, and John Raimo, eds., *Biographical Directory of the Governors of the United States, 1789–1978*, 4 vols. (Westport, CT: Meckler Books, 1978).

Speech of Mr. Black, of Georgia, on the Right of Members to Their Seats in the House of Representatives. Delivered in the House of Representatives, February 12, 1844 (Washington, DC: Printed at the Globe Office, 1844).

Stansbury, Arthur J., *Report of the Trial of James H. Peck, Judge of the United States District Court for the District of Missouri, Before the Senate of the United States, on an Impeachment Preferred by the House of Representatives Against Him for High Misdemeanors in Office* (Boston: Hilliard, Gray & Co., 1833).

Statement of the Measure of the Contemplates Against Samuel Bryan, Esquire, Register-General of the Commonwealth of Pennsylvania (Philadelphia: Printed by Francis and Robert Bailey, 1800).

Steffens, Lincoln, *The Struggle for Self-Government: Being an Attempt to Trace American Political Corruption to Its Sources in Six States of the United States* (New York: McClure, Phillips, 1906).

Stephen, Sir James Fitz-James, Bart., *A History of the Criminal Law of England*, 3 vols. (London: Macmillan, 1883).

Stoddard, Lothrop, *Master of Manhattan: The Life of Richard Croker* (New York: Longmans, Green, 1931).

Stolberg, Mary M., *Fighting Organized Crime: Politics, Justice, and the Legacy of Thomas E. Dewey* (Boston: Northeastern University Press, 1995).

Stratton, David H., "Two Western Senators and Teapot Dome: Thomas J. Walsh and Albert B. Fall," *Pacific Northwest Quarterly* 65 (April 1974), 57–65.

Strong, Theron George, *Joseph Choate, New Englander, New Yorker, Lawyer, Ambassador* (New York: Dodd, Mead, 1917).

Stroud, Richard H., ed., *National Leaders of American Conservation* (Washington, DC: Smithsonian Institution Press, 1985).

Swindler, William F., "High Court of Congress: Impeachment Trials, 1797–1936," *American Bar Association Journal* 60 (1974), 420–428.

Swinney, Everette, "*United States v. Powell Clayton:* Use of the Federal Enforcement Acts in Arkansas," *Arkansas Historical Quarterly* 26 (Summer 1967), 143–154.

Taft, George S., *Compilation of Senate Election Cases from 1789 to 1885* (Washington, DC: Government Printing Office, 1885).

Talmadge, Herman E., with Mark Royden Winchell, *Talmadge: A Political Legacy, A Politician's Life: A Memoir* (Atlanta, GA: Peachtree Publishers, 1987).

Tarr, Joel Arthur, *A Study in Boss Politics: William Lorimer of Chicago* (Urbana: University of Illinois Press, 1971).

Taylor, Hannis, "The American Law of Impeachment," *North American Review*, 180 (January-June 1905), 502–512.

Taylor, Telford, *Grand Inquest: The Story of Congressional Investigations* (New York: Simon and Schuster, 1955).

The Testimony in the Impeachment of Adelbert Ames, As Governor of Mississippi (Jackson: Power & Barksdale, 1877).

Thayer, George, *Who Shakes the Money Tree? American Campaign Financing Practices from 1789 to the Present* (New York: Simon and Schuster, 1974).

Thayer, William Makepeace, *From Log-Cabin to the White House* (Boston: J. H. Earle, 1881).

Theoharis, Athan G., ed. et al., *The FBI: A Comprehensive Reference Guide* (Phoenix, AZ: Oryx Press, 1999).

Thomas, David Y., "The Law of Impeachment in the United States," *American Political Science Review* 2 (1908), 378–395.

Thomas, Lately, *A Debonair Scoundrel: An Episode in the Moral History of San Francisco* (New York: Holt, Rinehart and Winston, 1962).

Thompson, Clifford, ed., *Current Biography 1998* (New York: H. W. Wilson, 1998).

———, *Current Biography 1999* (New York: H. W. Wilson, 2000).

Thompson, Dennis F., *Ethics in Congress: From Individual to Institutional Corruption* (Washington, DC: Brookings Institution, 1995).

Thompson, Fred Dalton, *At That Point in Time: The Story of the Senate Watergate Committee* (New York: Quadrangle/New York Times Book Company, 1975).

Thurber, James A., and Roger H. Davidson, *Remaking Congress: Change and Stability in the 1990s* (Washington, DC: CQ Press, 1995).

Tilden, Samuel J., *The Writings and Speeches of Samuel J. Tilden* (New York: Harper & Brothers, 1885).

Timperlake, Edward, and William C. Triplett II, *Year of the Rat: How Bill Clinton Compromised U.S. Security for Chinese Cash* (Washington, DC: Regnery, 1998).

Trefousse, Hans L., "Ben Wade and the Failure of the Impeachment of Johnson," *Historical and Philosophical Society of Ohio Bulletin* 18 (October 1960), 241–252.

Trefousse, Hans L., Abraham Eisenstadt, and Ari Hoogenboom, eds., *Before Watergate: Problems of Corruption in American Society* (New York: Columbia University Press, 1978).

Trevelyan, George Macaulay, *History of England* (New York: Longmans, Green, 1927).

The Trial in the Supreme Court, of the Information in the Nature of a Quo Warranto Filed by the Attorney General on the Relation of Coles Bashford vs. Wm. A. Barstow, Contesting the Right to the Office of Governor of Wisconsin (Madison, WI: Calkins & Proudfit, and Atwood and Rublee, 1856).

The Trial of John Peter Zenger, of New York, Printer: Who Was Charged with Having Printed and Published a LIBEL against the Government, and Acquitted. With a Narrative of His Case (London: Printed for J. Almon 1735).

Tucker, David M., *Mugwumps: Public Moralists of the Gilded Age* (Columbia: University of Missouri Press, 1998).

Turner, Frederick Jackson, ed., "Documents on the Blount Conspiracy, 1795–1797," *American Historical Review* 10 (April 1905), 574–606.

Turner, Lynn W., "The Impeachment of John Pickering," *American Historical Review* 54 (April 1949), 485–507.

The United States Government Manual, 2000/2001 (Washington, DC: Government Printing Office, 2001).

Utter, Glenn H., and Ruth Ann Strickland, *Campaign and Election Reform: A Reference Handbook* (Santa Barbara, CA: ABC-CLIO, 1997).

Van Nest, G. Willet, "Impeachable Offences under the Constitution of the United States," *American Legal Review* 16 (1882), 798–817.

Van Riper, Paul P., *History of the United States Civil Service* (Evanston, IL: Row, Peterson, 1958).

Van Tassel, Emily Field, and Paul Finkelman, *Impeachable Offenses: A Documentary History from 1787 to the Present* (Washington, DC: Congressional Quarterly, 1999).

Vare, William S., *My Forty Years in Politics* (Philadelphia: Roland Swain Co., 1933).

Volcansek, Mary L., *Judicial Impeachment: None Called for Justice* (Urbana, IL: University of Illinois Press, 1993).

Walden, Gregory S., *On Best Behavior: The Clinton Administration and Ethics in Government* (Indianapolis, IN: Hudson Institute, 1996).

Walsh, Thomas J., "The True Story of Teapot Dome," *Forum* 72, 1 (July 1924), 1–12.

Ward, Sir Adolphus William, et al., eds., *The Cambridge History of English and American Literature,* 18 vols. (New York: G. P. Putnam's Sons, 1907–1921).

Warmoth, Henry Clay, *War, Politics and Reconstruction: Stormy Days in Louisiana* (New York: Macmillan, 1930).

Weeks, Kent M., *Adam Clayton Powell and the Supreme Court* (New York: Dunellen, 1971).

Wendt, Lloyd; and Herman Kogan, *Lords of the Levee: The Story of Bathhouse John & Hinky Dink* (Indianapolis, IN: Bobbs-Merrill, 1943).

———, *Big Bill of Chicago* (Indianapolis, IN: Bobbs-Merrill, 1953).

Werner, Morris Robert, *Tammany Hall* (Garden City, NY: Doubleday, Doran, 1928).

Werner, Morris Robert, and John Starr, *Teapot Dome* (Clifton, NJ: A. M. Kelley, 1950).

Wesser, Robert F., "The Impeachment of a Governor: William Sulzer and the Politics of Excess," *New York History* 60, :4 (October 1979), 407–438.

Westphall, Victor, *Thomas Benton Catron and His Era* (Tucson, AZ: University of Arizona Press, 1973).

Westwood, Howard C. "The Federals' Cold Shoulder to Arkansas' Powell Clayton," *Civil War History* 26 (September 1980), 240–256.

Wharton, Francis, ed., *State Trials of the United States during the Administrations of Washington and Adams, with References Historical and Professional and Preliminary Notes on the Politics of the Times* (Philadelphia: Carey & Hart, 1849).

White, Theodore H., *Breach of Faith: The Fall of Richard Nixon* (New York: Atheneum, 1975).

Wilhelmy, Robert W., "Senator John Smith and the Aaron Burr Conspiracy," *Cincinnati Historical Society Bulletin* 28 (Spring 1970), 39–60.

Williston, Samuel, "Does a Pardon Blot Out Guilt?," *Harvard Law Review* 28 (1915), 647–654.

Wolff, Wendy, ed., *Vice Presidents of the United States, 1789–1993* (Washington, DC: Government Printing Office, 1997).

Wooddy, Carroll Hill, *The Case of Frank L. Smith: A Study in Representative Government* (Chicago: University of Chicago Press, 1931).

Woodward, C. Vann, *Responses of the Presidents to Charges of Misconduct* (New York: Delacorte Press, 1974).

Wright, Marcus J., *Some Account of the Life and Services of William Blount* (Washington, DC: E. J. Gray, 1884).

Zelizer, Julian E., *Taxing America: Wilbur D. Mills, Congress, and the State, 1945–1975* (Cambridge, UK: Cambridge University Press, 1999).

Zelnick, Bob, *Gore: A Political Life* (Washington, DC: Regnery, 1999).

Zink, Harold, *City Bosses in the United States* (Durham, NC: Duke University Press, 1930).

Zuber, Richard L., *North Carolina during Reconstruction* (Raleigh, NC: State Department of Archives and History, 1996).

Dissertations and Theses

Bates, J. Leonard, "Senator Walsh of Montana, 1918–1924: A Liberal under Pressure" (Ph.D. dissertation, University of North Carolina at Chapel Hill, 1952).

Benson, Harry King, "The Public Career of Adelbert Ames, 1861–1876" (Ph.D. dissertation, University of Virginia, 1975).

Beyer, Barry K., "Thomas E. Dewey, 1937–1947: A Study in Political Leadership" (Master's thesis, University of Rochester [New York], 1962).

Brammer, Clarence Lee, "Thomas J. Walsh: Spokesman for Montana" (Ph.D. dissertation, University of Missouri, Columbia, 1972).

Byler, Charles A., "Trial by Congress: The Controversy over the Powers and Procedures of Congressional Investigations, 1945–1954" (Ph.D. dissertation, Yale University, 1990).

Cognac, Robert Earl, "The Senatorial Career of Henry Fountain Ashurst" (Master's thesis, Arizona State University, 1953).

Cummings, Hilary Anne, "John H. Mitchell, a Man of His Time: Foundations of His Political Career, 1860–1879" (Ph.D. dissertation, University of Oregon, 1985).

Dodds, Archibald J., "'Honest John' Covode" (Master's thesis, University of Pittsburgh, 1933).

Dunar, Andrew J., "All Honorable Men: The Truman Scandals and the Politics of Morality" (Ph.D. dissertation, University of Southern California, 1981).

Dunnington, Miles W., "Senator Thomas J. Walsh, Independent Democrat in the Wilson Years" (Ph.D. dissertation, University of Chicago, 1941).

Foot, Forrest L., "The Senatorial Aspirations of William A. Clark, 1898–1901: A Study in Montana Politics" (Ph.D. dissertation, University of California, 1941).

Forth, William S., "Wesley L. Jones: A Political Biography" (Ph.D. dissertation, University of Washington, 1962).

Giglio, James M., "The Political Career of Harry M. Daugherty" (Ph.D. dissertation, Ohio State University, 1968).

Gregg, Leigh E., "The First Amendment in the Nineteenth Century: Journalists' Privilege and Congressional Investigations" (Ph.D. dissertation, University of Wisconsin, 1984).

Hill, Janellen, "Spiro T. Agnew: Tactics of Self-Defense, August 1 to October 15, 1974" (Master's thesis, Arizona State University, 1974).

Hjalmervik, Gary L., "William Langer's First Administration, 1932–1934" (Master's thesis, University of North Dakota, 1966).

Horne, Robert M., "The Controversy over the Seating of William Langer, 1940–1942" (Master's thesis, University of North Dakota, 1964).

Johnson, Gordon W., "William Langer's Resurgence to Political Power in 1932" (Master's thesis, University of North Dakota, 1970).

Jones, Robert F. "The Public Career of William Duer: Rebel, Federalist Politician, Entrepreneur and Speculator 1775–1792" (Ph.D. dissertation, University of Notre Dame, 1967).

Keighton, Robert Laurie, "The Executive Privilege and the Congressional Right to Know: A Study of the Investigating Powers of Congressional Committees" (Master's thesis, University of Pennsylvania, 1961).

Lowry, Sharon K., "Portrait of an Age: The Political Career of Stephen W. Dorsey, 1868–1889" (Ph.D. dissertation, North Texas State University, 1980).

Mach, Thomas Stuart, "'Gentleman George' Hunt Pendleton: A Study in Political Continuity" (Ph.D. dissertation, University of Akron, 1996).

Martin, Jennie McKee, "The Administration of Governor Barstow" (Bachelor's thesis, University of Wisconsin, 1921).

Mattingly, Arthur H., "Senator John Brooks Henderson, United States Senator from Missouri" (Ph.D. dissertation, Kansas State University, 1971).

Miller, Frank L., "Fathers and Sons: The Binghams and American Reform, 1790–1970" (Ph.D. dissertation, Johns Hopkins University, 1970).

Raper, Horace Wilson, "William Woods Holden: A Political Biography" (Ph.D. dissertation, University of North Carolina, Chapel Hill, 1951).

Sherman, Robert Lindsay, "Public Officials and Land Fraud in Arizona" (Master's thesis, Arizona State University, 1978).

Sinow, David Martin, "The Foreign Corrupt Practices Act of 1977" (Master's thesis, University of Illinois, Urbana-Champaign, 1982).

Smith, Charles P., "Theodore G. Bilbo's Senatorial Career: The Final Years, 1941–1947" (Ph.D. dissertation, University of Southern Mississippi, 1983).

Smith, Willard Harvey, "The Political Career of Schuyler Colfax to His Election as Vice President in 1868" (Ph.D. dissertation, Indiana University, 1939).

Thompson, Margaret S., "The 'Spider Web': Congress and Lobbying in the Age of Grant" (Ph.D. dissertation, University of Wisconsin, 1979).

Government Documents, United States Government

Bazan, Elizabeth B., and Jay R. Shampansky, *Compendium of Precedents Involving Evidentiary Rulings and Applications of Evidentiary Principles from Selected Impeachment Trials,* Congressional Research Service (CRS) Report for Congress, 3 July 1989.

District of Columbia, Supreme Court, *Title United States v. Harry F. Sinclair and Albert B. Fall. Indictment: Violation Section 37, Penal Code, Conspiracy to Defraud the United States. (Presented May 27, 1925.) Atlee Pomerene, Owen J. Roberts, Special Counsel of the United States* (Washington, DC: Government Printing Office, 1925).

Doyle, Charles, *Impeachment Grounds: A Collection of Selected Materials,* Congressional Research Service (CRS) Report to Congress, 29 October 1998.

Final Report of the Independent Counsel for Iran/Contra Matters. Lawrence E. Walsh, Independent Counsel, 3 vols. (Washington, DC: U.S. Court of Appeals for the District of Columbia Circuit, Division for the Purpose of Appointing Independent Counsel, 1993).

Final Report of the Independent Counsel in re: Bruce Edward Babbitt. Before: Sentelle, Senior Circuit Judge, Presiding, Cudahy, Senior Circuit Judge, and Fay, Senior Circuit Judge. Carol Elder Bruce, Independent Counsel (Washington, DC: U.S. Court of Appeals for the District of Columbia Circuit, Division for the Purpose of Appointing Independent Counsel, 2000).

Final Report of the Independent Counsel in re: Eli J. Segal. Curtis Emery Von Kahn, Independent Counsel (Washington, DC: U.S. Court of Appeals for the District of Columbia Circuit, Division for the Purpose of Appointing Independent Counsels, 1997).

Final Report of the Independent Counsel in re: Janet G. Mullins. Joseph E. diGenova, Independent Counsel (Washington, DC: U.S. Court of Appeals for the District of Columbia Circuit, 1995).

Final Report of the Independent Counsel in re: Madison Guaranty Savings & Loan Association. Kenneth W. Starr, Independent Counsel (Washington, DC: Office of Independent Counsel, 2000).

Final Report of the Independent Counsel in re: Madison Guaranty Savings & Loan Association: in re: William David Watkins and in re: Hillary Rodham Clinton. Robert W. Ray, Independent Counsel (Washington, DC: U.S. Court of Appeals for the District of Columbia Circuit, Division for the Purpose of Appointing Independent Counsels, Division no. 94–1, 2000).

Final Report of the Independent Counsel in re: Ronald H. Brown. Daniel S. Pearson, Independent Counsel (Washington, DC: U.S. Court of Appeals for the District of Columbia Circuit, Division for the Purpose of Appointing Independent Counsel, 1996).

Final Report of the Independent Counsel in re: Samuel R. Pierce, Jr., Arlin M. Adams, Larry D. Thompson, Independent Counsels, 6 vols. (Washington, DC: U.S. Court of Appeals for the District of Columbia Circuit, Division for the Purpose of Appointing Independent Counsels, 1998).

History of the Committee on the Judiciary of the House of Representatives, House Committee Print, 97th Cong., 2d Sess. (1982).

House Rules Manual, House Document No. 106–320, 107th Cong. (Washington, DC: Government Printing Office, 1999).

Memorial Address of the Life and Character of Michael Crawford Kerr (Speaker of the House of Representatives of the United States). Delivered in the House of Representatives December 16, 1876, and in the Senate February 27, 1877. Published by Order of Congress (Washington, DC: Government Printing Office, 1877).

Report of the Select Committee of the House of Representatives, Appointed Under the Resolution of January 6, 1873, to Make Inquiry in Relation to the Affairs of the Union Pacific Railroad Company, the Crédit Mobilier of America, and Other Matters Specified in Said Resolution and in Other Resolutions Referred to Said Committee (Washington, DC: Government Printing Office, 1873).

Shapansky, Jay R., *Congress' Contempt Power,* Congressional Research Service (CRS) Report No. 86–83A, 28 February 1986.

Speech of Mr. Black, of Georgia, on the Right of Members to Their Seats in the House of Representatives. Delivered in the House of Representatives, February 12, 1844 (Washington, DC: Printed at the Globe Office, 1844).

United States Information Agency, Office of Inspector General. *Report of Audit, Review of Planning and Management of Lisbon Expo 98* (Washington, DC: Government Printing Office, 1999).

U.S. Congress, Joint Committee on Congressional Operations, *House of Representatives Exclusion, Censure and Expulsion Cases from 1789 to 1973,* 93d Cong., 1st Sess. (Washington, DC: Government Printing Office, 1973).

U.S. House, *Conduct of George W. English, United States District Judge, Eastern District of Illinois: Hearing Before the Special Committee of the House of Representatives Pursuant to House Joint Resolution 347,* 2 vols. (Washington, DC: Government Printing Office, 1925).

———, *Conduct of Harold Louderback, United States District Judge, Northern District of California.*

Hearing Before the Special Committee of the House of Representatives, Seventy-second Congress, Pursuant to H[ouse] Res[olution] 239, September 6 to September 12, 1932, 3 vols. (Washington, DC: Government Printing Office, 1933).

———, *Conduct of Judge George W. English: Report on the Report of the Special Committee of the House of Representatives Authorized to Inquire into the Official Conduct of George W. English [House Report 69–653]* (Washington, DC: Government Printing Office, 1926).

———, *Conduct of Judge Harold Louderback. Report to Accompany H[ouse] Res[olution] 387,* House Report 72–2065, (Washington, DC: Government Printing Office, 1933).

———, *Impeachment of Halsted L. Ritter. [House Report 74–2025]* (Washington, DC: Government Printing Office, 1936).

———, *Impeachment of Judge Alcee L. Hastings: Report of the Committee on the Judiciary to Accompany H[ouse] Res[olution] 499,* House Report 100–810, (Washington, DC: Government Printing Office, 1988).

———, *Impeachment of Judge Harry E. Claiborne: Report to Accompany H[ouse] Res[olution] 461,* House Report 99–668, (Washington, DC: Government Printing Office, 1986).

———, *Impeachment of the President: Articles of Impeachment Exhibited by the House of Representatives Against Andrew Johnson, President of the United States,* House Miscellaneous Documents 40–91, (Washington, DC: Government Printing Office, 1868).

———, *Impeachment of the President: [Report] from the Judiciary Committee,* House Report 40–7, (Washington, DC: Government Printing Office, 1868).

———, *Impeachment of Richard M. Nixon,* House Report 93–1305, 93rd Cong., 2d Sess., 1974.

———, *Impeachment of Walter L. Nixon, Jr.: Report to Accompany H. Res. 87,* House Report 101–36, (Washington, DC: Government Printing Office, 1989).

———, *Impeachment of West H. Humphreys, Judge of the United States District Court of Tennessee,* House Report 37–44, (Washington, DC: Government Printing Office, 1862).

———, *Impeachment of William W. Belknap, Late Secretary of War,* House Report 41–345, (Washington, DC: Government Printing Office, 1876).

———, *In the Matter of Representative E. G. "Bud" Shuster: Report,* House Report 106–979,

(Washington, DC: Government Printing Office, 2000).

———, *In the Matter of Representative John W. Jenrette, Jr.,* House Report 96–1537, 96th Cong., 2d Sess. (Washington. D.C.: Government Printing Office, 1980).

———, *In the Matter of Representative Mario Biaggi,* House Report 100–506, 100th Cong., 2d Sess. (Washington, DC: Government Printing Office, 1988).

———, *In the Matter of Representative Michael J. Myers,* House Report 96–1387, 96th Cong., 2d Sess. (Washington, DC: Government Printing Office, 1980).

———, *In the Matter of Representative Raymond F. Lederer,* House Report 97–110, 97th Cong., 1st Sess. (Washington, DC: Government Printing Office, 1981).

———, *Investigatory Powers of Committee on the Judiciary with Respect to Its Impeachment Inquiry: Report Together with Additional, Supplemental, and Separate Views (To Accompany a Resolution (H. Res. 803) Providing Appropriate Power to the Committee on the Judiciary to Conduct an Investigation of Whether Sufficient Grounds Exist to Impeach Richard M. Nixon, President of the United States, and for Other Purposes),* House Report 93–774, (Washington, DC: Government Printing Office, 1974).

———, *Judge Walter L. Nixon, Jr., Impeachment Inquiry: Hearings Before the Subcommittee on Civil and Constitutional Rights of the Committee of the Judiciary* (Washington, DC: Government Printing Office, 1989).

———, *Judge Walter L. Nixon, Jr., Impeachment Inquiry Transcript of Proceedings U.S.A. v. Walter L. Nixon, Jr.,* 2 vols. Criminal Action No. H85–00012(L) (Washington, DC: Government Printing Office, 1989).

———, *Memorial Services Held in the House of Representatives of the United States, Together with Remarks Presented in Eulogy of Thomas J. Walsh, Late a Senator from Montana* (Washington: Government Printing Office, 1934).

———, *Memorial Services in the Congress of the United States and Tributes in Eulogy of Richard M. Nixon, Late a President of the United States* (Washington, DC: U.S. Government Printing Office, 1996).

———, *Proceedings in the House of Representatives, Fifty-Eighth Congress, Concerning the Impeachment of Charles Swayne* (Washington, DC: Government Printing Office, 1912).

———, *Report of the House Managers on the Impeachment of W. W. Belknap, Late Secretary of War,* House Report 44–791, (Washington, DC: Government Printing Office, 1876).

———, *Star Route Transportation of Mails,* House Report 1701, 47th Cong., 1st Sess. (Washington, DC: Government Printing Office, 1882).

———, *Testimony Relating to Expenditures in the Department of Justice: The Star Route Cases,* House Miscellaneous Document No. 38, Part II, 48th Cong., 1st Sess. (Washington, DC: Government Printing Office, 1884).

U.S. House, Committee on Banking, Finance, and Urban Affairs, Subcommittee on General Oversight and Investigations, *Relationship of Arizona Governor J. Fife Symington III with Southwest Savings and Loan Association: Hearing Before the Subcommittee on Oversight and Investigations of the Committee on Banking, Finance, and Urban Affairs,* 102nd Cong., 2d Sess., February 20, 1992.

U.S. House, Committee on Government Reform and Oversight, *Report of the FBI General Counsel on the Dissemination of FBI File Information to the White House, Issued on June 14, 1996, by FBI General Counsel Howard M. Shapiro; Investigation into the White House and Department of Justice on Security of FBI Background Investigation Files,* House Report 104–862, 104th Cong., 2d Sess., 28 September 1996.

U.S. House, Committee on the Judiciary, *Constitutional Grounds for Presidential Impeachment: Report by the Staff of the Impeachment Inquiry* House Committee Report, 93rd Cong., 2d Sess., February 1974.

———, *Hearings of the Committee on the Judiciary (Impeachment of President Richard M. Nixon),* 93rd Cong., 2d Sess., 1974.

———, *Impeachment: Evidence on the Resolution Concerning Charles Swayne, Judge of the United States District Court for the Northern District of Florida,* March 21, 1904, (Washington, DC: Government Printing Office, 1904).

———, *Markup of House Resolution 461, Impeachment of Judge Harry E. Claiborne,* 99th Cong., 2d Sess. (Washington, DC: Government Printing Office, 1986).

U.S. House, Committee on Post Office and Civil Service, *Display of Code of Ethics for Government Service: Report to Accompany H.R. 5997,* (Washington, DC: Government Printing Office, 1980).

U.S. House, Committee on Rules, *Congressional Gift Reform: Hearings before the Committee on Rules, House of Representatives, on H. Res. 250,* 104th Cong., 1st Sess., November 2 and 7, 1995.

U.S. House, Committee on Standards of Official Conduct, *Ethics Manual for Members and Employees of the U.S. House of Representatives*, 96th Cong., 1st Sess. (Washington, DC: U.S. Government Printing Office, 1979).

———, *In the Matter of Representative Charles C. Diggs, Jr.: Report, Together with Supplemental Views to Accompany H. Res. 378*, 2 vols. (Washington, DC: Government Printing Office, 1979).

———, *Inquiry into the Operation of the Bank of the Sergeant-at-Arms of the House of Representatives, Together with Minority Views (to accompany H. Res. 393)* (Washington, DC: Government Printing Office, 1992).

———, *Manual of Offenses and Procedures: Korean Influence Investigation, Pursuant to House Resolution 252,* (Washington, D.C.: Government Printing Office, 1977).

———, *Report of the Special Outside Counsel in the Matter of Speaker James C. Wright, Jr.*, 101st Cong., (Washington, DC: Government Printing Office, 1989).

———, *Rules of Procedure: Committee on Standards of Official Conduct* (Washington, DC: Government Printing Office, 1987).

———, *Summary of Activities* 101st Congress, House Report No. 101–995, 101st Cong., 2d Sess. (Washington, DC: Government Printing Office, 1990)

U.S. House, Select Committee on U.S. National Security and Military/Commercial Concerns with the People's Republic of China, *U.S. National Security and Military/Commercial Concerns with the People's Republic of China. Submitted by Mr. Cox of California,* 3 vols. (Washington, DC: Government Printing Office, 1999).

U.S. House, Select Committee to Inquire into the Causes and Extent of the Late Defalcations of the Custom-House at New York and Other Places, *Report of the Minority of the Select Committee of the House of Representatives, Appointed on the Seventeenth of January, 1839, to Inquire into the Causes and Extent of the Late Defalcations of the Custom-House at New York and other Places* (Washington: Printed by Blair and Rives, 1839).

U.S. House, Select Committee to Investigate Covert Arms Transactions with Iran [with the U.S. Senate Committee on Secret Military Assistance to Iran and the Nicaraguan Opposition], *Report of the Congressional Committees Investigating the Iran-Contra Affair, With Supplemental, Minority, and Additional Views,* 3 vols. (Washington, DC:

Government Printing Office; three volumes, 1987).

U.S. Senate, *Answer of George W. English, District Judge of the United States for the Eastern District of Illinois: To the Articles of Impeachment Against Him by the House of Representatives of the United States,* Senate Document 104, 69th Cong., 1st Sess. (Washington, DC: Government Printing Office, 1926).

———, *Extracts from the Journal of the United States Senate in all Cases of Impeachment Presented by the House of Representatives: 1798–1904,* Senate Document 876, 62nd Cong., 2nd Sess. (Washington, DC: Government Printing Office, 1912).

———, *Final Report of the Investigation of Illegal or Improper Activities in Connection with 1996 Federal Election Campaigns, Together with Additional and Minority Views,* 10 vols. Senate Report 105–167, 105th Cong., 2d Sess. (Washington, DC: Government Printing Office, 1999).

———, *Final Report of the Senate Select Committee to Study Undercover Activities of Components of the Department of Justice,* Senate Report 682, 97th Cong., 2d Sess. (Washington, DC: Government Printing Office, 1982)

———, *Law Enforcement Undercover Activities: Hearings Before the Senate Select Committee to Study Law Enforcement Undercover Activities of Components of the Department of Justice,* 97th Cong., 2d Sess. (Washington, DC: Government Printing Office, 1982).

———, *Leases Upon Naval Oil Reserves and Activities of the Continental Trading Co. (Ltd.) of Canada,* Senate Report 1326, 70th Cong., 1st Sess. (Washington, DC: Government Printing Office, 1928).

———, *Proceedings of the Senate Sitting for the Trial of William W. Belknap, Late Secretary of War, on the Articles of Impeachment Exhibited by the House of Representatives,* 4 vols. 44th Cong., 1st Sess. (Washington, DC: Government Printing Office, 1876).

———, *Proceedings of the United States Senate in the Trial of Impeachment of George W. English, District Judge of the United States for the Eastern District of Illinois,* Senate Document No. 177, 69th Cong., 2d Sess., 1926.

———, *Proceedings of the United States Senate and the House of Representatives in the Trial of Impeachment of Robert W. Archbald, Additional Circuit Judge of the United States from the Third Judicial Circuit and Designated a Judge of the Commerce Court,* 3 vols.

Senate Document 1140, 62nd Cong., 3d Sess. (Washington, DC: Government Printing Office, 1913).

———, *Proceedings of the United States Senate in the Impeachment Trial of President William Jefferson Clinton,* Senate Document 4, 106th Cong., 1st Sess. (Washington, DC: Government Printing Office, 2000).

———, *Report [of] the Committee Appointed to Investigate the Charges of Bribery in the Recent Senatorial Election of Kansas, Preferred against Senator Pomeroy by A. M. York and B. F. Simpson,* Senate Report No. 523, 42nd Cong., 3rd Sess. (Washington, DC: Government Printing Office, 1873).

———, *Report of the Senate Impeachment Trial Committee on the Impeachment of Harry E. Claiborne, Judge of the United States District Court for the District of Nevada, of High Crimes and Misdemeanors,* Senate Document 99–812, 99th Cong., 2d Sess., August 15 to September 23, 1986. (Washington, DC: Government Printing Office, 1989).

———, *The Senate, 1789–1989: Addresses on the History of the United States Senate, by Robert C. Byrd,* 3 vols. Senate Doc. 100–20, 100th Cong., 1st Sess. (Washington, DC: Government Printing Office, 1991).

U.S. Senate, Committee on Governmental Affairs, *Hearings on the Nomination of Thomas B. Lance to Be Director of the Office of Management and Budget, and Nomination of James T. McIntyre, Jr., to Be Deputy Director of the Office of Management and Budget,* 95th Cong., 1st Sess., January 17 and 18, 1977, and March 4, 1977.

———, *Investigation of Illegal or Improper Activities in Connection with 1996 Federal Election Campaigns—Final Report of the Committee on Governmental Affairs,* 6 vols. Senate Report 105–167, 105th Cong., 2d Sess., 10 March 1998 (Washington, DC: Government Printing Office; 6 volumes, 1998).

———, *Matters Relating to T. Bertram Lance: Hearings Before the Committee on Governmental Affairs,* 3 vols. 95th Cong., 1st Sess. (Washington, DC: Government Printing Office, 1977).

U.S. Senate, Select Committee on Ethics, *Investigation of Senator Alan Cranston,* 2 vols. (Washington, DC: Government Printing Office, 1991).

———, *Investigation of Senator David F. Durenberger: Report of the Select Committee on Ethics and the Report of Special Counsel on S. Res. 311,* (Washington, DC: Government Printing Office, 1990).

———, *Preliminary Inquiry into Allegations Regarding Senators Cranston, DeConcini, Glenn, McCain, and Riegle, and Lincoln Savings and Loan: Open Session Hearings,* 101st Cong., 2d Sess., November 15, 1990, through January 16, 1991.

U.S. Senate, Select Committee on Investigation of the Attorney General, *Investigation of Hon. Harry M. Daugherty, Formerly Attorney General of the United States. Hearings Pursuant to S. Res. 157, Directing a Committee to Investigate the Failure of the Attorney General to Prosecute or Defend Certain Criminal and Civil Actions, wherein the Government Is Interested,* 68th Cong., 1st Sess. (Washington, DC: Government Printing Office, 1924).

U.S. Senate, Select Committee on Standards and Conduct, *Hearings, on Allegations Against Senator Thomas J. Dodd, Pursuant to Senate Resolution 338,* 2 vols. 89th Cong. 2d Sess. (Washington, DC: Government Printing Office, 1966–1967).

U.S. Senate, Special Committee on Official Conduct, *Senate Code of Official Conduct: Report of the Special Committee on Official Conduct, United States Senate, to Accompany S. Res. 110,* (Washington, DC: Government Printing Office, 1977).

U.S. Senate, Special Committee to Investigate Whitewater Development Corporation and Related Matters, *Investigation of Whitewater Development Corporation and Related Matters: Final Report of the Special Committee to Investigate Whitewater Development Corporation and Related Matters, Together with Additional and Minority Views,* (Washington, DC: Government Printing Office, 1996).

Government Documents—Individual States

[Arizona], *Record of Proceedings of the Court of Impeachment: In the Trail of Honorable Evan Mecham, Governor, State of Arizona. Arizona State Senate, Sitting as a Court of Impeachment* (St. Paul, MN: West Publishing Company, 1991).

[California], San Francisco Municipal Government, *Report on the Causes of Municipal Corruption in San Francisco, as Disclosed by the Investigations of the Oliver Grand Jury, and the Prosecution of Certain Persons for Bribery and Other Offenses Against the State; William Denman, Chairman. Committee Appointed by the Mayor, October 12, 1908. Reprinted with a Preface and Index of Names and Subjects by the California Weekly* (San Francisco: Rincon Publishing Co., 1910).

[Kansas], *Proceedings in the Cases of the Impeachment of Charles Robinson, Governor, John W. Robinson, Secretary of State, George S. Hillyer, Auditor of State, of Kansas* (Lawrence: Kansas State Journal Steam Press, 1862).

[Massachusetts]. *Report of the Trial by Impeachment of James Prescott, Judge of the Probate of Wills, &C. for the County of Middlesex for Misconduct and Maladministration in Office, before the Senate of Massachusetts in the Year 1821. With an Appendix, Containing an Account of Former Impeachments in the Same State. By Octavius Pickering and William Howard Gardiner, of the Suffolk Bar* (Boston: Office of the Daily Advertiser, 1821).

[New Jersey] New Jersey, Department of Law and Public Safety, *Final Report on the Investigation of the Division of Employment Security, Department of Labor and Industry to Robert B. Meyner, Governor, State of New Jersey. With Foreword* (Trenton: State of New Jersey Official Report, 1955).

[New York] *By His Excellency William Cosby, Captain General and Governour in Chief of the Provinces New-York, New-Jersey . . . a Proclamation: Whereas by the Contrivance of Some Evil Disposed and Disaffected Persons, Divers Journals or Printed News Papers (Entitled, the New-York Weekly Journal . . .) Have Been Caused to Be Printed and Published by John Peter Zenger . . . I Have Thought Fit . . . to Issue This Proclamation, Hereby Promising a Reward of Fifty Pounds to Such Person or Persons Who Shall Discover the Author or Authors of the Said . . . Journals or Printed News-Papers . . . Given Under My Hand and Seal at Fort-George in New-York This Sixth Day of November . . . in the Year of Our Lord 1734* (New York: Printed by William Bradford, 1734).

[New York] Court for Trial of Impeachment, *Proceedings of the Court for the Trial of Impeachments. The People of the State of New York, by the Assembly thereof, against William Sulzer as Governor. Held at the Capital in the City of Albany, New York, September 18, 1913, to October 17, 1913* (Albany: J.B. Lyon Company, Printers, 1913).

[New York] Legislature, Senate, Standing Committee on Judiciary, *New York's Impeachment Law and the Trial of Governor Sulzer: A Case for Reform. Prepared by the Staff of the New York State Senate Judiciary Committee* (Albany: The Committee [on the Judiciary], 1986).

[New York] *The Trial of the Hon. John C. Mather, One of the Canal Commissioners of the State of New York, in the Court for the Trial of Impeachments, Held at the Capitol in the City of Albany, Commencing Wednesday, July 27th, 1853 . . . Richard Sutton, Short Hand Writer to the Court of Impeachments* (Albany: H. H. Van Dyck, Printer—Atlas Steam Press, 1853).

[New York] State Supreme Court, Appellate Division, *The Investigation of the Magistrates Courts in the First Judicial Department and the Magistrates Thereof, and of Attorneys-at-Law Practicing in Said Courts: Final Report of Samuel Seabury, Referee* (New York: The City Club of New York, 1932).

[North Carolina] Legislature, *Articles Against William W. Holden*, Document No. 18, 1870–1871 Session (Raleigh: James H. Moore, State Printer, 1871).

[Ohio], *Record of the Proceedings of the High Court of Impeachment on the Trial of William Irvin: Consisting of the Senate of the State of Ohio* (Chillicothe: Printed by Thomas G. Bradford & Co., Printers for the State, 1806).

[Pennsylvania]. *The Trial of Alexander Addison, esq.: President of the Courts of Common Pleas, in the Circuit Consisting of the Counties of Westmoreland, Fayette, Washington and Allegheny: On an Impeachment, by the House of Representatives, before the Senate of the Commonwealth of Pennsylvania . . . Taken in Short Hand by Thomas Lloyd* (Lancaster: Printed by George Helmbold, Junior, for Lloyd and Helmbold, 1803).

[Texas] *Record of Proceedings of the High Court of Impeachment on the Trial of Hon. James E. Ferguson, Governor, Before the Senate of the State of Texas, Pursuant to the State Constitution and Rules Provided by the Senate during the Second and Third Called Sessions of the 35th Legislature. Convened in the City of Austin, August 1, 1917, and Adjourned Without Day, September 29, 1917. Published by Authority of the Legislature, T.H. Yarbrough, Journal Clerk, Senate* (Austin: A.O. Baldwin & Sons, State Printers, 1917).

[Virginia] *Debates and Other Proceedings of the Convention of Virginia, Convened at Richmond, on Monday the Second of June, 1788, for the Purpose of Deliberating on the Constitution Recommended by the Grand Federal Convention. To Which Is Prefixed the Federal Constitution. Taken in Short Hand, by David Robertson of Petersburg*, 3 vols. (Petersburg: Printed by Hunter and Prentis, 1788–1789).

[Wisconsin] State Senate, *Trial of Impeachment of Levi Hubbell, Judge of the Second Judicial Circuit, by the Senate of the State of Wisconsin, June 1853. Reported by T. C. Leland* (Madison: B. Brown, 1853).

[Wisconsin] State Senate, *Trial of Impeachment of Levi Hubbell, Judge of the Second Judicial Circuit, by the*

Senate of the State of Wisconsin, June 1853. Reported by T. C. Leland (Madison, WI: B. Brown, 1853).

Manuscript Collections

Henry S. Johnston Collection, Special Collections and University Archives, Edmon Low Library, Oklahoma State University, Stillwater, Oklahoma.

James Buchanan Papers, Historical Society of Pennsylvania, Philadelphia [Papers regarding the impeachment of Judge James Hawkins Peck].

Letters to and from Senator Burton K. Wheeler, American Civil Liberties Union Papers, Princeton University, Princeton, New Jersey.

Matthew J. Connelly Official File, Harry S Truman Library, Independence, Missouri.

Official Records of the Impeachment of George W. English, File 69B-A1 in Records of Impeachment Proceedings, 1st–90th Congress (1789–1968), General Records of the United States House of Representatives, 1789–1988, RG 233, National Archives, Washington, D.C.

Official Records of the Impeachment of Judge James H. Peck, File 21B-B1, in Records of Impeachment Proceedings, 1st–90th Congresses (1789–1968), General Records of the U.S. House of Representatives, 1789–1968, RG 233, National Archives, Washington, D.C.

State Governors' Incoming Correspondence, 1857–1888, Series 577, Florida Department of State, Division of Library & Information Services, Bureau of Archives & Records Management, Tallahassee, Florida.

Warren Hastings Papers (minutes and related papers related to his impeachment in Parliament in 1787), Add[itional] MSS 17061–62, 16261–67, Add[itional] MSS 17066–082, 24222–268, British Library (London).

William Dudley Foulke Papers, Library of Congress, Washington, D.C.

William Wirt Papers, Maryland Historical Society, Baltimore, Maryland [Papers regarding the impeachment of Judge James Hawkins Peck].

Zachariah Chandler Papers, Library of Congress, Washington, D.C.

Oral Histories

Abe Fortas Oral History Interview, 14 August 1969, Lyndon Baines Johnson Library, Austin, Texas.

Charles S. Murphy Oral History Interview, 25 July 1969, Harry S. Truman Presidential Library, Independence, Missouri.

Matthew J. Connelly Oral History Interview, 28 November 1967, Courtesy Harry S. Truman Library, Independence, Missouri.

"Memoirs of Thomas Woodnut Miller, a Public Spirited Citizen of Delaware and Nevada. An Oral History Conducted by Mary Ellen Glass" (University of Nevada at Reno Oral History Program, 1966).

Wilbur D. Mills Oral History Interview I, 2 November 1971, Lyndon Baines Johnson Library, Austin, Texas.

Court Cases

Addonizio v. United States, 405 U.S. 936 (1972)

Austin v. Michigan Chamber of Commerce, 494 U.S. 652 (1990)

Barry v. United States, 865 F.2d 1317 (D.C. Cir. 1989)

Barry v. United States ex rel. Cunningham, 297 U.S. 597 (1929)

Buckley v. Valeo, 424 U.S. 1 (1976)

Burton v. United States, 196 U.S. 283 (1905)

Burton v. United States, 202 U.S. 344 (1906)

Claiborne v. United States, 727 F.2d 842 (1984)

Claiborne v. United States, 465 U.S. 1305 (1984)

Colorado Republican Federal Campaign Committee v. Federal Election Commission, 116 S. Ct. 2309 (1996)

Federal Election Commission v. Massachusetts Citizens for Life, Inc., 479 U.S. 238 (1986)

Federal Election Commission v. National Conservative Political Action Committee, 470 U.S. 480 (1985)

Federal Election Commission v. National Right to Work Committee, 459 U.S. 197 (1982)

Finn v. Schiller, 72 F.3d 1182 (4th Cir. 1996)

Flanagan v. United States, 465 U.S. 259 (1984)

Florida Right to Life, Inc. v. Lamar, (11th Cir. 2001)

Hastings v. United States, 802 F. Supp. 490 (D.D.C. 1992)

Helstoski v. United States, 442 U.S. 477 (1979)

Hubbard v. United States, 514 U.S. 695, 115 S. Ct. 1754 (1995)

In re Grand Jury Investigation [Bert Lance], 610 F.2d 202 (5th Cir. 1980)

In re Grand Jury Investigation Into Possible Violations of Title 18, 587 F.2d 589 (3d Cir. 1978)

In re Sealed Case, 267 U.S. Appeals Court D.C. 178 (1988)

In re Secretary of Labor Raymond J. Donovan, 838 F.2d 476, 1986 U.S. App. LEXIS 29829 (D.C. Cir. Special Division, 1986)

Jurney v. MacCracken, 294 U.S. 125 (1935)

Kilbourn v. Thompson, 103 U.S. 168 (1881)

McCormick v. United States, 500 U.S. 257 (1991)

McGrain v. Daugherty, 273 U.S. 135 (1927)

Morrison v. Olson, 487 U.S. 654 (1988)

Newberry v. United States, 256 U.S. 232 (1921)

Nixon v. Shrink Missouri PAC, 528 U.S. 528 U.S. 377 (2000)

Nixon v. United States, 506 U.S. 224 (1993)

Pan American Petroleum & Transport Co. v. United States, 273 U.S. 456 (1927)

Pendergast v. United States, 317 U.S. 412 (1943)

Powell v. McCormack, 395 U.S. 486 (1969)

Tenney v. Brandhove, 341 U.S. 367 (1951)

United States v. Addonizio, 442 U.S. 178 (1979).

United States v. Bramblett, 348 U.S. 503 (1955)

United States v. Brewster, 408 U.S. 501 (1972)

United States v. Eilberg, 465 F. Supp. 1080 (E.D. Pa. 1979)

United States v. Eilberg, 507 F. Supp. 267 (E.D. Pa. 1980)

United States v. Eilberg, 536 F. Supp. 514 (E.D. Pa. 1982)

United States v. Eisenberg, 711 F.2d 959 (11th Cir. 1983)

United States v. Gillock, 445 U.S. 360 (1980)

United States v. Helstoski, 442 U.S. 477 (1979)

United States v. Johnson, 383 U.S. 169 (1966)

United States v. Mandel, 591 F.2d 1347, *vacated,* 602 F.2d 653 (4th Cir. 1979) (en banc), *second rehearing denied,* 609 F.2d 1076 (4th Cir. 1979), *cert. denied,* 445 U.S. 961 (1980)

United States v. National Treasury Employees Union, 513 U.S. 454, 115 S. Ct. 1103 (1995)

United States v. Nixon, 418 U.S. 683 (1974)

United States v. Oakar, (No. 96–3084A), U.S. Court of Appeals for the DC Circuit, 1997

United States v. Rostenkowski, 59 F.3d 1291 (D.C. Cir. 1995)

United States v. Shirey, 359 U.S. 255 (1959)

United States v. Worrall, 2 U.S. (2 Dall.) 384 (1798)

Vermont Right to Life Committee v. Sorrell, (No. 98–9325), 19 F.2d 204 (1998)

INDEX